Forgotten Valor

Brothers Elzie and Jesse Moore
From childhood through the Great War
1903-1919

by
David G. Moore

Cork Hill Press
Carmel

CORK HILL PRESS™

Cork Hill Press
597 Industrial Drive, Suite 110
Carmel, IN 46032-4207
1-866-688-BOOK
www.corkhillpress.com

Issued simultaneously in hardcover and trade paperback editions.
Hardcover Edition: 1-59408-457-2
Trade Paperback Edition: 1-59408-108-5

Library of Congress Card Catalog Number: 2004107145

Printed in the United States of America

1 3 5 7 9 10 8 6 4 2

For Benita and for the descendants of Helen and Jesse Moore

Contents

In Flanders fields the poppies blow
Between the crosses, row on row,
That mark our place; and I the sky
The larks, still bravely singing, fly
Scarce heard amid the guns below.

We are the dead. Short days ago
We lived, felt dawn, saw sunset glow,
Loved and were loved, and now we lie
In Flanders fields.

Lieut. Col. John McCrae

I do not have the words to describe how awful war is.

Jesse A. Moore

Acknowledgment

Thanks to Benita for countless hours of research and editing. Without her there would be no book.

Author's Note

The story is true. I have used a literary license, if needed, to reveal what I believe to be a reasonably accurate account of events. A few fictional characters were created to better understand the events surrounding the lives of Elzie and Jesse.

Finally, one could logically challenge my objectivity in my search for truth; for I am the ninth child of Helen and Jesse, the nephew of Elzie.

CHAPTER 1

THE PRISONER

August 10, 1918.
Headquarters. 5th Division.
Saint Die, France. The Saint Die Military Sector.
Office of G.2., Intelligence.
Interrogation Room.

The major appears to be an unlikely warrior. In peacetime he lives in New Jersey and is employed as a banker in New York City. Slight of frame, academic in appearance, and painfully deliberate in purpose, he approaches his assigned military work in a consistent methodical manner. Just as millions of other Americans have responded to their nation's call to arms, he has volunteered for service in the Army of The United States. He previously has served his country during the Spanish-American war as an officer in the Service of Supply, but now he is assigned to G.2. as an Intelligence Officer in the 5th Division. He performs his wartime assignment well, but he does not cherish the task.

Major Frank Johnson is bilingual, fluent in German and English. He has just finished final interrogation of three German soldiers captured in a night raid, August 7, 1918. Although not widely known, but suspected by the rank and file, the 5th Division is preparing for its first American military offensive, scheduled to occur during the middle of August, 1918, in the Vosges Mountains of Lorraine, France. The military objectives are to liberate the French village of Frapelle, to secure hill 451, and to penetrate nearby German fortifications. It promises to become a difficult mission, and proper preparation is essential. The Americans, anxious to prove themselves in battle under American command, need all available intelligence at their disposal. The information acquired from the German prisoners is critical to the success of the military operation.

The interrogation room is situated on the top floor of a three story stone building located on the northern outskirts of Saint Die, France. The eight glass windows, shutters wide open, provide the light necessary to conclude the three day, and night, inquiry of the recently captured German soldiers. The smell of burned kerosene, caused by the all night burning of lamps, permeates the entire room, and the fresh air smells good. The room is furnished with two hard back chairs and one long table. Two armed guards stand beside the closed door. Major Johnson sits on the east side of the table, with the early morning sun to his back, as Corporal Hans Weis, the German prisoner, sits directly opposite the major, on the west side of the table. Major Johnson is writing, making a concerted effort to conclude his notes of the interrogation. Corporal Weis is sitting in his chair, erect and still, and the two guards are standing at ease. The sounds of the ink pen scratching the paper as the major writes, and the various annoying sounds of military movements heard from outside the stone building, are the only sounds heard by the four men. The major continues to write his notes. Everyone in the room is exhausted.

After approximately twenty minutes of writing the major places the cap on his ink pen, lays the pen on the table, and stands to stretch. He walks to the window, looks outside without talking to anyone, and then returns to his seat. Without making eye contact with the prisoner the major begins to speak. "I have no more questions for you so this interview is over. I don't know if you fully realize it or not, but for you, this war is over. Sometime tomorrow, you will be sent behind the lines to a prisoner camp for the duration. I can't tell you any more about your fate, because I don't know any more than that. I do want to say that this interview has been easier than most because of your command of English and because of your direct response to my questions. I have made note of those facts to be placed in your file. Do you have anything else you would like to say before I leave?"

The corporal, a battle-hardened infantry veteran of four years of fighting, mostly in the nearby region of the Vosges, calmly sits, listening attentively to his interrogator. He still wears his dirty and torn, gray German uniform. Although he looks to be in his early forties, he says he is twenty-eight years of age. His face has been made leathery by constant exposure to the elements. He weighs 176 pounds and measures 5 feet, 11 inches in height. The interview clearly reveals that he has been a good German soldier and a worthy opponent in this Great War. Corporal Hans Weis, a baker before the war, is proud of his German heritage, but tired of fighting. The major's words—for you the war is over—are bittersweet. He intuitively senses that Germany, having failed to rout the Allies in the 1918 spring offensives, is about to lose the war. Although he is tired and battle weary, and most eager to see his family, he has concerns about postwar life in a defeated Germany. He is a proud soldier and now he suffers from the humiliation of having been captured by the American Army.

The soft spoken corporal speaks clearly as he attempts to preserve his dignity by his mild but firm manner. On the surface, he remains a proud man. He answers, "No, sir, other than to thank you for your fairness and kind treatment. You Americans are very hard to understand. You fight like demons but you have a sense of fair play. You are a complicated sort."

"Thank you, I will take that as a compliment. I have made arrangements to get you breakfast since we talked all through the night. The guard will escort you there. Would you like a cigarette before you leave?"

"Certainly I would. American cigarettes are without equal. Your coffee is terrible, but I love your cigarettes." The major, smiling for the first time in several days, because he, too, dislikes Army coffee, lights the cigarette for Hans, and watches as Hans inhales deeply.

The major becomes amused. "I can see you like our cigarettes."

"Major, I do have one question if it's all right for me to ask."

"Ask."

"Why did you not ask me about the German raid on the 61st Regiment about six or seven weeks ago?"

"I did ask you about it. We talked about it. Do you have something else to add?"

"I do not want to be rude or disrespectful. I am talking about the attack near La Sadey."

The major looked puzzled. "I guess I don't know what you're talking about. The only attack near La Sadey was part of your night raids which occurred near the center of our line which was almost four kilometers from La Sadey. Or possibly, you're referring to our counterattack. I'm not aware of any attack on our outpost." The major abruptly stopped speaking, feeling stupid for what he had just said and showing his ill at ease for saying it. He just violated the first rule of interrogation. He had unnecessarily revealed information. He knew he was tired and he had just made a careless mistake. However, he also realized that he must proceed with caution, as the German might be providing new information, and he could not allow this informational opportunity to pass. "Of course, I remember. I'm sorry, my mind was elsewhere. Please continue."

The German corporal realized the major was unaware of the events at La Sadey, so he continued to speak, only with more sincerity, more purpose. "Major, your army needs to be aware. You lost five brave soldiers that night, and all of them died a heroic death. May I tell you what happened?"

The major sat in his chair, stunned. Stunned first because he was not aware of what the German was talking about, and second, because the German was volunteering the information. "By all means, tell me what happened."

"As you know, we Germans have been fighting the French in this area for the last four years. At first we were very successful, almost occupying Epinal. However, we failed to gain Nancy, which was our objective, so I suppose we were not totally successful. We did occupy Saint Die in 1914, and, in fact, our soldiers slept in this very building."

Almost in anger the major replied, "What's all this got to do with the 61st and La Sadey? You're talking ancient history. I think you're stalling. Now either get to the point or shut up. I've got other things to do."

"I am sorry I disturbed you. I am getting to the point. Since 1915 there has been limited fighting in this area, but there has been fighting. Many soldiers, on both sides, have died. Now the Americans are in this war, and we do not know much about the American soldiers or how well they fight. We call you Americans, cowboys. Did you know that? We love to read about your wild west with cowboys, Indians, and outlaws. Buffalo Bill's Wild West Show is very big in Germany. Many Germans have seen that very entertaining show, and most of us thought of your soldiers as cowboys in military uniform."

"You got two minutes, Hans. Either you say something or I'm gone."

"Be patient, I am saying something. On that particular night, near La Sadey, our unit was sent in to get American prisoners, more specifically, we were ordered to capture the Americans in the outpost. To complete our task we had over two companies while most of the fighting was occurring elsewhere, so we knew our assignment was important. We needed to capture the Americans so we could find out about the American Army and the American soldier. These American soldiers were recent arrivals to the line, so we figured, without battle experience, we could complete our task without much difficulty. We were wrong. Now do you want to hear the story, or do you still want to leave?"

"I'm listening."

"Our orders were to deceive the soldiers positioned in the primary trench to make them believe that they were our target, when in fact are true objective was the outpost. But to our surprise the trench was not manned. It was deserted. I do not know why but there were no soldiers in the trench, no weapons, nothing. The soldiers in the outpost were out there isolated, without support. It makes no sense, but it is true. Thus, the outpost was ours to capture, or so we thought."

"Why had the 61st abandoned the primary trench?"

"I do not know the answer to that. About one hour before our advance we hit the trench with some artillery, but not much. I know for sure that soldiers were there just a few hours earlier. When we advanced we used only machine gun fire and small arms fire for cover. No one in the trench returned fire. I'm sure they were gone. We saw some soldiers in the distance retreating down the dirt road, and we fired on them; and as far as I know, they never came back."

"How many did you observe in retreat?"

"I do not know. I saw about a dozen or so, but I have no idea how many were there when we attacked. I am not positive but I think they were wearing French uniforms. I know that makes little sense, although that is what I saw."

"Where were you personally positioned after the retreat, I mean after you saw the men in retreat?"

"I was part of the decoy force ordered to attack the primary trench. If you allow me to continue, I can explain what happened. We thought we had to attack the trench to prevent the men in the outpost from retreating to it. You could not see the outpost from the German trench, but we knew where it was. We had deliberately circumvented the outpost in our raid that night. Our plan was to attack the primary trench while others surrounded the outpost and cut off their escape route. We assumed the Americans knew what we were doing, so we prepared for the Americans to counterattack, and in the meantime, we sent another platoon to help secure the outpost. The Americans did not counterattack because they were not in the trench. In fact, the Americans did not return until the next day."

"What day of the week, and what time of day was your attack?"

"We made the attack at dawn and the Americans did not return until dawn the next day. Of course the Americans in the outpost remained, because we had them surrounded. I do not remember what day it was. It was six or seven weeks ago. That is too long to remember the day of the week. I do not even know what day it is today."

"Okay, go on."

"We surrounded the outpost and demanded that they surrender. They had no choice but to surrender or die. We had them and they knew it. We had them totally surrounded. We targeted them with two cross firing machine guns and over fifty infantrymen surrounded them. Instead of surrendering, they chose to fight and opened fire on us even though it was useless for them to try to escape. At first, I could not understand why they refused surrender. It made no sense to me because we had them totally cut off. Apparently, they believed otherwise. What followed was a brilliant tactical move by the Americans." Pausing in the telling of his story, Corporal Weis stretched his arms and asked, "May I stand?"

"Yes."

"May I have one more American cigarette?"

"Yes. You can have the whole damn pack if you finish this story in less than fifteen minutes. And remember this. If you're just stalling, I promise you, you'll be sorry."

The corporal stretched his arms and body, sat down, lighted the cigarette, and continued the story. "The Americans continued to fire at us, forcing us to return fire using our machine guns and mortars. If only they would have surrendered, they would be alive today. We had no option except to close in on them, even though our orders were to take prisoners. Then, they surprised us by putting heavy small arms fire at those of us between them and their primary trench, making us believe they were all going to make a run for it. As we prepared to stop them, they surprised us again by attacking in the opposite direction. By that I mean they attacked the center of our attacking force. It was a brilliant tactical move. If they got through our line they might have reached a nearby woods in a deep ravine which was, more or less, a hundred meters from their outpost position. We had to stop them, even though some of our fire might hit our own troops. Do you understand? If we fired at them we risked hitting our own troops, and if we did not fire they might escape. Five of them attacked the center of our line, and the other six or seven fired at us in support of the ones attacking. The five almost made it to the woods, coming as close as perhaps twenty meters. It was a daring, calculated maneuver which almost worked. They attacked a larger force and almost succeeded. Had they reached the woods we would not have got them out without great cost to our own men. They were very brave and smart men, and most certainly we had underestimated them. Their attack was bold, well conceived. These Americans were well trained and they knew the terrain very well. We were forced to assume a defensive position and had to use our mortars to stop them as we were reluctant to use our machine guns, for fear of hitting our own men. The fight was over in less than twenty minutes, from the time they charged our lines until they were brought down. At that we only killed the five men who attacked. The others, the men who remained in the outpost, got away." Hans hesitated in his description of the fight. He sighed and then said, "They died good soldiers, those five who attacked us."

The major was overwhelmed by the personal narrative, by the exact details, but he tried not to reveal it to the German corporal. Likewise, the major was fascinated by the corporal's expressed admiration for the American soldiers. The major carefully calculated his words before he responded. "I thought for a minute you were going to tell me something new. We already knew about this. It's in our records. What I want to know is, if it was as you said, why didn't they surrender? Did you tell them they could? Or, did you Huns just kill them for the sport of it?"

The major's comment sparked indignation from the corporal. "I'm in no position to say this, but I resent that comment. We Germans admire bravery in soldiers, regardless of their allegiance. We Germans do not kill for the sport of it anymore than Americans do. They were given the chance to surrender three separate times; and I know this for sure, as I am the one who communicated with them, in English. We told them they were surrounded and had no chance of escape. The third time I spoke to them someone yelled back and asked for time to talk it over. We granted them five minutes, and when the time elapsed, they said no; and that is when they opened fire on us. They were good soldiers and we did not want to kill them. I told you we wanted to take them prisoners, not kill them."

"Well you did kill them, and I'm not sure I believe your version of the story. Besides, we know this stuff, anyway. We know they were good soldiers, and we know that they died fighting Germans."

"I know that you are angry, and I guess I do not blame you; but you should be proud of the men instead of angry at me." Hans pointed to a medal on his uniform. This is an Iron Cross of the second class awarded to me by the fatherland for my participation in the battle that day at La Sadey. All of us there on that day, all of us who survived that is, were awarded one. I assure you that our Army does not award Iron Crosses for just anything, and most certainly not for random killing." Corporal Hans Weis sat erect in his chair, looked away from the major and tried to regain his composure. The major maintained eye contact with the prisoner as he shifted his sitting position, but he said nothing. The two guards remained in position, although their facial expressions revealed their interest in hearing the rest of the story. There was a long silence.

The prisoner broke the silence by clearing his throat. "You need to know the rest of the event, and I, probably for my own purposes, need to tell. Do you want me to continue?"

"Continue, but get to the point, be specific."

"First of all, it is most important for me to say, I apologize, rather we apologize for the manner in which the young soldier died. Our entire company watched as he fought to his death. Will you please tell your commander that we regret his manner of death, and that we had no other alternative."

"Explain yourself."

"I'm talking about the bullet to the head while the young soldier, the one who led the attack, was in captivity. Once he had his hand on the pistol we had no choice, whatsoever."

"Explain yourself."

In wonderment, the corporal looked across the table at the major and the major stared intently at the German prisoner. "You really do not know how that soldier died, do you? We left the American bodies positioned exactly as they were. We even left the pistol in his hand so you would know what happened. We paid tribute the only way we knew how to pay tribute to those brave soldiers, by leaving everything as it was for you to discover, and you did not even know it."

"Of course we know what happened. It is written down in our records. I just don't have the files in front of me. Explain yourself, and I will cross-check it with our records; and then I will know how honorable you really are. Remember, the truth is rewarded, and lies are punished."

"At this point in the war, major, I do not care about rewards and punishments. Life, honor, truth, family, home, are the important things. I do not care how you threaten me. As you said, the war is over for me. Do you want to hear the truth, or not?"

The corporal's words, the words describing what he believed to be important, hit very close to home for the American interrogator. In fact, the major agreed with the corporal's philosophy, as to what was important. The corporal had spoken to the very heart and soul of civilized man. He spoke to the very essence of what used to be important issues for the major— important not in the military sense, but in the scope of humanitarian values. This prisoner's assessment of what was important made the major realize that he had become so concerned with military issues that he had temporarily forgotten the real issues of life. Instead of answering the corporal, he pondered his words and their meaning. He wondered why it took a simple statement from a German prisoner of war to remind him of what he, also, believed to be important. He wondered if he personally had been so affected by a few months of war, what was the effect on others after four years of war? He wondered what he would be like after the war. Can war change man that much, and if so, what price man will pay for this war. He temporarily forgot about the interrogation, rather he indulged in introspection. For almost fifteen minutes the major sat in his chair, looking at the corporal, thinking about life, honor, truth, family, and home. Finally, he broke his silence. "I would appreciate it very much if you would share with me what you believe to be the truth. Tell me what happened."

Just as the major had engaged in reflection, so had the corporal. He had time to organize his thoughts and an opportunity to think about what might have been. "I will tell you, major, because I want you to know. I will tell you, not out of pride in our actions, but out of admiration for the brave soldiers that died. Do you remember I told you that we were ordered to take American prisoners, so we could find out about their training and what kind of soldiers they would be? We needed to find out about this new foe we were fighting. Let me tell you, we took no prisoners, but we found out what we needed to know about the American soldier. The American soldier is a good soldier, a formidable foe. Major, if only we could have fought you four years ago, when we were fresh and the war was new. Had it been that way I would not be sitting here now talking to you. Instead, I would have met you on the field of battle, not as a worn out soldier, but as a young, fit warrior fighting for the fatherland. Unfortunately, as we all know, that is not the way it happened, and here I sit."

"I still don't understand what you are talking about. Do you admire them because they refused to surrender and chose to fight you? Or is it something else?"

"We admired them because they were brave warriors in the face of certain death. We admired them because of the manner in which they died. We admired them because they were not cowboys, they were soldiers. As I said earlier, you Americans are hard to understand. This is not your war, but you believe it is, and you fight with everything you have. You fight to win as though your country would be destroyed if you lost. We do not care about your country. We care about our homeland, our life. My home is less than one hundred kilometers from where we sit, and there I have a wife and a child. We used to own a small bakery, and we had a good life. Now, I do not know how things are at home. Do you understand me? I do not know how things are at home, but I do know this much. If we lose this war, my life will be different. You fight for a cause which I do not even understand. I fight for the fatherland, my family, and my way of life. I do not understand you Americans."

"I really believe I could answer your questions if we had the time, but we don't have the time, and I have much to do. So if you have no more specifics about La Sadey, I will be on my way."

"I have a final note to my story. I am talking about the bullet to the head of the lead soldier, the one who got the pistol. Have you forgotten already?"

The major had forgotten. He had become preoccupied with his own personal thoughts and too tired to conduct a proper interview, but now, he had no choice. His answer to the question was a softly spoken, "Please continue."

"I told you that five Americans attacked the center of our line and we were forced to use mortars against them. During the attack the remaining Americans in the outpost managed to retreat to their primary trench, and thus they escaped us. However, our mortars brought down the five attackers. We secured the outpost, set up our defensive positions, and checked to make certain that all five were dead. We found four dead and one alive. The soldier alive was the young soldier who led the attack. He was wounded, groggy, but alive. He had suffered various wounds to the body and a concussion to the head. Our medical man stopped some bleeding in the leg, checked him over, and we prepared to take him back to our line. He was a young, robust soldier, a private, with green eyes and dark hair. When I first saw him he was gritting his teeth, indicating he was in a lot of pain. Two of our soldiers were helping him to his feet and three other soldiers were standing nearby to help with his evacuation. I was one of the soldiers standing nearby. We had no stretcher so we were going to carry him. When we got the American to his feet, he looked around as though he was surveying his situation, and then he saw the dead bodies of his comrades. His expression changed from showing pain to showing anger. It was then he made his move. Somehow the American was still strong enough to take an automatic Steyr from an unfastened holster of one of the men helping him. The American, and believe me it occurred within the blink of an eye, shot and killed the two men who were helping him up. I and the other two men grabbed and struggled with the American for control of the Steyr in his possession. During the struggle the American shot another soldier before the remaining two of us finally managed to get the gun under the American's chin. It was now strength against strength, his strength against our combined strength. We prevailed and it was my finger pressing on his finger which caused the pistol to fire a final shot. The fired bullet entered through the chin into the head of the American. As far as I know there was no bullet exit wound, but there was no doubt that the American was dead. He fell limp to the ground, face up. This all happened within a few brief seconds, in fact, before the others could arrive to assist us. The American had fired the Steyr pistol five times killing two of our soldiers, and wounding two more before the bullet went into his head. After the first shot was fired everyone in the field observed the struggle. There we stood, over thirty of us, looking into the face of this fallen, courageous American soldier who led the attack and who refused to be taken prisoner. We lost over twenty good German soldiers that day but it was the dead American we all were watching. I will forever remember that moment in time."

"How do you remember that kind of detail, even to the color of his eyes?"

"I will never forget the detail. I will never forget his eyes. Remember, major, I was the soldier struggling with him to get the pistol. It was my hand over his hand when the pistol fired the last time. I was the one responsible for his death. It all happened so fast. During the struggle the American, although seriously wounded, was still so very strong, so agile, so quick, and so angry. For a brief second, during the struggle, our eyes met and I saw into his soul. I didn't know the man, but I feel as though I did know him. I believe his anger was caused, not because we had wounded and captured him, but because we had killed his comrades. I know he was angry at me because I was part of the force responsible for the death of his comrades. I saw it in his green eyes. When he fell dead and landed on his back with his eyes still opened he was still looking at me. His expression was still the same. I will never forget the face and the eyes of that young American soldier."

"What happened next?"

"Our company captain arrived and we described the incident to him. At our urging, the captain ordered the site to remain as it was so the American Army could see what occurred that day. Then we went back to our trenches and prepared for the inevitable counterattack. We did not go back with prisoners, but we went back with knowledge of the American Army. Later that night we collected the bodies of our dead comrades under the cover of darkness, as did the Americans. As you know, the American counterattack came at dawn the next day. We offered token resistance, and then retreated. There was nothing more to do, since we had determined the information we had been sent for.

"That is the end of my story. Now you know why I felt obliged to tell you. In my judgment, the action by the American soldiers in the outpost was the bravest I have seen in this war. I will never forget the battle at La Sadey."

"Thank you, Hans. Here are your cigarettes, as promised. I will make sure the 5th Division Command knows the details as you described them. By any chance, did you look at his identification tags? Do you know the name of the American who led the counterattack?"

"No, I do not know the name. I remember his face, but no name. I just think of him as the young, brave American soldier."

The interrogation ended at 10:15 that morning. Corporal Hans Weis was given breakfast and escorted to the holding pen for German prisoners of war, and the next day he was sent to Claumont, France, headquarters of the A.E.F., for additional interrogation. Major Johnson spent the remainder of the morning finishing his written report of his interrogations. After completing the report he went to G.2. Headquarters to examine the intelligence report of the military activity at La Sadey. He read and studied the brief report about La Sadey. The report made no reference to enemy engagement near the outpost. Five Americans were listed as killed in action by enemy artillery.

The German prisoner's description of the military engagement at La Sadey generally coincided with the written American report of that battle with one major difference—the American records made no mention of the outpost. However, there were other missing pieces to the puzzle. There was no description of the retreat from the primary trench, or explanation of the lapse of a full day before the counterattack. There was no reference to the attack on the Germans by the men in the outpost, although American bodies were found in the position described by the corporal. There were many details missing, and it was clear to the major that the military report on La Sadey was careless paper work, poor intelligence work. The German story was undoubtedly true and had gone unnoticed, at least not noted by the proper American authorities. Conversely, it was also true that these past events at La Sadey were of little military value in preparing for the Frapelle Offensive. The major's personal dilemma—should he pursue making the proper authorities aware of the event, or simply, write his report and file it?

Major Johnson departed G.2. Headquarters for General Headquarters thinking about the events of his recent discovery. He walked toward the center of town and arrived at the banks of the Muerthe River in the center of Saint Die in less than twenty minutes. He could not help but notice the natural beauty of the area, perhaps the most beautiful countryside he had ever observed. He walked without haste and paused as he passed the clearly marked exit to the Saint Die cemetery which he could see situated high on the large hill. In early July he had walked through the cemetery and was familiar with its surroundings, and its history. Now the cemetery took on a different meaning as he wondered how many American boys would die and be buried in this area. There was no doubt that his recent debriefing of the corporal had affected his state of mind. For the first time, Major Johnson thought of the war in personal terms of life and death of individuals. His professional, impersonal approach to the war had ended.

Major Johnson walked beside the banks of the river until he reached Rue Des Trois Villes; and then he walked the cobblestone sidewalks to the center of town near Rue Thiers where he sat on a public bench, close to the shallow river, and watched the early afternoon activities in the town of Saint Die. He was fatigued, but not sleepy. His mind was too alive with new thoughts to sleep.

The town appeared busy, active with people, but not crowded. Major Johnson noticed something unusual—the people he observed were women, older men, and children. How strange it was to observe so many women, some operating businesses, and some shopping, carrying their netlike bags filled mostly with fresh baked bread and food, while the town was void of their men. He also noticed the absence of laughter and frivolity although the people were friendly and polite. He speculated that the war had taken its personal toll on the citizens of this town, although the people did not openly show it. This all made him think of what the German had said about the importance of safety and home. The major wondered what life at home was like for his family. It was almost as though every new sight sparked new thoughts and new uncertainties. Answers to his mental queries seemed illusive.

Major Johnson also observed many American soldiers passing by as they efficiently attended the many tasks necessary for an army preparing for battle. In preparation for the upcoming offensive the town was full of American military personnel. Looking at the individual faces of the soldiers reminded the major that waging war required the efforts of many, and he conjectured that many of these men would soon be engaged in battle, and their survival, in some small way, might depend on his gathering of accurate information. Suddenly his military responsibilities took on a new personal importance—the importance of life. The faces of young and eager soldiers very much made him think of the soldiers who died in the outpost. His thoughts about the limits of his responsibilities were jumbled and lacked clarity. For longer than one hour he remained seated on the bench deliberating about his responsibility to the living soldiers to prepare data for the Frapelle Offensive, versus his responsibility to the dead soldiers to reveal the true story of their fate. Eventually Major Johnson made a decision—he needed to tell the La Sadey story, or at least to personally make the story known to the higher command.

The major gathered his written reports and with deliberate speed he personally delivered them to the office of Colonel Parsons, the Assistant Chief of Staff for G.2., the Intelligence Section of the Fifth Division. Personal delivery of reports was out of the ordinary, a bold move for the major, bordering on violating the chain of command protocol. Arriving at the office in less than five minutes, he was met by the aide to the colonel. The major spoke with a tone of authority. "I need to personally speak with the colonel."

The aide looked surprised. "The colonel is busy right now. How urgent is your need to speak with him?"

Although it should not have, the question caught the major off guard. He hesitated and then responded. "I consider it most important, not urgent. I would not be here if it were otherwise. May I speak with the colonel?"

"I will check with Colonel Parsons, please take a seat." The aide went into the colonel's office and the major remained where he stood. In less than a minute the aide returned and offered the words the major wanted to hear. "The colonel will see you."

The major entered the office and found Colonel Parsons sitting at his desk, writing. After the military formalities the major had the colonel's full attention and he wasted no time in presenting his report and explaining the purpose of his visit. He presented the colonel with a detailed explanation of the German's story concerning the outpost and the counterattack. He then presented the previous military files of the event, pointing out the discrepancies in the report. Colonel Parsons gave no direct response so, without hesitation, Major Johnson walked to the posted wall map of the Saint Die Sector, used the colonel's pointer, and said, "Sir, if you look at the map, I think the whole thing begins to make sense."

The major glanced to see if the colonel were interested in what he was saying, or disturbed with him for saying it. The colonel sat expressionless, so he continued. "If you observe, La Sadey is the extreme position of our trenches protecting the Bonhomme Pass, which grants access to the city of Saint Die and other vital positions. La Sadey, itself, has no strategic value whatsoever, other than it is the end point of our trenches. The mountains there are nonpassable, and they are patrolled, but not usable for troop movement. Even if the Germans secured La Sadey, it would be of no value to them because there is only one way in and one way out on this narrow dirt road. We could easily block any attack from that direction. In short there is no reason for the Germans to attack La Sadey, other than harassment. Yet, on the 21st of June, the Germans attacked that area with two full companies.

"Now look here at La Croix-Aux-Mines, the very center of our trenches and the strongest part of our line. It was here that German artillery pounded us for eight hours, and we assumed this was to be the location of their attack, which it was, sort of. French artillery returned fire and we moved in our reserves and prepared for the worst, but it never came. The Germans made a few feeble attacks along the center of the line and they retreated. It was all a diversion. For some reason we never figured it out. Our intelligence estimated the Germans only had eighteen casualties with no deaths in the entire two day operation at the center of the lines, and yet, at La Sadey we estimated they suffered forty casualties including twenty-seven killed."

The colonel appeared agitated. "I have not heard of any fighting at La Sadey. Are you positive you have correct details?"

"Yes, sir, I do. The name La Sadey also threw me in the beginning, and here is why. German maps refer to the area as the La Sadey sector, the French identify it as the Violu sector, and we call it La Cude. At first I couldn't even find a report until I looked at all sector maps and found what I needed in the La Cude file." In response the colonel smiled, shook his head, but said nothing.

Major Johnson paused in his presentation long enough to take a deep breath. "I admire those ten men in the outpost. Acting on their own initiative they counter-attacked and deprived the enemy of its objective. I doubt if they even knew how successful they were. They did more than stand against the enemy, they shaped the German's image of the American fighting man. That particular thought is not from me, but from the German prisoner. Imagine the psychological effect on the enemy. We can't begin to measure that. I can't forget how that German held these men in such high regard. As you can tell, colonel, I consider the firefight that day to be significant and I believe our men engaged in heroic action. Yes, sir, I think the German prisoner had it right."

The colonel listened intently, not saying anything until after the major concluded his final thoughts. "Major, you present your case well. I get your point and understand exactly what you are saying; and I appreciate your initiative in figuring out the sequence of events. In fact, you're probably correct in your assessment. But, I don't understand why you're telling me this now. Do I need to tell you how important our intelligence gathering work is for the next few days. We've got a full division preparing for our first offensive in this area, and thousands of American soldiers are depending on us to supply them with useful information. Thus, we need to be gathering useful information for the offensive, preparing for the future, and not gathering information about what happened two months ago. Why don't you wait until the offensive is over, and then deal with this? What's the urgency?"

Colonel Parsons had asked the very question that had concerned the major—the question of time allocation and responsibility. The major gave no immediate response. Rather, he appeared to stare at the map on the wall.

"Major, do you have an answer?"

"When you phrase it that way I don't know what to say. I understand how important this operation is, but I also understand how important truth is. The major then looked directly into the eyes of his superior. Moving toward the desk he gave an impassioned plea. "Sir, it greatly bothers me that this event went unnoticed by us. After this offensive, I suspect there will be another offensive, and another, and by then we will be too busy to deal with it, just as we are now. Sir, the urgency is, those soldiers, the ones who died in that outpost, deserve better. Besides, after this offensive, neither one of us may be here to set the record straight."

The colonel was touched by the uncommon display of emotion for the fallen soldiers from his major. He deliberated briefly, and then said, "This is personal, isn't it?"

"Yes, sir, I suppose it is. I did not know any of the men, although I would like to have known each one of them, individually. Sir, I believe when we send American boys to their deaths in some remote battlefield, we owe them. We owe the truth to their families. In that sense, I suppose it is very personal."

"You look exhausted, major. How long since you slept?"

"Twenty-nine hours, sir."

"How many more remaining prisoners do you have to debrief?"

"None, sir. Or at least none when I left the station late this morning."

"These are your orders. Immediately, you are to get some sleep. Then study the reports concerning the La Sadey, La Cude incident. Locate the C.O. of Company L., 61st. Regiment, and explain your theory to him. Have him assign you a squad of men to accompany you, and you get out to La Sadey, reconstruct the battle, and determine the facts. Attempt to identify the men in the outpost who made it safely back. Put your theory to the test. If everything rings true, we will modify the records, at least as much as we can modify them, and give the soldiers some kind of recognition. Does that satisfy you?"

"Yes, sir."

"You do understand that we are just beginning to fight this war and events like La Sadey are going to happen many more times, over and over. Unfortunately, that is the nature of war. We can't prevent them, and we can't know the details about each and every one of them."

"Yes, sir, I clearly understand that."

"I want a written report on my desk by tomorrow night. That is all the time we can spare. Do you understand?"

"Yes, sir, thank you, sir."

"One other item. You do know that General Pershing, himself, recently gave a directive that no medals or citations are to be awarded unless the event in question was directly observed by an American officer at the time? Since this event went unobserved at the time, there will be no medals awarded. Are you all right with this?"

"Yes, sir. I want the families, and other soldiers in the 61st., to know what happened. No need for medals."

"I will read your report tomorrow night. If you can verify these events, to my satisfaction, I will write letters to the families myself. I will make sure that every man in the 61st. knows what happened, and I will do it before the offensive, because, in your words, I may not be here afterwards. Now, will you get out of my office?"

"Yes, sir."

CHAPTER 2

MOTHER IS AWAY

George sat on the oak-board porch swing patiently waiting for Mary, his wife of fifteen years. The wraparound elongated porch, covering three sides of the house, created an illusion of largeness to the modest, five-room white, frame house which was situated on the northwest corner lot of Milton. The air temperature was still much too cool to sit on the porch, especially at this early hour, but George was tolerant of the frigid air. From the open porch he surveyed his surroundings and his possessions. If he glanced to the right from where he sat, he could see the small barnyard, the outbuildings, and most of the one hundred sixty acres where he worked as a farmhand. If he looked straight ahead he viewed his beloved Milton, a place where George had lived most of his adult life. Here, in Milton, he intended to live the remaining years of his life. Near here, in the Montezuma Cemetery, he intended to spend eternity. George had been a pioneer to Pike County and now his roots were deep and clearly established. The small town of Milton had a proud history, and George and Mary McCullah were a part of that history.

The bay horse was hitched to the buggy, the house was in order, and preparations for the trip were complete. George and Mary had worked since 3:30 a.m. completing the morning farmyard chores, anticipating the Sunday visit to Mary's brother and family. This was a sad day as Mary was burdened with the responsibility of delivering tragic news to Erastus, her younger brother. George realized the magnitude of the tragedy, and he sensed the probable impending change in his and Mary's life, but he knew he had few options, and most of all, he wanted to support Mary in her time of sorrow. Both he and his wife were overwhelmed with a compassionate sense of helplessness.

George patiently continued to wait on the swing.

At 5:20 a.m. Mary emerged from the front door of the house and George could sense she was with purpose. She spotted George on the swing and almost impetuously said, "Let's go. I want to get this over with."

George quickly took heed, recognizing this tone and behavior were uncharacteristic of Mary. Swiftly moving from the swing, he took Mary by the arm, walked with her, and assisted her into the buggy. Mary had tears in her eyes. After Mary was seated and ready to go, George gave a final glance at the homestead confirming everything was in order before their departure. They started their journey in silence. It hurt George to see Mary emotionally distraught. He lacked the words to ease her pain. He lacked the wisdom to identify the deeds which heal. Instead, he was vigilant, available, and supportive of her decisions. George thought Mary to be the kindest and most sensitive person he had known. But he also knew that, beneath her sensitivity, she was a strong woman hardened by time and experience. He knew she would endure. So George remained silent, a proven course of action in turbulent times. He reasoned that if Mary wanted to talk, she would. If Mary needed help, she would ask. He waited for her inner strength to emerge, as he knew, eventually, it would.

George, age 64, and Mary, age 51, were married later in life than most people of that time. By any standard they had a successful marriage, due in large part to their maturity. Their life had never been easy and past experiences had taught them to appreciate what they did have. They were tolerant of other people and accepting of each other. Each made a deliberate effort to make life better for the other. April, 1903, their marriage would be put to the test.

Upon leaving Milton, George and Mary immediately approached the most dangerous part of their journey. Still partially dark, travel would not be easy, as the roads were not totally dry; and the spring thaw had been most destructive of the road surfaces. It was unwise to travel without daylight but they needed an early start to what promised to be a long day. George needed to concentrate, to be aware of hazards and to be alert to danger, and that was fine with him. For George, concentration was easier than discussion. Previous knowledge of the road and terrain increased his travel confidence, just as poor personal communication skills discouraged conversation. To reach Alsey they would travel five miles to Montezuma, ferry across the Illinois River, and pass through Glasgow. The total trip was about fifteen miles distance or two hours time, if things proceeded according to plan.

Eventually, Mary broke the silence. She spoke without looking at George, continuing to stare toward the woods, as though she were thinking aloud rather than communicating thoughts. With a soft, mellow voice Mary remarked, "This is such a beautiful time of the year when the earth seems to come alive. The grass is as green as it can be. The redbud trees outline the woods. Blooms from the wild fruit trees give color, dimension, and depth to the forest, as the blooms from the hickory trees reach for the sky. What a magnificent sight! Do you see that when you look at the forest, George, or am I just a silly old woman looking for some beauty in this harsh world?" Without giving George time to answer, her voice firmed, echoing frustration as she continued. "This is such a hard land. It is so hard to make a living here. It is hard to endure the elements. No doubt that life here is hard. It is a hard place to be a child and equally hard to be an adult. How can one area produce so much beauty, so much suffering, so much love, so much misery? This whole world, in all its grandeur, makes little sense to me." Mary briefly paused in her speaking. She then asked with a desperate tone of voice, "What am I going to say to Erastus and the family?" Her voice stiffened as she pleaded, "Help me, George, what am I going to say? What do I tell my brother? How will their family deal with this? What will become of the children? Oh my God, what about the children?"

Tears flowed down Mary's cheeks and George could hear the silence created by the absence of any answers to Mary's questions. Continuing their trek down the damp, winding, sunken road to the river, silence prevailed, aside from the sound of the horse's hooves pounding the moist, softened surface of the dirt road. Although comforting words were needed, none were given.

George had perceived it was time to render assistance; but he could not find the words. He felt inadequate. He possessed physical and emotional strength, but he had no words. He knew no way to ease the suffering which was consuming his dear wife. So, he did not break the silence, he offered no comforting words. Although George also hurt and felt the pain created by the situation, he did not convey his feelings. They continued the journey, neither offering encouraging words to the other.

After a brief lapse of time, which seemed like hours to George, he responded. "I don't know what to say to you, Mary. As you know I am not the best with words, but you are. When the time comes you will reach into your heart and find the perfect words, as I have seen you do hundreds of times. Just tell them what happened. Assure them they are loved. Tell them we will help."

Without turning her head toward George, Mary wiped away the tears and spoke. "You are wrong, George. You are good with words, and your advice is correct. I must tell them exactly what happened and not attempt to explain the meaning of it all. You are right. Each of them must be told and allowed to grieve in his own way. It is in the future that I must be strong and willing to help. What I do in the future is far more important than what I say today. Thank you, George."

George felt dismayed. "You are welcome, although I don't know what I said."

Mary's thinking was becoming clearer. Her thoughts were no longer disjointed, and emotion was yielding to reason. Her mood rendered reflective thought.

The gently sloped road became muddier as they neared the river. The air was dry but you could feel the emerging humidity as the sun sucked the moisture from the wet ground. The horse and driver both became apprehensive as the road lost its crown and the ditches ate away the sides of the road. The tension was relieved as the horse and buggy rounded the last curve and George could see the bottomland was not under water. Minutes later George lost all remaining anxiety when he heard the groans of the steam engine that powered the ferry. He assumed the ferry must be operating, and, therefore, the river crossing was possible. He looked toward Mary, and with assuring relief in his voice, he said "Mary, it looks like we will be able to cross the river. It looks promising."

Offering no comment Mary continued to stare at whatever was situated on her right. Her contemplative silence continued.

Near the water's edge stood an elevated, two-story, stone building, which housed the John Mills family. John Mills was the owner and the operator of the ferry. A single lower room of the building was used for ferry business and also served as a small general store for both travelers and inhabitants of Montezuma. People, often gathering near the building to visit, described this location as the social center of Montezuma. Access to the building and ferry landing was across a man-made, elevated, narrow strip of land which connected the village and the landing site. George spotted the entrance to the strip of land, but saw no people. Squinting and shading his eyes, he looked for John or a glimpse of the ferry, and he could see neither. Twisting in his seat, looking around the town for signs of activity, he saw none. Trying to understand the lack of activity, he wondered if it were still too early, or worse, if something were wrong. George became concerned, first about the ferry, and then about the residents.

George yelled, "John, John!" and he got no response. At the top of his lungs he yelled "John," and five people emerged from the front of the stone building, two people appeared on the street, and dogs started barking. George felt foolish.

"Quiet, George, you will wake the whole town!" Mary said as she broke her silence and finally looked directly at George. She did not want to attract attention. Just as she spoke she saw the movement of people and quietly said, "Never mind now, it's already too late."

John stepped to the front of the five men, looked at George, and at the top of his voice yelled, "George." The tension was broken as the five men burst into laughter and the dogs barked again. Even Mary had a slight smile on her face as George looked embarrassed; and now he stared into the distance. "What exactly do you want, George?" John said in a more normal voice, but still with a smile on his face. "I thought maybe someone had died the way you said my name." The comment from John immediately sobered the expression on Mary's face, and this fact did not go unnoticed by all within sight of Mary. All were aware of the circumstances and no one knew what to say, so no one said anything. Each of the five men pretended to engage in some essential activity, rather than dealing with the awkward situation created by John's words. George drove the buggy to the landing site, and Mary rode in silence, looking off to her right.

"Where is the ferry?" George asked upon arrival. "Is it running or is the river too high?"

John, embarrassed by his earlier comment, meekly responded, "No, it will be running shortly. We just fired up the boiler a couple of hours ago. Today is the first operation of the ferry since the flood. I sent little John across to check out the cables and the landing site. If everything is okay, we will bring him back in a few minutes, and then we will have you on your way." No more words were spoken, and John, after looking across the river for a few minutes, went over and stood by the boiler.

Additional people were beginning to gather at the landing, giving the site a more normal appearance. Apprehension abated for George. George slowly got out of the buggy, made a few stretching motions, and said to Mary, "I am going to stretch my legs. Do you want to stretch?" Mary did not answer, but moved her head in such a way that George assumed a negative response. In an effort to divert her attention, George commented, "Look at the mud in that water! You know that is someone's topsoil on the way to the Gulf. It is too bad I can't pull it out and use it here. I know a few farms that could use that rich soil." His attempt at diversion failed. Mary never responded, and George, still feeling inadequate, just watched the sadness in Mary's face, seemingly unable to do or say anything to relieve the sorrow. George slowly walked the bank of the river and generally moved toward the location of John.

John watched George walk toward him, and he glanced to confirm the location of Mary. Once John determined that Mary was out of hearing range, he moved to meet George, and when he was close enough to whisper, he said, "I am so sorry that I made that remark in front of Mary. I spoke without thinking, and I am ashamed of myself. What can I do to make amends?"

John's apology was indicative of small town awareness and sensitivity, and apparently, the residents of Montezuma already knew the details of the recent tragedy.

Briefly hesitating, George answered. "There is nothing you can do or should do. You did nothing wrong. The problem is that everyone knows about Mary Dosia except the ones who need to know. That is where we are headed now, to tell the family. You would think in this day and age of telegraphs, telephones, railroads, and all the modern wonders, that we would not be so isolated, and this would not be such a problem. But, it is a problem. The timing is wrong." John did not understand this last comment about timing, but he continued listening to

George. "I guess that is the price we pay for living where we do. Yes, we pay that price and many other prices too." George rambled and continued to talk without his usual presence of clarity, as he jumped from topic to topic. It was most evident to John that his friend George, also, was deeply affected by the death.

Little John gave the signal and the ferry was brought back to the landing. George paid the twenty-five cents fee before he and Mary boarded the ferry. The buggy was firmly anchored on the ferry as George stroked the bay horse. George, Mary, and two other people crossed the Illinois River to the east side. They were now in Scott County and one third of the distance to Alsey.

The friends and acquaintances on the west side of the river watched the crossing, watched the getting ashore, and watched until George and Mary were out of sight. When John could no longer see the buggy, he remarked, "Today will be a sad day in Alsey." He then went about his business.

George and Mary continued their journey. George started to think of the children and how the death would affect each of them. Much to his surprise, and more to his aggravation, he could not remember each child's name and age. In a mental effort to chronologically list the names, he apparently made a sound.

"What?" Mary rudely said in response to the unintended sound.

"Nothing."

"What do you mean nothing? I know you said something."

George reluctantly answered. "I guess some of my thoughts took on a sound. Don't you ever do that? Besides, I'm not used to it being this quiet. Usually you are talking and you can't hear my sounds. I think a man has a right to make a sound if he wants."

These unusual grumblings by George amused Mary and with a constrained smile she took his hand and said, "George, you make all the sounds you want. If all your thoughts are as strange as that sound, I am glad I do not know what you are thinking."

George was surprised by Mary's comment and he quickly responded. "My, my, you sure went from sad to flippant in a hurry. If you must know, I was thinking of the children, trying to remember the names and ages. Now, do you feel better?"

"George, I did not mean to hurt your feelings. Let me help you with the names and ages. It will help me too. Remember there were nine children and two have died."

George impatiently said, "I know that."

Mary continued, "Remember the oldest was Gussie, who died at age ten. Archie, who is about...nineteen. Hardin is...sixteen. Goldie is almost fifteen. The next was Roy who died at age four." Mary hesitated at this point, and then said, "Oh my brother's family has had its share of grief. My heart goes out to all of them. Those poor children!" Mary hesitated again and wiped her eyes. "Next in order is Sylvia, who will be nine this July. Jesse just turned seven. Elzie is three and Frieda is less than one year. Imagine, George, the predicament of my younger brother. He is forty-seven years old, seven children at home and two of them are small children; and now his wife is dead. What will he do?"

Shifting from helping George remember, Mary was now thinking out loud. "It seemed to me they were just getting on their feet with the recent move to Alsey. A nice three-bedroom house on land with plenty of space for garden and animals. Erastus has plenty of work and a barn for his mules. I remember when Jesse was born they lived in a two room log cabin in Pearl. Not enough room for a family there. They moved to Glasgow just before Elzie was born, and things started to get better. Now a nice house, a beautiful family, a little happiness, and then Mary Dosia dies."

With a doleful expression Mary remembered her perception of Mary Dosia. "I am really going to miss that woman. I am going to miss her smile, her warmth, and her compassion. She always helped anyone in need, and look where that got her. She was such a good person and came from such a good family. That poor lady was so attractive, so classy. She lived her married life without material things, and never complained. She and Erastus were such a good-looking couple. She was so proud of her children. The family meant everything to her." Suddenly Mary internalized her thinking and she almost felt guilty as she concentrated more on her personal loss than the loss felt by others. Mary held little doubt that the death of her sister-in-law would create a partial void in her life. Mary felt such self-centered thoughts were not proper, but she continued to think them. She also continued to feel guilty about it.

Approaching the outskirts of Glasgow and viewing the town as a whole, George was reminded of the small town similarity in west central Illinois. On a normal day this hour was the perfect time to arrive in town, just as the people were preparing for church. However, today was not a normal day. Mary, not anxious to visit, asked George not to stop if possible. Between the two of them they knew just about everyone in town, and probably everyone knew them. Those who were outside waved and shouted greetings but one family flagged them down and wanted to talk about the flood and its affect on Pike County. George was gracious but brief, Mary sat without saying a word, and they managed to exit the town without giving explanation for their presence in Scott County. Apparently, people on this side of the river were not yet aware of the tragedy. They would arrive at Alsey in just twenty minutes.

"Finish telling me about your brother's family," George requested.

"There is little more to say. You know as much as I do."

"What about Mary Dosia? She always looked so young to me."

"Well, George, she was young. You should know her age."

"Well, I don't!" George responded. "We have spent time with them, but I do not remember sharing personal information or asking for personal data. It seems to me that we always talked about the children or we listened to the personal philosophy of Erastus."

"That is not a nice thing to say, George. Shame on you!"

George smiled and said, "No shame on me. I just stated the truth."

"Well, if you must know, Mary Dosia would have been thirty-six this July. She married my brother March 21, 1881, when she was almost fourteen."

George somewhat shocked by Mary Dosia's age at marriage, but more shocked that he was not aware of the information, simply said, "Wow. Tell me some more."

Mary looked disapprovingly at George, and said, "No."

No more was said until they were within sight of her brother's house near Alsey. Distressingly Mary said, "Oh my, there they are." No more words needed to be said. Both Mary and George were consumed by thoughts of the tragic death, and the dilemma it would present for the family.

At a distance Mary and George could identify plenty of activity and movement at the house. Kids were playing in the front yard, two men were working in the garden, smoke rose from the kitchen chimney, and the animals strode about the barnyard. As they approached the house, they could identify Sylvia on the porch holding Frieda; and they determined the children in the front yard were Jesse and Elzie, playing kick-the-can. Jesse recognized them and ran to greet them. Elzie followed.

Jesse yelled out, "Hi, Aunt Mary. Hi, Uncle George. Have you come to give us a hug and to see Mom and Dad? Dad is in the garden and Mother is away."

Before anyone could answer Elzie said, "Hi, folks. Dad is mad about his potatoes."

Jesse said, "Oh, Elzie, what he means is we didn't get the potatoes planted on Good Friday and Dad is worried they won't grow right. You know Dad and his garden."

George started to ask about the garden but before anything else could be said, Jesse and Elzie were in the buggy hugging their aunt and uncle. Hearing the commotion, Goldie came from the kitchen, was joined by Sylvia who held baby Frieda, and they walked to greet Uncle George and Aunt Mary. Hugs and greetings were exchanged before Mary started to cry.

Jesse, visibly concerned, said, "What's wrong, Aunt Mary?"

Mary looked at Goldie and said, "I must see your father right away!"

"Dad and Hardin are working in the garden. I will get them immediately. Is there something we can help with?"

Mary snapped right back and said, "No! And don't go get them. I will go to them. You gather all the children and meet us on the front porch, but first I want to visit with your father. Is everyone here today?"

The tone of Aunt Mary's voice concerned all the children.

Goldie thought a minute and then answered Aunt Mary's question. "All but Arch and Mother. Arch has moved away from home and Mother is in Pearl, helping with a measles epidemic. She won't be back until the measles are gone and until she no longer is contagious. She may not be home for another two weeks." Pausing just long enough to breathe she continued, "Will you and Uncle George stay for dinner? We are having fried chicken, mashed potatoes and gravy, hominy, and some of Mother's canned beets. We got some sorghum to go on the biscuits, and Dad is going to make some ice cream later this afternoon. Will you stay, please?" Speaking with pride, she added, "I'm doing the cooking."

Aunt Mary looked at Goldie with a blank stare. Jumbled, tragic thoughts seemed to paralyze her ability to communicate. Uncle George sat motionless, trying not to establish eye contact with anyone.

Elzie put his hands in the air and yelled, "Please stay, please stay. Tell Goldie you'll eat with us."

Sensing the potential tragic impact of her news on this young family, was more than Mary could bear. Her heart hurt with grief and the sight of the children made it hurt more. Their mother was dead and none of the children even considered the possibility that something was so seriously wrong. From now on all their lives would be different and they had no inkling. The children remained naive, innocent, and wonderful, but George and Mary's visit today would soon change that. Her thoughts shifted from the family to herself. Mary wondered if, as the bearer of bad news, she would be held responsible for the ensuing sadness, or if they would be angry at her for bringing the news.

Mary's brief, self-centered thoughts were abruptly halted when Sylvia asked, "Aunt Mary, are you okay? Whatever is wrong, I promise you, that if you stay for dinner, everything will be fine." Looking out the corners of her eyes, and giving an impish smile, Sylvia continued, "Goldie is not as good in the kitchen as Mother is, but she is a decent cook."

Interrupting the conversation George took command. "Yes, we will stay for dinner. Now do as your aunt said. Gather everyone and wait on the porch. Mary, you go find your brother and I will stay with the kids.

As Mary scurried to talk with Erastus, Elzie looked at Uncle George. "Do you want to play kick-the-can? I'll be it."

Jesse chimed in and said, "Yeah, it's fun, come on, Uncle George!"

With a grateful smile for his potential inclusion in the game, and a heart full of love and sorrow, George replied, "I'll play with you after dinner. Now let's all go sit on the porch."

Once she arrived at the garden site Mary sent Hardin to join the other children while she and her brother talked. Mary and Erastus stood near the strawberry patch and visited for what seemed like an eternity to the children. Jesse peeked around the corner several times to see if he could determine what was taking so long. It appeared to him that Aunt Mary was doing all the talking and that his father was passive, just listening. Jesse kept everyone on the porch informed of his observations and George had difficulty keeping the children contained as, naturally, they were curious. They wanted to hear the conversation, too. Almost one hour later Aunt Mary walked to the front porch, but Erastus stayed in the same spot where he had stood while Aunt Mary was talking to him. He looked as though Aunt Mary was still talking to him or at least her words were still in the air and he was gradually absorbing them. Erastus looked different. He was standing in the garden, not working, just standing. His lean, muscular frame was slumped, as though a part of him hurt or as though the task in front of him was too great for him to bear. His father's behavior alarmed Jesse as he had never seen his father look or behave quite like this, and the young child sensed that something very important was very wrong.

Elzie started to move toward his father. Hardin picked him up and headed for a chair on the porch. Hardin looked directly into the eyes of Aunt Mary and said, "What's up, Aunt Mary?"

Without a word Uncle George got out of his chair, motioned for Mary to sit there, and moved his arms and hands indicating the children should sit around her. All followed the silent directions and, without words or disturbances, they patiently waited for Aunt Mary to speak. Momentarily Aunt Mary had tears in her eyes. Eventually she regained her composure, gently blew her nose, cleared her throat, and in her soft gentle voice she started to speak. "I want each of you to listen very carefully as I have some sad news for you. Your father should be telling you this news, but right now he can't and you have an urgent need to know."

Before Mary finished her last word, baby Frieda started to cry, and Sylvia rocked her to silence. No one said anything but it was almost as if Frieda was physically expressing the feeling for each of them—a feeling of apprehension and uncertainty.

Mary continued. "As each of you know, your mother left here two weeks ago to assist your friends across the river in Pearl. Pearl had a terrible German Measles epidemic and they needed help. Seven days after Mary Dosia arrived in Pearl she, herself, came down with the measles. Your mother became very ill, and I am so sorry to say this—your mother died one week ago today."

Almost to a child, each had the same reaction. A brief shock from the thought— Mother is dead—to a painful realization that she was dead. Grief consumed them. Almost as if they were functioning as a unit, they buried their heads in their hands and sobbed. No words were offered and no movement was attempted. Each child cried as though he were alone, totally unaware of his siblings' grief. Their loss was personal and there was no immediate comfort in knowing others were also suffering. Sylvia was the first to realize she was not suffering alone. Recognition of the obvious agony all around forced her to think about the plight of her family. With a seriousness of purpose and with a quivering voice, she looked directly at Aunt Mary and asked, "What is going to happen to us?" Sylvia's question demanded the attention of the other children, and they all looked to Aunt Mary for the answer.

Aunt Mary felt a sense of futility, almost impotence. She felt the need to offer guidance or direction, but she had none. She had no answers. Attempting to temporarily satisfy the children's need for assurance she decreed, "Everything will be all right. We'll make it." Without clear thinking Aunt Mary kept on offering assurances, until even she realized her expressions were meaningless. Aunt Mary did not know the answer to Sylvia's question of what was going to happen to them.

Uncle George spoke directly to Aunt Mary, but the children knew he was talking to them when he said, "Mary, there is more to tell and I think now is the time to tell it."

Heedful of the suggestion because it gave necessary direction, Mary continued with her sad news. "After your mother died she, of course, needed to be buried. The river was flooding, still cresting, and there was no way to get her body back home, and no way to communicate with you. The elders of Pearl decided to bury her on the Boone Slope of Green Pond Cemetery, beside four other adults who had died from the measles. Your mother is buried on a beautiful site in the Green Pond Cemetery. However, that is not all. That same night Pearl got a four-inch rain, on top of already saturated ground, and the temporary grave markers were washed away. Also, the coffins were disturbed, and because it was so wet no one checked the graves the next two days; and now no one remembers the order of burial. It's all so confusing. We don't know exactly where your mother's grave is. We know the area, we just don't know the exact grave. So, temporarily, your mother is in an unmarked grave."

Mary paused. She realized she should not have shared with the children, the details or the problems with the grave. She felt ashamed and insensitive. In an effort to compensate, she said, "The undertaker will work with your father to figure it out. As soon as they know, we will all go to the cemetery together, visit your mother, and pay our respects." Not one child verbally responded. The shock muted their voices, dulled their reactions. Mary continued speaking. "I'm sorry to bring you this news, but you needed to know, and you needed to know now. I had to tell you before you found out some other way. Hopefully, after your father has had a little time alone, he will do a better job of communicating with you than I have. God, I hope he does."

The combination news of the death and the mismanaged interment over-whelmed the children. Personal emotional reactions prevented the young minds from logically processing all the information, and not one of them gave a verbal response to Aunt Mary.

Mary added, "There is one other very important thing. You older children need to explain the circumstances of your mother's death to the younger children, either now or later. It is important that each child understands that your mother died a hero, helping other people to live. She gave her life helping those in need. There is no greater sacrifice. She will always be a hero in Pike County. She will always be in the hearts of the people of Pearl. She is a hero to us, and she will always remain in our hearts."

The children grieved individually. No one knew what to say or how to comfort the others, so no one said anything. The shock of the news seemed to force each child to withdraw to his inner self. Mary Dosia Moore, the mother of these six children, was dead. Nothing else seemed to matter. Their mother was not coming home, ever again.

Erastus did not join them for dinner. About midway into the meal the mood of mournfulness totally permeated the room, as all individuals eventually gave in to their feelings of despair, and conversation totally ceased. Each child quietly finished the meal and respectfully excused himself from the table. Sylvia took Frieda to the porch, Hardin took a walk, and Elzie followed Jesse outside. Aunt Mary offered to help Goldie clean the table and do the dishes, but Goldie insisted on doing it herself. Mary and George moved to the living room hoping others would join them, but no one did.

George whispered to Mary, "I think we should leave. Tell the children good-bye and assure them we will be there if they need us. Mary, I think the best we can do, as you said earlier, is to leave, and allow each child to grieve in his own way." George paused. "Maybe they will draw strength from each other."

"I suppose you are right. If we leave, I hope you are right."

Moving from the chair as he spoke, George said, "What about Erastus? Is he going to be all right?"

Remaining in her chair and displaying a reluctance to leave, Mary took an audible breath and said, "That is the real question, and I don't have a clue to the answer. I have not talked with him since this morning. I am very concerned about my brother."

George and Mary left the house that afternoon with little fanfare. The excitement and exuberance of their arrival was a memory, and the farewell by the children was a polite and gracious good-bye. After a two-hour journey home, Mary and George arrived in Milton before dark. It had been a long and sad day for both of them. They went to bed early, each thinking of Erastus and recalling memories of Mary Dosia, but mostly, they thought of their nieces and nephews.

The Moore household in Alsey was very quiet that night. Each child continued to grieve in his own way.

Erastus sat alone on the bench by the garden until after midnight.

Hardin took another walk and returned home at bedtime.

Goldie had washed and put away the dinner dishes and sat alone at the kitchen table for the remainder of the afternoon. There was no need for an evening meal.

Sylvia spent the rest of the day in the living room taking special care of baby Frieda.

Jesse went to the bedroom and sat on the side of his bed. He placed the tips of his fingers to the matching tips on the other hand and slowly moved his fingers to touch and then not to touch. He sat in the same position for hours, repeating that process, while thinking.

Elzie was everywhere. The unfortunate youth was confused and did not know what to think, as he had never seen his family like this. He was very much alone.

The Moore children seemed to draw from their individual inner strength, not from the strength of others. Each child went to bed early that night, unaware of the others, except that Frieda was with Sylvia and Elzie was with Jesse. Arch still did not know his mother had died.

The night passed, morning arrived. Although the Moore family was awake and active by dawn, the thoughts of the children were anything but usual. At this time, they simply did not know how to communicate with each other, although each wanted to communicate with the others. Hardin, Sylvia, and Jesse were attending to their morning chores. Everyone functioned independently and appeared to be oblivious to the others until breakfast. Withdrawing into themselves was their method of coping, until a better alternative presented itself.

Goldie was cooking in the kitchen plus attending to Frieda in the bassinet, while Elzie was dressing near the kitchen stove, trying to preserve his body heat and warm his clothes. Erastus was nowhere to be seen. The children suffered and continued to grieve alone, not because they chose to, but because they had to. They found no guidance, no direction.

Elzie was still awkward at dressing himself, and he knew help was available if necessary; but he also realized he should not ask for help on this particular morning. Elzie, at age three, understood he too needed to be strong. He was most proud he could tie his own shoes. Even at his early age he sensed the importance of independence and self-reliance. On this particular day Elzie wanted things to go right, just as he wanted to contribute to the process and make things be right. He kept thinking about his mother and wondering how she was. Although Elzie knew his mother was dead, he did not fully understand the concept of death. In his own limited way he tried to analyze death. He had no concept of afterlife, no concept of the difference between the physical and spiritual, and no concept of eternity. He had never seen a dead person nor observed the process of dying. Elzie knew his mother was alive in his mind, a fact that confused him even more. He assumed death was not good, because people did not want to die, and death made people sad. He hoped as he got older he could better understand things. Advanced for his age, he grasped the reality of the situation better than others recognized. He wondered how old you had to be before you understood everything. He felt so confused.

Respecting the wishes of his older brother to be alone, Elzie had only asked Jesse a few questions the previous night. He had wanted to ask more, but he thought it wise to wait. He believed, eventually, Jesse would be willing to visit with him. He desperately needed guidance from his siblings. Others had thought him asleep last night, but he was awake as his sisters talked. Elzie heard Goldie and Sylvia talking about a better place, some kind of lasting life, and Mother was going to live forever in a kingdom. These expressions had really baffled Elzie, and he needed to comprehend the thinking of the others. Elzie could endure, as deep inside, he knew he would understand everything as soon as he and Jesse could be alone, sometime today, probably in the hayloft of the barn, or on the porch swing. Because then, Jesse would explain it all, as Jesse always did.

Goldie clanged the bell which signaled breakfast was ready. Hardin was the first to come inside. By the time his hands were washed, everyone else was inside. Eventually, after the remaining children had cleansed, they assumed their designated places at the table and they started to eat, without discussion. Erastus' and Mary Dosia's chairs sat empty. Frieda, seated in her high chair, was between Sylvia's and Goldie's chairs instead of next to her mother's empty chair. Everyone noticed the change. Although the food tasted good, no one enjoyed the meal. They satisfied their physical need for food, without observing the traditional time of conversation. Finally Sylvia spoke, and with a sorrowful voice, said, "I believe the meal yesterday and this one today are the only meals I have ever eaten without either Mother or Dad. Where is Dad anyway?"

Hardin quickly answered. "The mules are fed and his chores are done. I was hoping he was inside. I don't know if he even came in last night. Has anyone talked to him or seen him this morning?"

No one gave an answer. Finally, Elzie said, "Not me, what about you, Jesse?" Jesse nodded his head in the negative, and immediately Elzie said, "What about you, Sylvia?"

Without looking at Elzie, Sylvia responded, "No, Elzie, no one has seen Dad. Now eat your breakfast."

"I was just trying to help," Elzie apologetically said. "Don't get mad at me."

All, having finished their breakfast silently remained at the table unsure of what to do next. Sadness and grief abruptly turned to uncertainty and insecurity. In a few minutes Goldie spoke. "Maybe Dad has gone to tell Arch, or maybe he is taking care of some important things. I know he will be back. I just don't know when. Whatever he is doing he probably is doing it for us. We must go on as though he was here. In the meantime we must be responsible and wait for him to return. He's hurting too, you know. Maybe he has to sort it out for himself. I know he will work out something. We should continue as I said. Do all of you agree?"

Everyone verbally agreed or nodded consent. Goldie started to clear the table, Hardin went outside, Sylvia left the room, and Jesse and Elzie stayed at the table. Almost in desperation·Elzie looked at Jesse and said, "What do we do?"

Jesse smiled at Elzie and said, "Come on, little brother. We are going to finish our chores and then play—maybe in the hayloft or maybe we will explore something."

Elzie jumped to his feet and said, "Oh boy, let's get the chores done."

Goldie smiled, recognizing that Jesse was heeding her advice. Jesse reached for Elzie's hand as they passed through the door heading for their adventure. Goldie watched them leave and said, "You boys have fun, and thank you, Jesse."

Elzie answered, "You're welcome."

It was Friday, five days later, before Erastus returned home. About midafternoon, while playing alone in the barnyard, Elzie saw his father in the barn. Erastus was sitting on the milking stool, rubbing down the mule harness, something he usually did on Sundays. Elzie screamed, "Dad's home, Dad's home!" Elzie was so excited he could not decide whether to fetch the others or go to his father. It made little difference as his loud screams alerted the others, and they all arrived at the barn about the same time. The children were relieved, crowding near their father, desperately trying to touch or hug him.

After a few minutes of joyful reunion Erastus said, "Let's all go to the kitchen and talk. We have some things to talk about." As they walked toward the house Erastus carried Elzie on his shoulders and held Jesse's hand.

Following behind, Goldie whispered to Sylvia, "I told you Dad would come up with something."

Hardin looked at his two younger sisters and said in an older, brotherly manner, "You better hear what he has to tell us before you celebrate."

Goldie poured ice tea as the others sat in their usual places around the table. Frieda started to cry and Sylvia comforted her, although Sylvia was beginning to wonder if Frieda had some intuitive ability to sense a crisis. Goldie said, "It is so good to have you home, Dad. We all are so relieved."

Elzie followed the statement with a joyous, "Me too!" and continued with,

"Where you been? I've been worried."

The comment broke the tension and all laughed. Elzie looking perplexed said, "What's so funny? I have been." That brought more laughter.

Erastus began to speak in a tone that created a renewed seriousness. "I know that all of you are distraught, and the last few days have been very difficult for each of you. Be assured, I miss her too. I don't know if we can make it without your mother, but we must try. She would want us to try." Erastus, eyes watering, managed to maintain his composure. Sensing his pain and observing the sensitivity of the others, Goldie reached for the hands of those next to her, and others followed her lead. Erastus deliberately kept his hands folded on the table, thus not completing the circle of holding hands.

Elzie commanded, "Dad, hold my hand." Erastus, keeping his hands immobile, refused to answer his youngest son, a gesture that did not endear him to the others.

In a firm, patriarchal style the father spoke. "Enough tears, enough weakness. We must be strong, stronger now than ever before. Hard as I try, I don't understand why your mother died. It makes no sense to me. She should be alive and here with us today, but she is not. And there is nothing we can do about it. Do you understand that? We cannot bring her back."

There were no outward responses from any of them, as it appeared that their father was speaking more to himself than to them. The room was silent enough to hear their breathing.

"At first I felt guilty that I was alive and she was dead. I kept looking for some explanation. I wanted to blame somebody so I blamed myself. However, I gradually did realize something; it was not my fault that she died, nor was it anyone's fault. There is no grand explanation, other than she got the measles and died. We have to accept it and get on with our lives. We cannot bring her back, so we must learn to live without her."

Erastus' acceptance of their mother's death bewildered the children. His tone was too final and his demeanor too abrupt. Hardin harshly responded, "Personally, I am not ready to accept her death, and I don't think the others are either. We are not ready to go on without her. We need more time."

Erastus retorted, "Well we don't have more time. We have got to deal with it, and deal with it now. In order to do that, we are going to make some changes, starting today."

Hardin interrupted by saying, "What changes?"

Erastus responded in a firm manner. "Just listen." Sylvia started to say something and before she could complete a full word, Erastus spoke in a harsher tone. "I said, just listen."

The conversation was creating tension, and the room was filling with apprehension. Erastus gained full control as the children were now intimidated. Erastus continued. "I spoke to Arch and he is not coming home, much to my displeasure. He says he is going to move to Alton, so we count him out. Three weeks ago our family was nine in number and now it is seven— three too small to help with much of the work. The house is too large and there is too much work to be done, and we can't handle it."

Jesse interrupted. "I can help with things and Elzie is getting bigger everyday."

"I asked you to listen. Listen until I finish, and then, we will talk." Jesse sank into his chair as Erastus continued. "Someone has to do the work around here; and since it will be necessary for Hardin to work with me, because it takes at least two of us to properly work the team of mules, there is not any one left to do the hard physical labor to keep this place going. We must move to a smaller place!"

Not one of the children had anticipated this line of thinking. This statement came as a shock, and they could not assemble their thoughts fast enough to either rebut or agree. They did not like the decision but they understood the decision was already made—their fate was determined. Thoughts turned to possible consequences and the children had many questions about how the move would personally affect them, but none dared to ask. The notion of living in a different house did not much bother them as they had no history of permanence. Each child had been born in a different location, and, in fact, Hardin remembered living in eight different houses. However, previous moves were proactive so as to capitalize on an opportunity, and this move seemed to be reactive. Also, they had never moved without Mother. They knew this move would be different.

Goldie, trying to control her anger, said, "Why didn't you confer with us before you made such decisions?"

Erastus, making no effort to control his anger, spoke in a loud and demanding voice. "I asked you not to interrupt. I am the father and I make the decisions." Erastus then paused and looked around the table to determine if there might be more challenges to his authority. There were none. Erastus was now empowered with full authority, granted by both his family position and lack of additional objections.

"So here is what we're going to do. We'll stay here until the garden is gone, sometime in October. Then we're going to find a different place to live, probably near Montezuma. All the family is across the river and I like Pike County better anyway. That is where my roots are. This is really your mother's house, she picked it out, and I just can't stay here without her." This comment about mother's house evoked additional resentment in the children, and Erastus perceived this resentment. After briefly hesitating, he continued. "I know you think me to be mean and selfish, but I think this is best for all of us. I'm not doing this for myself, I'm doing it for us." Almost as though he was attempting to convince himself as he talked, he became more adamant. "And, we are going to make more changes too. These changes are going to be harder and you have got to work with me on this. My mind is made-up, so no reason for any discussion."

Erastus shifted in his chair so that he was looking into the face of Hardin. Partially asking, he stated to Hardin, "You are almost seventeen now."

Hardin, temporarily restraining his anger, responded, "I will be in September."

"Good," Erastus said. "You are going to learn how to be a teamster, like your father. I always thought Arch would be the one to work with me, but since he is gone, it is going to be you. You were always good with the mules anyway. Yes sir, I am going to teach you everything I know and I am going to teach you right. We start tomorrow afternoon."

Shifting his position again to look directly at Goldie, he continued. "At fifteen you ought to be able to run the household like your mother taught you. Right?"

Goldie responded with a mild utterance. "I suppose, but..."

"Good," Erastus said, more to stop Goldie from talking than to give approval. "Sylvia, you are to take care of Frieda and assist Goldie around the house."

"Oh, Dad, I'm only eight and I can't do that; and besides, what about school? What about my life?"

Taking the high ground, Erastus responded. "We all must make sacrifices and do what needs to be done. This is not easy on any of us, but it has to be done."

Sylvia turned to Goldie and said, "I think I'm going to Alton with Archie."

"One more word like that and I am going to get a hickory switch and use it on you. Do you understand?"

Before Sylvia could answer, Hardin said, "She didn't mean it, Dad, she was just talking."

In the eyes of the children, the direction of this conversation was worsening. Their innocence departed the room and was replaced by insecurity and resentment. Hardin and Goldie realized their father was determined, uncompromising and nothing they said would change his mind. They had no choice. An atmosphere of doom and pessimism engulfed the kitchen. Although they were a family sitting together around the table, they did not feel like a family. Somehow each child had lost the emotion of grief and thoughts shifted to a focus of the self. Sylvia became disturbed, angry at her father for planning her life and angry at her mother for dying. Hardin became upset for not having a role in making the decisions, which were so abruptly imposed. Goldie was terrified of the responsibility she faced in her future. Jesse remained fearful of his uncertain future. Elzie did not understand all the implications, other than he knew something was very wrong. Baby Frieda continued to cry as if she sensed the uneasiness of the entire group. Erastus started to move from his chair, and Jesse, in a very uneasy voice, asked, "What do I have to do?"

Immediately Elzie followed with the words, "Yeah, what do I get to do?" Erastus did not answer either question. Gradually, all eyes focused on the father. Silence ensued and unasked questions abounded in the minds of the older three.

In a most unusual act of defiance Goldie sarcastically said, "Surely you don't have jobs for the little ones in your grand scheme of responsibilities." Erastus gave a look of contempt to Goldie without responding to her question. "Well, do you?" she asked, less certain of the answer this time.

"I told you things were going to change," Erastus replied in a much milder tone. Then he hesitated. "Tomorrow morning, Jesse and Elzie are going to leave here to live with Aunt Mary and Uncle George." Without any pause he continued, but his voice stiffened. "I have talked with Mary and George and they have agreed to take them in. Aunt Mary is expecting them by lunch time, tomorrow." The three older children all started to talk at the same time, and although no one could be understood it was clear they were angry with Erastus. In an attempt to restore order Erastus put both hands in the air and shouted, "Please let me finish. Jesse and Elzie will be treated fine, and George is going to teach both of them to farm. They will learn a good way to make a living, and maybe, they will have a better life because of it."

Hardin grunted and attempted to leave the table.

Erastus shouted, "Sit down." Hardin sat down, and the others remained seated, passively defiant.

Jesse's initial reaction was one of confusion. He wondered why Dad was going to whip Sylvia for talking about leaving, and in the next breath he was sending Elzie and him away. After brief reflection Jesse exploded, "Elzie and I don't want to be orphans."

Elzie said, "What's an orphan?"

Answering quickly Erastus said, "You are not going to be orphans. Get that thought out of your mind. All of you. This is a temporary solution to our current problem. Perhaps one day we will all live together again. Besides, if we live in Montezuma, we will see each other all the time." Tears starting to flow down his cheeks, Erastus openly cried. This was a totally new experience as none of the children had ever observed their father weep before this day. Until this moment, it had never occurred to the three older children, that Father might be doing what he believed was necessary for the survival of the family. Eventually, all were crying except Jesse. Jesse sat and looked at his father in disbelief until he felt the hurt so much and became so angry, he could not sit there any longer.

Jesse got up from the table, displaying an obvious hurt and an angry facial expression—an expression none of them had observed before. He looked more like a mature adult and less like a child of seven. Without specifically looking at anyone, Jesse took Elzie by the hand, and said. "Come on, Elzie, we don't live here anymore." Without the slightest hesitation Elzie obediently followed Jesse, as he had always done.

Erastus voiced no objection to their departure from the room.

Jesse and Elzie went to their room, talked to each other, and tried to understand the events of the day. The others stayed in the kitchen and talked, although Jesse and Elzie never knew what was said. When no siblings came to their room to visit or to comfort them Jesse assumed they all agreed with Father. Jesse and Elzie stayed in their room, and before going to bed that night they made final preparations to move to Aunt Mary's. They hurt more that night than any two young children ever should. Both cried themselves to sleep, as did everyone else in the house, that April night in 1903.

The following morning the crow of the rooster awakened everyone at dawn except Jesse who was already awake and dressed. That morning Jesse assisted Elzie as he got dressed and both went outside early. Jesse first completed his unfinished chores from the previous day and then completed his normal morning chores. Amazingly, Jesse appeared undaunted. Elzie followed Jesse everywhere he went from the time they awakened until they sat for breakfast. As Jesse behaved, Elzie behaved. Erastus fed his mules and then hitched two mules to the wagon in preparation for the trip to Aunt Mary's. Everyone else performed their usual morning routine, and, to the outside eye, it appeared to be a normal day at the Moore household, but to the members of the Moore household it was a day of family dissolution. All sensed that these were the last hours of the last day that six siblings and their father would live in the same house as a family.

Lacking usual conversation, the breakfast meal was an unsettling experience. After breakfast Jesse and Elzie went to their room, gathered their belongings and placed them in an old orange crate. Jesse carried the crate to the hitched wagon, returned to the kitchen, and announced, "We are ready to go." Jesse's composure was astonishing. Both Jesse and Elzie granted good-byes to their brother and three sisters; and then they proceeded to the wagon to wait for their father. Promptly, Erastus came to the wagon and the three of them left on their journey.

CHAPTER 3

A NEW HOME

To say the least, the short journey to Aunt Mary's was an anxious experience. Both boys suffered feelings of insecurity. They understood that from now on their lives would be changed, but they could not imagine the future impact of that change or the difference it might make in their lives. Understandably, they felt apprehensive, displaced, but true to their nature, neither boy outwardly demonstrated any such feelings. Instead they traveled as though they were on a routine journey, and they cloaked themselves in a shroud of confidence and resolve.

During the journey Erastus appeared determined, showing more concern for the details of travel, less concern for the welfare of his boys, which probably indicated that he was the most true to his character.

Elzie viewed his world through the eyes of a three-year-old child, which he was. His anxieties were less about the future, more about the present. Although precocious for his age, his thinking skills were limited, and at this moment Elzie felt an emptiness where a feeling of belonging once resided, and he felt concern for his well-being. Often his insecurities were triggered from observing the emotional behavior of those around him. If Jesse became angry, Elzie became concerned. If his father became unusually quiet, Elzie became suspicious. The changing moods of the adults were reflected in the changing moods of Elzie and this day was no exception. There could be little doubt that the events of the last few days had taken an emotional toll on Elzie, the three-year-old child.

Elzie was old enough to realize that something was drastically wrong, but too young to comprehend the situation. Traditionally, he sought direction from those around him, although his questions usually went unanswered, except by Jesse. The irony was that sometimes Elzie's questions, the simple questions of a three year old, gave good perspective to most situations. From Elzie's view few adults took time for him, and much of what he said was discounted. Fortunately today he was with his older brother.

On the other hand, Jesse was forced into the role of decision maker and interpreter. He assumed responsibility as protector of Elzie, often losing the luxury of thinking and caring only about himself. He tried to do what was right both for himself and for his little brother, plus he had to make sure Elzie intellectually understood what was happening. This was a major responsibility for any seven-year-old child; let alone, a seven-year-old child in the identical insecure position in life as the one he was protecting. Ironically, Jesse cherished his role of big brother and gained strength from it.

Cognizant that the present situation was not under his control, Jesse cautiously waited for potential problems to arise, and he remained determined that he would deal with them the best he could. He had been forced to become practical and somewhat wise for his age. He hoped for the best and understood that the best might not be. Early that day he had decided, that if their new home situation did not work for him and Elzie, he would, somehow, deal with it.

The arrival was awkward as neither the boys, nor the adults, knew what to expect. It needed not be so. Aunt Mary was seated on the front porch eagerly awaiting their arrival. Upon seeing them, she rushed out to welcome them, a behavior which surprised but delighted both boys. Relieved, it appeared they were wanted. After the initial greetings and casual conversations, Jesse and Elzie were told to unload their belongings and play outside. Erastus and his sister needed to visit. The boys did as told, but they did not feel much like playing. Mostly they passively observed the nearby people and activities in Milton. Milton had all the features of an exciting place to them, and they liked that. Gradually they began to feel at ease, but not too at ease, because they still had not seen Uncle George. They worried about his feelings, and wondered if he wanted them in his house.

A few hours before Uncle George returned from the fields, Erastus left for Alsey. Upon his departure Erastus displayed no obvious emotion and said farewell by patting Elzie on the back and shaking hands with Jesse. The moment was emotional for the children, because they felt abandoned, alone in an uncaring world, as they watched their father ride away. Sensing their hurt, Aunt Mary put one arm around each of them and said, "I have some apple pie and lemonade. Do you think you could eat it without spoiling your appetite for supper?"

Elzie's response was, "Yep, it won't spoil my appetite."

Jesse, looking at the ground, said, "I hope you want us, Aunt Mary. We really can be good kids."

"Oh, my dear child, of course we want you. Now enough of this nonsense. Let's go eat the pie."

Jesse and Elzie ate the apple pie, drank the lemonade, and visited with Aunt Mary. Jesse gradually felt better, and because Jesse felt better, Elzie felt better. The remainder of the afternoon passed without incident and good feelings began to develop. Aunt Mary had done and said the right things, although the situation still remained somewhat awkward for all three. Aunt Mary, happy the children were there, was unsure of how they felt. She did not know them well enough yet to perceive their unspoken emotions. Jesse felt better about being there, but was not yet certain it was home. Elzie's feelings ran parallel to Jesse's feelings. Had Aunt Mary known this, she would have worried less.

The initial evening with Aunt Mary and Uncle George evoked more anxious feelings in both Jesse and Elzie. Not only were the surroundings unfamiliar, the personal emotions were different. Jesse realized gradual adjustment to the surroundings was probable, but he had doubts. He could not understand his feelings that made him so insecure; but the feelings were real, and they were strong. He knew these feelings had to be controlled or changed, but he simply did not know how to control them. His emotional feelings consumed all his thought, and he feared his behavior would reveal his thoughts of insecurity. Ashamed of his feelings, he did not want Aunt Mary to know his fears.

The inner most depth of Jesse's soul sensed the uncertainty and fears of the tomorrows. Knowing that his life was bound to be different, the truly important question now was, different in what way. He carried a heavy burden, not knowing what to expect.

Elzie's fears, usually more observable than Jesse's, remained somewhat tempered by the mere presence of his brother. The positive relationship between Jesse and Elzie was to be the cornerstone of their young lives in their new abode.

In her usual manner of graciousness and kindness, Aunt Mary informed the boys, "Supper will be at 6 o'clock. We are having meat loaf. I hope that meets with your approval."

Both boys answered at the same time. "Yes." They both smiled and were delighted as both loved meat loaf and neither was accustomed to granting approval for meals.

Aunt Mary, noting their delight, said, "Wonderful. You still have an hour to play but make sure you are washed for supper. I will show you where you will sleep after we eat. Uncle George will be here before long, and he is anxious to see both of you." Her soft spoken but firm manner reassured them of what they both knew: Aunt Mary was a kind lady.

After Aunt Mary went inside, Elzie said, "Why is Uncle George anxious to see me? He just saw me a few days ago."

Smiling, Jesse responded, "I think she meant that he is happy that we are here. I think Uncle George likes us." Elzie reflected on those thoughts and quickly accepted them, without comment.

Indeed, Uncle George was happy to see them. He even told them that he was delighted they were living there, a most unusual expression of sentiment for Uncle George. When it was time to eat, the boys were told where to sit at the table and made to feel comfortable with the mealtime procedure. There was little conversation during the meal, because Uncle George preferred it that way, although it seemed strange for the boys who were accustomed to laughter and conversation during all meals. The supper was delicious, and the boys' appreciation actually was more than obvious by the manner in which they consumed their food.

Wanting to show appreciation and not knowing exactly what to say, Jesse expressed what was on his mind. "Aunt Mary, you sure are a good cook. I hope, one day, you will teach me how to cook."

Before Aunt Mary could respond, Elzie exclaimed, "Yep, mighty fine food, but awful quiet. I don't want to learn how to cook, just eat."

"I appreciate the compliment and I would be happy to teach you what I know about the kitchen. From what I observed at dinner it won't be hard to teach Elzie how to eat." Jesse and Uncle George laughed at Aunt Mary's humorous words, spoken in such a serious tone.

Elzie looked around the room expecting to see something humorous. "What's so funny? What are you guys laughing at? I'll be glad when I get old enough to understand jokes. Either tell me what's so funny, or stop laughing." They stopped laughing, but continued to smile. The smiles annoyed Elzie.

After supper George sat in the parlor and read the *Milton Beacon*, a small weekly newspaper. George read every word of every issue because the paper emphasized local and regional events and it served as his primer to county events. He also faithfully read it because he paid a yearly subscription cost of one dollar and fifty cents. As George read, the other three cleared the table and washed the dishes, a routine to which they would accustom themselves. After the kitchen was back in order, all four adjourned to the porch with George and Mary seated on the swing and the boys seated in separate rocking chairs. The initial conversation between Mary and George was mostly commentary about topics Jesse considered casual or insignificant. He had hoped they would talk about their expectations of Elzie and him. They did not. Neither boy was at ease with the reserved or quiet nature of the evening, as both were more accustomed to activity and a greater noise level. Naturally, the boys complied with the preference of their aunt and uncle, and while on the porch that evening, neither Jesse or Elzie initiated conversation or engaged in playful activity. Each person, although recognizing the uneasiness of the others, was at a loss for words that might alter the situation. Foremost was the need for cooperation, but for the children there also was a strong need for the heart's ease, to feel oneself at home. Not grasping what to do, no one did anything to relieve tensions. Uncle George withdrew to the comfort of thought as Aunt Mary fiddled with her sewing basket, organizing her thread. Jesse rocked in his chair, observing his new guardians as Elzie fidgeted and revealed his discomfort. The evening progressed with little interaction until the awkwardness of the situation became foremost. All four individuals now strongly sensed what they had previously suspected—a dramatic change in their personal lives was occurring and they were not comfortable with the change. The squeak from the chain of the porch swing and the wood-on-wood noise from the rockers, dominated all other sounds, interfering only slightly with all the unspoken thoughts. Submitting to his new found insecure feelings, Elzie first began to sniffle and then quietly he started to cry. His tears were ignored, or at least not acknowledged. A few minutes into the tears, Elzie professed, "I miss my mother. I want my family. I want to go home."

Quickly, Jesse reacted. "Elzie, we are home. We are your family. Stop your crying or you will make Aunt Mary feel bad." Turning his whole body toward Aunt Mary, as if to emphasize the importance of his question, Jesse asked, "Is there a place Elzie and me can go, to talk? We will be okay tomorrow, I promise." Jesse's statement revealed that he understood the permanence of their situation; he understood there was no other home for them.

In the kindest manner possible, Mary affirmed, "Of course there is a place for privacy." Stumbling for the exact words to ease their pain, she continued to talk. "Don't you boys worry. It's going to take time, but we're going to make it work. Elzie, you cry all you want. This is home for both of you, and we are going to do everything within our power to make it feel like your home."

Aunt Mary had found the right words to defuse the situation. The words provided immeasurable comfort, especially to Jesse. He needed to hear that they were wanted; and the words "wonderful children" assured him they were wanted. Reluctant to speak, but with a need to express himself, Jesse, while holding Elzie's hand, said, "Aunt Mary," followed by a long pause, "Elzie and I will do our best to make this work. We will try not to be burdens, and we are sorry for the pain we cause."

Immediately Elzie spewed, "I'm sorry, Aunt Mary. I need to do what Jesse told me to do, to be strong. I'm just a kid, but I'm going to be strong, just like big people, sort of like Uncle George."

Elzie's comment touched Uncle George in a most positive and personal way. Just as Aunt Mary started to speak, Uncle George, in a loud and clear voice, stated, "No apologies are necessary, and you don't cause pain."

Uncle George's declaration surprised Aunt Mary. She placed her hand on her husband's arm, looked directly at the two boys, and said, "Your Uncle George said it all, and nothing more needs to be said." She then stood and moved toward the door. "It is getting late, and time for bed. A good night's sleep will help us all." She went into the house, and the boys followed. Aunt Mary showed them to their bedroom, pointed out the essentials, and reminded them to put out the lamp before they went to bed. "This is your room." Closing the bedroom door, she said, "We will work out the details tomorrow. Good night, boys."

"Good night, Aunt Mary. Thanks again," Jesse politely responded.

Both boys remained totally quiet for several minutes while they sat on their bed and thought about their new world. They absorbed the sounds and smells of their new home. They looked around the room, touched different objects, trying to become familiar with the room. Jesse opened the window and they listened to the night sounds, and, eventually, they gained the courage to go to bed. Their young bodies exhausted, they felt tired but not sleepy.

"Aunt Mary is a nice lady. Don't you agree, Elzie?"

"Yep."

"Uncle George is a good man, huh?"

"Oh yeah, I like him."

"This is a nice house, isn't it?"

"Yep."

"I suppose we should consider ourselves lucky."

"I guess."

"Are you okay, Elzie, or do we need to talk some?"

"I'm okay. You forgot something."

"What?"

"You forgot to say that I'm a good boy."

"You are a good boy!"

"You forgot to say something else."

"What?"

"You forgot to say that you are a good brother."

"Well, I try to be. Thank you. Let's close our eyes. What I need is sleep, not talk. Good night, little brother."

"You're the one who started to talk, not me. Good night, big brother."

Awakening just before dawn, Jesse slowly turned his head to absorb the details of his new abode. The slightly dark room, more spacious and better maintained than his Alsey room, looked mysterious to his young mind. Unsure of his relative location in the room, he first looked to spot the door, got his bearings, and then he observed the furnishings before he noticed his younger brother was already awake sitting in front of the window, looking outside. "Good morning, Elzie," were his first words, spoken very softly. Elzie turned to acknowledge Jesse's greeting, but in lieu of words he nodded his head and smiled. He resumed looking out the window. Moving to sit on the side of the bed, Jesse monitored Elzie, wondering what thoughts his little brother must have. He worried if Elzie could adjust to their displacement. Then, for the first time since arriving at Aunt Mary's, his thoughts became self-centered. He worried about himself and wondered if he could adjust. The first faint daylight of this new day had rekindled concerns. Jesse still had doubts.

It was dawn and the bedroom window faced west. As the rising sun eased higher the view out the window became clearer, more distinct. Objects revealed detail and shadows began to take shape. Birds took flight and began to sing, and the sky was becoming lighter and bluer. There was an absence of clouds except on the distant horizon. The morning dew on the grass glistened, and the gentle breeze generated slight movement from the tree leaves. The day was coming alive. It was a beautiful sight, this new April day.

Continuing to look out the window, Elzie, almost in a monotone, spoke the surprising words, "I think I'm going to like it here."

Caught off guard, Jesse was speechless. A few minutes passed before he asked his brother, "Why did you say that, Elzie? Why do you think you're going to like it here?"

Speaking with the innocence of a child, but showing the wisdom of an adult, Elzie answered. "Do you remember how I love to go exploring? Do you remember how I like to do new and different things?"

"Yeah."

"When I look out the window, I see new things, different from yesterday. I see all the things to explore, and everything looks different. It looks like fun out there. Come, look out the window, and you will see what I mean."

Jesse was flabbergasted with Elzie's perspective. Elzie continued to look at the barn and Jesse continued to wonder what Elzie was seeing. Was Elzie simply day dreaming, or was he prophetic? What strange configurations outside that window could make Elzie think he was going to like it here? Perhaps Elzie was more resilient than Jesse, and this was Elzie's way of announcing it.

Elzie was becoming concerned about Jesse's silence. "What's wrong, Jesse? Did I say something wrong?"

Still thinking about the seemingly mature thoughts of his little brother, Jesse did not move or respond. Elzie, more in a manner of a child his age, continued, "Am I bad for saying that? I do miss Mom and everybody. Last night I was scared, but not now. I am just trying to do what you told me to do, to be strong. Are you mad at me? Please, don't be mad at me."

Jesse replied, "I am not mad, I am proud of you. I just underestimated you, that's all."

Shifting moods, Elzie quipped, "Proud of me? Wow. What did I do? What does underestimate mean?"

"You adjusted. You thought more like an adult, less like a kid. You did what I should be doing."

"What's underestimate?"

A gentle knock on the door disrupted their conversation. Aunt Mary said, "I hear you guys, are you up? Are you dressed yet? Breakfast will be ready in a few minutes."

"We'll be right out." Jesse answered, now thinking more about food than conversation.

Elzie yelled, "Good morning, Aunt Mary. Jesse is proud of me. We will be right out. Is Uncle George up? What's for breakfast?"

Both could hear Aunt Mary chuckle before she answered, "You will have to come to the table and see for yourself."

The kitchen was spacious. Following the same arrangement as the previous night Uncle George sat at the head of the large kitchen table with Aunt Mary seated on the other end, and the boys were seated on opposite sides. Accustomed to more people at a smaller table, the boys appreciated the more than ample space for sitting and eating. Elzie waved both elbows in the air, acknowledging the extra space. The food, already on the table, included fried eggs, a bowl of oatmeal, sugar, potato cakes, large slices of hot baked bread, dried fruit, butter, blackberry jelly, coffee, and hot cocoa for the kids. Both boys looked at the amount of food with wonderment, as they waited for permission to eat. Elzie looked at Jesse and blurted, "I told you I was going to like it here."

Uncle George firmly said, "You may take all the food you want, but you will eat all the food you take. We don't throw away food in this house. We use all leftovers, like the potato cakes are made from last night's mashed potatoes. Now, let's eat."

Elzie responded "Okay," as he reached for food, and Jesse, accepting what Uncle George said, wondered how many more rules he would have to learn. Jesse was cautious as he ate, fearing he or Elzie would do something wrong. Jesse was still not certain and it showed.

In an effort to make the boys more comfortable, Mary said, "Eat hardy, boys, we have a big day ahead of us."

Following the meal, Uncle George spoke. "I have my lunch, so I will see all of you this evening." He patted Jesse on the shoulder, which Jesse interpreted as a pat of endearment. "Don't you guys wear yourselves out today. Save enough energy to take a walk with me this evening."

Elzie smiled and cheerfully responded, "Don't worry, Uncle George, we will. We're kids and we got lots of energy."

Jesse interjected, "Don't you want us to go with you? Are you going to teach us to farm today?"

Aunt Mary answered the question. "No, you boys stay with me today. We have many things to go over and many things to do." Uncle George left, and the boys cleared the table and helped Aunt Mary wash and dry the dishes. After completing the kitchen tasks, Aunt Mary directed the boys to make their bed and to straighten their room, emphasizing the importance of order and cleanliness. Once they finished they were to meet Aunt Mary on the back porch. They were given to understand, from now on, they were responsible for cleaning up after themselves. Jesse considered that a reasonable demand. It was a good beginning to the first full day in their new home.

Aunt Mary went outside as the boys went to straighten their room. Elzie shut the door behind them, and immediately said, "Did we have all these rules at the other home? What's that smell, anyway? I smelled that last night. What's to straighten out? This is the cleanest room I've ever been in."

"Whoa, Elzie, don't get in a huff. They are not bad rules, just things to live by. They give us direction and that is good." Jesse did not share his earlier qualms concerning rules with his brother. He thought it better to comfort Elzie. "I think she wants us to make the bed and put things away. Sort of keep the room like we found it." Loudly inhaling through his nose, he then said, "I think it is just a musty smell, from not being used. Look around you. This is quite a room. Nice iron frame bed with a feather bed on the mattress, thick feather pillows, two chairs, and a hall tree for our clothes." While pointing at the hall tree, he continued, "By the way, I'll take these two sides for my stuff and you take the other two. Okay? And look at that! I'll bet you don't even know what that is."

Elzie fired back, "I do to, it's a pee pot. You pee in it at night, and somebody else empties it in the morning."

"It's called a chamber pot, and if you pee in it during the night, you, not somebody else, you, empty it in the morning."

"What if we both pee in it?"

"Elzie, don't be difficult. Let's do what we need to do here and go meet Aunt Mary. Okay?"

"Okay. Let's do it, and then go get the rest of the rules to live by."

The boys straightened their room, made the bed, looked everything over, and went to find Aunt Mary.

Aunt Mary was patiently waiting by the coal shed. "There you are. I thought, maybe, you couldn't find the outdoors."

Neither boy answered, thinking they had done something wrong.

Smiling, Aunt Mary said, "Humor, boys, humor, that was supposed to be humorous. You are going to have to get used to my humor."

Neither boy knew how to respond. Elzie eventually said, "Okay, we'll get used to it."

Changing to a more serious tone, Aunt Mary proceeded to take the boys on a tour of the barnyard, carefully identifying each building and its purpose. She was very articulate, explaining what needed to be done and why. Speaking to them more as adults, rather than children, she commanded their attention, and more importantly, commanded their respect. In addition to identifying the buildings, she identified the flower beds, the fruit trees, the raspberry bushes, and the general layout of the yard, always pointing out the effort and work needed to produce food and beauty. She consistently used words in the collective sense, such as, ours, we, family, and all of us, rather than the individual sense, such as, mine, I, or yours. In a brief period of time, Aunt Mary successfully conveyed the thought that the boys were part of the family, and not outsiders living at the house. Her inclusive speech helped Jesse and Elzie feel more at ease, and Jesse felt a little more certain.

The barnyard and grounds tour was exciting to Elzie. It revealed several wonderful hiding places and opportunities for exploration; although, not everyplace looked inviting.

"That chicken house was terrible, dirty, smelly. I don't want to play in there."

Amused by Elzie's remark, Jesse responded, "I suspect you and me will learn how to clean it out."

"Who wants to learn that? I didn't mean I want to learn how to clean it out. I meant I don't want to play in it. You underestimate me."

Aunt Mary was enchanted with the verbal exchange between the boys. "Oh, to be young again."

"What's that mean?"

"Oh, nothing, I suppose. Let's move on."

Elzie did not like the answer, but he said nothing. It seemed to him that he always had to answer questions, and nobody, except Jesse, gave him a straight answer. Adults would often remark, "One day you will understand." He thought that might be true, but he certainly was tired of waiting for "one day."

After the barnyard tour, the three sat on the porch and drank hot cocoa, which Aunt Mary had especially prepared for them. Aunt Mary, continuing to speak in the same serious tone, asked, "Do you have any questions or thoughts about what we just saw?"

Elzie said, "I do. When we looked in the cellar building, I saw three bathtubs. How often do we take a bath around here?"

Aunt Mary, in a matter of fact manner, said, "Once a week in the winter, on Saturday, and twice a week in summer, on Wednesday and Saturday. Are there any more questions?" Elzie wanted to ask if April counted as winter or summer, but thought he better not. Neither boy asked other questions so she continued. "This is my home and now you boys are a part of it. I know you don't want to be here, but it's the only real alternative we could come up with. I know it's not easy being separate from your family, and living apart from them in a different place, but I'm determined we can make it work. You both are going to have to help us, if it is going to work. The death of your mother changed almost everything for you. I don't want to replace your mother and I won't try to." Aunt Mary took a deep breath and sighed before continuing. "As you know, George and I don't have much money or many possessions, but, I think we lead a comfortable life; and George has agreed we have enough to help you boys along. We will provide you with a place to stay, feed and clothe you, and try to provide the proper environment for you to live and grow up in. We won't be your parents, but we'll try to create an atmosphere where you are free to grow."

Collecting her thoughts, Aunt Mary resumed her presentation. "George and I are considerably older than your parents, and we are pretty set in our ways, as I'm sure you have noticed. I can't promise it will be easy for you. We are going to try to adjust to you living here, just as you must adjust to us. There is little doubt things will be different for you, as well as for us. I hope you understand this. I don't know, but we may not be easy to get along with. If conflict arises, we must resolve it, always remembering, Uncle George is the head of this house. If I ever have to choose between something that is right for George or right for you, I will always choose George. Do you understand this?"

Jesse, carefully listening to every word and every inflection in her voice, answered, "Yes, ma'am, I do and I respect that. I think you and Uncle George are the most wonderful people in the world. It is really nice of you to take us in. I know you didn't have to. Elzie and me will work hard, we'll try to be good, and we'll try not to disappoint you. Isn't that right, Elzie?"

Looking perplexed, Elzie said, "Whatever Jesse says."

Almost in anger, Jesse snapped back at his brother. "That isn't good enough, Elzie. Tell Aunt Mary you agree."

"I agree, but I don't know what she said. I listened, but I don't understand everything she said. Maybe I'm too little. Anyway, I agree."

Elzie's honesty touched both Jesse and Aunt Mary. Jesse looked at Aunt Mary for guidance, and she granted it. "I'm sorry, Elzie. I was so concerned about what to say, I forgot to think about how to say it. You take all the time you want and, Jesse, you must help him."

"I will, Aunt Mary. It'll be easy cause Elzie is a good kid. He learns fast."

Elzie looked at Jesse and casually said, "Thanks, Jesse." Then looking at Aunt Mary, he tilted his head upward, and said, "I told you he was proud of me."

Elzie's remarks amused Jesse. Aunt Mary, mimicking Elzie, tilted her head upward, and said, "I am proud of you, too. In fact, I am proud of both of you."

This comment prompted Elzie to sit back in his chair and savor the moment and ultimately declare, "I'm proud, too."

Indeed it was a needed light moment and after a brief pause, Aunt Mary continued with her thoughts. "As I assume you know, there is a lot of work to be done around here, just to keep the place going. We expect you boys to help with the work. We will designate daily chores for each of you, and we expect them to be done. If for some reason you can't do them, you get someone to do them for you. We depend on each other, and the chores must be done and done right. This next week we will show you how to do certain chores and then we, all together, will decide who does what chores and when. This is important, and you both must be responsible. Will you both agree to this?"

Very quickly Jesse answered, "Yes, I had chores at my other home. What you ask is reasonable."

More deliberately, Elzie answered, "Okay, I think I understand."

Aunt Mary continued. "This evening, when Uncle George is home, we will talk about school, your life here, and other things. Also, Jesse, as you know we have plans for you to do some farm work with your uncle. So if you boys have any questions or doubts, you bring them up tonight. Will you please think about what we have talked about, and remember that we only know your concerns, if you express them?"

"We'll both try, Aunt Mary."

"I think that to be a good answer. Now, it's time for dinner, so let's go see what we can find to eat. After dinner, maybe you boys will explore Milton and tell me what you find. Can you do that on your own?"

Without a moments hesitation, Elzie exclaimed, "Sure we can. It'll be fun."

Dinner was exactly at noon, and it was slightly past 1:00 before the kitchen was back in order. Jesse, having thoroughly enjoyed the food, was content to visit more with Aunt Mary, but not Elzie. He had consumed his food thinking about the promise of exploration. He was now ready to see Milton and all the intriguing components of his new world, and he made sure Jesse did not forget the proposed schedule. As Aunt Mary observed Elzie's anticipation, she could not help but admire his spirit and, also, admire the positive relationship between the brothers. Encouraging their departure, she stated, "You boys be home by four o'clock, and not one minute later. Your Uncle George left this nickel for you in case you get thirsty, and happen to be near downtown."

"How do we know when its four o'clock?" Jesse queried.

"There is a town clock that chimes on the hour. Just listen for the chimes."

Feeling a little stupid, having heard the chimes last night and this morning, Jesse sheepishly said, "All right, we won't be late. Thank you for the nickel, I mean thank Uncle George when you see him." He felt stupid again for that comment, but he excused it because his mind was preoccupied. He wondered if the clock chimed on the hour, how would they know it was four o'clock until it was too late. However, he was not about to ask another stupid question, confident that eventually they could figure it out.

"Thank him yourself. Now be off with you."

The two brothers were off to explore the town of Milton. Confidence oozed from both, as they were exploring together, had a nickel in their pocket, were eager to see the town, and had a nice place with nice people to return to. Anticipation of what they might see excited them, and innocence of youth provided the courage to have the adventure. All the ingredients for an exhilarating episode were in place.

Milton was easy to explore, easy to find one's way. The town was laid out in a grid with nine streets running north and south, and six streets running perpendicular to those streets. The large, spacious square situated in the middle of town provided the main commercial center, although a few businesses were located on the edge of town near the four entrances to the town. Jesse counted thirty-eight separate business establishments and with the many people walking about the town the area seemed abuzz with activities. Elzie politely spoke to all the people he established eye contact with, and had they had the time and the courage they probably could have engaged in conversation. Instead, they explored the full length of every street before they returned downtown for their refreshments, complements of Uncle George. They purchased two bottles of Coca Cola and drank them as they walked around the square for the third time. By any measurement this first outing in Milton provided the children with a wonderful experience, that spring afternoon of 1903. They returned home at 3:58 p.m., two minutes before the designated time. Elzie regretted that they did not use their final two minutes.

After the evening meal and after several reminders by Elzie to Uncle George, the three males took a long walk. The boys quickly discerned Uncle George's obvious affection for his much appreciated town. He spoke with pride as he tried to acquaint the boys with their new hometown, but unfortunately, he also spoke as though he were talking to his peers. "Allow me to ramble as I tell you about Milton. Please listen carefully as I believe this is important stuff for all who walk these streets. Have I scared you yet? Does it sound like school?"

Elzie was excited as he deliberately answered what he believed to be a serious question. "Heck, no, I'm not scared, I want to know all about this place. I want you to know that this is the most exciting place Jesse and me have ever seen in all our lives. You should have seen all the people downtown today. There were more people in one place than I have ever seen. More people here this afternoon than in church on Sundays, and that's a lot of people."

Jesse interrupted. "We want to hear about Milton, Uncle George. Elzie, be quiet so we can learn. Okay?"

"I was only answering his question."

Once again Elzie made George smile. "Elzie is on target, you know. We have

703 residents who live in Milton, and again half that number of outsiders might visit our town on any given day. Believe me when I tell you that's a lot of people, although not the number that the early city fathers hoped for. Originally, the city was laid out in 1835 for 25,000 people, but that never happened. First the canal was built which linked the Illinois River to Lake Michigan and we thought Montezuma would become a major port on the river, but it failed to materialize. They used to say that by water, through canals, Montezuma was exactly half way from New York City to New Orleans. I guess that didn't make any difference. But the real blow to Milton came when the railroads chose not to lay track in Pike County."

Jesse interrupted again. "Uncle George, you're hard to understand. Do we really need to remember all that stuff. It's interesting enough, we just can't understand it."

Elzie supported Jesse. "I don't even think it's interesting. Tell us some good stuff, something I can understand. Remember that I'm just a kid."

"Sorry, boys, I'll try to make more sense to you. We'll discuss the hard stuff in a few years when you are older. Let me start over. The people here are good, hardworking people. Nobody here is really rich or poor, just somewhere in between. We look out for each other and we take care of those in need. We abide by the rules and play fair. We may not have brick streets or electricity like Pittsfield, but we keep our place clean and respectable. We all have a stake, a responsibility, in keeping our town the way it should be. I tell you this because you both now live in this town and you need to act accordingly."

Elzie had to know so he asked. "What does accordingly mean, and what do Jesse and me do for fun? Is it against the rules to have fun here?"

Uncle George became amused at the question, but before he could answer Elzie's concern, Jesse spoke. "Yes, we can have fun, he didn't mean that. Wait until we get home and I'll explain to you when we are alone. It's complicated, Elzie."

"I guess it is. Did Uncle George underestimate me too?" That comment brought more laughter which only aggravated Elzie, but he soon got over it. As they headed toward home Uncle George continued his lesson about the importance of knowing the particulars about the place you live, and the more he spoke the better he became at communicating on the boys' level. They all learned something that night while on a walk in Milton. The evening was a delightful experience for all three, and far beyond the intent of sharing information, George's affection for the boys increased beyond measure.

Brothers, Jesse and Elzie, went to bed that night with very different emotions from the previous night. This night they were comfortable with their aunt and uncle and they felt wanted, certainly they felt more secure than the previous night. They liked the environment of their new home. They were closer to accepting their imposed fate following the death of their mother, and closer to accepting the fact that their young lives would never be the same again. Jesse felt a twinge of guilt for his happiness.

With both boys in bed and lying on their backs with their hands underneath their heads, they pondered the day's events and the recent changes in their lives. Almost one hour elapsed before Elzie philosophically stated, "Today was one of the best days of my life, but I still miss Mother, Dad, Arch, Hardin, Goldie, Sylvia, and Frieda. I hope we all can live together again, maybe with Aunt Mary and Uncle George." There was a long pause. "But if we can't, we can't."

Impressed with his brother's thoughts, Jesse responded. "I agree, and you said it better than I could say it. Once again, I'm proud of you. Keep up the good thoughts. Good night, little brother."

"Good night, big brother."

In December, 1906, Jesse and Elzie attended a birthday party for a daughter of Aunt Mary's friend. Upon returning home, Elzie appeared despondent, and Aunt Mary was determined to discover the reason. After several probing questions, Elzie revealed his feelings. "Life isn't fair. Those kids got it made, they got everything. I got nothing compared to them. She got more presents for her birthday than I've had in my entire life. She doesn't even have to do chores. Life isn't fair."

Jesse grabbed Elzie by the arm and gave him a not so gentle tug. "Come with me, we're going to our room and talk," Jesse said in anger.

Uncle George grabbed the other arm of Elzie and said, "No, boys, we are going to stay here, and we all are going to talk."

Sensing real trouble, Elzie said, "I'm just doing what you always tell me to do. I'm telling the truth. Those kids got it made, and that's a fact."

All four became seated around the table before Uncle George began the conversation. "Elzie, I want you to listen to me. Okay?"

"Okay."

"I know life doesn't always seem fair and, in fact, life isn't fair. Get used to that. But, if you're going to compare advantages, you need to compare apples to apples. There are different kinds of advantages, and sometimes, what appears to be an advantage may not be. We all have some advantages and some disadvantages. The true advantage in life is understanding that."

"What does that mean?"

"I mean some people have more money, a better house, or more things. Some people are more loved or have families that look after them. Some have more talent or better jobs. Some have better health. Some are more able than others to endure or survive. The list goes on, and no one has all the advantages, or all the disadvantages. You need to recognize your own advantages. Let's try that. Why don't we make a list of the advantages we have."

Without hesitating at all and in a sarcastic tone, Elzie answered, "I know one disadvantage I have. I don't have it made, like some I know, and I can't think of any advantages. So there's my list, where's yours?"

Uncle George's face showed a flush of anger, revealing a strong emotion previously unobserved by Jesse or Elzie. Uncle George jerked Elzie out of the chair, placed the boy over his knee, and spoke with aggressive determination. "I'm going to show you one advantage I have," and he proceeded to spank Elzie. "I'm going to teach you a lesson you won't forget. You will act civil in this house." Not wanting to seriously hurt the boy, but to make him feel the pain, Uncle George spanked hard, but Elzie refused to outwardly cry or to express remorse. Uncle George spanked harder and harder.

Partly out of compassion but mostly out of concern, Jesse intervened and pleaded, "Please stop, Uncle George. Let me have Elzie, and I'll talk to him, and he'll listen to me. Please."

Hearing the brother's plea, and observing Aunt Mary's expression of displeasure, Uncle George stopped the spanking and commanded Elzie, "Go to your room and think about your behavior. You stay in your room and there will be no supper for you tonight. We'll talk about this in the morning after you've had a chance to think about your behavior." Elzie went to his room. "That kid is as stubborn as a mule, just like his dad."

Disturbed by Uncle George's treatment of Elzie, Jesse tried to intercede. His manner of speaking was respectful, although one could identify his displeasure in his tone. "Allow me to go in and talk to him. He usually listens to me, and we'll talk about advantages. Elzie is a good kid, and he didn't deserve such harsh treatment. He just got a little too sassy for his own good, but he did not deserve that."

"Go!" Uncle George said. All that evening Aunt Mary could hear the boys talking, but what they discussed she did not know. Neither boy ate supper, nor did they come out of the room. Before retiring for the night, Aunt Mary and Uncle George discussed the days events. Her final words before going to sleep were, "I'm not sure who learned what lesson today."

The next morning both Jesse and Elzie came to the breakfast table with a list of advantages.

Although, in future years, there were similar experiences of youthful disrespect and misbehavior by both boys, there were no more spankings from Uncle George. However, there were several nights in the bedroom, without supper.

Since Jesse was the older of the two boys, he was judged by a different standard and more was expected from him. Prior to living in Milton, Jesse had completed two full years of education at a rural school in Scott County, enjoyed learning and attending school and had been a good student. Unfortunately for Jesse, the adults who exercised influence and control over him, saw little value in formal education, other than reading, writing, spelling and arithmetic. Traditional local beliefs dictated that self-instruction could be equal to formal learning for the common man, especially for one who would earn a living with his back. At best, education was thought to be a luxury, not a necessity. Subsequently, Uncle George and Aunt Mary determined that Jesse's needs would be best served by encouraging him to learn farming rather than attend school. Before Jesse finished his third year of full-time school attendance he became a part-time farmworker and school became secondary to earning a living. The school term at Milton was seven months, and attendance was not compulsory. Recognizing the needs of the rural community and the need for farm labor during the planting and harvest seasons, the local school board adopted a liberal policy of attendance. The policy allowed each student to miss a reasonable number of school days, with the understanding that the student would continue to learn on his own time. Students could accomplish this without jeopardizing their academic status in school. The student who selected this option would not be promoted to the next higher grade but would be permitted to attend occasional classes and was expected to learn on his own. This course of study was determined by Aunt Mary and Uncle George to be adequate for Jesse. So, attending school on a part-time basis, Jesse planned to independently advance each year with his classmates and to complete his grade school education on schedule.

Because of the age difference and slightly different circumstances, Elzie was expected to attend school and Jesse very much supported this decision. The family wished for Elzie what none of them had acquired—a formal elementary education. Although Elzie was a bright and articulate boy, he was never overly fond of school. Be that as it may, he preferred school to the alternative of full-time work, especially full-time farmwork. Elzie's major objection to school was not the learning per se as much as the learning process. He intensely disliked the laborious memory work and repetitive rote learning required by the curriculum. He particularly disliked his major textbook, the *McGuffey Reader*, the standard reading book in most schools. Elzie was a thinker, a dreamer. He was not an outstanding student, nor was he a poor student. He was a reluctant student. Elzie particularly thrived in the school's social setting. He was a most likable kid and he significantly benefitted from the many peripherals of school learning. How one socially functioned in school was thought to be an indicator of how one would socially function in life. If true, Elzie could look forward to a productive future social life.

There were, however, incidents. The opening day of school, September, 1909, Elzie made an unusual request of Jesse. "I know you usually go to school the first day. Are you going today?"

"Yeah, why?" Jesse answered with skepticism.

"I want you to be there when school gets out at noon today. Be at the front gate exactly at noon."

"Why?"

"Because, today, I'm going to make my stand."

"What are you talking about?"

"Each year I have run home from school because big Jake, the meanest kid in school, has told me he is going to kick my ass at high noon on the first day of school, and he means it. But, I can't keep running. Besides, all the other third graders will be there to watch him tell me. Everybody's expecting a big show, and I'm not going to run away this time."

"What do you want me there for, to protect you?"

"No, well sort of. I'm going to fight big Jake today and I plan on whipping him, and he's got these two big friends who are going to be mad, and I'm afraid they're going to jump me afterwards. If you're there, they won't. What about it? Will you?"

Jesse did not answer right away. "It's against my better judgment, but I guess I will. Are you sure you have to fight him, and there's no other way? Did you tell the teacher?"

"I'm sure I have to fight him, and, no, I didn't tell any teacher. What a silly question that was."

"Okay, Elzie, I'll see you at noon, but I'm not going to fight big Jake for you."

"Don't want you to."

Jesse arrived at the front gate outside the school by 11:50 a.m.. Seeing no crowd, he felt relieved. At 11:55 a crowd had gathered with big Jake standing at the front of the group, and Jesse knew Elzie had been correct in his assessment. He hoped his little brother knew what he was doing. Jesse positioned himself so that he was not part of the crowd, but so the friends of big Jake could see him. Exactly at noon, the front door to the school opened and Elzie emerged; and in a rather audacious manner he walked to where the crowd had gathered. Big Jake aggressively stepped forward and pointed his finger at Elzie. "I told you if you didn't run home on the first day of school, I was going to kick your ass, didn't I?"

"Yep."

"Well, are you going to run?"

"Not this time." In a flash and catching Jake off guard, Elzie leaped forward with his right arm raised and his elbow collided with Jake's nose. The blow broke Jake's nose and Jake let out a terrifying scream. Elzie quickly placed his right leg behind Jake's leg, pushed him to the ground and jumped on top of him. Elzie started hitting Jake in the head and face delivering several blows in a short time.

Jake's face became bloodied and Elzie stopped hitting long enough to shout, "Say uncle, and I'll stop. If you don't I'm going to keep hitting you until you say uncle."

Jake was in pain and, without hesitation, he yelled "Uncle!" but Elzie did not relent. He continued to straddle his opponent while he held his clinched fists near Jake's face. Elzie spoke so everyone could hear him. "If you don't run home from school today, I'm going to kick your ass again. Got that?"

"Yeah, I got it."

"What about next year? You going to run home then, too?" Jake gave no answer so Elzie starting hitting him again.

This time Jake screamed. "Yeah, uncle, uncle! Let me up, I'm hurt. My nose hurts big time."

Elzie demanded, "Say uncle, one more time before I let you up." But before Jake could say anything, Jesse grabbed Elzie under the arms and dragged him off Jake. Jesse looked directly at Elzie, proclaiming, "That's enough." He then looked at Jake, astonished by the damage done in less than two minutes of fighting, and spoke directly to the injured Jake. "Take your friends and get out of here." Jesse then walked Elzie through an astonished crowd and away from the site of the ruckus. As they walked away, the crowd cheered, shouting Elzie's name in praise. Elzie turned and waved to his admiring crowd, which only aggravated Jesse all the more. Jesse grabbed Elzie's arm, pushed him forward, and Jesse continued to direct Elzie as they headed in the direction of a nearby farm pond. Jesse, stunned by Elzie's aggressive antics, was angered that he had agreed to be involved in such an unsightly scene. Once they were seated on the bank near the pond they sat in silence, because both were too angry to speak. Eventually they communicated, and in fact, the brothers spent considerable time discussing the incident, but they resolved nothing. Elzie stood by his position that he had no choice but to fight, and Jesse argued there were other alternatives. Jesse accused Elzie of playing to the crowd, of grandstanding. Elzie denied it, defending his behavior as necessary and proper considering the circumstances. Jesse was disappointed with the violent behavior of his little brother, and Elzie was disappointed by the lack of understanding from his big brother. Their discussion on that day resolved nothing.

CHAPTER 4

EARLY ADVENTURES

The sky was cloudy, the temperature cool for a September day. As Jesse approached the house he saw his brother sitting on the front steps. "Hi, Elzie, what's new?"

"Nothing is new, everything is old and boring. There is nothing to do around here. Besides, it seems that I never see you any more." His tone of voice revealed far more than his words expressed. Elzie was not happy. "It seems to me that all I do is get up, do chores, go to school, do more chores, and somewhere in between those exciting activities I eat and get ready for tomorrow. I can't believe I thought Milton was an exciting place. We never do anything together any more. What happened to our time together? What happened to our adventures?"

Elzie almost became hopeful when he got no immediate answer, because Jesse always answered his questions. As he watched and waited for an answer his hopes increased that a positive alternative to his humdrum life was forthcoming and he believed this because of Jesse's facial expression. In place of a quick verbal response Jesse tilted his head to the side, looked upward, and engaged in thought. The mere sight of Jesse in his usual thinking, problem-solving position satisfied the younger brother that Jesse was not ignoring him, rather he was preparing his answer. Jesse remained in a pensive position for several minutes without saying anything. "Well, what's the answer?" Elzie asked as his patience wore thin.

Jesse looked directly at Elzie and answered in a mellow tone. "I don't know, I just don't know."

This certainly was not the answer Elzie wanted. "Well, take more time to think about it, but come up with an answer. I'll sit right here until you come up with a good answer. No hurry, take your time, I don't have to be anywhere for a good twenty minutes."

This display of confidence brought a smile to Jesse's face. "If there is an answer it will take a lot more time than twenty minutes. I'm afraid the answer is one that neither of us wants to hear. I suspect, little brother, the answer is best found somewhere in one simple fact—by and large, that's the way we live and it's pretty difficult to change it. Chores and work are a major part of our lives, and excitement isn't."

"Hogwash, there's got to be a way!"

Elzie's words had effectively expressed his sentiment, and Jesse's response had properly analyzed the problem. Although, at first, things seemed exciting at Aunt Mary's, little time had passed before the exhilaration of living in Milton had faded for the boys. Indeed, life on North Street demanded considerable work and effort from both boys which definitely infringed on their leisure-time. The older they became the more they were expected to do and, it seemed, the more work there was for them to do. Had they been older they might have realized that their drab lifestyle was characteristically normal for most rural, young people, especially for the likes of commoners.

Aunt Mary and Uncle George possessed little wealth, although to their credit they did share what they had. Although each boy had a few prized possessions, neither personally had much to call his own; and, fortunately, they did not yet know that. They knew little about life outside of Milton. In fact, both were most appreciative of what they did have. They lived in a comfortable home, ate very well, and most physical needs were satisfied. They had sufficient clothing for winter or summer, although the clothing was not always store purchased. They had few personal luxuries, and additional items were not expected.

Each boy prized a cigar box full of their cherished private items. The content of these cigar boxes was so personal that neither brother knew what the other's box contained. A valued and practical gift from Uncle George, each owned a pocket knife which he carried on his person. Aunt Mary had given them a book, *The American Boys Handy Book*, What to do and how to do it, by Daniel Beard. This illustrated book was a compendium of practical children's activities, how to build and do things. Although Beard's book held a lure for most children, it was held in highest esteem by both Jesse and Elzie. One copy held in joint ownership, they literally used the book till it was destroyed beyond practical use.

Dime adventure novels intrigued Elzie. Owning only two dime novels, he traded for other novels enough times to read over twenty dime novels by the time he was twelve. The books served to stimulate his active imagination, and from these novels he compiled a priority list of places he wanted to travel and he secretly kept his list in his cigar box. In contrast, Jesse was fascinated by the *Farmers' Almanac* which he considered as accumulated practical knowledge from man's experiences.

He not only studied it, he followed the conventional wisdom of the Almanac when possible. Second only to the above books were the cutouts from Sunday funny papers, if available, especially Happy Hooligan and Buster Brown. Both maintained their own file of cartoons.

With little doubt, however, a good sense of humor not only served them well in their lives, it fed the souls of both boys. Both honed their own brand of humor, and although Jesse's humor was dry and Elzie's was more demonstrative, both immensely enjoyed the other's humor. Often feeding on each other's quick wit they looked for and found amusement in everyday events, and few days passed without finding something funny about the most mundane circumstances. Jesse's preference leaned toward puns, often in homonyms. His humorous remarks usually provoked moans from others, rather than chuckles or laughter. Uncle George was the exception in appreciation of Jesse's humor, often laughing profusely, sometimes before others even understood the humor. At an early age, Jesse seemed to have an unlimited capacity to find humor in the most mirthless situations. Not always willing to share his thoughts with others, he sometimes would amuse himself and laugh aloud as others were left wondering. More than once Aunt Mary remarked, "Jesse just told himself another joke." Not surprisingly, Jesse was most discriminate, seldom using his humor at inappropriate times.

On the other hand, Elzie's humor was more obvious, in the form of jokes, riddles, or embellished descriptions of events. Some might even refer to his wit as biting, excessive. Not always, but sometimes, the laugh was at the expense of others and could antagonize. At other times his jokes could be off-color. One winter evening as everyone was seated in the parlor, Aunt Mary saw some mice and was aggravated by their presence in the house. Elzie, after watching Aunt Mary chase the mice, said, "Leave them alone, Aunt Mary, it's just a male and a female mouse playing inside where it is warm."

Jesse, of course, questioned the statement. "Just how do you go about identifying the gender of mice?"

"I only know for sure because I heard them talking. I overheard the female mouse giving an invitation to the male—come around the corner and I'll show you my hole." Uncle George and Jesse roared with laughter, but Aunt Mary who could be prudish became indignant with the inappropriate remark.

Observing his aunt, Elzie responded. "I'm sorry, Aunt Mary, I'll behave myself. I'll go over to the stove and study what Uncle George told me were the three main parts of the stove."

Looking at Elzie, partly disgusted and partly curious, Aunt Mary said, "What are you talking about?"

"Uncle George told me there are three main parts of a stove that every man should know—lifter, leg, and poker."

Uncle George and Jesse dared not laugh, at least not respond until an aggravated Aunt Mary left the room. Then they snickered. Jesse said to Elzie, "You just won't learn when to back off, will you?"

"Nope, I guess not. I thought it was sort of funny. By the way, do you know the three main vegetables of the garden?"

"No, I don't, but I'm sure you will tell us."

"Yep. They are, lettuce, turnip, and pea."

Sometimes, conversations such as this, would continue for hours. Humor became a part of their personalities, and for both Jesse and Elzie, humor became a source of entertainment at uneventful times. Humor served them well and helped them cope with life's frustrations.

Oddly enough the daily, routine chores were not resented by either boy. Chores were chores and had to be done. Aunt Mary had philosophically convinced them that constant physical effort was required just to maintain a decent level of existence. Nevertheless, chores remained a necessary activity, not a cherished one. Jesse cynically spoke of the restrictive nature of daily chores by telling Elzie, he could travel anywhere in the world he wanted, as long as he left after the morning chores, and got back in time for the evening chores. The more extensive morning chores, usually involving all of the animals, were equally allocated while the evening chores were assigned more by matching work to interest of each boy. Elzie enjoyed the yard work, the flowers, and the general maintenance of the buildings. Jesse preferred the garden and farmwork. Winter chores, fewer in number but more difficult to complete, were done when they needed done.

Daily chores provided good lessons about individual responsibility and cooperation. The boys learned that life required hard work, and hard work had its rewards. They came to understand that chores were everyday, forever. Perhaps, most importantly, daily chores helped them understand who they were, and helped them recognize their station in life.

Life did consist of more than work, although at times the boys would have been a hard sell to this idea. The boys, not always pleased with their lives, continued to grow, enjoying good health. Experiences nurtured curiosities. Opportunities for successes and failures allowed them to further define who they were and what they wanted in life. As they matured and absorbed conventional wisdom, they learned many additional lessons about life. In effect, they learned about life by living it, and they were quick learners. They became aware of wealth and poverty, sickness and health, happiness and misery, work and play, love and hate, and of the many paradoxes of life. Perhaps all children learn these lessons, but these boys learned them at an early age.

As time progressed the world of Jesse and Elzie invariably broadened. They visited nearby communities where they observed the differences and similarities of other towns. The circus came to Milton and they observed a variety of animals, watched circus performers, and engaged in conversation with different people. They attended a riverboat show in Montezuma where they were exposed to vaudeville and professional entertainers. For the first time they sat in the seat of an automobile. They attended a nickelodeon. They ate their first meal in a restaurant. They switched on, and off, an electric light. Indeed, the limited experiences only created an appetite for more experiences, and both developed a craving for life beyond Milton.

In November, 1903, Erastus had moved his family to a farmhouse on the outskirts of Montezuma, just as he said he would. However, the family did not remain long in Pike County, moving again before winter's end, and this time they moved to New Berlin, Illinois, some fifty miles east from Milton. In effect, the two boys became more isolated from their father and siblings. Ironically, by 1907 the three oldest children married and moved from the father's household, leaving only two children at home: Frieda, age five and Sylvia, age fourteen. Any plans Erastus held for a self-sufficient, rural family operation were cast to the wind. Although Erastus remained in the New Berlin area, he did not develop strong ties to that community, and he always maintained an open eye for other opportunities. On rare occasions Erastus did brave the arduous journey to visit the boys in Milton.

The family move to New Berlin had forced Jesse into total acceptance of his new station in life, but strangely he did not resent the family's move. Jesse remained cautious and somewhat suspicious of his father's motives. He had decided, at an early age, he would never again allow himself to become dependent on his father or older siblings. He thought he loved them, but realized he could not depend on them. The events following the death of Jesse's mother convinced him that he, and he alone, should be responsible for his own well being. He tried to live his life, accepting due blame or due credit, as a responsible person. This philosophy became his creed, and, for some personal reason, he never shared these thoughts with anyone, not even Elzie. Conversely, the younger brother showed more confidence in his father's resolutions.

One warm, summer evening of 1907, Erastus arrived at Aunt Mary's house with presents for Jesse and Elzie. Aunt Mary answered the door. "Why, Erastus, how good to see you. Nothing is wrong is it?"

"No, no, I've just come to see the boys. Are they here?"

"Yes, they're here. But I have to locate them, they are doing chores."

"Doing chores, huh? How are those boys? I'll bet they both are pretty good workers by now. Tell them I'll be out by the wagon and tell them to hurry, as I need to get to Montezuma and do some errands by dark. Looks like it's going to be a clear night so there will be plenty of light, but tell them to hurry anyway. Tell them I got something for them."

Erastus did not wait long before Elzie arrived, and it was most apparent that the boy was pleased to see his father. A short time later Jesse arrived. Elzie yelled, "Hurry, Jesse, hurry. Dad has a present for us, and I can't look until you get here. Hurry!"

At first their father said nothing, rather he admiringly looked at both boys, noticing how much they had grown. His enormous grin revealed his pride in his youngest sons. With both boys eagerly standing beside the wagon, Erastus reached into the wagon and pulled an elongated bundle, wrapped in blankets, from the back of the wagon. "You boys care to guess what this is?"

"Looks like a bunch of blankets," Elzie said, showing his disappointment.

"It's a bunch of blankets with something inside for each of you." Carefully unwinding the blankets, Erastus pulled out two rifles. "I thought it might be time for you boys to own rifles. Here is a rifle for each of you. They both are the same: bolt action, .22 caliber, repeating rifles." Both boys, overwhelmed by the gifts, were speechless. Jesse cautiously held his rifle and admired it. Elzie fondled his rifle, operated the bolt, and held the rifle in firing position. Reaching back into the wagon, Erastus pulled out a wood case covered by a seed sack. Lifting the sack, he said, "Here are five hundred rounds of ammunition and a cleaning kit for each of you. Here is the manual which shows you how to shoot, care for, and clean the rifles. Take care of them, they are brand new. Find out from Uncle George where you can go to shoot them, and for God's sake, don't hurt yourselves or anyone else. Do you both understand?"

Elzie was the first to reply. "Thank you so much, Dad."

Jesse was more formal, more reserved. "Yes, we understand, and we will be careful, but why are you giving them to us?"

"I'm giving them to you because you are my sons." Now his tone became almost accusatory. "Is that a good enough reason?"

Guilt consumed Jesse. "Yes, it is. I'm sorry I asked, I did not mean to be ungrateful."

"Don't worry about it. Just be careful and enjoy the rifles. Become good shots. Treat that rifle with respect."

"Thank you, very much. This is a wonderful thing, Dad. We won't disappoint you."

"I know you won't. Well, I should be going, and I suspect you two need to get back to your chores. By the way, we need to get together and talk sometime. We need to talk about our future. Tell your Aunt Mary I said good-bye, and I hope to see you boys before too long. Take care, and remember to be careful."

Elzie was so enthralled with his gift that he hardly saw his father leave. Jesse waved good-bye for both of them, although he remained curious as to why their father needed to talk to them about their future. The following days the boys did exactly what their father had ordered—they became good custodians of their rifles. At age seven and eleven, Elzie and Jesse were proud and responsible owners of new rifles, a present they had never expected. They taught themselves to shoot, Elzie shooting right handed, and Jesse, equally capable of using either hand, preferred to fire on the left. Both were good shots, at least in comparison to others they had observed, but they had no idea how good they really were.

Aunt Mary was not enthralled with the gifts. She believed the boys were too young to have rifles, but once she determined the responsible boys and the rifles were a good fit, she soon changed her mind.

The boys knew the location of a wide, flat-bottomed gully far from town suitable for target practice. Surrounded by woods and two earth embankments to absorb the bullets, the location was isolated and secure. For a firing range they paced distances which they believed equal to fifty, one hundred, and two hundred yards. For targets they placed erect sticks, about one inch wide and one foot in length, in rows on the ground an equidistance apart, and then worked out a scoring system to measure accuracy. When it was completed the boys had a reasonably accurate and safe firing range, and they took great pride that it was of their own design.

Near the shooting range Jesse built a crude lean-to shelter and, nearby, a sizable rock perimeter, fire pit with an iron grill mounted over the pit. In appreciation, Elzie assumed responsibility for maintaining the range and camp site. The range-campsite was an impressive project, perfect for the purposes of the brothers, and other amenities and comforts were added as time passed. This near perfect location not only became their private playground and shooting range, it became their favorite escape place, suitable for any season.

In early October of the same year, the boys planned to camp at their practical, pristine site for the weekend. In fact, the proposed outing was an outcome of their earlier conversation about spending too little time together, and now their plan was coming together. They named their outing "the big adventure, number one." Their timing was impeccable as this crisp autumn day provided the perfect natural setting in the woods. The near perfect temperature was cool, not cold. The dry ground was covered with recently fallen leaves. The oaks and maples still held their beautiful red and yellow leaves in contrast to the other deciduous trees which had already dropped their leaves. The sometimes thick undergrowth of the forest was diminished by recent freezes, and the summer smells of decay and dampness were gone, replaced by the many fresh smells of fall. The wind was strong enough to move the air without swaying the trees. The sky was clear, and light penetrated areas of the forest which had been deprived of sun for months. The eye could see distant parts of the forest, revealing the forgotten lay of the land with slopes and rises, hills and valleys, and flat lands; and the massive tree trunks stood in contrast to the smaller ones. The boys knew the forest well, but the view each season presented a different perspective. This beautiful October day was a glorious day in the woods, presenting a magnificent view of nature, particularly from the campsite. The boys were primed and the time was right.

This proposed outing was a momentous event to Jesse and Elzie, one which they had planned with all due diligence. They had secured permission from Aunt Mary, they had made arrangements for their chores to be done, and they had taken all necessary precautions. Most of their free time from the previous week had been spent in final preparations for this exalted adventure, and they were impassioned. They had anticipated, they had exercised responsibility, and they had fantasized about what might occur that weekend; and now the weekend was upon them. Surely, nothing could foil this adventure.

Arriving at the site early Friday evening, they first prepared and ate their meal, and then spent the evening sitting around the campfire, talking and telling stories. Both sensed extreme pride not only to be on the planned outing, but to be there on their own. They were content to passively savor the blissfulness of the moment, quite willing to sit around the fire without direction or purpose. They took pleasure not having to submit to others daily regimen, or required to find sleep at a given hour. "I think I'm going to put another log on the fire, I'm not ready to sleep yet. How about you?" Without time for Jesse to answer, Elzie continued, "I love the night sounds. Look at those stars. I like being here, it just feels good. Do you like it as much as I do?"

Jesse only slightly hesitated before answering. "Well, I don't know how much you like it, but I suspect I do. However, I'm beginning to think that we like it for different reasons. I like the freedom of being on our own, not responsible to other people. I like the time to think, or being able to swear, or taking a leak, whenever and wherever I want. I think I just like the independence. Now to me, you're different. You love nature for what it is, you appreciate it more than most. You seem to like everything in the wild, and you probably function better in the wilderness than I do. Am I right or wrong?"

"You're right that I love the outdoors, but I think you do too, and I don't think I do anything better than you." Elzie smiled as he continued, "This time you underestimated Jesse."

That comment merited a laugh from Jesse. "Yeah, perhaps. I do love the outdoors, but you just appreciate things out here more than I do. You know trees and plants and wildlife better than me. You're just naturally more at home out here than I am. In fact, nature may be your true home. And as for doing things better, let me tell you something, little brother. For your age, you are more advanced in many more ways than I was at your age. Plus, you have a spirit about you that is different from anyone I know. You love excitement, you seek adventure, and yet, you're usually self-contained. I wouldn't be out here had you not talked me into it, and I certainly wouldn't be out here by myself. You would. I think you would be here most the time if you could. Already at your age, you swim better than I do, you're a better hunter than I am, and physically you're getting pretty strong. When it comes to shooting, you're the best I've ever seen. You have a natural eye for shooting. I was telling Uncle George, the other day, what a good shot you are. He agreed with me. We decided, that if you can see something, you can shoot it. Can't say that about many people." Jesse paused, and Elzie said nothing. "The list of your outdoor talents goes on, but I'm going to stop before you get a big head."

Although it was dark and Jesse could only see the outline of his brother, he had no doubts that Elzie was sporting a huge smile and about to capitalize on what was just said. Elzie proved him right when he said, "I've already got a big head. Don't stop now, I'm enjoying this." Just as Elzie spoke, Jesse heard a strange sound from the woods.

"Quiet, Elzie, listen to that sound!" Somewhat spooked by the unusual sound they both listened intently. "What animal is making that noise?"

"I hate to say it, but that's not one animal. Listen, that noise is all over that area." Both reached for their rifles, and Elzie shouted, "Who's there?" There was no answer. "If you're somebody playing a joke on us, you better come forward or I'm going to shoot your ass off." There was no answer. Elzie fired high into the woods.

"God damn it, Elzie, don't fire at it. We don't know what it is. Might be cattle or something." Jesse quickly struck a match and lighted the lantern. He inched closer to the sound with the lantern in front as far as his arm could reach. Suddenly he turbulently jumped back. Exactly at the place he was attempting to see, a flutter of noisy movement had erupted and he dropped the lantern just as he saw the shadowy outline of several large creatures scurrying away from him.

"Oh shit!" Elzie exclaimed. "It's a pack of wolves. Get back here."

Having just stood so close to the wild wolves, then realizing the danger of such, almost unnerved Jesse. He had been foolish. He knew better than to do that. The wolves were apparently gone, but not the shock and fear. He wondered why the rifle shot had not scared them. Something was not right. Looking at Elzie, he said, "Are you sure they were wolves?"

"Yes, I'm sure. I saw at least four or five."

The mere thought of a pack of wolves horrified Jesse. "Put more logs on that fire. Keep that fire bright! We'll just have to wait and see if they come back. Let's sit close to the fire where we can cover each others backs. I don't like this, no, sir, I don't like this one little bit. Usually, wolves would run from us."

"I've never seen more than one wolf at a time. Have you?"

"No, I don't think so," Jesse answered with concern.

Jesse's obvious fear enervated the younger brother. After brief thought, Elzie attempted to diffuse the anxiety. "Don't worry, we need to think it out, that's all. We know wolves act different in groups. Maybe they're braver or maybe they only act braver. You remember Dad's saying, you act like a pack of wolves, and he says that when we act mean in a group and do things we shouldn't do." Elzie paused a moment. "I agree, I don't like it either. What are we going to do?"

"First, let's see if they come back. We needn't panic. I don't think even a pack will get near the fire. Let's think. We got ourselves in this mess and we'll get ourselves out. Let's think."

The next few hours, neither boy saw any more wolves or heard any disturbing sounds. Convinced the wolves were still there, and the wolves were still watching them, they stayed alert, listened, and attempted to identify, or distinguish all the different night sounds. The entire experience was disconcerting. Speaking very softly so as not to miss any sounds from the woods, Elzie asked, "Do we need to go back to the house?"

"Not me. I'm not walking in those woods at night with wolves out there. I'm going to stay right here until daylight. It ought to be light in two or three hours. If you got any sense, you'll stay here too."

"I've got sense, and I'm going to stay right here with you. But I think I'm going to lean up against the tree."

Glancing at the tree, Jesse responded, "What a good idea. Only instead of leaning on the tree, let's climb it, find a good, strong branch and sit on it. Nothing can get to us there. We'll take our rifles. We'll feed the fire, make it big before we go, and we'll climb the tree. Yes, sir, we'll climb the tree. You like the idea?"

"I love it, let's do it."

Elzie and Jesse stayed in the tree the rest of the night, only climbing down at first light. Once their feet were back on the ground and it was fully light, they regained some confidence, but their spirits remained dampened. They proceeded cautiously, but for the sake of their own dignity they had to do something. Jesse scrambled eggs and fried potatoes for breakfast, as Elzie looked around and gathered more wood. There was not much conversation while they ate. As soon as the tins were cleaned, Elzie said, "What do you think we should do now?"

"I don't know about you, but I'm ready to go home. I've had enough of the outdoors for a while. I want to go home and sleep in my bed in a nice quiet room."

Clearly disappointed, Elzie tried to hedge. "How about if we stay the day and go home before dark?"

"Nope, let's clean up, put things away, and go home."

"Ah, come on, let's stay one more day, please."

"End of discussion. I'm going home. Stay if you want."

Elzie had the last word. "Some he-men we are."

The boys gathered their essentials and started for home. Sometime during the walk back to Milton Jesse knew all was well with his little brother when Elzie said, "Maybe we can do this again sometime, when the wolves aren't around. Maybe we can talk some more tonight about what you're good at, and what I'm good at. How about it? Is that a deal?"

"It's a deal. I want you to know I'm proud of you, again. Proud of the way you acted last night, and proud of the way you bounced back today."

"I'm not sure why you're proud, but I'm glad you're proud. You're an okay big brother." Once the reassuring words were spoken, both became silent. It became a long, quiet walk home, with needed time for introspection.

Upon arrival the boys found Aunt Mary scrubbing the kitchen floor. Elzie was the first to speak. "Surprise, guess who's home."

"Well I can't imagine, unless it's the mighty campers of Milton. I bet you boys missed my home cooking, or maybe you missed the chores. Either way, you're too late. The chores are done and breakfast is over. Come to think of it, there is some corn bread left. I was going to mix it with the slop for the hogs, but I guess, if you want it, you can have it."

"Don't give it to the hogs. I don't know about Jesse, but I'm starving, especially for corn bread. Is that it over there?"

"Calm down, Elzie, she's not going to throw it out. Before we eat we've got to explain why we're home so soon."

"That would be a good idea. Why don't you boys sit down and I'll get you a glass of good cider. I want to hear about your adventure, your escapades."

Sitting at the kitchen table, the boys vividly described, in great detail, their encounter with the wolves and their emotional feelings during the event. Their seriousness of purpose and animated descriptions convinced Aunt Mary that this event had been a crisis of major proportions, at least in their minds it was. Showing her sensitivity, Aunt Mary worked with the boys to analyze the good and bad decisions made during the crisis. Her conclusion was, "You boys handled the situation. You did right, both in what you did last night and in coming home today. I do encourage you to go back soon and spend another night there, so that your memories will be good ones. You need to wipe out the fear and replace it with the good thoughts of camping. It's what Uncle George calls, getting back on the horse after you fall off. I hope you will go back soon. You are brave children and you exercised good judgment."

With new found confidence, Jesse said, "We're not afraid and we'll go back. Thanks for the advice. Some adventure, huh? We're a pair, aren't we?"

Mary ignored the self-degrading comment and continued with her take on the event. "I'm sure there will be many more such experiences for both of you. It's part of growing up. Learn from your experiences. You both learned a lot about each other from this, and I've learned something too—that, together, you guys can deal with unexpected events. You know how to survive, by working together. You're a good team. But you do realize there is another view of your night in the woods. To the outside eye there is humor in your adventure, and when you think about it, it is a funny story. People are going to tease you about last night. My advice is to laugh with them, and don't get angry. Take the teasing like a duck takes water, and just let it roll off your back. Will you do that?"

Surprised by the teasing concept, Elzie said, "I'll try, but I don't know what I'll do if some pansy punk makes fun of me, but I'll try."

"We'll both try," Jesse responded. "Come to think about it, it was sort of funny seeing Elzie scurry up that tree."

Aunt Mary chimed in, "How many wolves did you say you saw, Elzie, fifteen or sixteen? And did you say each was about the size of a horse?"

"Quit it, you guys, that isn't funny. If you want something funny, Aunt Mary, you should have seen Jesse jump when those wolves ran. I'll bet he jumped three feet, straight up, or maybe that was the hair on his head standing that high."

The following weekend Jesse and Elzie went camping in the same place. They saw no wolves. In effect, they got back on the horse, and most of the good natured teasing rolled off their backs.

Most activities of the youthful residents, humorous or not, were never secret for long. Jesse's and Elzie's adventures earned them a local reputation, and with the reputation came considerable teasing, from the towns folk, for misadventures. The good spirited teasing, more than not, was prompted by envy or admiration of the boys' various activities. Because of their youthful endeavors and accomplishments, they became high profile brothers. People were eager to hear their stories, partly because Jesse was such a great storyteller, and partly because of the many vicarious thrills created by the stories. The boys were forthright and honest, identifying errors as well as successes. They learned to be responsible for their own safety and well-being. They came to know their own limits; plus, wisely, they learned the limits of each other. To many folks the brothers were exciting young people. Yet the boys continued to regard their lives as most mundane. From their perspective, life had too few adventures and too many instances of unpleasant or dull experiences, for they were young and there were many more exciting hills yet to climb.

One particular adventure became ingrained in memory. The outhouse at home on North Street was in need of work because the human waste had been allowed to accumulate too high in the pit. Thus, the outhouse needed a different location and a new pit had to be prepared. Uncle George also demanded that some of the waste should be retrieved and used for fertilizer. Both jobs fell to the boys, with neither boy anxious to tackle the task. They did it because it had to be done, but mostly because Uncle George told them they had no choice. Needless to say, neither looked forward to this endeavor.

With advice from Uncle George the boys dug the new pit, built skids to move the building, and successfully transplanted the outhouse to its new location. The bulk of the work was completed in five days, but the remaining task, the undesirable task, of spreading the waste and filling the old pit, was yet to be completed. The final phase of the task had to be done in proper sequence, which meant they had to haul the waste before they filled the used pit. They stalled, as they tried, in vain, to figure a more desirable method to complete the task. Pure and simple, neither wanted to participate in such a displeasing undertaking. They even considered filling the pit first, and telling Uncle George they forgot about spreading the waste until they already had put the dirt back in the pit. But, wisely, they decided that ploy might not work.

Sitting side by side under the backyard crab apple tree on that cool November morning, Jesse announced, "Well, we've got to do it, there just isn't any other way. If Uncle George comes home tonight and this still isn't done, it's going to be hell to pay and we know it. So, let's get at it. You get the buckets and I'll get the ropes and gloves. I think it might be better if we only fill the buckets half full and make twice the trips. I don't want that crap to splash all over me. What do you think?"

"You don't want to know what I think."

Jesse thought he needed to ease his brother's mental suffering. "Ah, come on, Elzie, it won't be that bad. I'm just glad it's not hot today and glad we don't have to do this every year. Can you imagine the smell on a hot summer day?"

Directing his anger at Jesse, Elzie reacted in a loud, clear voice, "You make me so mad. I'm worse than mad, I'm pissed. Pissed at you and pissed at your damned attitude. You're the only person in this state, make that the whole world, who is grateful he gets to clean out a shit house, because he doesn't have to do it again real soon, or because the temperature is pleasant. Sometimes I think you're crazy." Changing to sarcasm, he continued, "Oh yeah, its not so bad, why just have the right attitude, and cleaning the shit house can be fun. I take it back. You're not crazy, just stupid. I'm pissed."

There was a brief pause in Elzie's discourse which allowed Jesse to interrupt. "I can tell you are. Stop your cussing. Anything else you want to tell me before we get started?" Before Elzie could answer, Jesse continued. "Let me give you some free advice before you say anything else, you stupid ox. I'm not crazy or stupid, like some people I know. You have such a smart mouth and my advice is you better keep your mouth shut. Remember, I can still whip your ass with one hand behind my back, and you're due, little brother, you're due." Wisely, Elzie said nothing, rather he started walking toward the barn to gather the buckets and tools.

Resentfully, both commenced the task. The strong, putrid smell almost made Jesse sick, but there seemed to be no way to avoid this horrendous odor. The odor permeated everything nearby, in every direction, until soon even their clothing took on the offensive odor. Jesse complained, "It's hard for me to believe that any of this stuff came from my body. There's got to be a better way to fertilize a field." Elzie chuckled at Jesse's comments. "What's so funny? If you enjoy this job so much that it makes you laugh, I have a good mind to leave and just let you enjoy the hell out of yourself."

"It's not that I like this job, as much as I'm just amused that I got a brother who thinks his shit doesn't smell. But I'll bet you're right. It's not your shit that smells. I'll bet it's Aunt Mary's shit that smells. We ought to have Aunt Mary out here doing this. You want to go get her?"

"What I want is for you to shut your mouth."

The pair continued working together transporting human waste, neither saying anything. Once a reasonable amount of cool down time elapsed, Elzie started in again, but Jesse ignored him. Elzie would not relent and made one final effort to rankle his brother. Speaking while sporting a sheepish grin, Elzie said, "I've never seen you so mad, Jesse. I'd kind of like to know what I said, in case I ever want to get you mad again."

"Keep it up, buddy, keep it up."

Elzie saw the need to back off. "Now don't get in a huff, I'm just talking to hear myself talk. All that aside, I do have a serious question. Can I ask it, without you wanting to fight me?" There was no response. "I want to ask you about that attitude stuff." There was still no response. "You know, you're always saying I got a bad attitude. How do you get a good attitude?" Pondering the seriousness of the question, Jesse looked directly at Elzie, but said nothing. Realizing that Jesse was still peeved, Elzie continued cautiously. "I really want to know. When we were working in the garden the other day you kept talking about all the good food we were going to get out of it; and all I could think about was all the work we had to do to get the food. Isn't that the kind of attitude stuff you were talking about? How do I get the proper attitude so that I like to work?"

Still not certain if Elzie was serious or flippant, Jesse chose not to answer the question. Elzie spoke again. "All kidding aside, I want to know. Is it possible for someone to change his attitude?"

Jesse temporarily stopped working and looked at Elzie. He decided it was a serious question, and as an older brother he should try to give Elzie an answer. Changing his ruffled demeanor Jesse answered in a sincere tone. "Elzie, I don't think anybody likes to work all the time, but we have to work to live, especially people like you and me. It's got to be done, and we're the ones who must do it. No way around that simple fact. So, I just take it as part of life. Make no mistake, if I could go through life without moving outhouses and hoeing gardens, I would. I suspect that before our lives are over you and me are going to do a great many things we don't want to do. But, we're going to do them because they have to be done. Living isn't free! We pay the price everyday of our lives and sometimes it's a mighty high price that we pay. It's just that simple! I think the key is finding enough pleasure in life to make work bearable. Sometimes, even work can be enjoyable. If that's what you mean by attitude stuff, I guess that's my answer. Yes, I think you can change an attitude. It's not easy, but it can be done."

"Are you telling me that if I think a good attitude, I will have it?"

"I think you have played that too dumb card one to many times."

Knowing that he was still on thin ice, Elzie treaded carefully. "No, I really don't understand for sure."

Not totally convinced Jesse proceeded cautiously with further explanation. "No, I'm not saying that at all. I'm trying to say, and maybe I'm not expressing it well, that you and me are not rich folks."

"Well, I know that."

"Just wait a minute and give me a chance to answer your question. Don't get smart!" Elzie appeared somewhat unbelligerent so Jesse resumed speaking. "Whatever we have in life we're going to work for it, and I suspect very few things will be handed to us on a silver platter. So what's the alternative to hard work? For us, there is no alternative and that's my point. If hard work is our only avenue to a decent livelihood, why not accept work, instead of resenting it. I don't enjoy work any more than you do, I just resent it less."

Elzie looked perplexed. "It's as I said, huh? Just think it's easy, and it will be. Nope, I'm not old enough to do that yet."

"You're old enough, you just don't want to understand. Let's try again. Your attitude isn't always bad. No one likes all kinds of work, but you like some work. You like tending the yard and working the flowers. You like cleaning your rifle. You like hiking long distances."

"Yeah, but that stuff is fun, not work."

"Exactly what I mean. You view it as fun, so it's not work, it's fun."

"So you mean I've got to start thinking that work is fun. Mm, that's going to be hard to do. Say, Jesse, I've got one more question. Do you really think you can whip me with one hand behind your back?"

Disgusted with Elzie's last question, Jesse gave no answer. Instead he said, "We're not that far from done. Let's finish it and be done with it forever."

Under his breath, Elzie muttered, "Or until it fills up again." Trying to ignore the odor, they both worked hard until the worst part of the task was behind them. They had lowered the level of waste by two feet, and all that remained not completed was to fill the old pit with the dirt from the new pit. They drew water from the cistern, cleaned the buckets and themselves, and fetched the shovels to finish the job. With less than a dozen shovels full of dirt in the pit, Elzie leaned on his shovel and slowly spoke in a challenging fashion. "I really don't think you can whip me with one hand behind your back, big brother. What do you say we find out? Indian style. My right foot against your right foot and my right hand in your right hand, except I get to use both hands. First one with both knees on the ground, loses."

"You mean to tell me you want to do it right now?"

"Yep, why not? Let's add a little pleasure to our work. You know, a proper attitude."

This time Elzie had gone too far. His last words infuriated Jesse. "Okay, little brother, with one change. I'll use the left hand if you don't mind. And if you lose, you take it like a man."

"All right with me. And when you lose, you can take it any way you want. Get ready, and we'll start when I say go." They squared away and Elzie put the contest in motion. "Ready, set, go!"

They wrestled and Elzie was on his knees in less than a minute.

Jesse issued his own challenge when he yelled, "Say uncle, and I'll quit."

Reacting to the humiliation and exerting with all his might to pull Jesse down, Elzie yelled back, "I'm not on the ground yet. I said knees but I meant body." The older, stronger brother only smiled and in a mighty burst of strength, he jerked hard and Elzie helplessly rolled prone to the ground, and unable to stop his body's momentum his lower half rolled partially into the old unfilled pit. As he struggled to escape he slipped deeper into the waste until he finally stopped his struggle and desperately clung with his arms to the side of the pit as his bottom half remained engulfed in the sludge of human excrement. Elzie screamed, "Give me your hand, get me out of here, hurry... uncle, uncle!" Jesse was laughing so hard, he almost lacked the strength to retrieve his younger brother, but he managed to get him out of the pit, safely back on solid ground.

Continuing to laugh, Jesse said, "You sure do stink. You want to go two out of three?" Then he laughed harder.

Once on his feet Elzie frantically struggled to remove his clothing. He was debased and incensed. Jesse only watched and laughed, offering no assistance. Finally, Elzie stood stark naked on bare ground on that cool November day, and without any fear at all he walked directly to Jesse, stood face to face, and proclaimed, "If you say one more word or laugh one more time, you're going in the pit. I don't care how strong you are, you're going in the pit. If you tell anybody about this, and I mean anybody, I won't talk to you for ten years." Jesse gave no acknowledgment but did turn away so that Elzie could not observe his expression.

This retreat satisfied Elzie and he walked away with the small amount of dignity he had left. Elzie threw water on his clothes, picked them up, and walked the most direct route to the house, not looking back, not looking anywhere.

Jesse finished shoveling the dirt, smiling the whole time. With the task soon completed he went to the house so that he could describe the events to Aunt Mary, or anyone else who would listen. He decided to risk the ten year silent treatment. He relished his mental image—the image of a bare ass Elzie, dragging his clothes and walking to the house with his head down. Jesse felt no guilt or shame for his involvement in the affair. For some reason he felt his younger brother had it coming.

CHAPTER 5

DISRUPTION

Not all events occurred according to plan. Another lesson Jesse and Elzie would learn well.

The winter of 1907-1908 was not an especially harsh winter in the traditional sense, but it was a most difficult, almost devastating season for the McCullah household on North Street. After completion of the fall harvest, Uncle George fell seriously ill. The local doctor remained stymied, unable to determine the cause or exact nature of the illness other than to verify that George was seriously ill; and, therefore, the doctor was unable to successfully treat him. Many remedies were suggested, in vain. Laxatives, change in diet, tonics, bed rest, and many other possible cures were attempted with little success. Uncle George found no repose. Some friends, offering explanations, thought he was just tired, a product of working too hard all of his life. Having worked as a farmhand since the age of fourteen, Uncle George had never enjoyed a vacation or successive days off work other than scattered days in the winter season. Perhaps he was merely worn out. Having turned sixty-nine years of age the previous August, some were convinced his malady was no more than old age. Whatever the illness, it was eating away at his life.

The aunt and two nephews had sat at the kitchen table delaying their discussion almost one hour, waiting for Uncle George to fall asleep. With apprehension and great uneasiness, Aunt Mary presented her analysis of the situation and offered a scenario for the future. She spoke softly. "Boys, I have a heavy heart, and I need to share my burdens with you. I'm not for sure, but I think your Uncle George is dying." It so hurt her to even say the words that a long pause fell between her sentences. "He doesn't eat right, he doesn't sleep well, and he has no energy or strength. He's just bone tired, with a constant fever, a bad cough, and sometimes a sore throat. And equally painful to me he suffers from what the doctor calls mental fatigue. He doesn't always remember what he should, his mind is weakening. Sometimes he appears fine; other times, especially when he has a high fever, he might not even know me." Aunt Mary stopped talking and kept her watery eyes focused on the tabletop instead of the boys. Although both boys already had perceived the seriousness of Uncle George's condition, this was the first time Aunt Mary had openly expressed her concern, openly displayed her emotions. Each boy wanted to offer verbal support to Aunt Mary, but since neither knew what to say they physically responded. Elzie put his hands on her left hand, and Jesse held her other hand while the three of them agonized in silence.

Regaining her composure, Aunt Mary continued. "Thank you, boys. I'm afraid I will need to lean hard on both of you from now on. Aside from the hurt and pain we now feel, we have a more pressing concern of the most practical nature—we are about to run out of money. When George doesn't work, he doesn't bring home any money. Our meager savings are now depleted, we have no money to live on, and we still have one more year of house payments, before the house is ours. If need be, the Bank of Milton has agreed to extend our mortgage, not indefinitely but extend it, and no matter what we must pay off our debt. Your Uncle George most likely will lose his job, as though that makes any difference, because Douglas Farms needs to hire a replacement to do the winter work. Even if George gets better, we don't know if he still has a job. So, boys, you see our dilemma; we've got to bring in some money."

Without hesitation, Jesse said, "Elzie and I will get jobs. We will find a way to make it, I know we will."

Elzie concurred. "We will find a way." Then his tone changed. "You're not going to give us away, are you?"

"No, no, Elzie. Perish the thought. Rest assured, you poor boys have made more than your share of adjustments. That's not what I meant. I need you to help me think this out. I'm not used to making these kinds of decisions without George. I'm trying to think of what options we have, at least for a while. We need to act right now, but consider alternatives for the future. I hate these kinds of decisions. Do you boys have any suggestions or thoughts?"

Caught totally off guard by the overwhelming question, the boys looked at each other, but offered no constructive thoughts. Elzie offered assurance, "I don't know exactly what we should do, but I know, for sure, we can make it. Let's think."

Aunt Mary responded in kind. "I sort of have an idea for now, but it's up to you boys to agree or disagree with it, and I don't know if it's a good idea or not. Douglas Farms was very impressed with you, Jesse, when you went to work with George to learn farming. They have agreed to give you George's job until he comes back, if he does come back. They didn't talk about pay, but I'm sure they will be fair. No matter what, that would be some income. Think about it!

"Elzie, that means you would need to do more of the chores and maintenance around the place, but at least you could stay in school. Mr. Wilson, the owner of the produce stand, has said you could work some for him after school, especially in the spring, and full time in the summer. That would provide more income. Think about it!

"I'm not sure what I can do, but I have an idea. I would need to buy some chicks, but Mr. Holcome, General Merchandise, said he would buy all the eggs and chickens I could sell him, as long as the demand is there. Lucy Morton, of Eagel Hotel, will send me laundry to do. There might be other jobs for me, I'm not sure yet. That would provide some more income. I've never worked outside the home before so this is all new to me.

"Now, realize, this is only temporary, at least until the house is paid for and we make some money. Then we might come up with a new plan. Well, what do you think, boys?"

Jesse was impressed. "I don't need to think about it, because it's a good idea. I can do it and, maybe, also help you with the washing and chickens."

Before Jesse finished his thought, Elzie shouted, "Heck, yes, that will be easy. As far as I'm concerned, it's a deal. You never know, Uncle George might get better anyway."

"Bless your hearts. Both of you are wonderful children."

Jesse held out his hand. "It's a deal, now let's shake on it"

All three shook hands to affirm their solidarity. The symbolic gesture served to diminish concern, to provide some emotional relief, if but for the moment. They felt satisfaction because they had a plan. The family had looked directly in the eyes of economic despair, and they had escaped its clutches, at least temporarily. Although the threesome did not feel victorious, they did not feel defeated. They had a reprieve.

Jesse started to work the next day at Douglas Farms, as a full-time farmhand. Elzie took on the extra chores and worked part-time at the produce stand. Aunt Mary took in laundry and eventually purchased more chickens. Somehow they managed and endured, all the while praying Uncle George would recover. Nonetheless, it was not to be as the evil hand of fate had only started to play out. The family problems were only delayed, not eradicated.

Uncle George passed away in his sleep, May 1, 1908, at age sixty-nine. Aunt Mary scheduled no official wake for Uncle George. On the second night following his death a visitation was held at the funeral home, which over two hundred people attended, and burial with grave side services was conducted the following day at the Montezuma Cemetery. Aunt Mary preferred it this way, instead of the traditional three day public mourning. She appreciated the community support and expressions of condolences, but from past experiences she understood she might become most uncomfortable in such a setting. Aunt Mary preferred to grieve alone in her own way in her own house. On May 4, 1908, family and friends said good-bye to George McCullah. He was not remembered for great deeds or outstanding accomplishments; rather he was remembered for his personal dignity, his positive attitudes toward life, and his deportment. It was a fine epitaph, worthy of George.

The temperature the day of the funeral service was pleasant and the cloudless sky displayed a brilliant blue. It was a fine day to commemorate the life of George McCullah. From the high ground of the cemetery one could see miles in every direction, but most unusual, one could observe miles of the Illinois River as it flooded its banks, presenting a majestic view of the awesome power of nature. Fitting for the occasion, nature and civilization found undisturbed harmony— nature seemed unrestrained by civilization, as civilization appeared undaunted by nature. George McCullah would have approved of this day.

Mourners exited their wagons and buggies on the main road to Montezuma, and entered the cemetery on a grass roadway, about two hundred yards in length. The vista of the many vehicles and numerous mourners was a touching tribute which illustrated the profound loss caused by the death of one respected individual from the small community.

At the conclusion of the funeral and before the actual burial, the family exited the cemetery first and the other mourners followed, as was customary. The funeral experience at the cemetery, somewhat steeped in tradition, fascinated Jesse and Elzie. People were hovering over Aunt Mary and Erastus and there was a deluge of support and sympathies. Although the boys attended the service, they felt more like they were on the outside looking in, free to observe the inner workings of the community grieving process. Unsure of their role at the cemetery, the boys deliberately remained unobtrusive. Although they too were grieving, they also were fascinated with their up close observation of the rituals involving death and funerals. The real impact of the death was yet to come, and for now they were content to observe.

Jesse and Elzie remained at the cemetery following the services. Gradually, the crowd dispersed allowing the gravediggers to complete the interment, and the boys watched the burial without questions or discussion. They were showing respect in their own way. The boys had observed, first hand and up close, the entire process of the funeral from the death to the burial. With no disrespect intended, this day became a learning adventure in which they continued to remain unsure of their own feelings as they explored the entire experience. The adventure would not be complete until they were granted the time to absorb, to understand their feelings. They needed to verbally communicate with one another.

Elzie was the first to speak. "Have you ever seen anything like that before?"

"I've seen funerals before, but I've never been involved with one."

"That's what I meant. I didn't know Uncle George had so many friends. You know there were people here that I've never even seen before."

Jesse thought a minute before speaking. "Yeah, me too. I suppose that's the way of funerals. People come to observe the final end of life. They come to support the remaining family."

"How do they support you? What do they do?"

"I don't exactly know, other than they show respect, express sympathy. They show they care, and I think that is important to the family. We were certainly impressed."

"Did you see all that food people kept bringing to the house? Who is all that food for, do you know?"

"I think it's for us. I know for sure that people are coming over this afternoon to eat and visit with Aunt Mary. I overheard her say she was worried about how she would stand up through it all. That's why we've got to be home by four o'clock." Jesse admiringly pulled his watch, a recent gift from his father, from his pocket and studied the timepiece. Elzie patiently waited for some verbal conclusion from Jesse. Jesse stared at the watch, said nothing.

"Well?"

"Well, what?" Jesse replied.

"Well, what time is it, or do we have time to do what you were thinking about, or were you just practicing telling time?"

"Actually, I was thinking about Mother. I wonder if she had a funeral. All I remember about that awful time is Aunt Mary telling us that Mother died, Dad disappearing, and then moving to Aunt Mary's. I don't even know for sure where she's buried. I mean, I know the cemetery and general area, but not exactly where. Do you remember when Mother died?"

"Of course, I remember when she died." A brief, pensive silence followed his strong declaration before he sniffed, cleared his throat, and conceded in a most sorrowful manner, "No, I don't remember when she died. This is awful to say, but I can't even remember what she looked like. I know I used to know. I told Aunt Mary I couldn't remember, and she said I was too young at the time and wouldn't remember. Do you think she's right, or is it just me. Do you remember what she looked like? Do you remember her?"

Jesse was somewhat shocked by Elzie's blunt confession. It had never entered Jesse's mind that Elzie could not remember his mother. The older brother understood he must carefully choose his words before he answered. "Yes, I remember Mother, but I was older, and to be honest I can't remember as well as I used to remember. I sometimes have trouble remembering personal details about Mother, or remembering particular events. I remember a few things, not everything. I wish I remembered more about Mother. I've wondered if it's okay with Mother that I don't remember. I worry and wonder what she would say, if she knew."

Elzie, now more concerned about Jesse than himself, responded with reassuring confidence. "She would understand, I know she would. That's the way mothers are." A short pause indicated he was still thinking. "Do you think we'll remember Uncle George, or in five years will we wonder the same stuff?" The thought about future memory amused both of them to the point it changed their dispositions. Laughing, Elzie said, "I might not even remember you in five years, you big lummox."

"Where did you learn the word lummox?"

"I learned it from you, you big lummox. I heard you studying vocabulary the other night. Pretty good, huh? You study it, and I learn it."

"Call me lummox, one more time, and you're going to be sore all over." Elzie mumbled something beyond Jesse's hearing. "What did you say, little brother? If you're talking to me, speak up."

"I'm not talking to you."

"Well, what did you say?"

Looking at Jesse with a snicker on his face, and in an effort to save face, Elzie, sort of mumbled, "I said I don't want to get sore." Without additional words, Jesse accepted the explanation, knowing full well Elzie did not say that.

Deliberately shifting attention elsewhere, Jesse said, "Come here a minute! I want to show you something before I ask you a question." Looking directly at Uncle George's grave, he continued. "Do you see that the lots are laid out to contain four graves? Look at the corner markers, here and here. There are four graves in each lot. Uncle George here, on the corner, and then three empty graves sites. Now look right behind you. Do you see the corner markers? They look a little different. They are erect and have the name, James Moore, written on them."

"Okay, so what? James Moore is our grandpa. What are you trying to say?"

"Look! There are no headstones, like the other graves. Who is buried here?"

"That's a silly question. Grandpa and Grandma are there."

"How do you know that, and who is buried in the other two places?"

"Nobody is buried in the other two spots and I know it because Aunt Mary told us, but I see what you mean about no markers. If someone doesn't mark the graves, one day we might lose track of who is buried where."

"Exactly, now here is my question. Does it really make any difference? No one ever comes here to look anyway, or seldom comes here. Are headstones for the living or for the dead? Mother doesn't have a headstone. My question is, do we need headstones or is just being buried enough?"

Momentarily pondering the question, Elzie arrived at an answer. "I don't think we need them, but we should have them. I want to know who is buried in the cemetery. At least, I want one when I die. I want people to remember that I am buried there, and I want to be in a cemetery like this one."

"Why?"

"Why, what?"

"Why do you want people to know where you are buried?"

"Because I want it. Isn't that a good enough reason?"

"That's a good enough reason, little brother. I'll tell you what. If you die first, I'll make sure you have a headstone. However, you won't die first, because I'm older. I'll die first, so you better get a backup."

"You don't know that, and I won't need a backup. What about you? Do you want a headstone?"

"I haven't made up my mind yet. Still thinking. That's why I asked you the question. I wanted to hear your thoughts."

"When you make up your mind, let me know. I'll do what you want: get you one, or not get you one. By the way, you better get a backup, too."

"You always want the last word, don't you?"

Smiling, Elzie answered, "Not always."

Again looking at his watch, Jesse nonchalantly mentioned, "It's time to return home. I really don't think anyone will miss us, but I suppose we need to remain respectful. Speaking of respectful, do you realize how little time we have spent thinking of Uncle George? He was a good man, gone now, forever. I think he knew how we felt about him, even though, I don't remember ever telling him. Gosh, I hope he knew. I wonder how many people, in this cemetery, went to their grave before other people told them how they felt about them. I just made up my mind about something important. From now on, for the rest of my life, I'm going to make sure the important people in my life, know that they are important. I'm going to start with you, little brother. You mean a lot to me!" Looking down, he said, "Uncle George, you were important to me and I hope you knew it. If you didn't know it, I'm sorry, because you were there when we needed someone. Good-bye, Uncle George. Good-bye, friend."

Elzie, having listened to and absorbed the meaning of every word, responded, "Jesse, you think and say some of the strangest things. What bothers me the most, is, you usually make sense. I think Uncle George knew, just like I knew before you told me. I'm not sure we need to tell people. I think they know by the way we act." At this point he paused as though he was questioning his own thoughts. "On the other hand, I don't always know how I feel, so how can somebody else know. Now, I have confused myself. This thinking about life and death stuff, is too tough on my little brain. Maybe you have to live a long time before you know the answers to all this stuff. Maybe we're both too young. It's probably not important anyway. I'll tell you what. I'm going to make you a deal. Why don't you and me agree to come back here to this same place, the cemetery, when we're old enough so that we have some answers instead of all questions. Let me see. In 1910, I'll be ten, and by 1920, I'll be twenty. Why don't we agree to meet here in the summertime, say July 4, in 1920? We ought to have a lot of answers by then. Better yet, let's carry it out and agree to meet every ten years, thereafter, like 1930, 1940, and so on. Can you imagine how smart we will be by then? If we don't know the answers by then, we aren't ever going to know. Now that's the end of this heavy thinking stuff, period. Now let's sit down, watch the river flood for a while, and then go home and be respectful."

Amazed by the flow of Elzie's words, Jesse retorted, "I may be strange, but certainly not as strange as you. I'm not sure where, but somewhere in that head of yours, you harbor some good thoughts. I like it, it's a deal. Right here on July 4, 1920. Who knows, maybe we'll even meet here in 1940, if I'm not too old to think by then. I'll be forty-four, you know." The thought of himself as that old brought a smile to his face, but only momentarily. "One more thing before we watch the river. As you know, with Uncle George gone, things are bound to be different around here."

This last comment bothered Elzie. He was concerned, not only by what was said, but by the way it was said. He knew that was no afterthought. "Different, how? What do you mean?"

"I'm not sure how, I'm just sure that things will be different. Things are bound to be different, and we can't get caught off guard by the change. I suspect we're going to be more responsible for ourselves, although, I don't know exactly how. If life gets harder, we'll get harder. I think we can handle whatever happens. I just don't want to get caught off guard. We've got to prepare ourselves for change, that's all."

"Okay with me, cause I like change. And for Pete's sake, let's stop thinking, okay? Now, let's watch the river."

The boys watched the flooding river from the high ground of the cemetery for the better part of an hour; both thinking in solitude most of the time rather than conversing, as the younger boy still remained very preoccupied about his brother's last expression. Finally, they started for home. The boys were late without valid reason, and they knew it. Most uncharacteristically, neither showed concern, and the slow walk home required almost fifty minutes, making them even later. As they sauntered home they discussed the possible changes in their lives, and how they might deal with them. At first, the unsettling thoughts greatly disturbed them until they almost became uncomfortable with the idea of change. Fortunately, the more they conversed the more they took comfort in knowing they always had one another. The conversation helped both of them, for they had

80

considered in the abstract the uncertainty of life. Convinced they could handle whatever life brought them, they now became less concerned about change in their lives, or so they felt. They continued walking and talking, remaining in no great hurry.

When they finally arrived home, an agitated Aunt Mary explicitly expressed her displeasure with their tardiness. Contrary to what the boys had assumed, they had been missed. They had been insensitive to people they should have considered important. Both had disappointed Aunt Mary, at a crucial time. To their credit, they felt considerable shame and offered no excuses.

The years 1908-1910, indeed, were transitional years for the boys. Jesse became a full-time farmhand and by age twelve he became the major wage earner in the household. He soon developed a high proficiency in farm labor and, before long, he became a sought after commodity, with opportunities for employment at various farms. He learned to love farming, both the farmwork and the lifestyle, and dared to dream that one day he might actually own a farm.

Elzie continued as a reluctant student, working part-time at the produce stand, never developing a strong commitment to any future vocation.

The death of Uncle George did put an end to the carefree boyhood days of Jesse and Elzie, just as they suspected. Their jobs and additional responsibilities restricted the time each had for the other, and certainly reduced the spontaneous playtime the brothers so cherished. The bond of brotherhood was still intact, but the frequency of personal contact was diminishing. Although lamented by both, the brothers were drifting in different directions. Of the precious little time they now had together, they spent more time talking of past experiences than living new experiences. Jesse recognized that their lives, as close brothers, were changing and he lamented it. Elzie resented it. Both were powerless to alter the change.

Aunt Mary made plans to host a family dinner Thanksgiving Day, 1909. Any holiday get together was most unusual, let alone a family holiday meal. In addition to those currently living at the house, seven others including Erastus, Uncle Ben, and their families were expected for dinner. The proposed event was greatly anticipated by all concerned, especially the children as they seldom enjoyed such opportunities. Needless to say any day with family was considered a special day for Jesse and Elzie, but little did they suspect that on this day Aunt Mary was about to reveal her weaker side.

The mood Thanksgiving Day was festive, reflecting the considerable effort in its preparation. Nine place settings at the table, using the good china on a linen tablecloth, revealed how special this occasion was. No one, other than Aunt Mary, had ever seen the china before. Elzie remarked he had never seen the table with the two added leaves, and Jesse commented he had never seen Aunt Mary cook for nine people. For the first time, since the death of Uncle George, there was frivolity in the McCullah house. The gathering and meal exceeded all expectations, even enjoyed by Erastus. At the meal's conclusion as the children were preparing to leave the table, Aunt Mary made a request. "Jesse, will you take all of the children outside to play? We old timers have some visiting to do."

This request, most unlike Aunt Mary, deeply concerned Jesse. "Is everything all right, Aunt Mary?"

"Of course it is. You children go on outside and play, and let me know when you are ready for more pumpkin pie." Aunt Mary had not revealed the entire truth. Everything was all right for the present, but things might change, depending on the conclusions reached by the adults while the children were outside playing. Of course, Aunt Mary did not express that to Jesse. Jesse only suspected something was askew.

The children did as told and played outside in the yard, the barnyard, and at times in the barn. Carelessly the children frolicked as one would expect children to do when presented the opportunity. Little did they know that as they played, the fate of their playmates, Jesse and Elzie, was to be soberly debated by the adults in charge.

Erastus stood at the window and watched the outside activity. The other adults watched Erastus until, eventually, he initiated conversation. "You have done a fine job, Mary. The boys are something to be proud of. They're polite and well mannered. When the boys first came here, I thought I might need to take Jesse down a notch or two but, now, he appears to have mellowed some. You haven't spoiled those kids have you?"

"I can assure you those boys aren't spoiled. If anything, they might use a little spoiling. They have had a hard life for children their age, and have been forced to grow up, long before their time. We probably have robbed them of part of their childhood."

Erastus became visibly indignant. "Nonsense, they haven't had it any tougher than the other kids. None of us has had it easy, and if you think we have, well, you better think again. Do you think I wanted to send them to you, away from the rest of the family? Remember you were pretty anxious yourself to have someone around here to help with the chores. I suppose you think I've had it easy, raising four kids on my own. I suppose..."

Firmly interrupting in a louder voice, Mary responded. "Just hold your horses, Erastus. Nobody is saying anything about you or the way you raised your family. Don't be so sensitive."

"I'm not sensitive. I just resent your implication. Nobody has been robbed of any childhood. We've all lost something."

In a much needed calmer manner, Ben spoke. "I think you both are right. Things aren't the same since Mary Dosia died, and that's the truth of it. Both of you had no choice but to go on with life, and you did. You did what had to be done. Mary, you and George did a wonderful thing, offering to take the boys. Maybe you're disappointed with what you had to offer them, but I don't see why. They are fine boys, and in no small part, it's due to you. I think you both can look back at the last six years with pride. I hope you both see it the way I do, because that's the way it should be viewed. Do you agree with me, or should I waste more time, and elaborate more?" Ben paused to wait for answers. There were no reactions. "I'll take your silence to mean you both agree. Now, let's get down to the business at hand. Let's do what we've come here to do. Lets make some decisions."

Mary, choked with emotion, walked to the window to observe the children play. She remained there, motionless, for several minutes, while the others watched her, and said nothing allowing silence to prevail. Her mood was somber, foreboding.

Turning from the window and looking at the other three adults, Mary took a deep breath and exhaled slowly. "I guess there is no other way to do it, other than say it clear and plain. I can't make it any longer, I don't have the strength to endure without George. Financially and emotionally, I just can't make it. Let me be absolutely clear about one thing. It's not because of the boys. I couldn't have made it this long without the boys. Jesse and Elzie have done far more than their share. They provide more of the income than I do, and they do everything that I ask. I just don't know what to ask. If George were here, he would say I'm not coping with my frustrations. I suppose that's the crux of the problem. So, I've asked you here today to give me some advice and direction. Something has got to change and I don't have any idea what I should do. I don't want to drag the boys down with me. Something has got to change."

This expression of personal crisis had been difficult for Mary. Erastus, Ben, and his wife, Elitha, all had suspected something was not right, but none expected anything of this magnitude. "What can we do?" Elitha asked. "How can we help?"

"That's my point," Mary rudely snapped. "I'm at wit's end, I don't know what to do, I need advice, I need some thoughts from you, I need help. I just can't go on. I've tried to ask myself, what's happening to me. Am I over reacting or am I just a silly old woman who can't make it on her own?"

Erastus answered first without knowing exactly what to say. "Let's be calm, let's think this out. If I understand you right, you feel depressed and overwhelmed. Is that right? Is there something else wrong, are the boys getting to you?"

"Heavens no, the boys are wonderful and supportive. It's to their credit, I've made it thus far. I don't know, for sure, what's wrong. I think the problem is, George is gone. I haven't prepared myself to live without him."

After brief reflection, Erastus spoke in a commanding voice. "I understand, I went through the same experience myself. It takes time, Mary. Time is the healer.

There will always be a void. It just takes time to build a new life. Be patient, Mary, just be patient!"

"I have been patient, but to no avail," Mary answered before she broke down and cried. Albeit, others were nearby it seemed she cried in solitude, as the others had nothing to say, had no response, because they did not know what to say or to do. After the tears stopped there was still silence until Mary regained her composure and spoke. "It would appear that I'm not going to get many ideas from this group, so here goes. I do have some thoughts, and I need input from each of you. These are selfish thoughts, so prepare yourselves and, above all, please be honest with me." Mary hesitated in her speech, long enough to assess their reaction. "Well, here goes. I hope you won't think less of me for what I am about to say. I am a lonely widow, and I lead a most unpleasant life. I am alone in this world with no adult company, and I think that's the problem. Everywhere I go, I'm by myself. No one stops by to see me any more. When George was alive, all kinds of people stopped by to visit, or we were asked to go places, but not now. Everyone in Milton looks at me with pity, and I just can't stand it. I am a person, not one half of a couple. I feel so selfish for saying this, but I want a life. I want to be around people."

Elitha moved closer to Mary, held her hand, and said, "Mary, you are not selfish, and we understand your plight. What is a women to do? There is no role for a widow, this day and age. Well, there is a role, but not a very desirable one. Heaven knows, it's not easy being a widow. Perhaps we all can be a little more sensitive, and make more of an effort to include you."

"That's exactly what I don't want, more pity. What I need is to naturally be a part of something, not to be part of something because of kindness." Removing her hand from Elitha's hand, she looked at her brother and said, "Erastus, you know me as well as anyone. What do you think?"

"Mary, I don't know what to say. I understand your problem, but I don't know what to say."

"I know what I want to do, and there is no other way to say it, other than to say it. I want you, Erastus, and your family to move in with me. I want us to be a family. I will cook and clean, provide a good environment, and do what I do best, which is, take care of the family. Of course you would need to help with the finances. I certainly would like the feminine companionship of the girls. I think we all would benefit. What do you think? Be honest."

Mary, holding the rank of older sister, surprised everyone with her proposition. She had always been the wiser, more mature, more independent person. Others came to her for advice or assistance, rather than her asking others for help. Uncharacteristically, Mary appeared frail, not in control, unindulgent. This was not the lady they had known and her words, her manner shocked the group, in particular her brother. Realizing the urgent need of a response, Erastus spoke slowly as he answered, collecting his thoughts as he spoke. "Well, I don't know what to say. Ah, ah..." Then his expression began to change. "Ah, I think I like the idea. Do you really think it will work? The more I think about it, the more I like it. Is there enough room for all six of us to live in this house?"

"Therein is the problem, and that is why I wanted Ben and Elitha to be here."

Ben, surprised by his inclusion, said, "What do you mean? What are you talking about?"

"Hold your horses, don't get huffy, Ben. I'm not going to impose on you. I only need a little help, if you'll just allow me to explain, I will."

"Please do. What do Elitha and me have to do with this?"

"It would be very crowded for all of us to live in this house, but it would be possible. I thought we would explain to Jesse and Elzie, and get their thoughts. I know how much Jesse thinks of you, as he has said many times that he admires you as a farmer, and he wants to learn from you. I also know you have an old house behind your place that no one has lived in for years. I hoped we could give Jesse a choice. If he wants to stay here, we can make it; or if he wants to be on his own, he'll have the opportunity. He is capable and for all practical purposes he already supports himself. Jesse is very handy and could fix up that place in no time. He wants to be a farmer. This wouldn't hurt him, it would help him. Anyway, I need your approval before I offer him this option. Who knows, he may want to stay here, although I doubt it."

Looking perplexed, Elitha asked, "Why do you doubt it?"

"Because I know Jesse."

"I'm not sure that answers my question. How old is Jesse, anyway?"

"He'll be fourteen next February."

"My God, Mary. Thirteen years of age and on his own. That should never happen."

Erastus interrupted. "I agree with Mary in that I think he can handle it. Unless, of course, you want him to live in the same house with you."

Ben spoke before Elitha could answer. "We have enough in our family. I think the old house is a good idea, as long as, Jesse knows it is not permanent. Make sure he understands that he is on his own and that we are not responsible for him, we are just helping him make the transition to live on his own. Can he take care of himself? Can he cook, do his washing, get himself up on time, and manage his affairs? I don't want to raise another kid."

Mary answered with a soothing voice of confidence. "I can assure you, he can do all those things and more. Jesse likes to please. He anticipates things that need to be done, and then does them. He is always repairing something or improving something. George would say Jesse walks the place each night in search of prob-

85

lems, thinks about the problem for a while, and then solves the problem by making a minor repair. He uses scrap material as well as anyone can. George was surprised at his talent because no one taught Jesse how to do repair, he just figured it out. What I like about it too is, he never wants credit. Some things he fixes and you don't even know it's fixed until you get ready to use it. Yes, he is a good fixer, a real handyman, that Jesse."

Erastus interrupted Mary. "He got that from me, that's my blood in him." This remark amused the others, but no one contradicted Erastus.

Upon hearing the positive comments about Jesse's abilities, Ben became more attracted to the idea of Jesse living in the old house. "We have a lot of things around our place that need fixing. Maybe we can work out an arrangement of fixing-work for rent. Might be real possibilities here." The longer Ben talked, the more he liked the idea, but he did not want to sound as though he would benefit from the move. Instead, he praised Jesse. "I can tell you this much. That kid is a good farm hand and everybody knows it. He could get a job today on most of the farms in Pike County, if he wanted it. If he does choose to move, it won't be long before one of the larger farms will snatch him up. Mark my words. He'll have his choice of farms and places to live."

Mary spoke offering closure. "I would like to make a suggestion. Why don't all of us think a little longer about what I have proposed. Ben, you and Elitha need to talk. Erastus, you need to give this considerable thought, as this basically involves your children and their futures. You have the two girls, the two boys, and, also, yourself to think about. None of us should take this lightly. Why don't we meet here this Christmas, for dinner, and make our decisions then. Also, I think it best if we keep this discussion among ourselves. For sure, none of the children need to know. Let's keep it on the q.t. Are we in agreement?"

All were in agreement, at least there was no open disagreement until Elitha appeared uncomfortable and squirmed in her seat. Her perplexing expression revealed qualms. In fact, she was somewhat embarrassed by her husband's selfish expression and not yet sold on the idea. Observing her expression, Ben asked, "Elitha, do you want to say something?"

Elitha hesitated and then spoke. "I have one more question, or perhaps a request. I don't know these boys as well as the rest of you. Ben seems to know Jesse. Erastus is the father, and they have lived with Mary for the last six years. Could we take a few minutes to talk about the boys? Do you know what I mean? Let's talk about their weaknesses and their strengths. I believe we need a discussion that reminds us all, who they are. After it's all said and done, we want to do what's best for them, as well as what's best for us."

Almost in a defensive manner Erastus snapped at Elitha. "Let me set you straight on a few things. These are my boys and I'm not going to do anything to hurt them. Life doesn't always follow a golden path to a perfect world. Sometimes your life changes without your consent. People die, or you run short of money, or disasters occur; and as common ordinary folks, you damn well better adjust. If you don't adjust, you don't survive. The sooner all my children learn that, the better off they will be. Life, even when everything goes right, isn't easy, and we all know life isn't fair. If Miss Goody Two Shoes thinks we are too harsh, so be it. Who cares?"

After listening to the unwarranted attack on his wife, Ben started to respond to Erastus, but Mary shouted, "Enough, Erastus. There is no reason to vent your frustrations on us. We know you have had a lot of bumps in your life, just as I hope you realize that no one here has lived on easy street. There are no silver spoons here. Now if you calm down and think a minute, you'll realize that Elitha has a valid point. The more accurate information we have, the better our decisions. Now, are you calm enough to contribute to this process, or are you going to verbally attack someone every time you get your feelings hurt?" Erastus sat in his chair, feeling uncomfortable and slightly embarrassed about his previous remarks. He said nothing. Mary waited long enough to embarrass him a little more, but not long enough to make him angry. Mary realized that although she agreed with her brother, she did not like the manner in which he expressed it. She continued speaking. "Good. Let me preface our discussion by saying Jesse and Elzie are two of the finest boys I know. That is not the question here, as they are good kids, period. Initially, it was not easy for them to move here with us. Seldom complaining, they endured. Eventually they began to contribute to the process, doing far more than they were asked to do. They worked hard and expected little in return. I think this alone says worlds about them." Mary's voice was softened with emotion. It was obvious she deeply cared for both.

Sensing Mary's emotional feelings, Ben interjected additional facts, hoping to lift the burden of explanation from Mary's shoulders. "Both have jobs and seem to be responsible enough. I think we'll all agree they are good boys. What exactly do we need to talk about? What do you have in mind, Elitha?"

"What are their interests, or personalities, or problems? Can Jesse make it on his own, or do we just want to believe he can; and, if Jesse leaves, what effect would that have on Elzie? We need to talk about that kind of stuff."

Erastus showed his impatience. "How can we know the answers to questions like that? You women!"

"Enough, I said. You know something, Erastus? For someone so sensitive to what people say to him, you sure are insensitive in what you say to other people. Will you just sit there and listen for a minute? You know something else, Erastus? I think you have worked with mules too long. You're beginning to act like them, and maybe you think like them. Now, do you want to talk and listen, or do you want to end this discussion right now?"

Mary's reprimand of Erastus worked. He sat, red-faced, in the chair and uttered, "You talk, and I'll listen."

"Thank you."

Beginning to understand the importance of the conversation, Ben asked Mary, "Do the boys have problems that we should be aware of?"

"None that I know of. They certainly don't have any physical problems. They're healthy and both are strong as oxen. Both are talented boys, quick learners, and not afraid of hard work. When I say talented it makes me think, I really don't know exactly all of their talents. As you know, they really haven't been exposed to a lot of things. Jesse loves music, I do know that. Elzie draws all the time. Whether he has talent in that direction, I don't know. What I do know is, they seem to learn quickly, and whatever they put their minds to learn, they learn."

Elitha asked, "Do they get along well with other people?"

"Yes, they do, but in very different ways. Jesse loves people. He learns from them. He wants to be in the crowd, not as the center of attention, but as a member of the group. Elzie, on the other hand, is more aggressive, and likes to be the center of attention. Crowds gather around him. Yet, Elzie is more of a loner. He can walk away from the group and be satisfied to be alone. Jesse is less confrontational, unless pushed too far. Jesse seldom loses his temper, instead he pouts. He gets alone and sulks. It's hard to know what Jesse is thinking. On the other hand, Elzie is quick tempered, will blow his stack at the time, and then usually get over it. Yet, people, kids and adults alike, appreciate each of them for who he is. No problem of popularity or social acceptance with those boys."

"I don't know the boys like Mary does, but I have observed some things. When the boys are at our house, little Ben follows them everywhere. He loves to be around both of them. As a matter of fact, I like for Ben to be around both of them. I like their influence. They know when to work and when to play. Jesse has such a positive attitude, making the best of each situation. And I'll tell you one thing for sure. That kid can get the most out of the ground, because he knows when and where to plant everything in the garden; and last year he gave me some tips to make the garden ground more fertile, and sure enough, they worked. I've got the best garden this year I've ever had."

"Oh for God's sake, Ben. He's just telling you what I've taught him."

"That may be, Erastus. Nevertheless, I learned it from him, not you."

"You want to know what I think?" No one answered so Erastus told them anyway. He pointed his finger in the air, started shaking it, and said, "This conversation reminds me of a bunch of old women at a sewing circle gossiping about someone. All this chatter makes no difference whatsoever. The boys are either ready for the world, or they are not ready, and all this talking makes no difference.

If they're ready, they'll make it, and if they're not, they'll learn to be. This is a hard world, and we don't make it in life by talking about it; we make it by living it. Like it or not, that's the way it is. That's all I've got to say."

Angered by this insensitive dissertation, Elitha spoke in disgust. "You want to know what I think?"

Ben and Mary simultaneously answered, "Yes."

"For the life of me, I can't understand why Mary wants an old goat like you to move in with her. I would rather live with a jagged rock, than you."

The back door squeaked as it opened and Elzie stuck his head around the door jamb. He shouted, "It's time for pie. Can we come in, it's cold out here and Frieda is shivering?"

Mary answered immediately. "Well, speak of the devil. Of course you may come in." Once consent had been granted all five children filed in, gathered around the stove, and placed their hands as close to the heat as possible. "Oh my, you kids look so cold. Why didn't you come inside sooner?"

The children looked at each other without offering an answer. Erastus smiled. "I told you it's a hard world—you get cold and eventually you find heat. You learn to do what needs to be done."

Frieda looked at her father with bewilderment. "I would have come in sooner, except Jesse told us you guys were talking about us, and we had to wait outside. Besides, we were having fun, we just got cold. There wasn't anything hard about what we did. It was fun. Did you folks have fun?"

"I'm not sure we had fun, just been visiting. Jesse, why did you think we were talking about you?"

"I'm not sure, Aunt Mary. I just thought you were. Were you?"

Mary looked at the other adults for direction, but finding none she avoided the question. "We've got some good news. Our three families are going to celebrate Christmas, here, together. We are going to have a special Christmas dinner. Doesn't that sound exciting?"

The children smiled at one another in appreciation of the good news. Elzie spoke for the group. "Sounds good to me. I'm anxious, I'm ready for Christmas." Then he looked at his brother and smiled. "You were right, Jesse, they were talking about us." He then looked directly into Aunt Mary's face, but he lost his smile. "Have we done something wrong, again?"

Christmas arrived and the promise of a special dinner with the three families was honored. On completion of the dinner, the children were encouraged to play outside, so that the adults might visit. In fact, the children did not need to go outside, as final decisions about the move had already been made. Erastus had agreed to move with his two daughters into the house on North Street in Milton, expecting to be there by April, 1910. Without any input from the boys, it had been determined that Jesse was to live in the old house at Uncle Ben's place, and Elzie was to stay put. Mary, Erastus, and Ben had agreed this was the best solution for all concerned. Elitha had dissented. For the second time in seven years, Jesse was to be displaced, his life disrupted.

That fateful Christmas day at the McCullah house on North Street in Milton, Illinois, was destined to become a sad, distressing day for all concerned. Erastus had employed his usual tact and had already informed Frieda and Sylvia of his intent for the family to live with his sister, Mary. He presented his explanation for the move in an arbitrary, factual manner, soliciting no input or consent from the girls. He also explained that Jesse would live elsewhere, offering no other data. Jesse and Elzie had not yet been told of the change. As should have been anticipated the girls used the first opportunity to inform the boys of the move. Jesse learned from his sisters that he was to live elsewhere, with none of the children knowing where. When Uncle Ben and family arrived at Aunt Mary's, the children retreated to the hayloft to discreetly discuss the planned event. In the hayloft it was determined that little Ben, also had known, and knew that Jesse was to live alone in the house near Uncle Ben's. The children became angry and hurt, but assumed they were powerless to prevent the change. Jesse, the most affected child, convinced the others that they should say nothing, but wait for the adults to offer some explanation. He remained steadfast, convinced there was more to the story than the children knew. His thinking was that Aunt Mary had not yet spoken, and she would not allow this to happen without good reason. Sylvia, the oldest child, dissented and favored immediate confrontation with the adults, but Jesse's thinking prevailed. Eventually, all agreed they should continue the day as normal and wait for some kind of adult explanation. So the remainder of the time until dinner the children's play was subdued, their spirits dampened. They were still children that Christmas day, but children with heavy burdens.

The adults did not realize that all of the children were aware of their future plans; and, mistakenly, Aunt Mary assumed that the plan was still a secret. Christmas dinner came and went with very little conversation among the adults and no conversation by the children, other than to politely answer adult questions; and nothing about Jesse's move was discussed. Clearly, the meal was not joyous and very quickly the adults, other than Aunt Mary, suspected the children were all aware. After dinner, before dishes were done, Aunt Mary suggested they all sing some Christmas songs. Jesse responded at once. "I would rather not if it's the same to you. Elzie and I prefer to do the dishes. The rest of you go ahead and enjoy yourselves."

No one answered or offered additional alternatives. The adults sat at the table dumbfounded. Aunt Mary soon became distraught, not knowing what to do or to say. All the children got up from the table and helped Elzie and Jesse clear the table and carry the dishes to the kitchen. Each child, by his restrained behavior, demonstrated disappointment with the adults for not explaining. The adults got the message, and as soon as all the children were finally out of the room, Aunt Mary spoke. "The cat is out of the bag. I think it would be best if all of you left. I need to talk to Jesse, right now." Within five minutes of Mary's request the company had departed.

Before the company had completely left the property, Aunt Mary was at the kitchen table and directed Elzie and Jesse to sit with her. Prior to her explanation she extracted from the boys how much they knew and exactly when they found it out. The boys were cooperative, willingly told her what she had asked, and anxiously awaited her explanation. Aunt Mary felt shame as she methodically explained the reasons and the logic of the new living arrangements. The reasons she listed were identical to the reasons she had given to her brother, but without the emotion. She told the boys the truth.

Elzie became incensed, speaking to Aunt Mary as he had never done. "I think the whole thing stinks, I'm ashamed to be part of this family, to hell with all of you. If Jesse goes, I go. I don't care how lonely you are, Jesse doesn't deserve this kind of treatment. I don't understand what makes grown-ups so mean." He got up from the table, his chair falling to the floor, and left the house, slamming the door. Aunt Mary watched him leave, offering no rebuttal, not correcting his behavior.

Jesse refused to show anger, stoically accepted Aunt Mary's explanation, asked to be excused, and proceeded directly to his bedroom. He sat on the side of the bed, placing the tips of his fingers to the matching tips on the other hand, and slowly moved his fingers to touch and then not to touch. He remained alone, undisturbed and sat in the same position for hours, constantly repeating the finger process as he pondered his situation. Before midnight of that Christmas day, Jesse came to terms with his new displacement, and found sleep while fretting about his future. He was not happy, not pleased with Aunt Mary, but he acquiesced and came to terms with the decision. He went to sleep knowing and accepting that, come morning, he needed to prepare himself for life in a different place, a different house.

Elzie's reaction to the news that Christmas day was very different from his brother's. Elzie was angry. So angry that when he left the house that day, he thought about never returning and, in fact, he did not return home that night. The next morning Jesse found Elzie in the hayloft, cold, depressed, and still angry. No one ever knew for sure what Jesse said that day to Elzie in the hayloft, but whatever it was, it calmed his younger brother. Later that morning they both returned to the house, ate a late breakfast, and completed their chores.

January 2, 1910, two months ahead of schedule, Jesse was packed and prepared to move to the old house behind Uncle Ben's house. Elzie waited on the porch as Jesse went inside to say good-bye to Aunt Mary, who had remained indoors seated at the kitchen table. "I wanted to say good-bye, Aunt Mary, and to thank you for all your kindness and consideration these last seven years. You have done so much for me and Elzie, and I know our living here has forced you to make many personal sacrifices. I will never forget that when Mother died, it was you and Uncle George who took us in, and I now accept it is time for me to move on. You are a wonderful lady and I care for you. Thank you and good-bye."

Mary found no words worthy of the occasion. She mustered a weak smile and said, "Good-bye, Jesse. I pray for your happiness and success." He turned and walked out the door to the porch.

"You know I'll go with you. You and I can do anything together," said Elzie.

"I know that, but it's better this way. Aunt Mary was wise in her decision for you to stay here. You stay in school and make something of yourself. Actually, you, Sylvia, and Frieda might have a pretty good life here, if you let it happen."

"I doubt it."

"Besides, we won't be that far apart. In the wintertime, if you look you can see where I'm going to be. Look, you can see the house from here!"

"I don't want to look. It's not that, anyway. What bothers me is I think you got a raw deal. I don't like what they did, and I don't like the way they did it. No matter what you say it wasn't right."

"Well, I don't think that and you shouldn't either. You never know, it might be an opportunity in disguise." Reaching out to shake Elzie's hand, Jesse continued to take the high ground. "So long for now, little brother. I'll be in touch. You be strong. Remember, I care for you." Jesse picked up his belongings—one cloth suitcase in his right hand, a cigar box tucked under his left arm, and a rifle in his left hand—turned, and walked toward Uncle Ben's house cloaked in a veneer of confidence, never once looking back. Not far beneath the veneer could be found the true feelings of a frightened, insecure lad of fourteen, but it was most important to Jesse that Elzie not comprehend his true feelings. Elzie observed his departing brother and thought him a strong, determined man of inspiring perseverance, as he watched his older brother until he was out of sight. As Elzie watched Jesse unhesitatingly walk away carrying his meager belongings, he shed tears. Jesse did not know his brother cried that day, and that was the way Elzie intended it.

As Jesse walked away from his old home to his new house, and away from his brother, he also shed tears. Elzie did not know his brother cried that day, and that was the way Jesse intended it.

As scheduled, Erastus moved to Milton, April 1, 1910, early enough in the year to plant a full-term garden. The move to Milton turned out to be absolutely beneficial to Erastus and Mary, enhancing both lifestyles. Mary secured adult companionship and gradually lost her melancholy. Erastus found sufficient work and gained a housekeeper.

Six weeks from the day he left Milton, Jesse turned fourteen years of age, and continued to live on his own. He never looked back, never felt rebuked, never resented his displacement. To no one's surprise Jesse pursued life on his own, living less than three months in the old house at Uncle Ben's, and approached his new beginning with optimism, tempered only with caution. He had departed Milton with dignity, always believing that his absence from North Street was best for all concerned. He harbored no resentment or anger, having come to understand the economic and social needs of his Aunt Mary. He always believed Aunt Mary to be an honorable person, a lonely lady simply caught in the web of survival.

Uncle Ben had been correct in his assessment of Jesse's job opportunities. During the spring of 1910, Jesse had numerous job offers, and he chose the job which he believed offered a promising future and reasonable security. Jesse found good employment as a farmhand on a large farm near Jacksonville. Jesse was about to start a new chapter in his life. He felt up to the challenge. He dreamed of a better life, and he forged ahead with great expectations.

CHAPTER 6

SIBLINGS GO TO TOWN

Finally, the determined day was upon them. Jesse's joy abounded, tempered only by concern about inclement weather.

Daylight lingers and the darkness of night is brief during late June in central Illinois. A truism on most farms is that once the crops are planted and cultivated the hectic pace of work slows, and the urgency of tasks temporarily diminishes as the fate of the crops is left to the mercy of Mother Nature. This year, 1912, holds the promise of a banner crop. The corn is already knee high, the wheat is golden, and the hay is ready for a second cutting. With the wheat harvest rapidly approaching there is still much harvest preparation to be done, but never at the expense of daily chores or general repairs. Early summer is always a most apprehensive time for the farmer as he hopes for the best and fears the worst.

Routine farmwork is never completed as the end of one task is the start of another. Reliable workers are not only crucial for a successful harvest, but necessary for a successful yearlong operation. Knowledgeable, industrious, and loyal farmhands are always at a premium and are deemed a major farm asset. Jesse A. Moore, age sixteen, industrious and loyal, is becoming more knowledgeable about agriculture every passing day. He is a valued farm worker, a major farm asset.

Today is a glorious day, or at least the beginnings of one. By 8:32 a.m. Jesse has finished his morning chores and he is now free to prepare for the upcoming family adventure. He washes his hands one more time before he approaches the big farmhouse to confirm his departure with his employers, the owners of the Lukeman farm. To be absent from the farm on Saturday morning is most unusual. Jesse locates Mrs. Lukeman, sitting on the back porch, snapping beans, and he greets her with an unusually happy toned, "Good morning, Mrs. Lukeman, is the Mister around?"

"My, aren't we gussied up and spiffy this morning. I almost didn't recognize you. You look nice, Jesse. Are you ready to go?"

"Thank you. Yes, I'm ready, I just wanted to check with the Mister about a few more things, and then, I'm off."

Entering the porch from the kitchen Mr. Lukeman appears delighted to see Jesse. "Do I hear some young man out here bothering my wife?"

After a slight chuckle, Jesse answers in a similar tone. "Yes, you do, but not for long. I'm going to get out of here so she can finish those beans. She has to finish snapping them before she cooks them. If she cooks them, then I might get some." Grinning, he looked at her waiting for acknowledgment, which he soon received when she nodded her head and winked a confirmation. "Mr. Lukeman, I have a few things to talk with you about before I go to town. First, I want to thank you again for the use of the wagon. I will be careful, and all three of us greatly appreciate it. Next, I have a small problem, and I need you to advise me. Actually, I guess it is more of a favor, than a problem. As you know, I'm on my way to meet Elzie and Frieda in Jacksonville. Their train arrives at 11:30 this morning. We were hoping to make this a two-day event, and I wondered if you would mind if the three of us came back here tonight, and they spent the night here, with me. We will be late getting back, but we will try to be quiet, and I promise that they won't be any problem. And if you will agree to that, then I have another request. We all will need to eat, and I wondered if they could eat breakfast with us tomorrow morning. Of course, I would pay you folks for the food. If you think this is not a good idea, then, would it be all right if we slept in the barn, and we can forget about breakfast until we get back to town? If any of this is too imposing, I can make other arrangements in town. Do you have any thoughts, Mr. Lukeman?"

Before the Mister could answer, Mrs. Lukeman responded. "Now don't you be silly. We both would be delighted for them to stay and to eat breakfast. There will be no payment for food on this farm. Besides, we are eager to meet your family. End of that discussion, what's your next question?"

"Thank you, folks, you are such kind people. Elzie and Frieda will be delighted. My next question is, since I'm going to be in town with the wagon, I wondered if you need supplies of any kind?"

"We don't need supplies, but I do have an errand for you. We, also, are going to town tonight because we can't miss a Saturday night on the town. Can we, dear?" He waited for a rebuttal but Mrs. Lukeman denied him the pleasure of a reply. "We can pick up any supplies, but, I'm afraid we might not make it in time to get to Andrews Lumber Company. They close at five o'clock, and tomorrow is Sunday. I have this list of materials to order, materials needed for the new granary. Mr. Jackson, the yard boss, has worked with me on this, and he knows generally what

I want. Make sure you give this final list to him. Tell him I need delivery by the first of August at the latest."

"Sure thing! Mr. Jackson, before five, delivery by first of August. Anything else?"

"Not for me. What about you, Edna. Do you need anything?"

"As a matter of fact I do. Jesse, I need for you, your brother, and your sister to have a good time. Don't worry about anything here. I think we can manage a day and a half without you. Enjoy yourself, you deserve it."

"Thank you. We will, and we'll see you in the morning. One more thing, Mr. Lukeman. Earlier this week, I was working near the bottom land, of the northwest corner of the 320 acres. Do you know where I mean?"

"Yes."

"I noticed the tree limbs are poaching out over the tilled area. I know we have got to cut them again, but it made me think. You have about eight acres of woods there, around the creek, that I think has the makings of good pasture land. Next winter, we could fence it in, do a little clearing, connect it with the forty acres of existing pasture, and put six more head of cattle in there. If we can keep the undergrowth down for the first year, I don't think we will have to trim it back so often, and we will have more pasture. Anyway, you think about it and let me know. I'm going to run now. Don't you folks get too wild on your Saturday night on the town. Talk to you later."

The Lukemans watch in admiration, as Jesse prepares for his journey to see his family. "He is a fine young man, Edna. I feel most fortunate to have him in our employment. It's like the additional pasture land. That's a great idea. He's always thinking. I hope we can keep him."

"I concur. He is a fine young man forced into adulthood, far too soon. However, I do have qualms, not about him, but for him."

"What in the world does that mean?"

"I'm not sure what I mean. The young man is so polite, so well mannered, and I know how you appreciate his work. I worry that he works too hard, or that he spends too little time away from work. I guess I don't know what I mean."

"Now that is one, unusual concern about a hired farmhand—you think he works too hard for us. That's one for the books."

"That's not what I meant, and you know it."

"I'm just kidding, don't get in a huff about it. Of course, I've noticed what you're talking about. I even spoke with him about it a few weeks ago, when we were cutting our first hay crop."

"What did he say?"

"To be real truthful I'm not sure what he said. Actually, he got amused with my concern. He answered my inquiry in terms of life's comforts. He talked of the pleasure of having food when he was hungry. He spoke of finding warmth when it was cold. He spoke of a roof over his head, or clothes on his back. It all made sense at the time, but he never answered my question."

"What exactly was your question?"

Grinning as he answered, "I guess I'm not sure what I asked him. I think it was something about, what made him happy. He claims he wants to be a good farmhand, and that he has a lot to learn. He has a high regard for an Uncle Ben, the man that taught him most about farming. He likes to farm. He says he enjoys what he is doing, and once he learns what he needs to know, he'll back off and enjoy life a little more. Now, how do you argue with that? Already, he's the best hand we have, and he's the youngest. I think he's got it right. I think he's got a good future."

Continuing to snap beans and not looking up, Edna responded. "I guess you're right, but I will bet you, if he's as dedicated to work as you say he is, we won't be able to keep him around here for long, at these wages, anyway."

"Maybe, maybe not. I like the young man, I hope he stays. I believe he is happy here. You do know I let him off work this afternoon. I do what I can."

A small cloud of dust follows the wagon on the gravel road which will lead a proud Jesse to meet his younger siblings. He handles the horse with ease, his stout body erect, and he exudes confidence as he turns to wave good-bye. Today is slated to be a fun day, not a workday. Today holds great promise for the youngest three members of the Moore family.

Earlier in the week after he secured permission from his father, Jesse purchased and sent train tickets to Frieda and Elzie who were to take their first train trip on their own. Eagerly anticipating their arrival, Jesse intends to show his siblings the sights of Jacksonville. Jesse regrets seldom seeing the little ones, as he refers to them, and he views this trip as a unique opportunity to make amends. In his letter of invitation he referred to the upcoming weekend as an adventure, an old fashioned, family outing, and that is exactly what he hopes it to be—a family adventure.

Having turned sixteen in February and having been separated from family for over two years, Jesse often finds himself dealing with the void created in his life by the absence of loved ones. Since moving to the Jacksonville area, Jesse has enjoyed little contact with family members, a situation for which he finds some shame, although he considers his neglect as having been necessary, certainly not intentional. He hopes this weekend will rectify the situation. In addition to Jesse's eagerness for the arrival of his brother and sister, he also feels anxiety. He worries that they might become bored, or homesick, or if they will delight in his planned activities. It is important to Jesse that the little ones enjoy the visit, that the bonds of kinship be renewed, and he knows that nothing can assure that outcome. Rather, it must simply occur.

Immediately upon arrival to town, Jesse responsibly goes to Andrews Lumber Company to conduct his farm business. Afterwards, he goes directly to the East State Street rail station, arriving one hour before the scheduled arrival of the train. Although he has been to Jacksonville several times before, he feels unprepared to show others the sights of town. So to properly acquaint himself with the city layout he diligently studies the posted street map. He need not remind himself that it is considerably more important for the younger ones to enjoy the visit than it is for him. He wishes for this trip to be their adventure, first and foremost. He smiles as he looks at the beautiful blue sky and senses the light north breeze on his skin. It would appear that the heavens have favored him as a high pressure front has moved in over the entire area indicating, for now, the weather will cooperate with the scheduled adventure. Jesse's excitement grows.

The train whistle blows loudly as the eastbound passenger train from Pearl, Illinois, slows as it nears the station. "There they are!" Jesse proclaims to no one in particular when he first sees his brother and sister. They stand together on the car platform waving and smiling as they locate their big brother working his way to the exact location where he thinks the train car will stop. Speaking as though they are able to hear him, knowing full well that they can not, he exclaims, "Oh, what a glorious sight. You are such beautiful children." Realizing they are approaching hearing range, Jesse tones down his rhetoric, not wanting to embarrass himself or either of them. He observes the smiling conductor who stands behind the two young ones with one hand on each of their shoulders. Frieda, now almost as tall as Elzie, is a pretty girl made prettier this day by her facial expression of delight. Elzie, stockier than Jesse remembers, stands proud and appears excited. It becomes apparent they not only enjoyed the train ride, but that they arrived well cared for. Jesse's concern or apprehension for their well being abates. "Welcome to town, Frieda and Elzie!" Jesse shouts. If anyone at the station bothered to look, it was more than obvious that this was a joyous reunion.

They wasted no time becoming united. Frieda, without uttering a word, hugged Jesse as only an adoring younger sister could hug an older brother. Elzie, watching the crowd watch his brother and sister, put out his hand to Jesse for a handshake, partly to acknowledge his presence, but mostly to protect himself from a possible big brother hug in front of the admiring crowd. Sensing Elzie's concern, Jesse shook his brother's hand and politely spoke. "Did you have a good train ride, brother?"

Frieda answered Jesse's question before Elzie could. "We had a great ride. We didn't stay in our seats much. We walked all over the train, and the conductor explained what everything was." Her words reminded her that she had failed to thank the conductor, and she looked for him, sighting him standing several feet from where she stood. She yelled, "Thank you, Mr. Conductor. You're a nice man. Maybe we'll see you tomorrow night. Our train departs at 7:09."

"You're welcome, young lady. Have fun with your brothers."

"I will. Good-bye." Looking back at Jesse, she continued. "Elzie really liked it too, even though you can't tell it now by looking at him. He thinks he's too big to show excitement."

Defensively, Elzie answered. "Frieda, act your age! People will think we're from the sticks. Jesse it is good..."

"I am acting my age. I'm acting like a ten year old and you ought to act your age, like a twelve year old, and we are from the sticks."

Amused by the exchange of words, Jesse said, "Well, it's good to see some things don't change. I'm pleased to see you both. You both have grown so much. Frieda, you're so pretty. Elzie, you're filling out. You're bigger and you look stronger." With a restricted grin on his face, Jesse said, "There's an outhouse over there. Do you want to wrestle, Indian style?"

"That's not funny. I didn't come all this way to take abuse."

Now with a full smile, Jesse answered in a softer tone. "I know it. I was just kidding. I couldn't help myself. I'm so happy to see you."

Baffled by the conversation between her brothers, Frieda inquired, "What are you guys talking about?"

"Nothing, we're just being silly. Here, let me take your satchel. I'll bet you folks are hungry, and I know a few places that look like they might have good food. What do you say?"

Elzie answered immediately. "Sounds good to me. I'm hungry."

"Oh, Jesse, I want to see the city first. Please! Elzie is always hungry."

Demonstrating a sense of fairness, Jesse took control. "How about a compromise? Let's grab a quick bite here at the station, and then, let's go downtown to look around. We have much to see in little time. Is that agreeable?"

Elzie nodded in agreement. Frieda said, "Okay with me."

The adventure commenced immediately. The threesome dined with haste, and the walk downtown started at twelve minutes past noon. The three of them walking the streets of Jacksonville was a sight to behold—a sixteen-year-old farm boy, his twelve-year-old brother and his ten-year-old sister, taking in the sights of what they considered to be a large city.

Less than five minutes into the walk they passed a small grocery store, and Jesse surprised them, and himself, by saying, "Wait, I'll be right back. There is something in here you have got to try." Jesse came out of the store with a pack of cookies and a quart of milk. "This is a new type of commercial cookie, called Oreos. I'll bet you love them. But we have to eat them now, because I've got to return the milk bottle."

The three hastily ate the cookies, save the few they put in their pockets for later.

When Jesse went back into the store to return the bottle, Elzie snickered. "Guess I'm not the only one around here with an appetite. I think you liked those cookies. Isn't that something having cookies already baked and packaged. Hope we can get them at home."

They continued toward the center of town. It seemed with each step they took the activity, the busyness, intensified and the noise level progressively increased. The brick paved street was congested with traffic from automobiles, trucks, horses and buggies, horse drawn wagons, and horses with riders. Electric trolleys riding steel tracks positioned in the middle of the street passed with regularity. The wide, brick sidewalks were crowded with fellow pedestrians, but it did not much affect the Pike County sightseers. By simply following the sidewalks the threesome could just walk along and gaze without concern for safety or direction, and they could observe more of everything if they walked at a slow sauntering pace. Every store showed activity, from either customers or window shoppers admiring storefront window displays. Indeed, Jacksonville was a bustling place that Saturday afternoon, and it was the people as much as the sights which gave this beautiful, organized town its real character, real identity. Some in the crowd showed purpose, some did not. Men and women of all shapes and sizes, various styles of dress, together or alone, blended into a larger crowd with no particular identity. Seemingly unaffected by the crowd, the threesome continued to function, to view everything they saw with wonderment and, somehow without knowing it, they became part of this crowd, part of the hustle and bustle.

Soon the concept of time eluded the threesome. Their legs seemed to function mechanically so that their minds could concentrate more on sights and sounds. At that, their eyes failed to perceive it all. Nor could their minds properly record all they saw as many impressions were fleeting, lasting only until they became overwhelmed by a succeeding impression. Spontaneously, the excitement of the moment was shared with remarks of: look at that, or what is that, or that reminds me of, or did you see. Even when they all looked in the same direction they might view different objects, as one might see the whole structure, one might see the details of the building, and the other might see the activity near the structure. The one common, changeless feeling of the group was excitement. By the time they completed the walk down East State Street and around the square, they were exhausted.

Frieda, somewhat in jest, remarked, "I'm tired. I've never looked so hard in all my life. My neck hurts, let's sit down, so I can see what I've been looking at."

Frieda's wording amused them, although her meaning was understood. Jesse threw back his head, gave a loud laugh, and said, "Let's go to the park in the center of the square and sit on a bench, so we all can see what we have been looking at." Jesse led the way to a bench, carefully crossing the traffic with his arms partially outstretched to protect and to direct his younger siblings. Frieda and Elzie, amused at Jesse's protectiveness, chose not to say anything, just yet. They found an empty park bench which seemed to be the perfect bench in the perfect spot, to see the town square and its activities. They continued to absorb, the excitement never abating.

"After you two are rested I have an idea of something to do, and if you agree, we'll do it sooner than later. About three blocks down, on West State Street, is Merrigan's Ice Cream Parlor. Good ice cream, I understand. How about we go there, get something to eat, and then take the trolley for a look at the town from a trolley car? Then, after we finish looking, we can come back here and decide what else we want to do."

Frieda's response was instantaneous. "Wonderful."

Elzie was more deliberate. "I told you I wasn't the only one with an appetite, but that's good because I'm hungry. What can we order when we get there?"

"Well, little brother, you just tickle me to death! You can order anything on the menu, and I just hope that holds you until supper time."

"If I can order anything I want, it will hold me, I promise. Let's go to the ice cream parlor, and then let's see the rest of the town by trolley. Say Jesse, have you ever ridden in a trolley?"

Not certain if Elzie's question was born of concern, or one of curiosity, Jesse answered in a confident way, even though it was not the truth. "Of course, many times."

As they crossed the busy street to exit the square, Elzie jumped in front of the others, outstretched his arms as if to protect and direct the other two, and led them across the street. Frieda, amused by Elzie's antics, gave a big smile as she looked at Jesse to observe his reaction. It took a minute but Jesse did receive Elzie's subtle message. Quickly, Frieda started imitating Elzie, making it appear as though the two younger ones were helping the older one across the street. Jesse could not hide his amusement, and followed the younger two, playing the game as though he appreciated the assistance. After they crossed the street, Jesse placed his hands on his hips and said, "Elzie, you are a clown. I had forgotten how silly you are, and now I see you are influencing your sister. What a pair!"

"You're absolutely right, Jesse. I do silly things. I'll stop doing silly things like that, if you'll stop doing silly things like helping me across the street, which inspire me to do sillier things."

"Point taken."

The parlor was crowded, mostly with young people, which suited them fine. Frieda and Jesse ordered banana splits. Elzie ordered a banana split and a cherry malt. They ate what they ordered which satisfied Frieda and Jesse. Elzie ordered an additional double dip chocolate ice cream cone. He ate it all, and wondered if he should have ordered more.

The trolley ride was a smashing success, consuming almost three hours. They rode the trolley to the end of the line and back to the square four times, seeing four different sections of the city. Once they completed their trolley marathon, they slowly walked around the square twice, ate again, and went window-shopping before they returned to the city square and sat on the same bench. They felt exhausted, but it was a satisfying exhaustion.

Before Jesse had left the farm he had in mind a special surprise for this occasion. He planned to purchase an article of clothing for each of his younger siblings, so without revealing his intentions he tricked them into looking at merchandise in different stores to discover what they needed. The ploy worked and afterward they went shopping for real. Frieda selected a new dress, a hat, and shoes from Andre and Andre Department Store. Elzie received a new suit and a no collar, pin striped shirt from Myers Brothers Clothiers. Jesse purchased dress pants for himself from J. C. Penney Company. Jesse felt pleased with the purchases, but he felt more pleasure from the fact that the younger ones were so appreciative of the gifts. The shopping event was a special treat, a positive experience. All three needed the clothing, plus, until today they had never been shopping together.

The task now at hand, of how to spend the remaining time and still keep the eagerness and excitement alive, was not a simple one. Jesse wisely determined that either Elzie or Frieda should decide the Saturday night agenda, and the other choose the Sunday afternoon activity. Jesse presented his plan, carefully explaining the need for total cooperation. He expected disagreement, thinking they would select unusual or foolish activities. His fears were unwarranted.

"As I see it, you first need to decide who gets Saturday night and who gets Sunday. Next, you need to agree that both of you will cooperate and participate in the other's selection. Any thoughts, objections?"

Frieda said. "Does it make any difference to you, Elzie?"

"No."

"Fine, I'll take Sunday, you take tonight."

A surprised Jesse offered more input. "Good. Here are a few choices or we can do something else, if you prefer. There is a movie theater on East State. The feature is *An Unseen Enemy*, starring Lillian Gish. From the promotional pictures it looks pretty good to me. Or the Opera House has a stage show. I don't know the particulars, but they sure get a crowd. Or there is a band concert, right here, in the park tonight. Or we can go to the new park in South Jacksonville. I've not been there, but I understand they have a nice lake and I assume they host some type of Saturday night activities. Also somewhere near the park they have a Chautauqua tent. Or we can do what a lot of the natives do on Saturday night: just stay downtown and watch the people. Or, we can do something else if you prefer. Your choice, Elzie. Whatever you want. What do you say?"

Elzie had intently listened to every word. "Wow, that's a lot of choices. Everything sounds good to me. My call, right? Well, I choose to stay downtown, and people watch. Maybe, if we have time and energy, come back here to the same bench for the band concert."

"Great. Is that all right with you, Frieda?"

"Sure is. Tomorrow, maybe, we can go out and look at some of the institutions. We can do most of the other stuff in Pittsfield. We can only see the institutions here, in Jacksonville."

Somewhat confused by the word, institutions, Jesse asked for clarification. "Exactly, what do you mean by institutions?"

"You know. All that stuff we saw from the trolley today, like the blind and deaf schools, the colleges, the crazy house, and stuff like that."

Jesse was surprised by the unlikely wishes of his little sister. "I don't know exactly how to go about looking at them, but I'll bet we can find a way. Is that all right with you, Elzie?"

"It certainly is. Everything sounds good to me. How about you, Jesse? Does all of this sound like fun to you? You should have a say, too."

Jesse had underestimated the maturity of his siblings. Their choices surprised but pleased him. "Sounds great to me. As a matter of fact, you two picked better than I would have. I'm proud of both of you, proud as punch. So let's go do it."

That Saturday night in late June, siblings Frieda, Elzie, and Jesse stayed downtown, walked around the square and watched the people. Their choice to stay downtown was a wise one. They looked in different stores and shops, they conversed with strangers. In essence, they blended into the crowd, thoroughly enjoying all the social interaction. Every moment was consumed with activity and, again, they lost all awareness of time, knowing the evening would end, not wanting it to end. Frieda experienced an adult world through the eyes of a child. Elzie enthusiastically interacted with strangers. Jesse experienced true joy from observing Frieda and Elzie participate in situations uncommon to them. The 9:00 music concert was scheduled to begin shortly after the downtown stores closed, but the threesome deemed mingling and people watching so enjoyable that they remained on the storefront sidewalks until most of the crowd dispersed. By the time they arrived at the concert seating area all seats were gone, and they were forced to watch the concert from afar without benefit of seating comfort. Fortunately personal comfort made no real difference to them. At that, they were sufficiently near to clearly hear the entire band concert, and after some of the crowd departed early they managed to secure seats close to the stage. Following the concert Elzie initiated conversation with fellow concert attendees while Frieda and Jesse mostly tagged along as passive observers. At 10:15 they returned to the wagon for their nighttime journey back to the Lukeman farm. Before they left town, they purchased cold meat sandwiches, a large bag of popcorn, more cookies, three Coca-Colas, and a sack of warm peanuts. They all shared the snacks, but Elzie managed to eat most of the peanuts.

By any standard the day had been a major success, far beyond what they had envisioned. This memorable day would be remembered by the younger ones as a day they were treated as mature individuals, and they functioned as adults, alongside their big brother in the exciting town of Jacksonville, Illinois.

The return trip to the farm required less than one hour. All were very tired, but instead of sleep or restful silence, they reminisced about their exciting day. Shortly before arrival at the farm, Frieda posed a final question. "What was the most impressive thing you saw in Jacksonville, today?"

Although he was unprepared for such a question, Jesse answered first. Stammering with a few uhs, he finally got some words together. "I saw many impressive things, and I'm not sure I can pinpoint any particular one as the most impressive. Maybe the whole thing. I liked the city, the way it was laid out, and the way everything was so efficient. Yeah, I liked the city. Maybe, someday, I might live in Jacksonville. What about you, Elzie?"

"Well, I was impressed with that seven-story bank building. Also, just seeing all the people and visiting with strangers was something else. You know, I figured I saw more people today, in one day, than I have seen in total, the rest of my life. What's the population of Jacksonville?"

"Not positive, I think it's somewhere in the neighborhood of twenty thousand."

"Seemed like a lot more to me. If Jacksonville is twenty thousand, I wonder what it would be like in Chicago. Yeah, one day I'm going to see Chicago, and before I die, I want to visit New York City. Wouldn't that be something! What about you, Frieda? What impressed you?"

Frieda, sitting in the back of the wagon, thought for a minute, and moved to the front so that both brothers could clearly hear her answer. They were arriving at the barn as she spoke. "My two older brothers were the most impressive thing I saw."

They all slept well that night. Breakfast with the Lukeman family and other farmhands was at 7:00, one hour later than other weekdays because Sunday was a reduced workday. Food was abundant and tasty. The Lukemans were gracious hosts and the two guests, polite and respectful, presented themselves well. Jesse was proud. Engrossingly, Elzie admired his brother as Jesse interacted on equal footing with older adults. Elzie saw his brother in a totally different capacity, surviving on his own in the world of work. Naturally, Elzie was impressed, but he was not surprised.

Adding to the kind treatment, Mrs. Lukeman had prepared a picnic lunch for the Moores, and others had prepared the wagon for travel. By 8:15 the threesome eagerly hit the road on another adventure. As they exited the farm site, Frieda remarked, "I feel like royalty. No wonder you like it here." The comment pleased Jesse.

Although the day was already somewhat planned, they decided the hour was still early enough for some latitude in their schedule. Subsequently, they agreed to start the day at the square, where yesterday had so joyfully ended. What they encountered upon arrival at the square overwhelmed them—there were no people, no stores were open. Intellectually, they understood that Sunday activities were different from weekdays, as most people went to church, rested, or spent time with the family, but they had expected reduced activity, not the absence of it. They sat on the same bench as the previous day and became amused with themselves, and amused with their expectations, amused with their naiveté. Spontaneously, their behavior erupted into silliness as every word, all movement became funny. Consumed by the foolishness of the moment they sat and laughed, not at each other, with each other.

Elzie, after controlling his laughter, said, "Not much difference here from Milton on a Sunday morning. I wonder what it's like this morning in the center of New York City? Probably not much different." He tilted his head and thought about his last statement. "Now how would I know that? What a stupid thing to say. Have mercy on me folks, I guess I really am from the sticks." That remark induced more laughter, more silliness.

In total innocence Frieda said, "Look at the iron arch over East State Street! I didn't even see that yesterday. It's kind of like a gate to the square."

Jesse responded. "Yes, it's just like the other one on West State Street."

Elzie said, "Yeah, just like the one we saw there yesterday."

Turning to look, Frieda saw both arches. "Oh my gosh. Are you sure we're in the same town as yesterday?"

Elzie seized the moment by pointing to all the obvious things in his view, and proclaiming they were not there yesterday. His antics were outrageous, but funny. Frieda and Jesse laughed and enjoyed themselves immensely, watching their brother demonstrate his quick wit and sense of humor. The scene was a wonderful sight, if not inspiring, seeing the three youngest Moores, sitting on a bench in a deserted, downtown Jacksonville, laughing uncontrollably.

Elzie jumped to his feet, pointed his finger to the sky, and announced, "I've got it figured out, I can explain it all. Last night we all had the same dream. Yesterday never happened, we only dreamed it did, and today is really yesterday." That induced more laughter. "And, although I liked my dream, from now on, you guys stay out of my dreams. My dreams are personal and I don't want you guys knowing what I dream." They laughed so hard, they fatigued their bodies. The laughter served a purpose as they were openly making fun of their own innocence. Indeed, the whole situation of laughter on the bench was an incredible, therapeutic experience of family bonding.

Eventually, they calmed themselves, returned to the wagon and headed west traveling West State Street. With little Sunday morning traffic it was easier than yesterday to absorb the sights, more convenient to exchange thoughts. The relaxed atmosphere of travel gave birth to a mellow, less intense mood that was not frivolous, nor serious, but simply more conducive to sight-seeing. They passed the courthouse and a large school building, admiring both impressive structures but not taking time to explore them. Once across Prairie Street they entered a residential area with large, beautiful, elaborate houses lining both sides of the street. Although yesterday they had passed this exact location, they had not noticed the many individual magnificent houses with multiple architectural styles, and today they could not help but stare at them in awe. It was Frieda who realized and pointed out that a major part of the beauty was the overall setting including the tree lined street, the proper building setback, and the spacious lots capable of showcasing the architectural masterpieces. All three were taken by such residential beauty and, quite simply, never before had they personally observed such grandeur, such symbols of wealth. Jesse expressed what the others were thinking when he stated, "We can look, but we dare not touch. We're out of our element in this neighborhood."

At the intersection of State and Webster Street, near the grounds of the Illinois School for the Deaf, they rested under a massive sycamore tree in a park they supposed to be public. Since it was the summer months they logically assumed school was not in session, although they observed a few people promenading on the grounds, entering and exiting the buildings. In no way could they determine if the people they observed were hearing-impaired, and in fascination they continued watching but remained unable to discern. Observance of conceivably deaf people resulted in a stark realization for all three, provoking discussions about how life would be different for a deaf person. Questions with no answers provoked additional thoughts and questions. They were intellectually stimulated, dealing with some thoughts for the first time in their young lives. These fresh thoughts quickly lead to a compassion for deaf people, and an appreciation of their own ability to hear. Out of respect for those who might be deaf, and not knowing how to communicate with the deaf, they discussed and selected not to explore the grounds. Frieda waved at the people they were watching, and a few of the people waved back, but it did not help her to determine their level of hearing.

The journey resumed. Traveling east on College Avenue, they saw more beautiful houses before reaching the campus of Illinois College. Seemingly, the campus had unrestricted access. Uncertain if it were proper for them to walk on the campus, they ultimately decided, mostly at Elzie's insistence, to cast caution to the wind, and they followed Elzie as he shadowed the sidewalk to the center of campus. Elzie's action verified that he was the most aggressive of the three. He impatiently yelled, "Come on, hurry up, we're not going to hurt anything. The worst that can happen is they tell us to leave, unless, of course, I get mad and beat the guy up and then have to spend the night in jail. Just kidding, I'm not that stupid, at least I don't think I am." Jesse and Frieda continued in pursuit of Elzie, and Frieda became convinced that an aggressive nature was not all bad. She appreciated Elzie's leadership on the unofficial tour of the entire campus. Jesse expressed his attitude when he said, "Go on, Elzie. We'll hold with the hare and run with the hound. You're the man."

In the middle of the campus they came upon a permanently displayed sign which revealed that Illinois College was the first college in the state of Illinois, established in 1829, and that they were standing in front of Beecher Hall, the first college building in the state. They were duly impressed. Intrigued by all they saw they naturally wondered about the academic world, but unable to imagine the collegiate life, they found themselves with few answers and with additional thoughts to ponder. College was not a new concept to them, but it was a remote concept.

Manifestly, the siblings revealed different attitudes based on their individual observations. Frieda, in particular, appreciated the campus, and several times she verbally noted its overall beauty. Elzie was impressed with the massive trees, each tree tagged and identified. Jesse saw unused buildings in a delightful setting, and he understood he lived outside this world.

Continuing to travel east, admiring what they could discern, but unable to absorb all they viewed, the adventure continued. Soon after they crossed the Church and College Street intersection, they came upon a single house of such proportions that they could not view it in its entirety without moving their heads. Halting the wagon on the street directly in front of the house, they gaped at the mansion. The manicured grounds, encompassing almost one full square block, were enclosed by an elaborate wrought iron fence, and granted an impression more similar to a country estate than a house situated within a town. The brick mansion with stone corners and stone steps was the largest private abode any of them had ever seen. They were awed, not only by the building's vastness, but also by its beauty, and quite naturally, they wondered what it would be like to live in such a house. Quickly, they concluded that such concepts were well beyond their imaginations. Jesse suggested that unless one were wealthy, one could never truly understand the lifestyle of the wealthy, an idea totally rejected by Elzie. Frieda agreed with Jesse, although neither could help but wonder how wealth would change their lives, their futures.

Continuing east, passing the city library and turning south on Main Street, they set a course for the village of South Jacksonville. Soon they crossed a bridge over a small man-made brook, a most picturesque sight reminiscent of a rural area. Activity within the town seemed to increase the further from the center of town they traveled. More people emerged from their houses and more automobiles took to the streets. Elzie remarked, "Jacksonville is like an ant hill. The inhabitants all come out at the same time, and you can't tell what anyone is doing." His analogy was amusing, if not somewhat accurate.

Once the trio arrived at the corner of Main and Morton Streets, they were presented with a commanding view of the extensive grounds of the Jacksonville State Hospital for the Insane. Inside the confining wrought iron gates dozens of people were stirring about, engaging in a variety of activities. The mental institution seemed to be a microcosm unto itself. Ironically, the activity inside of the gates appeared little different from outside activity. This observation intrigued them. As far as they knew, none of them had ever observed a mental patient before today. Now they were watching scores of institutionalized patients and they detected no difference apart from the fact that the patients were confined. This was not a comforting thought. Elzie summarized his feelings when he said, "That is one scary idea. How do you tell who is crazy around here? I sure hope someone knows how to tell. Do you think the people on the inside know how to tell the difference? Sure glad I don't have to prove I'm not nuts." Realizing that his last statement opened him to ridicule, Elzie turned, facing Frieda, pointed his finger at her, and said, "You say nothing." Frieda gave no verbal response because her all-knowing smile preempted any need for words.

Jesse, without conferring or without consent from the others, turned west on Morton because he wanted to investigate the size of the hospital grounds. They encircled three sides of the perimeter before they stopped near an open gate which granted entry to the grounds. Jesse estimated the size of the enclosed grounds to be 160 acres, excluding the nearby state-owned farm land. Although each one desired to pass through the gate into the grounds, each was reluctant to do so. Elzie was not as aggressive this time, and the other two took the cue from him. Whether their restraint was caused by respect for the institution or by fear of the unknown, even they did not know.

Just as they were preparing to depart the site a patient walked to where they were standing and initiated conversation. "Hello, folks, it's a beautiful Sunday afternoon, isn't it?" The three siblings were dumbfounded and offered no response. "Pardon me, folks, my name is Orville and I'm a trustee. It's all right if we talk."

More from embarrassment than from politeness, Jesse extended his hand and said, "My name is Jesse and this is my brother, Elzie, and my sister, Frieda. We are visiting Jacksonville and we were admiring the beautiful grounds here. We did not intend to be rude." First Elzie and then Frieda extended their hands for a hand-shake. Jesse's words and Frieda's pretty smile put the patient more at ease, and the four of them visited for several minutes. The trustee was a gracious person, and all three liked the man. He presented himself as well mannered, neat appearing, and polite. Their brief exposure to the trustee at the Jacksonville State Hospital, for-ever changed their attitudes toward mental illness. They did not understand men-tal illness, but for the first time, in their young lives, they knew they did not understand it. This new awareness was an unexpected bonus of the adventure, if it served no more than cause for future reflection. The young inquisitive minds were active with many new questions, but few answers.

The journey continued. They were well into the day with much more yet to see, so time was at a premium. Traveling to South Jacksonville, they briefly looked around, took Vandalia Road to Nichols Park, and picnicked on the bank of Mauvistierre Lake while they watched the boaters, the swimmers, and the swans and other waterfowl. It was here and now, at the park on this Sunday afternoon, where they found the multitudes. Although not as crowded as the downtown square of the previous night, the park was abuzz with people of all ages in a festive, relaxed mood. Presumably, Nichols Park was the place to be, particularly exciting for the youngsters from Pike County. The siblings were tempted to spend their remaining three hours here, but chose instead to visit more sights in Jacksonville. Nichols Park was a splendid public park and the decision to depart was not an easy one for the young visitors.

Once the threesome crossed the earth bridge to the children's play area, they again were tempted to indulge their youthful urges, but selected instead to stay the course. At the urging of Frieda they returned to downtown via Clay Street. She had an ulterior motive for the route, but she did not share it. As they slowly traveled north they soon entered another section of town which sported a differ-ent, less affluent type of housing. The houses, although certainly more spacious than the average house in Milton, were less pretentious in design, more modest in size, and were situated on smaller lots, which was in direct contrast to the houses they observed on the west side of town. Once again, they became aware of the many degrees of wealth and of different lifestyles.

They continued north passing a riding stable and multiple large, undeveloped parcels of open ground before Jesse figured out exactly where they were. Frieda knew. When Frieda initially viewed the campus of the Illinois Female College, she stared in breathless wonder. In Frieda's mind this campus was the most beautiful, most enthralling sight of the day. Her insistence on walking around the campus and her reluctance to leave, almost perturbed the other two. Earlier in the adven-ture Frieda wished to absorb as much of the town as possible, but now she wanted to linger at this location, wanted to explore all sections of the campus in more detail. Fortunately, the boys realized this was Frieda's moment, a time to look and dream, a time when their little sister chose to keep her thoughts private. They willingly acquiesced. Besides, as Jesse reminded them, this was Frieda's day to choose the activity for the group, so even Elzie remained cooperative, congenial. Twice Frieda read aloud the sign, "Illinois Female Academy, Founded in 1846," but she said nothing else. Obviously, she was impressed by the age of the school. To a ten year old, sixty-six years of existence represented an eternity. But what commanded her attention the most was the word female. She pondered how college life would be different from her school life in rural Milton.

The train was scheduled to leave the station at 7:09 p.m. Regrettably, it was now 5:36 p.m., and their time in Jacksonville was near its end. They had not toured much on the east end of town, and nothing on the north side. Understanding there was insufficient time to visit another campus, Frieda requested that at minimum they should ride by the Illinois School for the Blind. She was pleased when Jesse concurred and Elzie made no objection. They headed east on State Street, arriving in time to see a class of young blind students, younger than Frieda, who were all sitting under an elm tree, listening to an older man play a string instrument thought to be a viola. She, as well as the other two, was emotionally moved by the image of blind students enjoying music in the outdoors. This time no one shared his observations or made personal reflections. They simply watched for a while before they circled the wagon and returned to the train station from whence they started. On the road back they shared their highly charged personal thoughts concerning living conditions for those who were either deaf or blind. Without anyone stating it directly, they realized how fortunate they all were to be in good health. Jesse, speaking directly to Elzie, said, "Perhaps Uncle George knew what he was talking about. We all have certain advantages, disadvantages." Slightly pausing he continued. "Given a choice I would take health over wealth any day."

Elzie understood Jesse's message, but he gave no response. He was thinking. Elzie felt the need for some closure, or some way to give summary. "I liked what we did today. I liked what we saw and how I felt when I saw it. I saw a lot and learned a lot about myself today. You know, I think I learn more from doing something like this, than I do studying about it in school. Jacksonville has a lot to offer and I didn't know that. I assume each town is different and offers different things for different people. It's a big world out there, and in many ways I'm kind of sheltered. Do you understand what I am saying?"

Frieda answered, "I do and I agree."

"Well that is something to write home about—Frieda and I agree on something." Elzie grinned before a seriousness recaptured his thoughts. "Somehow I never thought of myself as being different, but I think I am. We're all different in our own way."

Jesse smiled and Frieda said, "You're different all right. But in all fairness, it is a good different. Thank goodness for that."

Jesse intervened before Elzie could answer his sister. "Elzie, as usual, you intrigue me. You are a bright and sensitive person with so many good thoughts, and they flow out of you like water out of a pump. I guess my little brother is growing up faster than I thought. I propose that sometime in the future the three of us find a comfortable place in the woods, and we sit down and discuss this stuff." Jesse's suggestion offered promise of a future group adventure, although they all understood that it was unlikely to occur. "Thank Frieda for the activities of the day, not me. After all, it was her idea. Well, here we are folks back at the train station. Get your things ready."

After checking with the ticket agent, Jesse, Elzie, and Frieda sat in the waiting room, drank Coca-Cola, and waited for the train. Frieda spoke first. "Jesse, I've had such a wonderful time. All I know to do is to say thank you, and that isn't enough. Someday, I hope to find a way to repay you."

"Yeah, me too. This was nice."

Jesse was humbled by the sincere expressions from his younger siblings. "I've had a wonderful time, too. It's thanks enough just having you two as my brother and sister. Maybe, someday, we will do it again."

"Good idea. Maybe when I go to New York City, I'll take you and Frieda with me, and you never know, I might buy you some clothes, like you did for us. Only in New York City I bet we need a map to get around. I might even rent a horse and buggy and take you guys out on the town. On second thought, heck with a horse. I'll get us a fancy automobile."

Frieda, smiling as she spoke, said, "Fat chance, Elzie. By the time you get that much money, Jesse and I will be too old to enjoy the trip." That made all three laugh. Elzie began to mimic what he envisioned Jesse to be as an old man, speaking without teeth, talking about New York City. They laughed again.

"Oh shut up, Elzie. You make me laugh so hard that my sides hurt."

Elzie frowned at Frieda and said to Jesse, "Thanks again, big brother. Any messages to Dad or Aunt Mary?"

"I don't think so. Just tell them that I'm all right. One of these weekends I hope to come and visit with them."

Frieda now spoke in a more serious, deliberate tone. "Before we leave, Jesse, I have one question. Do you have any idea what you need to do to go to college—say, like go to Illinois Female Academy?"

Jesse was taken aback by the question. He recognized it to be a serious question deserving his consideration, but he found no words to answer the question. To him college was still a foreign concept. The thought of Frieda's going to college had never crossed his mind. "To be honest, Frieda, I don't know. I'm the wrong person to ask. What I do know is that people like us usually don't go to college. That takes money, and lots of it. I don't think they even start attending college until they are older than I am now, and then, it takes four or five years to graduate. That would mean you don't earn any money until you're twenty-two or twenty-three. I don't know if that is realistic or not. Why do you want to go to college? What do you want to be? Do you have something particular in mind?"

Before Frieda could answer his question, the train pulled in the station, prompting Frieda to say, "Saved by the train whistle. Forget I asked. It's not important anyway. It was a silly question." Her comment ended the discussion of college.

Elzie and Frieda, now appearing more sophisticated than when they arrived, said their good-byes with a hug and a handshake, boarded the train and located their seats. Jesse stood on the track platform, watched and waved good-bye until the train was out of sight. It had been a wonderful weekend with brother, Elzie, and, sister, Frieda, and now it was over. Jesse stood alone on the platform beaming with pride, for he was proud of his siblings, and proud that his plans for an adventure with them had materialized. The weekend exceeded all expectations.

Twenty minutes before Jesse arrived back at the farm the younger ones arrived at the train station in Pearl and were met by their father and Aunt Mary. Elzie and Frieda talked for hours that evening before their excitement abated.

When Jesse arrived at the farm, there was no one there to meet him. He took care of his chores, and then sat in the backyard, thinking and looking at the stars. He sat there for most of one hour until a loneliness, a melancholy descended.

Alas, the adventure was over, it was time to prepare for the usual routine of life on the farm, as a hired farmhand. Tomorrow the working day commenced at 5:00 in the morning.

CHAPTER 7

DISCONTENT

Almost no one would argue the point—Jesse Moore was an excellent farmhand, an asset to any farming operation. Ask the same people if they believed Jesse was satisfied with his personal life and you would get dissension. In fact, few knew him well enough to give a valid answer to the complex question. Jesse, himself, was uncertain of the correct answer.

A few sources of discontent were easy to remedy. Jesse sometimes worked with individuals he did not appreciate, and he learned to be more discriminate about his associates. Trust and confidence in friends became more important and he learned to be more selective about what he said to whom. He became aware of deceitful manipulation by a few, and learned to appreciate the sincere efforts of the good intentioned. Both positive and negative work experiences taught him valuable lessons and he became wiser in the ways of life. He did not become cynical, although he suffered from a loss of innocence. He found the solution to many personal problems was simple—he avoided particular people and certain situations. In this regard he became wise for his age.

It was a given that desirable changes in his life would require considerable time and effort. Frequently, Jesse felt alone without family or quality friends. Personal events, such as birthdays, might come and go without acknowledgment. Whether this situation was of his own doing, or not, made little difference to him. Of more importance, given time and purpose, he believed it was within his power to remedy such problems.

Much to Jesse's delight he continued to immensely enjoy the simple things ever present in his rural existence. When the elements and time would permit he pursued solitude by taking long walks on the country roads or in the nearby woods, and over time his walks gained importance as a source of relaxation and mind-clearing pleasure. As he walked the isolated areas he often practiced his whistling and singing, and because he had good pitch and a pleasant voice, he actually became quite a melodious singer. Soon those who worked around him began to request songs, and even though he could not read music, once he heard the song, he usually could reproduce the sound.

Life required diligence, a lesson Jesse repeatedly had to relearn. Even while pursuing the simple pleasures he was reminded of how vulnerable an individual might be. One cold, blustery January evening Jesse determined he could endure the elements for the solace of a walk. While walking and showing little concern for the nasty elements, Jesse slipped on a patch of ice and fell hard to the frozen ground. Initially he felt more embarrassment than concern for safety, but as he tried to stand, his concern grew greater, then foremost. The fall had severely injured his ankle. He was alone in the elements and when intense pain prevented him from putting any weight on the ankle, his attention immediately shifted to his overall safety. It was very cold and he might be incapable of walking home. After searching in vain for nearby shelter, he desperately looked for alternatives to his, potentially, life threatening predicament. The thought of prolonged exposure to the elements terrified him, but he did not panic. Most concerned about the intense cold, and a little angry at himself for getting into this mess, he accepted that the full responsibility for any solution rested on his shoulders as it was most unlikely that help would arrive. When he spotted a stack of replacement fence posts about twenty yards from where he fell, and although he was uncertain how he could utilize them, he knew he had to get to them. In pain he crawled to the stack, analyzed the possibilities until he determined he really only had one option—he had to get back, rather than making shelter. He selected a post suitable as a crutch. He had trouble maintaining his balance as he tried to stand, but achieved an upright position on the fourth try. He adjusted his outer clothing, attempting to preserve his body heat and still efficiently use the post as a crutch. Estimating the distance to the farm at less than a half mile, he started the walk back, cold and in pain. The distressing, difficult walk back required the better part of an hour, and by the time he arrived he was more concerned about frostbite than the ankle pain. He had survived.

Jesse spent the next six days in bed while the ankle healed, walking about only when necessary. Fortunately, the injury from the frostbite was minimal. A doctor stopped to see him on the fourth day and informed him the ankle was not broken. Jesse missed seven days of work, lost seven days pay, and had to pay the doctor two dollars, all of which immensely aggravated him. Foolishly, his carelessness had not only endangered his life, it also had put his livelihood at risk. Jesse had become complacent about his own well-being, and now he would pay the price. He vowed to become more diligent.

As his young life progressed, Jesse developed and nurtured new passions. He learned to cook, actually becoming quite a good cook. He took a lot of pride in his personal appearance, never going to town without cleansing his body and changing his clothes. He kept his shoes shined, his pants pressed, his shirt ironed, and his hat blocked. He developed a passive interest in local politics and read local newspapers, whenever possible. Passionately he worked to improve his social skills, becoming both a good listener and an interesting conversationalist. He learned to be polite, well mannered and became more sensitive to others, less focused on his own problems. He honed his carpentry skills, volunteering his labor to those in need. Aspiring to become a good person, he was well on his way.

The walking, the whistling, and the singing never ceased. They were critical to his well being, or so he believed. Learning to relax became easier with time, but learning to play was never easy. Never exposed to spectator sports, he basically was unaware of professional or collegiate sports, and he considered team sports the domain of the more affluent. He decided that structured play, at least by his definition, was a luxury more suited for the wealthy or a child's activity learned at an earlier age, and of marginal value for responsible adults. He distinguished play from relaxing activities, considering certain games, as checkers, to be relaxing activities. He did learn to relax, and somewhere in the process he was beginning to find inner peace.

Another unfortunate accident befell the young farmhand in November, 1913. Toward the end of a workday three workers, including Jesse, became involved in benign horseplay as they were moving hay with pitchforks. With no regard for safety they engaged in competitive work with one another, each trying to toss hay farther and faster than the other two, resulting in the tosses becoming less accurate, more careless. After making one strenuous toss Jesse, turning and backing at the same time, moved directly into the path of a coworker's pitchfork. The outer prong of the pitchfork struck and penetrated Jesse's face, less than one inch below the outer corner of the left eye. Fortunately the prong struck at an angle, glanced off the cheekbone and slid sideways, rather than penetrating the eye. Once the pitchfork was retracted the open wound bled profusely, and although, Jesse used his handkerchief to cover and apply pressure to the wound, he was unable to stop the bleeding. He became more frightened when the flowing blood got into his eye, resulting in limited, blurred vision. Quickly Jesse got prone on his back, and remained in that position until the bleeding eventually subsided. One slow and anxious hour passed before the blood clotted over the wound. Carefully, Jesse rinsed out his eye and eventually determined that there was no detectable damage to his vision. He sat up as a coworker washed around the wound with soap and water before he carefully applied an iodine disinfectant. Jesse returned to his quarters, wrapped a bandage over the wound, and remained in bed the remainder of the day. A scab began to form that evening.

Jesse refused to see a doctor, engaging only in light work the next two days, and by the third day he was back to a full work schedule without any loss of pay. The wound required a full six weeks to heal. Thereafter, on occasion, the wound would ooze a milky liquid, but there was never any additional pain or decreased vision from the wound. Simply put, Jesse was most fortunate and he knew it. Two scars formed as a result of this happening—one physical, one psychological. The physical scar visually showed and the psychological scar ran deep, always reminding Jesse that careless horseplay was foolish. Hereafter, he did not intend to be a foolish person, if he could prevent it.

Jesse's life was in transition. He spent less time worrying, more time learning to enjoy himself. Probably, his favorite activity was going downtown Jacksonville on Saturday nights. He loved the active nature of a busy downtown and immensely enjoyed socializing with the townsmen. Also, downtown Jacksonville offered structured entertainment to Jesse's liking. Frequently, he attended one of the two movie theaters or one of the two opera houses. He used the library and seldom missed the Saturday night public music concerts. Although he carefully watched his spending, he enjoyed shopping, especially shopping for clothing and personal items. Frugal by nature and seldom spending in excess, he allowed himself the gratification of acquiring what he needed plus a few luxuries, but always in moderation. Even though he was a modest person, pride prevailed on occasion as sometimes he did not wear his hat in order that he might show off his black curly hair, or he splashed on extra cologne, or he made the extra effort to make himself presentable. Jesse relished personal compliments, but remained uneasy with excessive personal attention. Downtown Jacksonville was the right place for him to be in a crowd and still maintain his privacy, his personal identity.

Quite by accident, while searching for a place to eat early one Saturday night, Jesse saw a poster advertising an ice cream social, starting at 5:00 p.m., at the Central Christian Church, on the corner of College and Church Streets. He decided to attend. The event was held on the lawn outside the church building with dozens of people of all ages in attendance eating, laughing, and enjoying themselves. Not recognizing one familiar face, Jesse approached with apprehension; but in a short time, regardless of knowing no one, he decided to participate in the ice cream social, found the entrance, and paid the 25 cents food cost. He had made a wise decision, if for no other reason than for the food. At the all you could eat affair the three different flavors of homemade ice cream were delicious, the home baked cakes and pies were scrumptious, and the food was complemented with milk, lemonade, or coffee. He was not positive but he thought the cherry pie and the angel food cake might have been the best he had ever tasted. He downed three complete helpings and drank four glasses of milk before a most attractive young lady offered another refill of milk. Politely she spoke to Jesse. "You have quite the appetite, sir. Would you care for more cake or ice cream?"

Most embarrassed about his food consumption, Jesse responded. "Oh my, no thank you. The food was so good that I forgot where I was and I lost track of how much I have consumed. I guess I thought I was in hog heaven for a while. Allow me to pay another 25 cents, and that might not be enough."

"Don't you be silly. This ice cream social is all you can eat. Actually, I wanted to meet you, and not knowing what to say, I ended up saying something stupid. Forgive me?"

The young lady and Jesse continued to converse, and within minutes more young people gathered around his table and visited with him as though they were long lost friends. It became a wonderful experience for Jesse as he very much enjoyed the conversation, and much to his astonishment the strangers appeared to like him. Giving up his Saturday night on the town, he stayed until they stopped serving food at 8:00, and assisted his new friends with the cleanup, and capitalized on an opportunity to visit with an assortment of interesting people. Following the cleanup Jesse accepted an invitation to a young adult follow-up outing at the park. The entire group of friends rode to the park together in one large wagon and once there, they shared stories, sang songs, played games, or socialized as they individually chose to do. Time passed quickly and at 12:30 a.m. the park superintendent politely requested that they leave because the park had closed at midnight. Although Jesse was embarrassed about his group overstaying the time, he had no regrets. The experience was just what he needed—a splendid evening interacting with fine, young people.

February 16, 1915, Jesse had turned nineteen years of age, and for some unknown reason this birthday induced questions about his future, about who he was and where he was going. No obvious conclusions were reached, other than he still was in a transitional period of his life, for which he felt unprepared. Aside from a small amount of personal property, he owned nothing, had no savings, and saw little promise of future security. His assessment of his financial situation was best summarized by his questioning of a fellow farmworker. "How do you and your family live on the money we make? I can hardly do all the things I want to do, and I have a modest lifestyle. How do you do it?"

The answer from his friend was, "We manage," and this answer did not help Jesse in his query. "I'm sorry, Jesse, I don't have a better answer. We just make do with what we have, that's all. But you need to remember that my wife is a special person and we're happy. So I suppose the answer to your question is, of course, I would like more money, but we do live on the money I make. What exactly is your concern? Do you want something particular, are you thinking about marriage, or do you just want to acquire wealth?"

"No, I do not expect riches. I do wonder why someone would want to marry someone like me. I have no money, no property, and no real prospects of gaining such. I have nothing to offer but the promise of a lifetime of work, of struggle."

Somewhat in relief, the friend looked at Jesse and smiled. "You have a lot to offer, you have yourself. People like us never start out with stuff, we accumulate as we go. We live on love, we make our own happiness. I assume you have not met the right girl yet, for if you had, you would not have made that last statement."

This conversation made little sense to Jesse, although he was intrigued by the idea that he had not yet met the right girl. He thanked his friend and then continued to harbor concern about his future.

Do all he might, the wealth issue never went away, as well illustrated by a single event in May, 1915. After considerable effort in searching for a means of transportation Jesse found a fine Standardbred trotter and a used buggy for sale, priced well within his acceptable range. Convinced that a horse and buggy would significantly enhance his social life, plus initiate the process of modest wealth accumulation, his heart was set on the acquisition. He and the seller shook hands on the deal, contingent on financing. The following day Jesse went to a bank in Jacksonville for the purpose of securing a $62.00 loan. Since this was his first banking transaction of any type, he naively assumed the process would be brief and simple. Upon arrival at the bank, he spoke with a teller who advised him of the proper procedure of filling out a loan application before visiting with a loan officer. He read and carefully followed the instructions on the loan application form, answering all questions to the best of his ability. He turned in the form and nervously waited for his interview with the loan officer, not because he believed his application might be denied, but because he was eager to secure the loan and to close the deal. He waited over one hour in the bank lobby before a tall, older man, dressed in a three piece suit, invited him into the office. Dressed in his best apparel, a little nervous and uncomfortable in the surroundings, Jesse initiated the conversation. "Thank you, sir. I hope this is not an inconvenient time for you."

The bank employee answered in a business manner. "No, it is not inconvenient. That's why I'm here, to review loan applications." The banker sat at his desk concentrating on the loan application without uttering a word. Several quiet minutes passed before the banker glanced up, looked at Jesse, and then looked back down to continue studying the application. Finally, he spoke. "Why do you think we should lend you the money?"

Jesse was totally unprepared for such a question and offered a poor response. "Because I need the money to buy a horse and buggy."

"That's not what I mean. Why should the bank grant a loan to a person we don't know? You list no assets. It appears you have no permanent place of employment. This form shows you holding three different jobs in the last four years. What do you do, work when and where you feel like it?" He really gave Jesse no time to answer, and the tone of his voice and personal demeanor indicated he did not expect an answer. "What kind of collateral do you have?"

"I'm not sure what collateral is."

"Collateral is property you put up to secure your loan."

"I assumed the horse and buggy would be the backing for the loan. If something happened to me, or I didn't make the payments, you would get them, wouldn't you?"

"Well, maybe. But that is not sufficient collateral. It is obvious to me that you know very little about finance, and even less about the loan process. Let me explain. If you borrow money from a bank you must have some collateral, like another horse and buggy or other property that you give the title to the bank for security until your loan is repaid. That way we reduce our risk if you fail to repay the loan. We lend money to help people buy something, not buy it for them."

Somewhat indignant, but still determined to pursue the loan, Jesse responded. "I have been on my own since I was fourteen. I support myself, I have worked everyday of my life, and I owe no money to anyone. That's my collateral and it should be worth something. I'm an honorable person, and I will pay back any money I borrow from the bank. If you can't get a loan, how does a poor person ever buy anything, how does he ever get any collateral?"

"Save some money and purchase some collateral. Then we can do business. Until that time, your loan is denied. Come back and see me after you have saved some money, or acquired some assets. Now, is there something else I can help you with? If not, good day."

Jesse offered no response other than quickly exiting the office, feeling dejected and humiliated. Once out of the bank building he crossed the street, went to the park, sat on a bench and thought about his ordeal. He did not appreciate the way the arrogant banker had talked down to him. It had been a humbling experience, his pride was hurt. What hurt the most was the reality that he would be unable to purchase his horse and buggy. Jesse sat and sulked until a most amusing thought broke his feeling of self-pity. He imagined he was farming and the banker, dressed in his business suit, came to him for assistance in growing food. Jesse's imagined response was, What do you have for collateral, and how have you got your food all your life? Come back and see me when you know something about growing food. The mental image was a delight, made Jesse smile, and forced him to temporarily forget his own humiliation. In a final thought of defiance, Jesse reasoned that although he might not understand bank finance, he would bet the banker did not understand much about the financial problems of the less fortunate, the poor.

Although he needed to get back to his work, he took time for one more act of defiance. Unaware he was being observed, he looked directly at the imposing seven-story bank building and shouted, "I don't want your money, anyway. If I ever need a loan again, I'm going to take my business elsewhere." That meaningless act of defiance made him feel better until he spotted a nearby lady looking at him. He tipped his hat, smiled at the lady,and then said, "You've got to let those buildings know how you feel." He knew it was a silly statement, but it offered some humor to an otherwise awkward situation.

Jesse believed he would never forget the humiliation he suffered on this day, and he hoped he would never be forced to endure such again; but he also believed that there were few guarantees in life, especially for those without assets.

The farm community was elated with the fall harvest of 1915, as bumper grain crops fetched unusually high prices. Ironically, farmworkers shared little in the prosperity other than benefitting from more work. Generally, the farmworker did not share in the profit and Jesse found himself in no better financial condition than he was at the time of the bank loan fiasco. If anything, the general farm prosperity served Jesse as a source of personal discontent. For the first time that he could remember he questioned his future as a farmhand, not only in terms of unappreciated hard work, but also he questioned his station in life, his future earning potential. Uncertain about his source of discontent, and convinced the issue was more than money, he felt some change was needed, but he remained most uncertain regarding the nature of any possible alterations. He considered moving to a completely different location elsewhere in the state or he even thought about another region of the country. He considered learning a different trade such as carpentry or working with metals. The possibility of town employment such as the restaurant business or factory work crossed his mind. For almost a week he thought of little else other than an alternative, a new direction in his life.

Lot, or fate as he called it, was to play a role in Jesse's decision. After three other employment offers from nearby farms, Jesse allowed himself three days of work-free time before he committed to stay on another year with his current employers. Since, as usual, room and board were part of the pay for farmhands, it was essential that he make his decision soon, but before he committed he made arrangements for travel to Milton to visit with and seek advice from Aunt Mary. The trip would provide an additional bonus as Jesse always treasured family visits.

The occasion was festive, a Saturday night supper prepared by Aunt Mary, attended by Jesse, Elzie, Frieda, Erastus, and Aunt Mary, and he found the old home place pretty much the same. After the meal Jesse and Elzie reminisced about their earlier adventures, and Frieda listened in envy. Aunt Mary and Erastus listened and laughed, often inserting into the discussion what they believed to be the correct description of events. The story of their youthful encounter with the wolves while they were camping was the highlight of the many musings on the past. Frieda particularly delighted in the telling of the many stories most of which she had never heard. "You guys have all the fun. How come we never do exciting things like that any more?"

Elzie was quick to answer. "We do. It's just that the stories are funnier and more exciting in the telling, especially a few years after they happen. We have exciting events too. Do you want me to tell the story about what happened to you in the chicken house last week?"

"No, I don't, it's too embarrassing. You just shut up. You can tell it five years from now, and maybe by then, if you are right, it will be funny to everyone, even me."

The other three were not aware of the chicken house escapade, and although they wanted to know, they were not going to ask. Frieda obviously was uncomfortable with the event. Elzie just smiled and said, "Okay, five years from now and I tell."

Erastus intentionally changed the subject. "Elzie and me have accepted a big work project for the coming winter months. We have a contract to clear out the stumps and level the ground suitable for farming on forty acres of land south of Montezuma. They just finished cutting the timber and we can start anytime we are ready. The way farm prices are now with the war in Europe, I expect there will be a lot of land to clear in the future. Grain farming seems to be the way to go, nowadays."

Jesse abruptly said, "Maybe, if you own the land, it's the way to go. But, if you are just a farm laborer, I'm not so sure."

This expression of doubt by Jesse about farming caught everyone off guard. Aunt Mary directly asked what the others were wondering. "Why, Jesse, do you not like farming any more? I can't believe that I just heard those words from your mouth."

Jesse looked about the room and realized everyone was waiting for an explanation. He had little choice other than to explain his statement. "No, don't get me wrong, I love farming. Actually, I believe I'm now at the point where I'm a pretty good farmhand. I seem to enjoy it all. I like working with the animals, I like the field work, and I like the preparation and maintenance work. No doubt that life on a farm is a good life. I really like living in the rural area, and if you will excuse some corniness, I like living next to nature. What I do not like is the poor pay and the absence of any opportunity for advancement. There is no promotion for a hired farmworker, other than top hand which really doesn't mean much. No matter how hard you work, you get little pay. Might be if you're good you might get job offers on other farms, but seldom do you get offers of more money. To be honest I make enough to live and that is about all. I can't seem to save anything. I don't know how other people support a family on a farmhand's wages. To add to the anguish of low pay, I see no future in farming unless you own the land, and we all know the chance of my ever owning farm land, in this day and age, is remote. Simply put, I think I've got to look to the future, and as I see it, the financial future for a farmworker is not bright. Right or wrong, those are my feelings." Jesse stopped speaking hoping someone might offer different insight, but no one else said anything.

Reluctantly he continued. "Please, do not misunderstand me. I feel no despair. Happiness is all around me, and in fact, I'm as happy now as any time in my life. I just feel so uncertain about the future. I often think of Uncle George and the lecture he gave me and Elzie, explaining to us the advantages we have in life. Basically, if I remember it right, I agree with what he told us, and more importantly, I have been influenced by his philosophy. I do have more than my share of advantages, and I know it. For sure, life has a lot of bumps, but those bumps are not what bother me. What I feel is more like a concern for the future. One day, as you all know, I want a wife and family. I guess I'm concerned if I will be able to adequately provide for them; and right now, I don't know how I'm going to do that." Pausing in his speech, looking around the room, Jesse observed that he still commanded the attention of all, a situation which made him most uncomfortable. He ceased talking, slightly lowered his head, almost as if in shame. By sharing his personal concerns he felt he had destroyed the joyous mood of the group.

Aunt Mary spoke. "Please continue, Jesse. We want to hear your thoughts. We are not critical of you. It's more that you so seldom complain that we are just surprised by what you say. Please continue."

"About now, I guess I must sound pretty selfish. I hope not. The other day I had an experience that influenced my thinking. Let me describe it to you." Jesse proceeded to describe his recent encounter at the bank, and he was very articulate in describing his emotional reactions created by the condescending banker.

Erastus and Aunt Mary understood Jesse's feelings, both having had similar experiences in the past. Frieda felt compassion for her brother, and Elzie felt anger toward the banker. Aunt Mary offered an explanation. "I'm sorry to say, but that is the way of the world. It seems to me that those with less in life have a bigger cross to bear. That might be how we get our strength, at least strength enough to survive. Remember this may have happened for a purpose. Things do have a way of taking care of themselves. I do believe things are better now, and the future for you younger people is a little more promising than it was for us. I know this may be hard for you to accept, but I do believe it to be true. Don't allow yourself to get discouraged, Jesse. Just knowing you, I'm sure things will work out for the best."

Regardless of her good intentions, Aunt Mary's words offered very little comfort.

Erastus spoke. "I don't know anyone who saves money. What's so unusual about that? Stupid banker." Erastus offered no advice, but he did have an offer of work. "Elzie and me have more work than we can get done. I must hire one laborer, or maybe two, to help with the clearing. I have the mules and the tools but we need more muscle. If you want it, the job is yours. No doubt it will be hard work, but at job's end there will be a nice paycheck. I can't tell you exactly how much until I determine my cost, but I expect to pay somewhere around three hundred dollars per man for four months or so of hard work. I think it would be great to work with you, Jesse, so give it some thought. Ben told me the house behind them, the one you fixed up, is still empty, and for a little work around the farm, I would guess you could live there. Everyone here would love to have you back, if it suits you to be back."

Elzie interjected his feelings. "I hope you will give it some serious thought, big brother. Sure would be nice to work with you." Hesitating, and smiling, he looked around the room. "You might learn a thing or two. Dad said we will work a little with dynamite and it will be an opportunity for all of us to learn about that stuff. Besides, I would like to have you around as we learn because, generally, you are not as reckless as the rest of us and, specifically, I mean Dad. Dad and I need you to watch out for us. Is there anybody in this room who will disagree with that?"

Erastus disagreed. "Although there might be a tiny element of truth in your feeble attempt at humor, I want you to know I'm quite capable of working with explosives. If you keep talking and having doubts, we'll never get him to work with us. Come on, Jesse, we'll make it a family project."

Jesse would not commit, although he did agree to consider the possibility. Later that night Elzie and Jesse went to Pittsfield to meet Sylvia and to have a Saturday night on the town. Frieda went to bed early that night, quite perturbed that she did not feel welcome to join her older brothers. The next morning she asked Elzie about the boys' night on the town. He first answered with a sheepish grin, then he spoke. "It was a pretty fun night. Wait five years from now, and I'll tell you all about it." Frieda was furious.

By Sunday evening Jesse had made up his mind. He was going to work with the family clearing the land, even though he did have concerns about the type of work, and serious reservations about working for his father. He informed his father of his decision and that he would work for him, but only after he had given two weeks notice and had finished all obligations of his present job. Erastus agreed and Jesse entered into a contract with his father.

The Moore boys and their father completed their task of land clearing by late February, one month ahead of schedule. The work had been difficult, but rewarding. Jesse received full payment of $317 on March 1, the largest single sum of money he had ever possessed. He paid his meager debts which he had accumulated during the winter, purchased replacement clothing, and gave Aunt Mary $50.00. He opened a personal savings account at a Pittsfield Bank, depositing $205.00, which earned 2% per year.

In Jesse's mind the most rewarding product of the work was the new found relationship with his family. He enjoyed working with Elzie, spending time with Frieda and Aunt Mary, and learning from his father. Also, he personally benefited from the work experience by developing some new skills such as working with dynamite. Of particular importance to Jesse, he learned to better appreciate his father. For the first time since the death of his mother Jesse developed an emotional tie to his father.

In early March Jesse, still living in the old house behind Uncle Ben's place, started work as a farmhand at one of the larger farms in Pike County. From the beginning of his new employment he made it clear that he would work only through the planting season. He had other plans for the harvest season.

The previous November Jesse had made inquiries about opportunities of employment, other than farmwork. Although there were no particular agencies which directed him to employment, he found resources for employment placement and job descriptions at the public library. He did find employment opportunities, but none with a promise of a better future. With Jesse's present skill level most of the available jobs were in retail, sales, or farmwork, and the first two had no appeal to him at all. During his search for a different career he came across a flyer offering work for an experienced farmhand. The bulletin alone made little impression on Jesse until a later conversation with another farmhand revealed some interesting elements. The farmhand told a story about his brother-in-law who had hired on for such a trip and who remained in eastern Colorado at work's end. The brother-in-law had written home about the good wages, the opportunities out west, and most specifically about the many exciting experiences. Jesse was not naive enough to believe it was the opportunity of a lifetime, although he was interested enough to gather more information. He seriously wondered if a totally new environment might not serve him well. He decided to take the plunge and signed on. His instructions were to report to the Central Railroad Station, Saint Louis, Missouri, June 21, 1916, 11:00 a.m., for group transportation to Elk City, Oklahoma.

From the first meeting with his fellow harvest workers, Jesse suspected that his employment would become more than a work adventure; it would provide an exposure to people and personalities never before imagined by the somewhat unsophisticated young man from rural Illinois. Undoubtedly, his traveling companions were vastly different from his church associates, giving Jesse hope that the enterprise would provide a giant step in his journey of learning about the world and himself.

The designated starting place for the harvest crew was a temporary campground, located west of Elk City, Oklahoma. The campground housed hundreds of people, male and female, ranging in age from fifteen to forty, all with a common purpose of working for Harvest Productions. Indicative of the well organized operation, it required more time for Jesse to locate the registration center than it did to register and to receive his work assignment to one particular work crew from a field of nine crews. The following morning Jesse joined seventy other workers, plus several pieces of machinery and operators, plus several horse pulled supply wagons, and headed north to begin their first harvest. From the first hour of the first day Jesse recognized that the entire effort was the most organized endeavor he had ever witnessed, and that he would observe farming on a larger scale than ever imagined. The first thing every morning a supervisor assigned daily tasks to the workers, informed them where and when to start work, location and time of meals, quitting time, and where to sleep. The worker simply followed the instructions, never needing to understand the entire operation, with emphasis on volume of work completed, less on quality of the job.

Jesse's first work assignment was the pitchfork gathering of the recently cut wheat as others loaded the wagons which hauled the crop to one of the four steam powered threshing machines. The system was efficient, as the total harvest at the first farm, which Jesse estimated over 800 acres in size, was completed in less than four days. The cutting crew had finished its work and arrived at the second farm by the end of the second day, and apart from the first week of work Jesse never saw the lead cutting crew again. Most generally he worked with the same people, about twenty in number, but on occasion Jesse would help throw the small bales or he would assist the sackers. Sometimes, depending on the pace of the threshing crew, Jesse used a pitchfork and assisted with the gathering of the straw, or sometimes he fed straw into the balers. All the tasks involved dirty, fatiguing, and monotonous work. Any activity directly alongside the machines was less desirable because it was dirtier work with dustier air to breathe. The length of the workday varied slightly, ranging from twelve to thirteen hours, and much to Jesse's chagrin he basically performed the same menial tasks, day after day.

Lodging varied from basic to adequate. Although sleeping in barns was the most usual accommodation, tents and bunk houses were sometimes available, and on rare occasions, part of the crew would sleep in a farmhouse. The farmer under harvest contract provided food which varied from good to great, and in Jesse's estimation meals were the highlight of each day. He not only enjoyed the delicious home cooking, he delighted in the variety of regional foods and the slightly different preparation of standard dishes. Breakfasts were the hardiest meals. The noon meals were served in the fields, as were the snacks and beverages, and there always was an abundant supply of cool water. The evening meals, often with time for social interaction, were usually served near or in the farmhouses where one could, within limits, take as much food or as much time as he wanted to eat. If the occasion presented itself, Jesse tried to compliment the cooks, or anyone associated with food preparation. No doubt he appreciated the good food and the convenience of always having the food prepared for him.

The harvest crew worked seven days a week except for wet days. On wet days the machine operators, wagon drivers, and supervisors attended to maintenance tasks while the forkers, as the workers were called, were awarded free time, and there were as many different uses of free time as there were workers. Nonetheless, unstructured time often brought out the base, underside of a few crew members. For the first time in his life Jesse observed individuals engaging in unregulated behavior, totally free of societal constraints. He assumed that the youthful working crew, away from family and friends, often engaged in behavior they would not have partaken in had they been subjected to the usual accountability. He did not deem all activities as wicked, merely unrestricted, unmonitored by authorities. Although uncharacteristic of Jesse, he participated in a few of the unsavory activities, but never to a great extreme. Fortunately, he quickly thought better of foolish behavior and refrained. Jesse never described or made public his judgments about his activities or those of others. He only stated that as a result of his work experience, or his enterprise as he called it, he personally became more aware, more sophisticated, and more worldly—an outcome he deemed positive. It is, however, noteworthy that during the entire trip he never developed close ties or friendships with fellow workers, nor did he cherish the group as a whole. He believed many of the individuals and their personal activities were better forgotten, and thus, he did.

It was late November before the crew finished its last harvest near the small town of Brandon, Manitoba, which fortunately was situated less than forty miles from the farm where Jesse's sister, Goldie, and her family lived. The work crew was paid in full, given five days of furlough, while Harvest Productions concluded its business and arranged for return transportation. Jesse immediately set forth to visit his sister whom he had not seen since she married in 1907. Goldie's husband, Bert, had been lured to Canada by the promise of farm employment and other opportunities. Bert was a likable fellow who possessed a good work ethic and he valued family, which were all admirable qualities by Jesse's standards. Jesse believed his sister had made a good choice for a marriage partner and was eager to see them, to meet the family, and to hear about the opportunities in Canada. Jesse was a little embarrassed by the fact he was seeing them now in Canada when he had not seen them the last four years when they were living in Illinois less than thirty miles apart. Arriving at the Canadian farm late in the afternoon, Jesse joined the family for supper. It was a joyous reunion.

The untimely death of their mother had been difficult for all the Moore children, but particularly hard on Goldie. Not quite fifteen years old, Goldie remained at home and cared for the family for four years until she was married in 1907. Because both had made many personal sacrifices, a unique bond existed between Jesse and his oldest sister, and the visit reinforced their valued kinship. At first they discussed individual family members, expressing concern for some and confidence in others. Beaming with family pride they concluded their family discussion on a positive note, believing they all would be stronger individuals as a result of earlier struggles. Later the conversation shifted to personal choices in life, paths not taken, and the conversation did not proceed as Jesse had imagined. Bert took the initiative by asking Jesse some interesting questions about the future of agriculture. Jesse first judged the inquiries as polite conversation, but later determined otherwise. One of Bert's questions concerning agriculture forced Jesse to respond when he would have been more comfortable not sharing his thoughts.

Bert inquired with a serious tone of voice. "I want you to try and answer a nagging question for me. Hopefully, your recent experiences will give you some insight. As you know, I moved here by invitation to work on this farm, and I assumed life might be better here, but now I'm not so sure. My question is, do you see any major changes coming to farming and, if so, what are the changes?"

"Oh my, Bert, I don't know if I'm capable of answering that question. I think I lack the experience, the foresight, to draw valid conclusions."

Goldie spoke before Bert could respond. "Nonsense, Jesse, answer the question. You're good at thinking, at analyzing. I want to hear your answer to Bert's question." Her comment cinched it. Jesse had to answer.

"Thank you, Goldie, you flatter me. I will try to give you my thoughts, if I already have not. I suspect your questions are a result of something I have already said, or implied."

Bert responded, "Now you flatter me. I've observed no concern on your part. It's concern on my part that worries us. Life as a farmhand is not easy for the man or for his family, in Canada or at home. We came here looking for a better life, and I'm not sure we have found it. You know that Canada has been at war for two and one-half years, and that has not made it any easier for us. And I would guess before this war ends the United States will be in it, too. These are not easy times to raise a family. So back to my question, what do you see as to the future changes in farming, and how does a common farmworker fit into that change?"

Jesse straightened his sitting position, placed his hands on the table, and hesitated before speaking. "First of all let me affirm what you already know. I love farming, I want to be a farmer, however, I must make a point of distinction. I'm talking about working as a farmhand, not a farmer who owns his land, because those are two separate categories. There are a lot of men out there who want to farm, and as you know, almost anyone with a strong back can be a farmhand. As far as I can tell there is little premium placed on being a good farmhand, at least no premium where money is concerned. All farmhands make about the same wages. I kept thinking that with this war in Europe there would be more need for good farmhands, but that has not happened. What has happened is that the same number of workers farm more land and we produce more grain, but the price per bushel stays the same. Now the emphasis is on large scale production of grain and animals. I'm not sure where the same farmer fits into all of this."

Bert spoke with an inquisitive tone. "I understand and agree with your description of the change in farming. What I don't understand, why is that not good for farmworkers?"

"That's the real question and the answer bothers me. I will try to answer, but you need to give me some latitude, okay? The last six months I have been with the traveling harvest crew, and I am very honest when I say, I have received little pleasure in my work. It was not individual farmwork as much as it was group work which required little skill or knowledge about the farm, and there was an absence of any pride in what one was doing. My experience as a farmhand served me to no advantage. On any given day, I could have been replaced with anyone willing to work. However, you need to remember that was not true for everyone. If you were a good machine operator, you could not be replaced as easily. Let me explain that statement. First, years ago steam engines mechanized farm equipment, and we have adjusted to that. Now, large self-contained farm machines powered by internal combustion engines, fueled by gasoline, are coming, and coming soon. One day every large farm will have one. The machines are getting better and better, and the better the machines get, the fewer of us they need. For example, the new baler now picks up the straw, or hay, and not only does it put the straw into bales, which are easier to store, it ties the twine around the bale. And it is my understanding that they are developing tractors that not only power the balers, but they pull them too. That is a one man operation, which used to be a four man operation. But in my opinion, the clincher is not the baler or the tractor, it is the new gas-power combine. It will do the entire process of harvesting, and it too is a one man operation. The man who ran our thresher spoke of this machine and says it's on the drawing board right now. Sure, nowadays we still use work animals and we do much of the work by hand, but I suspect someday soon that farmhands like you and me will not be much in demand, especially on the larger farms where the jobs for farmhands presently are. I think if we want to stay in farming, we need to recognize that the future will be different. I have no definite idea of how all of this will pan out, but I think as a twenty-year-old farmhand, I need to be looking around and considering other jobs, maybe another line of work. But you never know for sure, I could be totally wrong."

After Jesse finished speaking neither Bert nor Goldie agreed or disagreed. It was the answer they expected, but had hoped not to hear. So Jesse changed his tone and added a ray of hope. "You do understand that I am speaking more for myself than for you. I believe there will always be opportunities for farmworkers of your caliber. You're too valuable because you're a good farmer and you like mechanics. Heck, you'll probably be the farmer operating one of those new combines, or driving the tractor, or repairing the equipment when it breaks down."

Goldie understood what Jesse was doing, and she appreciated it. She deliberately changed the subject back to family, and they visited a while longer, ate apple pie, and laughed about past experiences before going to bed after 2:00 a.m., long past their accustomed bedtime. Jesse regretted giving an honest answer to Bert's question.

The next day, Jesse said his good-byes to Goldie, Bert, and the family. He was off to see Winnipeg. After spending two days in the Canadian city as a tourist, he rejoined his harvesting group for the trip home, arriving in St. Louis December 1. From St. Louis he caught a train to Jacksonville, not to Milton. When he saw the people on the streets, when he saw the familiar structures of his chosen town and when he took his first big breath of Jacksonville air, Jesse understood that Jacksonville was his home, now and perhaps forever. His first full day in the rural area of Jacksonville he landed a job as a farmhand at the Davis Farm, five miles east of Jacksonville. His housing was a small, furnished four-room house with a kitchen and a good coal stove. His work ethic and experience as a farmhand were appreciated, not in pay, but in the owner's attitude toward Jesse. The returning farmhand had found another temporary place to live and work, a good place to ponder his future. In retrospect, he was pleased he had gone on the harvesting trip. He had his adventure, had earned extra money, and felt he had learned a little more about himself, and perhaps, a little more about the world. What could be better?

Two days later, on Saturday afternoon, Jesse paid cash for a horse and buggy. The black buggy, a two seater with a top, was perfect for Jesse. The horse, named Babe, was a graceful, spirited, black, two-year-old filly with a smart trot. After Jesse left the sale barn on North Main Street he rode to the public square, riding around the square seven or eight times, until he found the perfect stopping place, which happened to be situated directly in front of the bank building. He intentionally remained near the horse and buggy, visiting with the people downtown until the stores closed at 9:00 p.m. Jesse was so proud of his recent purchase that he strutted about the area like a peacock. His day was made complete when the banker walked by him and could not help but observe Jesse's newly acquired horse and buggy. It should not have been, but seeing the banker was a sweet feeling for the vindicated farmhand.

The following day Jesse attended the Sunday afternoon activities at the Central

Christian Church. To his delight his recent absence had been noticed, and he willingly told about his enterprise, making certain he described only the activities suitable for the group. Jesse, a good story teller, enjoyed the attention and was the man of the hour, a totally new experience for him. He savored the moment.

Continuing his frequent trips to town, Jesse immensely enjoyed a variety of social situations. Although he socially functioned well, he always endeavored to refine his social skills, becoming a courteous person, and learning to gracefully accept compliments. His personality blossomed. His new found confidence allowed Jesse to demonstrate his quick wit and display his keen sense of humor, both in expression and in appreciation of others. When he became amused, he would throw his head back and give a loud roar of contagious laughter, inducing laughter from others. Although he was good in a crowd, he remained sensitive to the individual, maintaining eye contact when speaking to others, and remaining fully attentive to what others were expressing. He became proficient at small talk, and yet, seldom was his conversation self-centered. He was interested in people, enjoyed conversing with them, and others quickly perceived his interest in them.

These newly developed personal qualities and self-confidence, coupled with his handsome presence, helped to make Jesse a person in demand, with people in general, and specifically with the young single females. He walked erectly displaying his strong stout frame and his natural good looks; and upon entering a room with people, his physical appearance commanded attention. More than anyone, Jesse was in awe of his social success. He was proud of the person he had become.

Jesse felt such freedom with his new mode of transportation and a little extra money in his pocket. He could travel to town to see whomever he wanted whenever he chose, or, within reason, could do what he wanted. From his perspective it was the dawn of a new age in his life. He liked who he was, where he lived, and the people in his life; and he felt as though he was on top of the world. There was only one important item still missing in his life, and it was his heart's desire to rectify that situation as soon as possible.

Capitalizing on his opportunities, the young, unattached farmhand frequently courted many young ladies. He was available, and it was no secret. While attending a downtown band concert he met an attractive young lady who was to become indirectly responsible for an acute change in his life, although neither one knew it at the time. Her name was Stella Kelly. Stella, age eighteen, a slim attractive girl, made deliberate efforts to meet Jesse that night, after having observed him at earlier church events. The young couple watched the concert together, conversed throughout the evening, and each appeared to enjoy the other's company. Mindful of appearing too aggressive, Jesse ended the evening early but proposed that they meet again for a ride around town, and perhaps an evening meal at a local restaurant. Stella, not wanting to appear too available, counter proposed that Jesse should join her and her family for an evening meal the ensuing Saturday night. Jesse accepted, as he seldom refused a home-cooked meal.

On a cool, clear moonlighted Saturday evening, December 15, 1916, Jesse arrived at Stella's house. As he approached the Kelly house, Babe pranced, and Jesse praised the horse for showing her stuff. The well-lighted house was easy to locate, and as Jesse reined in his horse he noticed a curtain was pulled back in a front window, and someone was looking out. Acting casual Jesse pretended not to notice the observer. The observer was Helen, Stella's younger sister, and she did not realize that Jesse had detected her presence at the window. She continued to watch in interest, in admiration.

Stella, still dressing, yelled at Helen, "Get the door will you, and be polite." Helen opened the door, but said nothing, looked at the stranger, and although she knew who he was and why he was there, she waited for him to declare his purpose. Helen was taken by the man's good looks.

Jesse was dumbfounded. Standing in front of him was the most beautiful woman he remembered seeing, and it was not Stella. He was so surprised that he, too, stood looking at her without saying a word. After, perhaps a minute or so elapsed, Helen sporting a huge smile, said, "Yes?"

Embarrassed, Jesse responded. "Does Stella live here?"

With a bigger smile, "Stella who?"

Momentarily, Jesse could not remember Stella's last name. "My name is Jesse Moore, and I was to meet Stella here tonight for dinner."

Edward, the father, entered the living room, saving the day for Jesse. In a pleasant manner the father introduced himself and invited the visitor into the house. As Jesse entered the room, Helen stood on her tiptoes and whispered to Jesse, "Kelly. Her name is Stella Kelly." Jesse tried to pretend he did not hear her, but he could not withhold his smile. He appreciated Helen's sense of humor.

After Stella's entrance into the living room and a reasonable amount of small talk, the five of them sat at the kitchen table and dined. Elizabeth and Edward, the parents, sat at opposite ends of the table while Jesse and Stella sat on the same side opposite Helen. Jesse was on his best behavior, most congenial. The evening meal consisting of fried chicken and more side dishes than could be placed on the table provided almost two hours of pleasurable eating and polite conversation. For Jesse this was the perfect evening—an evening of good food, and great conversation with interesting people. Elizabeth and Edward Kelly were reserved, kind, and gracious hosts. Stella talked excessively, often revealing her nervousness. Helen sat quietly observing the entire process and hearing every spoken word without ever making eye contact with Jesse. Jesse, almost to a fault, could not keep his eyes off Helen, a fact noticed by all at the table. He was smitten with Helen's beauty and elegant demeanor.

After dinner was completed the group adjourned to the living room for more visiting, which suited Jesse just fine. He was not eager to take the promised buggy ride with Stella, preferring instead to visit with the family. Jesse faced a dilemma that would put to the test his newly developed social skills. His predicament was, how could he show his interest in Helen without alienating her sister, or upsetting the seemingly harmonious family, or without making himself appear to be an opportunist. It was the perceptive mother who gave Jesse a possible solution. "Jesse, it's already after ten o'clock and it's a brisk night outside. If you don't mind, I prefer that you and Stella not leave for a ride at this hour. Why don't we pop some popcorn, and visit a little longer, that is, Stella, if you don't mind sharing Jesse's company with your father and me."

Stella started to respond, but Jesse spoke first. "That's fine with me. In fact, I should not stay too late as I must get up early to do the chores." Helen smiled, Stella frowned.

After popcorn and additional visiting Jesse left for home with an open invitation to come back. Most assuredly, he was not in haste to depart, but good manners dictated he should. Stella watched from the porch as he rode away, and Helen watched from the window. Jesse felt no ambivalence about the sisters at all. In his mind Stella was totally out of the picture. Jesse thought about Helen all the way home, and all the next day, and most of the next week. Jesse, positive he wanted to see Helen again, remained uncertain how he should arrange it.

That evening meal with the Kellys, the meeting of Helen, marked a turning point in Jesse's life.

CHAPTER 8

ADVENTURES

The fourth, annual Milton Harvest Festival, fondly referred to as the Corn Carnival, was scheduled for the last week of September, 1913. In 1910, the first year of the festival, over 4,000 people attended and last year's attendance exceeded 9,000. This year, as the town readied for the surge of outsiders, the organizers prepared for an expected 10,000 people, a total equal to twenty times the normal population of Milton. For Elzie the potential enclave of people promised excitement.

The carnival was not the major draw, as most events at the corn festival catered to the interests of the rural community. All local grains, especially corn, were on display as were vegetables, fruits, canned goods, and cooked or baked foods. Temporary animal shelters were constructed to house livestock, and a large show arena permitted proud owners of livestock to display their domesticates for judging. Winning or placing in any of these events was prestigious, resulting in county-wide recognition.

But the harvest festival was more than a carnival, more than an agricultural display at harvest time. It was a festive time for merriment and much of the available entertainment was of little or no cost. The festival provided opportunities to meet different people or renew old acquaintances. Competitive athletic events and skill-displaying activities attracted large crowds. A beauty contest which crowned a queen attracted candidates from near and far. Numerous fun contests involved children. Many adults, motivated by pride, displayed their work skills by competing in the hitching contest, the wood chopping contest, or similar manual skills. The celebration commenced with a grand parade of school children, and each evening large crowds attended music concerts, inner-dispersed with public speakers. Most people in Pike County were seduced by the lure of the Annual Milton Harvest Festival, and it was, by any definition, a jovial occasion of varied events held in a rural community composed of a population starved for social interaction.

Not all happenings were planned. An attractive girl of sixteen, named Rosa, worked with her father in a concession stand selling cotton candy, a recently developed form of candy made of spun sugar. Rosa emanated a striking appearance. Her shoulder length hair was dark black, her eyes appeared deep brown against her olive skin, and her bewitching facial features were highlighted by a dark mole on her left cheek. She wore a low cut white blouse with the shoulder straps high on her arms, which thus revealed the upper cleavage to her well defined bosoms. Her full cut, multicolored skirt reached about six inches below the knees; and as she moved about, the skirt clung to her youthful body, silhouetting a most attractive, voluptuous figure. Rosa's flamboyant style accentuated her most intriguing quality, her personal mystique. Of course, most men at the carnival noticed Rosa and probably an inordinate amount of cotton candy was sold to the crowd because Rosa was the friendly vender. Rosa, friendly to all, was socially more aggressive than the average Pike County female, but specifically she was flirtatious with older men. On occasion, Elzie walked past the cotton candy stand, and if he made eye contact with Rosa, she always smiled and winked at him as though they shared some secret from the rest of the world. Her flirtatious behavior almost intimidated Elzie, or at minimum, she reduced his normal outgoing personality to one of a shy, reserved individual. Elzie often watched Rosa but never verbally communicated with her until late on Friday evening. Normally a slow time at the produce stand and a busy time at the carnival, Rosa walked into the produce stand, surprising the young worker. Elzie was cleaning, preparing to close the stand. Caught off guard he simply stood motionless with the broom in his hand, and looked at her without saying a word. She initiated the conversation. "I was told that a gal could come to this place, and get a cup of coffee and some good conversation. Is there any truth to that?"

Delighted to hear Rosa speak directly to him, Elzie smiled, winked at her, and boasted, "Yep, it's true. We offer good coffee and the best conversation this side of the Illinois River. Sit yourself down, and I'll get the coffee for you, Miss Rosa. My name is Elzie, with a z. Actually, my name is Elza, but as far as I know, no one has ever called me that. They call me Elzie. I was named after a river town, about forty miles south of here, but the town has a different spelling. They spell it E-l-z-a-h. I don't have an h in my name."

Rosa, sporting a big grin, seated herself near Elzie. "Elza, I have but one question. Is that an example of the good conversation? I hope the coffee is better than the talk."

Feeling foolish about his introductory remarks, Elzie gave no answer, but poured a cup of coffee and handed it to Rosa. She held the cup in both hands, close to her lips, and slowly started to sip, looking at Elzie the entire time. "You know, Elza, I think I got a bum steer. This coffee is cold and too strong for me, and my name is Rosa, not Miss Rosa. I was named after a flower, and everybody calls me by my name, Rosa."

Elzie was flabbergasted. He did not know how to respond. Knowing that unless he did something he would likely lose his opportunity to talk with Rosa, he still was at a loss for words. He hesitated and looked at her. "I have a request. Can we start over again?"

Rosa placed her cup on the counter, walked to the door, turned around, saying, "Hi. My name is Rosa, and I was told I could come to this place, get a cup of coffee and some good conversation. Any truth to it?"

Pleased with her response, Elzie picked up the broom, took one swipe and then carefully placed it back in the same spot. "Welcome, Rosa. My name is Elzie, and yes, we have coffee and I try to visit with anyone who wants to visit. Unfortunately, it is late, the fire is low, and the coffee is strong, but if you will please come in and sit down, I will be happy to make a fresh pot, and I will try not to say anything foolish."

"It's a deal, and I will try not to be rude."

As he stoked the fire in the stove, Elzie tried to make polite conversation. Rosa listened.

"Elzie, I have seen you around all week, but you haven't said anything to me. Why not? Most males try their best to talk to me. Or is it that you are too young to notice the opposite sex? Whatever it is, I kind of like your shyness."

"First of all let me assure you that I am not too young, and second, I'm not shy. Whenever I see you, you are either working, or you are surrounded by people. Correct that. Surrounded by men. I do believe this is my first opportunity to talk with you, and I desperately don't want to spoil it by saying something stupid, like I did earlier."

"Well, don't you worry about that. This time around, we'll hit it off."

"Let me put on some fresh coffee, and in the meantime, here is some good Pike County cider. Mr. Wilson, my boss, wants the stand closed by 10:00 p.m. so I need to close the doors and then cleanup the place a bit. It should take about fifteen minutes. If you would wait, maybe finish your cider, then we could sit down and have that quality conversation. We can talk in here or go outside if that would make you more comfortable. Please say yes. Say you will wait, please."

"I will wait, and we can talk in here, no need to go elsewhere. But only on one condition will I wait."

"Name it."

"If you let me help you cleanup."

"Deal. Here's the broom." Elzie was so excited that he almost forgot the sequence of events in closing the stand. Rosa watched, finding amusement in Elzie's scurried movements before she, an efficient worker accustomed to manual labor, assisted. Once they finished the cleanup the young ones remained in the enclosed produce stand talking for hours spurred on by a positive chemistry between the two youths. Elzie had embarked on another adventure. Although the evening started on an awkward note, it became a felicitous night for both. The hour was 2:30 a.m. before Elzie walked Rosa back to her tent. For both of them it was a night to remember.

Milton was a town with few secrets. On the succeeding day others who knew that Rosa was at the produce stand asked Elzie to describe his activities of the previous night. Elzie refused. He smiled, and only said, "It was a most pleasant evening, and Rosa is a girl to be admired." Not one person, apart from the partakers, ever knew the details of what transpired that night, although there was no absence of speculation. Aunt Mary heard the gossip and expressed disappointment with Elzie, not with spoken words, but with body language.

Erastus was not as gentle. Three days hence, before Elzie left for work, Erastus asked Mary to leave the room so that he could speak with his youngest son. "I don't know what happened the other night, and I don't think I want to know, but you should know that everyone in Milton is talking about it."

Visibly upset, Elzie fired back. "Nothing happened the other night, if you are referring to Rosa. I thought you always advised me, never listen to gossip. Well, what changed your mind?"

"You are my son, and I'm trying to protect you. You've got to be more careful about the kind of people you associate with."

Erastus' choice of words disturbed Elzie. "Kind of people?"

"Yeah. You know what I mean. The kind of people who travel with carnivals. They're different from us."

"Different huh. I'm not sure what you mean, but if Rosa is different, I think it's a good different. Let me tell you a couple of things about Rosa. I don't know her very well, but I know some things. Her mother died when she was five years old. She has two younger sisters and they all live with her aunt, somewhere in Ohio, and during the season she travels and works with her father on the carnival circuit. They don't have much money and she does this to help out the family. Does this story have a familiar ring to it?"

Peeved, Erastus snapped back. "I don't think you should compare her to us."

Elzie refused to totally back off. "I'm just saying that not everyone in this country has an easy ride. I'm not comparing anyone to anything, but I can if you like. Some people might think that we have it tough, and compared to Rosa, I've got it made. I need to stop talking, because I'm getting mad. Is there anything else you want to talk about? If not, I'm going to work, and I'll try to stay clear of wicked people, if I can ever learn to tell for sure, exactly, who the wicked people are."

Erastus was indignant. His youngest son made more sense than he did, and his back was against the wall. Feeling a strong need to get in the last word, Erastus shook his finger at Elzie, and said, "You watch your mouth. Could be you need to be taken down a notch or two."

Having listened to the entire conversation from the other room, Aunt Mary quickly entered the kitchen talking as she walked, preempting any opportunity for a response from Elzie. "Elzie, you've got to get going so you won't be late to work. If any of the yellow delicious apples look especially good, will you bring home a peck?" As Elzie left the room mumbling something under his breath, Aunt Mary continued talking so that Erastus would not respond. Erastus' sister was successful in her effort to avoid additional confrontation.

The next few weeks were difficult for Elzie. Although Rosa was forever gone from his life, he constantly thought about her, remembering the few hours that they had spent together. He felt in limbo, having been somewhere, but going nowhere. What gnawed at him the most was his father's rush to judgment concerning Rosa's personal character. He hoped that under similar circumstances he would be less judgmental, more tolerant than his father. It concerned him that he might be like his father in many ways.

Working the produce stand was the ideal job for Elzie as he lived close to work, his labor generated decent income at 15 cents per hour, and his working hours were flexible. Another benefit was working for Howard Wilson, a nonpresumptuous, reserved, and understanding individual, who also possessed an exceptional working knowledge of the surrounding land. Mr. Wilson had taken a liking to young Elzie, admired his spirit of adventure, and motivated the lad to learn more about nature. In the eyes of the elderly bachelor, Elzie was the embodiment of what a youthful spirit should be and he willingly assisted the youth in his quest to become a proficient outdoorsman.

Wintertime business at the stand usually slowed, but regardless of the number of customers or sales, Mr. Wilson worked six days a week. Although Elzie's winter work hours were fewer, he often spent time at the stand visiting and sapping Mr. Wilson's mental storehouse of practical knowledge; and Howard Wilson was a willing teacher, zealous to impart what he knew. Mr. Wilson kept at the stand his twelve-volume reference guide to plants and animals of Illinois, and he taught Elzie to effectively use the reference material. More importantly, he instilled in Elzie the worth of knowing such information.

Compared to years past the winter snows of 1913-1914 were gentle, infrequent snows. Although by early February most of the ground still remained covered by the white, frozen substance, the roads and paths were free of the wintery covering. Fifty-five days past the winter solstice, the sun was high enough in the sky to induce daytime thawing in below-freezing temperatures. Each day was becoming longer and the sun rays were gaining in intensity. The final phase of winter, when all of last year's growth was either dead or dormant and before any of this year's growth started, was the ideal time to see the land in its bare natural formation. Lack of vegetation discloses many land features unnoticeable any other time of the year. Of particular interest to Elzie, this was the only window of opportunity to visually identify the small openings to the hundreds of scattered caves in the high bluffs on the Illinois River. Before his annual trek to the bluffs in search of previously unknown caves, Elzie checked with Mr. Wilson about his work schedule. "If all goes well, I won't be back for one week, if that is all right with you. Think you can make it around here and endure one week without my charming personality?"

Understanding that his employee was attempting humor, Howard Wilson replied in kind. "I'm sure I can make it. Might be kind of pleasant around here without you." Elzie gave no response other than to acknowledge agreement with a slight head movement. "Of course I'm going to miss you, but it's not your personality I'm going to miss. I'll miss all your complaining about how hard you work." Mr. Wilson changed to a serious tone. "I do have a few concerns about your outing. Does your Aunt know where you're going?"

"Of course she knows. I may be foolish at times, but not stupid. She knows the exact area, and she understands what I'm doing. She thinks I'm a little crazy. What do you think?"

"I'm not sure, Elzie. I know you are going to the bluffs to explore caves, and that sounds all right, but why are you staying out there for a week, instead of coming home each night? It is winter time, you know. What are you going to do with all of your inactive time? You can't explore at night in the dark. Where are you going to sleep? How are you going to get your supplies in there? What happens if you have a problem and need help?"

"I guess you have concerns. I just explained all of that to Aunt Mary. First, let me say that I have thought about all that stuff. I've been planning this trip for several weeks, and my supplies, what there are of them, are already there in the big cave. Remember the cave I discovered last year? Well that cave is my home cave, and my friend John from Montezuma, knows exactly where it is. When he's working the ferry on the other side of the river, he can see the cave opening and the landing in front of it. There is a tall hickory tree on top of the bluff, and he can see the tree without any obstruction, and everyday, around noon, I'm going to put out this old, long white cloth on a particular branch, and I'm going to take it down, about an hour before sunset. That's my signal that everything is okay. If I don't put it up or take it down, then he will come and check on me. I think we worked out a good system. Don't you?"

"I guess it sounds all right. John is reliable, isn't he?"

"Sure he is. He's the one who helped me get all my supplies into the cave, he knows what he's doing. He's a reliable friend. Mr. Wilson, you should see that cave." Elzie spoke with so much enthusiasm that he was hard to understand. "The opening is so small that I have to crawl through it, and once you get inside, it has more standup room than your house does. Temperature in the cave stays about the same all year, warm in the winter, and cool in the summer. Isn't that something? I still have much of the cave to explore. I don't even know how far back it goes, but it goes a long way. I've got a good lantern and enough coal oil to last a month. I've got a dozen candles and three boxes of matches. I aim to explore that cave. You can even build a fire in the cave, and the smoke goes straight up, just like in a chimney. Yes sir, I've got a lot to learn about caves. I'll bet you that I'll feel at home in that cave in no time, maybe not as comfortable as in a bed, but I'll make do." He slowed his pace of speaking and took a deep breath. "Actually, me and John thought we were the first to discover the cave, but it turned out not to be true. About three weeks ago we found a bunch of arrowheads in the cave, and John found what we think is an old Indian spear head. Found some bones too. Not sure if they are coyote or dog bones. So it's pretty clear that we are not the first to find the cave. In the beginning it made me mad, because I thought we had discovered something no one else ever knew about.

"I hope I don't get sidetracked. I can't get too involved exploring the cave because I've got plenty of time to explore it, since I know where it is. The most important thing is for me to scout the area and find as many openings to other caves as possible. You know that any good scouting must be done this time of the year, or you will miss a bunch of caves. It's exciting stuff because you never know what you might find. Who knows? I might find a cave bigger than Milton. You never know about those openings as some are big on the outside, and inside they end in a few feet. Some caves you can never stand up in and some are bigger and taller than rooms. I'm going to mark each entrance to the good caves, and I intend to explore them another time. Now tell me, Mr. Wilson, doesn't that sound like fun to you?"

"No, it does not. I like my bed, my comforts. But it sounds like it might be fun for you." A pause in speaking and the look on his face indicated some concern. "I do have a couple of warnings, if you don't mind. Remember to always watch your head in those caves. As you know those cave ceilings don't always run a constant height and with poor light you might bump into something and knock yourself silly. You could be knocked out for quite a while. What you need is something like a helmet to protect your head. Do you have anything like that?"

"No, I don't. I'll be careful. I have a rule that I always follow. Before I go into any opening I mark the outside with a red flag, and I tie my twine to something on the outside; and I unwind my twine as I go in, so if someone was looking for me, they would spot the flag and then follow the twine. Pretty smart, huh? I actually use the twine to find my way back out in case I get lost. Some of the caves have many turns, and I don't want to get lost. So I use twine for both reasons."

"Sounds reasonably prudent. I just hope you don't snag or break your twine. The other item I am reluctant to mention, but it must be said. Watch out for snakes in those caves, especially rattlesnakes. I assume you know that many snakes go in the caves for winter hibernation."

"Wow! If you're trying to scare me, you did a good job. I didn't think there were many of the timber rattlers left in this area, and I sure didn't know they went into the caves. How do you know that, have you seen them?"

"No, just stories. About fifty or sixty years ago those rattlesnakes were all over the place around here. Every farmer carried a bull whip and was obliged to snap them into, if he saw one. In fact, your father probably has killed more snakes with a bull whip than anyone else around here."

"I know. I've heard him say that, but recently I haven't seen him kill any rattlesnakes, and what makes you think they go into the caves for winter?"

"Sometime back in the 1840's or 50's, that's how the old timers got rid of them. Late one fall someone saw a bunch of snakes crawling into the same cave. When it was the dead of winter, they went into the cave and found hundreds of them, all balled together, way back in the cave. They didn't have much movement about them, but there was no doubt they were still alive. So the people got organized, found their hiding caves, poured kerosene all over the snakes and around the caves, and lighted a match. Burned them to death. They say that's how they got rid of most of the rattlesnakes in this area. Since then they have spent an additional fifty years killing any stray rattlers whenever they see them. Not much love for rattlesnakes around here. I suspect they got most of them, but don't know if they got all of them. So you be careful."

"Mr. Wilson, sure wished you hadn't told me that. I promise I will take extra care, and if I see anything that even resembles a rattlesnake, I will get the hell out of there in a hurry. I promise you, and I promise me."

Adventure time arrived. Early the next morning Elzie, with his backpack, rifle, and fishing gear, walked from Milton to the bluffs, requiring three hours of time and considerable energy to get there. The last two miles of the road he was forced to detour from the path to the edge of the woods to escape the raw north wind. The last hour of the journey, across rugged, uphill terrain, fatigued him, but he never wavered in his quest, becoming more determined each step of the way. Eventually he located the entrance and crawled into his designated home cave, took inventory of his supplies, and prepared the surroundings for his week of survival. Already well past midday before he finished his preparations, Elzie left the confines of the cave to admire the river from the heights and to become familiar with the land near the cave opening. He was surprised to realize how little time he previously had spent watching the river, considering all the time he had spent on the bluffs. Today, because of the north winds and his current vantage point, he could hear the familiar, and some unfamiliar, sounds of the river. It was a new experience. The river viewed from high was a magnificent sight.

Upon reentering the cave he immediately used his lighted lantern to examine the space and contents of the front section of the cave. After satisfying himself that there were no "critters" around, and after thoroughly checking the ceiling height, he prepared his in-cave campsite and made preparations for future cave explorations. Anticipating the explorations he studied the map he had drawn, specifically the relative locations of the newly found cave openings. Feeling no need for a fire he burned one candle for light. He prepared his first meal with the heat of the candle and spent the next few hours sharpening his ax and two knives on his whetstone, cleaning and checking his rifle, and rechecking all his supplies. He fell asleep before 9:00 p.m., although he was not aware of the exact hour. On this cold February night, Elzie was where he wanted to be, doing what he wanted to do, and proud that he was going it alone.

Elzie's adventure of camping alone in an isolated cave in the dead of winter was a marvelous personal experience. He became dispassionate to the hardships, and enamored with the workings of nature. Although he sensed he was vulnerable, he was never afraid, and he emerged from the week one step closer to manhood and many steps closer to understanding who he really was.

Returning from his week-long adventure, Elzie arrived home, cold and dirty, ready to communicate with another person. The young adventurer was happy to be home, and Aunt Mary was so relieved that in recognition of his safe return she prepared a meal of Elzie's favorite foods. After Elzie's quick consumption of hardy portions he vividly recounted his adventure to Aunt Mary, who, with proud admiration, listened and absorbed his every word. His description was so detailed and his level of excitement was so high, that Aunt Mary could almost visualize the events. Like most of the Moores, Elzie was such an accomplished storyteller that any event he experienced, he usually could expressively describe, and often he embellished the tale.

Later that evening Mary conveyed Elzie's description of his experience to Erastus. She concluded by declaring, "Your youngest son is a treasure. I have never known anyone who enjoys the excitement of living more than Elzie does. He has a passion for life, he craves exhilaration. The boy has a dogged resolution to get the most out of life."

Erastus thought about it for a minute, and then replied. "Yeah, I guess so. I hope he also gets some kind of resolve for work."

May 29, 1914, marked the end of the Milton school term. Fifteen students, including Elza Hubert Moore, were slated to graduate from eighth grade. To the best of memory Elzie was the only one on either parent's side of the family to finish more than six years of schooling.

Becoming more independent each passing day, recently Elzie had found little time for casual visiting with Aunt Mary or Frieda. He was selfish that way. This night was unusual in that all five of the residents of North Street were at home sitting in the same room conversing with one another. Even Erastus was attempting to be congenial. "Fine supper, Mary. One of these days your cooking is going to make me fat." That comment evoked smiles from everyone as they looked at the slim, stout man of fifty eight years, pat his firm midsection. Frieda could not resist the opportunity to make light of her father's comment.

Putting her finger to her head, she declared, "Mighty fine supper, Aunt Mary. If you keep feeding me like this, one day I'm going to get intelligent."

Elzie joined the fun. "Great food in this house. I'll bet if I keep eating here, I'll grow to be a seven foot giant."

Most uncharacteristic of Aunt Mary, she stood up and pointed her finger upwards while proclaiming, "Woe be it to the cook in this house. Her food is making us all silly. If I continue to eat with you guys, I may win the corn festival beauty pageant, retire from cooking, and live like a queen. All right, brother, it's your turn. Top that one."

"I can't top it. Nobody can match wits with a bunch of crazies. You guys don't know my burden—to be the only sane one in a loony bin. Teach me to give a compliment around this place."

Elzie started to twitch his body, throwing his arms around, and speaking gibberish to the ceiling. Frieda followed suit in a similar manner. Aunt Mary refused to wholeheartedly join the drama, although she did slightly jerk her head in repetitive motions and mumble something unintelligible. No longer able to contain himself, Erastus roared, laughing harder than anyone could remember him laughing.

"It does my heart good to see such joy in this house. I haven't seen Erastus this amused since we were kids." Looking at her brother, Mary continued. "Do you remember when we were kids and stayed down at the river, and..."

"That's enough. I don't want you to start telling foolish stories about our youth, especially in front of my kids."

"Ah come on, Aunt Mary, don't stop now," was the plea from Elzie. "Tell us some stories about Dad as a kid."

Aunt Mary winked at Frieda and said, "Later, children, when your father's ears are well out of hearing distance. Then, we'll tell some real Erastus stories." She waited for her brother to respond which he did not. Mary continued, but in a more serious vein. "I wish Mary Dosia was here to see you all right now. She would be so proud."

"Yeah, me too," Frieda said. "Do you know that Elzie and me can't remember what Mother looked like. I know that you both have described her to us, but that's not the same. If we only had a photograph. I wish we had a picture of her, that would help."

Erastus retorted, almost defensively. "People like us didn't have their pictures taken. That's for folks with money."

"It used to be, not any more," Elzie stated. "They took my picture at school just a few weeks ago. They do it once a year."

"Yeah, he's right. They take school group pictures."

The thought of his youngest children in a photograph prompted a question from Erastus. "Where are the photographs? I've never seen them. Have you, Mary?"

"No. Where are they, Elzie, Frieda? I'd like to see them."

Impatiently Elzie answered. "I don't know, we didn't get personal copies of it. It's probably in the school library. Yeah, that's it. Dad, if you want to see a photograph of your youngest son, you'll have to go to school, look on the wall of the library, and you will see a photograph of me, mounted on the wall of the Milton School library. You'll find me about three feet to the left of Abraham Lincoln, and two feet below George Washington. If you look long enough, you most likely will find Frieda's picture too. She will be next to the commoners. Right, Frieda?"

"If you say so, Elzie, or perhaps I should call you President Elzie."

"Fine with me."

Frieda looked directly at her Aunt. "Aunt Mary, I have a question of a personal nature. I want you and Dad to carefully listen to what I have to say, and then give me an answer. I know my mother is dead, and I know you are not my mother, but you are the closest thing I have to a living mother. As I'm sure you have heard, President Wilson has declared the second Sunday of May as Mother's Day. I know the day has already passed this year, but still, I would like to do something nice for you, for Mother's Day. I don't think my mother would mind, and I wondered if it would be all right with you and Dad."

Erastus answered first. "I have no objections."

Aunt Mary was visibly touched. "That would be nice, honey, as long as we keep everything in perspective, but you don't need to do anything special. You already have by what you just said. Thank you."

Surprisingly, Elzie spoke. "I agree with Frieda, and we need to do something special for you. You name it, and we'll do it."

Mary, humbled by the comments, briefly reflected. "There might be one thing, but it might be too much of a sacrifice."

Elzie boldly stated. "Just name it, and we'll do it."

"Okay. Elzie, I want you to attend your graduation ceremony. Frieda, I want you to go with me to Elzie's graduation and, if possible, convince your father to come with us. Now if that's too much for any of you, I understand." Aunt Mary paused in her speaking, and no one else spoke. Aunt Mary restated her wish. "I would like for all of us to go see Elzie graduate from eighth grade."

This time Frieda answered. "That's a wonderful idea, Aunt Mary. Okay, Elzie? You said just name it."

"Oh, Frieda, I don't know, I suppose so. I think I agree with Dad. This will teach me a lesson—one should never attempt to be nice in this house."

On Friday, May, 29,1914, Elza Hubert Moore reluctantly walked across the stage and received his diploma.

Although completion of eighth grade offered little personal satisfaction to Elzie, it did become a symbol of something far more significant—it represented his passage to manhood. No longer was his life regulated by school bells and school terms. Never convinced that school after a certain undefined point taught practical skills, Elzie was ready to teach himself or to learn by experience all that which he deemed important. Knowing and understanding who he was and where he came from, he never entertained thoughts about entering into any of the professions, and he never had the slightest interest in the academics. He was Elzie Hubert Moore, from Milton, Illinois, descended from hardy pioneer stock, and part of the common class of man. His future was to be shaped, not by education or family wealth or business savvy, but by the strength of his back and the sweat of his brow. Right or wrong, Elzie had been taught to think in that manner and he believed it to be an absolute truth. Success came from hard physical work, personal endurance, not from opportunities resulting from formal education. He was ready for the challenge of life and the thought of failure never crossed his mind.

Elzie frequently used the expression, "What you intend to do, is less important than what you do. What you do, is who you are." For him this expression was less a criticism of other individuals, more a statement of a personal philosophy. Some people were baffled as to its meaning, but to Elzie the meaning was crystal clear. If asked to explain the expression, he arrogantly refused, saying, "No explanation needed. Think about it." No doubt about it, Elzie at times was flippant and roguish, and he took no shame in it.

In a far off continent across the Atlantic Ocean a political earthquake was shaking the very foundations of European governments, and its strong aftershocks were felt throughout the world. June 28,1914, the hier-apparent to the throne, Francis Ferdinand, the Archduke of Austria-Hungry, and his wife, Sophie, were assassinated in the Bosnian town of Sarajevo. The assassin was a nineteen-year-old Serbian named Gavrilo Princip. World leaders feared this act might become the spark that would ignite a global war. Their fears were justified.

Isolated and protected by the Atlantic Ocean, Americans felt secure, free from involvement in European affairs. American conventional wisdom espoused that any future European conflict would be regional in nature, thus America could escape involvement if the United States Government would pursue and maintain a policy of neutrality. Within the United States most everyone talked about the events, most every newspaper and magazine wrote about the impending conflict, but most Americans thought of themselves as outside looking in, not involved nor wanting to be.

For some reason young Elzie became intrigued by the developing world events which conceivably could lead to war. From the beginning of war discussions the lad became frustrated in his attempts to understand all that was happening, to understood the chain of political events, or how the many events related to one another. For the first time to his memory, Elzie became interested in political events, but his pursuit to understand the complex issues met with little success. He could find no one around him who understood the issues well enough to explain them to him. Not to be deterred Elzie visited the library in Pittsfield, read two different newspapers, talked to the librarian, and read the current edition of *Harpers* magazine about the European crisis. He even attended a public lecture about the impending war, and when that failed to enlighten him he hung around the barber shop, listening and absorbing the local take on international events. Every endeavor to understand the complex political issues was in vain. He felt that most everyone had an opinion about what was occurring, but no one understood why it was occurring. It was paradoxical that now, when he wanted to learn, he could not.

August 6, 1914, was a pleasant summer evening in Milton, Illinois, and many residents were outside their houses, enjoying the mild weather. All appeared well in their isolated part of the world. Aunt Mary and Frieda were sitting in the porch swing, Elzie was relaxing in the wicker rocker, and Erastus was already in bed. The serenity enhanced the pleasant summer evening as the only sounds were the night sounds or an occasional barking dog, and everything seemed right with the world. Aunt Mary broke the verbal silence. "You're so quiet tonight, Elzie. Are you preoccupied or are you relaxing?"

"A little of both. Relaxing as I think about the problems of Europe."

"Well that's a new one on me—my fourteen-year-old nephew, sitting on the front porch thinking about the political situation in Europe. What is this world coming to? No pun intended."

"I know what you mean, Aunt Mary. Sometimes I surprise myself too. I just can't clear my mind of it. I guess you folks have already heard that Germany invaded neutral Belgium, and that France is sending troops to stop them, and Great Britain declared war yesterday. They are mobilizing their forces in preparation for the war against Germany."

Frieda answered first. "Yes, I heard, but I'm not real sure what mobilizing means. To get ready, I guess. I know Germany, Austria-Hungry, Russia, France, and Serbia have already mobilized. Guess Great Britain is not ready yet. How long does it take to get ready to go to war after they decide to? Seems to me like it's just a bunch of talk. Why would you go to war if you didn't have to, why don't they work it out? Surely, there's a way."

"How would you answer her, Aunt Mary?"

"I don't have an answer, because I don't know much about it. It's not my place to figure it out."

"Well, whose place is it?"

"It's their place, it's their war, not ours. Let the politicians figure it out. I suspect the politicians got them in their predicament in the first place."

"Aunt Mary, I don't want to be disrespectful, but I'm not sure I agree. I don't know who or what caused the mess. I can't seem to make heads or tails out of anything that is going on, and it's not because I haven't tried. I just don't understand. I've been reading, listening, and talking, but so far it's got me nowhere. Reading about the events is like hitting your head against a wall. It doesn't do any good. Maybe you're right. Maybe it's their mess and it doesn't really affect us. It still aggravates me that I can't figure out what is going on."

Frieda spoke without hesitance. "If I wanted to know something that confusing, I know who I would ask."

"Who?"

"Miss Simmons."

"You mean the old maid history teacher?"

"I think we're talking about the same person, although I wouldn't describe her that way. If you decide to ask her, I don't think you want to use that wording. Don't ask, if you don't want to. To me, she's the smartest person I know, and I'll bet there aren't too many things she doesn't know."

"How do you know her, anyway?"

"I know her the same way you do. She lives down the street and teaches at the high school. Just because she's not my teacher, doesn't mean I don't know her. Ask anybody in town. They will tell you the same thing—she's one smart woman. You know what I think, Elzie? I think you don't want to ask her because she's a teacher, or probably more important, because she's a woman. Is that why, Elzie?"

"I didn't say I didn't want to ask her, I just called her what she is, an old maid school teacher. What would she know about war anyway?"

"Just forget what I said. You think just like dad. Go ask some of your male friends to help you understand. Men!" Frieda left the porch, went into the house, and slammed the screen door.

"Frieda sure got huffy, didn't she?" Aunt Mary looked as though she was pondering the question. Elzie repeated. "Frieda sure got huffy, didn't she?"

"I heard you, I was thinking. It's my understanding that you've been asking questions all over creation about the impending war. Why don't you talk with Miss Simmons? Is there some reason you don't?" Elzie did not give an answer. Aunt Mary repeated the question. "Elzie, is there some reason?"

"I don't know, might be."

Aunt Mary gathered her things and prepared to go inside. "Good night, Elzie, I hope you find someone who can answer your questions. Just for your information, I'm about to get in a huff, too." She closed the screen door a little firmer than usual.

Elzie watched in astonishment. After Aunt Mary was well out of hearing range, he spoke aloud. "Women."

It was now up to Elzie to ponder Frieda's question. Somehow he had just alienated two of his strongest supporters. He knew the reason he did not want to talk with Miss Simmons, and it was not because she was a woman. It was because she was a teacher. He somehow felt that talking with a teacher might mean he was wrong about not going on to school, and he did not want anyone to think that, because he was finished with school for good. Knowing he had to back down someway, and knowing he wanted to preserve his pride, he worked out a plan and would execute it tomorrow after work. Before he went inside he looked around the porch and spoke, even though no one was there to hear him. "High school is for sissies and rich folk. I'm neither, and for your information, I'm in a huff, too."

Elzie had somehow missed the point. Frieda was not upset with him about school, she was upset because he was reluctant to talk to a female teacher, which indicated to her that Elzie believed females were intellectually inferior to men. The truth of the matter was, he probably did believe such, just as most contemporary, local men believed women were inferior. But he also knew that he might be wrong, so he decided that from now on he should give the issue of male and female equality more thought, and he should talk less, and think more, about women and their abilities and their rights. Sometimes, Elzie's attitudes concerned

Elzie, too. However, he was not about to share these thoughts with anyone, at least not Frieda.

The next day after work Elzie went directly to Miss Simmons' house. He adjusted his clothing, checked his appearance, swallowed his pride, and knocked on the door. An elderly, rather sophisticated looking woman, Miss Simmons, the old maid school teacher answered the door. "Good evening, Elzie. What can I do for you?"

"My name is Elzie Moore, and I live over on North Street. I don't go to school anymore."

"I know that, Elzie. What can I do for you?"

"I wondered if you had some chores you might want done, or some repairs that need to be made. I'm pretty handy and I work cheap."

"Well, I must say, this is a surprise. I have known you for about ten years, and I have never known you to seek work, nor have I known you to initiate conversation with me. This must be a special occasion. The last time I heard your name was in regards to a particular event. I believe you skipped school for a week to live in a cave."

"Yep, that was me."

"That was I, not me. You know better than that." Miss Simmons paused, waiting for a response that never came. "Exactly how cheap do you work?"

"Dirt cheap, let me tell you what I had in mind. I would like to work in exchange for some tutoring. Even up, one hour of work for one hour of tutoring."

"Tutoring in what?"

"Everybody in town knows that you are the smartest person around, and I want to talk with somebody really smart. I desperately need to know all about the current problems in Europe. We already know that they have declared war, and I want to understand all about it. I want to know why they are at war, and what it means to us. I've asked everybody I know, and no one seems to have the foggiest idea. Frieda, my sister, said you could explain it to me."

"So you have a desperate need to know, huh. Why don't you come back to school this year and learn about it there?"

"I don't want to offend you, Miss Simmons, but I don't learn all that much in school. My teachers would just have me learn the facts, and then write them on paper, about fifty times. I don't want to learn the facts as much as I want to understand them. That's why I'm here."

"First of all, young man, you must know the facts before you can make generalizations from them. Second, the reason no one explains the current problems of Europe to you is probably because none of us understand all the problems; and more importantly, we do not know the full implications of Europe at war. I doubt if Kaiser Wilhelm, himself, understands all that is going on. It's for sure that nobody here can explain what you want to know, and no one could explain it in the amount of time equal to a few chores and repairs. The best that could happen, is that you could eventually acquire some information which would allow you to gain insight into the problems of Europe. And be assured, that is no easy undertaking."

"Wow! It sounds worse than fractions to me."

"It could be. Do you still want to work for me, or as you put it, work even up?"

"Yes, ma'am. I want to figure this stuff out."

"In that case, I have two tasks for you. My front gate is squeaking and does not latch securely. Can you repair that?"

"Sure. Once I get my tools and some oil, I'll fix it in a flash, unless it's broken. If it's broken, it'll take a little time."

"Next, I have a pile of wood that needs to be cut in proper size for kindling, not too big and not too small. Can you do that?"

"Of course."

"Well then it's final. We have a work in exchange for tutoring arrangement. You complete the two tasks and then we will determine the time for learning. If it is agreeable with you, we will study on my front porch. And you must remember, this will not be easy, and it will require considerable effort on your part."

"It's a deal," Elzie proclaimed as he extended his hand for a deal-binding handshake. Thank you, Miss Simmons. I will not disappoint you on the work, and I will attempt to be a good student. He departed immediately, returned in less than ten minutes, and completed the tasks in less than two hours. Elzie informed Miss Simmons that the tasks were completed, and requested a time to start the tutoring.

"My, you work fast. I'm not accustomed to students so eager to learn."

"That's cause you don't teach fun stuff in school. How about if we start now? I got coming, one hour and thirty three minutes of tutoring."

"First, we need some ground rules. I want you to use proper English. I don't wish to hear any more, 'I got coming,' expressions. Second, please keep your attitudes about school to yourself. In my presence you will be a gentleman in pursuit of knowledge. Third, you will need pencil and paper, and I expect you to do some reading on your own. Are these terms agreeable with you?"

"Yes, they are, I think. I'm not expressing an attitude but I need to ask a question. Why do I need pencil and paper? I don't have to write down everything you say ten times or so, do I?"

Miss Simmons was amused, but still answered with her firm manner. "No, you do not, Elzie. However, you will need to take notes, write down the names of research books, and write other pertinent data. Writing is a way to organize your thoughts, especially when you first start to learn. All information is useful, and some is vital. I believe the best way to learn is to write notes. I will not abuse you as a student. Does that sufficiently address your concern, or do I need to give more justification?"

"Nope. Your answer was just fine."

Miss Simmons continued with her instructions. "I feel better since I have your approval on the proper way to learn. In the future I assume you will trust me to employ the proper teaching techniques. However, we cannot commence tonight as I must prepare my thoughts to properly work with you. Information does not come easily, it requires effort on both our parts. We will have our first session, this Saturday, at 6:00 p.m., if that is convenient for you."

"That is most convenient. I'm going home tonight and start studying European geography. In my pursuit of knowledge, I will be a gentleman, even at home. It goes without saying that I trust you to teach the best way. Thanks again, Miss Simmons." As he was leaving the porch, he stopped, turned and spoke. "I like you, Miss Simmons. I like the way you talk. Hope I learn to talk like that. See you Saturday."

Elzie was home in less than five minutes. Frieda, sitting on the porch, was intently reading a newspaper until Elzie appeared. "Elzie, I have something here you'll want to see. Brace yourself, because this is big stuff. It's the article that describes the military action at the start of the war. Maybe this will answer some questions." Frieda held the newspaper high and in front of her so that Elzie could read the headlines.

WAR IS DECLARED. GERMANY INVADES BELGIUM. FRANCE RESPONDS.

August 7,1914, in Milton, Illinois, Elzie reads about an ongoing military engagement which started the day before yesterday.

Unable to contain himself after reading the newspaper account, Elzie returned to Miss Simmons' house to share the news with her and to solicit her reaction. He was very disappointed once he determined that she already had known about the newspaper coverage, aware even before he was there earlier; and she had not informed him. Miss Simmons, unwilling to discuss the events until she acquired more accurate information, sent Elzie home and reminded him they were scheduled to meet Saturday. Elzie interpreted Miss Simmons' behavior as dispassionate, when in fact it was not. She wanted more information to better understand the fast-moving, series of events. Elzie did not yet understand the complexity of the events, nor did he comprehend the academic effort necessary to understand them. He would soon learn. He was off on an intellectual adventure, one that he never dreamed he might one day take.

Saturday night did arrive, although to Elzie the arranged time for learning was slow in coming. In his pocket he carried a list of questions he had compiled, and this night he expected to get a concise answer to the nagging question of why the European countries were going to war. Once Elzie received a simple answer to his pressing question of why, he intended to present his list of additional questions. He arrived at his tutor's door exactly at 6:00, with paper and pencil in hand, and a smile on his face. "Good evening, Elzie," Miss Simmons said as she opened the door with a smile equal to Elzie's giant grin. "I was not certain you would be here since this is Saturday night, the night of youthful activities. I am most pleased to see you; plus now, I know you are truly interested. Please, have a seat."

"Ah heck, Miss Simmons, I wouldn't miss this for anything. I'm ready. Why are they fighting? I suppose you heard, excuse me, you have heard that Great Britain is now in it, too. Mr. Wilson thinks it all will be over by Christmas, but he's not so sure who will win."

"I hope Mr. Wilson is correct, but I doubt it. Remember, I told you there is no easy explanation as to why they are fighting, and I certainly can't give a one line response to your question. We must pursue two different lines of inquiry. First, we need historical perspective. Did you study the geography, as you said you would?"

"Yes, ma'am. I know every country in Europe, the capitals, and population of each country. I have it all right here written down. Do you want to see it?"

"No, you keep it and use the information as we go. All countries have different histories, and we need to examine those differences. For example, the country we call Germany is relatively young, having proclaimed itself an empire in 1870, after defeating France in a rather brief war. Germany today feels they are not getting proper respect from other nations for their recent economic growth or for their powerful political position in central Europe. Germany feels they have something to prove. Did you know this information before?"

"Heavens no. I'm not old enough to know stuff like that, yet."

That response forced a brief smile from Miss Simmons. "Age has nothing to do with it. If you want to understand what is going on in Europe, we will need to work with this kind of information. You will study facts and more facts. We have much to learn, and at that we will only scratch the surface. Remember, true understanding is based on knowledge. Do you still want to continue?"

"Heck yes. By the time you finish with me, I'll be the smartest fourteen year old in Milton."

"No delusions or false promises, Elzie. That isn't going to happen. Education is a lifelong pursuit with no shortcuts, and remember, we are only concerning ourselves with a limited topic."

"You sure say it like it is, don't you?"

"I do not. I say it as I see it. Please allow me to continue without interruption.

151

Before you leave here this evening we need to identify the belligerent nations, and those likely to become belligerent. After we identify these areas you need to study about them. You need to learn about the people, the cultures, the religions, the ethnic groups, the languages, and something about their history. You need to learn everything about them that you can, so that we determine why these nations are willing to go to war. Are you willing to do that?"

"I guess I'm willing, except I don't even know how to start. Where do I find that kind of stuff?"

"We start here." Miss Simmons handed the student a handwritten list of European nations with notations indicating probable political alliances during the war. She handed a rather large, intimidating looking book to Elzie. You will begin with this European contemporary history book. It is my personal copy, so you take proper care of it."

"Do you want me to read the whole thing?"

"No. Read only about the belligerent countries, and read only what you want to read. The amount of effort you put into this project is up to you, not me. Now for our second item. You remember I said we need historical perspective. Well, we also need a current perspective. That is to say, we need to grasp how the people today, especially the people of Europe, view what is happening as it happens. That's more difficult to acquire. I imagine if we could personally speak with the leaders of each country, and we asked them why they were going to war, I believe each leader would give different reasons. The reasons would be based on his own interpretation, or his perspective. Furthermore, I believe no one leader would be totally right, or totally wrong, in their assessment. His perspectives would be different.

"Now comes the difficult part. First, we must determine what the leaders of each country believe to be the causes of the war, and believe me, there will be as many reasons as there are countries. Then we need to evaluate the reasons to determine if they are valid, or only thought to be valid. You must take the position of a neutral party and judge each nation fairly. Out of that process will come the answer to the question, 'Why are they fighting?' You need to read everything available, especially newspapers and magazines. Talk and listen to people who have a different view or perspective. You also have a unique opportunity to acquire information made possible by new technology, the motion picture. If you attend the movies, you will see newsreels about the war. You will see pictures of the leaders, the lands, and I suspect the war itself. Don't count solely on this information, or any one source of information to be totally accurate, but do factor it in."

Miss Simmons illustrated with a specific example. She proceeded to explain all the data for France that she thought Elzie should know. He was to use this model for gathering data about other countries. She presented historical perspective first, then current perspective, as she saw it.

Elzie could not keep up as he attempted to write on paper all the information he feared he would not remember. It was too much to write or absorb. He put down his pencil and shook his writing hand as though it were cramped. "I don't know what to say, Miss Simmons. I don't know if I am capable of doing this or not. Can't we just get a book and get the reasons out of the book? I remember a book in school that listed the causes of the Civil War."

"If it were only that easy. The Civil War was over fifty years ago, and the book you are referring to was written years after the war ended, after historians had sorted out the information. There is no such book about this war. The road to understanding is a long road, you must remember that."

"I hope I have the patience to walk that road. I'm going to try and try hard, I promise you, Miss Simmons."

"That is as much as anyone can ask. You do your best, and that is all any of us can do, our best."

"I will be here for more work tomorrow afternoon. I already owe you more time on our work for tutor agreement, and I'm sure you will need to help me a bunch more."

"I do not want you here tomorrow. Tomorrow is Sunday, the day of worship and no one should work. You no longer need to do work for me, as my reward is watching you learn, and I will continue to help you as much as you want, time permitting. Saturday is not a good time, though. I initially said Saturday night to see how much you really wanted to receive help. You have now convinced me. Would it be agreeable with you if we planned to meet the first and third Tuesdays of the month at 5:00 p.m.? In the future I prefer that we meet at the school where I have access to maps and additional material, unless you have objections."

Elzie hesitated and started to answer making the sound, "Uh..."

Before he spoke a full word, Miss Simmons spoke. "Fine. We will meet in my room at the school, 5:00 sharp, a week from this Tuesday. I expect you to have done some studying and some good thinking, and we will start the session with questions from you. Agreeable?"

"Uh, I guess so. You want to meet at the school, huh. Will there be other students around?"

"No guarantees, but I assume not. Why? Are you ashamed of wanting to learn?"

There was hesitation before the answer. "No good reason. I just wasn't thinking, that's all. Thank you, Miss Simmons, and I promise that in the future I will be better prepared."

Elzie made several trips to the school for tutoring before the formal learning process terminated. The sessions ended not because he understood the war, but because his desire to formally learn about the war diminished, or at least his desire to study decreased. As Miss Simmons had suggested, the road to knowledge was a long one, and his journey was taking its toll on the young student. He never completely understood the causes of the Great War, although he never stopped trying to gain insight. Elzie felt he had learned from Miss Simmons much more than academic information. He developed some higher level thinking skills, he changed his perception of the world about him, and perhaps most importantly, he held the process of learning in higher regard. He believed that as a result of studying with Miss Simmons he had become a more tolerant person, perhaps a better person. He forever remembered her words, do the best you can, no one can expect any more. Elzie was pleased that he had followed Frieda's advice to talk with Miss Simmons.

Clearly, one attitude changed. The young student never again questioned the intellectual capacity of the opposite sex. Surprising almost everyone, Elzie made an announcement one night while at the dinner table. "Far as I'm concerned, women should have the right to vote."

CHAPTER 9

MORE ADVENTURES

As so often happens in life, a single, random occurrence influenced Elzie. While he and Erastus were delivering a load of freight to the general store in Pearl, Illinois, Elzie met a traveling man. It was but a brief conversation before Elzie realized that he and the older man shared similar interests, specifically in firearms. The stranger was a marksman, had in his possession a high powered rifle with a scope, and was willing to demonstrate the weapon's power and accuracy. The only hitch was the man intended to leave Pearl early the next morning, and if Elzie were to observe the demonstration, it had to be this evening. He sought consent from his father who was unwilling to delay his trip home for such frivolous reasons. Erastus showed his disgust and returned alone, leaving his son to walk the five miles back to Milton.

Elzie was nobody's fool when it came to shooting a low powered rifle or shotgun, but he had never handled such a sophisticated weapon as this one, a model 1903 Springfield rifle, .30 inch caliber. He carefully monitored the older man as he handled, loaded, aimed, and fired the rifle into a hillside about 250 yards away. His opportunity to handle the rifle finally presented itself when the older man said, "Would you like to try it? It's got a pretty good kick if you are not prepared for it, but it shoots like a charm. You line up the cross hairs in the scope, and gently squeeze the trigger. I estimate the tin can down there near that stump to be about two hundred yards. Do you think you can hit it?"

"I don't know for sure if I can hit it, but I know I could with my rifle."

"Doesn't your .22 have an open sight?"

"Yep."

"Are you telling me you can hit a target two hundred yards away using a .22 rifle with an open sight?"

"Sure am."

"That would be a pretty good shot even with this rifle. You take a shot and we'll see how good you are. If the tin can is not enough of a challenge for you, there is a red label on the can. Do you see it?"

"Yep."

"Try to hit it."

Elzie assumed a lower position with the left knee directly on the ground, pointed the rifle, sighted the target in the scope, and held the position for a few seconds without firing a shot. He stood and then looked at the bolt and slightly lifted the rifle as though he was trying to get a feel for the weight of the rifle. "This rifle is quite a bit heavier than mine. Maybe twice as heavy."

"Probably so. Unloaded it weighs eight pounds, eight ounces. Yours probably weighs about four or five pounds. Is it too much for you?"

"Nope. Do I line up the cross hairs on the target or do I need to shoot a little higher?"

The man was impressed with Elzie's question. "Directly on the target at two hundred yards. Your question, however, just explained to me how you could hit a target two hundred yards away with a twenty-two. Take your time, line up the target exactly in the cross hairs."

Elzie followed the instructions and fired. The shot was a direct hit which exploded the can, forcing it first to move upward and then landing several feet away from his original location. "Wow! This is some rifle," Elzie exclaimed with pride and some astonishment.

"It's more than the rifle. That was one hell of a shot. Let's leave the rifle here and go check the can. I want to see where you hit it." As they walked to the location of the target the man asked questions of Elzie, and Elzie responded in short direct answers. Elzie enjoyed answering the knowledgeable questions and appreciated the interest the man was showing in him.

After examining the target up close, Elzie spoke first. "Look at the size of that hole. I've never seen a bullet hole that big. Not much left of the can, is there?"

The man showed greater enthusiasm. "I don't think I've ever seen a shot that good. Look at the red label on the can."

"I don't see it."

"That's what I mean. You don't see it because it's not there. You shot right through it. Hell of a shot, kid. Let's set up some more targets and on the way back, I'll pace it to measure the exact distance. I guessed it at two hundred yards but it might vary some." The pacing revealed two hundred six yards. Now Elzie was impressed.

"How did you come so close on distance? I could never do that."

"Yes, you could, it only takes practice. You first learn a given distance, say one hundred yards. You practice identifying that one hundred yards on everything you see, until you get good. Then you just double or triple it. You never see five hundred yards, only one hundred yards, five times. I practice everyday. After a while you get pretty good at it; but it's harder if you don't have level ground, because then you have to make adjustments. It just takes practice, that's all. I'll tell you one thing. If you ever want to be a good distance shooter, say three, four, five hundred yards, you need to know how to estimate distance."

The two remained at the site for more than three hours, talking and firing the rifle. With the given constraints of time, an attentive Elzie learned more from the stranger about rifles than he had imagined possible. Before leaving they cleaned up the site and visited some more. "One of these days I'm going to buy a rifle just like yours."

"The United States infantry really likes this rifle too and I understand why— bolt action, five round clip, and possible to fire eight to twelve rounds per minute of aimed fire. Some say the only rifle better is the German Mauser, and not everyone agrees it is better. The Mauser is the rifle the Germans are using in the war. I guess it's a matter of choice. I've never fired a Mauser, so I don't know. Speaking of German guns, have you ever fired a handgun?"

"Yeah, but only a single action revolver belonging to my dad. I can't hit much with it, certainly not at any distance. He uses it for snakes and critters, and he doesn't hit much with it either."

"Handguns have an all together different use, and you don't use them for distance. I have one here I bought about five years ago, and it's the best handgun I've ever seen. It's a German automatic Steyr pistol. It's lightweight, six rounds in the clip, and one in the chamber, always ready to fire, after you flick off the safety. If you need to fire six or seven in a hurry at close range this is the gun you want. I don't know for sure, but I'll bet a lot of German officers are carrying it right now. It's quite a handgun."

"May I look at it?"

"Sure. Let me take the clip out first. What I really like is you can always tell if the clip is in or out, by looking at the indicator, next to the safety. It doesn't tell you if its got bullets in it, but it shows if the clip is there or not."

Not familiar with handguns Elzie awkwardly, but carefully, handled the automatic pistol. "It's a nice gun, but I'm going to save my money and buy a Springfield."

"Good choice, young man." The stranger stopped talking long enough to look at his watch. "It's been a pleasure talking with you. Take care of yourself and I hope you're not in trouble with your old man."

"I'm not, good-bye, sir." Elzie left Pearl at twilight which meant his five mile nighttime walk to Milton would be difficult, but he had no regrets as the time with the man was time well spent. On his journey home his mind was so occupied with thoughts about the rifle that he lost awareness of both distance and time. He could still sense the exciting feeling of holding and firing the Springfield rifle, and although he knew he wanted one, he also knew his chances of acquiring one were quite slim. Regardless of probability, he dreamed of owning a high powered, 1903 Springfield, .30 inch caliber rifle with an adjustable sight.

During the years 1915, 1916, the political world was vibrant with unfurling events that were destined to affect the lives of all who lived in those turbulent times. Few doubted that the future of mankind would soon be reshaped by this devastating, ongoing war, yet few dared to even speculate regarding the nature of this change. Mankind possessed no method of measurement, no accurate predictor of change. As always the political future of the world remained an intriguing mystery, but this time the warring nations and their governments risked more than slight change. They risked obliteration.

Conversely, the lives of many Americans remained the same, not yet visibly touched by change; and to many, especially those in the more isolated areas of the United States, the changes seemed remote, nonexistent. Although the events of war were very real, they appeared to many Americans as no more than abstractions to be intellectually understood, not to be experienced. The remote events were similar to reading a novel where the vicarious experience was only imaginary. Elzie, the young adventurer, felt that life elsewhere was similar to an active Saturday night in the city, and instead of him visiting the city, he was home sleeping through it all. He lived in exciting times and, yet, he lamented his drab life, his uneventful existence.

Regardless of how remote global events may have appeared to be, more than not they sent political shock waves throughout the world. Unbeknownst to the young adventurer from Pike County, many such far away happenings were shaping his personal view of the world. In particular, one prodigious international incident occurred May 7, 1915. A British passenger liner, the Lusitania, carrying 1,919 civilians including 139 Americans was torpedoed and sunk by a German submarine. Ultimately, it was determined that 1198 lives were lost in the sinking, including 128 Americans. *The New York Times* reported the disaster:

LUSITANIA SUNK BY SUBMARINE, PROBABLY 1260
DEAD;
TWICE TORPEDOED OFF IRISH COAST; SINKS IN

FIFTEEN MINUTES; CAPT. TURNER SAVED, FROHMAN AND VANDERBILT MISSING; WASHINGTON BELIEVES THAT A GRAVE CRISIS IS AT HAND.

President Wilson demanded an apology from Germany, and got one, but the attacks continued on other civilian ships. Early in 1915, the Germans had warned that all ships entering a war zone around Great Britain risked an attack without warning. The submarine, a new weapon of naval warfare used exclusively by the Germans because they were the only country who produced it, complicated the question of neutral rights in wartime. International law required that a ship give warning before an attack, but submarines, slow on the surface and vulnerable to ramming, could not risk giving warnings. Germany contended the British blockade in the North Sea bottled up the German Navy, and that submarine warfare was their only recourse. The use of the submarine was a perfect example of nebulous right or wrong in the confusion of war, each side believing its course of action to be justified. In the eyes of many Americans, Germany was making war on civilians and neutrals, and by doing so it was clearly becoming the evil power.

As Allied propaganda continued to influence American attitudes, many Americans were becoming indignant, intolerant of German action. Sympathy with the Allied war effort was gaining momentum, and hostility toward the Central Powers was increasing. Another article read:

GERMANS ARE HAPPY
Submarine Crew Which Sank Lusitania Is Praised For Pluck
And Daring.

VICTIMS' BODIES FILL WAREHOUSE
ADDITIONAL DEAD LIE IN HOTELS
Funerals of Most of them Will Be Held Sunday
Children Clasping One Another Still Unidentified.

GERMAN SUB MADE NO EFFORT TO SAVE ANYONE
"We saw it for a moment before it dove."

TWO MORE LINERS SAIL TODAY
Capt. John Black, of the British Steamer, Translyvania, says,
"I have been hunting for a submarine ever since this war began.
I only hope I can see one on this trip and it comes close enough
for me to ram it."

Most Americans viewed unrestricted submarine warfare as the end of a regional conflict and the beginning of a global war as politicians and newspapers called for an end to American neutrality. For many Americans the events of the war had made a critical turn, becoming a personal war involving Americans. There was little doubt that the press, the most important source of information about the war, had shaped Elzie's attitude just as anti-German sentiment was becoming prevalent throughout America. Newspapers and magazines capitalized on public interest and devoted more space to war events, with more descriptions of battles and tactics, and more editorials favoring the Allies. Previously unknown terms like trench warfare and stalemate became common words for Americans. Weapons and tactics were discussed. Throughout America the family dinner table became the forum for war discussions, and the Great War in Europe no longer remained a remote concept.

Nothing outraged the public more than the use of poison gas as a weapon of war. Once gas was used in combat at Bolimov in January, 1915, it became a standard weapon for both sides. April 22, 1915, at the Battle of Ypres, the Germans used chlorine gas in a major engagement which affected 150,000 men. Weaponry now took on a new dimension in the form of chemicals.

By 1916, Elzie had totally forgotten his lessons from Miss Simmons about the need for objectivity while studying war. Elzie had made the full progression in attitude from neutrality to zealous Allied advocate.

The spring season of 1916 seemed different. It was slower arriving and less conducive to outdoor activity. The past winter which had brought colder temperatures and less precipitation than normal, refused to relinquish its final grip. When spring weather finally arrived it was more tenacious than usual with more temperature extremes, more and stronger storms. Most unusual for the first week of April, Milton was blanketed with nine inches of snow and the following two days saw 80 degree temperatures accompanied by strong south winds. During the last week of April, four consecutive days of stormy, windy, rainy conditions brought farming and most outside work to a halt. Elzie, becoming most impatient with the confines of inside activities, decided to camp overnight in the forest. He packed his supplies and prepared his attire for the wet conditions, including the securing of his rifle in a weatherproof case. The campsite, frequently used by Elzie as a home base for a host of outdoor activities, was well stocked with tools and equipment necessary to function in the woods and to endure bad weather. Close to the central location of the camp was a small hillside with a gradual slope where Elzie had dug out a cavern into the hillside, about five feet deep, three feet wide, and four feet high. He shored the inside of the hole with timber, diverted the flow of surface rain water, and built a wood awning over the entry. Simple in design, the cavern became a convenient location for storing supplies, a refuge from the elements.

It was late afternoon when Elzie was sitting near the fire when he sensed that something was very different, not in appearance but in sound. Over the years Elzie had taught himself to use the sounds as well as the sights of the forest, to better function in the rugged terrain. At this exact moment Elzie could hear absolutely nothing, and he never remembered hearing that before. The air was dead calm, leaves were without the slightest movement. The forest, usually alive with the sounds of nature, appeared void of life as no wild creatures could be heard or observed. Suddenly, the temperature increased, the air became heavier, and perhaps for the first time in his life Elzie sensed absolute solitude. As the daylight began to diminish, not as in twilight but as in blockage of the sun's rays, Elzie looked to the sky where he viewed a totally unfamiliar cloud formation containing multiple flashes of lightning. The southwest sky exposed a wall of dark clouds, gray and black in coloring, and the entire cloud formation was rapidly approaching overhead. Suddenly, the cloud bank spewed a spout of continuous dark clouds that funneled all the way to the ground, and the downward funnel moved erratically but not in separation from the massive, low cloud bank. Never having observed a cloud formation of such turbulence, and realizing there was possible danger ahead, Elzie nearly panicked until he spotted the awning over the entrance to his cavern and he realized he had his shelter. He quickly tossed the supplies to the outside and crawled into the opening as fast as he could, carrying only his rifle with him. This frenzied behavior was unlike Elzie, but instinctively motivated by a fear of nature's fury, he cowered. His instincts had served him well.

Instantly the silence broke. Violent wind emerged and then raged in gusts. Wind driven rain pelted every object in its path forcing Elzie to squirm as deep into the cavern as he could manage. Flashes of bright light from multiple lightning bolts briefly lighted the landscape, and on two occasions even the inside of the hole was momentarily illuminated. One thunderous bolt of lightning after another cracked the air with some strikes hitting so close that the nearby ground quivered. Multiple bolts brought forth thunderous bangs followed by the ominous sounds of trees splitting and large limbs falling, crashing against the ground. The terrifying experience became more frightening when the sounds of rain, wind, and thunder suddenly gave way to a totally dominating loud roar which actually created a continuos ground vibration. Enduring for several minutes, the monstrous roar blocked all other sounds, and was accompanied by a pitch black darkness. Suddenly the vibration terminated, the roar departed as quickly as it had approached, and darkness slowly yielded to increasing light. The sound of thunder diminished as it faded into the distance, the rain lessened in intensity before it completely stopped. The storm had ended, and although brief in duration, the experience seemed like an eternity to the hunkered down frightened lad.

Bright light reemerged as Elzie awkwardly squirmed, edging closer to the entrance of the hole until he was outside the cavern and free to stand. Now he had an unobstructed view of a clearing sky with a distinct line of dark, gray clouds passing to the northeast, almost the exact opposite of what he saw before the storm, except this time he had an unobstructed view of clear, blue sky. Overwhelmed, he realized the trees that normally would obstruct his vision were not only downed, they were gone. In disbelief he stood and gawked. His campsite was totally destroyed with no indications that there ever had been a campsite. An irregular and uneven swath in the forest, about thirty feet wide and one hundred yards long, now existed where trees had firmly stood minutes before. Adjacent trees were toppled with their roots exposed, some were snapped in half, and many were simply gone. Debris was everywhere, some was unidentifiable. Less than twenty feet from the entrance to the cavern lay a ten foot section of crinkled tin from a porch roof or from a house proper. The longer Elzie looked, the more destruction he saw. His once familiar campsite, his home away from home, was nonexistent. The wooded area he had come to know so well was obliterated, forever altered. Nothing appeared the same, not even remotely. Elzie stood in one location, turning almost in circles, attempting to absorb the changes, but he could not as there was little to recognize in the altered landscape.

In a brief period of time Elzie experienced a wide array of emotions ranging from fear to relief, to shock, to awe. Now he sensed a sadness, a true loss. His emotions fed other emotions which produced a mental state of anxiety, not of panic but of helplessness. With disbelief he stared at the severely damaged forest silhouetted against the now deep blue sky, and he felt compelled to verbally express some thought. Ever so softly he whispered. "A storm of storms. I have survived, but I've lost a part of me. I have no epitaph other than it is gone, forever." Before the last word passed his lips Elzie sensed a feeling of concern which quickly engulfed his full being. Until this very second he had not thought of family, of others, about their well-being, or about his home in Milton. Without the slightest hesitancy he turned and started to run toward Milton, imagining as he ran all the possible scenarios of disaster in Milton. He convinced himself that his immediate presence at home might save lives or ease suffering. He ran until his lungs burned before he slowed his pace, pushing his body to its maximum limits of endurance. Convinced that his arrival time in Milton was of the essence, he felt selfish and guilty because initially he had thought only of himself and of his private place, rather than of his family's safety. Suddenly he realized he had left his rifle, his most precious possession, but it concerned him little. Motivated by fear of the unknown he ran harder, pushing his body to a previously untested level, until his body began to function without pain, almost mechanically. So preoccupied was he with his immediate return that he never looked at the landscape as he moved through it, never noticed all the features of the land and its growth that he had so carefully learned in the past. Had he noticed the landscape he would have observed less destruction the closer he got to Milton. By the time he could see Milton he had run four miles on rugged terrain in less than twenty-two minutes. The structures of Milton were still standing, but Elzie was so preoccupied with reaching his destination of home that he failed to observe even the slightest detail, until he could see that his house was still standing, and he saw Frieda was in the front yard picking up small fallen branches and twigs. Frieda saw Elzie and stopped her activity until he was within hearing range. "Hi, Elzie. Some storm, huh. Are you okay? You look worn out."

Fatigued, out of breath, and without answering, Elzie sat on the ground breathing heavily as he leaned against the tree. Looking around the area, he mentally confirmed that everything was in order. Before recovering his full breath he started talking. "Where..." Then he took a deep breath and exhaled. "Where's Aunt Mary? Is she all right? Where's Dad?"

"Calm down, Elzie. It was just a thunderstorm. Last I knew Aunt Mary was in the kitchen and Dad went to the square. There he is now."

Erastus was approaching at a fast pace. "What the hell is the matter with you, kid? I was standing on the square and you ran by me like your pants were on fire. I yelled at you but you didn't stop. Are you all right?"

Frieda spoke first. "I think he got scared in the storm. You said it would be spooky in the woods during the storm. I've never seen Elzie scared before. Are you a scaredy-cat, Elzie?"

With his breath restored, his mind relieved, and in no state to take abuse, Elzie answered. "Oh shut up, Frieda. I'll scaredy-cat you." He then proceeded to describe with incredible detail the storm and the destruction it had brought to the woods. Frieda and Erastus listened intently. Because of Elzie's natural propensity to exaggerate, neither would have been inclined to believe him, were it not for his vivid descriptions and obvious anxiety. This time they knew there was no exaggeration. He convincingly imparted the detail of his experience in the woods, continually emphasizing the intensity of the storm and the destruction brought from the sky. Elzie planned to return to the campsite the next day to assess the full damage. Tonight he was ready to stay home, and he did.

Before closing her bedroom door to retire for the night, Frieda spoke some final words to Elzie. "I can't wait until five years from now to talk about the storm in the woods. Maybe by then it will be funny. Think so, Elzie?"

Apart from the storm episode, the years of 1915 and 1916 provided mostly positive experiences for Elzie. He renewed his close relationship with Jesse, he developed a good working relationship with his father, acquired a greater appreciation of Aunt Mary, and learned to enjoy his younger sister, Frieda. Perhaps Elzie was maturing or, perhaps, others were learning to appreciate him for who he was. He no longer was identified as the younger brother of Jesse, or as the older brother of Frieda, or the son of Erastus, as much as he was identified as Elzie, the individual, the man. He was coming into his own, he was making the passage to manhood.

While walking with Jesse and Uncle Ben after a successful early morning hunting trip, Elzie began to tease the other two. "Good thing you guys are good farmers and you have plenty to eat other than the game you shoot. Otherwise, there would be a bunch of hungry people around here." Elzie sported a big grin as he waited for some reaction to his indicting, if not boastful, statement.

Uncle Ben was up to the challenge. "Why, you young whippersnapper. I think I hunt rather well for an old man. When I was your age I was as good as you are now, maybe better. I used to hunt for one hour, and then I had to spend the rest of the day cleaning all the game I shot." He looked at Jesse, gave a wink, and continued. "Matter of fact, I think a count of the rabbits we shot this morning might be in order. What do you say? Let's lay them out, right here, right now, and count them."

"Now, Uncle Ben, you know there is no need to do that," Jesse said with a sheepish grin. "I know we each have six rabbits, unless of course you want to weigh them to determine poundage. Elzie's pouch looks sort of light to me. We know that you and me waited for the big ones to come along before we shot, but I'll bet that Elzie just fired at the first ones he saw. Maybe we should weigh them. What do you think, Elzie? You want to weigh them?"

Not to be outdone, Elzie looked behind where Jesse was walking and winked at an imaginary person. "I'll bet in the old days, when Uncle Ben was a kid, rabbits were as common as flies, and probably weighed five pounds apiece. That's the only explanation that makes any sense to me. Besides, I wasn't talking about the number of rabbits, or the size of rabbits, as much as I was talking about the shots fired to get the rabbits. With those shotguns you and Uncle Ben made so much noise that I thought the Germans had invaded Pike County. A couple of times I thought you guys were using rapid-fire cannons, you made so much noise. In my estimation, a hunter should be evaluated by the number of rounds fired compared to the amount of game killed. Shots and game should be equal in number, and I'm talking about a rifle, not a shotgun that scatters buckshot all over creation. One bullet through the head, is my idea of a hunter."

Uncle Ben responded. "That's my idea of a good shot, not a good hunter, but I do see your point about a shot to the head. If you can do that every time, there is no concern about buckshot in the meat. Looking first at Jesse, then Elzie, then back at Jesse, Uncle Ben made sort of a grunting sound. "I have an idea. How about a little friendly competition here, say a hunting-shooting match between Jesse and hotshot Elzie."

"Wait just a minute, I'm no match for Elzie when it comes to shooting a rifle."

"Now, Jesse, you wait just a minute, you haven't heard the proposed rules yet, because I intend to even the odds. Rules are: 1. Elzie uses the rifle and Jesse uses the shotgun. 2. Both of you have three shots, and that's all. 3. One hour time limit. 4. You hunt at the woods near my place, so that Elzie doesn't have the advantage. What do you think, lads?"

Elzie gave a loud laugh before he proclaimed, "Heavens no, that's unfair to Jesse. If you let me change rule two, we have a match. Jesse gets four shotgun shells and I get three bullets, and if he wants to use the full hour time limit, that's okay with me, as long as I don't have to. Agree to that, big brother, and we got a match."

Jesse stopped in his tracks and looked directly at Elzie. "What you said is bad enough, but the way you said it is worse. I think you just talked yourself into a match, little brother."

Uncle Ben was delighted. "Tomorrow morning, be at my house at 6:30. Bring your game to the old shed at 7:30, and I will announce the winner." Uncle Ben laid down his gun, quickly moved behind Jesse and started to rub his shoulders. "Come on, Jesse, I'm going to get you in shape." He rubbed faster. "We're going to whop this kid at his own game. Come on, Jesse." Elzie almost fell to the ground in laughter and Jesse roared with his belly laugh. It was so unusual to see Uncle Ben act silly, and both brothers immensely enjoyed it.

The next morning both contestants were on time. Ben checked their gear and sent them out, exactly at 7:30. Elzie sprinted to the woods, Jesse walked in haste. Having been informed of the contest, Frieda was also there, cheering for Jesse. Elzie loved it. Within minutes the shooting began, three shots for Elzie in the first half hour, and four for Jesse using the full time limit. There was no sign of Elzie when Jesse arrived at the shed carrying his four rabbits, but Uncle Ben and Frieda were there to greet him.

"I got four. Has Elzie checked in yet?"

"Yes, he has and you are not going to believe what you see." Jesse looked on the table and saw four rabbits, three shot in the head and one in the butt. Jesse looked at Uncle Ben with astonishment. "Don't look at me, I don't know what to say. He brought them in about twenty minutes ago and said, 'Sorry the one has a bullet in the butt, but I couldn't get two rabbits to line up evenly so that I could shoot both in the head.' Then he walked off saying, 'Clean em, Uncle Ben!'"

Jesse sat in a chair and laughed and laughed. An annoyed Frieda watched until she felt compelled to express her thoughts. "I don't know what is so funny. Elzie cheated, and I don't think that is funny."

"Why do you say he cheated?"

"Well, it's obvious to me, with four rabbits and three shells. No one can do that."

Jesse straightened his sitting position and prepared to answer. He was very serious when he spoke. "I know I can't do it, but I'm not so sure about Elzie. Be that as it may, you're missing the point, Frieda. Elzie would not cheat. He is as honorable as anyone I know. He would never cheat. However, he might exaggerate, or more likely, you are seeing an example of his sense of humor. As you well know, Elzie is very creative and he loves to get reactions from people, especially reactions to situations that he has created. That is exactly what we have here. Somehow, and I don't know how, but somehow, he got four rabbits with three shots, or at least he did it without cheating. If you really want to know what happened, just ask him, and he will tell you, after he teases or taunts you for a week or so. It's Elzie's way. He exposes himself to others, sometimes at his best, sometimes at his worst. Elzie is Elzie. You should be proud of your brother, not mad at him. What do you think, Uncle Ben? Am I right or wrong?"

"You're right, except I can't figure out how he did it either. I guess it doesn't make any difference anyway." Uncle Ben pointed his finger toward the ceiling, announcing, "With four rabbits apiece, it is a tie, a draw, there is no winner." He leaned over to Frieda, smiled and whispered, "I think Jesse's rabbits are fatter."

"I do too," was her girlish reply.

Unknown to the others, Elzie was eavesdropping outside the shed and heard every word. It was good for him to hear Jesse's explanation. He worried that someone would be angry with him, and now he felt better knowing otherwise. Elzie was pleased with his prank, but he was more pleased with his family. He agreed with Jesse's description of him at his best and at his worst. It was a fair description.

No one ever asked Elzie how he achieved his feat, and he never told. The competitive three shell hunting episode was soon told, and retold in the Milton area until the story became legendary.

In the Moore family Elzie held no monopoly on impulsive behavior. Catching her family members off guard, Frieda announced that she was planning a party for the first week of June, and she intended to invite approximately twenty friends. Hosting a party was most unlike Frieda. She professed the party was for no special occasion, but Jesse and Elzie concurred that the party was in celebration of her having completed eighth grade. They were partially correct. Still uncertain about her future school plans, Frieda felt a need to socially communicate with school friends before the opportunity faded. Likewise she sensed that additional time with Jesse was limited, or that her precious time with Elzie was about to change course. For whatever reason, she wanted the party, and she scheduled the event for the first Sunday in June. Frieda, the youngest child, made few demands on the family and she rightfully anticipated that her family would cooperate. Even Erastus consented. Much to her brothers' surprise, Frieda was insistent that Jesse and Elzie attend.

Plans for the party were finalized by week's end. The party was to be out-of-doors on the river shoreline near Montezuma, north of the ferry ramp. Activities, including a light lunch, games, and time for socializing, were slated to commence at noon and continue until early evening. Plans called for a group crossing of the river later in the day for a potluck picnic on the somewhat deserted eastern side of the river. Otherwise, there was little structure. Frieda made all the arrangements without assistance. The ferry operator agreed to gratuitously transport the group across the river and back. Parents were informed of the party plans, and Aunt Mary and Erastus agreed to be the chaperones. The party was intended to be a simple social gathering for Frieda and her young friends, not pretentious or extravagant in any way. Jesse and Elzie took pride in Frieda's organized efforts, her basic approach. Their youngest sister was growing up, and they felt flattered that Frieda wanted her older brothers at the party.

Accompanied by glorious weather the highly anticipated day arrived, and initially the gathering was more successful than Frieda ever imagined. As expected, Elzie was the life of the party, although Frieda was sort of surprised that her brother spent so much of his time with her friend, Sarah. Until this day Frieda had not directly observed Elzie's acute interest in the opposite sex, although she was definitely aware of female interest in her brother.

What would a party be without some good-natured, boisterous play or so Elzie thought? At day's end as the youthful entourage was ferrying back to the west side of the river, a few of the fellows were horsing around near the section of the ferry without guard rails, when Elzie suddenly fell overboard. Everyone knew that Elzie was an outstanding swimmer and few worried about his safety as they waited for him to surface so that they could laugh and tease him, as he so often teased others. Elzie had other plans. He had intentionally fallen into the water so that he could swim underwater, beneath the boat, to the opposite side of the ferry. Although this was a most difficult feat, he had previously performed it several times and he felt no real danger. Jesse, having seen Elzie pull this stunt before, figured out what he was doing and moved to the opposite side to help his brother aboard. Elzie would already have been back aboard had he not been hindered by his own amusement at the successful trick he had just played. Once Elzie was aboard the ferry and he saw that members of the group were still looking for him in the water, he added to the suspense by waiting one more minute before he shouted, "Oh, poor Elzie, where could that devil be? Oh, here he is." The group turned to see Elzie standing onboard, dripping wet and sporting the biggest smile his devilish face could accommodate. "Hello, folks. Why are you all looking down at the river?" Realizing that they had witnessed an Elzie joke, most laughed, and a few persons even stated they suspected he was up to some of his antics or trickery. Most were amused, but not Sarah who was crying, nor Frieda who was attempting to comfort Sarah. Elzie, realizing he had gone too far with the prank, apologized to Sarah and eventually won her forgiveness, but he could not immediately win the forgiveness of Frieda. Frieda's hero had temporarily fallen from grace. Elzie also had to endure a lengthy lecture from Jesse concerning sensitivity to the feelings of other people. Aunt Mary and Erastus did not see the incident, although later they heard about it, and Elzie got two more sensitivity lectures.

Eventually, Elzie deeply regretted the pain he had caused and learned a valuable lesson that day, and went so far as to confide to Frieda that his days of exercising irresponsible humor were over. Frieda believed him for the moment, but she remained unconvinced that her mischievous brother could willfully change his behavior, even if he wanted to change. Frieda believed that Elzie's free spirit controlled him more than he controlled it, and she never was certain if she really wanted her brother to diminish his expressions of such free spirit. What Frieda never knew was that Elzie was more disappointed in himself than she was. It emotionally bothered him when he hurt other people, intentional or not.

During the summer and fall of 1916 Elzie found a good friend in Sarah, the girl from the party. A popular and most attractive girl, Sarah was the pride of the Milton rural area from a wealthy, middle-class, farm family who, unlike Elzie, lived in a stately house. In some ways Sarah and Elzie were opposites, in other ways they complemented one another; and in many ways they were a good blend, each a positive influence on the other. Surprisingly, their friendship blossomed into a close personal relationship.

In late November after the crops were harvested, Sarah and her family intended to move from Pike County to the eastern part of the state. Sarah withheld this information from Elzie, not because it was a secret, but because she never found the courage to tell him. Elzie suffered a crushing blow when he heard through the grapevine about her family's plans to relocate. He was also hurt because he heard the news from others, rather than from Sarah.

Sarah's explanation to Elzie for not telling him sooner fell on deaf ears. In an effort to make amends Sarah proposed that she and Elzie have their own farewell picnic near the river, and that she would assume all preparations. When he rejected her offer she passionately pleaded for acceptance. "In a few weeks I will be gone. Let's end the friendship on a positive note, in a manner equal to the quality of our friendship. Please, allow me to say good-bye to you." She was convincing, and Elzie acquiesced, assenting to attend the picnic if Sarah would acknowledge that she should have told him earlier about the move. She so acknowledged and they planned the picnic for the upcoming Saturday afternoon.

Nature provided a flawless setting for the picnic as the site could not have been more beautiful than it was that day. The air was dry, the temperature was pleasant, the sky was blue, dotted with white, puffy, high clouds, and the breeze was gentle. The only dark clouds were those cast by the inevitable sad thoughts of knowing the end of their friendship was close at hand. At times it was difficult for both of them to treasure the moment, to appreciate their remaining time alone. Outwardly, Elzie managed to withhold his true feelings of sadness. Sarah's feelings were less concealed, revealing an undertone of joylessness as she was more pensive, less vivacious than usual.

The scrumptious lunch of meat loaf sandwiches and additional fixings was to Elzie's liking. After eating they washed the dishes in the cool river water and packed the straw basket with everything except for two small plates, two forks, and two glasses. "Sit down, Elzie, here by the river. I have what I hope is a special treat. Last night I baked my first apple pie, and up to this point, no one has tasted it. I don't mean that no one has tasted this pie, I mean that no one has ever tasted a pie baked by me. You are the first." Sarah's facial expression revealed that her humor was about to emerge as she turned her head toward her right shoulder, stuck out her chin, and formally declared, "If you like it, I want you to tell me so, and if you don't like it, I want you to tell me you like it anyway. That way nothing will spoil this special day. Besides, I can't stand personal failure. You must agree to those terms or you don't get any of, this one of a kind, this special, this delicious, good smelling apple pie. Remembering my stringent conditions, do you choose to try a piece?"

With a perfect imitation of her head movement, Elzie affirmed. "Yes, I can already tell, just by looking, it's probably the best pie I've ever had, and if it's not, I can't remember eating any other pies, so it has to be the best."

"Oh, Elzie, you're as silly as I am."

"Yes, I know I'm silly, but I wouldn't stretch it that far." To further illustrate, Elzie held his hands different distances apart to indicate different amounts of silliness. Her response was a smiling, shake of her head. Sarah cut the first piece of pie, handed it to Elzie, and he had it consumed before she had her piece cut. He passed the plate back to her, and said, "To give an honest evaluation, I think I need another piece." Elzie consumed three pieces of apple pie in the time it took Sarah to eat one piece. Intentional or not, his behavior made Sarah feel good. "Let's wait a few minutes before we eat the rest of the pie, and then I will fight you for it. Winner take all. Meanwhile, come with me, young lady, and I'll share something with you, never shared by me before." Pointing his finger in a mocking way, he proclaimed, "You are the first. We're going to sit on the rocks and listen to the river."

"You mean watch the river, don't you?" she said with a giggle.

"Nope. You watch if you want, I'm going to listen. You can look at the river any day, but it's only on certain quiet, calm days you can really hear the river. Sit here, close your eyes and listen. You'll be amazed at what you can hear. Try it, experience it for yourself."

Positive this was an Elzie prank, Sarah closed her eyes and pretended she was listening to the river. She became disappointed when nothing unusual happened, so Sarah peeked at Elzie and found him still sitting with his eyes shut. "What are you doing?" she asked with a louder giggle.

"I'm trying to listen to the river. The same thing I thought you were doing. If you concentrate you can hear a bunch of stuff. You can hear the current, you can hear the splashes on the bank, you can hear the fish jump, or on rare occasions you can hear a log or debris floating. Put those sounds with the sounds of nature, like birds, and throw in some man-made sounds, like the ferry noise, and you really have something. I call it, The River in Symphony."

"Oh, Elzie, you are so silly. Nobody listens to a river, and if they do listen, they don't name it"

"I should have known better." Little doubt, Elzie was peeved.

"Why? What do you mean?"

"I've got to be more careful about what I say. I can't seem to learn that. People always ask me what I do at the river, or why I spend so much time here. For obvious reasons I usually don't tell them. Now today when I let down my guard and try to share with you, I remember why I don't tell people. I don't talk about it because they would think I'm crazy, like you thought I was silly. I thought you might be different. Guess I was wrong."

Embarrassed, Sarah put her head down. "I'm sorry, Elzie, I didn't dream you were serious. I thought you were playing a joke on me. You know sometimes you do play jokes on people." She waited for a response that never came. "It's hard to tell when you are serious. Here, let's try it again, and this time I'll do it right."

Elzie tried to act as though his feelings were not hurt. Sarah knew better, just as she knew she was now on thin ice with Elzie, even if she did not totally understand why. Before she could think of something clever to say in jest, Elzie spoke. "Let's wait, and do it another time." Partially to divert Sarah's attention from the topic, Elzie moved and pointed. "Look way down river on the west bank, maybe a mile down, and you can see a big tree leaning out over the river. Do you see it?"

"I'm sorry I didn't listen to the river." When there was no response again, it almost aggravated Sarah. "Yes, I think I see the tree you're talking about. What about it?"

"I call it my bluff hickory tree. As you well know that high ground up there is called Pilot's Bluff, some say the highest bluff anywhere on the Illinois River.

About three hundred yards beyond it is the entrance to the best cave in the county. I call it, the Elzie cave. As far as I know, no one else knows about it, other than my friend, John, who never goes there. It is kind of like a hide-a-way, a place to be alone."

Sarah thought about mentioning how unusual it was to label by name so many things, but wisely, she did not. "Will you take me there, sometime?"

"Maybe, I'm not sure. Why do you want to go?"

"Because it means something to you, because it's your cave. I didn't have sense enough to listen to the river, but I do have enough sense to want to see the Elzie cave. Is that the same cave you spent a week in?"

"Yes, it is, but how do you know about that?"

"I know a lot about you. I know about your four rabbits with three shots. I know about Rosa. I even know about the time you went to Jacksonville to visit your brother. I saw you fight big Jake. I know a lot about you. I know how old you were when you moved to Milton. I know you went to Miss Simmons to learn about the war."

Feeling as though his privacy had been violated, he responded with true indignation. "How do you know all that stuff?" He was especially concerned that she knew about Rosa, but he did not want to repeat the name. "That makes me mad. I never told you all those things. How do you know that stuff?"

Sarah realized she had angered him again, and still having a little trouble with her own feelings, she bordered on exasperation. "For Pete's sake, don't get mad at me. I just know. We live in a rural area where everybody knows everything about everybody."

"That's nonsense. I don't know that kind of stuff about anybody."

"If you don't, it's because you don't listen."

"I'm glad I don't listen. I'm surprised that you listen to gossip."

"Oh, Elzie, don't be so sensitive. It's not gossip in the negative sense. It's simply being interested in someone and hearing about them. You're a doer, Elzie. You have the courage to strike out on your own, to do what you want, regardless of what others think. There are few people like that. Most of the people I know are not doers, they are talkers, like me. You doers give us talkers something to do, while you're out doing what we talkers would like to be doing. And if you think that wasn't a mouthful, you should try saying it."

"I don't want to try to say it, so there." He knew his harsh words bit deeply so he changed his tone and softened his position. "I'm not sure, but I think you just gave me a compliment."

"I did give you a compliment, you stupid ass, but you're so bullheaded I'm surprised you recognized it. And it doesn't count because I'm taking it back. I hate doers, and I'm glad I'm a talker, so there, yourself."

Elzie became amused at Sarah's anger. Mockingly, he said, "For Pete's sake, don't get mad at me. We live in a rural area, and I'm a doer, not a talker."

Sarah glared at her companion. "Elzie, you're mean, just plain mean."

Realizing he again had gone too far, Elzie tried to rectify the situation. "You're right, and I apologize. Forgive me, and I will take you to the cave. By the way, I loved your pie."

"No. I don't want to go to any cave with you." She deliberately turned her body so that her back was toward Elzie. For the next three or four minutes the young antagonists looked at the river, neither saying anything before Sarah broke the silence. "If I decided to go to the cave, when would we go?"

Feeling somewhat victorious, Elzie thought of many smart retorts, but wisely he chose not to use them. "At your convenience, my lady. We don't have enough time to go now. How about tomorrow?" He did not allow time for her to respond. "Wait a minute before you answer, because I'm not sure you really want to go. It's pretty rough getting there. It's about four and one-half miles from my house, across rough terrain. The cave is about forty feet down the side of the bluff and we must use a rope to get to a small landing, and then you have to crawl for about five feet through a narrow opening to get into the cave. And when you leave you've got to do it all again, only in reverse."

Sarah could not contain her thoughts. "You mean I have to crawl and walk backwards?"

"You may be a match for me in the smart aleck department. You want me to continue telling you about the cave, or not?"

"Continue."

"It is a magnificent cave. Don't worry about bringing anything, I'll bring the water and some food, and I have a few supplies already there. Yeah, that's it. We'll have a picnic in the cave, and this time I bring the food, not as good as yours, but food. What do you say? Think you can endure it?"

The word endure sounded more like a challenge than an invitation. However, Sarah would not allow herself to be lured into forgiveness by a challenge. She answered with uncertainty. "I'm not sure. I'll have to think about it on the way home today. What concerns me most if I do go, is not the problem of getting there as much as the problem of enduring you, especially if you get in one of your moods." Sarah was pleased with her answer. She had used the word endure, and had put the challenge back to Elzie.

A smiling Elzie gave an appropriate response. "No problem. If you decide to go I will be Elzie, the angel, at least as much of an angel as Elzie can be. I promise." Sarah confirmed she would go with Elzie to the cave, if Elzie agreed never to tell anyone that she went with him. She was rightfully concerned about propriety.

Sarah missed church in order to arrive at Elzie's house by 9:00 a.m., where she found Elzie anxiously waiting and unnecessarily worrying that she might change her mind about going to the cave. Elzie had prepared the food before hand, and now he divided the gear, making certain that Sarah's load was lighter. They immediately started their trek with eager anticipation, tempered only slightly by Sarah's personal reservations about propriety, and Elzie's concern about inclement weather. Dark clouds filled the sky and the wind blew like rain. Wet ground introduced an element of danger as Elzie was uncertain about how surefooted Sarah would be on rough terrain. Both individuals were determined that this day was going to be a good day, a good experience no matter what.

Small talk was never Elzie's forte, and today was no exception. "Sarah, you look different, and I can't figure out why."

"Well so much for the angel Elzie. I look different because I have on my work clothes. You said we were going to crawl through holes and stuff like that. What did you expect, my Easter bonnet? I know I don't look glamorous, I dressed for the occasion."

"I didn't mean that at all. In fact, you look better than usual."

"Good job, Elzie. You wormed your way out of that one. Give me enough time and I'll make you into a talker. Yes, sir, I'll straighten you out."

"You straighten me out every time I'm with you."

Looking mystified, Sarah replied. "I don't understand."

"Good," was Elzie's relieved reply. He knew he should not have made that brazen, off-color remark. "We're leaving Milton now, so say good-bye to civilization, and hello to wilderness."

"All right with me. Today I'm a doer and I've already paid part of the price. Mama and Papa are both mad at me for going to the cave with you."

"Why?"

"Well you must admit it is not exactly ladylike behavior. Papa thinks it is not proper for me to go to a cave with you, not to mention the danger of tramping around in the woods."

Elzie was offended by her words as he resented the implication that he was dishonorable. Elzie thought of many smart remarks about women and ladylike behavior but, judiciously, Elzie swallowed his pride and thought about Sarah from her viewpoint. "I understand. In my eyes you are always ladylike and proper, and I'll look after you in the woods. I don't worry about danger, unless we get careless, and we won't. I'm more at ease here than in a room full of people. Be assured, if you think it better that we not go, we won't go, or if at anytime you want to come back, we will come back."

Somewhat reassured, Sarah said, "Let's go on. Today we're doers. To paraphrase some navy captain, damn the dangers, full speed ahead." A handshake sealed the bond, and they were on their way.

The young outdoorsman was impressed with Sarah's agile movements as she walked the fields and woods, and crossed the creeks with such ease. He had anticipated an awkward female, uncertain of each step, but found instead a graceful girl with poise and confidence. She was as supple as he. He did monitor her for safety reasons, but mostly he admiringly watched her body movements. The young lad was more attracted to his hiking mate than he remembered. However, Elzie remained cautious, remembering that there was an element of danger for the novice in the woods and that the real challenge of the hike, descending the bluff, was yet to come. He would withhold final judgment concerning Sarah's physical ability until the test of descending was over, so he chose not to say anything that might divert her attention from the task at hand.

When they reached the summit of the bluff, Elzie suggested they take a break, rest and drink some water. "From here on it gets tougher. I tie this rope around that tree, throw it over the side, and we use it to lower ourselves to that landing down there. How do you want to do this? Do you want me to go first, do you want to go first, or do you want to go together? It looks worse than it is. Here, take a gander and tell me your wishes."

Sarah looked, and said, "Hum, if we slip, not much between us and the river, is there?"

Laughing, Elzie replied. "You're correct about that. If you let go of the rope, you'll fall into the river. You don't want to do that." The thought of Sarah slipping or falling sobered Elzie. "If you don't want to do it, it's okay with me. Probably not a good idea to bring you here anyway. My fault for suggesting it."

"Nonsense," she stated while looking over the side of the bluff. "I think I can make it by myself. Is there anything I need to know?"

"Nope. Just don't let go of the rope. You go first, and I'll stay here, lean over the side and talk you down. When you get to the landing, wait there for me."

Sarah grabbed the rope, made a last minute evaluation of the terrain, eased over the side, and descended to the ledge, seemingly, with the skill of a climber. Delighted with her effort, she declared, "Piece of cake. Your turn, big boy."

Elzie was ecstatic. He stood and applauded, then put both arms with closed fist high in the air and yelled, "What a woman!" In response, she smiled and curtsied. Without further ado he pulled back the rope, tied the supplies to it, and lowered them to Sarah. Once the supplies were down and secure, he quickly descended to the landing, released the rope, and turned to hug Sarah. "You are something, Sarah."

The praise was graciously received. "Thanks, I thought I could do it. What's next?"

"See that opening there? We crawl through it into the cave. Let me go first because it's pitch black in there, and I'll light a candle to give you a little light.

After I'm squared away in there, I'll yell, and then, you come in. Remember to mind your head. Are you ready to try it?" Sarah nodded and Elzie entered the cave. In less than two minutes she heard this faint voice. "All clear, you can come in now."

"Where are you?"

"What do you mean where am I. I'm in the cave," Elzie answered with an obviously agitated voice.

It was a ridiculous question and Sarah felt silly for asking it. "I know that. I meant how far away are you?"

A faint, almost inaudible voice answered. "I don't know for sure. Maybe about eight or ten feet." She did not like hearing that she would need to crawl such a distance, and with some reluctance Sarah prepared to enter. At once she saw the light from the candle, and soon spotted Elzie's smiling face. She was relieved, and by the time she reached the large cave opening she had regained her courage. "I'm sorry, Elzie, that my question sounded so stupid, but your voice sounded like you were at the bottom of a well. It scared me."

"It's the cave. It does strange things with sound. Here, you sit against the wall, light this lamp, get comfortable, and I'll light the torch and make a quick round to check for critters. I've never seen one, but I still think it's wise to check."

"Thanks for waiting until now to share that with me. It's just what I wanted to hear."

There were no critters and Sarah's other anxieties about the cave gradually abated. Elzie took Sarah by the hand and proudly toured her around the cave, explaining all he knew about the structure, and showed her the handmade amenities he had brought to the cave. "It's just as you said, Elzie. It's a perfect place. Thank you for bringing me here."

Elzie proceeded to build a fire. "You did wipe your feet before you came in, didn't you? A man needs to protect and care for his property, you know." He waited for a response to his obvious pretentious assessment, but no comments were forthcoming. While scooting a crude handmade log bench near the fire, Elzie made an announcement. "You sit on the sofa in the parlor and rest your weary bones. Dinner will be served in one hour."

"Such hospitality, I swear. Did you bring the good china and crystal?"

Her indulgent humor was appreciated by the nervous lad. Using a handmade iron grillwork over the open fire, Elzie warmed a delicious meal of rabbit stew and biscuits which he had cooked and baked earlier that morning. The biscuits were complemented with sorghum molasses, chocolate bars were available for dessert. After the meal the adventurers sat next to the fire and visited. Sarah used the opportunity to show her appreciation, her delight. "I must say that was the finest stew I have ever eaten in a cave. Whoever would have dreamed that I would spend a pleasant Sunday afternoon in a cave, eating rabbit stew prepared by Elzie Moore."

"I would have, that's who. I got you here and I may not let you go. I forgot to tell you that I don't know the way home from here, so I guess we'll have to stay here until someone finds us, about forty years from now."

Sarah reached for Elzie's hand. "Okay with me, although I don't know what others might think."

"Who cares what others think?"

"I do, and you do too. You may not admit it, but you do. You're a complex person, Elzie, very hard to understand. The real you is protected by a public you, and each passing day I realize that simple fact more and more. What about it? Am I correct?"

As Elzie often did, he used humor to divert attention elsewhere. "If you really admire me you would scoot over here, and admire me from close range. I'll bet I could give you good reason to admire me." Sarah moved closer, tenderly placing her head on his shoulder and holding his right hand with both of her hands on her lap, and Elzie responded by placing his other arm around her shoulders. He could feel the warmth from her body, and he smelled the faint aroma of perfume. As her soft hands engulfed his hand, she moved her finger, gently caressing his palm. His body was consumed with pleasure and excitement, and he dared not move for fear of losing the sensation. He hoped she would use that gentle touch to explore other parts of his hand or wrist, but he knew no way to make it occur without risk of her stopping the motion, altogether. He was sensitized by her close presence, her gentle touch, and he felt so inadequate. He did not know how to respond or how to demonstrate his pleasure, so for several minutes he remained motionless as she continued her gentle stroking. Neither spoke.

Eventually Sarah discontinued the gentle massage motion, and in place of it she firmly held his hand. Elzie decided to risk movement and while imitating her soft finger motion, he gently stroked the back of her neck, never staying in one location too long, until eventually he explored her ears, her hair, and finally her face. Sarah slightly moved her head as though she was guiding his touch. By now he was using four fingers to gently explore all of the her face, and the more gentle he was in touch, the more she moved her head which encouraged more exploration. Her breathing became more pronounced and, on occasion, she slightly groaned in a low whisper tone which excited Elzie all the more. Becoming braver he slowly lowered his fingers to her neckline, not stopping his descent until he felt the material of her dress. With the same degree of gentleness he slowly felt the upper part of her chest. Her skin was soft and warm. Discovering more courage, he moved the hand she was holding and placed it beneath her dress at the neckline, and using his thumb as an anchor he stroked her sensuous skin as far as his fingers could reach. Sarah slowly turned her head toward Elzie, slightly moving her body back, which allowed Elzie's hand to penetrate lower on her chest. Sarah did nothing to encourage him, nor did she stop him. Both were unskilled in the art of foreplay, but by now they fully understood the passion of it. They were sexually excited, uncertain about how to proceed or if they should proceed at all. Sarah reached to kiss Elzie and her movement allowed his hand free access to touch her warm firm breasts. She placed her slightly parted moist lips against Elzie's lips, and greatly adding to the intensity of the kiss, she delicately moved her head. Elzie was afire wanting to do more, not knowing what to do. Cautiously, but boldly, he moved forward in his quest. As they kissed Elzie's hand explored the breasts, not stopping his hand movement until he reached her firm nipples, which he circled with his finger. She continued to passionately kiss Elzie, several times momentarily withdrawing, but always resuming with more passion. At times they both made muted grunting sounds and the heavy uneven breathing by each only served to excite the other. Elzie's whole body was alive with excitement when suddenly Sarah pulled away, and said, "Stop! I can't do this anymore, I've got to stop."

Totally surprised Elzie answered by expressing the only thought that made sense to him. "Why, am I hurting you? Tell me what to do to stop hurting you and I will, but I don't want to stop everything."

"You are not hurting me, and I don't want to stop either, but we are going to stop. Elzie, I'm a virgin. I've never gone this far with a boy before, and I'm not going to go all the way now. Do you understand me? I have to stop." Sarah sat up straight, adjusted her dress, and Elzie knew she was serious, determined. "You know what people think of girls who do it? Do you want people to think of me that way?"

Frustrated, searching for any explanation, Elzie replied. "Why don't we just not tell anybody, and then no one can think that way."

"Sorry, Elzie, it doesn't work that way. You know it doesn't work that way."

"Please."

"No."

"How about if we just kiss and I keep my hands to myself, sort of?"

"You don't understand. It's not only you I have to stop, I have to stop myself, too. I want you, too, but I'm not going to have you, and that's final."

Elzie stood, and started walking around the cave, never going in any direction, and never arriving anywhere. For over two minutes Elzie paced like a caged animal as Sarah stayed seated with her head in her hands. "I'm sorry, Elzie, we just can't do it."

"I'm not totally insensitive, Sarah, and I know we shouldn't do more. My head understands it, but my body doesn't. I'll stop if we must. I do have one thought and you can say no if you want, but I hope you won't."

"What?"

"You remember awhile ago when I was touching you there? I've never seen or touched anything that beautiful before. If I promise not to go too far would you let me see your breasts? Just for a minute. I promise, if you let me see, I will stop when you say to stop. No exceptions, I will stop. Please, it will be the only opportunity we will ever have, and no one will ever know."

Sarah thought for a minute, and much to Elzie's surprise, she answered, "Okay, but when I say it's time to stop, we stop, and no one except the two of us will ever know what went on in this cave today. Do I have your word?"

"I swear on a stack of bibles."

"I would rather you just say yes."

"Yes, you have my word."

Sarah sat erect and took a deep breath as if she were positioning herself for inactive involvement. "If I sit here, can you see?"

"Yes, but wait a minute. Let me put more wood on the fire and light some more candles, so I can see better."

Her response was a firm, "No more candles."

"Okay, okay." Elzie stoked and fed the fire and Sarah timidly started to unbutton her dress. Slowly she lowered her dress to her waist and carefully pulled her upper undergarments over her head and placed them on the bench beside her. Elzie, fearing she might change her mind, acted at once. He fell to his knees beside Sarah, making certain his body did not block any of the light from the fire. "Oh, my gosh, you are beautiful." He was motionless as he stared at her breasts in absolute adoration. He refused to blink his eyes or to make any movement which might deprive him of even one precious second of viewing. Most embarrassed, Sarah sat with her eyes closed, only occasionally looking to affirm everything was still under her control. Eventually as Sarah became more at ease she found the courage to keep her eyes open. Adoringly, she focused on her lover's eyes as he admired her firm pointed breasts against the backdrop of her pale, white, exposed body. The young virgin sat passively and watched in awe, admiring Elzie's restraint, as he appreciated her body, her exposed breasts. Becoming less awkward with each passing moment, the situation slowly evolved into a precious sensation for both of them. Elzie, challenged to exercise restraint, became extremely sensually stimulated as he viewed the partially naked body of this beautiful young innocent maiden, and Sarah became more excited by watching Elzie admire her until both almost became overwhelmed. Certainly the visual images were stimulating, but it was the new, abiding sensation of physical, sexual excitement that was the most difficult to control.

Sarah spoke slowly with an uncertain voice. "You may touch them if you want, but remember, you still must stop when I say so." Calmly, Elzie gave no verbal response, only a facial response expressive of intoxicating rapture. Briefly, he glanced into her eyes before he engaged in the pleasure of touching. Gradually moving his hand with outstretched fingers toward her breasts, he gently touched the skin and proceeded to slowly explore the incredible female wonders with a soft, perpetual concentric motion until no part of either breast remained unexplored. Then, he touched her with the other hand, and using all of his fingers on both hands, he repeated the process only slower. With one hand always on one breast he used the other hand to explore all of the exposed skin, front and back, from her waist to the hair on her head. Elzie was learning the art of foreplay. He was gaining confidence. Sarah, giving occasional involuntary moans of approval, began to slightly quiver. Elzie, not realizing the significance of the quivers, and believing Sarah was chilled and that his opportunity was about to end, discontinued his soft, gentle fingertip motion. He moved both hands to her large full breasts, gradually concentrating his attention on her swollen hard nipples, changing from a stroking motion to gentle squeezing movement. Elzie's restraint waned until he could no longer resist. In one quick movement he placed her right breast in his mouth, sucking the breast as he tongued the nipple, and placed his hand on the other breast, stroking, squeezing, and gripping without any regard to ease. In a fluid manner he lowered his left hand, never losing its touch with her body, and continued downward over her naked arm to her clothed hip and leg. His hand remained for a brief while on the leg and with no obvious resistance he started exploring again, this time underneath her dress. He slowed his movement with his hand on Sarah's inner thigh, and immediately he engaged the fingertip circling motion. His hand moved closer to the forbidden area. He continued the motion, but stopped the progression long enough to allow any discouraging reaction from Sarah. With no discouragement he resumed with a gentle back and forward thumb motion on her inner thigh as his fingers gradually moved toward his intended goal. Once near the summit of her leg, he spread his fingers feeling the mound of hair through her panties. As he moved his fingers he felt a moisture laden area and began to gently, but firmly, push inward. He became so excited he feared he might lose control, and when Sarah slightly spread her legs and continued to moan he thought he would explode. Instead, he paused and remained in blissful embrace.

Regained in composure and somewhat encouraged by her previous cooperation he returned his hand to her most private area and slid his fingers under her panties, feeling her mound of hair as he progressed to her opening. Abruptly, she shouted, "Stop." In one commanding motion she grabbed and removed his hand, closed her legs, and firmly stated, "Stop, stop, stop." Elzie immediately ceased all movement, but remained in place as though he was waiting for a confirmation of the command. Very quickly he got it when Sarah spoke in a firmer tone than Elzie had ever heard. "I said stop, right now."

Elzie looked like a whipped puppy as he followed the command and backed away from Sarah. "I'm sorry, Sarah. Did I do something wrong?"

"No, you did something right, and that's the reason we must stop. I just about lost control, and then we would be in a fine how do you do. You stay right where you are, don't you move a muscle, and I mean it. I need to regain my self-control, gain some of my senses back."

"What is the..."

Before he could finish the word, Sarah spoke with absolute authority. "Don't you say one word. You're not going to use your golden tongue to convince me of anything. You turn around while I get dressed, and you stay that way until I say different. Do it now!"

Elzie followed the instructions, mumbling something unintelligible as he turned. He stood facing the dark part of the cave for what seemed to be an unreasonable amount of time. When he finally got the word that she was ready for him to turn around, he found Sarah standing behind the bench, fully clothed. He spoke immediately. "Let me tell you, one pays a high price for being an honorable man. Here I stand, all hot and bothered. In the future I'm going to think long and hard before I ever give my word. I don't think you know what my body is going through. I think you ought to turn around, face the dark wall, as I calm down."

That comment brought a smile to Sarah's face. "Now don't get all nettled. You're honorable, I'm glad you are, and you should be glad, too. Besides, if you must know, it wasn't exactly easy for me to stop either. Gosh, am I glad we did stop. I'm sorry I was so abrasive, but I knew no other way. You just stand there for awhile and regain your composure, and after you calm down there is something else we need to talk about."

"I'm almost normal again. What is it?"

"That sure didn't take long. You must not have been too excited." Sarah's words demanded a retort from Elzie, and the next five minutes they bantered back and forth, but this time with a humorous, not a biting tone. Sarah ended the bantering. "I think you are calmed down now, and before I get you riled again, we need to talk about something serious. You do remember there is another degree of honor involved here. You implied that you would be discreet, and not talk about what we did. Remember our discussion is between you, me, and the gatepost?"

This time, Elzie displayed the smile. "When did I say that?" Sarah turned her head and glared at Elzie. "Now, Sarah, don't you go getting nettled or riled." He paused in delight because he had thrown back the same words she had used on him, as she had done to him yesterday. "I'm just kidding, it's a joke. I may be a rascal, but I'm an honorable rascal. Besides, what we experienced today is personal, far too wonderful to share with anyone." He moved closer to Sarah with his arms outreached, and they embraced. He spoke with a devilish tone. "I've thought long and hard about it, and you've got my word." He then spoke with more seriousness. "Our secret will go to the grave with me, as will the memory of it. I mean it from the bottom of my heart."

CHAPTER 10

LOVE AND WAR

Without the slightest doubt Jesse knew Mary Helen Kelly was the girl for him. She was everything he wanted. He knew it, but he was not yet ready to share this feeling.

Therein was Jesse's problem. This young man of almost twenty-one, this farmhand of rural Jacksonville had to devise a plan, which not only provided for a proper courtship of the fourteen year old from South Jacksonville, it needed to contain the footings of a foundation for a future marriage. His task at hand was awesome, but with absolute confidence he felt equal to the challenge. He was determined to marry this girl.

Helen Kelly and Jesse Moore were mutually attracted to each other from the beginning and their relationship blossomed with a futurity. Wisely, Jesse understood the critical importance of a courtship without animosity from Stella or without causing hurt to anyone. In an honorable effort to be forthright he informed Stella that he desired to spark Helen, not her, and in a calculated, deliberate manner he convincingly presented his position. Jesse forever appreciated Stella's cooperation after she agreed and consented to cooperate. The future relationship was initiated on the right foot, the proper way.

Yielding to Helen's wishes, the Kellys invited Jesse to spend Christmas day starting at 7:00 a.m. Such a prolonged Christmas celebration was foreign to Jesse, but he was more than willing to participate. He had not celebrated Christmas since the ill-fated Christmas dinner with his family in Milton when they informed him that he needed to live elsewhere. Unable to eradicate that negative experience from his memory, he naturally approached this Christmas day with cautious optimism.

It snowed Christmas eve and continued to snow during the night until eight inches of the white fluffy substance had blanketed the entire Jacksonville area. Christmas morning strong north winds blew, causing considerable drifting of the snow and creating dangerous traveling conditions. A disappointed Helen and family waited for Jesse's arrival, but assumed that the invited guest could not endure the elements, and would not be able to make the almost four-mile journey to Jacksonville; but they did not know how persistent he could be. At 6:45 Christmas morning Jesse pulled up to the house on Michigan Avenue in a sleigh pulled by Babe. The previous night he had used the farm sleigh to check on the livestock and decided it would be the best means of transportation on Christmas day. Helen and family were elated.

Edward Kelly was shoveling snow off the porch when he caught his first glimpse of Jesse arriving in the sleigh. Edward was so pleased by the sight of Jesse that he dropped his shovel, went into the house, and summoned the others before he acknowledged Jesse's arrival. As Jesse was hitching his horse to the post the Kelly family all came outside and gave the Christmas guest the warmest greeting imaginable. Jesse could not remember any other personal welcome that measured up to this one. It was a great beginning to the day.

The Kellys had decorated the house for Christmas, inside and out. Three evergreen wreaths with red ribbons and bows were tastefully displayed on the snow covered front porch, and visible from the street were lighted red candles displayed on the sills of the four front upstairs and downstairs windows. The double windows facing the front porch revealed a tastefully decorated white pine Christmas tree covered with electric lights and topped with a lighted star. Garlands were hung throughout the living room, boughs of evergreen with large pinecones covered the end tables, and strings of popcorn hung near the doorways. In the center of the room a large floral centerpiece, lighted with scented candles and outlined by green branches of holly with red berries, occupied a major portion of a large table. Under the Christmas tree were packages wrapped in white, red, and green colored tissue paper, each with bright colored ribbon and bows. More numerous than the eye could absorb were small handmade Christmas decorations scattered throughout the room. Red stockings with personal names written on them, including one with the name Jesse, were hung on the wall next to the stove. The Kelly house was prepared for a family Christmas celebration, and Jesse was included.

The guest could find no words to express his admiration, appreciation of the decorations so he simply stared at the splendid array without speaking. Elizabeth and Edward said nothing, but derived considerable pleasure observing Jesse's reaction. Helen and Stella, the organizers of the decorations stood back and watched Jesse's nonverbal appreciation, and neither could contain her delight of Jesse's awe.

Facial expressions revealed it all. In an effort to express his appreciation Jesse searched for words of praise, but found instead inadequate expressions composed of strange sounds, half words, and incomplete sentences. His verbal stumbling amused the others. Elizabeth tried to rescue the temporarily inarticulate guest from further embarrassment. "Jesse is like me. He is sort of overwhelmed with the decorations, and I do believe he likes them."

Elizabeth had chosen her words carefully which gave Jesse the opening he needed. "Like doesn't begin to describe my feelings. I have never seen anything like this before. I've never seen a decorated Christmas tree, up close at least." Reaching to gently touch the string of lights on the tree, he continued. "I've never seen electric Christmas tree lights up close before and never in a private residence. Everything is just beautiful."

Helen responded. "We will never use candles on a tree again. Last year South Jacksonville School had a Christmas party for all the students and parents. We had a large, beautifully decorated Christmas tree in the center of the room, and lighted candles were used for tree lights. A friend of ours was playing Santa Claus when he bumped one of the lighted candles and the sleeve of his Santa suit caught fire. Within seconds his whole outfit was in flames, and when he fell against the tree, it tipped and burned. The whole tree was gone in a flash. People were standing right next to him and the tree, but no one could react fast enough to help him. The Santa Claus suit burned right off of him and badly burned the man. No, sir, I will never again decorate a tree with live candles. I didn't even want the candles in the windows until Dad convinced me that he thought it was safe."

"Oh, Helen, we shouldn't talk about such things on Christmas morning," Edward said, as he moved to put his arm around Helen. "I know it was a terrible sight, but we should not dwell on it or we'll scare Jesse to death."

"You won't scare me into leaving this house, I promise." Then with a twinkle in his eye and a big smile, Jesse looked directly at Helen. "Helen, I promise you that I won't get near a lighted candle, and if for some reason my clothing catches on fire, I will go outside to burn." The other three were amused by the ridiculous comment, but not Helen. Seeing no smile from Helen, Jesse continued, except this time he used no humor. "I'm sorry, Helen. I thought I was being cute, and all I really did was make light of something that was serious to you. I hope you forgive me."

Now Helen was embarrassed. "Apology accepted." Looking at her mother and grinning, Helen resumed talking. "If he makes fun of me again, I will take him outside, light a match, and personally set his clothing on fire."

Elizabeth smiled. "Sounds good. Okay if I provide the match?"

Stella spoke. "And you can bet I will be there to observe."

Edward came to his rescue this time. "Now, ladies, both Jesse and I will be good lads. No need to tar and feather us. We will behave, at least until after dinner. We men need to stick together in this household. Right, Jesse?"

"Absolutely, men need to stick together." Jesse was relieved. "Do you folks know what? I'm so looking forward to this Christmas day, that it might be worth it to be on fire. I do hope you'll wait until the day is over before you light me."

Helen liked his answer. "That's a deal. Come on, I want to show you the other two rooms, and I know you will want to see the kitchen. You won't believe what Mom has in store for Christmas dinner, and before dinner, and after dinner. You are in for a real treat, I promise." Less than five feet in height and slightly more than one hundred ten pounds, Helen moved across the room into the dining room with the grace of a dancer. Jesse followed.

The dining table, covered with a red table cloth and a floral centerpiece, was the main focus of attention. Twelve chairs, each facing a place setting, surrounded the neatly arranged table. Small handmade Christmas items placed throughout the room accented the table arrangement. The room displayed a complementary blend of function and festivity, creating an appearance of grandeur. Helen took Jesse's hand and squeezed it as she spoke. "Isn't it beautiful?"

Jesse emitted a broad grin, his blue-gray eyes sparkled. "It is the most beautiful table setting I have ever seen."

Helen directed Jesse into the kitchen where her mother was tending a stovetop dish. Elizabeth, slight of build and small boned, was an attractive lady of fifty-two years. Her medium length gray-brown hair parted in the middle, and her wire rim glasses resting on her high cheek bones presented an image of dignity. She was soft-spoken and moved her body with an air of gentleness. As Jesse glanced back at Helen he spotted a spectacular display of prepared food. At that particular moment nothing else, including Helen, could command his attention until he viewed the array of baked goods. Jesse released Helen's hand, walked to the table, and put his nose close enough to smell the pastries and audibly inhaled, followed by a prolonged sigh during the exhale.

"Oh my, Helen. Look at this! This is a sight of pure pleasure. Never have I seen anything that looked and smelled this good. I may never leave this room. Mrs. Kelly, what an early hour you must have started baking this morning."

"Indeed, I started early. You haven't seen it all yet. I have two more pies in the oven and another batch of cinnamon rolls baking. Helen, you will need to help me put the icing on the rolls when they come out of the oven. I've got too many things going now. In a few minutes they should be ready. As soon as we finish with the baking we will all go to the living room and open our presents. Okay?"

"Just yell when you need me. Come on, Jesse, I want to show you the rest of the goodies. Here are the dinner rolls. Don't they smell good? Look here! Cherry pie, apple pie, vanilla filled graham cracker crust pies, cinnamon rolls. I think we get to eat the cinnamon rolls as soon as the second batch comes out of the oven. Yummy! Here is the bread. Mom bakes two loaves of bread every morning." Helen moved to the other side of the kitchen. "Look at this table: oatmeal cookies, molasses cookies, sugar cookies, chocolate cookies, popcorn balls, fudge and divinity, and five-pound candy. We don't know the exact name of the candy; but since we fix it in five-pound batches, we call it five-pound candy. It has a vanilla taste with the consistency of fudge. It might be my favorite. And look here! It just so happens that I experimented and came up with my version of chocolate-covered cherries, your favorite candy I believe. I hope they are good. I took candied cherries, put them in a heavy syrup, and covered them with chocolate. We saved them for you to taste first. No one here has tried them yet, at least as far as I know, although Dad was eyeing them this morning before you got here. Oh, I almost forgot, there is peanut brittle candy too. Think you can find something here that will suit your taste? I hope so. We've been working four days preparing this stuff."

"Guaranteed. I feel like I have died and gone to heaven. I assure you that I will do my share of eating, and then some."

"Good. We haven't even talked about the food for dinner. Do you want to know?"

"If it's all right with you, I'll wait. I don't think my mind can handle anymore pleasure."

Mrs. Kelly smiled, and said, "Taste anything you want, just help yourself. It might not taste as good as it looks."

Helen pinched off a corner of the five-pound candy as Jesse reached for the chocolate-covered cherries. Helen's response to the taste of candy was, "mm, good." Jesse, after one bite, rolled his eyes and pointed his thumb upwards in a sign of approval. Helen liked that he chose to taste the candy he knew she made.

Still licking the sweetness of the candy from her fingers, Helen moved to the sitting room, and Jesse followed. "Here is where we all go to sit after we all eat too much. Christmas day we call it the recovery room. We decided not to decorate this room as much—just the garlands around the windows and the centerpiece on the table."

"Who makes the centerpieces or do you buy them? Each is a work of art in its own right."

Placing her hand near the object and gently stroking the floral art piece, Helen reflectively answered. "Dad does. He's the one in this house with the flair for it. Before he accepted the job as sexton at the Diamond Grove Cemetery he worked at the Heinl Florist greenhouse. He knows his flowers and how to arrange them. I wish I had his touch. I picked out the large red candle in the center. Does that entitle me to some of the credit?"

"It certainly does. That's a pretty red."

Helen gave an all knowing smile. "To me, all red is pretty. If I had my way, red would be everywhere. Needless to say, red is my favorite color."

"I will remember that. That tidbit of information may come in handy. Tell me more about you and the rest of your wonderful family. Everyone in this house is so interesting."

"Why, thank you. Later I will tell all you want to know, but now we need to gather around the Christmas tree. It's time to open the presents." Having made a complete circle they walked back to the living room. Every room had two openings, one into the room, and one out to another room. Although it was a small house, Jesse was surprised and somewhat impressed by the practical floor plan.

Jesse, Edward, and Stella visited in the living room and Helen went to the kitchen to assist her mother. In a few minutes Helen and Elizabeth entered the room carrying a tray of hot cinnamon rolls with icing and five cups of hot cocoa. Jesse ate three rolls and could have eaten three more had he not been concerned about the thoughts of the others. Helen enjoyed watching Jesse devour the rolls.

Edward placed a footstool near the tree as though he was setting the stage for an event before he made his announcement. "If everyone is ready we will proceed with the gifts." He paused and looked about the room. "Hearing no objection, we will start." Edward selected one gift at a time, read aloud the name and information on the tag, delivered it, and waited for the person to open the gift as the others watched. He methodically followed this procedure for almost two hours until all the presents were opened and were stacked beside the respective chairs for viewing. Jesse sat in awe of the process, never saying anything except when asked a direct question or to express gratitude for a gift given to him. Jesse had never observed such a gift exchange before. His appreciation for the entire process was obvious to the others, but it was diminished slightly by the fact he had only brought a gift for Helen, not for the others. No one else expected a gift and that helped some, but he still felt a twinge of guilt. Jesse had received eleven packages, mostly homemade items of food, plus one pair of socks, a set of handkerchiefs, and a beautiful neck scarf. Christmas morning, 1916, was a wonderful experience for everyone at the Kelly house on Michigan Avenue. Jesse knew this day would forever be etched into his mind.

The oldest Kelly daughter, Hattie Jackson, and her family arrived at the house shortly before 11:00 a.m. and another brief exchange of presents occurred. Jesse stood in the doorway and immensely enjoyed watching the family, especially the children. Following the second round of gift opening, the four women moved into the kitchen, the three children played on the floor of the Christmas room, and the three men adjourned to the sitting room. Neighbors, Mr. and Mrs. Hazlett, arrived soon thereafter and she joined the other females as he joined the males. The men casually discussed the local economy and politics, but mostly they talked about the war in Europe which added considerable passion to the conversation. Jesse tried to passively listen and generally spoke only in response to a direct question. Jesse intellectually benefitted from the conversation and was most impressed with their knowledge about the war. Jesse determined they were all of the Republican political persuasion but that no one totally agreed with the thoughts of the others, especially concerning American entry into the war. Before long Jesse lost his right to passively listen when Mr. Kelly asked him a direct and poignant question. "Jesse, what are your feelings about the war? Do you believe the United States should enter the war?"

Obviously uncomfortable with the question Jesse squirmed in his seat giving no immediate response. "I'm not sure how I feel. I'm certainly not as informed as any of you, and quite frankly I have not given it the thought that I should have. I favor the Allies and that is as far as I have gone, I'm ashamed to say. I feel deeply for the men in the trenches and I know I'm unable to even imagine what they must be going through; but for some reason I have not been motivated to learn about the war, or at least, I lack the level of knowledge that you folks have. It seems to be such a distant war. However, I do understand that if the U.S.A. becomes involved in this war, I will lose my right of noninvolvement, and at that time I will deal with it. I regret that I don't have a better answer to your questions." Mr. Kelly's reaction to his position was important to Jesse, and he felt he had given a most inadequate answer. Almost to the point of ignoring the others, and to the point of embarrassment, he looked directly at Mr. Kelly. "I'm sorry, Mr. Kelly. That was not a good answer."

"On the contrary, Jesse, you gave an honest answer. In light of our discussion today, I admire you for saying what you feel. You have the courage not to agree. Nevertheless, let me offer some advice. With the recent reelection of President Wilson, the man who ran on the platform that he kept us out of war, I am convinced that his policies will lead us into the war. If I am correct you had better give it some thought, because it is young men, like you, who will be called upon to serve your country. God, I hope I am wrong, but I suspect not."

Helen walked into the room and announced, "Dinner is ready. Mom told me to fetch the gentlemen folks and the young ones. It's time to gather at the table, and be sure you bring your appetites. Wait till you see the feast she has prepared." Political discussion ceased and the menfolk filed into the dining room.

Helen's comment was not an overstatement. The tabletop was utilized to maximum as was an adjacent smaller table. Once everyone was seated Mr. Kelly returned thanks offering a brief, heartfelt message. After his prayer he made mention of how fortunate they all were to be together, made a special welcome to Jesse, and asked that they all remember those family members who were not there. He then concluded with a final thought. "Meal time should be a joyous time and I request that we always keep it so. But let us remember in our hearts all those in the world who are less fortunate than us, for there are many and they need our prayers. Now with that said, let's eat this delicious looking meal."

Jesse was emotionally moved by the expressed sentiment of concern for others.

Elizabeth announced, "Everybody start a dish, take all you want, and pass it to the left. When it comes back to you, place the dish back in the same spot. Be careful as some are hot. After we finish passing the food on this table we will pass the food from the other table. If there is something else you want, just ask. Everyone should have a glass of milk and a glass of iced tea by your plate, and there is more to drink if you want it. Everything is to eat, so eat hardy."

Jesse had never seen so much variety of food at one meal, nor had he eaten such an organized meal. He smiled in anticipation. He leaned over and whispered to Helen. "I need sideboards for my plate. I've never seen so much food."

Helen giggled and spoke aloud. "My friend, Jesse, wants sideboards, Mom. Do we have any?"

Everyone laughed except Jesse. With a sheepish grin and his head lowered, Jesse said. "I only meant it in jest."

Edward Kelly came to his rescue, again. "And that's how it was taken. We don't have sideboards, but you can fill that plate as many times as you want."

Helen became amused with Jesse's awkwardness. "I'm sorry, Jesse, but it was funny." Jesse gave no verbal answer, only an approving facial expression. Nothing was going to interfere with his appreciation of this meal.

It required one and one-half hours for the family to finish the meal and everyone remained at the table until all others were finished eating. Jesse noticed he was the only one still eating. He was embarrassed again. This time no one laughed aloud, although they all were amused with Jesse's slow and deliberate pace of eating and, also, with his massive consumption of food. Good-naturedly he smiled and went along with the crowd. "Well, that may be the best meal I've ever had. I think I should stop and save room for dessert." His comment endeared him to all. He continued. "After we eat the dessert, I'm going to make a list of all the fine food we had at this meal, a menu, if you will, and show it to my little brother, Elzie. If you folks want to see a big eater, you should see my brother eat." His remarks created interesting mental images for the others at the table which encouraged more laughter.

According to family tradition the men gathered in the kitchen to do the dishes, the children played in the Christmas room, and the women adjourned to the sitting room. The women quietly visited as the men noisily talked with neither aware of the other group. It was as intended.

Before much lapse in time the children approached Helen and inquired about the sleigh in front of the house, knowing full well that the sleigh belonged to Jesse.

Helen conspired with the children to ask Jesse for a ride, and he was more than happy to accommodate. The open sleigh had seats for six people and, before the afternoon was over, everyone in the house that Christmas day took a memorable ride around town and through the park. Jesse, with his horse and sleigh, made his personal contribution to that joyous Christmas day. By dark the neighbor guests, Mr. and Mrs. Hazlett, and Hattie and her family, had returned home. Jesse stayed a while longer.

The first three months of the calendar year usually are slower times for the agricultural worker, save the daily chores and usual maintenance responsibilities. The early months of 1917 were no different at the farm where Jesse worked, so he took advantage of some free time to foster his relationship with Helen by seeing her every Saturday night; and sometimes more frequently, if he could make it to town on weekday evenings. He wrote her one letter every week, plus occasional postcards. Once it was determined that if he posted a letter or card before 7:00 a.m. in nearby Arnold, a very small town with a post office, Helen would receive it by mid-afternoon, he always sent notification by mail of his intention to visit her that evening. On occasion, Helen wrote a letter to Jesse, but generally she left the correspondence to Jesse, which was fine with him.

Saturday, February 3, 1917, Helen received a card from Jesse, postmarked Feb. 3, 1917, Arnold, Illinois. The front of the post card had a picture of the Bank of Montreal, Winnipeg.

> Dear Helen,
> This is a card I got when I was in Winnipeg. Notice how wide the streets are. I hope to be with you tonight if nothing hap-
> pens.
> I remain, Cy. T. B. Jesse.

Cy. T. B. was part of a personal code between Helen and Jesse. Both refused to explain the code to anyone.

The courtship was conventional, not pretentious. Much of the time the Kelly family was consulted or involved with any courting activities and, initially, there were few special activities involving only the two. Mostly Jesse visited Helen at the Kelly house where they spent alone time on the front porch or on walks in the neighborhood. Most outings involved a short buggy ride around town with Babe strutting her stuff. Jesse was proud of his fine looking horse, and Helen, although not especially attached to the animal, found pleasure watching Jesse handle the high spirited beast. Indeed, Helen and Jesse were a fine looking young couple as they paraded around town in the immaculately clean and shiny buggy pulled by Babe.

Friday, February 16, 1917, was Jesse's twenty-first birthday and the Kelly family planned a small celebration offering a homemade dinner of his choice. Helen baked an angel food cake and prepared homemade vanilla ice cream. In Jesse's words, "The meal was a feast fit for a king." They all sang happy birthday to him, and everyone presented him with a modest homemade gift. As they were singing to Jesse, Helen thought she saw a tear of joy in his bright, blue-gray eyes. There was little doubt that this was his happiest birthday ever.

The outside air was cool this February night, but that did not prevent Helen and Jesse from sitting on the front porch after his birthday dinner, because it was their only opportunity to be alone. In an effort to keep warm Helen wore a long wool coat, a wool scarf, and a muff for her hands. Jesse with his long underwear, layered clothing, cap, and gloves was always prepared for the cold. The young couple sat on the porch swing that crisp, clear, starry night, both oblivious to the elements. Jesse expressed his appreciation. "This is the perfect ending to the perfect day. I don't deserve such treatment. Thank you, Helen."

"You are more than welcome, Jess. May I call you Jess? The sound of Jess has a little more endearment to it."

"Then by all means, call me Jess. You are so fortunate, Helen. You have a good life, a nice house, and the most incredible family. Everybody in your family loves you so much, and they show it by the way they all interact with you. Little doubt that you are loved by many people."

"No argument here. I'm most fortunate, I know."

"Your family seems to have a special bond. Everyone cares equally for the other. Your parents are what I would describe as the perfect parents."

"Thanks, again. They need to hear you say that. Granted they are special people who deserve their happiness; however, let it be clear in your mind that both of them have paid their dues. Mother works her fingers to the bone everyday, just to make everything flow, and she has done that since... well, forever. Both of her parents died before she was seven and she doesn't remember much about either one of them. After Mother's parents died she went to live with her grandparents, who, as I understand it, didn't really want her, but accepted her out of obligation. Poor Mother lived and worked on their farm all through the 1870's and early 1880's, until she married Dad, in 1884, when she was nineteen. So to my mother her family is everything, nothing is more important to her. That's why she works so hard.

"And then there is Dad, poor Dad. No one could work harder. As you know he walks almost two miles to work and then walks home, in all kinds of weather, six days a week, never missing a day of work. He works very hard overseeing the cemetery. He married Mother just before he turned nineteen, and he, like Mother, values his family above all, although the last few years have been very hard on him.

In March of 1913, my brother, Roy, the only boy in the family, died at age eighteen. Three months later, while my sister, Meda, was visiting us at this house, her son, little Irvin, took ill and died. He was such a precious little thing. Mother said that Dad bought the lot at the East Cemetery, instead of the Diamond Grove Cemetery where he works, because he couldn't stand to see the graves everyday. Both Roy and Irvin are buried there.

"In between those two deaths, my grandfather, my father's father, died in April, 1913. The combined grief was almost too much for my father to bear. Poor Dad suffered so. Just as we thought he was coming out of it, his mother died in November of that same year. Think about that. Both of your parents, a son, and a grandchild all die within seven months of one another. It was too much for any man to bear, and thank God for my mother's strength because Dad sure leaned hard on her through it all." Helen stopped talking, momentarily, as she wiped the tears from her eyes. Jesse sat beside her not knowing what to do or what to say. He offered his handkerchief, and she accepted it without words, and they sat quietly for the next few minutes. Helen then continued. "You must think me silly for crying about something that happened so long ago. I know I was talking about how my folks suffered, but those deaths were my losses, too. There is not one day of my life without thoughts about each one of them. I didn't have many years to know any of them. I'm sorry, I keep getting sidetracked on my own feelings. Let me continue. There is more sadness. The following year, 1914, my older sister, Ella, Mom and Dad's second daughter, took ill. She lived in Los Angeles, California. She was twenty-six years old, married, with five children: two boys and three girls, the youngest girl named Helen, after me. Ella knew she was dying and asked Mom and Dad if they would come to visit her, but they didn't go because they couldn't get enough money to make the trip. I will never forget seeing my mother crying in the backyard as she hung up the wash. She and Dad had just determined that they could not make the trip, and they had no other recourse. When I asked if I could help, she replied, 'Please, Helen, I need to be alone, I need to cry.' I can still see Mother's face on that day, even though it has been two and one half years ago. Ella died in June, 1914, and the folks had never gotten to see her. Two days later she was buried in Los Angeles without anyone from Illinois at the funeral.

"It was hard on all of us, but I think it was hardest on Dad. After Ella died, Mother thought Dad suffered a broken heart, and she didn't know if he could recover or not." Jesse was emotionally touched by the anguish suffered by those he liked so much. He, too, sat in the swing with watery eyes, never finding words to comfort Helen. "I shouldn't have burdened you with all of this, Jess. I tell you this not to depress you, rather to make you aware of how special my parents really are."

"Help your parents, help bring them out of it. Grief is important, but prolonged grief is not good for anybody. Sadness can destroy the person, making them look at everything in life through the wrong eyes. I've seen it before, sadness causes the person to lose his spirit for living, and it can wreck his life, and sometimes it can kill him. Help your parents. Bring joy to their lives. Help heal your father's broken heart."

"I will try, although heaven knows I have been trying. I suppose it's the little things that can help the most. They both have been deeply hurt. I hope I never do anything to add to their hurt."

Jesse reached for Helen's muff-covered hand. "Both of your parents are special, I know that. I suppose we all need a little extra understanding at times. It seems to me that life is full of sadness, and we have few options, except to endure. It's easier to say than to do, I know. Sometimes, hearing about the problems in another's life helps one with perspective in his own life." Jesse proceeded to describe the tragic events of his young life, the first time he had ever shared or verbally recounted the events to anyone.

"Recently I have come to believe that if you bounce back from adversity, you are stronger as a person than you were before the adversity. That's my point. My struggles have made me a stronger, and hopefully, a better person. I am sure of one thing—my struggles aren't over. I've always thought that my younger brother and sister, Elzie and Frieda, are the ones who have had it the toughest because of their ages. That leads to something else. I'm not sure how we can arrange it, but I would really like for you to meet Elzie, Frieda, Aunt Mary, and my father. I think you will very much like all four of them. Maybe sometime we can make a trip to Milton, and I will show you my old stomping grounds. Would you like that?"

"Heavens, yes, I would like that; however, we should tread with caution in what we plan. I don't know what Mother and Dad would think about me going to Milton with you, even if it's only for one day. We need to go slow on things like that. Let me think about it for a while before we plan anything. Speaking of the folks, I think we should go inside. It's getting late."

"Of course. I hope I have not created a problem by staying too long. I will tell you this, for sure. This is the best birthday, ever. Thanks again, Helen."

"You're welcome, again. Now, let's go inside and bring a little joy in their lives. Help me wish my folks a happy anniversary. Tomorrow, February 17, is their wedding anniversary. They will have been married thirty-three years. Isn't that something? Matter of fact, tomorrow I'm going to bake a cake for them. I'm going to put one candle for each year on that cake. I wish I could do more, but I don't know what it would be."

Helen and Jesse developed a special bond this night. They found common ground through sharing and describing emotional experiences with one another. Each discovered a sensitivity in the other which allowed them to grow closer as a couple. This evening became one of many that Helen and Jesse would pass the night away visiting and sharing thoughts.

Jesse must have enjoyed himself. The next night he drove to Jacksonville to see Helen again.

As time passed their relationship grew, strengthened. Helen adored Jesse, thinking him near perfect. He was a handsome man marked by graciousness. She was proud of her man, and just as she knew she was too young to marry, she knew Jesse was the man she wanted to marry. To Jesse, Helen was without equal. His growing admiration of Helen accrued to major proportions. Indeed the young girl from South Jacksonville was a rare find. Helen had the courage to be herself and the wisdom to be proud of who she was. Wise for her age she most valued honesty, integrity, and commitment, as she placed little emphasis on wealth and material things. She felt disdain for those she referred to as highfalutin. Above all she valued family as much as Jesse did, and most of their personal beliefs were on a par with one another.

Marriage was not discussed. The relationship continued to flourish without guarantees of personal commitments and without restrictions. The seed of marriage was planted and was growing, but not yet mature.

The delightful weather in the spring of 1917 enhanced the courtship. In Jesse's mind everything was more beautiful and life was more pleasant when he was with Helen. Without fail every Saturday night Jesse made his way to Michigan Avenue to visit Helen, and every Saturday night Helen cleared her schedule to receive Jesse. More than not, the evening commenced with a buggy ride which provided time to be alone and the opportunity for each to catch up on the recent activities of the other. Sometimes they went to the movies, or simply went downtown to be near the hustle and bustle of the commercial center. Frequently they rode the buggy around the town for much of the evening, seldom with any destination in mind. If public band concerts were scheduled, they attended. Structured activities were far less important than was the personal time together. They were so under cupid's spell.

Sunday morning was church time, not courting time. Church attendance had always been important to the Kellys, but church was especially significant to Helen who consistently held strong in her Christian beliefs. For years Helen had aspired to become a Sunday school, nursery teacher, an opportunity to teach which would allow her to combine her love of small children and to demonstrate her spiritual beliefs. Her teaching aspirations were deeply entrenched into the person she had become. However, after Sunday worship services were finished, the day became a time for family leisure. Somewhat a Kelly tradition, Sundays, from April to November, were designated as family picnic days in the park. For Helen and Jesse Sunday afternoons purveyed uninterrupted time together without shortchanging valued family time. Sunday afternoons in the park were wonderful. On one occasion Jesse even convinced a reluctant Helen to go boating on the lake with him and, although Helen was uncomfortable near the water, Jesse's skillful manipulation of a rowboat made the boating experience enjoyable. Sometimes they found simple pleasure in watching the children on the playground, or in observing other comparable activities. Reaching a new plateau in their courtship the greatest degree of personal satisfaction for the young couple came less from the prescribed activity, more from the time spent together. Sundays at the park were the source of many precious memories for both Helen and Jesse.

Jesse felt on top of the world, believing that his life was better than he had ever envisioned. The pace of life accelerated for the young farmhand trying to balance workload, personal responsibilities, and courting; and complicating that fact, Jesse was determined not to disappoint anyone who counted on him. In addition to his now busy routine, he undertook a special project. Putting his carpentry skills to use, he remodeled his living quarters and enclosed the surrounding yard with a four-foot high, white picket fence. He added a covered back porch to the house and enlarged the sitting area of the front porch. By previous agreement the owner of the farm supplied the materials and Jesse provided the labor; and upon completion of the project both were most satisfied with the end product. Their efforts had rendered an attractive cottage-like, self-contained living quarters in a beautiful rural setting. Jesse installed a convenient kitchen sink pump for water and built a new and extravagant three-seater outhouse with one opening reserved for guest. He prepared a rather large vegetable garden plot and several small flower beds, all of which he also managed to get planted, save the earliest produce and floral seeding. Since the house was near other farm buildings, yet far enough away to have its own identity, it created a unique living atmosphere more indicative of ownership than farmworker. Indeed, the homestead was an impressive sight. Jesse did not reveal his reasons for wanting improved living quarters, if in fact, he had an agenda. If asked about his motivation, he would reply, "It is time for improvements." No one questioned that.

———

The official policy of neutrality by the United States Government held to the belief that the past, senseless slaughter of millions of soldiers and civilians should be reason enough to force the belligerent nations to the peace table. President Wilson issued a plea for peace without victory, but his efforts were misdirected. Instead of peace talks early in 1917, and after two and one half years of horrendous fighting, both warring sides engaged in a policy of all-out war to achieve final, absolute victory. In effect, this policy of all-out war held the dire consequence of inevitable American involvement in the war.

In January, 1917, Germany chose to risk moral condemnation from the neutrals and resumed unrestricted submarine warfare, unleashing its deadly submarines to sink all ships, enemy or neutral, which carried supplies for the Allied cause. This calculated action by Germany assumed the Central Powers could, and would win the war before the United States could enter the war, certainly before the United States could raise, train, and ship an army to Europe. Unrestricted submarine warfare immediately resulted in a loss of American lives and American ships and obligated the United States Government to break all diplomatic relations with Germany. Of course, the American people were outraged by the German action and supported President Wilson when he asked Congress to change the official position of the United States Government to "armed neutrality" with permission to arm American merchant ships. By March, 1917, the U.S. Navy was ordered to arm and provide gun crews for merchant ships.

Early March, 1917, a German document, known as the Zimmerman note, was made public. In the document the German Foreign Minister, Arthur Zimmerman, urged Mexico and Japan to enter the war on the side of the Central Powers if the United States entered on the side of the Allies. The document promised Mexico, in return for supporting Germany, the opportunity to regain its lost territory of New Mexico, Texas, and Arizona. The disclosure of this document created a storm of outrage among Americans, creating American moral indignation.

Later that month a revolution in Russia overthrew the autocratic Czar and created a constitutional government in its place. Thus, in the minds of many Americans the war was now a war clearly defined by type of government, pitting the democratic Allied Powers against the autocratic Central Powers. United States entry became more justified.

On a cold, damp Monday night in Washington, D.C., on April 2, 1917, President Wilson went before Congress to ask for a declaration of war. He read from a paper he had prepared himself. He stated, among other points:

We have no choice. We cannot choose submission.

We must bring the German Empire to terms and end the war.

The United States will fight for the ultimate peace of the world.

The world must be made safe for democracy.

The speech was received by Congress with enthusiasm. It was reported that later the same night President Wilson made a personal comment to a close friend.

"My message today was a message of death for our young men." It was reported, "He then put his head down on the table in the Cabinet Room, and sobbed." The public was unaware of Wilson's personal reaction.

At 1:18 p.m., Friday, April 6, 1917, the United States was formally at war with the German Empire.

Elzie heard the news that night in Pittsfield. He cheered the action and celebrated with friends on the lawn of the courthouse. If there were people in Pittsfield against American entry into the war, they were not visible that night.

Jesse heard the news early Saturday night on his way to visit Helen. His reaction was mixed as he was proud of his country, but uncertain about his role in the war. He was met at the door by Mr. Kelly. "I told you, Jesse. The reelection of Wilson meant we were going to war. I pray to God we know what we are doing." Most of the evening was spent discussing the possible consequences of America at war. Mr. and Mrs. Kelly, although most supportive of their country, were concerned about the declaration of war, fearful of the possible negative effects on the nation and its citizens. Jesse remained cautious with guarded feelings. Helen listened to the discussion, never expressing her opinion. Indeed, everyone in the Kelly house, as in most households, felt a deep personal shock in that American boys would soon go to war.

It was no secret that the United States Army was not prepared to fight a war. On April 1, 1917, the Regular Army was comprised of 127,000 men, supplemented by 67,000 National Guardsmen under federal control, and 102,000 National Guardsmen under state control, none of whom were equipped for service in Europe. The United States had a peacetime army. It was hoped that by August, 1918, the United States Army could have 2,000,000 men in Europe, trained and equipped to wage war. May 18, 1917, President Wilson signed into law the Selective Service Act which required that on June 5, 1917, 7:00 a.m. to 7:00 p.m., all males living in the country, between the ages of twenty-one and thirty-one, register with local draft boards. Draft numbers were to be assigned at registration and, later, numbers drawn by lottery would determine the order of drafting. Almost ten million men throughout the country registered on that day.

On Tuesday, June 5, 1917, Jesse A. Moore, twenty-one years of age, registered with the local draft board in Jacksonville, Illinois, along with three thousand other men. The morning of June 5th was pleasantly cool and sunny. Jesse arrived in town before 7:00 a.m. to find others already in line. The crowd of men emanated jubilance. Most were anxious to register, many were eager to serve, few were disinterested, just as most registrants thought this day more of an opportunity, less of an obligation. Jesse, still uncertain of his own feelings, patiently took his place in line waiting for the registration to begin. Once the doors opened registration progressed efficiently, allowing Jesse to complete the process in less than one hour.

He filled out a twelve line registration card, swore under oath the information was correct, turned the card in to the officials, and was assigned draft number 59.

Registration Card   No. 59.

Name: Jesse A. Moore   Age 21.
Address: RD 7. Arnold Ill.
Registration Center: Jacksonville, Illinois.
Date of Birth: Feb. 16, 1896.
Place of Birth: Pike County, Ill.
Names of Parents:
  Mother: Mary Dosia Moore
  Father: Erastus L. Moore
Occupation: Farmhand.
Employer: Earl Lukeman Farms. RR.
Race: Caucasian.
Marital Status: Single.
Children: None.
Health: Excellent.

————————

Jesse had never before received a telegram until Friday, June 8, when he received one from Elzie.

> Need to talk. Meet me early Sat. night, June 9, Winchester Court-
> house, if possible.
> Elzie

Winchester, Illinois, was about half-way in distance between Milton and Jacksonville. Assuming the meeting was important, Jesse canceled his plans to see Helen and arrived at the Scott County courthouse by 5:15 p.m., to find Elzie on the courthouse steps waiting for him. By the time Jesse had hitched his horse and buggy Elzie was near the hitching site with outstretched hand. They shook hands. Elzie spoke first. "Thanks for coming, Jesse, I really appreciate it."

"What's wrong? Why are we here?"

"Nothing is seriously wrong. I just needed to talk to you without anyone else around. You know how Dad can be."

Relieved, Jesse said, "Am I glad to hear that. Your telegram scared the hell out of me. Let's go get a coke and find a place to sit and talk."

Elzie rendered a big smile. "I'll go you one better than that. If you're hungry we'll eat a meal at the Winchester Hotel. My treat."

"I sure won't argue with that." The brothers walked to the nearby hotel restaurant, were seated at a window table, and both ordered the daily special of Salisbury steak with milk to drink and carrot cake for dessert. Elzie wanted to eat before they got to the business at hand, so the brothers consumed the food and engaged only in casual conversation.

Elzie was proud that he was taking his older brother out for dinner. "Pretty nice, huh? Two country boys eating dinner at the best restaurant in Winchester. Pretty high on the hog, isn't it? I think a guy could get used to this in a hurry."

"I'll say. We're in the lap of luxury all right." Both allowed themselves to enjoy the rare occurrence of dining out together.

He could wait no longer. Immediately after the meal, while still at the restaurant table, Jesse spoke. "What is this all about? Why am I here?"

Elzie became very deliberate. "Nothing is wrong, okay, so don't work yourself into a dither. First I have some questions, and then I need some advice. Sorry to make you come all this distance, but you are the one I need to visit with. I'm sorry to say, Jesse, that since you've left Milton, I don't have anyone to talk to, or at least anyone I respect enough to get advice from. I miss our visits."

"I miss them too."

"Okay, enough of that. I'll just get right to it. Are you going to join the Army and fight in this war?"

Jesse did not hesitate. "No, I'm not going to enlist. If they draft me I will go, but only if they draft me. I suspect you know I registered for the draft this week."

"Yeah, I know, everyone did. How come you're not going to join up?"

Leaning back in his chair Jesse paused a moment. "You're getting pretty personal, aren't you?" Elzie looked at Jesse without responding. Personal or not he wanted to know the answer. "It's a long story, Elzie. I'm going to tell you something and I want you to keep it under your hat. I've met this girl, Helen, and I'm going to marry her, except she doesn't know it yet. At this point in my life she is my only real concern. It's not quite that simple, but that's the gist of it. I'm happier now than I have ever been before and I'm not ready to lose her, which I might do if I do something silly, like join the army. If push comes to shove and I have to go, I will, but not before. Now, surely, you didn't bring me all the way over here to find out if I was going to join up, at least I hope you didn't."

"No, not at all. I just wondered, and I knew, whichever way you answered, there would be a good reason. Pretty good reason at that. Well what do you know about that, my big brother is in love. How about that? It should not have, but that caught me off guard. I want to meet this girl. She must be something. Actually, Jesse, I'm happy for you, and as usual, you have a well thought out plan. I should have known."

"Elzie, what's this all about?"

"Jesse, I want to join the Army, and I can't figure out how to do it. They tell me I'm too young, but we both know better. I'm old for my age. Anyone under twenty-one has to have consent from his parents, and Dad won't even talk about it. As you know, I turned seventeen about three months ago. Too damn young, that's all anyone says. By the time I'm twenty-one this war will be over and forgotten about. I can't wait, I want to go now. I'll be one hell of a soldier, and you know it. Stupid rules make me mad. Let me explain. I went down to the draft registration the other day, and they wouldn't even talk to me. I've talked to people on the board, and they say there is nothing at all they can do for me. So there you are, I can't find a place to enlist. I'm too young, and everyone in Pittsfield knows how old I am, and most of them know that Dad has said no."

Looking at his younger brother, Jesse saw a brother in need of assistance or, more specifically, in need of direction. The compassionate Jesse wanted to help, but he was concerned if he was the right one to give advice; and he knew any assistance he gave might have dire consequences for both of them. He sensed how much Elzie wanted this, just as he sensed nothing he could say would change Elzie's mind. He carefully chose his words. "Before I give you my thoughts, allow me to ask you some questions."

Elzie, convinced Jesse had a solution, said, "Fire away. Ask all the questions you want."

"Why are you so eager to enlist, to fight in this war, anyway?"

"I can't believe you asked me that. You already know the answer. We are at war! Our country is at war with an evil enemy, and my country needs me, even if they don't want me. My God, Jesse, to me the question should be, why would one not want to fight, rather than why one would want to. There is more to this war than meets the eye. You know there is a right and wrong issue involved in all of this. A man has got to stand up for what he believes to be right. I've heard you say it a hundred times—we are our beliefs. If we don't stand up for what we believe, what good are we?

"There are other reasons too, and they are no less important. The foremost reason is because we are at war now, this very minute. Who do you think should fight this war for our country? I am the perfect candidate. I would be a good soldier, and I want to defend my country. Think about it. If not me, who. Would our army be better off with men who have wives and children, or with someone who doesn't want to be there, or worse yet, with some pansy-ass person who happens to be the right age? I am what a soldier should be. I haven't met anyone better with a rifle. I'm as good in the wilderness as anyone around here, and as you know I'm no pushover either. To be real truthful, there aren't too many around here who can kick my ass, and I can go on with my list, if I need too. The best answer to your question is, just because, that's why. I'm the right person at the right time. Now if that doesn't tell you why I want to be a soldier boy, then I'm not capable of expressing it."

Elzie's answer was direct and passionate. Jesse knew he was not going to change Elzie's mind. "You're capable all right, that's not at issue here. Perhaps too capable. You know those Germans over there are trained to kill, and it's my understanding they are very good at what they do. It's not like hunting for a squirrel in the woods. Those boys shoot back. It's not a walk in the park, Elzie. It's not a game. This is the real thing."

"I know that, I'm not stupid. I know what war is, at least as much as any civilian can know. My eyes are wide open.

"Besides, there are other things to consider. How happy do you think I will be if I stay in Milton, living with Aunt Mary, walking behind those mules of Dad's, when others are off risking their lives? That's just not me and you know it. I need to do my part." Elzie hesitated to regain his composure. "To be honest there is more to my wanting to go, and I think you know what it is. This is my chance to do something with my life, to see the world, and to have adventure, and all the while I would be helping my country. It would just kill me, Jesse, if I lived all my life in this isolated area, doing what everybody else does, never doing anything, never getting ahead. It just isn't fair. This is my chance, perhaps my only chance."

Jesse was moved by the genuineness of his words, the open honesty which flowed from his younger brother. "I will say this. You certainly present your case with passion."

"Will you help me figure this out, then?"

"I'm not sure there is a solution. Let me be perfectly clear about one thing. I would rather you not join the military, period. I wish you wouldn't do it. With that said, I do understand why you want to. I don't think you should join, at this age anyway, but at this point in time what I think is not important. You are an adult, capable of making your own decisions, and only you should make the decisions that affect you. Here is what I would do, if I was you. First, I would keep working on Dad, and then work on Aunt Mary to help you. Remember, if you can convince her, you have won half the battle, and she carries a lot of influence with our old man. Second, think about waiting until you're eighteen. I know for a fact that some eighteen-year olds have enlisted, but I have not heard of seven-teen-year olds. At this point the American war effort is just getting started and by the time you are eighteen there will be recruiting stations all over the place. They will be begging you to enlist. Third, if you just can't wait and you feel you must join, join somewhere else, not in Pittsfield.

"I hope I don't hate myself for giving this advice. Please go easy, Elzie, and don't do something stupid or something that will embarrass you. Get a plan and think of the consequences if the plan doesn't work out. If you're going to do it, do it right. I repeat, do it right."

The answer was not all that Elzie had hoped for, but it was something to consider, a different perspective. "Well I hate to say it but, as usual, you make sense. I will do as you say and not be rash. I can tell you one thing for sure, I won't lie unless I just have to. I don't want to begin on a falsehood. However, let me make one thing perfectly clear to you. I'm going to be a doughboy and fight in this war, and that's final."

CHAPTER 11

MARRIAGE

Times were changing as America prepared its sons for war. Wheresoever one traveled in the United States, one found discussion about American involvement in the Great War.

Sunday, June 10, the Kelly family picnic at the park was canceled because of rain and, in its place, Elizabeth Kelly served a picnic lunch on their back porch. About mid afternoon two visitors, Edward's younger brother, Curtis, and his friend arrived unannounced at the Kelly house. The visitors from Nortonville had come to Jacksonville on this day to hear the Lieutenant Governor of Illinois speak about Illinois' role in the Great War. Curtis was Helen's favorite uncle and Jesse was eager to meet him, having heard much about him from Helen. Similar to Edward in appearance and demeanor, Curtis was a grocery store owner in his early thirties. His friend, Jeb, was an older gentleman with a definite air of distinction about him. The welcomed visitors shared in the leftovers of the porch picnic as the Kelly family was brought up to speed about the most recent happenings in Nortonville.

As was customary the group eventually segregated with the men in one room, the women in another. Jesse became so intrigued by the visitors that he temporarily lost his normal sensitivity to the needs of Helen who at first was hurt when she realized that Jesse was part of the men's conversation by choice, rather than politeness. It was Elizabeth's comment that brought proper perspective to the situation. "Helen, you should be proud, not angry. Jesse likes to talk with your father and his brother, and apparently they enjoy him. I see nothing but good in that." Elizabeth was correct and Helen soon recognized it.

Helen gave a slight grin of approval. "I have an idea, Mother. Why don't the three of us sit at the kitchen table and have some sugar cookies and milk. Then we'll see who gets envious."

Mother responded, "Good idea, only I think we should share the cookies and milk, don't you?"

"I do, and if you don't mind, I'll take the cookies and milk to them. That way they won't know what a real brat I almost was."

Stella interjected her thoughts. "I wouldn't do it if I was you. I would make them come in here and get it themselves. I don't care if they know that I'm a brat."

Helen started to respond to Stella's comment until a quick look from her mother precluded her words. Stella, convinced the girls were deliberately excluded from the conversation, intended to push her point until Elizabeth interceded. "We are not brats, and they are not excluding us. I doubt if any one single act, good or bad, by any one of us would change their opinion of us. Besides, who knows, the conversation in the kitchen may be better anyway."

Meanwhile, the conversation in the living room had turned to the serious side. "Tell me about the speech, Curt," Edward requested.

"There is not much to tell as it was really more of a rally than a speech. He talked about how important Illinois is in the war effort, because of our industry, our agriculture, and our large population. Everything seems to center more on patriotism, less on issues about the war. Why we are in the war is no longer a point of discussion. Instead they want everybody to help in the war effort and, for the present, they are defining ways for all of us to help. For now they mostly want men to enlist and for the rest of us to buy war bonds. I'm sure that later they will be more specific. As I said, right now it was really a rally."

Jeb felt obliged to contribute. "Curtis says it well. We came today hoping to acquire a better understanding of the issues and to obtain answers to a few questions. What the government wants now is support, not questions. I think we've waited too long to take issue. I think if you asked the wrong questions today your name would be Mudd."

Usually most reluctant to appear argumentative, Jesse, nevertheless, felt compelled to insert his opinion. "Isn't that the way it should be? Our country is at war, and now is not the time for petty politics. Before long American boys will be shedding their blood in France. This last Tuesday I went and registered for the draft along with thousands of others. I hope if I serve there will be support for me from the people at home."

Somewhat surprised, the other three listened intently to Jesse. Edward Kelly spoke first. "Heavens, Jesse, there will be plenty of support, and you can rest assured of that; but I hope to God that you don't have to go. That is not what Jeb meant at all." While pointing at his younger brother, "Curtis may well have to go too, if the war lasts that long. We don't oppose the war. We want to better understand why we are at war."

Jeb was apologetic. "I'm sorry, young man, if I offended you. That was the farthest thing from my mind. Please forgive me."

Jesse was humbled. "No apology necessary. I overreacted. Yesterday, I met with my younger brother and I advised him on ways to enlist in the army so that he could help fight this war. I believe when I spoke I was thinking of him rather than thinking about the right and wrong of the war. I'm the one who should be apologizing to you."

Almost in a fatherly tone, Jeb continued. "Good for you. You should be thinking about your brother and about yourself. Heavens knows that it will be boys like you who will pay the real price in this war. Old men like me will sit at home and worry, but we won't make the kind of sacrifices that millions of young American boys like you will make.

"Allow me to explain my qualms. I'm not real sure how we got into this war in the first place. I do understand the events, just not the reasons behind the events. I'm sure if you have been around Edward at all, you have heard him express his reservations about President Wilson's trade policy, and I agree with him. We have financially linked our country to the Allies because we have traded with them, at the exclusion of trade with the Central Powers. This trade was less by design, more by opportunity. Our trade ships could not get by the British blockade or we would have traded more with Germany. Adding to the confusion, American banks ended up lending money to the Allies to purchase the goods we had to sell. Once this happened our financial institutions had a stake in the Allies winning the war. Now here is my real concern. Somebody, and I don't know who, makes a lot of money during any war. Every time a bullet is made, or a uniform is made, or anything else that is used for war is made, somebody makes money. My question is, how much influence do these people, the ones who make the money, have in our government?

"War stories sell newspapers. How much of what we have read in the paper is factual, or is part of the news distorted like it was in the Spanish- American War? Yellow journalism, I think they called it. I wonder if some stories are exaggerated to sell newspapers. This is another concern, and I do not know the answer. I do know that different newspapers give different accounts of the same story. How do I know that I am reading the real story if their purpose is to sell newspapers? What obligation do the editors have to the truth? I do believe I have a right to wonder about such things, but I'm not sure if I need to worry about them.

"For the last three years our major communication link with Europe has been through the transatlantic cable system which links London to New York. I hope we have been presented with the truth about the war, but I seriously doubt it. Surely, I have the right to question about these concerns. Do you think my concerns are legitimate, Jesse, or do you think that I'm way out of line? I want you to answer me because I'm not sure. I'm not stating a position as much as I am asking questions."

Fascinated by Jeb's thoughts and queries Jesse sat with his hands folded and was not forthcoming with any answer. Curtis answered. "I don't know how I feel. I certainly agree with your right to ask the questions, if that is what you want in the way of an answer."

By now Jesse had the courage to respond. "I don't think I know enough to even attempt to answer your questions. You may as well be talking high finance as far as I'm concerned. These are all new ideas to me. If you don't object I will simply listen, and later when I have time, I will think more about the answers."

Edward supported Jesse. "Wise answer, Jesse. Jeb is more scholarly than the rest of us, and I agree with you. Better to be quiet than to be foolish."

Jeb became uncomfortable with that comment. "You gentlemen give me more credit than I deserve. These are not my ideas. They are reworded questions that have been raised elsewhere. The war for profit idea is straight from the Socialists and Eugene V. Debs. Yellow journalism has been around as long as we've had newspapers, and just as everybody seems to know about yellow journalism, few seem to care about it. I realize the importance of propaganda, so do you. Regardless of where they came from they are valid questions, and I am merely looking for some answers. I regret that I have sounded all knowing as that was not my intention. I'm just looking for answers. If in fact we are fighting the war to preserve democracy in the world, I hope we also preserve democracy at home as we fight the war. Perhaps things have always been this way, and they always will be this way."

"What do you mean?" asked a most interested Edward.

"I'm not sure what I mean. I guess it was not a good thing to say. I'm just not certain that war is always the best way for nations to deal with unresolved issues. There have got to be better ways, and I'm just not smart enough to figure it all out. All we can do is hope that someone out there understands all that is going on in this world and that person has the wisdom to lead us in the right direction."

"Amen to that."

Jeb continued. "Final thought, if you will. This idea is not original with me, except that I have thought about it so much I have come to identify it as my own. The thought... Why do we allow our elder statesmen to make war and then send our young men to fight them? I can't help but to wonder this as I look at young Jesse. Men like Jesse and his younger brother are the men who must fight this war. God bless them, everyone of them, but why?"

Helen entered the room in time to hear the last two sentences. She stopped all movement and looked first at Jesse, then her father, her uncle, and Jeb. "I don't know what all of you were talking about, but Jesse doesn't have to fight in any war.

Jess, I need a buggy ride, right now." Most uncharacteristic of Helen she abruptly turned and exited the room in a huff, and without realizing it she exited carrying the same cookies she had brought in for the men. Helen did not like what she had heard.

Helen and Jesse took a buggy ride and were gone from the house until dark. Jesse dropped Helen off at the front of the house without coming into the house himself. Although Edward asked, Helen refused to give any explanation of where they had been or of what they had discussed; and the sensitive Kellys had the courtesy not to push the point. Helen retired to bed early that night, and her parents stayed up later than usual, fretting about Helen's well-being. No one ever determined what transpired between Helen and Jesse on that rainy Sunday afternoon.

Monday through Friday that week Helen received a postcard from Jesse. Friday's card, dated June 29, read:

> Dear Helen,
> I expect to arrive in town shortly after noon on Sat. I hope the
> weather is nice. Give my regards to your parents.
> I remain Cy. T.B.
> Jesse

Saturday, the 30th of June, was a beautiful day. Jesse had plans for this day which included several hours of alone time with Helen. Indeed, he was a chipper young man when he arrived at the Kelly house. Helen had never been to the farm where Jesse was employed, and today Helen was going to see his house and look at the land that Jesse worked with such pride.

Mrs. Kelly met Jesse as he arrived at the door. "Good afternoon, Jesse. Helen will be right down. I must say that she is rather excited about your outing today and she has prepared a special picnic lunch. Her dress and shoes have been laid out for three days. I would guess she is looking forward to this day, wouldn't you?"

"As am I, Mrs. Kelly. As I'm sure you know, your daughter is a very special person and I care deeply for her. If she's happy, then I'm happy."

"I hope that deep care you speak of also involves honor and respect for her. She's very young, Jesse, and she thinks the world of you. She is special to us, too, and we would not want her to get hurt. Once innocence is lost, it is gone forever. You remember that."

"I understand and you have my word. I would never intentionally do anything that would hurt Helen. I hope you and Mr. Kelly realize that."

Mrs. Kelly felt reassured. "We do, and thank you for expressing it." Hearing Helen on the stairs Elizabeth Kelly announced the presence of her youngest daughter. "Oh, here she comes. There is a gentleman at the door, and I think he would rather see you than talk to me. Should I ask him?" Before any answer was given, Mrs. Kelly realized that Jesse was politely waiting outside. "Oh my, where are my manners? Jesse, please come in."

Elizabeth watched from the porch as Jesse and her youngest daughter rode east on Michigan Avenue. Elizabeth felt mixed emotions. She was happy for Helen, although she felt concern that her not yet fifteen-year-old daughter cared so much for a man six and one-half years her senior, honorable as he might be.

Heading in the general direction of the farm, they traveled east to the Arnold turnoff before traveling several country roads. Jesse knew the land well and his knowledge was revealed, not only in his descriptions of the land, but in his admiration of particular parcels. He identified the fields best for grain production, or suitable pasture areas, and he was cognizant of drainage patterns and the perk factor of different soils. He seemed to know future possibilities of the land, as well as its limitations. Helen was impressed.

"I'm bringing you this way so you can see the land, the exact land that some call the best farm land in the state. It is flat prairie land with rich topsoil several feet deep. I do believe this land will grow anything. Wish I owned about a hundred and sixty acres of it, but that will never happen now. Farmland is too expensive. Had I been born twenty-five years earlier, you never know, I might be a rich farmer today."

Helen giggled. "I for one am glad you were not born twenty-five years earlier. Had you been, I'll bet we would not be here together. Would you rather own one hundred sixty acres, or have me as your sweetheart?"

"Silly question, I would rather have the land." Jesse tried to look straight ahead without changing his serious facial expression, but he could not do it. Instead he looked at Helen, and said, "There are several Helens in the world, but there is only one, one hundred and sixty acres. Did I say that right or did I get something mixed up?"

Helen looked at him, squinting her eyes, and gently shaking her fist. "Listen here, buster. I want you to know that I would trade you in for one good building lot in town. Come to think about it, any lot in town would do. You had better mind your p's and q's."

"Yes, of course, I will. Thanks for the warning. Let's get back to the land that I don't own any of, before I get in real trouble. It's wonderful farm land, but do you know what it lacks? It lacks rugged beauty. If you want to see beautiful land with rivers and forests and hills, you won't find it in this county. You'll find that kind of land in Pike County or maybe Scott County. However, here I will stay. I love this land too. I even think the air is better here. We're about five miles from Jacksonville, and yet, on a clear night you can look across this flat land and see the overhead glow from the electric lights of Jacksonville. I know that is hard to believe, but it's true. Every night before I go to bed I look and I'll bet I can see the lights three or four nights a week. If you stay up long enough, you can see the dimming glow as the lights are gradually turned off. At least, I think that's what I see. I've decided that your house is due west of my house, so each night I look and pretend I'm seeing your lights. Kind of sweet, or kind of stupid, I don't know which."

"Sweet."

"Look ahead, there she be—that's my home you're seeing. Do you see the big house surrounded by all the outbuildings?"

"Yes."

"Well, that's not my house." Jesse paused and waited for a response to his humor, but none was forthcoming. He continued his description. "See the barn? About fifty yards beyond the barn is a small, white frame house with a fence around it. That's my private palace. Actually it shows up pretty good, and that's because I just put a fresh coat of whitewash on it." Jesse continued talking describing all the different farm objects to her. It became quite apparent that Jesse was proud of his agricultural work, proud of his agricultural knowledge. Helen intently listened, mentally absorbing all that she could as she was beginning to understand that her beau was truly a proud farm boy.

Jesse hitched the horse and buggy in the barnyard. The couple walked around the farm site for almost an hour, partly to show Helen the farm, but mostly to show Helen to anyone within seeing distance. Although he was proud of where he worked, he was more proud of Helen. "Usually, it's pretty active around this place, except that today is Saturday and most everyone is in town. Pretty nice place, huh? I should know the answer to this question, but I don't. Have you ever lived on a farm?"

Shaking her head, she answered. "No, I haven't. We have lived on the edge of town, never in the country. As you were talking earlier I was thinking how little I really know about the farm. Sorry."

The answer somewhat surprised Jesse. "No electricity, no paved streets, otherwise I suspect it is not a lot different."

Surprised by his comment she revealed her feelings in her retort. "I suspect there is a lot of difference." Once Helen observed Jesse's reaction to her words, she realized that her one spoken sentence had been too blunt. Without intent, she had offended Jesse and felt ashamed. In a dramatic fashion she stepped to the forefront, put her hands in the air, and began to mock herself. "What about grocery stores or shopping? What about if you want to visit someone? What about schools? Where are the parks and benches? Where are all the people? What about walks at night without streetlights? How can you sit out on the porch with all these flies? What about all these animals? I've never come out my front door and looked at a cow before. No, I would say there is more than a little difference, I would say there is a big difference. Like the difference between day and night."

"I'm sorry, Helen. I thought you would like it here. Boy, was I wrong."

"Now you look here, Jesse A. Moore. If you can point out the big house and then tell me you don't live there, surely I can poke fun, too. There is supposed to be humor in my words."

At first Jesse continued to look at Helen, not at all certain there was intended humor. Finally he smiled and said, "You had me going there for a while. Your words sounded pretty serious to me, but if you say it was humor, humor it is. Now before I take one more step, I want to hear you say something nice about my house, even if your words are humorously nice."

"I love that house. It looks like a building that houses a great man. Do you have any idea who lives there, because I know I would like him?"

"I'll bet you would at that. Come on! I want to show you the house." Jesse gave Helen a tour of his small house, pointing out all the improved features resulting from his efforts. His pride was more than obvious, as was Helen's admiration for him when he showed his humble abode without embarrassment nor boastfulness. After almost an hour of looking at the house and surroundings, Jesse encouraged Helen to sit on his porch as he fetched cool water from the well. "Some say they can't taste the difference in water, but to me this is the best water I've ever had. How did you like my house? I don't mean that I own the house, it's just the house where I live."

"I like the house fine, it's you, it's perfect. Jess, are you nervous? You don't seem yourself today."

"I'm about as nervous as a man can get. I've got something important to ask you, but now I've got another issue at hand, an inner conflict to consider. I'm worried about the honorable factor."

"What in the world are you talking about? Make sense!"

"This morning I promised your mother I would be honorable. I think, I certainly hope what I'm about to say is honorable. Well, anyway, here goes." Jesse straightened his sitting position and cleared his throat. "If you don't mind, I would like for you to wait until I have finished before you say anything. As you know I am very fond of you. More to the point, I'm in love with you, and I want to spend the rest of my life with you. I know that you are not quite fifteen yet, and that I'm twenty-one which normally would be a big difference, except in our case I don't think it is. I'm not rich, except I do have a little money saved and I have a strong back and I'm willing to work hard to provide for you. If you say yes, this is where we would live at least for the time being. If after a while you don't like it, we can move anywhere, even to town if you wanted to, I guess. I know we haven't talked about such things, but I want a large family, and for some reason I think you do too. I hope so because I sure want a family—with you as the mother and me as the father. It would be all right with me if we had a dozen kids, because I think we would be good parents and I can only imagine how great our kids would be. In brief, I want you to marry me and I'm not done talking yet, but I want you to know that where we live, and how many children we have is not cast in stone. The idea that I want to marry you and have children with you is cast in stone." Jesse paused and took a deep breath. Helen started to say something and he interrupted her. "Wait, I have more to say.

"This war has got me in an uproar, and I'm afraid if we don't marry now, something might happen that would spoil our opportunity. That's the reason I'm springing it on you now without any warning. I think we need to get married right away, without making a big deal about it, before someone talks us out of it. Things in this world are changing so fast. I learned a long time ago that you can't take even the most simple things in life for granted. None of us are ever sure what tomorrow has in store for us. If you agree to marry me, I want us to do it soon, and there is one more thing. I believe I am an honorable person, at least I try to be. I state here and now, if you agree to marry me I will honor and respect you for the rest of our lives. That is the one thing of real value that I can offer you—love and honor for life. I will love you forever, and I will forever honor you."

Jesse leaned back in his chair and placed his hands on his lap with his fingertips on one hand touching the fingertips on his other hand. "I think I have finished now. I hope I said everything the way it needed to be said. Now it's your turn to talk."

Flattered but speechless, Helen sat motionless in her chair. Almost two minutes passed before she found the emotional courage to give a response. "I... I... I don't know how to answer. I am so happy and I love you too. That's not it. My answer to the question of marriage is yes. I love you and I will marry you. Your other proposal is not as easy to answer. I simply have not thought of an immediate marriage. No, that's not it either. Now you've got me nervous and I'm not talking right either. I want to marry you, but I don't know what my folks will say, I just don't know. I have said from the beginning and you understand that I can't hurt them, especially at this point in their lives when they have had so much hurt already. This is going to be a shock to them, and they may need some time."

"Would it be better if I asked them, sort of formal like?"

"I don't know, I don't think so. Since we have decided to do it, get married I mean, I think I should be the one to ask them for their permission or certainly for their blessing. I'm worried less about that, more about the timing of it all. I can't go home and say that I'm going to get married this week. I'm almost certain that they have considered the possibility of our marriage, just not the urgency of it. Tell me again why it needs to be soon."

A hopeful Jesse smiled. "To me it's simple. I don't want to lose you, and I learned a long time ago that no one knows what tomorrow holds. That's the best I can say it."

"I'm not sure, let me think a minute. First, let me ask you a question, and I want a truthful answer. Are you thinking about enlisting in the army?"

"I am not. That's the furthest thing from my mind. However, as you know, I just registered for the draft so I suppose I could be drafted, and if drafted I will go willingly."

"Am I correct that if someone has a dependent, the army won't draft you, at least that is what they say?"

"I don't know the answer to that question. I have heard it said, whether it is true or not I don't know. That's not the point. I would not get married to avoid the army, and I'm surprised you might think that. Times are changing and we don't know the future. I would guess, if this war goes on long enough, the government will take any man they want when they want. Again I say, that is not the point. I want to marry you for the best of all reasons—I love you and I want you to be my wife. I want it now."

Helen was not certain that she totally understood the urgency, but she was not going to ask again. She felt her question had somehow hurt Jesse, and she was not going to push the point any longer. Helen felt wedged between two different hurts. She would hurt her parents if she married, and hurt Jesse if she did not marry him right away. She was unprepared to make such a choice. "Let me think, Jess, let me think." The couple sat on the porch, Helen in agonizing silence and Jesse patiently waiting for Helen to sort out some details. After almost ten minutes of thinking, Helen broke the silence. "When did you have in mind?"

"I was hoping for this Monday, July 2. Before long, maybe in a week or so, the wheat harvest will begin and as you know I will be very busy. If we married Monday, we will have some time together before the harvest. Everyone gets the Fourth off work, and if I play my cards right, I think I can get some extra time off. I hoped that Monday morning I could come to town early and we would get our license and get married in the afternoon. At least that was my plan if you agreed."

Helen gave no immediate response. After what seemed like a long time to Jesse, but actually less than five minutes, Helen spoke. "The answer to getting married on Monday is yes with one qualifier. After our picnic lunch today I need to go home and explain it all to Mom before Dad gets home from work. I'm hoping that Mom will help me with Dad. If I can convince them, and I will put my all into it, then we will do it on Monday. If I cannot convince them, then when we meet tomorrow we will work out another alternative, providing that you agree to such an arrangement. That's the best I can do. I promise you I will do all I can, except you need to understand that I just cannot out and out hurt them. Do you understand?"

"I do," he answered before he granted a huge smile. "Oops, did you hear what I just said? One might think I'm practicing the words, I do, so that when the day comes I say them just right." Jesse moved next to Helen, warmly embracing her. After listening to Helen express her devotion to her parents, Jesse now had more reason to love her. Helen was truly a compassionate, sensitive person. "Without question today is the happiest day of my life. I know I keep saying that everyday, but it's true. Each day with you makes me happier than the day before, and today is the best of the best. I believe a celebration is in order."

Helen was so pleased with Jesse's words that she could hardly contain herself. "Me too, I'm overflowing with joy! I'm so happy I can't even talk right. Yea for you, yea for me, yea for us." Helen broke free of Jesse's embrace, jumped off the porch, put her hands in the air and yelled at the top of her petite lungs, "Yea, yea, yea!" At this moment no one was around to hear the proclamations of joy, except for the dairy cows in the barnyard, and two of the cows looked at Helen as though they were annoyed. Helen looked directly at the cows and then spoke. "Yea, yea, yea, we are happy, like it or not, yea, yea, yea!"

An amused Jesse followed Helen off the porch and joined in. "Yeah, yea, yea, yea. Let it be known that Helen and Jesse have announced to the world and to a few cows that as of two-thirty this afternoon they are engaged to be married. Marriage, yes, exact day of marriage, still uncertain. Nevertheless, yea, yea, yea."

The young couple chose to celebrate by eating their picnic lunch on the bank of a nearby creek. A grand feeling, an emotional high consumed both of them. Starry-eyed and exuberant Helen and Jesse sat together eating their picnic lunch under the shade of a tree on the bank of a flowing creek on that lovely June day in 1917. Blissful and with innocence they celebrated their happiness, their commitment. No artist could have painted a more beautiful image.

They returned to South Jacksonville a full four hours before sunset so that Helen could undertake her dreaded task of explaining the plans to her parents. At Helen's request Jesse did not remain in town, returning to the farm instead. He fully intended to tend his garden, but instead he took a long walk following the bank of the west branch of Mauvaisterre Creek. Although he could not have been happier, he felt that he should be by Helen's side as she talked to her parents. He now questioned the wisdom of his earlier decision allowing Helen to ask permission alone, and yet, he strongly believed in Helen's ability to determine what was best. His ambivalent feelings tugged at him the entire evening, leaving him anxious and concerned about Helen. He was a man in love tormented by the thought that his betrothed might be hurting or in need of him.

Before retiring that night Jesse found peace with his conflicting thoughts. His confidence in Helen prevailed and, if she wanted to be alone when she explained to her parents, she would be alone. He would know by tomorrow the outcome of Helen's conversation with her parents. From his chair on the front porch he looked for the glow of the lights from Jacksonville, deriving considerable pleasure from knowing that Helen was somewhere beneath the glow. Jesse was a man in love, on the threshold of marriage, full of hope. His final thoughts before slumber were of Helen Kelly, soon to be Helen Moore. With all his being he sensed true happiness.

As it turned out Helen had made a wise decision. After Helen had drawn on and used all of her powers of persuasion, and they were considerable, her parents consented to the Monday wedding. Helen's plan had worked. She first convinced her mother, and her mother helped convince her father. When Jesse arrived at Michigan Avenue on Sunday afternoon he received affirmation, not by words, but from Helen's radiant smile. Mr. and Mrs. Kelly were waiting in the living room allowing Helen the opportunity to greet Jesse before they went outside to welcome him to the family. Jesse had never felt such elation.

Preliminary wedding plans were discussed the same afternoon. The happy couple selected not to officially announce the plans, preferring to keep the wedding private and simple. Since Jesse's family in Milton was unaware of the upcoming marriage, Helen believed it best not to inform friends and family in Jacksonville, leaving only her parents aware of the plans. Jesse encouraged Helen to tell her other family members, but Helen stayed the course insisting on a private wedding without notification to anyone. Helen, concerned that some family members might discourage the wedding because of her age or the suddenness of the event, really felt she was protecting Jesse's wishes of a quick wedding by not encouraging additional input. It had been difficult enough for Jesse to explain the urgency of the marriage to Helen, and for Helen to explain to her parents; thus she was unwilling to give the explanation to others. However, more than anything else it was an effort by Helen to protect her intended from unnecessary questioning. Indeed, they were a couple in love, each desiring to protect the other.

The naive couple, almost totally unaware of the marriage procedure, set forth on that afternoon to plan details of the wedding. Both had attended other weddings, but neither was familiar with all that went into the planning. Mr. and Mrs. Kelly assisted them with the plans and arrangements. Helen and Jesse, accompanied by Mrs. Kelly in the event that Helen needed written consent, would acquire the marriage license from the courthouse on Monday morning. Legal age for marriage in Illinois was eighteen or with parental consent. They preferred a religious ceremony instead of a civil ceremony, if possible. Helen and Jesse wanted Mr. and Mrs. Kelly to stand up with them, but Mr. Kelly declined, feeling he should not miss work. Two burials were scheduled for that Monday and he felt obligated to be at the cemetery. His decision to work on that day revealed more about his responsible nature and personal commitment to the job than anything else. Mrs. Kelly, honored that her youngest daughter wanted her to be at the wedding, consented and made arrangements for their friend and neighbor, Mrs. Hazlett, to be the other person in attendance. Mrs. Kelly wanted to provide a bouquet of flowers for the bride, but in keeping with the theme of simplicity, Helen rejected the kind offer.

An embarrassed Jesse realized he had no ring for Helen. The more they discussed the wedding the more unresolved necessary details seemed to emerge until, fortunately, their mutual unpreparedness actually became a source of amusement. Finally, after an hour of considering appropriate clothing and all other necessary details, they found closure when Helen announced, "Ready or not, we are ready." By 3:30 Sunday afternoon the hasty preparations were completed. Tomorrow was to be their wedding day.

Later that afternoon they visited with Helen's church minister and, although he believed it to be a hurried decision, he agreed to perform the ceremony at his home on the following day, July 2, 1917. With the ceremony now planned the engaged couple returned to the Kelly house for supper and spent the remainder of the day sitting and visiting on the front porch. Shortly before 8:00 p.m. Jesse left for home; but, before he departed, the couple reaffirmed their love for each other as they bade their final farewell as an unmarried couple. Happiness, compounded by hope and great expectations, filled their young, innocent hearts. They believed that no obstacle in life was too great and that no challenge in life could break their bond of love, because they dared to dream that life would always be as splendid as it was this day.

Jesse's solitary ride back to the farm in no way diminished his optimism. He intuitively sensed, maybe for the first time in his life, that the shattered pieces of misfortune might be in decline. Alone on the country roads without another soul nearby he yelled loud and clear, "It is about time. I'm so lucky I can't believe it. Tomorrow I will be a married man, Helen will be my wife. Yea, yea, yea."

Monday morning Jesse, Helen, and Mrs. Kelly arrived at the courthouse by 9:30 a.m., and the fact that Mrs. Kelly had accompanied them was most fortuitous as parental consent was required before the license was issued. Their marriage license read that both parents had consented. With official permission in hand they immediately returned to the Kelly home for a quick lunch before dressing for the ceremony.

The bride to be dithered about her bedroom until 2:00 when she emerged downstairs looking radiant, dressed in her navy blue linen suit, matching hat and high heels. The groom, at ease on the surface but nervous in fact, patiently waited until his first glimpse of Helen made him glow with excitement. Attired in a brown cloth suit with matching tie, shoes shined to perfection, he looked every bit the part of a nervous groom. Mrs. Kelly shed tears of joy when she observed the bride and groom as each first saw the other.

The marriage party of four persons arrived at 620 West College Avenue, the home of Pastor F. A. McCarty, the minister of the Central Christian Church. The nuptial ceremony commenced at 3:00 and the couple was joined in holy matrimony by 3:10. The ceremony was simple, exactly as they wished. Elizabeth Kelly and Mrs. C. M. Hazlett officially witnessed the ceremony, Mrs. F. A. McCarty observed.

With no planned reception the simple wedding concept carried into the evening and the newlyweds ate their first meal as a married couple at the Kelly house. By early evening they were en route to their future rural abode. The parents of the bride watched as their youngest daughter left their nest with her husband to experience the bliss of marriage. Although Mrs. Kelly was saddened by the thought of Helen leaving, she was happy for her and intended to support her daughter in her marriage anyway that she could. Mr. Kelly was sad, but philosophical. Once the newlyweds were beyond her sight, Elizabeth lamented, "Helen is so young. I pray to God that she's not too young."

"Do you have doubts, Elizabeth? Have we made a mistake? Should we have put our foot down and said no?"

"Heavens, I hope not. I don't think so. Jesse is such a fine man, and he cares for Helen as much as humanly possible. Helen simply worships him. I was just thinking of Helen's age and inexperience in life. I really believe they are well suited for each other, it just won't be easy, that's all. I don't need to tell you that, we have found many times over that life doesn't always flow in the direction one thinks. No, I have very few doubts. I just worry, as I suppose any mother would worry. They will make it, and we will be here to help, if needed."

"Of course we will be here if they need us. Surely they know that. Be that as it may, I will always wonder what might have been for Helen. She was always a little special, always my little girl. Deep in my heart I thought that one day she might become a teacher. She did well in school and she so loved younger children, almost as much as they loved her. One can't help but wonder."

Elizabeth totally understood her husband's feelings. Perhaps she shared the same sentiment, but if she felt it, she did not express it. "We can't think that, Edward, we must look ahead from where we now are. Maybe Helen has a greater destiny now, than you or I can see. Who knows what lies ahead? Helen will do right, whatever she does, and I believe she will make a great wife, a great mother."

"I hope so. With all my heart I wish happiness for them, but I wouldn't put much stock in destiny."

"Well stated, Edward. Perhaps in their case, happiness and destiny are one in the same."

Although eagerly anticipating the experience of living on a farm, Helen was as unfamiliar with rural living as she was with her new house, only having visited the site once. Clearly, many new experiences were in store for her. Scattered rain showers accompanied the couple as they rode to their new home, which required Jesse to give his full attention to the road, and also made Helen aware of one disadvantage of country living—no paved roads. In all fairness the elements were only a minor distraction for the bride and groom, as few conditions could have diminished the much anticipated splendor of their first evening together. They arrived at the farm with less than one hour of remaining daylight. The low clouds indicated a dark night ahead, and although Jesse had the house in proper order for his bride, he needed to acquaint Helen with her new surroundings, in and outside the house. Jesse realized how critical his brief refresher tour of the homestead was to be for Helen when she asked about the location of the outhouse, and the whereabouts of a lamp if she needed one. Fortunately, most obstacles for Helen were viewed with humor which made the night even more special. Jesse fondly referred to Helen that night as his town bride, and Helen referred to Jesse as her country boy.

Before retiring Jesse completed his necessary farm chores while Helen unpacked and put away her personal belongings. This was Helen's private time to prepare herself for her first night of marriage, an event she anticipated but with some concern as innocence and naiveness generated apprehensions and self doubts. However, once the couple retired to bed, and Jesse demonstrated gentleness and understanding, Helen found more ease. Both were physically excited, but awkwardly timid. Passion yielded to tender love and rendered an expression of pure love when their marriage was duly and affectively consummated. Few words were spoken, none were needed. They found sleep that night in the arms of one another. All was as it should have been.

The following morning Jesse and Helen prepared breakfast and washed the dishes together. Just as it became obvious that Jesse would be required to help Helen adjust in her role of running the household, it also became apparent that Helen would be an eager and fast learner. Helen was not inept, just unaware. As the bride looked around the kitchen trying to become aware of her new surroundings, she casually stated, "What a beautiful oilcloth on the kitchen table. Did you pick that out?"

"I picked it out for you. It's brand new, used the first time this morning. I figured you would like it because it's red. Red is your favorite color, isn't it?"

"It sure is. How did you know that? Have I told you that before?"

"Only about a dozen times. Really, you didn't have to tell me. Everything you see that is red, you say it's pretty."

"Well, Jess Moore. You're rather confident and think you know all about me, don't you? You know there might be a few surprises in store for you." Looking back at the oilcloth, and touching it with her fingertips while sprouting a big grin, Helen continued. "It's not the prettiest cloth I've ever seen, but I'll made do. It's actually an off red, if you must know."

Jesse threw back his head and gave a loud laugh, almost a defiant laugh. "I'm glad that you will make do, and I'm also glad we're not going to have our first disagreement over a shade of red. I've got to learn when you are funning me and when you have got your dander up."

"It won't be hard to learn. I promise that you will know when my dander is up."

"Good. I'll take that as words to the wise. What do I do when you get your dander up?"

"Simple. You do nothing. It's too late then."

"Fair enough, I have been forewarned."

"The secret is not in remembering the warning, but in not getting my dander up in the first place." Helen had said the words in jest, and she waited for Jesse's response. When there was no response, she added, "Another thing you need to remember. My bark is worse than my bite." This time she got an amicable smile from her husband. This conversation reminded Helen that she had married a sensitive man and, most likely, any inconsiderate words from one he loved, could and would hurt him. She needed to remember such. "After all I wouldn't want you to think you are living under a reign of tyranny."

"No worry here. In fact, I feel like I might be living under a reign of happiness." Jesse rose from his chair and put his fist into the air above his head in a gesture of triumph. "Now since this is our first day married, I thought a treat might be in store, so get yourself ready." He took out his pocket watch and briefly studied it. "In exactly one hour and fifty one minutes you and I are catching a train to Pearl, Illinois. From there we take a brief buggy ride to Milton, and therein is the treat. You are going to meet four members of my family, and I assure you that each one will make a lasting impression, all for different reasons. You will meet my father, my Aunt Mary, brother Elzie, and sister Frieda. I sent them a telegram yesterday, before the wedding, and they are expecting us for lunch. Now get ready, we don't want to miss our train."

"Oh, Jess, must you do everything so lickety-split?"

"That's a strange question coming from you. You're the one who does everything lickety-split. I don't do things fast as much as I just do things on the spur of the moment. In this situation, I wanted to surprise you. There is certainly a lot to learn about the other person, isn't there?"

"Why didn't you tell me last night? Can you miss work? What do I wear? How long are we going to stay? If I'm going to meet them, I need to make a good impression."

"Exactly one hour and forty-nine minutes. I wanted to surprise you. Yes, I can miss work. Wear anything. You look beautiful, no matter what you wear. We'll come back tonight. You will make a good impression. I'm more worried about the impression they make on you. Exactly one hour and forty eight minutes."

They made it to the train station with one-half hour to spare. Neither had ridden a train before, and they were excited as they talked and looked around the waiting room. The train arrived, they boarded, and Helen sat by the window. Just as the train was leaving the station and the people on the platform were waving good-bye to others on the train, Helen saw her nephew, Ed Jackson, looking at her with eyes of disappointment. Without thinking about the circumstances, she proudly waved at her nephew, but got no response from him. He looked so sad and it looked as if he was saying her name, Aunt Helen. Jesse, having met her nephew on Christmas day, also waved without a response. Helen spoke in a distressed voice. "What's wrong with Ed? I know he sees me."

Jesse started to laugh. "He sees you, all right. What he doesn't know, however, is that you are married. He thinks you are going out of town with me as a single girl."

"Oh poor Ed. No wonder he looks disappointed." Helen also started to laugh. "What happens now is going to be most interesting. Will he tell his mother? If he does, will Hattie tell Mother? We have an interesting story line here. I guess we'll find out when we get back." The misunderstood situation remained funny, amusing Helen all the way to Pearl.

Much to Jesse's delight Frieda and Elzie were waiting for them at the train station in Pearl. Before Jesse could introduce his bride, Frieda was hugging Helen. Elzie waited his turn and politely introduced himself with a handshake followed by an amicable hug. "You must be quite a woman to be able to snag my big brother. He's a good catch, you know. Come to think about it what I really want to know is how did he snag you? He's the one who made out like a bandit."

Helen was pleased. "Thank you, Elzie, but it is only fair to tell you that Jess has already warned me about the Elzie charm. I've been warned to take everything you say with a grain of salt."

Elzie was amused. "She's wise in addition to being a looker. Normally Jesse's advice is pretty good but in this case I have expressed my true feelings." Elzie looked at Jesse. "I like her already. Are there any more like her left in Jacksonville?"

Frieda took charge, holding Helen's arm as they walked to the wagon. Helen and Frieda became instant friends, much to Jesse's delectation. Watching the female interaction Jesse suddenly realized that Frieda and Helen were the same age, which meant Elzie was older than Helen. This thought not only amused him, it made him see his siblings in a different light. Frieda was a young lady, Elzie was an adult.

Aunt Mary was waiting on her porch at the house in Milton. As usual, Aunt

Mary was a gracious lady, who immediately won Helen's heart. There was absolutely no doubt that Aunt Mary approved of Helen which pleased Jesse to no end. Jesse spoke to his brother. "So far, so good. Where's Dad?" Elzie could not help but smile as he was having similar thoughts. They both wondered what Helen would think of their plain spoken, sometimes coarse, father. They were about to find out.

Erastus entered the house by the back door, mumbling as he entered. "What's all the racket about? It's 12:00, lunch time, let's eat." Soon he saw Helen and walked directly toward her. "Hello, young lady, my name is Erastus. You can call me whatever pleases you. I'm the father of this group of wild ones. I'm a brother to that woman over there. What do I call you?"

Jesse stepped between them and said, "Dad, this is my wife, Helen. We were married yesterday in Jacksonville. Helen, this is my father. He's cantankerous by nature, so don't you let his manner offend you. He's that way with everybody until he gets to know you, and then he is really cantankerous." Everyone laughed except Erastus.

Aunt Mary had prepared a fine meal. Erastus immediately went back to work after eating, Elzie stayed and visited for over an hour, and the other four visited all afternoon. At 6:30 Elzie drove Helen and Jesse to the Pearl train station, and they were back in Jacksonville, out to the farm before dark. It had been a long, exhausting day, but well worth the time invested. Helen appreciated all the effort on the part of her husband for her to meet with his family. "I like your family very much. How come you don't spend more time with them?"

"It's just not convenient, really not possible given where I live. I'm very close to Elzie, of course, we grew up together. Frieda is precious, and I will always love that girl. Aunt Mary is Aunt Mary. They don't come any better, although she has gone through some mighty tough times. Right before I left Aunt Mary's house in 1910, she almost had a nervous breakdown. I've never figured out how much of the strain was caused by me and Elzie. Quite a bit, I suspect. I will always be indebted to Aunt Mary and Uncle George because they took me and Elzie in when we were just kids. They were the ones who really raised us. I'm not sure what would have happened to us, had it not been for them. But Dad is the one Aunt Mary is closest to. I've never understood it, but she gains strength from being around my dad. They are good as brother and sister."

Helen was intrigued by all he said. "Erastus is such an unusual name, I've never heard it before. Do you know how he got the name?"

"Erastus means beloved in Greek. It's a biblical name, like mine. Erastus was a missionary sent by Paul to Macedonia. It's also a family name. My grandmother's maiden name was Paul, and she had a brother named Erastus, who died in the Civil War. Do you see the connection? Erastus Paul. We assume that is where the name came from. I understand her family was very religious, but my father is anything but religious."

"Explain what you mean by anything but religious."

"I mean he is not a religious man, not a churchgoing man. I don't mean he's a sinner or evil, because he's not. He believes, he is just not religious. Dad is just different. He has his own way of looking at things. Everything has got to be his way, regardless of what others think. For years I resented him giving us away at such young ages, but I guess he didn't have much choice. Dad was never the same man after Mother died. Her death took a lot of the good out of him, or so Aunt Mary says. No doubt, he's a hard man, made harder by constant struggles in life. He's had a hard life you know. He's getting older now, and he has a lot of aches and pains; and he still works hard with those mules, although he is doing more metal work now, which is not very easy, either, but it's easier than working with the mules. Let me think. He'll be sixty-two in November. You know when you think about it, it's sort of sad. Take for example, you and me. We are young and healthy, just starting out, and we expect our lives to get better. We see a bright future. On the other hand, his life is just the opposite. He believes that his life is behind him and views the future as bleak. Each day is better and better for us, and each day for him is not as good as the previous day. I know he shouldn't feel that way, but he does. He's a hard man to understand, and not easy to describe. In time I think you'll understand. We'll see.

"Enough talk about him. You still have more family to meet, but probably not right away. You still have two brothers and two sisters to meet. You'll like my sisters, but I'm not so sure about my brothers, especially Arch. Time will tell.

"By the way, Helen, do you know what tomorrow is?"

"Sure I know. Tomorrow is the Fourth of July, Independence Day. The second full day of our marriage. Why?"

"Because tomorrow, after my morning chores are done, I don't have to work for the rest of the day and tomorrow you are in for another treat."

"Oh, good. What?"

"I'm not telling, other than it's a fun thing and you don't have to meet anymore family. I'll give you a few hints, but I won't tell you even if you guess. Hint number one—we are going to a small town and it is within a ten mile radius of here. Hint number two—it's better than a carnival and it requires a picnic lunch. Hint number three—it lasts all day and well into the evening."

"Hum. Please tell me."

"Nope. I'll tell you in the morning. I'm not spoiling the secret."

Helen snuggled up to Jesse, and pleadingly said, "Pretty please, with sugar on it."

Jesse relented as he intended all along. "Okay, if you insist. We're going to

221

Franklin. They have burgoo and an all day, fourth of July, celebration— carnival, fireworks display, entertainment, and the whole shooting match. What do you think? We'll stay until we're ready to come home."

"I think it sounds fantastic. I love burgoo. I've had more activity in the last three days than I have had in the last three years. Jess Moore, you're going to wear me out, maybe."

The young couple arrived at Franklin by 11:30 a.m., almost too late to get any of the locally popular burgoo. Helen was disappointed that the servers were dipping from the bottom of the last kettle. "Be careful, Jess, sometimes you find bones at the bottom of the kettle. No matter where you go, they always seem to run out of burgoo about half way through the day. Why don't they make more?"

Jesse took the question seriously. "That's a good question and I'm sure there is good reason. You know some are here at sunrise because folks say the best tasting burgoo is from the top of the kettle, although I wouldn't know. I know some come early, buy a panful to eat later. Burgoo is good stuff. Also, I suppose the cooks don't want to make more than they will sell, not knowing how many people will be here. You know it takes twenty-four hours to cook that stuff. I'll bet they started the fires two nights ago, and started cooking early yesterday morning; and who knows how long it took to put all the ingredients together in the first place, and that doesn't count the time it took to secure the wild game. Just for curiosity, let's count the kettles."

Helen had already counted. "I counted forty kettles."

"There you go. I estimate each kettle to hold about thirty-five, maybe forty gallons, and if you multiply forty kettles by thirty-five or forty gallons, you got some burgoo."

"What's in burgoo anyway? I know that it is meat and vegetables in broth, but I mean what are the exact ingredients? Do you know?"

"I don't think anyone but a burgoo maker knows for sure. You do know that there are special cooks who make burgoo and I suspect they do not share the recipe with just anyone. It's my understanding that burgoo was first made in Kentucky and some of the pioneers brought the recipe with them when they came to Illinois. I assume the ingredients are reflective of the food native to that area. I know the meat is squirrel, rabbit, and chicken, and probably more than that. There are all kinds of vegetables. I suspect there is some syrup or molasses thrown in. When you think about it, it's probably just as well that we don't know the ingredients."

Helen smiled at the last comment. "Probably so, but whatever is in it, I love it. Jess, you sure do know a lot of things for a country boy. I'm so proud of you. You are a self-made, self-taught man. I admire that, more and more every day. I think you have found what many people are searching for—a truth of who you are and what you want in life. I feel very fortunate that you chose me as the one you wanted to marry."

"That is most kind of you to say, and you can continue to believe it if you want. Actually, I feel just the opposite—like a man that doesn't know much at all. Most of the things I know are common sense things that anyone can learn if they want to."

Helen admired his modesty. "Say what you want. You are a knowledgeable person."

"The truth of the matter is that I'm the lucky one. No doubt about that at all." Although the couple was in public view, and they both felt that their affection should be restrained in public, they, nevertheless, embraced. They were young, they were in love, and they were happy. Embarrassed or not, they hugged.

Helen made a declaration. "Jess, you are my North Star. If I can always have you in sight, I will always know where I am and where I should be going. I don't want you to respond to that, I just want you to know it." Jesse did not verbally respond, but he acknowledged the statement by gently squeezing Helen's hand.

As expected, the day was splendid. The crowd at the Franklin Burgoo numbered in the thousands, and both saw people they knew. It was with great delight that each used the words my wife or my husband as each introduced the other to friends and acquaintances. In a manner of speaking the Franklin Burgoo served as a coming out party for the newly married couple, or at least it accomplished the same purpose. Helen and Jesse Moore were not only married, they were announcing their new status to the world. It was a most satisfying feeling.

They waited for the fireworks display to end before they started home, about 11 o'clock in the evening. Expecting a tedious return to the farm because it was dark and the roads were somewhat unfamiliar, they were pleasantly surprised when the mass exodus of people in wagons, buggies, and automobiles lighted the way. Lights of various types extended on the road as far as the eye could see. Jesse was the first to exclaim the wonder. "Well this takes the cake. In all my years of traveling country roads at night, I have never seen the likes of this. This is like having streamer street lights to drive country roads. What an impressive sight this is. Helen, have you ever seen anything like this before?"

"I have in town before but never in the country. Maybe it's an omen, a sign of an easier life and better things to come." With a slight giggle, she continued. "Maybe it's not an omen at all. Maybe it shows us how many people like Franklin burgoo. Whatever it shows, it means that our trip home will be easier. You know what? I just had an idea. Why don't we make a wish together. I wish that in fifty years, providing we are willing and able, we come back here again and remember this night. Not that we shouldn't come back sooner, just that we should come back to Franklin on July 4, 1967. What about it? What's your wish?"

"Your wish is my wish. We'll do it." The last two miles of the trip they were alone, no other vehicles in sight, and the only artificial light came from the lantern on the buggy. They made it home, and thus they completed their third day of marriage.

Jesse was now behind in his farmwork. Thursday and Friday he worked well into the night catching-up with his neglected daily responsibilities, plus preparing for the upcoming wheat harvest. He had suffered no lost pay for missing work, and for that consideration he was determined not to shortchange the farm owner. Helen used the time to become familiar with her new home and to add a feminine touch to the interior of the house. Jesse noticed every little change, and his expressed appreciation encouraged Helen to do more. Each expended considerable effort to please the other and to learn the newfound boundaries of married life. Both were adjusting to their new roles of husband and wife as they laid the first bricks of a solid foundation for the future. It was a grand beginning, mostly because of concerted effort.

Helen and Jesse chose to spend their first Saturday night as a married couple on the town square in Jacksonville and appropriately used the opportunity to show off one other to the local folks. After the stores closed for the evening they rode to Michigan Avenue for a brief visit with the Kellys before returning home. It had been a long day, they were exhausted, and the thought of being home was comforting.

Once back at the farm Helen walked alone toward the house as Jesse pulled into the barn to unhitch the buggy and bed down the horse. When Helen neared the house she heard an unusual sound and thought she detected some movement in the shadows, inside the fence. There was a strong breeze and a full moon that night, and the blowing treetops created the illusion of movement on the ground. Helen was spooked. She cried out, "Who's there?" but there was no answer. Holding the lantern higher she looked again before advancing further, and this time with a firmer voice she said, "Identify yourself before I shoot." Before she could say anything else, she heard additional sounds, similar to whispering voices, emerge from behind the house. With due efficiency she backed away from the house, turned and scurried to the barn where she found Jesse putting Babe into the stall. With calm firmness, she stated, "Someone or some persons are messing around right outside our house. I told them I was going to shoot them and they skedaddled, I think. Anyway, I'm not going back there without you."

"I'll be right with you. Don't worry, it's probably just some animal that got past my fence." Jesse reached for his bullwhip which he kept mounted on the wall of the barn. "Just in case it's a mean animal." As they walked toward the house, Jesse twice snapped the whip which made a loud and distinct crack each time. Just hearing the crack of the whip made Helen feel better as she struggled to keep up with Jesse's pace. Helen waited at the gate as Jesse twice circumvented the outside of the house and occasionally snapped the whip. He could find nothing. "If there was some critter here, he's gone now. Let's go inside and look around, although I'm sure everything is all right. No telling what you heard. There are many strange noises in the country, especially at night. Don't worry, you'll get used to them." With lantern held high Jesse led the way into the house with Helen following closely behind. Everything appeared in order until they looked in the kitchen, when Jesse spoke with relief in his voice. "Well look at that."

"What?"

"Look on the table. If I'm not mistaken that is a chunk of Limburger cheese and a packet of saltines, and they are not there for us to eat." He bent over to smell the cheese. "Yep, no doubt, it's Limburger all right. I believe you surprised someone who came here to play a trick on us. I wish I knew who it was, and I would love to have seen the look on his face when you said you were going to shoot him."

"I'm not so sure. I saw something outside, not inside. I hope you're right. What's that stuff for anyway?"

"I'm not absolutely sure, but I assume they were going to melt the cheese on the stove, which leaves a horrendous smell, and I suppose they were going to crumble the crackers in our bed."

"Why?"

The naive question from Helen amused Jesse, but he attempted to answer. "Sort of like a... you know, a shivaree. It's a country tradition intended to disrupt newlyweds about bedtime. Sometimes they make a lot of noise so that the couple can't get on with their business. It's all kind of a mock serenade. It's a playful thing, not a mean one. Usually it's done by your friends."

Before Helen could respond a loud commotion erupted outside the house. Helen had never before heard such inharmonious sounds as pots and pans were unrhythmically banged together while another person was hitting the side of the house, another was stomping on the porch, and another was making moaning sounds to imitate the supernatural.

Jesse sat down at the table, looking as though he was absolutely delighted. "Yep, it's a shivaree all right. You may as well sit down and enjoy it, because I don't think it's going to stop right away. Tradition says that when it's all over, you can cook them breakfast if you want."

"Well, we might just start a new tradition. When it's all done we might just send them home without breakfast. They're making so much racket, I can't hear myself think. Why don't you go outside and tell them to stop?"

"No, that's not a good idea. There might be someone out there waiting to throw some stuff on you that you don't want on you. We better wait until they stop, unless you want to invite them inside."

"No sirree. I want that group in here about like I want a hole in my head. I'll sit down with you and wait, although I promise you I won't get the pleasure out of it that you seem to be getting." After about fifteen minutes the noise subsided, Jesse took Helen's hand and said, "We'll wait ten minutes or so, give them time to get out of here, and then we'll check outside to make sure everything is still in order. Now that wasn't so bad, was it?"

Sarcastically, Helen answered. "Oh no, it was wonderful. I will never forget those glorious sounds and I will always remember how comforting they were. Why, I should write this down so that I can tell my grandchildren about this wonderful experience." Jesse became amused with her comments. Helen walked from the table to look out the window, and just as she raised the window shade, a man making obnoxious facial expressions jumped in front of the window scaring Helen half to death. Then the noise resumed, only louder this time. She lowered the shade, walked back and sat down at the table. "I gather they aren't finished yet." Jesse roared with laughter until he noticed he was annoying Helen, at which point he turned his body so that she could not see him and continued laughing in a more restrained manner. He could not help himself, although he knew he was aggravating his wife. In a few minutes the noise ceased for a second time. Jesse and Helen quietly sat there for about fifteen minutes looking at each other without saying one word until Helen broke the silence. "I'm certainly not going to look out the window again. You tell me when you think it is safe to move."

"Not yet." The couple continued to wait in silence, never knowing when the annoying sounds might start again. The longer they waited the sillier they felt. Surely by now the visiting marauders had departed. "I better go outside and look around. No telling what mischief they have been up to. Do you want to wait here or go with me?"

"Go with you, I'm not about to stay in here by myself."

Carefully Jesse opened the back door. "So far, so good. Here, give me your hand and we'll take a closer look." They looked around the outside of the house and found nothing drastically out of order. They stood by the fence and looked in the distance, seeing nothing out of the ordinary.

"Look, Jess! There are no lights on at the big house or any other place for that matter. How anybody could sleep through that racket is beyond me." Helen looked in different directions until suddenly she was greeted with a loud clamor of pans just about face level. The noise so startled her that she anchored her hand on the top board of the four-foot picket fence and in one continual motion she hurled her body to the opposite side of the fence. Indeed, the leap was a remarkable feat for a woman less than five-feet in height. Landing on her feet but falling to her knees, she shouted, "Ow, that hurt." Looking back across the fence, she announced fair warning. "If I find the fool that scared me, I'm going to take those pans and pound his head with them. She attempted to climb back over the fence, but became most aggravated by her futile efforts and her inability to easily access the enclosed yard. Talking aloud the entire time, she followed the fence to the front gate. "I don't know who you are, buster, but you wait until I get there. I've got a surprise for you." She uttered additional words, except she mumbled so much that she was difficult to understand. However, there was no doubt that everyone within hearing range received her intended message. Jesse met her at the gate and, without saying anything, he walked with her to find the culprits. They found no one. Wanting to vent her anger Helen now had a club in her hand as she determinedly continued her vengeful pursuit. Fortunately, the intruders had left. Shortly, she noticed light coming from the big house, the barn, and other structures which made her realize that probably most everyone from around the area had been involved in the prank. She gave a big smile to Jesse and gently squeezed his hand. "I think we can go back in now. I suspect the party is over, don't you?"

"Are you okay?"

"Sure, I'm okay. I might have been a little angry a while ago, but now everything is fine. As a matter of fact, everything seems sort of funny now, and on second thought I might really tell my grand kids about this night. I told you that you would know when I got my dander up, didn't I?" Once they entered the house Helen hugged Jesse and spoke softly into his ear. "Now that wasn't so bad, was it, honey? I may be a townie, but I think I'm learning these country ways rather quickly. Don't you?"

"I do. I think I married a fast learner and I also think I don't want to get you angry, especially when you have a club near you."

"And I think I married a wise man, and he is getting wiser everyday."

Jesse placed the lantern on the kitchen table. "Oh Helen, look here!" Openly displayed on the kitchen table were a variety of items, including a skillet and a large pan, obviously intended as wedding presents. "They must have brought these items in here, after they lured us outside. Wasn't that nice of them?"

Helen was very pleased. "I feel bad now. They came here bearing gifts, and I threatened them with violence." With a grand smile Helen picked up the skillet, waved it and proclaimed, "If there are any more shivarees, now I've got the perfect weapon. I won't need to search for a club, anymore."

Jesse laughed. "If we do have any more visitors tonight, I'll bet they won't be the same ones as before. I'll bet you that all of them are still running from my enraged wife." They hugged again.

Their embrace was cut short by a knock on the door, followed by the sound of a familiar voice. "Hello, in there. Don't shoot me, and put down any clubs or pots and pans that you might be holding. I come in peace. This is brother Elzie. May I come in?"

Helen and the brothers visited until the wee hours of the morning and Sunday morning Elzie first helped Jesse with his catch-up farm work and then wisely used most of the remaining time to better know his brother's wife. Helen and Elzie quickly developed a positive chemistry. Jesse, of course, was pleased with the positive interaction between his brother and his wife. He was proud of his brother, and Helen was the cornerstone of his new life.

The identities of the participants in the shivaree were never identified to the young couple, although they determined that farmhands from as far as ten miles away had participated. Elzie professed ignorance about the event, never revealing any helpful information.

About mid afternoon on Monday Jesse unexpectedly returned home from the field. It was most uncharacteristic of him to leave work in the middle of the day, but he wanted to see Helen, if only for a few minutes. He found her on her knees scrubbing the kitchen floor, and instead of disturbing her work he opened the screen door, put his head inside and announced, "There may be someone in this world who has had a better first week of marriage than I have, but I doubt it. I know for certain that no one could be happier than I am." He closed the screen door and went back to the field.

Quickly, the reality of life set-in with a normal daily routine. Characteristic of most farmhands, Jesse worked hard and long hours from the beginning of the wheat harvest to the completion of the corn harvest. It was a good year for crop production, but not a year without farm problems. As expected, 1917 was a transitional year for many of the larger Illinois farms, and specifically for the farm where Jesse worked. Agriculture was shifting more to mechanized farming, a transition destined to demand fewer traditional farmworkers and to create more demand for equipment and mechanics. With higher commodity prices and more equipment needed, additional land was placed under cultivation. This fateful shift to large farm, grain production was already in progress and many were convinced that the handwriting was already on the wall. No one was certain of the exact effect these technological advances would bring, only that they would bring major economic and social change. Without owning land and with little prospect of ever owning any, Jesse, naturally, was concerned about his future in farming as well he should have been.

Unlike life in the city, living conditions on the farm were little different from one hundred years earlier, thus adjustment to rural living was never easy for Helen. With her husband working long hours she was often alone and she felt isolated. Knowing that her husband preferred to live on the farm, Helen seldom complained and actually made serious strides in her adjustments to the rural life,

Helen Moore – 1917

ultimately concluding that she could learn to like it, if given enough time. More difficult for Helen was the role-change to housewife. Her young age and lack of preparation for household responsibilities made her life more difficult. She worked to overcome all obstacles, to learn, and her determination was aided by her sense of humor, her ability to laugh at her own mistakes. With the experiences of each day she gradually grew wise in the ways of a rural housewife.

Knowing that Jesse loved the taste of white rice, and also knowing she had never prepared the dish, Helen set out to cook a surprise dinner with rice as the main staple. She heated the water and emptied the full three pound sack of rice into the pan to simmer. As the rice cooked it swelled and before long the pan was over-flowing, requiring her to place some of the rice in another cooking pan. The rice took longer to cook than she had expected, and the longer it cooked the more it swelled. Two hours later when Jesse arrived home for dinner she was still cooking the rice, only now she had five pans on the stove all full of rice and was looking for a sixth container for the surplus. She was so consumed with the problem of the expanding rice that no other food was prepared and the table was not yet set for eating. Without expecting to do it, Helen had prepared six and one half quarts of rice and nothing else.

When Jesse came into the kitchen and saw the pans of rice he was astonished. "Why in the world are you cooking all that rice? I didn't even know you liked rice."

Helen, angry at herself but amused at Jesse's response to her dilemma, replied, "I knew you liked rice and I wanted to please you. The more the better, huh? Grab each of us a bowl and get the sugar and cinnamon out of the cupboard. We're ready to eat."

Baffled, but without argument, Jesse followed the instructions. They ate their evening meal of rice with sugar and cinnamon while engaging in the usual con-versation. Helen played the innocent, Jesse went along. After they finished, Helen asked, "Are you ready for dessert?"

"I don't know. I always thought that rice with sugar and cinnamon was dessert. What dessert do you have in mind?"

Helen could not finish her sentence without laughing. "For dessert I have in mind white rice with milk on it." Jesse roared with laughter. Following several minutes of mutual silliness, Helen explained to Jesse what had happened. Then they engaged in a nonsensical process of making more silly remarks with Helen giving ridiculous descriptions as she made fun of herself. It became a humorous, fun-filled evening, with all discussions always coming back to the rice episode. They had successfully turned what could have been a catastrophe into an amusing event. The recently married Helen and Jesse Moore ate rice with sugar and cinna-mon, sometimes pouring milk on it, for the next three days. They made the best of it, for what else could they have done?

CHAPTER 12

THE BOAT RIDE

Sandy Creek Road was deserted except for the traveling couple. The early morning air was heavy with moisture, the low thick clouds filtered most of the early morning sunlight, and both factors significantly affected travel on this off the beaten path. The dirt-sand road was full of natural hazards, difficult to travel with good light, somewhat dangerous with less than good light. The decision to journey the dangerous Sandy Creek Road from Jacksonville to Montezuma was prompted more by considerations of time rather than safety or comfort. The gravel road through Winchester would have been easier, the passenger train to Pearl would have been faster but Jesse, reluctant to spend the money, selected to journey by horse and buggy. At this precise moment the wisdom of his decision was in question, but Jesse carefully monitored the road and forged ahead. He had confidence in his dependable horse to stay the course and not to balk at danger. Helen remained passive, unconcerned, and enjoyed viewing the unfamiliar countryside, placing full confidence in her husband whom she believed had traveled this road many times in his bachelor days.

The temperature was unseasonably cool. Three days past the daytime highs had been in the mid eighties but the previous night an early frost had descended on west central Illinois. The rapid change in temperature allowed little time for the person to acclimate, making it seem colder than it really was. Helen broke the silence. "I'm still cold. It's too early in the year to be this cold. Hope this doesn't mean an early winter. It's a dark, dreary day, isn't it?"

"That it is, though remember what they say about the weather in the Midwest—if you don't like it, just wait a few hours and it'll change. I'm like you though, I hope it changes soon and for the better. I don't want an early winter either. Why don't you scoot on over here and we'll share some body heat." Helen liked that idea and nestled next to Jesse. He smiled. "Come to think about it there might be some advantages to a long, cold winter."

"Oh, Jess, you're either silly or a hopeless romantic. I can't decide which."

"I suspect there is a reasonable amount of both qualities in me. That's good, I think."

"No need to wonder. It's good."

Although he had solicited the compliment, Jesse still appreciated Helen's response and never tired of her praise. "I'm sorry to drag you out on a day like this, but I think it's necessary. Elzie had a certain urgency in his letter, and I promised we would come today if at all possible. I really don't think he would ask us to make the trip without good reason. He's pretty sensitive on things like that."

"I just don't know him very well. I still can't tell for sure when your brother is kidding or serious. Gosh, I hope nothing is wrong."

"No one knows when Elzie is kidding or serious, that's all part of his charm. I don't think anything is wrong, I think something is up."

"What's that mean?"

"Oh, nothing in particular. I'm not sure, but I wouldn't be surprised if he just wanted to say good-bye. I think my little brother is about ready to join the Army, but when I think more about it there must be something else on his mind or I think he would have made the trip instead of asking us to."

"He's not old enough to join, is he?"

"No, he is not."

"Then how is he going to join?"

Not wanting to reveal his minor role in the conspiracy of enlistment, Jesse played the innocent. "Beats me, but knowing my brother if he really wants to join, he'll find a way. Oh, look! There's the sandpit, northwest of Glasgow. Now I know exactly where we are." His words were followed by a sigh of relief. Jesse's tone revealed his previously unspoken concern about traveling the Sandy Creek road with Helen. "We're only about fifteen minutes from the river providing it doesn't rain. We made better time than I thought we would."

"Providing it doesn't rain. What's that mean? It's looked like rain all morning."

"We can't make this road, if it's wet. At least I don't think we can. The creek floods, the sand shifts, and the road becomes hazardous. Don't worry, it's clearing off and even getting a little warmer. We've got it made."

"Well I'm glad I didn't know all of this when we left. What would we have done had it rained?"

"We would have dealt with it. There is no way of knowing if it's going to rain, or not. It's no big deal, we made it didn't we? The road gets better now, and we're less than one mile from the main road. From here to the river the road is straight, due west. Oh look, Helen, the clouds are breaking up, the sun is trying to shine. You know what I think? Nature, in its own majestic way, has just welcomed us to the Illinois River."

They were in luck. The ferry was docked on the east side of the river which meant less waiting time at the crossing. Jesse waved to the ferry captain and sensed relief knowing that the ferry would wait for them to cross. Helen had no such feelings.

Initially saying nothing, Helen stared at the ferryboat not liking what she saw. The boat was flat with a deck less than two feet above the waterline, and although there was an iron guardrail protecting passengers and cargo, it all looked a bit too precarious. To Helen the moored, stationary boat, gently swaying up and down in the water, appeared unstable, downright dangerous. Much of the deck was wet from the previous crossing, and with Helen's strong fear of water she did not cherish the thought of crossing the river, particularly on this boat. "Are we going to cross the river on that thing?"

"Of course, it's a ferryboat. How did you think we were going to cross?"

"I never thought about crossing on a raft. I assumed we would cross on a nice safe bridge, or at least on a big boat with sides." Looking for reassurances, Helen spoke in a softened tone. "You do remember that I don't swim, don't you?"

"It's not a raft, it's a ferryboat, perfectly safe I assure you. I will be right beside you all the way. Look, Helen, Elzie and Frieda are waiting on the other side." Seeing his siblings on the shore was a pleasant surprise. Jesse yelled across the river in his loudest voice, "Hey, Elzie, hey, Frieda." The tone expressed more than his words. Helen became amused at Jesse's excitement, momentarily losing her apprehension about the river-crossing.

Frieda placed both hands in the air and waved, Elzie yelled back. "We've got hot coffee, all kinds of food, and homemade donuts. Hurry-up, over there."

The ferry operator showed his annoyance when he shouted back as if Elzie were prodding him. "You hold your horses over there, don't be so impatient." He looked back at Jesse. "Everybody around here is always in a hurry. Some things just take time." Jesse said nothing while he looked at the ground, acting as though he was uninvolved. The entire exchange amused Helen.

With the operator's assistance Jesse loaded the horse and buggy on the ferry. Once underway Helen stood in the middle of the boat tightly gripping Jesse's hand, but well before the ferry reached the opposite side of the river she released his hand, walked alone to the railing, and intently watched the flowing river. Jesse did not know, nor did he ask, if she had overcome her fear or if she was simply making a statement of confidence to him.

The younger brother and sister had prepared a temporary campsite on the river bank approximately two hundred yards upstream from the ferryboat ramp. The semi-isolated site, located on a beautiful stretch of beach was a perfect location for a picnic. Appreciative of the rare opportunity to be together they quickly ridded themselves of all initial small talk and shared in a quality conversation as they picnicked on the riverbank. The mood of the gathering soon changed to the lighthearted when Helen tried to express her gratitude for the prepared snack, specifically the homemade cake donuts. She directed her words to Frieda. "These donuts are really good. Can I have the recipe?"

Elzie seized the opportunity and jumped to his feet. "I'll have you to know that I fried the donuts. It's not the recipe, it's the masterful way by which they were prepared." He then took off his hat and bowed. "The recipe is a family secret and I promised the person who gave me the recipe that I would not share it without his permission. So, what about it, Jesse, do I have your permission to share your recipe?" That silly comment evoked a chuckle from Frieda.

Jesse joined the obvious charade using a pseudo inflection in his voice. "I have an announcement for all to hear. I hereby do grant to my younger brother, Elzie H. Moore, permission to share my donut recipe with my wife, Mary Helen Moore. Furthermore, I bequeath to brother Elzie the right to share all of my recipes with anyone he so chooses."

Helen rolled her eyes. "Oh, brother, it's going to be a long day."

Frieda giggled, pointing her thumb at her brothers before talking only to Helen. "Whenever you're around these characters, you just never know. Believe me, everyday can be a long day."

Once the antics were over they again became quite content to sit passively on the shore and visit with one another, to watch the river, or simply to enjoy the beautiful surroundings. Helen was learning to appreciate Jesse's younger siblings more and more. To no one's surprise Elzie was the center of attention as he often displayed his sharp wit, his keen sense of humor. He took such delight in the group's spontaneous reaction to his humor that it was difficult for him to remain straight, not tease or joke.

Shortly after the noon hour Frieda reminded Jesse that out of respect he and his wife should visit Aunt Mary. All agreed. As they prepared to depart Elzie insisted his brother look at his newly acquired, recently repaired, johnboat. Partly out of pride, partly to be considerate Elzie offered Helen and Jesse a ride on the river. "How about it folks, let's take a brief cruise? Come on, big brother, you don't want to miss this opportunity. Why don't you go with us, Helen? It will be fun. Frieda went for a ride with me this morning and we had a great time. About a month ago I found an old, abandoned john boat. I fixed it up and it's just like new. I know you usually don't use a john boat on the river, but with me as captain, what could possibly go wrong?"

Jesse looked as though he was considering it, but Helen gave the first response.

"Oh, I don't know, Elzie, I'm not very comfortable in boats. Truth of the matter is, aside from the ferry I've only been in a boat a few times, and that's been on a small lake with Jess. I'm too faint of heart...no that's not right. Truth is, I'm scared to death of water. I better not, thanks anyway. Why don't you and Jesse venture on out without me?"

"Well, okay, if you really don't want to. If you prefer, you and Jesse can go alone. Today is a good day for a boat ride with the river being so calm and all. Conditions are perfect. Are you sure? You may never have another opportunity to take a ride on such a beautiful riverboat." His words evoked smiles. "It's also an opportunity to converse with the pilot of the boat as you cruise the river. What an offer! Come on, Helen, be bold, be daring, there is no time like the present."

Jesse wanted to communicate with Helen before she had a chance to answer. "If you want to go I will go with you, but if you really don't want to go, don't go."

The words, be bold be daring, had the sound of a challenge to Helen, plus she felt reassured by Jesse's remarks. Reluctantly she relented. "Compromise. How about the three of us take a five minute excursion, just to say I've ridden in Elzie's boat? Is that all right, Frieda? Or better yet, can we get four in the boat?"

Frieda quickly reacted. "No, you don't want four in that boat, three will be a full load. I'll wait on the bank. Elzie, you be careful, no foolishness, okay? Helen is only going because you pleaded with her."

Helen appreciated that Frieda championed her, although she was somewhat bothered by the words, that boat. "Yeah, no foolishness, or I'm not going."

Elzie, looking directly at Frieda, symbolically crossed his heart and raised his right hand as though he was taking an oath. "No foolishness whatsoever, whatever foolishness is."

They policed their campsite and gathered the few possessions they had with them, although Elzie insisted they leave some of the partially consumed food for the wild animals. Helen appreciated the gesture and helped to distribute the food, leaving more than Jesse thought necessary although he said nothing. As they walked the shoreline to the boat's location, Helen, in passing, made reference to the beautiful setting of Montezuma. "Looking at that town from here is really special. What are there, maybe fifteen or twenty buildings, some of them pretty good size?"

Elzie could hardly wait to answer. "I'm not sure of the exact number of buildings, but to me the exact size of the town makes no difference. I love this place. Next to Pittsfield, it's the most exciting place in Pike County. Wait a minute, I take that back. Montezuma is the single most exciting place in the entire county. There is always something going on at this place. This is where the river and the people come together. This is home, I love it here."

Elzie's words of praise for Montezuma did not fall on deaf ears. Helen, although somewhat surprised, admired her brother-in law's emotional expression of a personal attachment to a village which undoubtedly belonged to the past century, mostly kept alive by river traffic, and according to Jesse the river traffic was decreasing each year. Obviously, Montezuma had more of a history than a future. Helen's innocent comments of beauty were intended to reflect an observation of quaintness, not intended to reflect modern or modish, and certainly not intended to reflect an exciting place. What she saw in Montezuma was not at all what Elzie saw.

Jesse remained still and quiet as though he was attempting to reconcile the contrasting thoughts. Frieda, almost as if she were making an effort to acknowledge Helen's comment as a profound statement, spoke for the three of them when she expressed heartfelt concern, "We worry about the future of this beautiful place. Really, it is home to all of us. It's almost as if Montezuma's charm is a deep secret and the people in the county haven't discovered it yet. For the last few years more people have left this town than have moved to it. Already there is talk about bringing a hard road to this area and that talk does not include possible routes through Montezuma. We may be looking at a dying community. I sure hope not. If Jesse doesn't object I will repeat that which I have heard him say many times. No one knows for sure what tomorrow will bring. We can hope, but we must prepare for disappointment."

Helen's innocent recognition of a beautiful site had sparked emotions that reached the hearts and souls of her companions, almost as though they considered this area as hallowed ground. Without knowing it she had exposed part of their roots, their pride of who they were, and they were speaking as sons and daughter of a bygone era, a forgotten place. Since Helen had initiated the discussion, she felt it wise to change the topic. "Did Jess really use those exact words? It sounds rather eloquent to me."

Responding on cue, Elzie laughed. "Eloquent, huh. I guess it must be in the ears of the listener. Eloquent, my foot." Jesse laughed.

At first sight of Elzie's upside down boat covered by a dirty, canvas tarpaulin, Helen began to harbor second thoughts. The low sided, flatbottomed boat with one rather large, dubious repair on its bottom looked to be in frightful condition. The wooden boat looked older than the combined age of the four of them. The minor repairs Elzie had mentioned earlier looked more like a major job. Helen grimaced and looked at Elzie. "Is this the beautiful river boat you were talking about? Can it even hold three of us? Does it float?"

Before Helen could express more reservations, Elzie had the boat in the river and was pointing his finger, giving directions. "Rest assured, it floats like a cork. Helen, you're in the front, excuse me, I mean the bow. Jesse, the stern, and Mr. Captain will sit here and row." Elzie extended his hand and Helen cautiously assumed her designated position. She had more doubts once all three were aboard and the boat sat even lower in the water. "Give us a good shove, Frieda, and we'll commence our river cruise." Frieda did as instructed, Helen clung to the sides for dear life, and the three of them were on their way, cruising the Illinois River.

An elderly gentleman working the ferry ramp wandered over to the shore from which they had just departed and shouted toward the boat. "Good luck, young lady, in that boat with Elzie Moore at the helm." Elzie smiled, waved at the man and Jesse laughed aloud. Helen had no words.

Once underway Helen found some comfort when the watercraft seemed to function as one might expect. The conditions for boating were near perfect; the sun was brightly shining, the temperature was pleasant, and the river was calm, save a mild current. Temporarily, Helen displaced her fear of water and attempted to absorb all that the eyes could behold. It was a resplendent view. Perhaps this was her reward for having been bold and daring.

As the young passenger shifted her sitting position she noticed that the bottom of her foot was damp. Looking for the source of the dampness she spotted a small amount of water in bottom of the boat. The least lateral movement by any of the three passengers caused the water to slosh from side to side, giving an impression of more water than there was. Helen intently watched the water movement and could only think about the previous repairs made to the boat, the same boat that she was now aboard in the middle of the Illinois River. "Jess, there is water leaking into the boat. My feet are wet."

Knowing that Helen needed some reassurance, Jesse started to respond. "There is no..."

Elzie interrupted. "Oh, my God, how did that water get into my boat? Do you think there is a leak in my boat? Oh, heavens, what should I do? I am so dismayed."

A smiling Jesse said. "I think you better get us back to shore, Elzie. No foolishness, remember?" Helen intently listened. Elzie dramatically grunted as he moved the oars in the water, rowing for the island. Jesse still amused said, "Not that shore, you character you. The other shore where we started from." Elzie kept a straight face, turned the boat around and started to row at a torrid pace.

After about two minutes of hard rowing Elzie stopped rowing and lifted the oars into the boat. "You know, Jesse, when you look at it I think the island is closer." Not permitting his brother the opportunity to respond, Elzie untied his bait bucket from the oarlock and handed the bucket to Helen. "You better bail the water until we get closer to shore. By the way, you do know how to swim, don't you?"

Before she indignantly answered, Helen grabbed the oversized bucket and started to dip out the small amount of water. "No, I don't, and you know it. Now get this boat ashore, and I'm not kidding."

Knowing better but not considering the consequences, Jesse joined Elzie in his teasing. "Oh, no, Elzie. This shore is closer I am sure." Jesse put his hands in the water and in a frenzied movement he pretended to row the boat in the opposite direction of Elzie. Helen said nothing. Both men continued their silly movements, Helen continued to bail without effectively removing any water, and the boat remained in the middle of the river. Desperately, Helen first looked at Jesse and then Elzie for direction but Jesse refused to make eye contact, and eventually, Elzie could not help but to let the cat out of the bag. What was initially a mischievous sparkle in his deep green eyes now revealed an absence of seriousness, and gradually his facial expression exposed his fraudulent behavior. Helen's facial color changed from a pale white to a red. She coldly stared at Elzie, totally stifling his outburst of laughter. Jesse, noticing the brief silence, glanced at Helen long enough to see the anger in her eyes, lowered his head and kept it bowed, and although he did not totally cease his hand paddling, he greatly reduced the intensity of it. The next few minutes the boat drifted in the light current, as both men looked at the bottom of the boat while Helen stared daggers through both of them.

A most angry Helen poked Elzie on the left arm, and without saying a word she pointed toward the shore. Elzie obediently rowed toward the shore where Frieda was waiting after she had guessed what her brothers had done. Jesse continued to either look at the shore or the river, refusing to make eye contact with his perturbed wife. Once near the shore Jesse tossed the hitch rope to Frieda, and as she steadied the boat, Helen carefully disembarked climbing right over the two men. Once Helen was ashore, Frieda defiantly shoved the boat back into the water, forcing Jesse and Elzie to dock again, which allowed the girls time to walk away. By now Jesse was deeply concerned once he realized that his moment of teasing might, in fact, cost him more than he wanted to pay. He quickly walked after his wife, using every second of time to mentally compose an apology. Elzie followed at a safe distance.

Meanwhile, Helen and Frieda talked. "Are you okay, Helen?"

"I suppose so. Mostly, I'm embarrassed for being so naive. I'm also a little perturbed."

"Take my advice. Don't let them get away with it. What's good for the goose is good for the gander. Punish them, taunt them. Make them think you're really angry. Otherwise they'll just do it again." Helen intended to take heed to the wise advice; and just as Jesse started to speak, Frieda stepped forward, pointed her finger at Jesse and clearly stated, "Jesse, if I was you, I would say I'm sorry, and nothing else."

Jesse showed real concern as he looked around Frieda to see his wife. "I'm sorry, Helen, I exercised poor judgment. It won't happen again."

Elzie stepped forward. "I'm sorry too, Helen. It's my fault, and I hope you aren't too mad at us. Will you forgive us?"

Helen stepped in front of Frieda and spoke to Elzie. "You're right when you say that it is your fault, but it's not your fault alone. Elzie, I'm not mad at you, I'm disappointed. I learned a valuable lesson here today." She turned and looked directly into the eyes of her husband. "You're the one I'm mad at. And if you don't like it, that's too bad." The more she talked the more perturbed she became. "As far as I'm concerned you both can take it or lump it. Just go away." Almost in an orchestrated fashion, Helen moved backward and Frieda moved forward.

"Helen and I will take the buggy and go back to Aunt Mary's by ourselves. We know that you two wanted to visit today, so this is probably as good a time as any. You won't be missed and, personally, I think you deserve each other. Dinner is at 3:00, we don't care what you do until then. Maybe by then Helen will have recovered from her humiliation." Pouring salt on the wound, she continued. "Shame on you, shame on both of you." Frieda and Helen turned and walked toward the wagon.

Jesse yelled, "Good-bye, Helen. I'll see you in a couple of hours." He got no response.

Elzie yelled louder. "Bye, girls, we'll see you in a little bit. Thanks." He got no response either.

Once the girls were out of sight they had a good laugh. Frieda was pleased. "Helen, you're good. That will teach my brothers to fool with you."

"Thanks for the help, Frieda. But if I was good, it's because not all of it was acting."

A dejected Jesse sat on the river bank as Elzie secured his boat before joining his brother. The pair remained seated on the bank in silence, with Elzie occasionally tossing small rocks or other minor debris in the river, but neither initiated conversation. Almost fifteen minutes elapsed before the younger brother stood, stretched, and emitted a loud grunt insinuating he was about to do something. Instead he stared at Jesse who was by now somewhat annoyed by his brother's meaningless behavior. "What?" snapped Jesse.

Elzie had induced his brother into breaking his silence. "I've got an idea. I'll find two sticks of equal size and, of course, you get to choose which one you want, and we'll throw them into the river. Whichever stick floats out of sight first, wins."

"I'm not in the mood for games."

"This is not a game. It's a noncompetitive, decision-making process." Elzie was so delighted with his nonsensical description of his made-up activity that he waited, expecting a reaction from his brother. He got no response. "If you win, we continue to sit here and sulk until you're ready to talk. If I win, we temporarily forget about how insensitive to Helen we both were and start to talk right away." Elzie did not even wait for an answer, but started his search for equal size sticks and quickly returned with one in each hand, rubbing one stick against the other pretending to clean them. Then he balanced the sticks in both hands as though he was preparing for a precise Olympic stick-throwing contest. "Take your pick, you big brute, and you get to throw first."

Unable to conceal his grin Jesse grabbed one of the sticks and threw it as far as he could, almost to the middle of the river about thirty yards in distance, and the stick started its descent down the Illinois River. "Top that, you little brute." Elzie slowly moved around the shore area as though he was unconcerned that Jesse's stick was already moving downstream. Finally, he pretended to stretch his body, leaned way back, and then gently tossed the stick about fifteen yards into the river. Although Elzie's stick had lost about twenty-five seconds of floating time, it started to float downstream about four times the speed of Jesse's, and in less than one minute Elzie's stick had outdistanced the other.

Adding some flair to the event Elzie placed his hands, forefingers to thumbs, around his eyes to give the impression he was watching a race through field glasses, before he started to cheer as though his encouragement would entice his stick to try harder. "Come on stick, go, go, go. Give it all you got." In less than two minutes Elzie's stick was out of sight, and Elzie proudly proclaimed, "The winner is — Elzie's stick by eighty-five lengths. In last place, if it ever finishes, is — the big brute's stick."

"I don't suppose you would care to tell me how that happened?"

"Sure, I'll tell you. Training and diet, and maybe, the changing current had something to do with it. You've been picking corn too long, brother. You've forgotten all that you taught me about the always changing river. Remember—always check the current."

"You are something, little brother. I don't think I ever could teach you anything about the river, and I ought to know better than to play river games with you. You were born with knowledge of this river. I wouldn't be surprised to find that Mother gave birth to you while on the river. You are a true Pisces. I declare you the winner, fair and square. Does this mean I've got to sit down, stop my fretting, and talk to you?"

"Indeed it does, but first let's go to the general store and get a Coke. Nobody is there, but I know where the key is. I'll pay him tomorrow, he won't care, I do it all the time. We'll bring the drinks back here and find a comfortable place to sit before we begin some serious talking."

The late September sun had warmed the air making it a fine day to be outside near the river, next to nature. Although there were many people at the river, the brothers located an isolated stretch of beach. Jesse sipped his Coke, Elzie chugged his. Sitting together on the riverbank brought back good memories, reminding

Jesse of past days when he and Elzie would play there. "Elzie, you look fit. Your life must agree with you."

"I don't think a good life has anything to do with me looking fit. I look fit because I am fit. For several months now I have been working hard to get in good physical shape. I've been running, swimming, doing push-ups, sit-ups, chin-ups, and any other-up you can think of. I've been working hard at it."

"Why?"

"I'm doing what you told me to do. I'm getting ready to join the Army, and I want everything to be just right. I practice my shooting every chance I get and I'm beginning to show improvement. Actually, I'm getting good. When I get into the Army I don't want anything about me to be a source of personal embarrassment. I'm going to be mentally and physically fit."

"When and how are you going to join?"

"That's my business and I'm going to keep it my business. It's better if you don't know. Let's just say the process is afoot. Rest assured I am doing it the right way, I won't do anything stupid or anything to embarrass myself or to embarrass anyone else. Once I enlist in the Army, people will be proud of me. That's enough talk about me, we have more important things to discuss."

"Oh, I would say that talking about you is pretty important to me."

"We're going to get serious now so clear your mind. First, thanks for coming today, Jesse, I know it was a big effort on your part. I'm sorry about what I did to Helen but, unless I'm a poor judge of character, everything will work out okay. She's quite a woman, and I can understand why you love her so. Perhaps one day, after this war is over, I can spend more time with the both of you. You never know, but by then you might have a kid or two. Who knows, one day I might even get married and have a few of my own. Boy, that's a sight to think about—you and me sitting on the porch, talking about our rheumatism as we watch our kids play. Heaven help us if that comes to pass."

"Yeah, that is quite an image. You never know, it might happen."

"Sounds funny, doesn't it? All this talk about us getting old. That's not the reason we're here. We're here to talk about Dad getting old. His problems have been coming on for quite some time. Do you know what I'm talking about?"

"Well, I'm not sure. Do you mean physically or mentally?"

"I mean physically. Far as I know there is nothing wrong with the old man's mind, just his body. I thought you might have noticed something a couple of years ago when we were clearing the land. That's when I first became aware of it."

"No, I didn't. He has slowed down some, but that's natural for a man in his sixties. I guess I don't know what you are talking about."

"Everybody always talks about how hard Dad works and how strong he is. Well, all of that is changing. He's not as strong anymore and it shows in his work. He sleeps a lot more now, gets real tired by the end of the workday. He's ready for bed as soon as supper is over. He's a little better on Sundays when we don't work, but not much. Even the most simple things are harder for him. It takes him more time to get dressed, and at the end of the day it takes him forever to change out of his work clothes. During this last year he sometimes did things I've never seen him do before. For example, the other day he went to bed without doing his chores. I've never seen that before."

"That is interesting. Did he say why?"

"Nope. I just went ahead and did them for him, and he never mentioned it, although I know he knew, because the next morning he went out and checked. But that's not all. He hardly works in the garden anymore. He goes out and looks at it, but he doesn't do much work. That's not at all like him, we both know he's not lazy. The man doesn't have a lazy bone in his body. He often puts his hand on his left hip, like the hip hurts him, and when I ask about it, he tells me he's fine. Aunt Mary says he has rheumatism, and maybe, kidney problems. I guess all of this sounds like I'm trying to pick at him, but I'm not. I tell you this out of concern, not to complain, and I hope you understand that. His problems with the freight work, specifically work with the wagon and mules, concerns me the most. He doesn't even get mad at the mules anymore, he doesn't push them like he used to. He has trouble loading and unloading the freight, and to be quite honest, I wonder if he could handle the hauling business without me. The other day he turned down an offer of decent money to help unload a riverboat, and I think it's because he worries that he can't do his share any more. Whatever the reason, we're working smaller jobs now and making less money.

"Something else concerns me too. Please remember this is private stuff for your ears only. I know he wouldn't want anyone to know about this. He's got man problems. When he takes a leak, it takes him forever. He can't seem to get started, and then once he goes, he can't stop the dripping. When I ask about it, he tells me it is none of my business. Sometimes his balls swell up so bad that he can hardly put his pants on. The other day he was hurting real bad and asked me to fetch him a cold, damp cloth. When I delivered the cloth I saw his balls, and I will never forget what I saw. His bag was swollen to about the size of a cantaloupe. It made me hurt just to look at it. And that's not all, Jesse, but I don't want to burden you with more detail, so I won't. I just don't think the old man is well, and he won't see a doctor. He refuses medical help, thinks they are all quacks.

"Given all of that, here is my real concern. What happens to Dad when I go to the Army? What if he can't continue to make a living? We hardly make enough money with both of us working, let alone the old man working by himself. What will happen to him until I get back? That's what I'm worried about. Do you have any thoughts?"

Jesse looked befuddled. He needed time to absorb all the information and to think about the consequences of what he might advise. Knowing that Elzie was not an alarmist, he took the question seriously and assumed the descriptions were factual—his father was failing and needed help. An equally pressing issue was that Elzie was assuming sole responsibility for his father, and he was not looking to other family members for assistance, while at the same time he was yearning to be free of all responsibility, free to join the Army. Jesse realized his answer to Elzie was critical and any impulsive answer might be imprudent on his part and, yet, Jesse was not eager to influence Elzie's self-determination. Speaking in a most deliberate manner he carefully worded his response. "I'm not real sure. I might have to think on that for awhile."

"Sorry to say, brother, I can't wait awhile for your answer. I need it now."

"Sounds to me like your mind is already made up."

"It is, and it isn't. If you give me a good enough reason, I can change my mind."

Jesse did not like the responsibility that Elzie had just placed on his shoulders. "I can't do that, Elzie, it's not my decision to make. Besides, I just don't know what to say, I can't come up with any good advice. I'm not real sure that Dad's problems should be any more of a concern for you than for the other six children. There is no clear-cut line for family responsibility, other than the line we draw for ourselves. There is no answer. I admire you for your sensitivity, but you must be the one who determines your own fate. Dad could become ill and die tomorrow, or he could outlive the both of us. We don't know about tomorrow, and it's probably a good thing that we don't. This time, little brother, I can't give advice. Sorry."

"No need to be sorry, you're honest with me. I guess it's time that I stand alone. You're absolutely correct in that only I should make this decision, and I will."

Before the visitors returned home on that day Helen and her brother-in-law had occasion to visit, permitting Elzie to make amends for his earlier behavior. Helen somehow sensed that Elzie was a very special individual, not only to the others but to her as well. She looked forward to knowing him better.

Helen was less forgiving of her husband. The long ride home for Jesse and Helen was considerably less enjoyable than their ride to Montezuma. Helen had been offended that day and it would take time to heal the wounds of her humiliation. Jesse regretted that boat ride as much as anything he could remember.

CHAPTER 13

A DREAM FINDS REALITY

It was the first week of October, a time to tie up all loose ends. Monday, Elzie worked hard the entire day stacking, loading freight so that his father could spend time hauling instead of lifting. After work he did his daily chores and used the remaining time for target practice. After supper he retired early. His day on Tuesday was similar except that he skipped his target practice in order to spend time making small repairs around the house. Wednesday was different—mid afternoon Elzie delivered the last load of freight to Pearl and ended his workday two hours earlier than usual. He did his chores, cleaned up the barn, and checked to confirm that everything else was in order. During the evening meal Elzie spent more time talking than eating, a first to his memory. Foregoing his usual evening activities he helped with the dishes and visited with his sister and aunt for almost two hours before the three joined Erastus on the front porch.

"Dad, I want to talk with you a few minutes before you go to bed."

"Fire away."

"As you know tomorrow is a big day in Pittsfield. A large contingency of Pike County boys are leaving for the army, and if you don't object I'm going to town, show my support and wave good-bye to them. As I understand it the whole county is turning out for the parade, the speakers, and all kinds of flashy things. My problem is, if I go I will miss work. We finished our big job today and tomorrow is slated for catch up day on the little jobs. Do you think you can make it one day without me?"

"Of course I can make it without you, I've made it over fifty years without help. My question is why would anybody want to go? Seems like a waste of time to me."

"I already told you, to say good-bye to the conscripts. You do understand that these boys are leaving for the Army and, of course, there is a chance that some of them might not come back. The least I can do is to show my support for them. I wanted to enlist with them, although it just wasn't possible. I tried to get in, I even went to the exemption board and offered my services, but they didn't want anything to do with me. It took me two trips just to get past the secretaries. Finally, I spoke with Mr. A. L. Kiser, the chairman of the board, and he told me they weren't taking anyone under twenty-one. All he would say is sorry, son, there is nothing I can do for you. They were too busy, setting up the draft and giving physicals, to deal with the likes of me. Actually, they weren't very kind to me."

Erastus was indignant, not because of the perceived unkindness toward Elzie, but because Elzie had tried to enlist in the Army. "When did you do all of this? You've been scheming behind my back, haven't you?"

"No, no, no, I have not been scheming behind your back. I haven't been forthright, that's all. Besides, I think all of you knew what I was up to, even if I didn't openly talk about it. To answer your question, I've been trying to get in the Army since April, right after we declared war on Germany. No need to worry because the big shots in Pittsfield don't want me. However, I am convinced that if this war goes on much longer, they'll have second thoughts."

Sensing the discussion was headed toward an argument Frieda and Aunt Mary listened, but refrained from conversation. Erastus was not restrained. "You're too damn young to go to war, and you know it. Even our government says you're too young, so that's the full story, period."

Elzie displayed amazing composure. "I understand that, but I want you to know those age guidelines are for the National Army, the army of conscription. I understand that if you enlist with parental consent, they'll take an eighteen year old in both the National Guard and the Regular Army. I will be eighteen, next March. What about then? If my country needs me are you still going to say no?"

If my country needs me were the perfect words to soften Erastus' position. "I don't know what I will say then, maybe I'll think about it. If our country wants you and really needs you, well that's a horse of a different color. Right now they not only don't need you, they don't want you. So, no promises, we'll deal with it when the time comes. Until then this issue is on the back burner and it's going to stay there. You might as well put that in your pipe and smoke it. End of discussion."

Uncharacteristically, Elzie calmly responded. "Fair enough, but I'm going to Pittsfield tomorrow to wave good-bye; and another thing, if my country really needs me I'm definitely going. Now, end of discussion."

Erastus grunted something unintelligible before he left the porch, and once he was out of hearing range, Aunt Mary whispered, "You handled that well, Elzie.

245

I'm proud of you."

"Thank you. Think how proud of me you would be if I was on that train tomorrow, or if I already was in the Army fighting for my country. That's where I want to be, that's my dream."

Having listened to the entire conversation, Frieda was sympathetic to her brother. "For what it's worth I agree with you, Elzie. If I was a man I would want to go too, although I think I would wait until I was the right age. I also understand why Dad doesn't want you to go. You're too valuable around here." Frieda paused as though she was having second thoughts. Up to this point, she had never seriously considered life without Elzie, nor did she like the implications of such thinking. "Who would help Dad, what about the chores, what about me?" Realizing that she sounded self-centered, she changed her tone of speaking. "Maybe you should start teaching me all the things that need to be done, just in case. You keep your chin up, everything will work out, I'm positive." Her thoughts were jumbled and she knew it. She was not clearly expressing herself and it was time to switch the subject. "By the way, is it okay if I go with you tomorrow? I would like to wave good-bye too."

"Sorry, Frieda, it's not okay. I've got some other things to do, and it would be better if you weren't there. Don't take me wrong, you are my little sister and I like being with you, just not tomorrow, okay? Now if you don't mind, I've got some things to do before I go to bed." She accepted his words, although his lame explanation for not wanting Frieda to go sort of concerned the younger sister as it was uncharacteristic of Elzie to make excuses.

Before bed Elzie worked at the kitchen table giving his rifle an unusually thorough cleaning. Once completed he placed his rifle, cleaning kit, and ammunition in the corner behind the kitchen back door, not the usual storage place. He oiled the blades of his pocket knife and put it back in his pocket before he polished his work boots, and placed them in the corner next to the rifle. Before retiring for the night he took a short walk on the streets of Milton but was in bed sound asleep by 11:30.

Elzie's internal clock must have been wound too tight as he awakened at 3:30 a.m., was up and about immediately. Efficiently he used his time to sort personal items, while maintaining almost complete silence the entire time. On his neatly made bed lay a cloth satchel packed with Elzie's personal toiletry items, a pair of socks, underwear, and a clean shirt. In an effort to conceal the satchel from unwanted eyes, he later carried it concealed under his coat as he went to the outhouse, temporarily storing it behind the coal shed. No one noticed. The remainder of the early morning hours he functioned normally in his usual routine of completing chores before breakfast. He helped his father hitch the mules to the wagon, and he watched as his father prepared to depart. Not knowing exactly what to say or how to say it, Elzie used a cliché when he handed the reins to his father. "Be careful and don't work too hard."

Erastus' answer was tart. "If I'm expected to make a decent living, I've got to work hard, and since I'm by myself today, I'll have to work harder than usual." Elzie waved good-bye, and his father acknowledged the wave with a slight nod of the head. The final farewell that morning was awkward to say the least as Erastus departed a little perturbed because Elzie had chosen to go to town rather than work; and, as usual, Erastus was not reluctant to show his displeasure. Elzie felt it unfortunate that such few words were exchanged, but he saw no alternative. The farewell was over and done with, beyond change.

Frieda and Aunt Mary had finished washing the breakfast dishes and were preparing to clean the house, the usual activity on Thursday mornings. Elzie asked, "Any coffee left?"

Frieda answered. "Plenty. I'll pour you a cup if you'll sit at the table and visit with us while you drink it."

"That's a deal."

Frieda knew the answer, but asked anyway. "Still going to Pittsfield, still don't want your little sister along?" Elzie rolled his eyes rather than verbally answering. Frieda understood the meaning.

Delighted that her nephew was taking time to visit, Aunt Mary made polite conversation. "What time are you leaving for Pittsfield? Are you going to stay all day, how are you going to get there, walk? I hope it doesn't rain on the festivities, although it looks as though it might. I hope not. Those boys deserve a grand send-off, bless their hearts. Just think of all the poor families who must bid adieu to a loved one today."

Deliberately avoiding comment on her last statement, Elzie answered with a tone of gaiety. "Yep, it'll be a big day all right. Good thing the Huns can't see a trainload of Pike County boys preparing to go to war or they might turn and run before our boys could get there."

The statement amused Frieda. "Fat chance, although come to think about it, most of the Pike County boys that I know are all so ugly that I'd run too. Ugly is what you meant, isn't it?"

Once again, a frown negated the need for a verbal response. "Aunt Mary, I think I'm going to leave in about an hour. I intend to walk, but since so many folks from Milton are going today, I fully expect someone to offer me a ride. I sure hope I get a ride, but if I don't I'll walk. I'll stick to the roads instead of the usual shortcut. Don't know when I'll be back. You'll know I'm back when you see me. Is there anything you need done before I leave?"

"Can't think of anything. How are you going to get back? If you walk, you be careful. Remember, it gets dark earlier now."

That exchange was as close as Elzie could get to announcing his intentions. At least this good-bye was preferable to the earlier one with his father. He hustled to his room and changed his clothes. He wore his dress slacks, a white shirt and tie. He dusted off his shined shoes before applying a little shoe polish on his belt to hide the worn places. Finally, he splashed on some face lotion, rubbed in hair oil, combed his hair, and went to the window to inspect his reflection. Pleased with what he saw he mumbled, "This is about as spiffy as I get."

Elzie scanned his room in a final check and found everything in order. It was now time to leave. The only items he carried on his person were his pocket knife, his billfold, thirteen dollars and change, plus the clothes on his back. Without additional fanfare Elzie fetched his satchel and started his trip for Pittsfield, turning twice to wave good-bye to Aunt Mary and his sister and, although the temperature was cool he carried his coat draped over his satchel in a successful ploy to conceal its existence. His notion that he would be offered a ride was on target as less than a mile from town he was picked up by a farm family traveling in a wagon pulled by horses. Arriving at the southeast edge of Pittsfield by 10:15 a.m., the stage was now set for the opening act of Elzie's big adventure. He had conceived his own improvisational drama of enlistment and now the curtain was up. Success or failure rested squarely on his shoulders.

Four and one-half blocks east of the square on Washington Street the young man from Milton graciously thanked his friends for the ride and explained his desire to walk alone so that he could mingle with the people. Mingling was not important but he feared that if he became part of a small group his behavior might become monitored. He was usually not this calculating, but today he felt it necessary so that nothing might interfere with his planned adventure.

Even at a distance it was apparent that Pittsfield was more crowded than usual. The diverse crowd from all over the county had gathered in town to demonstrate its support for the cause. Pittsfield seemed different, more reminiscent of an exciting summer Saturday night than of a Thursday morning, almost a frivolity merged with a seriousness of purpose. Most were enjoying themselves while pretending they were not. The restrained gaiety reminded Elzie more of the final hours of a wake, than of the beginning of the celebration. There was laughter, there were tears, there was noise, and there was solitude. Individual emotions were restrained as though the crowd were waiting for an opportunity to collectively express their true emotions. Whether it was unfathomable thoughts about the possible fate of the two hundred conscripts or subdued elation that made the crowd so strange that day, one could only conjecture.

All the commotion was to Elzie's advantage as the ubiquitous crowd made it easy for him to move about with a degree of anonymity. With his coat once again placed to conceal his satchel, Elzie's body quickly cooled in the brisk east breeze on that cold, cloudy, damp October day; but in due time he located a sheltered site on Monroe Street in front of The Pike County Democrat newspaper office. Here he pretended to read the newspaper on display in the front window as he plotted his next course of action. Once he determined his precise plan, he walked the four short blocks to the railroad station, entered the building and looked around like a tourist would. He visited a few minutes with the stationmaster and convinced him to watch over his satchel as he joined the festivities. Elzie had counted on the cooperation of the stationmaster. His plan was working.

The stored satchel granted Elzie more freedom to move about without questions. With more than one hour to spare he decided to locate his recently married sister, Sylvia, whom he expected to find working at the Hobnob Restaurant on East Adams Street. She was not working that day. Uncharacteristically aggressive Elzie asked the cashier about Sylvia's whereabouts and was elated when the cashier-owner offered to call her on the telephone. Although he had twice talked on a telephone, Elzie had never considered the possibility that he could reach his sister by phone. He felt foolish but chose not to share his feelings by acting as though it was routine to telephone his sister. When the owner offered him the use of the telephone he modestly declined, implying it was impolite to use one's business telephone. Elzie politely requested that the owner ask his sister to meet him on the west steps of the courthouse, and he immediately exited the restaurant not waiting for confirmation. Sylvia met Elzie at the courthouse steps in less than ten minutes.

Although slightly concerned by the mystery of the phone call, Sylvia was eager to see her brother. "Good morning, brother Elzie. I hope nothing is wrong."

"Not a thing is wrong, everything is right. I just came to town today to say good-bye to the boys, and I thought since I have a beautiful sister who lives in Pittsfield, I would say hello to her. Now doesn't that sound like everything is right, nothing wrong?"

A relieved Sylvia responded. "Oh, Elzie, I do believe you have visited the Blarney stone. Why didn't you talk to me on the phone?"

"You want the truth? It's bad enough being a country boy, let alone acting like one. I didn't know your telephone number, nor did I know how to use a telephone. I've never called anyone before and I didn't want anyone to know that."

Sylvia opened her purse, took out pencil and paper and wrote down her mailing address and a four digit telephone number. She folded the paper and handed it to Elzie. "I'm very sorry, that question was most inconsiderate of me, but it's easy to use the telephone. There is no shame in not knowing. The shame is in not learning. To use a telephone you pick up the receiver and put it to your ear and hold the telephone in the other hand and talk into the mouthpiece."

Disgusted, Elzie interrupted. "I know that. I'm a country boy, not a stupid boy.

I don't know the proper thing to say to the operator, that's all."

"All you do is wait for the operator to say number, please, and then you give her the number you want to call, and if the line is busy she'll tell you so; or after a certain number of rings she'll tell you that no one answers and she'll encourage you to call later. That's all there is to it. You talk to an operator like she was standing next to you. But you've got to know the number. I believe it's the same procedure anywhere in the country."

"Thanks, that bit of information might come in handy someday. Now, how about I repay you by buying you a cup of coffee and a piece of pie? How about the Hobnob Cafe?"

Obviously pleased, Sylvia slowly moved her arm in front of her to point the way before they walked across Adams Street, arm in arm, as though it were a formal occasion. Both delighted in their silliness. The restaurant was somewhat crowded with patrons whom Sylvia knew. Before they were seated at the counter, Sylvia stood by the counter stools, and in a very loud voice made an announcement. "May I have everyone's attention, please? I want the world to know that this gentleman with me is my youngest brother, and I am most fond of him. He may be the heartthrob of many women, but I have loved him the longest. Will you join me in my salute to a fine young man? To Elzie Moore, hip, hip, hooray." Instantly and with perfect timing, every patron stood, held up a glass of water and joined in the tribute. "Hip, hip, hooray. Hip, hip, hooray."

Elzie was overwhelmed, somewhat embarrassed as he looked at the crowd, and the crowd stared back at him as though they expected him to give a speech. Always quick on his feet, Elzie put his fist in the air and shouted, "Hooray for the soldier boys, for today is their day." The patrons applauded, and Elzie sat down and looked at a menu. After Sylvia was seated he looked at his sister with a glare before he said, "Got any more surprises? You just shot my idea of maintaining a low profile."

"One more." Sylvia looked at the waitress. "I get the check. Anything he wants to eat, he gets, and I get the check. Order up, big boy, this one is on the house." Elzie took advantage and ordered the noon special of ham and beans, corn bread, with side orders of slaw and macaroni and cheese. As he was eating Sylvia asked, "Why do you want to maintain a low profile?"

Caught off guard by the question, he stammered at first. "Well, just because. Today belongs to the boys who are going into the Army, and that's the way it should be. They deserve all of our attention." For some reason the explanation satisfied his sister. After Elzie finished his meal, he ordered apple pie and coffee. Sylvia was pleased, so was Elzie. Sylvia suggested that they spend time with one another as they watched the afternoon activities, but he declined her offer, citing personal reasons for wanting to be alone. His sister again accepted her brother's explanation, never suspected other motives and returned home alone. In his mind, and in his own way, Elzie had told his sister good-bye.

Every passing minute the crowd increased in number, excitement grew in intensity. The seventeen year old from Milton needed a fitting location where he could observe the ceremonies, yet not be noticed himself. Pulling his cap lower on his forehead, he walked, with lowered head, to the sidewalk on the south side of the square where he found an unobtrusive place to observe the ceremonies—the rear of the gathered crowd on the southwest corner of the square. Although he had stood in this exact spot many times before, for some reason he did not understand, today he gawked at the downtown area more like a tourist than a native.

Timing was everything; and the clock showed fifty-five minutes past noon and the activities were scheduled to begin at 1:00. The weather remained iffy. With limited success the low clouds were trying to break apart, which would not much affect the temperature, but a glimpse of the sun might enhance the ceremonial atmosphere. The courthouse lawn was massed with spectators, and the adjacent streets were pedestrian lined to capacity. Pittsfield had never hosted such a crowd to anyone's memory. Streets were blocked to all traffic, and most stores had closed at noon per the Mayor's request. Two-story buildings displayed large American flags between the second-story windows while other buildings used any appropriate place to display the colors. Photographs of President Wilson and General Pershing were in almost every storefront as were posters identifying the local agencies supporting the war effort. Telephone poles and lampposts were covered with patriotic material and posters. As was their way, Pike County citizens and businesses were paying tribute in the most suitable way they knew to the boys who were about to leave for war. The people of Pike County mirrored the thinking of most people living in the Midwest, and this spectacle was but one of the many impressive testimonials to the patriotic fervor found throughout America's heartland.

The scheduled activities and the attitudes of the residents reflected a profound change in America. For the first time in American history the citizens of this nation were not only willing to send their sons to fight a war in Europe, they were eager. On the surface it appeared that most Americans had lost their natural reluctance to fight a foreign war. If dissent to American involvement in the war existed, it was not visible in Pittsfield, Illinois, on this October day.

Promptly at 1:00 a twenty-five piece brass band, members dressed in black slacks, white shirts and black ties and positioned on the south steps of the courthouse, erupted with the thunderous music of *The Stars and Stripes Forever*. The overwhelming sound of their music commanded full attention and the ceremony was officially underway. The musical tribute was rousing, and almost everyone stood at attention, some with their hands over their hearts, as they faced one of the many American flags unfurled and displayed for this inspiring occasion.

Elzie observed the ceremonies from the sidewalk in front of the Parkway Hotel on East Washington Street. He removed his hat, stood at attention, and looked at Old Glory as his body stirred with pride, patriotism. On that day he stood tall, not only proud to be an American, but proud of his intent to join the great crusade. Today's tribute was also for him, even if others did not know it.

Each of the distinguished speakers spoke briefly in praise of the conscripts. The platform from which they spoke included not only the Mayor of Pittsfield, the State Representative from the district, and the chairman of the Pike County Exemption Board, but also a host of other local dignitaries. The War Savings Organization, the Red Cross, and the Salvation Army were also represented on stage. To the cheers of the multitudes a Civil War veteran closed the official ceremony at the courthouse square with a battle cry for the defeat of Germany. Truly, it was an auspicious beginning.

Following the opening ceremony the inductees were gathered for a group picture. This lull in activities provided the spectators an opportunity to position themselves for a cheering position along the designated parade route. The schedule called for a 3:00 group march of the inductees starting at the intersection of East Washington and North Monroe Streets and marching four and one-half blocks north. The parade was to terminate at the railroad station, and the train transporting the inductees was scheduled to leave at 4:20.

This transitional time allowed Elzie his opportunity to maneuver unnoticed in the crowd as he put into action the final phase of his plan. Discreetly making his way to the station, he retrieved his satchel and patiently waited in a judicious location under a maple tree at the southwest corner of the railroad station. He grew more excited as only a few more strategic moves and his plan would fall together, his dream would become a reality.

The anticipating crowd lined both sides of North Monroe Street. Suddenly, Elzie heard the band strike its chord, and the crowd erupted with thunderous cheering as the inducted men began their march. At times the crowd was almost loud enough to drown out the music as a concealed Elzie patiently waited for the band to near the train station where, once again, the rousing music prevailed. The emotionally moving music reached a high plateau for the proud marchers when the band started to play *Over There*. In unison the proud inductees shook their clenched fists in the air. This action of clenched fists so moved the crowd that they began to sing aloud the few words they knew of the recently composed ragtime song, intended to inspire Americans and to assure the British and French of American intervention. The crowd sang aloud, repeating the refrain almost as though they were singing a patriotic prayer.

"Over there, over there.
Send the word, send the word over there,
That the Yanks are coming, the Yanks are coming,
The Yanks are coming, over there."

There was reason this song inspired. The seemingly endless war now had the possibility of a conclusion if only the Americans could get there quick enough in sufficient numbers to turn the tide. This song announced to the world that it was going to happen.

As the marching men moved toward the station the cheering crowd fell in behind them, giving the frightening impression that a great horde of people would descend upon a small open space near the station. It did not happen. The crowd remained orderly, and fortunately the train was already in place to systematically receive the recruits. Since no major rail line ran through Pittsfield, the train was waiting on the spur line of the Wabash Railroad which linked Pittsfield to Maysville Station, the closest link to the major line. At Maysville Station the train would connect to another troop train carrying recruits from Quincy, Illinois. The final destination was an Army basic training facility at Camp Zachary Taylor, near Louisville, Kentucky.

Before boarding the train, the inductees were granted a few minutes for personal good-byes. Every inductee bid an emotional farewell to someone, as even the men who had no one at the station to personally see them off managed to find a proxy as on this day all the inductees were heroes, and hugs and kisses were free for the asking. In short order the inductees were called to attention, efficiently lined up in front of three different passenger rail cars, and prepared to board the train when their names were called. It was a bittersweet parting for the inductees as most were proud to go, but sad to leave. Unquestionably, this day would become a milestone in their young lives as from this time forward they were in the Army for the duration of the war.

As the men boarded the train, Elzie discreetly walked around the rear car to the far side of the train, and hoping to conceal his presence he stood close to a wheel of the rail car near the junction of the last two cars. Here he waited until he heard the train whistle and the train jerked in a slight movement as it started its forward motion. With satchel in hand Elzie quickly jumped to the steps on the rear platform of the last car, never facing the direction of the crowd. As the train slowly pulled away from the station he heard someone shout his name, but refusing to reveal his identity he never turned to identify the caller. Pride overtook him when less than three minutes out of the station and far enough away to still see the crowd, Elzie turned and gave a big wave good-bye to the crowd. He thought he saw some returning waves, although he was not certain. In his own mind he, like all the others, had waved good-bye to the adoring crowd. He had little time to savor the thrill as now he had to mentally prepare for his next obstacle, the merger of trains at Maysville Station which would shortly be at hand for Maysville was a short six miles ahead.

Maysville Station presented the greatest possibility of discovery, and it was still much too close to home for comfort. Failure this soon would be disastrous. Concealed from the other passengers he continued to stand on the platform at the rear of the rail car, rather than entering the car and risking detection. The train gradually slowed, eventually coming to a complete stop on a track which ran at an acute angle to the major line. From his outside vantage point he could see another troop train already on the tracks east of Maysville Station and, fortunately, there was no crowd of spectators at the station. For about five minutes there was no train movement, nor did anyone get off. Elzie had no option other than to patiently wait.

The small village of Maysville Station showed no more than twenty or thirty buildings, most of them private houses. Never having been here before the limited number of buildings surprised Elzie. He spoke to himself. "Not much larger than Montezuma, and nothing compared to the metropolis of Milton."

Out of the blue came the voice of a child. "What about Milton? My grandpa lives there." Elzie turned to see a small boy standing not five feet from him. Providentially, the discovery had been made by a child who was more interested in Elzie than in revealing Elzie's presence. A stunned Elzie looked around for others, but he detected no one else.

Compelled to answer, and desiring to answer in a suitable manner, Elzie put his fingers to his lips to indicate silence, and then proceeded to speak in a whispering voice. "Oh, nothing, I was talking to myself. Do you ever do that?"

Acknowledging the plea for quiet, the boy answered in an equally soft manner. "Yeah, all the time. Why are you out here instead of inside the train, and how come we've got to be so quiet?" It was a good question, which required a proper explanation.

Deciding that the truth was his best defense, he told it. "I'm running off to join the Army, and I don't want anybody to see me. I can't figure out where to hide because I don't know what the train is going to do next." Before he finished his last word, the train suddenly jerked and the movement almost knocked Elzie off the train.

The small boy giggled at Elzie's spastic movement. "Hold on, soldier boy, there's more to come. You're sure enough in the right place. Your train will go to the tracks and they will disconnect your engine because the engine goes into the big circle and returns to Pittsfield, and you go east. Hang on, you've got two more jerks before you connect. If you really don't want anyone to see you, you better stay on that side and stand close to the train car. It's easy to hide, I do it all the time." The boy placed his fingers to his lips just as Elzie had done. "Be real quiet and you'll be okay. So you're going to join the Army, good for you. Wish I could go with you. Shoot one of those dirty Germans for me, will you?" The boy put his fingers to his lips again, turned, and walked away as though he was out for a stroll and had seen nothing unusual. One could tell he enjoyed having been included in the conspiracy.

The boy's advice had been correct. The train slowly moved to the main tracks, lost it's engine, and was linked to the other train. There were two more sudden jerks before the train slowly started its forward movement, and as the train moved by the station Elzie could see the small boy waiting to wave good-bye to him. The boy gave a thumbs up and a big smile. Elzie shouted to the boy, "Thanks, kid." The young adventurer had not yet been gone twenty minutes from Pittsfield, and already he had made a new friend. He felt considerable satisfaction having some-one wave good-bye to him, and him only.

As the train gained momentum, Elzie felt a little more confident because his well thought out plan was finally coming together. His body relaxed, he sensed a decrease in anxiety. It was a good feeling.

Although the air was cool, he intended to stay outside on the car platform until the train was on the east side of Jacksonville, which he estimated to be about thirty minutes. Taking comfort in his conclusion that he was now safe from detection, he resolved that he should take advantage of the train ride, enjoy the terrain. Without understanding why, he seemed to view the countryside with different eyes, as he had done in Pittsfield. Oh yes, he saw the land as his home, but he also viewed it as the land of his heritage. Not knowing for sure how long he would be gone, he needed to capture a mental image of the land of his youth. He wanted a final image of the land of his father, and his father before him, and the only land that he had ever known. His perceptions of the passing land were grand, and he felt pride because of his past associations with the rugged land of Pike County.

The train was moving fast, and within minutes the train speeded across the low rail bridge on the Illinois River, offering Elzie a brief but different perspective of the river he knew so well. He was positive he identified the exact location of the river current even though the river looked different from a perspective of height. Although the river did not appear as wide as he knew it to be, the sight from above was spectacular. Now the east bank of the Illinois River represented a gateway to a new world. His emotions ran high, and Elzie felt as good as he ever remembered feeling. He wanted to make some proclamation, to state his feelings, but the appropriate words eluded him. He simply expressed his satisfaction through a big smile.

Before the train reached Jacksonville the low clouds suddenly released their moisture, immediately forcing Elzie to make an unforeseen decision. There was no question that if he stayed outside the car he and his best clothes were going to get soaked. Once he pondered his options it did not take long before he cast his fate to inside comfort. Surely the carload of Pike County boys would be sympathetic to his endeavor and would not betray him, plus he believed he could accomplish the task with little ado. He had no such luck. As he opened the door the outside noise carried into the interior of the car, attracting the attention of almost everyone inside. As he looked around he realized he knew almost everyone, by sight if not by name, except for two train officials and a rather large, stout looking man in an Army uniform to whom the officials were talking. Elzie could not identify rank or insignia, although he assumed the man in military uniform to be of some importance. The situation did not bode well as the three men had clearly observed the entry of the intruder. In a futile effort to disguise his unauthorized presence, Elzie engaged in conversation with other occupants. The large man in uniform walked straight to Elzie and spoke in a firm, but polite voice. "May I see your order number?"

"See my what?"

"See your order number. The slip of paper they sent you in the mail. The one you had to present to get on this train."

"Oh, that one. I guess I don't have it. Maybe they forgot to send it to me." The group around Elzie was amused by the interrogation and the evasive answers, but Elzie knew the large man was getting annoyed.

"Then what in the hell are you doing on the train? Are you alone or are there others?"

"No, I'm alone. I'm trying to join the Army. I'm on my way to basic training, like everyone else. I don't want any trouble, I just want to join-up. There's no place in Pittsfield to enlist until you're twenty-one. I'm not twenty-one yet."

The man looked less aggravated, more sympathetic. "Well, if that doesn't beat all. This is a new one on me. I've never had a stowaway before who wanted to join the Army. I'm not real sure what I should do." The man in uniform resumed his stare, but now it was more of a quandary look, less accusatory. "You stay here while I talk to John, the local organizer, and the conductors and we'll see what they come up with. You wait right here, you understand?"

Elzie worried that he had made a poor presentation to the man in uniform. This bothered him that he had botched his first opportunity to persuade an important someone of his sincerity. He felt stupid for what he had said, wishing he could talk to him again but instead he remained in the exact spot where the man had told him to stand. Obviously, this was not a man to cross. The lad feared he had bungled the one situation that had to go right, but now all he could do was wait, fret, and hope. For the first time since Milton he worried that his fate was not in his own hands, but was in the hands of a stranger. The train slowed but did not stop as it traveled through Jacksonville. At least they were not going to throw him off the train in Jacksonville.

He feared the moment of truth was upon him when he saw the man in uniform and the train conductor headed for him. Neither looked pleased. The conductor spoke first. "What's your name, son?"

"Elzie H. Moore, sir."

"Where do you live?"

"I used to live in Milton, but now I live where ever the Army wants me to live. I'm going to join the Army, sir. One way or another, I'm going to join."

"I do believe you will. However, I can't let you stay on this train. You're getting off at our next stop, Springfield." Elzie's heart skipped a beat. "If you want, I will try to help you get back home."

Discouraged and ill at ease, Elzie politely replied. "No, thank you, sir, I'm not going home. I'm going to join the Army, and I can't enlist in Milton. My mind is made up, that's all there is to it."

The military man responded. "That's what I thought you would say. I admire your spirit, son. As far as I'm concerned, I would take a whole trainload of men just like you, but I don't have a choice, and that's that. However, I can do the next best thing. I will show you where to enlist in Springfield. The recruiter there is an old Army buddy of mine from Jefferson Barracks, and I know for sure that if you tell him the same things you told me, he'll sign you up. Do you want that?"

These words were golden to the lad who was temporarily out of his element and in dire need of some positive feedback. Finally, instead of more obstacles, his dream was one major step closer to reality. Elzie answered with absolute elation. "Yes, sir, I want that very much."

Looking at the conductor, the man in uniform continued. "Do you have a problem with me helping him?"

"No problem, whatsoever. I do have a question for young Elzie. How did you get on this train?"

Feeling a little more confident, he answered with a spark of confidence, more characteristic of Elzie the boy than Elzie the stowaway. "It was no problem at all. I just got on." He winked at the other man, gave a toothy smile and said, "If you put your mind to it, you would be amazed at what you can do and my mind was set to join the Army." His borderline cocky response amused both men.

"In other words, you're not going to tell me."

"Correct, sir, if it's all the same to you."

The metropolis of Springfield looked huge to the country boy. The train reduced its speed as it passed a large cemetery and a residential area with houses situated perilously close to the tracks. Structures of all types bordered both sides of the railroad right-of-way as far as the eye could see. Beautiful trees in partial fall color towered above most of the buildings except for a large rectangular area in the center of town which was dominated by taller buildings, many with domes and spires. Within minutes the train came to a complete stop well past the depot area, blocking all street and pedestrian traffic at two different crossings. People on the street waited patiently and seemed accepting of the delay. The man in uniform tapped Elzie on the shoulder. "Let's go, son. We get off here because the train will wait here awhile as they prepare to pick up three more cars of recruits. I need to get you to the sign-up station and get back before the train departs." Only the two of them departed the train.

The train station and surroundings appeared busy. The crowd of people waiting on the platform or in the station seemed either anxious or sad, a familiar scene where so many local people had come to celebrate and to say good-bye to the drafted local boys. The ceremonies were over and now loved ones were bidding farewells. As in Pittsfield, this emotional scene forced one to realize that events similar to this one were occurring in hundreds of cities, in every state, throughout the nation. If one considered the magnitude of these combined farewells, it was profound. At least that was Elzie's thinking.

Elzie was told to take a seat in the corner of a small room in the large building situated adjacent to the train station. The man in uniform entered a nearby office, returned within minutes accompanied by another man in uniform. The man from the train spoke to Elzie in a paternal, but final tone. "Good luck, son. I hope my friend can help you."

The recruiter introduced himself, invited Elzie into his office. He sat behind a desk and Elzie sat in front of it. Before the expected inquiries the recruiter intently studied Elzie as though he was searching for obvious personal flaws. Seemingly he found none and with an official tone he officially commenced the interview. "Captain Brown informed me that you wish to join the Army. Is that correct?"

"Yes, sir, but I didn't know he was a captain."

"Well he is. What is your name?"

"Elzie Hubert Moore."

Upon hearing the name Elzie, the recruiter released a chuckle. "Do you get teased about your name?"

Pride consumed Elzie. "Not to my face, I don't."

The recruiter looked up as if he had been challenged, until he noticed Elzie's boyish smile. "Where do you live?"

"I used to live in Milton, Illinois, a small town in Pike County. My new address is where the Army tells me it is."

That last comment evoked the semblance of a smile from the recruiter. "How old are you?"

"I'm seventeen, I'll be eighteen next March on the sixteenth."

"You're not old enough to join the Army. Eighteen is the age requirement, and that's with parental consent. If we could overlook the age problem, would your parents sign for you?"

"I don't know. My mother is dead and my dad said he would think about it, but he's no where near to sign. I'm on my own, I don't think I need someone to sign for me."

"Well, you do. Why do you want to join? Why don't you wait until next year until you're old enough."

"I think I'm old enough now. Seems to me that if you're old enough to be on your own, you're old enough to fight for your country. I want to join because my country needs me, and my country needs me now. It's pure and simple."

"What do you have to offer your country?"

"What do you mean?"

"I mean what are you good at? Why would the Army want you when you're too young? There is good reason for the age requirement you know."

"It's hard to answer that question and not be a braggart. I was born to be a soldier, I'm disciplined with plenty of grit. I'm an excellent shot with a rifle, maybe one of the best in my county. I'm strong and not afraid to fight. I'm in as good of physical shape as anybody I know. I'm a good runner, a good swimmer, and a decent outdoorsman. I'm a country boy, and I know how to survive on my own. I believe I have what it takes to be a good soldier and that's about the size of it. Besides, the German army is a little too big for their britches, and I'm ready to help take them down a notch or two. Now you answer a question for me. What does the Army want from its men? Are there qualifications? You tell me, and if I don't already have them, I'll get them."

"I do believe you would. What do you want to do in the Army? What are you interested in?"

"I already told you. Simple answer, I want to be a doughboy, I want the infantry. I'm a loyal American and I want to fight the Huns."

"You've convinced me. I do believe Captain Brown was right about you. Let me tell you what we've got for you, and if you're still interested we'll make it happen. Fair enough?"

"Fair enough. I'll be obliged."

"I'm recruiting men for the Regular Army, Fifth Division. I'm not talking National Army, or National Guard, I am talking Regular Army. The Fifth Division is being formed in Texas as we speak. No doubt in my mind the Fifth will become one of the best fighting divisions, if not the best, in the whole United States Army. No draftees, only volunteers, and only the best of them. We won't wet-nurse any recruit. You'll make it on your own or you won't make it. The training will be hard, but effective. No question about it, it's not the easiest road to take, but if it's soldiering you want, it's the best road. Once you are properly trained you will be sent to the trenches in France. If you join up you'll serve with the best, fight alongside the best, be the best. I'm not going to pull any punches here. If it's action you want, action you'll get. That's as plain as I can put it. Do you still want to join?"

"Yes, sir, I do believe I'm Fifth Division material."

"Okay then, we'll fill out the papers, and I'll sign your father's name, making a note that it is with his consent, but that he is not available to sign. That is right, isn't it?"

"Yes, sir."

"You'll depart Sunday morning at 7:00 from this train station. We'll meet right out there in the center of this room. There will be over two hundred men on the train and we'll arrive at Jefferson Barracks, Missouri, close to 9:00 a.m. Do you have any questions?"

"I have one. What do I do until then?"

"You do anything you want to do. We don't provide quarters until you get to camp. Do you have any money?"

Elzie's answer lacked his usual confidence. "A little," and then he paused. "I can take care of myself, don't worry about me. If I can't manage on my own, I have no business being here. I'll be fine, it's not your worry."

The recruiter liked the qualities he saw in the young enlistee, and he was not prepared to lose the prospective recruit because of the departure time. With a benevolent concern in his voice, he offered a partial solution. "I'll tell you what, Elzie Moore. Do you have enough money to feed yourself until we leave Sunday?"

"Yes, sir."

"I close the office here at 9:00 p.m., and open at 6:00 a.m. If you want you have my approval to sleep on the floor while I'm gone at night. During the day you can see the sights of Springfield or whatever you choose to do. Just be out of the office during the day. Agreeable?"

"Yes, sir. Thank you, sir, it sounds perfect to me. I'll disturb nothing, and I will not be in your way."

"You better not. Now, let's finish this paper work. Tell me your full name, again."

"Elzie Hubert Moore."

"Address? Excuse me, former address?"

"Milton, Illinois."

"Date of birth, month, day, and year? Age, in number of years and months?"

Without the slightest hesitation, Elzie answered. "March, 16, 1900. Exactly seventeen years, six months, eighteen days."

The recruiter smiled and gave an approving nod to the eager and honest young man. "Occupation?"

"Day laborer, I'm a teamster."

"Can you read and write?"

"Yes. I'm not a scholar, but yes, I read and write."

"Height and weight?"

"Five feet, eight and one-half inches. One hundred sixty pounds."

"Father's name?"

"Erastus L. Moore. Spelled E-r-a-s-t-u-s, and as far as I know, no one teases my father about his name either. No one teases him to his face anyway."

This comment evoked another smile of approval. "I do believe you are going to like the Army, and I'll bet the Army really likes you." Handing the completed form to Elzie, the recruiter continued with his instructions. "Read this form and if everything is correct, sign your full name where it says signature of recruit, next to where I put the X." Elzie carefully read the form and signed his full name. The recruiter looked at the signature, stood, and extended his hand. "Congratulations, young man, you are now a member of a great fighting force, the Fifth Division of the Army of the United States of America. You will take your oath here, before you leave on Sunday. Report to me in the center room of this building by 5:00 a.m., Sunday, October 7. Any questions?"

Elzie beamed with pride as he heard those long awaited words. He stood, shook hands with the recruiter, and simply replied, "No questions."

CHAPTER 14

BASIC TRAINING

The troop train arrived and departed Springfield without benefit of daylight; and its passengers were an odd collection of men ranging in age from seventeen to twenty-six. In lieu of any official send-off ceremony, only a modest sized crowd gathered to bid farewell. The Springfield recruits boarded and departed with limited fanfare. As they embarked on this perilous mission to serve their country most of the recruits were dressed in their best attire, looking more like they were going to church than to an Army base. They were a patriotic group, a proud sort, a cocky bunch.

It required less than thirty minutes for the troop train to travel twenty miles west of Springfield where the emerging orange October sun then rendered sufficient light to clearly see the countryside. Too excited to sleep many of the Jefferson Barracks bound passengers marveled as they viewed the vast open landscape of farmland. The mature agricultural crops readily manifested the economic value of the rich black soil embedded in the flat, expansive land of Illinois prairie. A few parcels provided pasturing for dairy cattle, beef cattle, sheep, or draft animals, but most of the land served as cropland with large parcels of fenced land extending as far as the eye could see. An occasional farmhouse situated near a large barn and surrounded by a cluster of outbuildings intermingled with the parceled land view. Farmland was certainly not an unusual sight to the recruits, but this rich farmland was worthy of stares. Looking out the window from a fast moving train produced a hypnotic effect, creating the illusion that the land was moving, not the train; or perhaps, staring at the land was the recruits' mere guise to cloak their innermost thoughts. Whatever the reason the first light of the day brought temporary silence inside the railcar.

Unable to contain his admiration for such magnificent land, Elzie turned to the man sitting beside him and politely said, "My name is Elzie Moore and I'm from Pike County, about sixty miles west of here. Have you ever seen more prime farmland than this? Isn't it something?"

"Well, I'll be," the man answered with a grin that reflected pure delight. "My name is Sam Masterson and I'm from Pike County, Kentucky, and, yes, this is the best farmland I've seen. Back home we only dream of land like this." Extending his right hand to Elzie, he continued. "Pleased to know you. Wait till the folks at home hear I met a man from another Pike County. Isn't that something?"

Elzie gave a vigorous handshake to his new acquaintance. "Mine, too. I didn't even know there was a Pike County, Kentucky. I knew Pike County, Missouri, but not Pike County, Kentucky." Elzie paused in his speaking long enough to give a knowing smile. "Come to think about it, many of the people back home came from Ohio and Kentucky. Truth of the matter is my county was probably named Pike long after your county was. As they say, it's a small world, isn't it?"

"Indeed it is." Sam Masterson shook his head in agreement as his eyes moved from looking at Elzie, back to looking at the land. "How much would a fellow have to pay for land like this? Do you have any idea?"

"I do not. Undoubtedly it would fetch a good price. I just work the land, I don't own any of it. If it sold for two dollars an acre, it would be out of my price range."

"Yeah, mine too, I was just curious." Polite small talk continued. A brisk wind blew across the Illinois prairie causing a sway in the scattered trees, the high grasses, and the mature agricultural crops. Seemingly, the farm animals moved about unaffected by the gusty air movement. As both men observed the outside view they were reminded of the many rigors and pleasures of agricultural work created by the elements. Sam spoke in a mellow tone. "I'll bet it would be most pleasant here in the summer with a cooling breeze like that."

Elzie responded with a laugh. "I was just thinking how cold the air would be in winter. Kind of interesting isn't it—same land, different men, different thoughts." Characteristic of men with lives in transition, both were thinking more about home, less about their destination.

Creating a beautiful, almost eerie sight, the low sun cast elongated, distorted shadows on the vast open land. Then, when abruptly the terrain changed before their eyes, shadows and light were no longer of consequence. Hills and valleys replaced the flat land and isolated groups of trees merged into small parcels of forest. They were slowly ascending a mighty bluff and it was the view at the summit that temporarily erased from memory all other sights when on a haze-free day the recruits were visually exposed to the vast, majestic Mississippi River valley. The vantage point from the bluff presented a grand, magnificent view, one that almost defied description. Indeed, the river valley was a sight to behold.

Descending the bluff the train slowly made its way to the rail bridge across the Mississippi River. Every passenger stared in awe, both on the approach and during the actual crossing, at the monumental, spectacular river as the train slowly crossed the river directly into the city of St. Louis. The unique city was situated only a few miles downriver from the confluence of the Missouri and the Mississippi Rivers, which itself was only a few miles downriver from the confluence of the Illinois River. The width of the river at St. Louis was estimated to be almost a full mile, some thought it wider. Few recruits would ever forget the train crossing of the beautiful Mississippi River on that day. To the lad from Milton who had only known the Illinois River, it was an incredible experience.

As the train crept across the bridge Elzie first heard and then saw a low flying airplane following the river north. Within view and north of the rail crossing was another steel bridge hosting two-way traffic of trucks, automobiles, and horse-drawn wagons, and below the river bridge were multiple watercraft, mostly barges and pleasure boats. It seemed that most modes of transportation devised by man were within his view, all at the same time. Elzie shook his head in wonderment, deriving absolute pleasure from all he saw. And to think that the opportunity to see such was all compliments of the United States Army, only made it the better. The mere thought of such made Elzie smile, and smile some more.

The military camp of Jefferson Barracks was situated adjacent to the Mississippi River, less than nine miles in distance south of downtown St. Louis. Although not discernible to the eye, the camp was actually worlds apart from the civilian life that most recruits had known. Jefferson Barracks was a military base, and those who walked within its perimeter were to be governed by military rules.

Although the recruits did not yet know it, they were about to receive their military training at one of the finest military bases the United States government offered at the time. Unlike most of the recently constructed training camps this camp showed permanence and projected a proud military history. Established in 1826 on land provided by nearby settlers, this Army post was the oldest permanent United States military post west of the Mississippi River. Named for President Thomas Jefferson, the camp soon became the military gateway to Trans-Mississippi migration. Originally designated as an Infantry school of practice, the camp eventually became a staging area for the Army of the west. Soldiers from the post initially escorted settlers to the western frontier and fought in the first western Indian wars. In 1845 soldiers from the post were sent and fought in the Mexican War. In fact, most military officers in the comparatively small standing United States Army from 1830 to 1861 received their field training at this site immediately after their graduation from the West Point Military Academy. Two United States Presidents, Zachary Taylor and Ulysses S. Grant, and the President of the Confederacy, Jefferson Davis, had served as Commandant of Jefferson Barracks.

Sixty-five Confederate officers and hundreds of Union officers had served at the camp prior to the Civil War. During the Civil War Jefferson Barracks served as a major training center for the Infantry, an induction center, and a western command center. After the Civil War the post became the command center for the later Indian wars, 1865-1890. In the 1890's the camp was reestablished as an Infantry school. Rightly so, the Jefferson Barracks Post boasted of a long and proud military history.

By 1917 Jefferson Barracks had become more than an Infantry school with a history—it was an established military complex. In 1862 President Lincoln designated over three hundred acres of land next to the camp as a National Cemetery for soldiers who died in the service of their country. After the war both Union and Confederate soldiers were buried there, as were 3,200 unknown soldiers. The recruit train passed by this esteemed military cemetery as it entered the camp.

Also, Jefferson Barracks housed a rather large military hospital designed to meet the demands of long term combat injuries and, if needed, it was slated to become a major veterans' hospital at war's end. Presently used as a medical training facility, many Army medical doctors were scheduled to receive their stateside training at this medical complex. Likewise, in June, 1917, Jefferson Barracks became destined to play another vital role in the Great War when it was designated as one of the many camps for Regular Army basic training.

The train stopped directly in front of the camp but the men were kept in their seats until disembarking the train. The camp appeared to be exactly what it was—a highly organized military complex of two-story rectangular buildings, a perimeter tent city, corrals and stables, parade grounds, training fields, and many other things not yet identifiable, all extending as far as the eye could see in three directions while the Mississippi River defined the eastern boundary. Uniformed soldiers engaging in a multitude of activities abounded the premises. Field guns, wagons, and other military equipment were in transit, and everything seemed to function in a most orderly fashion.

Under the direction of officers the recruits were placed in alphabetical groupings and marshaled into columns. They marched almost a mile to a receiving building for the mustering in process. Here they waited in line at attention until each man completed the initial process of verbally giving personal information. Upon completion of the interview each man was given a large brown envelope, ordered to address it to his home and to place all money and personal possessions in it before sealing it. The process took on a note of finality when they were instructed to keep nothing they brought with them.

The recruits then entered another room, stripped off all clothing and wrapped their garments in a newspaper. They placed their wrapped clothing in a small cardboard box, addressed it for mailing home. Cost of postage was courtesy of the government. Taken to a different area they showered, scrubbed, and towel dried under the watchful eye of a hygiene inspector. For some it was their first indoor shower experience, and if deemed necessary, a few men were scrubbed with a broom by the inspectors. Needless to say, the spectacle of a broom scrubbing encouraged others to be more thorough in their own cleansing. Thereafter the recruits exited the shower room wearing a pasteboard around their neck, and one by one they were physically examined by a series of doctors and the printed lines on the pasteboards were filled in and signed by the appropriate medical personnel. The individual attention given to each man required time, and those waiting for their medical exam watched the process partly in fear, partly from curiosity. All men were struck with one realization—individual privacy was not an Army priority. Lack of privacy concerned some, especially those from the rural areas who had never been exposed to mass nakedness. A few resented the impersonal nature of the medical exam, most took it in stride.

Every recruit was fingerprinted, plus scars and distinguishing physical characteristics were noted. They waited in line until it was their turn to receive a total of seven shots, inoculations in the right arm, vaccinations in the left. Several men fainted. Although undoubtedly embarrassing, if one fainted from the needles there was no teasing from the men in line because most were uncertain of their own reaction to the process, and the men who had completed the shots were quickly routed from the room. This was Elzie's first experience with needles. He did not faint, but he did not much treasure the experience.

Upon completion of the medical exam and while standing stark naked, the recruits waited in another line until they received Army-issue clothing. They were instructed in proper Army dress procedure from hat to shoes. Once the men were in uniform and passed dress inspection they were given a bag full of additional clothing and personal toiletry items before they moved outside and stood in formation until all the men had completed the process. In uniform and in formation they may have looked like soldiers, but they were still a far cry from feeling like soldiers, and they were a farther cry from being real soldiers. No one needed to tell them that, they knew it.

The initial mustering process required less than three hours. The ordeal had been an efficient but harrowing process with more to come. From the receiving center the group marched to a recently constructed barracks which was to serve as their assigned housing. Outside the building a captain speaking from a podium welcomed the men to camp and introduced them to five youthful looking lieutenants. In turn, the lieutenants introduced less youthful noncommissioned officers. The men were divided by columns into five groups, and each group was assigned to a lieutenant. The five groups then were ordered to reassemble in a new formation after precise instructions were given.

Officially, the men were now United States soldiers in the making with the more physically demanding phase of basic training to commence the following day. But first, there were more preliminaries to endure. The recruits marched into a large hallway on the first floor of the large building, past rooms identified as kitchen, mess hall, officers' quarters, captain's office, and storage area. All doors were opened, allowing the recruits a casual glance. A massive room identified as latrine was located near the foot of the stairs and upon entering through the two sets of open double doors the room revealed a sight unimaginable to many recruits—modern facilities with indoor plumbing. For most men who had previously perceived indoor plumbing as a luxury the view of such a sparkling clean facility helped quell many previous qualms about living conditions. Open and in clear view were rows of metal urinals, rows of porcelain bathroom stools, rows of metal sinks, and dozens of faucets for flush and for control of hot and cold water, and in the rear of the room was an open gang shower area. Although they had just used similar facilities the men were taken aback that so much luxury was part of their living quarters. They were lectured about use and cleanliness expectations. Undoubtedly, many needed instruction for proper use of such modern facilities.

Additional wonders were forthcoming. Marching five abreast up a wide stairway of twelve steps to a landing and then another twelve steps to the second story of the barracks, they entered a large, open room containing one hundred sixty single bunks, evenly spaced in eight rows of twenty. Each recruit was assigned a numbered iron frame cot with springs. Orderly arranged on the bed were a rolled mattress, a tick pillow, a folded wool blanket, two folded sheets and one folded pillow case. While standing at attention the recruits were instructed in the proper method of preparing the bed and preserving the precise order of the dormitory setting. Punishments were described for those who could not follow the exact instructions. With the men still at attention the noncommissioned officers barked out additional instructions concerning procedure and housekeeping. Under watchful eyes the men made the beds as instructed. Thereafter each bed was inspected, critiqued, and remade if necessary. The overall lesson was obvious—the Army way was the only way, and they were expected to learn it and learn it fast.

Forms were passed out which required each man to write out the answers to the questions. The captain gave clear directions. "Complete these forms answering every question. If you need help, raise your hand. If you don't know how to answer the question, ask for help and someone will show you how to do it. If you cannot read, raise your hand and we will assist you." In response to the captain's instructions over thirty hands were raised. Questions were privately read aloud and answers were written for those who required assistance.

Afterward the men were awarded exactly ten minutes to take care of personal business, to acquaint themselves with their new home, and to reassemble in proper military formation. They were marched to the mess hall, given twenty minutes to gather their food, consume it, and return their dirty dishes to the proper location. Policy allowed the recruits to take all the food they wanted; but, they were required to eat all they took within the designated time. The point of the lesson was clear—they were expected to precisely follow all orders, directions that not everyone heeded. Observing the men as they ate were mess hall sergeants; and unbeknownst to the men their observations were later used to assign men to extra mess hall duty. Work in the mess hall was referred to as kitchen police, or K.P. for short, and certainly it was not desirable duty. The kitchens of Jefferson Barracks produced over twenty-five thousand pounds of garbage per day. It was said that only stable duty was worse.

After mess came intelligence testing, a ninety minute written exam or an oral test for those considered illiterate. In reality the exam was more a cultural test than an intelligence test, but it did disclose useful information about the recruits. Upon completion of the exam each man was given a one-on-one interview. Although the recruits were never informed of their personal scores, the combined tests were graded A to E establishing a simple reference point for future assignment.

The men were placed in squads and the remainder of the afternoon was spent on the parade ground where they attempted to learn military rank, military protocol, and marching formations. They ate their evening meal at 5:30, following the same guidelines set forth earlier. Once back in their barracks they were given additional instruction concerning Army rules, regulations, and procedures. Lights were out at 10:00 p.m.

It had not been a typical day of Army life, but it had been an insightful day. The mustering in process was over, and closure to the day's activities induced considerable personal reflection. For some recruits this was their first night away from home, and for a few the Army accommodations were far superior to home. For most, day's end merely represented another small step on a long journey, one day closer to becoming soldiers.

Before retiring Sam located Elzie. "Well, Elzie Moore from Pike County, we made it through the first day still intact."

"Yeah, we did. I don't mind telling you that I'm glad it's over. A long, hard day."

"Yeah, not an easy day, but I've seen worse."

Sam's perspective seemed to help. "Me too. Maybe a good night's sleep will help. I hope so. What I really hope is that there are no more shots." Sleep came easy that night.

The following three days provided more instruction and some Army indoctrination. Expectations were established, guidelines for daily living were presented, military standards were explained, and it was made clear that infractions of the strict Army rules were punishable. It became apparent to all recruits that the standing order of everyday military life was learn what needed to be done and do it right. Every activity required a rush effort to get somewhere and a patient wait to start the next activity. Unless specifically solicited by superiors, questions or challenges were discouraged and individual initiative was not valued. Priority was on learning to function as a group, developing personal discipline, and following orders.

To the untrained eye most of the recruits at Jefferson Barracks appeared amazingly similar. This unusual blend of men had been brought together to serve their country in a time of need, and they believed in the cause. All were United States citizens, all spoke some form of English, all volunteered for the Army, and all met the minimum physical requirements. Commoners by birth they were an all white, male group ranging in age from seventeen to thirty-six, no better or no worse than most Americans. Simply, they were Americans of the right age at the right time.

However, the enlisted ranks in the United States Army of 1917 did not represent a homogeneous group. Rather they were a true hodgepodge of American men sprouting from many different walks of life, from different regional cultures. Arrival at Jefferson Barracks was a cultural shock for most of them. Of course all Americans except the Native Americans were immigrants or descendants of immigrants; but, earlier immigrants, those arriving in America before 1880, were more of northern European stock while recent immigrants were more of eastern or southern European stock. Collectively the soldiers of new immigrant heritage were called hyphenated Americans because they were Russian-Americans, Italian-Americans, or some other nation-Americans. But in military service to the Army, heritage made no difference, and therein was the cultural shock, especially for those from rural areas. Some recruits had trouble speaking and understanding English, some could hardly read or write. A few, mostly from the cities, were inept in outdoor survival skills. Farm boys were thought to be the best infantry candidates, but it was not always so. Former civilian occupations just were not good indicators of future success in the army. Interestingly, a few recruits were stifled by the diversity of the group, some were energized by it.

By Wednesday of the first week three men were ordered to return home. By Sunday the number of recruits in Company L. had decreased from 170 to 149 men. No explanation was offered other than it was assumed that certain individuals were not cut out for military life. The Army felt little need to explain any of its policies to the enlisted man other than that personal failure was unacceptable. The actions of the individual were a reflection of the group. The men of Company L. accepted the reduction in number and pride became associated with making it, shame came with not making it.

Basic Training required each recruit to meet the following specified standards: 1. An acceptable level of physical conditioning. 2. A working knowledge of military protocol. 3. A proficiency in the art of fundamental soldiering with limited exposure to weapons and tactics. Generally, the proficiency level required in basic training was reasonable and attainable for all the men, although by any standard it was not easily obtained.

The physical challenges of basic training presented the greatest difficulty. Expectations were clearly presented with the intensity and rigor of exercise progressively increasing from beginning to end of basic training. The first day the trainees marched two miles without packs; but were expected to make twenty-five miles with full packs by camp's end. The physical endeavors were mastered one day at a time based on the premise that either the full company made it or no one made it. All physical feats were designed to build strength, increase endurance, and develop agility. The daily routine of vigorous training remained constant, varying only in intensity. The 24-hour day was structured: seven hours for sleep, one hour for eating, eleven hours for training, one hour for lecture, one hour for house cleaning and personal hygiene, and one hour for personal time. The other two hours were filled with extra duty, more individual training, or added personal time granted as reward or punishment. At the discretion of the drill instructor rest periods were given at various intervals. On occasion the schedule could vary, but seldom did.

Most instructional lectures were usually given to the company as a whole with individual instruction reserved for the smaller units of platoon or squad. In addition to routine military instruction, indoctrination and anti-German propaganda were presented daily. The Army deemed it necessary that all soldiers should hate as well as fear the German enemy, particularly the German method of waging war.

Once rifles were issued the trainee and his personal weapon were inseparable. Not only did the recruit learn to assemble, disassemble, clean, and care for his weapon, he also was held accountable for the condition of his rifle at all times. At minimum two rifle inspections were held per day. The issued rifle was the M1917 Enfield, .30 inch caliber, 5 rounds magazine capacity plus one in chamber, with an overall length of 46 1/4 inches, weighing 9 pounds three ounces, and with a muzzle velocity of 2,600 fps. With an adjustable sight the Enfield had a long range up to 3,000 yards, an effective range to 1,400 yards, and an accurate range up to 600 yards. Recruit Elzie H. Moore could not have been more pleased when he saw the rifle issue, as the Enfield was similar to the rifle he had fired in Pearl, Illinois. He cherished any opportunity to train with it and strove to become one of the best shots in the company. Elzie had been correct in his assumption that he and the Army were a good match.

Training was physically demanding, but positive results made it somewhat rewarding. The men accepted that physical conditioning was the focus of everything, everyday, for everyone. Many of the farm boys were physically advantaged because of their previous lifestyles, but they too were pushed to new limits. The youthful bodies of the beleaguered recruits, exhausted by evening but rejuvenated after a night's sleep, were gradually becoming the physical specimens demanded for service in the Army Infantry. Of course the recruits complained when pushed hard, but most complaints were rhetorical, self-indulging. These men were healthy young volunteers who had entered military service with eyes wide open. As the days passed the men learned to be soldiers, felt like soldiers, acted like soldiers. Few questioned the value or the method of the military basic training process. They became proud men training for Regular Army Infantry, and deep inside their hearts they knew they could endure the training, the punishment, or whatever was necessary to achieve that goal. They understood the urgency, the need.

Drill instructors were the gatekeepers of the American Army, and the gates at Jefferson Barracks were well guarded. To get the most from every recruit the D.I.'s had to push hard, and under their watchful eyes the men were exposed to the best training methods of the time. The D.I.'s were tough with a purpose—to prepare every man for combat duty, and there were no shortcuts. Perhaps D.I.'s were over zealous, sometimes abusive, but most recruits accepted their harsh methods as necessary.

At 9:30 p.m. on Saturday night, October 20, the senior D.I. spoke to all the men in Company L. He was unusually harsh in his tone. "You pussies disappoint me almost everyday, but if you disappoint me on Monday, I promise you will regret it. Monday we start evaluation of your physical fitness and will determine who has the balls to earn the rank of Private in this man's Army. The evaluation will last one week and we will test you on everything we have taught your sorry asses since the day you arrived at camp. Some of you are not going to make it, and those pussies who don't make it will have the opportunity to receive three more weeks of basic training. If you can't make it by then, you'll get more training until we get your puny, pathetic bodies in shape. From here on out nobody fails. You train until you make it. Do you understand?"

A collective, "Yes, sir!" resounded.

A voice from the crowd interrupted. "What if we make it the first try?"

The D.I. responded without hesitation. "I didn't ask if there were any questions, I asked if you understood. Whoever asked that question identify yourself." The recruit stood. "During your personal time tomorrow you have two hours of K.P. Are there any more unsolicited questions?" There were none.

"Good, we'll move on. You might be wondering what happens if by some miracle some of you pussies pass the tests the first time. The answer is simple. You become a private, and you report to my office for assignment; and once we get your paperwork squared away, we'll ship you out for advanced training in your yet to be decided designated area of specialization. Do you understand?"

There was a collective response of "Yes, sir."

"Tomorrow morning you start with full inspection and those who pass inspection continue. If you fail inspection you stay right where you are until you pass. As soon as you pass inspection you will be granted individual time, a rare opportunity to mentally and physically prepare yourself for the other tests. The longer it takes you to pass inspection, the less preparation time you have. I strongly suggest that you pass inspection the first time. I also suggest that you think about what I have said, identify your shortcomings, your weaknesses, and then by God work on them. Do you understand so far? Do I make myself clear?"

"Yes, sir."

"Monday we start with close order drill followed by marching in cadence. If you don't remember your left from your right, you better learn it before then, because no foul-ups will be tolerated. Afternoon activity is the rifle range where everyone will shoot to qualify at 200 and 500 yards.

"Tuesday we double-time with light packs one and one-half miles in fourteen minutes or less. Later that day we run the complete obstacle course and we keep running it until we sort out the ladies in the group.

"Wednesday is the endurance test, eighteen straight hours in the field with full packs and tents, and as you can well imagine it might be rather chilly out there. Meet all the requirements and you'll get your promotion. It's that simple, a piece of cake, unless you're a pussy that is.

"Thursday is second chance day, your final chance to make amends if you don't qualify in one area the first time. There is no make-up if you fail to qualify on the firing range. If you can't shoot by now that's all she wrote, you start basic all over." He paused for affect. "If you meet all of the requirements, Friday is your interview evaluation day and if you fail, Friday is your first day of basic training for another three weeks. One more thing. I don't want to discourage you ladies but most likely only a handful of you will make the grade, and the rest of you will need more training, and we'll be only too happy to accommodate you.

"That is all. Report immediately to the parade ground for night inspection. Dismissed."

Sunday morning the recruits were given additional time to prepare. Not the usual, every recruit became preoccupied with his own little world, attempting to properly prepare his space and equipment for the dreaded process of final inspection. Fewer than forty men in Company L. passed the first round of inspections, five of whom were from the first squad, second platoon. The elite group included Elzie and four of his military buddies: Tony Cimino, Alpio Souppo, Antonio Wolpi, and William Upton. The five men, obviously proud of the inspection results, walked together to the mess hall to eat their first military meal as individuals without imposed time constraints. These stout hardy men enjoyed their new found freedom, eating all they wanted and at their own pace. There was little conversation during the meal, other than an occasional complaint or comment. "Pity the poor slobs who didn't pass inspection."

"No pity from me. It's their own fault if they can't make their own bed by now."

"Wish I had a pass. I'd go in to Saint Louis tonight and find me a gal."

"Not me! I would hit the bunk and catch some z's." The conversation was meaningless because no one really talked about anything of substance, and no one really listened to the others. This relaxed meal was more about a rare military freedom of unstructured time, and less about profound personal expressions. It was all part of their reward.

However, once the meal was completed and a cup of coffee was in hand, the boys were anxious to seriously talk about the upcoming week. William spoke first. "I don't know how you guys feel, but I'm a little concerned about this week. Do they really expect us to pass all the tests? I feel fortunate to get by the inspection let alone the other requirements, especially the obstacle course. We've never done the complete obstacle course all at one time. I think that could tire me out in a hurry."

Tony gave the first reply. "Maybe, maybe not. I think what they really want is to get the physically fit men out of basic training in order to make way for new recruits. If you can do what they expect, why not get on with it and get some real military training. The sooner we get over there, the sooner we kick some kraut ass. I'm all for it, either we make it, or we don't. If we fail, we train until we don't fail. I say it's time to get on with it."

Antonio became amused. "Get on with it, my ass. They're not talking about a picnic in the park, this is going to be a grueling week. I know I can't make the endurance test. I've heard talk. First, you run one and one-half miles for warm-up, and you've got to do it in eleven minutes or less. Then, you carry full pack, and I'm talking almost one hundred pounds, and take a twenty-mile hike. They say you've got to do all of that in twenty-two hours. I don't know about you guys, but I don't think I've got it in me. Hell, what do I know? I thought I was in good shape when I arrived here. Wrong, wasn't I?

"What about it, Elzie, think you can make it?"

"Not sure, I hope so. I'm ready to give it a try."

"That's the spirit. Somehow, I knew you would say that. Let me be more to the point. Do you think the rest of us can make it or is it too tough? Do you think we need more training time? I don't mean do you think we ought to spend more time here, I mean do you think we need more fitness training. I can't believe anybody would want to repeat basic training."

Surprised by the solicitation of his opinion, and not knowing exactly how to answer, Elzie hesitated. Instead of answering the question he made reflections about the Army in general. "Oh I don't know about that. I kind of like it here. No, that's not right either. What I mean is I sort of like the Army so far. Three squares a day, a place to sleep, and a chance to develop some skills that will prove useful isn't all that bad to me. I know you've got to play by their rules, but it seems to me that following rules describes life, not just the Army. There are worse places to be. I suspect that basic training is the first important step, and I sure wouldn't want to fight the Huns without it." Elzie paused in his speaking after he realized how he must have sounded. Here he was the youngest, giving unsolicited commentary about the Army and not answering the question. He felt foolish. "Sorry about my rambling, guys, let me try again. I'm not sure what level of fitness we need to obtain in basic training. I assume the tests will reveal how good or how bad we really are. In my opinion nothing so far has been that tough, if you're willing to work at it. Yeah, I think we can pass everything. It won't be easy, but it's possible. The thing I worry most about is the rifle range."

Alpio gave a sarcastic laugh. "Tell me another story. You worry about the rifle range about as much as I worry about getting hungry for breakfast. Give me a break."

"I don't mean I worry about qualifying, I want to qualify as an expert. I know I'm a good shot, just want to qualify as expert, that's all. I might be a little better with the rifle, but I'm not all that sure about it. Besides, you guys are as good, if not better, in everything else. I've watched you train. All of us are going to score well on everything, or we'll do just what Tony said—we'll stay in training until we learn to do it. I think all of us will do okay. Maybe we can help each other."

Alpio softened his tone. "You may be right, kid, maybe we can help each other. I do know one thing for sure. We have got to pass it sometime and I sure as hell hope it's now. When I get into combat, I hope the guys beside me can pass it too. Don't want to be over there with any slacker. I want guys like you right beside me. I don't know all of you that well, but I'm like Elzie. I have watched you train, and I like what I see. I guess I agree with Elzie, I think we'll be okay. I hope we all make it the first try."

Elzie smiled. "Guess I'm not the only one who rambles."

Antonio slurped his last sip of coffee and kept his cup midair when he spoke as though he were using it as a band director's wand to point to the person to whom he was talking. "I can tell you one thing. All of you are going to be damn good soldiers, absolutely, no doubt. Interestingly, we five are as different as day and night yet the Army has given us common ground. Why don't we draw on our differences and help each other out? If one of us happens to be a little better in one phase of something, he should help the others, and we'll all do it for each other. With a little help from one another maybe we all can get through this week. We watch out for one another. Yes, sir, we'll form our own little triangle where the whole is far stronger than the total of individual sums. By God, it just might work. What about it?"

Elzie spoke loud and clear. "I like that little triangle stuff. I'm not sure how we will help each other, but as far as I'm concerned, it's a deal."

Antonio extended his hand palm down to the group. "To the little triangle."

The other four joined Antonio and placed their hands on top of one another. In unison they shouted, "Little triangle."

Out of this impromptu discussion came a lasting bond. All five recruits, men with raw physical talent, found confidence and security in a group pledge of assistance to one another. Buddy was the Army term given to a companion in arms, a soldier one could count on, one could depend on in the heat of battle. These five recruits now had a buddy for training and, hopefully, a buddy in the trenches. They became buddies at a time when buddies were all important. It was reassuring, it was special. If their plan worked, they would become Privates in the United States Army, one step closer to what they all desired—an opportunity to fight in the war.

As had been suggested, the tests were grueling. Four consecutive days of physical activities pushed the recruits to their physical limits, requiring them to apply all they had learned. Making everything more difficult the weather turned uncooperative. The beginnings of an unusually early winter descended on the Midwest, bringing strong northerly winds with cold temperatures accompanied by occasional rain and light snow. The combination of harsh elements and physical rigors forced several trainees to withdraw from the tests, but not the five. The members of the little triangle followed their plan and drew strength from one another. They persevered. Except for the results from the rifle range, the recruit had no way of knowing his field evaluation until the end of the week when the results were to be posted. Hope of passing waned as the week progressed, spirits became dampened.

The evaluation results were posted Friday. Many were disappointed as fewer than half of the recruits successfully met all the requirements. Fortunately, all the members of the little triangle made the grade and were ordered to report to the D.I.'s office for personal evaluation, and then ordered to the company captain's office for their assignments. Upon arrival at the captain's office each recruit was assigned an individual conference time to personally meet with the captain. The five buddies became separated during the process.

This one-on-one meeting with the company commander was a first occurrence, and the thought of talking directly to Captain Martin was very intimidating. The fears of the recruits were unwarranted as Captain Chester E. Martin merely wanted the opportunity to individually praise each successful recruit. Elzie H. Moore was scheduled for conference Sunday, October 28, 4:30 p.m. He was the last trainee to speak with the Captain.

Elzie found the Captain's office to be a disappointing, unimpressive area. He expected to see an ostentatious, posh environment, instead he saw a plain desk and two straight backed chairs. The Spartan appearance of the office made Elzie feel more at ease. Captain Martin was seated at his desk looking at some official papers as the sergeant escorted Elzie into the office. The sergeant announced, "Recruit Moore to see you, sir." Both men saluted and waited at attention, holding their salute until the Captain finished his reading and returned their salutes.

"Take a seat, Moore. That will be all, sergeant." Elzie assumed a straight sitting position in the nearest chair. Captain Martin intently looked at Elzie without uttering a word, only occasionally looking through the file on his desk. A long two minutes elapsed before the captain addressed Elzie. "It says here that you are seventeen. Is that correct?"

"Yes, sir."

"I noticed that the recruiter signed your enlistment papers instead of your father. Does your family know where you are?"

"Yes, sir."

"Are they proud of you?"

"I don't know, sir, I haven't heard from them. I assume they are. I sent them a post card, but I forgot to put my return address on it. Why, sir?"

"No particular reason, other than you are the youngest recruit in this company, and you entered the Army without proper consent."

"It was proper, sir. My father gave his consent, he just wasn't there to sign. I lived in a rural area where there was no recruiting station. I couldn't very well ask my father to travel fifty miles with me, just so he could be there to sign the papers. Is there a problem with my enlistment?"

"No problem. You're definitely in the Army now." The captain paused again to look more at the papers, and Elzie gave a quiet sigh of relief after hearing the captain's words. He had needlessly feared that his plan of enlistment might have backfired on him. "Do you like the Army?"

Surprised by the question, Elzie answered with a positive inflection in his voice. "Yes, sir." Captain Martin continued looking at the papers, almost as if he were stalling for some reason. Uncharacteristic of Elzie, he broke military etiquette and asked a question. "Is there something wrong, sir?"

"Nothing is wrong. On the contrary many things are right. You know by now that you met the Army fitness requirements and, indeed, you not only met the minimum requirements you substantially exceeded them. How do you account for that? Are the requirements too easy?"

"No, sir. They definitely are not too easy. I cannot account for it, other than I worked hard, but so did the other men. I want to make it clear that I worked no harder than the others. I have no explanation. Before my enlistment I spent a lot of time in the woods doing many of the activities the Army wants us to learn. I

Private Elzie H. Moore
Company L., 61st Infantry, 5th Division

suppose one could say I had a head start in training." Again there was a pause as the captain continued to look at Elzie as though he wanted more explanation. "Sir, I don't understand what you want me to explain."

"It says here that the other men like you. Is that correct?"

Uneasy with the question, Elzie stammered. "Sir, I don't know the answer to that question. I would guess that they like me no more than I like them. This is a good unit, sir. I dare say that once we get into combat you will see what good soldiers these men really are."

Captain Martin released a slight grin and nodded an approval. "I understand that you felt you were treated unfairly on the rifle range during qualifying, even though you qualified as a sharpshooter. Explain!"

"Sir, as you know we had to qualify at 200 yards with 30 shots."

"Yes, I know that. It takes a score of 150 out of 300 to qualify as marksman, and you shot 300. What's unfair about that?"

"Nothing, sir, but when I fired at 500 yards it started to snow so hard I couldn't see the target. The sergeant made me shoot anyway, and I only qualified as sharpshooter instead of expert. Had it been a clear day I would have qualified as expert. That's what is unfair, sir."

An impatient captain retorted. "Do you think every time you fire that rifle in combat the conditions will be perfect and, if not, the enemy will give you another shot? An expert is an expert under any conditions. I don't think you have any reason to whine."

"I'm not whining, sir, just explaining. I don't whine."

"I'll bet you don't at that. I can see why the drill instructors like you. You've got spunk, spirit. This Army likes spunk and spirit, if you can have it and still follow orders. Can you?"

"Yes, sir."

"Do you still want infantry, knowing that as an infantryman you are going to be in the thick of battle?"

"Yes, sir. That's why I want the infantry."

"Not artillery, or signal corps, or anything like that?"

"No, sir, infantry."

"That's what I thought you would say. Good for you. As you well know starting today you are a private, no longer a buck private. Once you walk out of this office no one will call you recruit. They will call you Private Moore. Monday morning you will participate in a limited graduation ceremony. I expect you to be sharp, be proud. You will march under the banner of Company L., the best damn company in this Army. Do you think that too?"

"Yes, sir."

"Good. After the ceremony you will have your picture taken in full dress uniform with rifle. This will be your official military photograph. Copies will be forwarded to you at your new camp. You are to send one of these copies to your family, and this time you will put a return address on the envelope. Do you understand, Private?"

"Yes, sir."

"Monday night at 10:00 p.m. sharp you will depart Jefferson Barracks on train number 107. Be at the station with your gear by 8:30. You will pick up your written orders there. Destination, Gettysburg, Pennsylvania. I am assigning you to G.2. Do you know what that is?"

"No, sir."

"G.2. is intelligence. There you will train to be an intelligence scout for the infantry. As a scout you will become the eyes and ears of the infantry. Does that sound good?"

"Yes, sir. This doesn't mean I have to leave Company L., does it? I'll still be in the infantry, right?"

"Would that make a difference?"

"No, sir. I will do what the Army needs. I was just wondering. I do want to stay in the infantry, if at all possible."

"It is possible, and you've made that point very clear. After Gettysburg you will be reassigned to Company L. By that time we will all be at Camp Greene, North Carolina, for advanced training. Private Moore, the Army is paying you a compliment, take it exactly for what it is, and don't get high minded. Learn well. Learn for yourself, learn for the infantry, and learn for Company L. Become a good scout. Once we get in combat lives will depend on you, and you damn well better know your stuff, because before too long we'll all be in combat. We need all the training we can get. Good luck, Private Moore."

"Thank you, sir. I will do my job, I won't let anyone down."

CHAPTER 15

SOLDIER BOY

Sunday, November 4, 1917.
Gettysburg, Pa.

Dear Aunt Mary, Dad, and Frieda,

Greetings from the State of Pa. Sorry that I have not written sooner, but as you might imagine I have been rather busy. You may now refer to me as Private Elzie Moore, Company L., 61st Regiment. How about that?

I didn't get any leave after basic or I would have popped in to say hello. I finished basic training at Jefferson Barracks, now I'm in a 4-weeks training program to become an infantry scout. Hope you folks are proud of me, because I'm sure proud of my new life. I love it here, and you can bet the farm that I'm going to be a good soldier. Once finished here I'll be assigned to another camp for advanced infantry training, and then hopefully we'll cross the big pond to France to take the Krauts down a notch or two. I'll try to keep you informed as to where I am.

Actually, Army life is a good life in many ways. Good food, good warm clothing, good housing. I get paid $30 a month, and once I get to France I'll make $33 a month. Who knows, if this war lasts long enough I might get rich. Already, I've met more people than I knew in my entire life before the army, and I've made a bunch of good friends. I'll bet by now that I have met men from at least 30 different states. It's interesting how in the Army you are drawn close to some guys. I've certainly learned a lot about people and I've got some great stories to tell, but I'll save the stories for when I get home. You folks be sure to make a mental note of all the events in Milton so that you can fill me in when I get back. Never thought I would say it, but I kind of miss the old home place.

I practice daily with the rifle, and at the risk of showing no modesty, I might say I'm getting pretty good. You might tell Miss Simmons that I actually train on the exact field where a Civil War battle was fought. A sergeant told us it was the same place that some Confederate General, named Pickett, made a famous charge.

The Army is not all roses. At Jefferson Barracks all recruits had to visit a dentist, and I don't ever want that experience again. Hope my teeth stay okay until I'm out of the Army. Army provides toothbrush and paste and I brush like hell, 4 times a day. Hope it works.

Hope all is well with you folks. If you get the urge, you might write me a brief note.

Enclosed is my official military photograph. Makes me look rather fierce, but still shows my natural charm, I think. If nothing else you might want to put it out on display to keep the rats away (especially any rats with Hun blood).

If anyone asks, tell them about me and assure them I am in good health and good spirits. Tell them I'm in the infantry, Regular Army.

Keep the home fires burning.
With fond regards from your nephew, your son, and your brother,

Elzie,

or if you prefer
Private Elzie Moore

P.S. Frieda. If you can find Sarah's address, you might send it to me.
P.S. 2. This is the longest letter I have ever written. If I was still in school I would call it a term paper, then I would grade myself an "A", maybe "A+".

Immediately upon completion of the letter Elzie posted the letter at the base post office, postage free. Although quite a few military perks were available, this particular one delighted him to no end. Once he mailed the letter, he unnecessarily became concerned about the content, fearing he had created false impressions such as that he was homesick, or worse yet, that he was lonely. He had never felt comfortable putting his thoughts on paper where everything was permanent and open to individual interpretation. Instead, he preferred to talk directly to people, where he could better explain uncertainties, eliminate any doubt as to his meaning. However, since the letter was already mailed its content was now an academic concern, and false impressions were beyond his control.

The following Sunday Elzie wrote another letter. To this point in time he had not received any mail.

Dear Jesse and Helen,

Just a note to say hello and to keep you informed about your little brother. For me, things couldn't be better. I was born to be a soldier boy.

I'm training to be a scout for the infantry. I spend 4 hours a day in the classroom (believe it or not, I love it) and 7 hours a day training in the field. Up to now nothing is too difficult, other than remembering it all. Most unlike basic training I now have some free time every afternoon and a little time for myself every night. I think all the free time is because of all the officers stationed at this camp. Officers need free time. There may be as many officers stationed here as enlisted men.

Next week I have to learn a few key German words and phrases, but rest assured that after the war I will intentionally forget all

German they teach me. So far I mostly have learned to identify German insignia, German infantry weapons, German machine guns, and I have learned a little about German tactics. I have my own copy of the German field manual (in English.)

I spend two hours every morning learning to crawl on the ground and sneak up on people who are trying to sneak up on me. It's a piece of cake. I guess it's so easy because of all the fun things we used to do in the woods and river. I'm just naturally kind of good at sneaking up. Remember the game, "ditch em?" My training makes me think of that game. Can you believe they are paying me good money to spend time in the woods and explore new land? If they only knew that we used to do this for fun.

I do believe Aunt Mary would be shocked if she heard the language around here, and more shocked if she observed some of the behavior. I don't know what it says about me, but I don't have any problem fitting in. When I get home I will need to watch my mouth and behavior. Helen, don't you read what I just wrote, it's for Jesse's eyes only.

Helen, I sincerely hope that you are not still mad at me because of our boat trip. I hope by now you have forgiven my foolish, insensitive behavior. In case Helen hasn't, Jesse, you work on her. Make her forgive me! It's important to me.

Jesse, I've been thinking a lot about our earlier conversation in Winchester. I want you to know that I did not embarrass myself. Thanks for the good advice. Also, I want you to know that you need to stay home and take care of Helen. One Moore boy in the Army is enough for our family.

I had a photograph of me in uniform that I intended to send you, but somehow, I misplaced it. If you want to see the photograph, Aunt Mary has one. As far as I know it's the only photo of me, apart from school pictures, and I hope someone misplaces those terrible pictures.

This is the longest letter I have ever written so I better close. I don't want to injure my trigger finger with all this writing. (humor) I often think about both of you, and I'm proud we are family. Jesse, I still remember the great trip to Jacksonville with you and Frieda. It was 5 years ago, but seems like yesterday to me. Just as we talked about then, I still intend one of these days to see New York City. By train I'm now less than 4 hours away. Helen, I also treasure our picnic on the riverbank. Hope you do too.

Tell everyone hello, and you don't need to write back. I can only imagine how busy, how happy you both must be. Thanks for always being there when I needed help. I'm glad you married Helen.

I will notify you when I get over there.

Your little brother,
Private Elzie Moore
Company L., 61st Inf.

The following Monday afternoon Elzie was pleasantly surprised. He received his first personal correspondence, a letter from Milton, Illinois.

Nov. 15, 1917, 20th century
Milton, Illinois, U.S.A.

Dear Private Elzie, (I prefer Elza) brother, nephew, and son.

Wonderful to hear from you and to know that your sense of humor is still intact (I use the word humor, loosely.)

Everyone is well here. We talk about you often. Aunt Mary placed your picture on the buffet so that we all can see our soldier boy whenever we want. It is quite a sight looking at a photograph of my brother all dressed up in his uniform. Some might say you look handsome.

We are so proud of you that we almost bust our buttons. I heard Dad talking to some friends about you the other day, and you should hear Aunt Mary brag about you in church. In fact, the whole town is talking about you. Don't know if it's true, but heard a rumor that Miss Simmons was singing your praises in the classroom today. The Beacon ran a front page story describing how you ran off to war. Everybody around here asks about you all the time. <u>My brother, the celebrity</u>.

With all that said, I still worry about you. You be careful!

Can't wait to hear your stories about all the people you have met. Wish I would meet somebody different once in a while. Sounds to me like you have a gravy life in the Army (excluding the dentist). I told Miss Simmons about the Civil War battlefield, and was she ever impressed! She showed me on a map exactly where you are. Aunt Mary bought an atlas, and we marked where all you have been starting with Springfield. You'll have to completely fill it in when you get home.

Not a whole lot of news from here. Do you remember the stray dog that kept chasing our chickens, the one you named Misfit? Well Dad renamed him. He calls him Kaiser Willy. I really believe that Dad is going to shoot him one of these nights. We had a wiener roast the other night with about 15 friends and family. Kaiser Willy showed up and stole some of our wieners. Dad sure was mad.

I don't know if you know it or not, but we don't call them frankfurters anymore. Now they are wieners. Sauerkraut is liberty cabbage, hamburgers are now Salisbury steak. More name changes around here than I can write about. Do you remember the group of Germans who used to have their own church? Well not anymore. They disbanded. I heard that all schools in Ill. must stop teaching the German language, if they have not already. Believe it or not, the effects of the war are already reaching our remote part of the world. During the Corn Festival this year they held a bond drive, and came up with a pledge for over $500. Surprised me. We sure seem to hate the Germans.

Weather in Pike County has been strange, unusually wet and cold. Dad says all the signs of a hard winter are in place. Crops matured early, squirrels gathered nuts early, and caterpillars have thick coats with big rings. Hope the signs are wrong. We bought some extra coal just in case.

I can't get Sarah's address. Seems she has moved again, some-where out east. Sorry. I will keep trying, but I doubt if I will have success. If you want I will write you a letter every week to keep you informed about the old place. Just let me know.

Got a letter from Helen the other day. I just love her. Jesse (she calls him Jess) has some news to tell you. Hint—It's a good surprise.

Must close for now, but remember that you are always in our thoughts. Aunt Mary sends her love, Dad says to say hello (Dad is just Dad) I'm sure you remember. Lots of people send their good wishes.

Your loving sister,
Frieda

P.S. Guess who inherited your chores. Thanks a lot!

Elzie read the letter three times, appearing to enjoy each reading more than the previous reading. He carefully placed the letter with his personal items so as to have it if he wanted to read it again. Good fortune seemed to run in streaks as two days later he received another letter, this time from Jacksonville.

11/19/17, Saturday

Dearest Elzie,

What a wonderful letter you write. Jess was so excited that he read it four times and then again before bed. We are so proud of you!

I am writing this letter instead of Jess, because he is so busy with work—harvest and all. When he does finally get home at night he is so tired that usually he eats and goes directly to bed. He works so hard.

Don't you fret yourself about that silly boat ride. I'm not mad.

Mostly, I was put out about me being so gullible. By the time you get home I hope to be a little wiser in the ways of the world, and not let so many silly things happen to me.

We do have some big news, but first the practical news. Sometime in December or January we will move to Peoria, Illinois. Jess has secured a job at Holts where they make armored tanks for the war. He has never worked in a factory before but he feels the money he will make is worth the gamble. I hope he likes it and that we can find a nice place to live. Peoria is a good sized city so we'll see what happens. Jess says the future for a farm-hand is bleak, and now is a good time to make the change. I sometimes worry that he is taking the job because he knows I don't cherish living on a farm. I hope that is not the real reason. He calls me his town girl.

Now the great news. I went to the Dr. last week and he said we are PG. Jess is so excited he can hardly contain himself. If everything goes well you might be an uncle next June. Jess told me not to say you will be an uncle because you are already an uncle 9 times over, but this one is different. This will be Jesse's child. Jess jokes and says this is only the first of 12. If it's a boy we will call him Jesse, Helen if a girl. Rather original, don't you think.

We talk about you all the time, Jess really worries about you. He says he knows that you are one of the finest soldiers in the Army, and when he heard you were going to be a scout, he put his head back and roared with laughter. He said that maybe the Army does know what it is doing. I think down deep he is envious of your adventure. I hope not too envious.

We hope to be less hurried in Peoria and we will try to keep you informed about our activities. Also, hope you will keep us informed about your exploits, if possible.

In love and admiration,

Helen and Jess

Elzie cherished the letter, placed it with his other valuables. He vowed that after

287

the war he was going to teach Jesse's child, boy or girl, how to hunt, fish, explore, and while doing it he was going to tell them war stories. Elzie hoped he could become an influence, hoped he would live up to his responsibilities, those characteristic of a good uncle. He grinned when he wondered if he would have enough energy to work with all twelve. He kind of liked the sound of the words, Uncle Elzie.

The following week training took a different direction, presenting Elzie with his first real military challenge. He studied the relatively new military theory of open field tactics, initially mostly presented in the classroom, very little in the field. Majors and higher ranking officers presented the instruction to the group as a whole, which included company grade officers, noncoms, as well as enlisted men. Learning while sitting next to officers was a rare experience for privates, one which kept Elzie on his best behavior. He rather enjoyed the learning process and was surprised how quickly he could grasp military concepts. He had a better mind than he thought.

Theoretically, this training taught intelligence personnel proper combat employment of open field tactics. In fact, no amount of training could totally prepare the soldiers for proper employment as the concept was untested in modern warfare. Only combat employment would tell the tale. Albeit, training was the critical first step. The very concept of open field tactics was nebulous, difficult to understand. The tactics were essentially an aggressive, offensive form of warfare to break the stalemate of trench warfare. Accurate intelligence about enemy troops in the field provided the foundation of the intricate system of fighting. Soldiers would be trained to simultaneously attack enemy positions from different directions, concentrating on the enemy's weak, or less defended, strategic positions rather than make a frontal attack against strongly fortified trench positions. The ultimate intent of the strategy was to bring about a different type of offensive fighting—to attack and break through designated enemy positions at various points along an extended defensive line, creating multiple flanks for the enemy to defend. At least, that was the thinking with many details yet to be worked out.

Success depended on a properly trained Infantry, the heart and soul of open field tactics. The plan placed emphasis on: 1. Infantry mobility and field flexibility, 2. Infantry firepower, 3. Infantry marksmanship, 4. Small unit tactics, 5. Accurate scouting, 6. Timely execution.

The next two weeks of training were even more to Elzie's liking as his schedule provided reduced classroom time, more field training. As he was fond of saying, "There's only one fly in the ointment, it's too damn cold in Pennsylvania." His training took on a new dimension when he learned to scout from advanced outposts. The concept of advanced outpost was actually very different from the more established forward observation post, because the outpost was an extension of the trenches, fortified, capable of resisting enemy attack, and vital to deployment of open field tactics. Infantry scout, Elzie Moore, was receiving training for deployment in the advanced outposts. This training fit Elzie like a glove.

Thanksgiving Day, November 22, 1917, the men stationed at Gettysburg were treated to an exceptionally fine traditional Thanksgiving meal. Duty and training were reduced to three hours per man, giving Elzie his first day in the military with over twenty hours of free time. It was wonderful, and he spent most of the day eating and sleeping. The following Monday Elzie was ordered to report to headquarters at Carlisle Barracks for evaluation and orders. He arrived at 2:00 p.m.

"Private Moore, reporting as ordered, sir."

"Private Moore, you will complete your training at this camp on Friday, November 30. Congratulations are in order. After that date you will have earned the designation of infantry scout. Of interest, but of little consequence, you are the youngest man to complete our training. I think that fact is worth noting."

"Thank you, sir. I may be the youngest in age but I don't feel that it makes any difference. The day I complete my training here, I will be a trained infantry scout, ready to fight."

"Not yet, you're not. Saturday, December 1, you will depart this camp for Camp Greene, North Carolina, for advanced infantry training. You will be reunited with the 61st. There you will put to the test the training you received here. You will pick up your orders, gear packed and ready to depart, at the Gettysburg train station at 6:00 p.m. on that day."

"Yes, sir."

"You have earned some leave time. You have been granted 36 hours of leave starting at midnight Thursday, November 29. You will report back at base by 12:00 noon on Saturday, December 1. Do you have any questions?"

"No, sir."

Tuesday, November 27, Elzie sent a Western Union Telegram to Frieda Moore, Milton, Illinois.

> Be at Sylvia's house 6:00 Friday night, November 30. I will telephone.
> Elzie

Frieda received the telegram Tuesday night. Aunt Mary thought the message was intended for Frieda only, not a request for all three to be in attendance. Erastus agreed to take Frieda to Pittsfield on that night and, although he wanted to talk to Elzie on the telephone, he would not openly express it. He was proud of his son, but felt it unmanly to express such emotions.

Elzie completed his training at Gettysburg Thursday evening, one hour before his leave was to commence. He had to hurry. He had to clean up, put on his dress uniform, and be at the train station in less than two hours, because he was catching a train—destination New York City, New York.

He arrived at Grand Central Station, New York City, 4:10 in the morning in full dress uniform with no luggage but with great excitement, a mind full of questions, and a determination to experience the wonders of Manhattan. The city of New York, almost made mythical by his own imagination, was now at his disposal. The fact he was totally on his own concerned him little as the sites of New York were his for the taking. Suddenly, a most practical concern consumed him. How does one begin to see a city, where does one start? He had no plan. How could he have been so naive as to believe the city would reach out and give him direction, point out its treasured sites. Caution was required since he had no concept of the city layout, or possible dangers lurking within its boundary. He was a country boy and the city was an unknown entity. The adventure was about to begin, but how and where?

His first task was to build self-confidence, but he was Elzie Moore from Pike County and he was more than up to the challenge. He welcomed it. As he knew it would, apprehension abated, his confidence increased. He was a young man in pursuit of adventure. He could explore this city. Within minutes his searching eyes found all he needed when he saw a large printed sign, Manhattan Guidebooks for sale here. From this point on, he only wondered how much of the city he could see within the time constraints, never doubting that he could see it on his own.

First things first for he was hungry. As he walked down the platform and through the gates into Grand Central Station, he could not prevent himself from gawking at the vastness, the ornate structure of the station. Temporarily putting aside his hunger he stood in the middle of the waiting room, turning and looking in awe at the magnificent building. To others who were watching or within hearing range he revealed his country boy status when he spoke aloud. "Damn, I think this building covers more square feet than all of Milton. I suspect there are more people in here at four o'clock in the morning than live in Milton. Damn, I like it already. Hayseed or not, let me at it." But before he could get at it, he spotted a nearby restaurant and his feet seemed to involuntarily move him in that direction. The rest of his body offered no resistance.

The restaurant was more elegant than he was accustomed to seeing. The adventure had started. After finding a seat at the counter, and looking at a menu with multiple entries, certainly offering more selection than he had ever seen, and with menu prices to match the elegance of the dining room, Elzie selected a staple of bacon, eggs, toast and coffee. Even considering his modest selection, the breakfast was expensive. He had sufficient money so the cost was no problem, other than he was unaccustomed to spending unwisely. When he asked for the check, the waitress lighted up and with a huge smile, she winked and said, "Don't worry about it, soldier boy. It's on the house. The manager said to tell you there is no charge. You go over there and give those Heinies hell. One breakfast for one Heinie's hell, fair enough?"

"More than fair. I intend to do that anyway. Thanks, Miss." Elzie left a fifty cent gratuity, gratefully waved at the manager, and exited the restaurant proud he was a soldier.

Outside the restaurant, near the exit from the station was the magazine stand. Elzie selected a map-guidebook for Manhattan and four post cards. The man running the stand was a plain looking individual, appearing more concerned with the morning paper than with customers. Impatiently, Elzie spoke. "How much, please?"

The vendor looked at the items, then at Elzie, then at the uniform. "I see you are a sharpshooter. How about that? Infantry?"

"Yes, and proud of both."

"As well you should be. Let me see. Since you're Infantry, the guidebook is free. Since you're a sharpshooter, one card is free, providing you send it to your sweetheart or your mother. So, that's a total of six cents you owe me."

With a gracious smile Elzie paid the man. "Thank you, sir, you're very generous."

"You're the generous one, you're serving your country. Wish I could. Good luck, and I hope you enjoy New York. I speak for a lot of New Yorkers when I say, thank you."

Somewhat overwhelmed by his warm reception, Elzie walked with pride as he exited to Fifth Avenue. What a reception he had been given. He felt appreciated, more at ease, and more confident. His courage to explore was boosted. The country boy, a soldier in uniform, felt welcomed in the city.

The sky was still dark this early hour, but the city was partially visible. Electric lights dimly illuminated the sidewalks, the paved streets, and the base of many tall buildings. Elzie felt no need to wait for daylight as time was passing, opportunities might be squandered. The young soldier located a street car, boarded it, and intended to ride until dawn, look at whatever sights he could see. Sometime during the process he figured he would use his map to determine his exact location. It was not enough just to see the sights, he wanted to know what he was seeing, where he was. First he had to pay. "How much, sir?"

Without looking up the conductor responded. "Nothing. Men in uniform ride free."

Throughout that event filled day, similar happenings occurred. The more than obvious New York appreciation of soldiers in uniform stirred a deep pride in Elzie. Today he felt more appreciated than he remembered experiencing before. As a soldier in uniform he was visible and welcomed on the streets of New York. Acknowledging the personal sacrifice of soldiers, the people of New York were gracious and kind. The unacquainted person in the crowd asked no questions and harbored no doubts about him as a person. His uniform was his passport to the city, and the role of military ambassador to the seemingly friendly souls of New York was played very well by the country boy from Pike County. The natural fluidity of his gregarious nature, born of his humble and simple life, emerged and flourished. Responding to the warm New York reception Elzie demonstrated a dramatic flair for the role of goodwill ambassador.

Seizing every opportunity to see and to experience, Elzie absorbed all that was humanly possible within his limited time. He savored the cool and crisp city air. He appreciated the drama of the city, the life within its walls. Most of all he liked the people, the reception they had given him. Elzie was humbled. Not only was he proud to be a soldier, he was proud to be an American. Recognizing the uniqueness of this day, he strove to accurately store all the memories, not only the sights and events, but the emotional feelings that came with it all.

By afternoon he was using the subway as transportation to reach and return from distant city locations. He traveled so much by city carriers that he lost his sense of direction in the city, and for the first time to his memory he was unable to identify north, south, east, and west. He merely followed numbered street signs or read his map. Exploring the city was truly an adventure.

Time was passing and the five o'clock hour signaled the adventure was near its end. Near Central Park on the corner of Park Avenue and East 60th Street, the visiting soldier boy was headed back to Grand Central Station when he approached a New York City policeman on foot patrol. "Excuse me, sir, I need to make a long distance telephone call. Could you tell me where I might do that?"

The police officer looked dismayed as he pointed across the street. "That building houses A.T.&T. I'll bet someone in there can help you."

Again, Elzie felt silly as even he had heard of American Telephone and Telegraph and, without knowing it, he was standing directly in front of the building. Elzie looked at the massive building, donned a sheepish grin, and then looked back at the policeman. "Thank you, sir. As you already might have guessed I am a country boy, just off the turnip wagon."

"No problem, soldier, that's why I'm here. Just go down to the corner before you cross the street."

Elzie grinned when the officer advised him to cross at an intersection. "Yes, officer, and.I'll look for someone to hold my hand."

Entry to the building was through a revolving door. The movement and operation of the door so fascinated the young lad that he twice missed his exit from the door, going around twice before he entered the office area. He hoped no one saw him. Upon locating the information desk, he directly walked toward it acting like he was a native New Yorker. Boldly he asked the receptionist, "Where do I make a long distance telephone call?" Without making eye contact, the receptionist pointed to a wall containing a row of several elongated, mounted telephones. Not at all comfortable with what he saw, he politely inquired, "Where else can I make the telephone call?"

This unusual question prompted the receptionist to make eye contact; and in a business, almost indulging manner she replied, "If it's privacy you want, you may call from one of the booths on the end. If it's help you want, go to one of the operators at the desks. The available ones are without customers at their desks."

Elzie did not appreciate the tone of the receptionist. "Oh, I need help all right, I'm just a soldier. I know how to shoot the telephone off the wall, I just don't know how to use the damn thing."

A nearby operator, hearing the discussion, quickly moved to the front desk before the receptionist could respond, and politely spoke to Elzie. "Please come this way, I will be glad to assist you." She walked Elzie to her desk, pulled out a chair and said, "Please, have a seat." Looking at Elzie with her dark brown eyes and a broad toothy smile she continued speaking, except she spoke so that only Elzie could hear her. "We much prefer that you talk on the phone rather than shooting it." The remark evoked a broad smile from the young soldier. "That's more like it. That smile becomes you, sir. Now, how may I help you?"

"It's easy to smile at you," Elzie replied as he looked at the very attractive lady across the desk. "Not so easy to smile when you talk to a battle-ax," pointing to the receptionist. "I want to make a telephone call to my sister in Pittsfield, Illinois, at 6:00 this evening. I want to impress her. You know what I mean—big brother visits the city, calls little sister. The problem is I don't know how to make a long distance telephone call. I need help."

The operator gave an approving look. "It's an operator assistance call anyway, of course I will help if I can. I think it's very kind of you to be so considerate to your sister. However, we might have a problem. I don't know if we can make the necessary connections for the call. Must it be exactly at 6:00?"

"Not exactly at 6:00, but close to that time. That's when she is expecting the call, except she doesn't know exactly where the call is coming from. That's part of the surprise. I told her to be at my other sister's house because she has a telephone." Handing the operator a piece of paper, Elzie continued. "This is the telephone number, my sister's name is Frieda. I mean I'm calling Frieda. The telephone is at Sylvia's house, my other sister. Did you follow all of that?"

"I think so. Not so fast. Let me get some details and then we'll determine if we can do it. Did you want to call at 6:00 eastern time or central time?"

"Oh, I forgot about that. Central standard time I think. What time does that make it here?" he muttered as he looked at the wall clock. "I always forget that time zone stuff. Hope I didn't mess up."

"That's 7:00 our time, we're still all right. If you want to be certain that you talk to your sister, we will call person-to-person. It will cost a little more, is that okay?"

"I have sixteen dollars. If that doesn't cover the cost, I won't make it."

"That will more than cover it. You said Pittsfield, Illinois. Where is that?"

"Well, do you know where the Illinois River is?"

The operator chuckled and then said, "No, no, that's not what I mean. What cit..."

Elzie interrupted. "You do know where Illinois is, don't you?" This time he had a big grin on his face.

"Yes, I do." Her facial expression indicated that she liked his sense of humor. "Just bear with me a few more minutes. In order to make the connection we must go through a larger city to see if they have lines to Pittsfield. Give me the names of the larger towns, the ones closest to Pittsfield."

"Nothing is real close. Jacksonville, Quincy, Springfield, and if that isn't large enough we have St. Louis or Chicago. Are they large enough?"

"Yes, they are. Let's try Jacksonville, first. This may take some time. Would you like to wait or come back?"

"How much time are we talking about?"

"I'm not certain. Could be ten minutes or could be that we can't make the connection at all. Won't know until we try."

"I'll wait, if it's all the same to you. I'll sit right here and watch you as you work. I don't have enough time to see much more of the city anyway. Besides, as I sit here I might be seeing one of the prettiest sights that New York has to offer."

Unable to contain her pleasure with his flirtatious remark, the operator responded. "Are all the boys in Pittsfield full of blarney, or are you special?"

"Nope, just me, I'm the only one full of blarney. I don't know about special. Might be, I never thought about being special before."

The next fifteen minutes Elzie sat in silence as the operator talked to various other long distance operators. She spoke in a businesslike manner, seemed most efficient, and still maintained her personal politeness. Her gracious manner did not go unnoticed, or unappreciated, by the young soldier boy. Then suddenly, the operator held her hand toward Elzie, and said, "We got it. Give me your full name, the full name of your sister, and I'll help with the surprise." Elzie pronounced and spelled the names, the operator wrote them down as she waited for the final connection. In less than a minute she raised her finger to get Elzie's undivided attention. "Yes, this is the operator from New York City, New York. I have Elzie Moore on the line, placing a person-to-person call from Times Square, the center of New York City, to Miss Frieda Moore. Are you Miss Moore? Do you have a brother in the Army? Would you like to speak to him? One moment, please." The operator looked at Elzie, but spoke into the telephone, still using her businesslike voice. "Mr. Moore, we have your party on the line."

If Elzie's voice and behavior were any basis for judgment, the conversation obviously was a pleasant experience for the siblings. They talked for nine minutes with much of the time consumed by laughter and frivolity. Without specifically listening to his words the operator observed Elzie and his many different reactions. She appeared to enjoy the experience almost as much as Elzie did. Elzie hung up the phone and reflected a few moments before he spoke. "Thank you so much. You did add to the surprise calling me Mr. Moore, and all. You made it sound like I was king of New York. No matter the cost, it was worth it. How much do I owe?"

"You're welcome. Four dollars and eleven cents. Elzie Moore, today you have done a good thing. You should be proud of yourself."

"I am sort of proud. I don't even know your name, and I refuse to call you operator anymore. Tell me your first name, and I'll pay my bill."

"Mary Ann."

"Mary Ann, you are the one who has done a good thing today. You are the one who is special. Thank you, so much. If there was not a war on I might stay in New York, just so I could get to know you."

"I presume the war will someday end. Maybe you will stop in the Big Apple on your way home to Pittsfield, Illinois. If so, you know where I work."

"Indeed I do. Until then, Mary Ann, hold that smile. You can bank on it, I'll be back to see you as soon as this war is over. Good-bye, thanks again."

"You're welcome, again. Good-bye, soldier boy, Elzie Moore."

CHAPTER 16

HOW PROUD THEY FELT

This late December day cheated the dawn when darkness changed to a dingy light under an overcast sky; but appreciative of any daylight the men of Company L. made no complaints as they struggled to complete the final few miles of a long hike up the mountainside. Instead they complained about the cold temperature, made colder by the howling wind.

"I'd like to get a hold of the fool who told me that North Carolina was warm. Come to think about it, it probably was the same fool who told me that training got easier after basic. Come to think about it further, I'm the fool for listening to anybody who talks about life in the Army. Remind me, when I get back to camp, I need to kick my own ass for being so stupid. What do you suppose we'll do after we reach the top? Turn around and come back down, maybe practice doing it again?" It was hard for the others to hear John's words with his wool scarf wrapped around his face as they walked single file up the mountain path. Actually, it made little difference if they understood his words, because the other men knew the essence of his expressions. He was complaining. He was cold, tired, in a foul mood, and ready for a respite from the cold and, in many ways, John was no different from the other soldiers other than he was more willing to express it. The entire company was ready for a break, ready for breakfast, and ready to get to where they were going, wherever that was. There had to be a final destination and, at this point, any place was all right if it meant food and rest. Everyone had cause for complaint, although John was the master complainer, not because he worked at complaining but, simply, because he was a natural. With little effort he could see the dark side of anything. Giving his complaints validity, he was not a malcontent. His grumbling was usually centered on something that was wrong but need not be. Others liked his negative expressions, almost as if he were speaking for the group. Every platoon needed a John, most had one. The complaint this time was that the men were tired of training exercises and believed they were adequately prepared as soldiers. They believed it was time for them to get into the fight.

"Pipe down, John. Save it for someone who cares," responded the lieutenant, who felt every bit as miserable as the men.

"I care, sir," said Elzie. "I like to listen to him."

The lieutenant recognized Elzie's voice and was not surprised by the remark. He responded in-kind. "Only an eighteen-pounder could possibly like to here John complain."

"I wish you wouldn't call me that, sir. I would not call you a brass looie to your face."

"Moore, just be quiet. Eighteen-pounder is a term of endearment. It's an under-age recruit, that's all. And you better not refer to me as a brass looie, if you know what's good for you."

"We've got a deal, sir. I won't call you a brass looie, and hopefully you won't call me eighteen-pounder."

Too tired, too cold to argue, the lieutenant threw his hands in the air and grunted something unintelligible. John became amused. "Don't fret, Elzie. When no officers are around, I'll complain all you want." Knowing that the lieutenant was not looking, John gave a thumbs up to Elzie.

Knowing the lieutenant was watching him, Elzie pretended he did not see the sign of approval, although he could not totally contain his pleasure. A slight grin slipped out, but before it could be detected, Elzie shouted, "Look, sir, I see a big fire ahead. Is that our destination?"

Much to the relief of everyone, including the lieutenant, they were finally in sight of a camp, a place to rest. The camp was obviously a temporary, crude camp, not designed for creature comforts. It served primarily as a training location to house reserve troops positioned for quick access to front line trenches. Located on the near side of the mountain crest, the camp positioned the men near the front line trenches, and yet kept them a reasonable distance from the action of simulated war. It was textbook training, designed to represent the real thing. While positioned in the temporary camp the troops could hear what was happening in the front trenches, but they could not see it. The troops were training under the sanctioned American system of soldier rotation—two weeks in reserve, followed by two weeks in the front trenches, followed by two weeks of rest usually near regimental headquarters. Each location demanded specialized training. That is the reason they were here, the reason they had marched all night—to practice wartime mobility, to learn the exact responsibilities and expectations of the soldier in all phases of the fight. The training was valid, but the soldiers were tired of hearing about the war, ready to become a part of it. They believed they were ready for battle.

The mere sight of the camp offered hope. The hike had been grueling, and they were exceedingly tired, ready for a rest. However, as expected, rest must wait until the routine tasks were completed. The men were shown a rolling patch of ground near a small, semi-frozen stream and ordered to set up camp. Each man knew what to do and under the watchful eyes of the company officers, they proceeded. First, they pitched their tents. Everything was on the buddy system, and every soldier carried one-half of a pup tent which when pitched together could sleep two men. The designated buddy was not to leave the other buddy's sight except in rare, ordered situations. From now until the completion of the exercise every activity was a two-man operation. Elzie's buddy was John, the complainer, and that was fine with Elzie because he believed John to have the makings of a fine soldier. Also, he liked him as a person and enjoyed his company. The feeling was mutual.

"How in the hell do we get these pegs in frozen ground?"

Elzie grinned. "Not sure. I imagine you just pound harder." Looking at the sergeant pitch his tent, Elzie continued. "Yep, you just pound harder. Surely you didn't expect anything to be easy, did you?"

"No, I didn't. Can you imagine how hard that ground will be for sleeping? Yep, cold and hard. I should be an officer and have someone else pitch my tent, a bigger one with enough space for a cot."

"What did you do back home in Texas? Did you have someone make your bed for you, or prepare your house for your convenience? Wasn't it cold there? Ground freezes there, too, doesn't it?"

"Well, for one thing, I didn't pitch a tent in the wintertime, and yeah, someone did make my bed, but that's not the point. The point is I don't like to do it, and I like saying that I don't like to do it. So there you have it. My advice to you, don't pay any attention to me. I sometimes think out loud and I make things sound worse than they are. Just because I've got to do something, doesn't mean I've got to like it. It's just my nature. You better learn to put up with me, because the way I see it you don't have a choice."

These were harsh words from a tired, cold soldier who thought he had a right to gripe. Elzie regretted that he had riled his friend. "Sorry, I didn't mean to ruffle your feathers. I have no problem with you. You think out loud all you want, I understand. But you need to remember that doesn't mean I won't growl back if you say something stupid. I'll put up with you, if you'll put up with me." Elzie extended his hand.

"It's a deal." The handshake bonded a pledge of tolerance.

After the campsite was totally established the men stood in line for breakfast.

Since this reserve camp offered no permanent kitchen, the food was prepared elsewhere, brought in, and reheated. Regardless, the food still tasted good. The men were allowed all the food their mess kits could hold and could go back for seconds if desired. They ate outside on the open ground, selecting their own setting and companions. Elzie and John visited as they ate.

It was understood that for the next four weeks the men would be required to survive with the equipment they had carried in their backpacks, aside from food and water. If additional items were required, they had to improvise as well as they could. A critical part of their training, they were expected to survive in the elements using whatever was available. In fact, this training was intended to teach group survival and required each man to assist his buddy or to help others in need. The men clearly understood the necessity of this training, but understanding did not make the task any easier. For Elzie survival in the wild was no great challenge, although he had much to learn about the problems of group survival.

Individual perseverance was not enough as the loss of just one man diminished the value of the fighting unit. Actually, the exercise had additional worth when the men honed vital information about one another's abilities and, perhaps most importantly, they learned how to depend on others. The soldiers learned to become individual infantrymen functioning as part of a squad, an extension of the platoon, and dependent on the company. Units had to work in concert. The standard order was to look out for oneself, remain vigilant for others. Most men in Company L. learned well, and service with this company became a source of considerable pride.

The scheduled two weeks of reserve status training transpired according to plan. By design the events of each day were different. Weather did not much vary—it remained wet and cold. The troops slept when they could, usually not at night, ate when they were fed or could find food, and practiced maneuvers when ordered. Their lives were not made easy, but it was a good sampling of what they might expect over there.

The final day of field training as reserve units was met with an unexpected but pleasant event—mail call, followed by three hours of free time. Private Elzie Moore, along with dozens of others, expected no mail and instead of waiting in line, prepared for what he most desired—rest and sleep. He chose to be alone, sat next to an open fire, and allowed his fatigued body to absorb the warmth of the flames. Temporarily having no purpose or direction felt good as he relaxed in the same manner that he had for much of his young life—alone, sitting next to a fire.

Elzie's solitude was interrupted by a fellow soldier. "Hey, buddy, here you are you lucky dog. I waited in line for nothing. I heard them call your name, figured I'd find you here by the fire." Elzie's buddy tossed the letter Elzie's way. "I hope it's good news. Come to think about it, any letter would be good news, I think.

Anyway, happy reading. Don't pay any attention to me, I think I've been too long in the field."

The letter was from Aunt Mary, postmarked December 27, 1917, Milton, Illinois. Holding and looking at the letter was cause for exhilaration. It made Elzie think of home, of family, and bygone years, something he seldom did. The postmark also made Elzie realize that he had lost track of time. Christmas had come and gone with no fanfare. He knew today was Tuesday, but he was uncertain about the exact date before it suddenly dawned on him. It was January 1, 1918. "Well, I'll be damned. It's 1918. Happy New Year!"

Elzie held the letter in both hands and continued to stare at it. It was nice to hear from home.

Dearest Elzie,

I take pen in hand to keep you informed about home and to offer assurance that you are thought of often and in the kindest way. Your presence is missed by all.

We assume you still enjoy your military experience and that you are learning how to best dispose of the evil Hun. Our thoughts and prayers are with you on your noble crusade to help make this world a better place.

Frieda and I are doing well, although your father is another story. Not that he particularly is physically unwell, but that a burden of sadness seems to control him. We suspect that a lifetime of hardships and misfortune has taken its toll on him. Perhaps a letter from his youngest son might serve to give him joy. If he could but read or write I am sure he would correspond with you.

Milton remains the same, but life here is more difficult as old man winter has spewed his wrath on our beloved county. The river has been frozen since early December, ice and snow cover the ground, and the winter wind is the strongest in my memory. We stay warm in the house but I do believe that our temperaments (especially your father's) need more outside air. Our section of the state has borne more than its share of illness this winter although, thus far, major sickness has eluded our humble abode.

Young men continue to leave our midst for military service. Many staples are in constant short supply. We at home are making many sacrifices for our boys in uniform and for the overall cause. We all will be pleased when this savage destruction called war comes to a right and proper conclusion.

We plan a special garden this spring, twice the normal size. People here refer to such as victory gardens, because those who plant them are expected to purchase less, allowing more for the war effort. Hope you are getting your fair share of food.

I must close for now. You take care of yourself, mind your manners, and be pleasant to your fellow soldiers.

Your adoring and appreciative aunt,
Mary McCullah

A letter from home, communication from what now seemed to be another world, was always welcomed. However, this letter hinted at a message aside from the usual home news, and it was not a good message. The news about his father's health stressed him, although he felt there was little he could do. Also, news that the folks in Milton were required to make sacrifices deeply concerned him. Strangely, this unadorned truth provoked a reaction in Elzie as, previously, he had thought only of war in military terms—of military camps, soldiers in uniform, or battlefields in Europe, not of sacrifice from those at home. The very thought of home front sacrifices gnawed at his inner being, and the more he pondered the concept, the more irritated he became until, eventually, his anger was totally directed toward the Germans. For in his mind the Germans had started the war and, therefore, the Huns were logically responsible for all the worldwide suffering and hardships, or any other ill effects of the war. It was one more reason on a list of many to hate the Germans.

By mid-afternoon orders came down to undertake final preparations for two weeks of training in the front trenches. Ordered to prepare field combat packs and to be ready to march by sunset, the soldiers, although somewhat frustrated by the short period of preparation time, were anxious for this particular training as up to this point training had been more about survival, or gear and weapons. This would become their first exposure to simulated wartime conditions. All believed they knew what the trenches were like, but few were certain. This was their opportunity to make practical use of training, and perhaps more significantly, to evaluate themselves in a combat environment, minus the enemy. Another company from the 61st was to occupy the opposing trench and pre-planned activities were scheduled to pit one company against the other. At the conclusion of the two-week period one company would be declared a winner which brought bragging rights and prestige, the other a loser which meant shame. The pride of each company was at stake.

Company L. was assembled and ready to move by sunset. The temperature that January night was brutally cold; and although the star lighted night might provide better vision, each recruit knew that without cloud cover the temperature would drop very fast, and many wondered how long they could endure without heat or shelter. Everything about that evening added fuel to self doubting thoughts. What kind of soldiers would they be? This exercise would test their mettle with even the best men expected to find challenge. Until they engaged in actual combat this was as close as they would come to the jaws of hell, so it was little wonder they were apprehensive and nervous on the inside, brave and bold on the surface.

The company marched over three hours in single file over all types of terrain without benefit of knowing where they were or where they were going. The night got colder, and each step became more difficult. Private Elzie Moore was the point man of the column as he followed the ever winding path traversing high ground to an unknown location. He felt relieved when he spotted multiple small campfires surrounding what appeared to be a field kitchen. Indeed, it was a glorious sight, a prepared camp for their use. Arrival at the camp meant it was time to eat, to rest and, hopefully, to get warm. It was a rare time when food was secondary to physical comforts.

Serving order in the chow line was first come, first served, so John and Elzie were first in line. While eating near one of the large fires John managed the first words. "I guess there is at least one advantage of partnering with the scout. By the time the poor slobs at the end of the line get fed, we'll be ready for seconds." Elzie gave no response and both continued shoveling in the food. Momentarily, he spoke again. "Are we there?"

"Are we where?"

"Don't get smart, you know what I mean. Are we at the trenches?"

"How in the hell would I know? I'm the same rank as you."

"Don't be a smart-ass. You led the whole damn column here. Now where are we?"

"I'm not getting smart, I'm as stupid as you are. All I know is they told me to follow the path. Captain told me I would know where I was going when I got there. Guess he was right, wasn't he? Does that smarten you any? If it does, we're both smart-asses."

"You mean to tell me that the entire company has been following you for the last three hours and you didn't know where you were going?"

"You got that right, I just do what I'm told. I'm not sure where we are, but I'm reasonably sure we're not in the trenches. I think we'll know when we get there. God, it's cold! I heard some brass talking last night, and they said this December was the coldest on record. I'm not real sure how they would know that, but I believe them, and I'll tell you something else. January isn't getting any warmer. There has got to be a point in temperature when we can't function outside any-more. Can you imagine how cold it will be trying to sleep in the trenches? No fires there, you know!"

"No, I didn't know, and I don't want to think about it. How do we stay warm?"

"Got me."

"Maybe they have some tents pitched around here. Maybe they'll keep us here until it warms up. What do you think?"

Elzie looked disgusted, or perhaps annoyed by the question. "I keep telling you that I don't know any more than you do, but I doubt it. I don't think that's the Army way."

Elzie's final statement brought an end to any more hopeful thinking from John. Both ate seconds, and afterwards they sat in silence, trying to absorb as much heat from the fire as possible without burning themselves.

About ten minutes elapsed before Elzie heard the growl of some unidentifiable man, no doubt an officer. "Private Moore, up front, take point." With only a brief pause in speaking, the officer continued. "Company L., prepare to move out." The order was greeted with a low roar of discontent, but the officer ignored it.

The column resumed its trek. Elzie was met by an unidentified junior officer who pointed in a general direction as he spoke. "Follow this road for about four or five miles until you arrive at the junction. You will see encampments on the way with fires burning. Just ignore them. You'll know when you get to where you are supposed to be."

Approximately twenty minutes into the march the column marched within sight of an encampment, and the vague orders began to make more sense. The camp consisted of forty or fifty tents, silhouetted by twenty or so large fires. Placed well to the west of the tents were multiple large, wood and dirt, parapets protect-ing what appeared to be nothing of importance. Scurried activity of perhaps a full company moving about in various directions transporting and stacking awkward objects gave a different indication. Something interesting was happening and the marching men wanted to observe it all, but pressed forward.

John, who was directly behind Elzie, was so curious that he risked punishment and broke the silence. He tapped Elzie on the back and queried in a rather loud whisper. "What the hell was that? What did we just see?"

Elzie risked the same punishment. "Got me. I suppose the artillery boys were pretending, some kind of training. Maybe they are laying a pretend barrage on German lines, I'm not sure."

"Jesus, Elzie. There wasn't any artillery there. That's a pretty big pretend."

"So it is. Maybe it's like infantry with pretend rifles. They might not have enough big guns for here and France both, so they make do with a little imagination. Sometimes you have got to make do with what you have. Now pipe down before we both catch it."

"I'll pipe down all right. But here's hoping those guys shoot some real guns before they get over there, especially if they're going over there with us."

"Yeah, I hear you."

A few minutes down the road they passed another encampment, this one with a billboard.

HEADQUARTERS

NINTH INFANTRY BRIGADE:
SIXTIETH INFANTRY
SIXTY-FIRST INFANTRY
FOURTEENTH MACHINE GUN BATTALION

"Hey, that's us. This is home base, buddy. Maybe they'll greet us with a brass band. On second thought, I'd rather be greeted in a warm building with a nice bunk."

This time John snickered. "Yeah, me too, except I know better. As you're so fond of saying, dream on!"

Before long they passed another camp, only this time it was more difficult to determine specifics as the camp was a considerable distance from the road and was not well lighted. However, the sign was well lighted.

NINTH FIELD SIGNAL BATTALION

The intriguing sights all made more sense as the pieces of the puzzle came together. They had marched through a simulated battle zone, and they, the infantry, were on their way to the front lines. The company marched another two miles until they reached crossroads, the designated junction for trenches. Here their C.O. was patiently waiting at the poorly lighted crossroads. "Company L., right?"

Elzie answered, "Yes, sir," assuming the voice belonged to an officer.

"Follow that road to the bonfire where the entire company will take a fifteen minute break. Double time, go!"

The camp offered no building with a hot stove and bunks, but it was a good place to rest. The bonfire was huge, allowing in one way or another all two hundred and fifty-six men of Company L. to gather around and receive some warmth. By now some of the men were so cold that they stood too close to the fire. One soldier caught his gloves on fire. Had this been another place, another time, the situation would have been humorous, but not tonight. Common sense did not prevail as a few men failed to determine a safe distance to stand from the fire.

As the men took their break they were quizzed by a medical officer about possible injury or frostbite. Eleven men, including one suffering from bonfire burn, were separated and sent to the temporary field hospital. The remaining men were ordered to assemble in squads. They were about to enter the trenches in relief of Company C. Noncommissioned officers issued exact, clear instructions. Company L. was to relieve Company C. in the trenches. The men were implored to be as quiet as possible. A seriousness of purpose by the noncommissioned officers was sensed by the men, and they took heed, granting full cooperation. Upon entering the trenches the only sounds were that of an occasional clank caused by men moving with full, field pack, or the chattering of teeth caused by the bitter cold.

With no source of light it was darker than dark as the men blindly entered the man-made, long, narrow furrows called trenches. Nothing was identifiable other than the smell of cold dirt. They advanced by touching the pack of the man in front and following his every movement until an unidentified superior touched them on the shoulder, and ordered, "here." Once the soldier was placed, he stood against the dirt wall, looking out into a dark, dismal, motionless, soundless stretch of land thought to be no-man's-land. Until all men were placed the soldiers waited and stared into the vast nothingness. There was nothing else they could do. Other than the faint voice uttering the repetitious word "here" and an occasional noise made by the slight stumbling of a soldier, no other sounds existed, nor were there visual images. Even though two hundred and some men entered the trenches together, each soldier felt alone. Time passed slower than time passes. The replacements waited until eventually all faint sounds faded into the distance, leaving absolutely nothing to hear. The feeling of unknowing aloneness became eerie.

It remained so quiet that some men believed they could hear their own heartbeat or hear the passage of air as they inhaled or exhaled. Everyone heard his own body noises, and wondered if others could hear him swallow, hear his teeth as his tongue touched the tooth enamel, or hear the ring in his ears. It was very strange, that sound of silence, in many ways more articulate, more explanatory than a scholar's words. Some took comfort knowing this was only a training exercise while some found no comfort at all. Not knowing what to do, the men did what they had to do—they waited—but for what they did not know.

A loud overhead explosion shattered the silence, a flash of light ended the darkness. Someone had set off a flare. Their world had gone from total darkness to bright lightness, until gradually the light dimmed into total darkness again. They waited for other events, but nothing occurred, so they did what they were forced to do—they waited some more. With no discernible beginning a distant, faint light slowly consumed the low horizon in the eastern sky. The men were witnessing the glory of dawn, and it was as comforting as any imaginable sight. For the first time they began to observe their surroundings, the trenches, no-man's-land. They acknowledged their delight to their fellow soldier by eye contact, a slight smile, or a nod of the head. All was well and knowledge of such provided considerable comfort to the courageous and to the faint alike.

As they peered to absorb all they could, the replacements saw much, but not enough. Suddenly in the openness of no-man's-land, a broad-shouldered, brawny soldier emerged less than twenty feet in front of their trench. He came out of nowhere, stood defiantly, undaunted by the cold temperature, and his full length unbuttoned wool overcoat revealed a British field uniform. His face was darkened with dirt and the Englishman wore wool gloves, a steel helmet over a wool stocking cap, and he carried a bayonetted Enfield rifle. The silence was shattered when he roared an unidentifiable sound equal in pitch to one of a giant. No question his presence demanded full attention. Then he spoke, not in a polite fashion, but in a harsh, accusatory tone. "Look at that tree behind me about one hundred meters away, the one in plain sight right in front of you. At first dawn I left the cover of that tree, crawled to your trench and, in my best judgment, not a single one of you saw me until I stood up. Think about what I just said! Had this happened in France, many of you bloody fools would be dead, and we don't want dead Yanks, we want live ones. Never let that happen again. Use your eyes, use your ears, be alert.

"When that flare went off we had ten men in no-man's-land and every single one of them reached your trench undetected, not one of you saw them. You must have been looking at the pretty color of the flare, because you certainly didn't see the enemy." The speaker raised his left hand high in the air, and ten men stood from various locations in no-man's-land. Each was in field uniform with helmet and rifle ready for combat.

"When you arrived you couldn't see anything, but someone could, because someone told you where to stop and all of you are evenly spread out. That person couldn't see either. He didn't need to see because he knew his trench from memory, from sound, from smell, or from whatever skill he possessed. Know your trench, use your training. Know your trench, know everything about it. Use your God given senses.

"Look around you, this is your home for the next two weeks. You will eat here, sleep here, and train here. The more you know about your new home, and the sooner you know it, the better off you will be. That simple fact is an absolute, don't forget it. Every trench is different, and I mean exactly that—no two are the same. Trenches, trenches, trenches. Learn everything there is to know about your trench, near it, above it, below it, or around it. Learn about it on your own, and don't wait for someone else to teach you. Learn by observation, never stop observing. Let me tell you a thing or two about trenches and if you listen it just might save your life. This war is fought from the trenches. All fighting is from the trenches, both defensive and offensive. You're either in a trench, going to a trench, or coming from a trench. If you move to another part of the trench, learn about your new position. Know your trenches.

"Take care of your trench. Everything you do affects not only you, it affects everyone else in the trenches. Filth kills soldiers as dead as a German bullet. Take care of your trenches because they become your home. You sleep there, you eat there, you live there. If you shit in your trenches, you live in shit. If you vomit, you live in vomit. Filth breeds filth, the dirtier your trenches are the more the rats will come and you will live with rats. This is your home. Your trench, like your rifle, will reflect the manner it is cared for. You are never too exhausted to take care of your trench. You take care of it, it will take care of you. That's another absolute.

"Your trench is your fortification from enemy attack. The better the fortification, the better the protection. In France there are almost 800 kilometers of Allied trenches; that is almost 500 miles in length. For every meter of trench our side has the enemy has an opposite one separated only by no-man's-land. If one side totally controls no-man's-land, the other side has lost and must dig a new trench and create a new no-man's-land. Lose your trench to enemy forces and you lose your transportation system, your supply system, and eventually your cities. Never, never let the enemy hold your trench long enough to learn about it. Do that and the battle is lost. Do not, I repeat, do not lose your trench. Other lives depend on you holding your trench. If you do lose your position in the trench, you must immediately take it back. My best advice is, don't lose it. Believe me, it is easier to hold than it is to take back.

"Remember there is no such thing as a standard trench, all are different in some way. Some are no more than shelter pits and some are so elaborate that they are impervious to bombardment. A few are temporary, some have been in place for four years. All trenches have a few things in common if they are constructed properly in the first place. Trenches must be deep enough to shelter a man and narrow enough to protect from artillery bombardment. Too shallow, too deep, too narrow, too wide are all problems. The trench must be constructed in a manner offering the best possible advantage in a given terrain. Trenches are built factoring in the ratio of troops to space. Too many men in one trench is as bad as too few. Trenches are not in straight lines, they are kinked at intervals to diffuse blasts or shrapnel, and to prevent attackers from controlling more than a short segment with a few men. Can you imagine the enemy kill power with an automatic weapon in a straight line trench? If the ground is impossible to excavate, then your trench is formed with a higher parapet made of logs or stones. You use whatever you have at your disposal; but believe me, dirt is better. Dig if you can.

"There is a reason why the trench is where it is; and usually that reason is tactical, because you can defend or attack from that position. If for some reason you need to construct a new trench, select your site carefully, consider everything you have been taught. In short, it's almost always better to leave the decision of where to build a trench to command, to the engineers, if possible.

"Barbed wire is your first line of defense. Always protect your trench with properly strewn barbed wire. Even outposts need wire. You always need wire, period, end of statement. In existing trenches where the wire is already in place, you simply maintain it. Check it daily, preferably in the early morning. If it's cut, fix it. If artillery destroys your wire or if for any reason you lose your wire, you replace it as soon as possible. If possible, it's best to let the engineers place the wire, repair the wire, but they're not always around. If your wire is down, I guarantee the enemy will find out about it, attack in that exact location. Never leave a body hanging on the wire, get him off immediately. A body is a perfect springboard over wire for attacking troops. Know all about your wire like you know your trench. In front of your wire is no-man's-land. After no-man's-land is enemy wire, protecting his trench. I have seen no-man's-land wider than two kilometers, I've seen it as narrow as twenty meters. No matter the size of no-man's-land, wire protects trenches. I've seen one row of wire, and I've seen up to ten rows and there is reason for both. If you don't have wire, your trench will become your grave.

"You never know enough about your trenches, you never stop acquiring useful information. Never, never, never. You have two weeks to learn about life in the trenches. Make every minute count. What you learn may save your life. Apart from actual combat, these two weeks of training are the most important you will get. Take it from one who knows. The last two and one-half years of my life have been in the trenches of northern France, and I'm still alive. Why? Because I learned my trenches, I checked my wire."

The British sergeant gave his first indication that he was cold. He wrapped his arms around his chest, hugged his body for warmth. For the first time he moved about without speaking, and used the opportunity to study the men of Company L. When he resumed speaking it was with different intonation. "I do believe it is rather chilly out here." Then he grinned. "Now you Sammies get at it. We need all the Yanks we can get over there, and we need them as soon as possible, but we need them trained and alive. Maybe you boys can help us Tommies, as you Sammies like to call us, in our endeavor to kick some Kraut ass. You do understand it is our intent to hang Kaiser Willy out to dry."

The two weeks of trench training was more than productive, it was eye-opening to the boys of Company L. To their dismay they had much to learn, they did need more training. They learned how to live within and to take care of the trenches. They learned to observe, to use their senses, to employ their skills. The British sergeant and the American training staff had done their jobs. The men quickly found out how unpredictable trench warfare could be and how little they knew about survival in the trenches. They came to accept that they alone could not shape their final fate in wartime. They were and always would be dependent on fellow soldiers, buddies.

Company L. won bragging rights in their competition with the other company, and their victorious attitude was reflected on their return march to Camp Greene. They traveled in daylight and in considerably warmer weather, making the distance back seem much shorter. Spirits were high and many of the young men felt invincible, up to any challenge. After all they were infantry, Company L., 61st Regiment, a regiment of regulars, and the Army had just put them through the toughest training endured by any unit. They felt ready to cross the big pond, ready to fight the war as wartime ambassadors from the United States of America in pursuit of justice. War seemed glorious, they ennobled the thought of going to war.

The United States Army attempted to take care of its own. February 3, 1918, Private Elzie H. Moore was presented a written explanation and cost of government life insurance. He was ordered to report to Captain Martin's office the following day. All military personnel were eligible for government insurance during wartime, regardless of where they served. Elzie studied the information and made his decision.

"Good morning, Private Moore. Take a seat!"

"Good morning, sir."

"I presume you have read the material on insurance and have made up your mind."

"Yes, sir."

"Well, what did you decide?"

"I want the insurance in the amount of $5,000."

"Okay, we'll do the paper work. I must say the amount does surprise me. I am correct that you are not married and have no children?"

"Yes, sir, you are correct."

"It must be the disability part of the insurance that you're after."

"Sort of, but not totally. If I get my arm or leg blown off, I can't earn a living after the war, so I might need the disability part, but to be totally honest that's not my main concern." Elzie refrained from saying more, hoping the captain would move on. The captain did not speak, but continued to look at Elzie. "Sir, what is it, sir? Do you want me to express my concern, or do you want me to shut up?"

"I want to know."

"My father is 63 years old and in poor health. Right now he works hard, earns $9 or $10 a month, and has trouble living on that amount of money. He has no other source of income, no property, and I really don't think he can support himself much longer. So, if something happens to me, my insurance will provide for him and, if nothing happens to me, I'll worry about his future after the war. This way I'm covered either way. I also am sort of responsible for my aunt, but I think she can take care of herself. I hope so. I'll worry about her after the war. Right now I want the insurance."

The captain looked at Elzie, delaying his comments as he absorbed what the young private had said. "Very well, private, it shall be. Life insurance in the amount of $5,000, payable on death while in the Army. Premiums will be deducted from your pay, monthly. Do you understand and is that agreeable?"

"Yes, sir."

"In case of permanent and total disability as a result of your service in the Army, you will receive $25 a month for life. Do you understand?"

"Yes, sir."

"Cost of your coverage is found on the information sheet. Have you looked at it?"

"Yes, sir, and I understand it."

"Entitlement to this insurance is a result of an act of Congress, October 6, 1917. Actually, it's a good value. There is really no latitude, no wiggle room, for you or the government. It's clear and simple. You just select the amount and everything else is in place. Now give me your full name, date of birth, and age."

"Private Elzie Hubert Moore, March 16, 1900, age 17."

"You mean to tell me that you're still not 18 years old? Damn it, now I don't know what to do. It states here that you must be 18 to get the insurance. You're supposed to be 18 to be in the Army, but you know all that."

"I'm not going to lie, sir. I didn't lie to get in, and I'm not going to lie now. I guess the insurance will have to wait until next month when I turn 18."

"The hell it will. If you're old enough to fight, you're old enough to get insurance, and you won't lie, I will. Give me a minute to rework some things." The captain changed the birth year on the form to 1899. "There, that will do it. Give me the name and address of the designated beneficiary."

"Erastus L. Moore, Milton, Pike County, Illinois."

"Any other names?"

"No, sir."

"Your policy number is 1290683, and it becomes effective February 12, 1918. Write down that information, send it home to your father. Sign down here, to the right of my name. Elzie signed, but lingered over the form. In response to Elzie's perceived concern, the captain offered paternal consolation. "Don't fret, private, this is nothing more than an exercise in paper work. After this war is over, you'll go home to a brass band."

At the conclusion of a routine training day John and Elzie were in the barracks cleaning their rifles. Both were tired and worked at a slower pace than usual. John spoke first. "I swear I know this rifle better than I know my wife."

"Good thing, because where we're going you will need it more than your wife." Elzie grinned and waited for John's reaction to his silly comment.

At this particular moment John was in a disgruntled mood. He ignored Elzie, continued to ramble in a monologue with no regard to those about him. "Did you see that grenade explode today? Did you see the damage that shrapnel caused? Those things could maim a man in a hurry. I wonder if the German stick-bomb is as bad. Knowing the lousy Germans, I'll bet their grenades are worse. I hate to think about it. You know something else? I hate those gas masks. With those stupid things on your head you can't see much of anything. Maybe directly in front of you, that's all. I'll bet if someone has a mask on, you could toss a grenade near them and they would never see it coming. Kind of like a bullet—you never see bullets coming either. At least with artillery you probably hear something. If I buy the farm over there, I sure hope it's from a bullet, and not from some damn exploding device. I don't want to see it, and I don't want to hear it. I think that's the best way." John, apparently now wanting social interaction, looked to Elzie. "What about you, Elzie? How do you want to get it?"

Annoyed by John's rambling, Elzie snapped back. "Are you crazy? I don't want to get it at all, and if I was nuts enough to think about it, I wouldn't tell you. I don't think there is a good way to be killed. I'm not going to think about it, and you shouldn't either. What's come over you? I know you complain a lot, but this isn't complaining, it's worry. Complaining about something might help, but worrying won't change anything. Now, snap out of it, stop it!"

John gave no response. Other men had heard the conversation and he looked around hoping someone might share his thoughts, but no one joined the conversation. In fact, that particular corner of the barracks became exceedingly quiet.

Unexpectedly, Captain Martin and two company lieutenants arrived at the enlisted barracks. Most unusual, they had come not in any official military capacity, rather they wanted to socially chat. After visiting with the sergeants at hand the officers ordered the men to resume their activities while they wandered through-out the barracks. They expected to banter with the men, but the enlisted men were ill at ease visiting with officers. Conversations were superficial, at best. Discouraged, the captain prepared to leave the enlisted barracks, but for some reason he stood by the door and offered a final comment. "Men, tomorrow we start our final phase. I don't think it will be long now. I do believe we are ready for initiation under fire. Now, before I leave, do you have concerns that should be discussed? Is everything okay, do you need anything? Questions?" Only silence followed the captain's words. "Very well, as you were."

As the officers were departing an unidentified voice sounded from the back of the room. "Sir, I have a question. If something happens to us over there, what would you do with our bodies? Would we be buried there?"

A lieutenant immediately shouted a reprimanding response. "What a stupid question. That's not what the captain meant. Who asked that?"

A private from the rear of the room stepped forward. "I did, sir. A few minutes ago I overheard a conversation about weapons, and it made me wonder about burial for anyone who didn't make it. I'm not looking for trouble, I just wondered."

Recognizing the significance of the question, the captain stepped in front of the lieutenant. "It's all right, lieutenant. I asked for questions, and I got one." The captain continued walking until he was directly opposite the questioner. "Private, I regret that I don't know the exact answer to your question. If someone is killed in France under my command, I have been instructed to set up a temporary burial ground, one worthy of interment for a fallen comrade. I am to keep precise records. That is all I know, I have not been informed about further plans. However, I can say with some confidence, I am positive that our government will not abandon any of us, especially those who fall while in the service of our country."

"Thank you, sir. That's what I needed to know."

Without speaking, showing no emotion, the captain's eyes scanned the room looking briefly but directly at the facial expressions of the young soldiers under his command. He detected no fear or overt concern from the men, other than intuitively he sensed there were additional questions that the men were reluctant to express. Acting more on impulse, less on military protocol, the captain ordered the men to relax and to find a seat. Likewise, he and his lieutenants assumed a relaxed sitting position in the middle of the room. Uncharacteristically, the captain spoke informally. "Company L. is one of the finest companies in the 61st. You men have faced the challenges of difficult training head on and with distinction. Repeatedly, you have demonstrated your willingness, your eagerness to participate in this war. No one can question your courage or desire. With that said I do understand why some of you may have questions about what your future holds. Every man in uniform wonders about such things, and there is nothing wrong with being concerned. But, as of this moment, I do not have the answers to such questions. I might add, no one has the answers, not even command. A war of this magnitude is simply not scripted. We have never before, save the Civil War, undertaken such a huge military task, and this war is on foreign soil. If you have pressing concerns, now is the time to ask. My answers will be honest, telling you what I can, or what I know, or what I think."

The room fell silent again. The reluctance of the enlisted men to share their thoughts with officers, or to openly express doubts was only natural. Inwardly, every man harbored fears concerning his possible behavior in future combat situations; and greatest among these fears was that some act or some spoken words might reveal these fears to other soldiers. No one wanted to be the first to expose his inner thoughts.

The room remained void of words. Calculating that he had misread the situation, the captain stood and prepared to leave. "Thank you, men, for your dedication and perseverance."

Before he could exit the room another voice from the crowd shouted, "Captain, sir, when do you think we might ship out?"

Immediately, even before the questioner was identified, the captain yelled his answer. "I'm not certain. There are numerous events already in play that I'm not privy to—transportation to coast, available troop ships, escorts, provisions, supplies, and necessary facilities over there, are but to mention a few. Personnel are working on it as we speak. I just don't know the exact date. However, I do know the procedure. At some point we will all be restricted to camp. All communication with the outside world will cease other than for military communication. We will prepare to depart. At some point we will receive transportation to our port of embarkation, we will board ships, and God willing, we will make it to France. After that, I don't have the foggiest idea of what happens. That information is on a need-to-know basis. It only makes sense that I don't know the exact details. We sure don't want to telephone the Germans when and where we are going. The fewer who know those details, the better. I do know that once we are over there, we can notify our families, if we want. Sorry I can't be more specific."

A private seated near the captain then asked a carefully worded question. "Sir, I have a question which has been nagging at me. I have asked others, and no one knows the answer, or at least they won't tell me if they do know. What about prisoners? Do both sides take prisoners? Nobody ever wants to be taken prisoner by the Germans, but what happens, if at no fault of our own, we are captured? What do we do?"

The question demanded an answer, but a prolonged hesitation preceded the captain's answer. The soldiers sensed it was not that he did not know the answer, but that he did not know how to express it. The captain carefully worded his response. "Our orders are not to surrender, not to be taken hostage. That order is perfectly clear. However, other orders direct us to take enemy prisoners whenever possible. So at least our side expects that there will be prisoners. I assume the other side expects the same. Enemy prisoners are interrogated by G.2. and then sent to detention facilities, presumably for the duration of the war. Useful information, things like equipment, training, numbers, and even tactics are extracted during the interrogation. I'm not certain of all the details, but I do know that our intelligence staff wants prisoners and wants them bad. The more we know about the enemy, the more prepared we are to fight them. If enemy intelligence does the same thing, which I assume they do, that explains our orders—no prisoners, no information." To the perceptive soldier the captain's facial expression, his mannerisms, the quality of his voice revealed far more than his stumbling, evasive answer. "I really believe that if we stay healthy and remember our training, we will all be fine. What happens if we are captured will be a nonissue."

The captain paused and before he could continue a lieutenant interrupted. "I know that during our Civil War both sides took prisoners, hoping to exchange them for other prisoners. This exchange did not work. Every time they exchanged a prisoner they, in essence, put another enemy soldier back in the field to fight. So they stopped exchanging them and put them in detention camps; and during war nobody wants to spend much money to comfort captured enemy. The result was that the camps weren't very desirable, becoming a prisoner was not a desirable fate. Isn't that correct, captain?"

Reluctant to answer such a loaded question, the captain spoke with an uncertainty in his voice. "Uh, yes, uh, uh, I suppose that was true at the time of the Civil War, but that was a long time ago. This war is different, in a different time, with different people. Now we..."

Interrupting again, the lieutenant continued. "Captain, correct me if I'm wrong, but all communication from command refers to prisoners in this war as deserters. Deserter is the exact word they use. I assume that means if you are captured by the enemy, our military considers you a deserter under fire." The captain looked at the floor, offered no correction. The captain's silence only affirmed the lieutenant's interpretation. "And as we all know, the Germans are barbarians. I shutter to think what a German detention camp would be like. No, sir, that's not for me. I don't want to be any deserter and end up in some German camp. Let the dirty Huns be the traitors, the Americans the heroes."

The other lieutenant took up the banner of American heroism as he joined the discussion. "It makes no difference anyway. I have a feeling that once the Germans find out exactly how good American Infantry really is, they'll turn their tails to us and run home as fast as those Heine legs will carry them. I can see the headlines now, 61st cannot catch frightened Krauts—they run too fast. Peace is declared in France and there are no Germans left to surrender. Kaiser Bill is trampled by deserting army. I don't know about you boys, but I'm ready to get there, kick some ass, and end this war. How about it?"

The room erupted with shouts of agreement, expressions of self-confidence and German ridicule. Men were laughing, shaking fists, and generally engaging in what would normally be regarded as disruptive behavior. The serious discussion had abruptly ended, the mood had shifted more to a pep rally mentality, a celebration. The men, convinced of their own combat prowess, were now more ready to fight than they ever were before. The confidence of a few men fed others, and before long they became cocky, confident their unit was invincible, if only they could get to the war. Previous qualms or fears about fighting in the war were lost to repression. After all, they were Company L., 61st Regiment, 5th Division. How else could they feel?

Sometime during the spontaneous medley the captain exited the barracks. The question and answer session had not taken the direction he had envisioned. The lieutenants, unaware the captain had left, stayed and conversed with the men, twitting the Germans, almost exciting the group to a frenzy. It was only the late hour, and not a lack of emotional agitation, that eventually squelched the prolonged outburst.

That night many men in Company L. went to sleep with thoughts of glory, individual heroism, a time when fabricated acts of bravery had no mental bounds. They were young, innocent soldiers, proud of who they were, what they were doing.

The pace of training intensified during the following two weeks. The trainees were subjected to more propaganda, more indoctrination. Formal instruction emphasized individual survival skills rather than unit tactics, and individual conditioning again became a priority. In the name of combat stamina more one-on-one activities, competitive events, and maximum endurance feats were scheduled. Priority on agility training resurged. Regardless of the day's primary training agenda, some time was devoted to obstacle course endurance or to demanding calisthenics. The bar was set high with much to achieve in a limited time. To those who noticed, it became quite apparent—the men in the 61st Infantry were rapidly approaching a conclusion to stateside training. Most men were energized by their recent training. It enhanced their fitness, it sharpened their skills, it gave them polish. Their training empowered them. How proud they felt.

On Saturday, March 16, 1918, Elzie turned eighteen. Initially he shared this milestone with no one, hoping to later reveal this all-important day while in the select company of a few friends. Today he was old enough to enlist in the Army. A twenty-four-hour leave was scheduled to commence at 5:00 p.m., and he had planned an evening on the town in Charlotte with five buddies. Saturday nights had always been special to Elzie, so it was only fitting that he should celebrate this Saturday night, his eighteenth birthday, on the town. The weather that day at Camp Greene was beautiful with temperatures in the upper seventies and an abundance of sunshine. It was a good day to turn eighteen.

During their evening meal, one hour before the train was scheduled to leave for Charlotte, an announcement was made.

> Orders just came down. All military personnel are restricted to camp. All leave is canceled, report to your barracks as soon as possible. Until further notification there will be no communication with anyone outside this base.

CHAPTER 17

SOMEWHERE IN FRANCE

My God, I do believe this ship is moving. Finally we're on our way. Good-bye U. S. of A., hello, France."

"You better hope, hello France. If this day is anything like the last ten days or so, we might sail for two hours and stop again. I'm about to decide that someone really doesn't want us to get there."

"Not this time, we're on our way for real. I can feel it in my bones, it's a good feeling. Yes, sir, we're on our way, with no more delay. Say, did you hear that? I'm a poet, and didn't know it."

"You're a poet all right, about like I'm a Methodist minister. After all, I thought about religion once. Bless you, my son."

"You quit making light of my poetic ability. Every poet has to start somewhere. Maybe this is my beginning. Who knows, maybe after this war is over I might become a sidewalk poet, and you just might become a Methodist minister. I can see it now—services conducted by the Reverend John Wagner. Come one, come all to hear the reformed sinner, once a complainer, now a preacher." Elzie looked toward the cloudy gray sky in an effort to conceal his amusement at what he had just said. He waited for John's retort until he could wait no longer. He had to glance at John; and when he did he found a disgruntled buddy, shaking his head while staring at the ocean. "Did I say something wrong, ole boy?"

"No, you said nothing wrong, you said something stupid. Sometimes you amaze me. You always find some humor in everything and if you can't find humor you find something else. If it's not funny, it's beautiful. If it's not beautiful, it's profound. We look at the same thing, but we always see different things. Sometimes I think you've got a screw loose. Either that or I'm screwed too tight. Which is it?

Are you too loose, or am I too tight?"

Elzie tried not to smile when he answered. "John, I'm not real sure. Whatever the answer, I think the question is beautifully worded, quite profound."

"Oh yeah, I almost forgot. Sometimes your humor resembles a smart-ass, like right now."

"Sorry, I couldn't resist. My brother used to tell me that I never knew when enough was enough. Maybe he was right, or maybe not."

"Oh, no, you're not going to start quoting that older brother again are you? Every time you do that you get real quiet, real philosophical. I think I would rather hear the smart-ass side. At least I can understand what you're yakking about when you're a smart-ass."

At first Elzie looked irritated, but gradually his expression changed. "Let me give you a straight answer to what I assume was a serious question about the difference between us. You've got to remember, I'm a country boy; and although I've been around the block, I haven't been around as many blocks as you have. You're older, wiser. I'm still learning, everything still fascinates me. If I can use the expression, I'm still looking at the world through virgin eyes; and to be honest with you, I like what I see through those eyes. Does that sort of explain it?"

"Nobody in their right mind could enjoy what we have been doing. We pack, wait, travel a little, wait, pack, wait, and then we wait some more. If you find something profound in that, then I'm going to puke."

"Well, puke away, big boy, because I've enjoyed it. More accurately, I'm in awe of the entire process. Think about it! Thousands of men catch trains, and somehow we all end up at the right destination. Once we arrive a place is provided for us to camp, there is food to eat. Eventually we will get to where we are needed. I don't know for sure, but I'll bet the whole 5th Division was in Newport News waiting to board transport ships. I wouldn't be surprised if they're still putting men on ships. Think about it! Somebody had to organize all of that. Once we boarded we sailed for a day and then waited at anchor. I was so innocent I thought we were waiting for the entire division instead of waiting for the escort ships. Little did I know, and the nice thing is I didn't need to know. Everything was taken care of for me. My only responsibility was to do what I was told, look around, and enjoy the scenery. Pretty good if you ask me! And what about that train ride through South Carolina and Virginia. Nothing to do but look and wave at all the girls who had come out to say good-bye to us. I have never seen so many skirts in my life, and as far as I know they were all waving at me. John, let me tell you, big boy, that's what dreams are made of—when arrangements are made, and all the girls waving at you.

"I'm about to cross the big pond and see France, maybe England, or who knows maybe Germany. My thinking is enjoy it while you can, because everyday brings a new experience. No other way to put it other than I like what I'm doing, and yeah, I do look forward to tomorrow. From where I sit, tomorrows look a hell of a lot better than yesterdays. Maybe as I get older, more experienced, I will change and see things in a different light. I hope that..."

Not concerned about who was listening or watching, Elzie continued his soliloquy. Admiringly, John intently listened until eventually he no longer absorbed the meaning of his friend's words. "Okay, okay, you've convinced me. Save some of this for another day. No need to go further."

Elzie abruptly stopped speaking. "Sorry, John, I just got carried away. I'll keep my big mouth shut."

"I don't want you to keep your big mouth shut, I just don't need any more convincing. It goes to show you that one never truly knows another person. Before today if somebody would have asked me to describe my friend, Elzie Moore, I would have described you as a fine soldier, a good man with a sense of humor, someone I was proud to serve with. Now I need to give them a longer answer and tell them that you are a philosopher, which is not easy to explain. You just complicated my life." John paused, waiting for Elzie's reaction, but only got a blank stare. "I'm not serious about that philosophy stuff, buddy. That was my attempt at humor. It sure doesn't make much sense to use humor if no one understands it."

Elzie approved. "Keep working at it, and one day you might say something really funny, but I suspect it will require time and practice on your part. You need to prepare your audience. No one expects humor out of you, we expect complaints. You've mastered that art. Keep working on the humor, big boy, keep working."

It was a spring like March day when the convoy of six transport ships, loaded to capacity with troops, and nine escort warships sailed from United States territorial waters en route to a French port. The infantry soldiers had come aboard with full packs weighing ninety-six pounds, excluding rifle. Elzie joked that if all the soldiers wore their packs and all went to one side of the ship, the ship would capsize. Without doubt the conditions aboard ship were most crowded.

Every soldier was assigned a hammock in a dorm-like room on one of the five decks. Packs were stored elsewhere. The hammock and the space around it belonged to one individual for twelve hours each day, and to another individual the remaining twelve hours. Three meals a day were served at staggered eating times, and enlisted men ate while standing at serving counters. There was no shortage of food, although there was a disproportionate amount of seafood. Other than space nothing was in short supply. Elzie and John were assigned adjacent hammocks from midnight to noon. They ate at 12:30, 5:00, and 9:00 in the p.m. All enlisted men were required to engage in one hour of daily, vigorous exercise. Daily inspections were frequent, and occasionally the men were required to stand watch in one hour shifts. Barring infractions requiring punishment, the remainder of the time was free time, or as the captain called it, "Ready time. Time to ready yourself, ready your equipment." Few additional demands were placed on the individual soldier.

Structured shipboard entertainment was available most days. Companies competed in physical activities, and by far the most popular spectator activity was boxing, although many individuals avoided group entertainment. Small groups of men visiting with one another was the most common sight.

Elzie enjoyed his schedule and spent as much time alone as possible. His greatest pleasure was observing the ocean. As an infantry scout he was issued field glasses and frequently he used them to study the ocean surface, or to watch the other ships in the convoy. He set aside one hour each night, regardless of weather, to stand on the upper deck near a rail and to stare at the vast emptiness of the ocean. He found real fascination with the open sea. In particular he enjoyed watching the irregular ocean swells and the ship's wake, especially spectacular on two, clear, moonlit nights. In daylight he enjoyed viewing other floating ships. Much of the time he simply stood looking out into the darkness, the emptiness of the open sea. Sometimes Elzie became so wrapped up in observing that the noises from the ship became as inaudible to him as the reflected light from the moon. The sounds of the ocean might become the only noticeable background sounds, if he willed it so. Alone time aboard ship became treasured time.

Two days in wait for escort, twelve days to cross the ocean was a long time aboard ship; and the first glimpse of land provoked immense excitement throughout the ship. Although precise location was never confirmed, the men in transit knew where they were—they were over there. Thereafter, the decks were lined with gawking men, each looking as though he had never seen land before or, perhaps, he thought this continent might look different. For whatever reason they continued to peer and gape, some relinquishing sleep or meals to maintain a favorable viewing position. The convoy slowed its speed, hugged the shoreline as it traveled south and east along the British Isles. A few innocents believed the slower speed was a deliberate diversion to accommodate the curious soldiers, but it was not so. Mindful of German submarines the navigational change was for safety and security. For twenty-five hours the convoy continued its slow advancement always within sight of land or at night, the silhouette of land. Interest in identifying location never abated, nonetheless place-names were never officially revealed. In place of knowing, soldiers improvised and referred to the land as somewhere in England.

The escort ships were replaced by smaller warships flying the Union Jack before the convoy nestled closer together and set sail to cross the even more dangerous English Channel. Unofficially, word spread that German submarines had been sighted in the channel, and the rumor was given credence when all shipboard passengers, other than lookouts and crew, were ordered below deck. It became an anxious time as soldiers helplessly waited below deck. All shared in the grave concern of possible enemy attack at sea until dawn when they were officially notified the convoy had made it to friendly shores without hostile incident. The 61st was ordered to prepare for disembarkation. Soldiers were to shave, shower, prepare the field uniform, roll the packs, and police the area. Strong jubilation ensued and sighs of relief abounded. Finally, they were over there, and cries of "Lafayette, we are here!" echoed throughout the ship to confirm their arrival, to acknowledge repayment of an old debt to the French.

Of the many transport ships in the convoy, it was by happenstance that the 61st was first to disembark. Characteristic of the military the first to do almost anything was prestigious. The proud soldiers, carrying full pack and rifle, marched in single file down the gangplank, reassembled in columns by companies and marched from the dock area to the reception area. Here the men stood tall when they read a large billboard printed in English:

Saint Nazaire, France.
Welcome American Soldiers.

Marching in cadence they were an impressive lot and these infantry soldiers beamed with pride as they marched in United States Army field uniform on French soil. The standard uniform included a single-breasted tunic with standing collar, breast and side pockets, bronze buttons and collar-discs bearing U.S. on the right and unit identification on the left. They wore khaki trousers with canvas leggings; for headdress they wore the khaki felt campaign hat with wide brim, peaked crown, and a light blue hat cord designating infantry. Every soldier carried full pack, a cylindrical knapsack with the entrenching-tool strapped vertically to the rear of the pack, the bayonet on the side, and the rolled greatcoat across the top. Around the waist was the webbing equipment including the canteen and five cartridge-holders. Little doubt, the youthful, energetic American soldiers looked well equipped and appeared well trained, and the mere sight of the American Infantry boosted the morale of the French, both civilian and military.

Marching to the martial music of a French brass band the column advanced to a small reviewing stand housing three staff officers from the 5th Division plus a slightly larger number of French dignitaries. As the 61st approached the reviewing stand the musical medley changed to tunes more familiar to Americans. Accompanied by standing salutes from the dignitaries, the musical instruments erupted into the melodies of the, "Star Spangled Banner," followed by the "Marseillaise," followed by "Over There." Hardly a soldier escaped the goose bumps of pride, and the men on parade rose to the occasion by marching even smarter. Directly beyond the stand a hundred or so French citizens lined the street, aggressively cheering, waving American flags. When the American soldiers passed in formation, several French women ran into the street, walked along side the troops and placed flowers on the hats and rifles of the men in the marching column. No soldier broke rank, but they were tempted as their eyes wandered to the many smiling French women. Their experience was truly a moment of glory for the recent arrivals, if all too brief. Within minutes the column was past the reception crowd and now faced another group of French citizens, more curious and more interested in observing the khaki-clad strangers to their country than in welcoming them. The marching column remained sharp.

In total, the column marched less than thirty minutes in front of an admiring crowd before they crossed railroad tracks and continued down a cobble stone street past an open storage area containing crates of provisions, stores of ammunition, bales of hay, horse-drawn carts, military trucks, containers of gasoline, and numerous other unidentified military supplies. American military personnel, French civilians as well as German prisoners, clearly identified by their attire, were working with the recently unloaded materials. Spectators diminished in number beyond the equipment area when the parade route became a gravel road paralleling the banks of the Loire River. The column marched the narrow gravel road for over an hour until they reached a well used, temporary rest camp quartering American soldiers. The temporary shelters, referred to as Adrian huts, were poorly constructed long, narrow wooden frame buildings, covered on the outside with tar paper, and the lack of doors revealed dirt floors, recently made muddy by rain. The column marched past the huts to an open area surrounded by trees where most of the men in the 61st took pleasure in pitching their more desirable, some said better constructed, pup tents.

Within the hour the field stoves were preparing food. A sudden, loud roar of engines from high in the sky captured the full attention of all when a squad of French airplanes flew overhead. Although every soldier knew it was not intended as such, the flyby appeared as a staged welcoming tribute to the arriving doughboys. The 61st Infantry had landed in France, and the French had made them feel welcomed.

Many sorts of changes ensued. The following morning the French sky unleashed its fury when a severe thunderstorm including two inches of drenching rain wreaked havoc on the American campsite. No one or anything remained unaffected. By noon the overhead sun appeared bright, giving rise to hopes that the campsite could be salvaged and tents could be restored. Unbeknownst to the men a restored campsite had little value for them as the newly arrived American troops were about to move again.

Captain Martin had just met with his company officers, and in turn the lieutenants were meeting with their noncommissioned officers, indicating that something of importance was brewing. In less than ten minutes the second meeting was completed and the sergeants emerged, dispersed among the men and barked out orders. "Gather around, men, I have orders, listen carefully. Break camp, secure and prepare all gear, we move out in two hours. Our destination is the 5th Division interior training facility, some place I can't even pronounce, let alone know where it is. They tell me the general location is a region of France called Lorraine.

"I know you knuckleheads might wonder why we're leaving this paradise facility so soon, especially after I told you yesterday that you would be here for two weeks. Let me tell you why. There is a war on and things change quickly during a war. While we were getting over here the Germans decided they would stir things up, and mounted an offensive against the British in northern France where they damn near kicked their British butts right out of this war. The French had to go help the Tommies and in doing that they thinned out their own lines. Well, guess what. We believe the Germans might be mounting a new offensive, only this time against the French lines and, yes, you guessed it—the Frogs need immediate American assistance. At this point there is no major fighting in the American patrolled sector of Lorraine, but you can bet your ass if the Americans aren't there, the Germans soon will be. So we're going, we're going to get there in seventy-two hours or less, and we will arrive prepared for any contingency. This is the real thing, so get your butts in gear."

In three hours the entire 61st Regiment crowded into the rail yard, one hour later the trains arrived. The French troop trains appeared significantly different from their American counterparts as they were smaller in all dimensions, including the locomotives. The troop cars were more like boxcars, contained no interior seats, no windows, and the doors were sliding cargo doors with retractable ramps open to both sides. Hommes 40—Cheveaux 8 was written on the side of each car. It was with a beguiled sense of humor that an English-speaking French train conductor gave the translation to an American lieutenant. Each car limited to 40 men or 8 officers. The accurate translation of 40 men or 8 horses became a source of great amusement to the privates; although needless to say, they did not verbally share their amusement with the lieutenant, at least not to his face. Thereafter, the men made jokes comparing officers to the rear anatomy of horses.

To the dismay of the doughboys, forty men with full packs were loaded into each car, but not with any comfort. In an effort to provide some sleep or rest, the men were ordered to sit and stand in four-hour shifts, and were forced to endure the cramped conditions for thirty-nine hours. Included in this time were four meal stops and six stretch breaks.

The most direct rail line to Vaucouleurs, Lorraine, the 5th Divisional training area, was tied up with freight trains delivering supplies to the training areas near the front. At first, rumor had it the troop train would be diverted to Paris, the city fondly referred to as Yankee Heaven. However, it was not to be, as the train traveled north to Le Mans, took a juncture east to Vaucouleurs. Other than orders to travel, the lower echelon of the U. S. Army was not given an itinerary, and most doughboys never really knew their exact location while en route. The small towns were identified in writing at the rail stations, but few recognized the names of the French villages. More importantly, it made no difference if they knew where they were as they understood they were in France, and they were traveling in the general direction of the trenches. That was all they needed to know.

The train ride to the divisional training area was interesting, not eventful. Arrival was disappointing. The train slowed, switched tracks, and came to a complete stop on a recently completed spur track, running parallel to the main track. To anyone who bothered to look it became obvious that the entire area was a work in progress; the designated divisional training area was little more than words on paper. The camp was surrounded by and inner dispersed with occasional, small French farms, all showing artillery damage. Prior fighting had produced a devastated landscape. Four recently constructed single story, wooden frame buildings served as the only indication that the unit was in the correct location. Just as the construction engineers had their work cut out for them, the infantry faced tough challenges if they were to secure the area from enemy attack. This isolated camp made the men wonder if the sergeant at Saint Nazaire knew what he was talking about when he spoke of relieving other American troops. There were no other American troops. Nevertheless, the 61st was here and regardless of conditions this was the place selected for their acclimation. There was much to do with little time to do it. Today was Saturday, April 13, 1918. Zero day was close at hand.

The Army called it site training, but final combat training would have been a more appropriate description. Officially it was designated acclimation time, a time deemed necessary for soldiers to adjust to the new environment after transport. The men had to be reconditioned and brought to maximum level of physical performance. In reality, acclimation time was the final phase of combat training.

The soldiers were housed in tents, totally functioning without benefit of manmade conveniences. Defensive positioning and guard duty became the primary function of infantry, and although guard assignment was not desirable duty, it was good training. An occasional sighting of German scouts or German patrols kept the men alert. This was the real thing, the enemy was in their backyard, and German occupied territory was only a few miles hence; and although a French contingent stood between them and hostile forces, German penetration was still probable.

Private Elzie Moore was assigned less guard duty, more scout duty. Daily, he scouted outside camp perimeters. Upon return he reported directly to the company commander. Patrol duty suited Elzie.

Elzie, John, and members of the little triangle bonded even closer while at Vaucouleurs. Elzie felt fortunate, he had good buddies. Needless to say, teasing, personal conflicts existed among the five buddies. Sometimes nerves were on edge. "Tonight would be a good night to let off some steam. Vaucouleurs waits for us, lads. What about it, any of you gentlemen want to go with me?" The other three men seemed more interested in eating than in answering the question, although John acted as though he was considering the proposal as he looked at Tony. "What about it, John? Want to go? They'll give a five hour pass to anyone who doesn't have duty."

"Oh, I'm not sure, I'm pretty tired. What do you have in mind?"

"I don't have anything particular in mind, other than a couple of beers and some girl watching. You never know, we might get some action. Besides it's better than sticking around here. I'm ready for a break. It won't be long until we're in the trenches, and then it'll be too late. You don't get five hour passes there. Better make hay while the sun shines. Besides, it would be nice to be around some friendly French people, not like the ones around here. They're a bunch of grouches."

The comment about the French annoyed Elzie. "What do you mean the French people around here? Grouches, my ass. Do they look or act different from other French people? Maybe you're just partial to frog dames or you like the frog dizzy shops in Vaucouleurs. As far as I can tell, these locals are just plain hardworking folks."

"Who said anything about whore houses? What's got into you, Elzie?"

"Nothing got into me. I just happen to like these people around here, and I don't like hearing them insulted."

"No insult intended. That's not what I meant and you know it. These French farmers are just different, not so in appearance or behavior, but in attitude. Other places we've been the French love us, but not here. They act like we're intruding. They just ignore us, and that's a description, not an insult."

Elzie's annoyance turned to sarcasm. "Well, isn't that just too damn bad. Why, what in the world could be wrong with them? We come all this distance to set up a camp in their backyard, and they aren't considerate enough to throw flowers and kisses every time we walk by. Remind me to speak to the captain about that, will you?"

"Go to hell, Moore. I hope you don't go to town."

John interceded. "What got you all fired up, Elzie? Tony didn't say anything wrong, he was only trying to set up a visit to town."

John's words caused Elzie to momentarily reflect, and when he spoke he used a different tone. "Yeah, I know it. Sorry, Tony, sometimes I'm too quick on the trigger with my words. I know you didn't mean anything." Elzie's flush face indicated embarrassment, he felt the need to explain. "It's just that the last couple of weeks I've gotten to know these people. I work quite a bit with them on the scouting stuff. They help me a bunch, they really know this area. Believe it or not, they haven't exactly been on a picnic these last four years. You know the Germans occupied this area for a while, and believe me, they hate the Krauts a lot more than we do. In that farmhouse right yonder there, they have already sent three men to this war. One is dead and they have not heard from the other two in months. Their farm has been used as a battlefield and now it is a training area for us. I'm not surprised that they ignore us. If it was me, I think I would do more than ignore us, I would resent us. I like these people."

John interrupted. "How do you know all that? Did they tell you that stuff? Do they speak English?"

"I know it because I've spent some time with them. They help me with scouting, and in return, I sometimes help them with a few chores around the farm. No they don't speak English. They have a granddaughter who studied English in school, speaks a little English, and the rest we can figure out with her dictionary."

John was the first to react. "Oh my goodness, Elzie Moore you've been holding out on us. I've seen that granddaughter, she's a looker. No wonder you're out scouting so much, you've got yourself a French girlfriend."

Elzie started to deny it, but others joined in the teasing. "You're not robbing the cradle are you? She looks awful young to me."

Almost indignant about the age issue the young soldier fired back. "She is not too young, she is seventeen. As a matter of fact she is only three and one-half months younger than I am. Furthermore, she is not my girlfriend. She is a friend who happens to be a girl, and besides I consider her whole family to be friends, male or female. So knock it off. I should have kept my mouth shut. I never learn. Forget I said anything."

Needless to say, the small group continued to taunt Elzie in a good-natured way until he warmed to their teasing and teased back about their trips to town in search of feminine companionship. John attempted to cap the discussion by facetiously asserting that Elzie was visiting with the family for the purpose of better scouting information. "I believe we all, except Elzie that is, should go into town tonight and leave Elzie to his military duty of scouting. The granddaughter might reveal some vital information to our company scout. Yes indeed, he might learn a lot especially if he works alone."

Tony managed to get in the final words. "How do you get to be a scout? Do you think this army needs more scouts? If they do, I volunteer." No more was said, although snickers abounded. Once the group disbanded, Elzie remained, pretending he had not finished eating. Actually, he had planned to visit the French family this evening, and hoped the others would go to town so as not to see where he was going, although it really made no difference. Moreover, he felt rather proud of who he was and what he was doing, and was quite unwilling to succumb to the teasing.

Reveille came early the next morning, especially for those who had gone to town the previous night. Everyday in camp brought different activities, but today the mode of procedure was most unusual. Scouts were sent out, but no infantry training events were scheduled. The day was more like a rest day, certainly unlike any other day since arrival at the camp. The hours passed with most soldiers using their time for sleeping, eating. If this day had a military purpose, it was not shared.

Some wrote letters home, most did not because personal correspondence for doughboys had lost much of its purpose. Since arrival in France all outgoing mail had to pass the censor's desk which resulted in a personal lack of privacy, and the censor's strict guideline of what could be written further served to discourage letters. A soldier writing home could make no reference to location or military activity, and no speculation about the war. In short, there was not much to write about other than to ask questions about home, and there was doubt as to whether the letters were even mailed. The need to maintain military secrecy about troops near the front trampled the soldiers' personal need to communicate with home. Military censorship was accepted, but resented.

By mid-afternoon the soldiers acknowledged the day as a bonus day, a rest day. "Have you guys seen the pictures yet?" a gruff sounding sergeant asked as he walked toward the small group of men from Company L.

"What pictures, what are you talking about?"

"We've got these photographs taken off of dead Germans. Presumably, the Germans took the pictures and then carried them around in their pockets. I guess they needed reminding of what bastards they really are. The captain wants all of you to look at the photographs, look at the stereoscope viewers, and then pass them on. Everyone is supposed to look at them."

"Hell, I thought you had some more French post cards, you know the ones with the French girls; or the thought crossed my mind that we might get lucky, and you would give us a few eight page bibles to read."

"Private, we have been ordered not to call them eight page bibles, and you know that. We call them French smut, and caught with one on you will get you an extra hour of guard duty. But, between you and me, if I see any I will send them your way."

"Thanks, sarge. What's so special about these photographs? Why do they want us all to see them?"

"You'll see. The photographs are part of your training. No explanation necessary. Look and learn, then pass them on."

The sergeant handed the men four large brown envelopes and a small wooden box with a stereoscopic viewer plus several photographic inserts. The packet contained nine envelopes, each containing twenty photographs of dead Allied soldiers killed by German infantry, with bodies displayed and laid out to be photographed. Attached to each photograph was a German handwritten description of how the soldier was killed, the place, and date of death. On the back of the photograph was a German's, presumably the killer's, interpretation of how the Allied soldier fared in death. A few photographs contained additional remarks, critical of the Allied soldiers' fighting abilities. Attached to each photograph was an English translation of the German writing. The photographs were grotesque, some showing mutilated Allied bodies with rearranged body parts. Some showed dislocated limbs, or distorted faces with eyes opened. One showed pieces of bodies stacked together. All the photographs provided a view of horror. Ironically, a few Americans viewed the pictures with a hideous fascination, but most saw them for what they were—mutilation of human bodies.

The pictures for the stereoscopic viewers were of the same type, but images were made larger for better viewing, more dramatic with more visible detail. Every soldier studied the photographs and, evidently, the morbid presentation accomplished its purpose. In the minds of these American soldiers the German soldier was unutterable vermin, worthy of the worst possible fate.

Before nightfall all units of the 61st Regiment were restricted to camp without explanation. Guards were doubled, soldiers were placed on alert status. Officers scurried in and out of meetings, activity near headquarters increased. Crated supplies and ammunition were shuffled to a different location. Something was astir and some upcoming event of significance was already in motion. Command secrecy prevailed as soldiers stayed on alert not knowing what to expect but preparing for any contingency. Ominously, no new orders were issued, no scuttlebutt surfaced as the fighting arm of the 61st remained on standby alert. At 11:30 p.m., seven hours after having been placed on alert, orders came down. "Prepare for immediate departure." The 61st was evacuating the base, and it remained unclear if they were running from something or hurrying to somewhere.

At 3:30 a.m. the men of the 61st boarded troop trains, by 6:00 a.m. the final train departed leaving the camp nearly deserted of soldiers. Portentously, the near sunrise departure left the camp intact, including all pitched tents and facilities. The eastbound convoy of trains traveled less than one hour before it came to a complete stop near a small rail yard. The train engaged in erratic forward movements followed by a series of stops, jerks, backward movements, and track switches which all served to disorient the military passengers before the rising sun eventually revealed the direction of travel. They were headed southeast, the general direction of the trenches. Before two more hours elapsed, the train stopped again, the passengers detrained and walked less than one mile to an encampment. Their train pulled away, another train stopped in its place and also displaced its cargo of soldiers. This process was intermittently repeated two more times or for at least as long as the soldiers could observe the process. Not all trains stopped. If soldiers wanted to make sense of the troop movement, they were challenged as the overall objective was difficult to comprehend, if not impossible. One fact emerged crystal clear—units of soldiers were systematically moving in different directions and some operation was underway. They were hurrying to somewhere, not running from something.

The new encampment consisted mostly of a massive field kitchen serving hot breakfast. After Elzie and his comrades ate and briefly relaxed, Company L. was reassembled and marched less than one hour across hilly terrain to the outskirts of a small village where another train was waiting. However, this train and its tracks presented an amusing sight, evoking laughter or at least a smile from even the grumpiest soldier. The train and track were narrow gauge, looking almost like a miniature railroad. Most American soldiers had never seen a narrow gauge train before, certainly not one of this proportion. The locomotive was about a quarter of the size of a standard locomotive, and the open transport cars, resembling grain wagons, looked even smaller.

The small gauge railroad normally used for military supplies was the new mode of transportation for the men of Company L. Boarding ten men and packs to each open car, the train moved in what seemed like slow motion for about one hour until it gained full speed, perhaps fifteen miles per hour. The ride soon became a fun-filled experience for the soldiers, resembling more a ride in an open automobile than a train ride and, if nothing else, the narrow gauge experience served to relieve the tension. They rode for twenty-six hours, stopping four times for food and rest.

About noon the troops detrained the narrow gauge confines and within the hour they boarded another train, a standard gauge train. The smaller French boxcars, which the soldiers had earlier made fun of, now seemed more practical, more efficient. The train traveled for three hours over a small range of foothill mountains, arrived late afternoon at a moderately large city situated in a beautiful mountain valley setting. As the train crept into the train station, the mystery of destination was revealed. Five different signs identified the location as Saint Die, of the Vosges. It was well known by American soldiers that the city of Saint Die was the final stop, used as an entry point to the southern portion of the four hundred miles of front lines.

After detraining, the soldiers assembled in columns and underwent a thorough inspection by company commanders. This inspection was more about company pride, less about instruction. With full packs Company L. smartly marched across three railroad tracks, made a right turn at the railway station, and came to a halt in the southwest corner of a plaza. Here they waited at attention until all fourteen companies of the 61st Regiment were in proper position. The men looked sharp, leaving little doubt that they were a disciplined military unit. On command they paraded in sharp formation across the Meurthe River bridge to Rue Thiers, Saint Die's business thoroughfare, where the column was joined by a French military marching band playing John Philip Sousa compositions. Much to their delight the soldiers marched through the center of the city to a grateful applause from appreciative French citizens. The doughboys were received as heroes, saviors of France. Indeed, it was a proud hour for the 61st.

Seldom do soldiers going to war experience a more moving moment than one of a civilian crowd cheering them on to victory. Hundreds of cheering French citizens, mostly female, lined the parade route for three blocks. Almost every upper story window was open and sported people of all ages waving French and American flags, or throwing flowers as the soldiers marched past. From any angle, from any perspective, the reception was a sight to behold.

Citizens of Saint Die had good reason to warmly receive the Americans. August, 1914, a German Army had overpowered the French forces in the area of Saint Die. The city itself was occupied by Germans for months until a French counterattack, late that same year, liberated the French city. Subsequently, German forces retreated into the rugged Vosges Mountains, established a defensive line of trenches, and eventually halted the French counterattack. The French soon developed trenches opposite the Germans, thus creating a Vosges stalemate battle line which still was intact and virtually unchanged when the Americans arrived in 1918. Because of the difficulty faced by both sides in mounting offensives in the Vosges Mountains, and because each hostile force controlled opposite entrances to the two mountains passes, no subsequent major offensives were conducted in the area. For three years the front lines in the Vosges had been deemed the quiet sector; and this designation was because it endured no large scale offensives, not because the area lacked ferocious fighting. Hostility in the Vosges represented stalemate for both sides, a place American Command considered suitable for American soldiers to experience their first taste of combat.

Many nearby French villages were still under German occupation. The arrival of 5th Division forces was intended to free French forces for use elsewhere, and likewise gave hope to the French that the fresh American forces would not only protect the Saint Die area from German attack but, also, might liberate much of the nearby area. Little wonder the Americans were received as heroes in a war torn area so desperately in need of hope.

Although the soldiers of the 61st Regiment did not totally understand the reasons for their warm reception, they demonstrated their appreciation in the manner they knew best—precise, sharp military marching formation. The column marched past a monumental structure constructed of red sandstone identified as The Cathedral of Saint-Die-des-Vosges, past a thousand year old, walled, city cemetery to the outskirts of town where they were ordered to set up camp. The high ground campsite rendered a glorious panoramic view of Saint Die, its red tiled roofs, winding streets, plus multiple unidentified structures, all enclosed within the valley. This centuries-old French village-city was indeed a grand sight of European splendor; and the overwhelming beauty was not wasted on American men far from home.

Just as the military camp's location offered a splendid view, it distorted sound. Soldiers could hear the distant sounds of war, yet exact identification of individual sounds was difficult. Distant explosive-like sounds, partially muted or distorted by the mountainous terrain, were thought to be artillery shells exploding on impact. Barely audible explosive pops were thought to be sporadic rifle or machine-gun fire. At times, Elzie was uncertain if he really heard the sounds or if they were imaginary. Expressions such as, did you hear that, what was that sound, listen, or that sounds like, became common refrains. Many sounds lingered throughout the night as did the intriguing mystery of positive identification. How could it be that men trained for eight months in the art of war could not clearly identify the sounds of war? The men conceptually understood that one never became totally prepared for war, and the sounds only served to remind them of their vulnerability. They had come prepared to fight a war, but they still had much to learn. One thing was certain—the men of Company L. were close to front lines.

"Private Moore, get out here now!"

Elzie awkwardly hastened, almost knocking down the front support pole of his tent. Before he was standing completely erect, he answered the summons, "Yes, sir."

"Report to the captain's tent, on the double."

Outside the captain's tent was an aide seated at a desk, shuffling papers. "Private Moore, reporting as ordered, sir."

The aide glanced at Elzie and then selected a paper from the file and talked as though he was reciting orders without any regard to their contents. "There is a meeting scheduled at 6:00 a.m. at the French command center for all infantry scouts. You get there by retracing the route we marched yesterday, back to the Meurthe River, turn left and follow the river until you reach the camp. You can't miss it. Captain is already there, check in with him as soon as you get there. Leave immediately, carry pack and rifle. Any questions?"

"No, sir."

"You've got less than forty minutes to get there, so get going."

Elzie hurried, using his long walking stride rather than a run. He passed the cemetery and cathedral without looking at either, other than to confirm his route. As instructed he turned left at the river and glanced at the water but never examined all the river's interesting characteristics which normally would have intrigued him. He arrived at the French camp, received his directions from the sentry, and made it to the meeting by 5:48 a.m. where the captain was waiting.

"About time," snapped an impatient captain. "Get in there and listen well."

"What's going on, sir?"

"We're moving up."

CHAPTER 18

FRONT LINES

Hell, I would have gotten more sleep last night if they would have left us on the trains. Get off the train, fall in, march, make camp, sleep five hours, break camp, move out, and get back on the train. I'm going to be worn out by the time I get there, hell, I'm ready to take a nap now. In case you guys don't know it, I'm aggravated all to hell, because I can't figure out why they marched us through Saint Die. Most likely, some general wanted to show us off, or perhaps to make the French feel better because we're here. Otherwise, it doesn't make any sense. You know what I think? I think some general is trying to figure out where the front lines are. I really think some unnamed person doesn't know what the hell he's doing, I'll bet he's lost. Elzie, why don't you go to headquarters, take charge, and show the brass how to get to the trenches, and then I'll take over and show the brass how to kill Germans."

"That's a good idea, John. The only problem is that I'm already in charge. It was my idea to stop in Saint Die. I wanted to see if there were any pretty French girls in need of a soldier boy from Pike County. Hope I didn't inconvenience you with my detour."

"Smart-ass!"

"You better be nice to me, John, because I know where we're headed. Be nice and I might tell you."

"How do you know where we're going?" John fired back. He looked Elzie's way and saw that he was sporting his all-knowing look which told John he did know. "I take back what I said if it's all the same to you, Mr. wonderful, kind, all-knowing, Private Elzie Moore from Pike County. Would you be so gracious as to inform me exactly where in the hell we're going?"

"Sure, Private John Wagner, from deep in the heart of Texas. All you had to do was ask. We're on our way to Gerardmer, about fifteen or twenty miles south of here. It is there where you, me and the other guys are needed to help General McMahon set up divisional headquarters. I didn't have the heart to tell him no. I hope that's okay."

"I don't want to sound impertinent, Private Moore, but how in the hell do you know that?"

"Early this morning when you were still sleeping, a little French birdie told me. It's the same birdie that told me we will link up with the French Army. I do believe, my friend, we are about to participate in this war. As a matter of fact if you want more information I will allow you to look at my map which shows the French and German trenches near Gerardmer. Any more questions I might help you with?"

The little French birdie was correct. The 5th Division was to be headquartered at Gerardmer, and was to relieve French forces in the Anould Sector. It was anticipated that the transition of forces would require about two weeks, and the 61st Infantry Regiment would arrive early afternoon, May 23. The precariously situated Anould Sector, the site of fierce fighting in 1914 and 1915, included areas of both German Alsace and French Lorraine. Early August, 1914, German forces defeated the French and occupied this strategic area until almost one year later when French forces liberated most of the same area. When the new front lines were established, a few of the French trenches were positioned in German territory, the only area where front-line trenches were found on German soil. Thus, when the lead regiment of the 5th Division arrived at the Anould sector, the 61st Infantry assumed a prestigious honor—its soldiers were among the first American combat forces to take position on German soil.

By early June, 1918, 5th Division forces were deemed ready, under French tutelage, for front-line duty. The American 5th Division joined the French 21st Division. American forces were placed under French command and, indeed, it became a most unusual sight watching American officers accompany and learn from their French tutors as American troops were placed alongside French troops. Combat groups became amalgamated units, half French, half American. Reserve and support troops were less integrated.

The doughboys were impressed with the speed and precision employed by command in establishing new divisional headquarters. Company L., a rifle company, manned the perimeter trenches as headquarters was fully established. For eleven consecutive days Third Squad doughboys served twelve hours guard duty, twelve hours reserve duty. Together, Elzie and a French scout, made joint, nightly patrols to the German trenches. During these scouting expeditions, the enemy was not engaged, no hostile incidents were reported.

Sunday, June 9, the men of Company L. were granted twenty-four hours duty free. The Third Squad buddies took advantage, enjoyed the day meandering the unrestricted areas of Gerardmer.

"This is a quaint little town."

The remark amused Elzie. "This little town has about seven or eight thousand more people than where I grew up. It's not so little to me."

Private Cimino had more than population in mind when he spoke. "I was referring to setting, not to size. I sort of like these French towns or villages or whatever they're called, they have a charm all their own. It would be more interesting to see them when they are unaffected by war. I'll bet the whole French countryside would be something special."

John had to respond. "Tony, you're getting as bad as Elzie, you're beginning to see beauty in everything. We're not over here to sightsee, you know. What has happened to you guys, have you lost your marbles? Quaint, my ass, what about all this horse shit in the street? You're not going to tell me that French horse shit has a pretty color, are you?"

"Nope, it's the same ugly color as horse shit at home."

"I'll need to watch my step with you guys. Next thing I know one of you will be telling me that I'm pretty because I'm in France."

Elzie laughed at John's remark. "No chance, you can relax. Nobody here is that far gone. At the risk of offending John, I am going to say something that he might construe as positive. Can you believe how fast headquarters was established? Since we've been here, engineers, military police, hospital units, artillery units, ordnance units, and God knows how many other units have arrived. I'll bet you that fifteen thousand, maybe more, military personnel are already here, and if I'm not mistaken it has all happened in less than two weeks."

Private William Upton joined the conversation. "I agree, it was fast. This morning I saw machine gunners from the 13th, some guys from the 9th Signal Battalion, and yesterday I talked to a fellow from the Quartermaster Corps. I wonder what brass has in mind. Something big, I'd bet."

John agreed. "I heard the 60th is headquartered a few miles from here, and the 11th is on its way. Including us, that's a bunch of infantry, and put that with the fact we are only a stone's throw from the German trenches. Something big is in the air, I can smell it."

"Look! I wonder what that is. Looks like somebody dropped a bundle of papers," Private Alpio Souppo said as he picked up one. "Well, I'll be damned, it looks like we got a letter from the Germans. Mail call. Why don't you guys pick up some, we'll see if they are all the same."

The leaflets printed in bold type on white paper were all the same.

TO THE DOUGHBOYS OF THE AMERICAN ARMY

Hello, boys, what are you doing over here? Fighting the Germans? Why? Have they ever done you any harm? Of course some American folks and the lying English-American papers told you that the Germans ought to be wiped out for the sake of Humanity and Democracy.

What is democracy? Personal freedom, all citizens enjoying the same rights economically and before the law? Do you live in the same type of house as some filthy rich Americans? Do you eat the same food or dine in the same restaurants? Do you have servants like they do? Do you drive automobiles as they do? Do you get equal justice under the law, or do the rich get away with crimes?

Why, then, fight the Germans only for the benefit of the Wall Street robbers and to protect the millions they have loaned to the British, French, and the Italians? You have been made the tool of the egotistic and rapacious rich in England and in America, and there is nothing in the whole game for you but broken bones, horrible wounds, spoiled health, or death. No satisfaction whatever will you get out of this unjust war.

You have never seen Germany. So you are fools if you allow people to make you hate us. Come over and see for yourself. Let those do the fighting who make the profit out of this war. Don't allow them to use you as cannon fodder. To carry a gun in this war is not an honor, but a shame. Throw it away and come over into the German lines. You will find friends who will help you along.

The printed message angered the men. Private Antonio Wolpi reacted first. "I don't know which pisses me off more—the fact they got into our secure area to distribute this crap, or the fact it was written by a German, maybe German-American, who knows some things about America, somebody who probably went to college in our country. I don't even know what the word rapacious means."

The others laughed, wadded up and threw away their copies, and left the additional bulletins to blow in the wind. "The Germans must think that we are really stupid to be influenced by a scrap of paper. I'm sure glad our side doesn't stoop to such devious tactics. I don't think we do, do we? Do we do crap like that?"

After nightfall on June 10, Company L. moved forward to La Croix-Aux-Mines. The military complex, positioned perilously close to the front-line trenches, was already up and running. Their cohorts, the French 93rd Infantry Regiment, were already stationed at La Croix-Aux-Mines and made no secret of their delight in the arrival of American troops. Indeed, the battle-weary French unit was in urgent need of reinforcement as there was little doubt these French solders were simply exhausted, burned out, used up.

Once fed the men of Company L. were given quarters in a well constructed dugout large enough to accommodate the entire company. The mess hall was also located in an underground shelter. This camp, located very close to front-line fighting, warranted a reasonable fear of artillery bombardment, thus, prudence demanded that all soldiers have access to fortified shelter or underground protection.

The Quartermaster Corps, already in operation, made available any item of standard issue equipment that might be needed and timing could not have been better. Most replaced field uniform and shoes. A large pile of discarded, worn out shoes illustrated how much the new issue was needed. In addition, a nearby field hospital was up and running if soldiers needed medical attention of any type. The hospital, arranged and equipped to handle large numbers of casualties, included three large tents and one sizable dugout. Recently having been converted from a French Army camp to the American 61st Regimental Headquarters, this complex was organized, ready to serve the needs of American combat soldiers.

"This cot is wonderful! I haven't seen quarters this plush since Camp Greene." John felt the softness of the bed and his facial expression eliminated the need for more praise. He sat on the side of the bed, gave a sigh of appreciation. The other men followed suit, took advantage of the comforts. "What about it, Elzie, do you know anything?"

"Do I know anything? What kind of question is that?"

"I mean do you know where we are, do you know what's up? You're always poring over those scouting maps, so I figured you might know something."

"I don't know if I know anything you don't know. I know we're awful close to the trenches. My maps measure the distance from here to the trenches in meters, not kilometers. That ought to tell us something."

John looked mystified. "Really, how come we don't hear anything? I haven't heard any sounds of war since we got here. How come this is such a good camp if we're so close to the lines? Maybe the Germans heard the 61st was coming, and they got the hell out of here."

Elzie was amused. "Maybe so, but I doubt it. My maps are really confusing. The French map calls this area the Violu Sector, Germans call it the Sadey Sector, and my American map calls it La Cude. My maps are mostly of the trenches, wire, land formations, stuff like that. So you tell me, do I know where we are or what's going on? You're welcome to look if you want."

"How come you've got German maps? Are they in German or English?"

"German. I think they are old maps used earlier in the war. You do know the Germans held this position for about one year. Who knows, we might be in a German dugout, one they built years ago." In a feeble attempt at humor, Elzie continued, "If we are, it sure was nice of them to leave it for us."

Sarcastically, John retorted. "Yeah, I'll bet they built it with us in mind." Others laughed. "Come to think about it, I'll tell you what I don't like. If they have been in this area for four years, and if they have maps showing our dugouts, that means they know exactly where to point that artillery. Now that's a sobering thought. I don't like it. I don't like it one little bit, and that's as clear as I can say it."

It was Elzie's turn to shed humorous light on the subject. "If that isn't bad enough, there is an area about three miles from here identified as Ancient Roman Camp. I don't remember my history very well, but I think the ancient Romans were here about two thousand years ago. Think about that! People have been fighting here for two thousand years, and I'll bet they made maps back then. The Germans might have maps all the way back to the time of Christ. They might not only know the terrain now, they might know the terrain as it was then. Yeah, their maps have more history than ours. Our nation is just over a hundred years old, so all of our maps are relatively new. Think of the disadvantage that puts us at."

"Elzie, why don't you go soak your head, or just be quiet, or get some shut eye, or something. I should have known better, expected some smart-ass philosophical answer. Put your maps away, be quiet, and let me sleep. I want to enjoy these comforts while I can." After a prolonged pause, John spoke again. "Was there really an Ancient Roman Camp near here?"

"Swear to God, that's what the map says. I'm not going to sleep yet, I'm going to take a walk first. When we arrived earlier I noticed a big church on top of the hill. I'm going to walk up and take a look at it. If any of you guys want to go, you are welcome." In light of the prior conversation about the nearness of German lines a casual walk through the village might appear audacious, almost defiant. He did not intend it so. It was more a matter of a young midwesterner wanting to look at the world whenever the opportunity presented itself. No one else showed interest.

The narrow, circling road to the top of the hill was steep with one dangerous hairpin curve, precarious to ascend. The spectacular view at the summit granted a panoramic view of the entire valley, and on this day the view was greatly enhanced by a cloudless, blue sky. Lamenting that he had forgotten his field glasses, Elzie concentrated hard, used his keen eyesight to study and to observe all he could.

The church, positioned in the middle of the square, towered above all else; and near the church four, three-story stone buildings shared the prominent hilltop position. Elzie assumed the structures to be government buildings since they looked as he thought offices in a small French village should look. Behind the church lay a large cemetery perfectly situated on a gradual slope. Indeed, the cemetery was an idyllic sight. Unable to resist the temptation he entered the cemetery through an open gate and wandered about the grounds. The first marker he attempted to read was a family monument with a surname in bold letters and several given names listed below in smaller letters. Dates were placed beside each given name, some as early as the 1600's. He finally put it all together—the marker revealed that one burial spot was used for several generations of the same family, all in one location. The thought of multiple bodies in one grave site just sort of overwhelmed him. Unfortunately, he could not understand the ins and outs of family graves as all inscriptions were in French and no one was there to explain the process.

For two hours he continued his fascinating wanderings around the cemetery, and when Elzie finally exited the cemetery an elderly gentleman politely attempted to engage him in conversation. Elzie could not understand a word the French-speaking man was saying but he respected his demeanor. It was clear the polite Frenchman was proud of where he lived, appreciative of an American soldier wanting to observe his generational home village. In spite of the inability to verbally communicate, Elzie and the Frenchman walked together, looked around the area as the Frenchman pointed out and talked about various structures. Regardless of the language barrier they were still able, somewhat, to transfer general ideas. Together they viewed the cathedral-like church, inside and out, and Elzie was formally introduced to other people, although he never knew the identity of those he met. When the two parted company almost three hours later, they shook hands and each bid adieu in his own language. As Elzie was walking away he heard the man attempt to speak in Elzie's language, although the American found it impossible to understand his broken English. Elzie believed the man said, "Thank you, American, Viva France, Viva America."

The trenches in the Vosges Mountains were like no others. An unusual curving configuration of trenches, spread out over one hundred miles in distance, reflected the ruggedness of the mountain terrain. Not always contiguous the trenches ended at the base of rugged peaks but resumed on the other side of the mountain at the point where troop movement once again became possible. No trench structure existed on higher mountain tops or other locations where enemy attacks were near impossible. In lieu of trench fortifications observation troops were strategically placed, thus all areas affectively were patrolled. Although a few mountain passes existed, most were not conducive to troop movement and, certainly, any strategic passes were heavily fortified. In short, the mountains themselves became a vital part of the defensive posturing.

Primary, front-line trenches in the Vosges were positioned near the crest of a hill in full view of enemy trenches on the opposite hill with no-man's-land situated in the valleys or lower areas between the hills. This well constructed defensive series of trenches had not fallen to enemy attack since its placement in August, 1915. The difficulty of digging deep trenches in mountain soil necessitated the building of elaborate protective structures, embankments to impede enemy penetration. Most common of these fortifications were earthen and sandbag ramparts, often surmounted by concrete or log parapet walls. If the terrain called for stronger fortifications, intervals of trenches were protected by a parapet of carefully placed, twenty-feet sections of pine logs to a minimum height of four feet. The log wall totaled about three feet thick and contained notched slots for machine gun emplacements. Infantry fired over the wall. To deter enemy penetration three rows of barbed wire, about forty feet apart, were strung forward of the trench fortifications. The only access to the trenches from no-man's-land was through the wire and over the fortifications. For additional security several sections of trench had an overhead netting to protect from hand-grenades or hand-tossed canisters of gas. No doubt, the Vosges front-line trenches were well conceived, built to endure.

Reserve trenches, sometimes called secondary trenches, were positioned on the reverse slope of the hill. Reserve trenches were dug deeper and wider, more elaborate in design, built with fewer ramparts and, commonly, were protected by only one row of wire. Almost one hundred yards of unfortified land separated primary from secondary trenches. In the event of a primary trench breech, reserve trenches offered a safe location for retreat which then could be used to fend off enemy attack. Mainly, secondary trenches housed reserve forces, provided a rest area for soldiers serving front-line duty, received supplies, and served as an entry point for replacements. Field command was positioned deep in the secondary trench. Reserve trenches received considerable artillery fire, but their infantry dwellers rarely engaged in hand-to-hand combat or exchanged rifle fire with the enemy. Danger always lurked anywhere in a hot zone, but infantry combat mostly occurred in front-line positions, not in reserve trenches.

A third type of trench, called an advanced outpost, also existed in the quiet sectors of the Vosges. Of shallow depth the outpost was protected by wire only. Situated well into no-man's-land this smaller third trench was intentionally not joined with the front-line trench. Advanced outposts stood on their own. Rectangular in shape and large enough to protect a squad of men, these advanced outposts served two major purposes: 1. to warn of attack, 2. to provide a forward position for scouts gathering enemy intelligence data. Although these outposts, located farther down the forward slope, were particularly vulnerable to mortar fire, sniper fire, or to enemy nighttime harassment raids, duty in the outpost was regarded no more life threatening than service in primary trenches. Both sides used the advanced outposts and seldom were these positions attacked other than when opposing troops made a rare direct frontal assault on a primary trench. However, if an enemy front-line assault did occur, men in the outpost faced extreme danger.

Fundamentally, German trenches in the Vosges were all laid out in a similar manner with a few notable differences. German defenses relied more on machine-gun protection, less on infantry fire power, basically because fewer German troops manned their trenches. Consequently, German trenches were constructed narrower, but equally fortified. The most significant difference in trench construction was found in the relative placement of German reserve trenches, being situated almost a mile behind the primary trench and built more like a front-line trench. Each line of defense, French or German, had its particular advantages, disadvantages.

The Americans understood they were under French command to receive front line experience while working in concert with the French 93rd. The amalgamated unit made for interesting bedfellows as the inexperienced Americans were eager for action while the experienced French were overly cautious, leery of front-line duty.

Company L. of the 61st Regiment was positioned southwest of the mountain pass in the La Cude-Violu Sector. Here, both German and French trenches were placed on steep hillsides with no-man's-land placed in an irregular shaped valley between two mountain ridges. Although sections of the valley varied in width, most opposing trenches along the La Cude-Violu line were separated by four or five hundred yards of open land. Moving up or down the hillsides was dangerous and any type of aggressive troop movement in this area was most difficult.

Defending the trenches in the La Cude-Violu area presented additional challenges. Although the front-line trench afforded a full view of no-man's-land, the uneven ground with numerous small, protruding ridges provided some cover for small units of prying enemy soldiers. Necessarily, the advanced outpost was positioned farther down the slope and was considered a precarious defensive position, but a highly advantageous position for spotting intruders. The safety valve for the men in the outpost was that in the event of enemy attack the men in higher-ground trenches could provide excellent cover for retreat. As long as the men in the primary trench held their position, the men in the advanced outpost were reasonably safe from enemy attack.

Any major assault near La Cude seemed unlikely, for it would gain little for either side. Be that as it may, La Cude was still dangerous ground. All men serving in a hot zone were aware that every soldier was under orders to kill or capture the enemy whenever possible, and that enemy forces could or might attack any site, any time of their choosing.

Positions were manned, Company L. was in place. First Platoon, Third Squad, was placed in the so called rifle pits overlooking no-man's-land. The situation was exactly what the men had been trained for, yet the men felt uncertain, apprehensive. No one said anything, instead, they gave full concentration to watching for movement in the battle-scarred terrain directly in front of them. Almost one hour passed before the soldiers felt comfortable enough to informally converse with one another. "John, this is the real thing," Elzie proclaimed as he pointed and handed his field glasses to John. "Take a look right over there, my friend. Those are Kraut trenches."

"With all the camouflage I can't see what you're talking about, but I believe you. What is that fortification down there?" John asked as he handed the field glasses to Tony.

Elzie smiled. "That is our forward position, our outpost. I didn't see anybody there, I can't tell if it's manned or not. Look, it has wire on three sides, a rear exit, and it looks like it might be pretty well built. Looks okay to me, at least from here it does."

"Maybe to you it looks good, but I'm not eager to spend the night out there. I like it here just fine. This right here is what I call a trench. As far as I'm concerned I'm a front-liner, right here."

William interrupted. "Did you see those French soldiers we relieved? Man, did they look whipped, looked like they had been through the mill. They were sure happy to get out of here. Most of them looked like old men, didn't they?"

John answered. "They were old men. Maybe old men before their time but, nevertheless, old men. Some of them probably have been fighting the Germans for four years. Think about it! We'd probably look old too if we had gone through what they have. We were told that duty here in the quiet sector was like a vacation for them, but it sure didn't look that way to me. I suspect they got all that wear and tear from fighting elsewhere. I'll bet they are glad just to be alive."

"One afternoon while on guard duty back at Gerardmer I heard the brass talking about some interesting stuff. I didn't think much about it until I saw those Frogs so happy to get out of here. I think I know why, and it's just about the way John said it. I heard the colonel tell his staff that Pershing thinks the French have a morale problem, that the French soldiers have just about had it."

"What are you talking about?" John impatiently said.

"Let me start from the beginning, and I will explain if you will keep your eyes peeled out there instead of looking at me. Anything happens out there I want to know it."

"Don't worry, our position is secure. Besides, who would want to look at you? We can talk, just keep your voice down. If something happens the siren will sound.

Don't be so up tight, relax!"

William was not totally convinced that all was well, or that is was all right to talk. He looked at Elzie; and since Elzie said nothing to the contrary, he reluctantly continued. "Here is what I heard. The colonel was talking about eighty American divisions in France."

"Awe, come on. We don't have that many divisions in the whole Army. Let me see...that's over two million men. No way."

"If you let me talk instead of interrupting me, I'll finish telling you what I heard." William was clearly aggravated with John as now he wanted to speak and spoke loud enough for others to hear. "The colonel was quoting Pershing. He was talking about us not having enough good officers, and not enough time to train them, but they have got to get them over here anyway, because the Allies can't hang on any longer. Something about a German spring offensive and only American troops could contain them. Now I didn't understand all of that but I did understand what came next. Pershing feels that both the British and French people are extremely tired of the war and their troops reflect this attitude, shown by their inability to thwart German attacks. The Germans have fewer men and still win the battles. He thinks the French are about whipped, and only the immediate use of American troops can turn things around. Problem being, American troops aren't ready yet. If I heard it right, ready or not they intend to bring our boys over anyway.

"In the meantime, Pershing wants us to support the French, cooperate with them, and encourage them in any way we can. Above all, the American Field Command is not to embarrass the French in any way, regardless of what they do. So, as I said, I think John was right when he said the French are worn out and just happy to be alive. I suspect much of what I just said has something to do with why they paraded us all over, like in St. Die. I think they might be..." All conversation abruptly ended when American small arms fire erupted further down the line. German machine guns returned fire, all soldiers' eyes stayed glued to no-man's-land. Sporadic gun fire continued for several hours. The doughboys remained on high alert for the remainder of the day.

The conversation was not concluded, nor did it need to be. The others understood the concept—the French Army was weakening.

The first day in the trenches passed without the men in Company L. firing a shot, but prolonged high alert status took its toll. Fear, anxiety never desisted, although as time passed the level of intensity slightly diminished. They endured the uneasiness, the nagging fear of the unknown. They had followed orders to stand firm, not to fire without a target.

The second day hinted at a routine—a twenty-four hour rotation of four hours on lookout duty, four hours off. Any opportunity to eat, sleep, or time to deal with body functions became treasured time. There was no free time.

Unnerving events became common, the unexpected became the norm. Life in the trenches could not be scripted. All was quiet when a stranger's voice echoed throughout no-man's-land. The men of Company L. could hear the words as clearly as if the speaker were standing next to them.

> Welcome to the war, American boys of the 61st. It's been a long trip for you since you left Camp Greene. We're pleased you're here, the poor French are in need of a respite. They are not very good soldiers. We hope none of you were injured by the French 70th Division when they ran away after you relieved them. We hope that you Americans are not counting on the French 93rd Regiment to back you in battle, because they won't be there if you need them, but we suspect you already know that. Your officers did warn you, didn't they?
>
> How are your loved ones at home since you left them to fight for France? We remind you that if you lay down your weapons and come over to us, you will be well treated.
>
> Farewell for now, we will visit with you later after you settle in.

A brief burst of Allied machine-gun fire erupted; there was no return fire. Undoubtedly an American machine gunner was venting his anger. John was also angry. "How did those sons of bitches know that stuff? Where did that voice come from? How in the hell did they do that?"

A nearby sergeant answered. "Got me. Sounded like he was right here didn't it? You know we can learn a lot from that. Mainly, sound carries funny in these mountains. We all need to be careful what we say, where we say it. You guys remember that. Those dirty Krauts know a lot more about this place than we do."

A private inserted his thoughts. "You know what bothers me more than that? That son of a bitch spoke with a southern drawl, not a German accent. I'll bet he's American, that son of a bitch. I'll lay down my weapon all right—I'll lay it down his throat or shove it up his ass, that son of a bitch. Better yet, I'll shove it down the throat of the Old Clown Prince, himself, if I could find him." These not so complimentary words perfectly expressed the sentiment of the others. Americans regarded the speaker as a traitor, and they had little regard for William, the Crown Prince of Germany.

Elzie spoke, more to raise the ire of John than anything else. "I think that southern drawl was a Texas twang. Only Texans can talk like that."

"Not true, and you know it. Texans don't do that shit. More likely, he learned his English in Pike County while swimming in the Illinois River."

Not privy to the background of either man, a baffled sergeant joined in. "I don't know what the hell you guys are talking about, and it's probably just as well I don't, so knock it off. We're here to relieve you. Go on back, get something to eat, or at least get the hell out of here." The sergeant then looked directly at Elzie. Just so that you know, son, I'm from Austin. So aren't a lot of others. You do know the 5th Division was organized at Camp Logan, Texas? You would be well advised to watch your lip."

The sun-warmed air, the high, blue sky made it feel warmer than it really was. Safe open space with sunshine was a rare commodity anywhere near the trenches, but the Third Squad had found such a spot. "That Mulligan stew isn't bad, hope they have some more back there. Anyone know what's in it?"

"You don't want to know. I heard it was made from regular ration issue and whatever extras may come to hand."

"Sorry I asked. While you scholars are in the mood to educate me, what about this stand-to stuff? How come when we're in the trenches we fix bayonets and stand to the parapet in full equipment? Are we going to continue doing that every morning, every night? What's the deal, anybody know?"

Elzie answered. "I'm not sure, I just assumed it was a roll call procedure, a way for others to check on us, check our equipment. Sort of like reveille and taps. I'm not real sure why we do it, there must be a reason."

"How come after we stand-to in the morning they want us to un-fix the bayonets? Think they worry we might stick someone?"

"I doubt that. If I had to guess, I would guess it was because they worry that during the day the sun might glint upon the polished steel. I know there is real concern about snipers in this area."

"Makes sense. As much as I hate to admit it, most of the crap the Army makes us do, does make sense."

Elzie released one of his now famous grins. "I wouldn't go that far."

John smiled after hearing Elzie's comment. "Amen to that. Speaking of education, I want William to finish his story. What else did you hear while you were eavesdropping at headquarters?"

"I really shouldn't respond to such a smart-ass comment, but I'll just consider the source. Are you real sure you're from Texas?"

John glared, pretended the comment was not worthy of an answer before he looked at Elzie and winked. "So sorry I offended thee, Sir William. Wilt thou forgive me?"

William's response was priceless. "No, but I'll tell you anyway. Really there's nothing more to the story, nothing that pertains to us anyway. Come to think about it I did hear something else kind of interesting. It doesn't really affect us, but I suppose one day it could. The colonel said Pershing was really pissed about some

Americans getting medals from French civilians for not doing anything other than being here. The colonel now has written orders—no more medals of any type for Americans unless the incident was directly observed by an American officer; and then, it must be in writing and okayed by General Staff."

"Someone is going to say it, it might as well be me," John said. "There won't be many medals given in this war, unless they are given for action far behind the lines. Since we've been at the front, I don't think I've seen many officers, let alone a field officer. Tell me more, this is good stuff. Best comedy entertainment I've had in a while!" The group had to be amused by John's comments. He was playing his role as a cynic, and he played it oh so well.

William continued as though he were enjoying his role as the straight man. "This one is even funnier. No, that's not right, it's sad, not funny. They don't want any more American soldiers killed until there is a separate American Command. Can you imagine such an order? No more American soldiers are to die until they can die under American Command. Too many American boys wrapped in blankets. They estimate nearly a thousand American boys already killed, and our Army has yet to mount its first offensive. When I first heard them talking, I sort of got mad. It sounded like it was okay to be killed under American Command, just not under French Command. Then I realized they were..."

His thought was not completed. The attack alarm sounded, every man assumed his firing position. Then they waited. On high alert, rifles ready to fire, they waited until nightfall before a sergeant approached their position. "Third Squad, Corporal Higgins."

"Right here," the corporal responded.

"Take your squad, move into the outpost, relieve 1st Squad. How many men do you have?"

"Eleven, plus me."

"Is your scout with you?"

"Here, sergeant."

"Do you have your maps?"

"Yes."

"Make contact with 1st Squad scout! Have him brief you, find out what he knows before you relieve him. They're up to something out there. Captain wants to know what's going down. Find out! Now move out, corporal, and for God's sake, be quiet."

The 3rd Squad took up position in the outpost, and by 10:30 p.m. Private Moore was sent out to scout no-man's-land. Exactly at 1:00 a.m. German artillery laid down a heavy bombardment northeast of the 61st position. Less than one hour later Allied artillery returned fire on German positions. It was quite a display of fireworks, particularly from the outpost vantage point. Then at 5:30 a.m. all artillery fire was lifted. American troops braced for an attack which never came. It had not been a good time to be in the outpost or no-man's-land but, fortunately, no shells had landed in their immediate vicinity. Just before dawn Private Moore returned to the outpost and reported having observed numerous German troops in and out of their trenches. The 3rd Squad was relieved, and they were more than happy to get out of the outpost.

Elzie whispered to John. "This time I know I've done it. I wasn't certain before, now I'm positive. Yes, sir, I have been to Germany and back. According to my maps I was more than thirty yards into Germany. How about that? I thought about leaving them an American dime in plain sight so they would know a Yank had been on their doorstep, but I thought better of it."

John grunted, "Big damn deal. Hope I never get there. Damn Krauts. Sure glad you didn't leave anything for them to see, that would have been stupid. No need to disturb a hornet's nest."

A lieutenant from another company joined the group of Company L. privates as they were taking their rest break. His presence was resented and put the privates ill at ease. The lieutenant sat beside John, took a sip from his canteen and entered the conversation. He spoke matter-of-factly without emotion. "Word came down this morning, 5th suffered its first combat casualties last night. As the 11th Regiment was moving into the line, German artillery scored a direct hit on Company I. Killed one private, wounded a few other enlisted men. Captain Mark Clark suffered a severe injury, guess he'll be out for the duration. Too bad he got it that way."

"What does that way mean?" asked John in an accusatory tone.

"Injured by artillery fire. All I meant was it was a shame that he didn't make it to the trenches. No one wants to get it on the way to the fight. We're going to miss Captain Clark. I hear he's a good man."

Without considering the consequences, John looked at his friends and fired words right back. "I don't know about you guys but I'm going to miss the private—the one who got killed. I know he was a good man." John's defiant words annoyed the lieutenant who wisely allowed the moment to pass. Others remained passive, knowing that John was on thin ice. John would not let go, continued talking as he walked away. "Think I'm going to get some shuteye, I don't like the company around here.

The lieutenant either did not understand or was attempting to further antagonize. "Sleep well, private, things are under control around here. The Jerrys know better than to mess with men like us." He smiled, nodded to the men, and walked away. The men stayed seated, pleased that the lieutenant was leaving.

Once the lieutenant was out of sight, John returned. "What an asshole! I'm happy he doesn't have any command in our company. If he did, I'd quit and go home. He is a typical half-assed, brass looie. That son-of-a-bitch told us about the dead private, and then talked as though a wounded captain was the real loss."

William, who was usually reluctant to voice contrary opinions, spoke in defense of the lieutenant. "He didn't mean any harm. He was just talking, trying to make conversation. I'd bet he is like the rest of us—a bit on edge, sort of nervous, kinda scared. I think it was all nervous chatter, trying to be part of the group."

"Maybe, but he's still an asshole!"

Elzie spoke for John's position. "I don't know about the asshole stuff, but he is wrong about something, and I know it for sure. The Jerrys are not afraid of us. Believe you me, they control no-man's-land, come and go when they want. At night they are out there all over the place. Those guys are battle-hardened veterans, probably not afraid of much. They know the terrain, I wouldn't be surprised if they already know the details about our trenches. I think they are just feeling us Yanks out. Remember, if I can get to their trenches, they sure as hell can get to ours. Those boys have been here awhile. They're not afraid of us. We're the new kids on the block."

"Why, Elzie Moore, is that fear I hear?"

"Nope, no fear, just respect. Mark my words, no-man's-land belongs to them, at least for the time being. You remember that." Elzie was correct, not because he was wiser, but because he had scouted no-man's-land, the German trenches. He had observed the German soldier at close range.

Shortly after dark on June 16, 3rd Squad reassumed their position in the advanced outpost. At 2:00 a.m. all hell broke loose when German artillery opened fire. Lines near La Cude took some incoming, but an area about six miles north took the hardest pounding. Presumably the 60th was under heavy artillery attack, perhaps under ground attack. The sounds of German artillery were terribly confusing. A few projectiles traveled in silence, some made an in-flight whispering sound, and others flew with a nerve-racking whine. Although one could hear shells in flight, one could not identify bearing or target until the missiles detonated or flashes were observed. Some explosions seemed to shake the earth itself while others detonated in air above target. The frightening sounds of an artillery barrage were awful sounds to endure, capable of unnerving almost any ground soldier.

Adding to the confusion, other sounds fused with the noise of artillery. Familiar sounds—the ra-ta-tat-tat-tat of machine-gun fire, sporadic pops of small arms fire, the intermittent sounds of small blasts, the explosion of hand grenades or other explosive devises—only added to the discomfiture. Flares, near and afar, kept the sky lighted, but the ability to observe was of little comfort. Soldiers endured two solid hours of raging artillery fire before the sounds of war abated and the sky darkened once again, before the warning alarm resonated over the entire area. Enemy attack was expected. The men in the outpost went full alert, preparing for the worst. They were fully aware that the outpost would receive the first blow of a ground attack. The sounds of artillery had tested their mettle, but now the thought of attack forced the men to muster what courage they had left. The 3rd Squad anxiously laid in wait three hours before the all clear sounded. Enemy forces had chosen not to make a ground assault against their position. Their sector was secure but the soldiers' nerves were on edge, their confidence was shaken. The Germans had successfully played with their minds.

What about other positions? With no knowledge about events elsewhere on the line the men hoped the German assaults had met with failure. They worried about a possible breech somewhere in their line and could only wait for confirmation, one way or the other. More doubts emerged, imaginations were fueled when a faint but unmistakable smell of mustard gas permeated their area. The use of poisonous gas became another concern, another source of fear.

The darkness of night passed, the early light of dawn created more anxiety when the attack siren blasted again. No enemy sightings were reported, but conventional military wisdom warned of imminent danger, a delayed assault, either here or elsewhere on the line. The entire American 5th Division, the French 21st Division remained hunkered down, prepared for a possible enemy assault. No American scouts were out, old intelligence data was of little value, so they did all they could do—they waited. No enemy was sighted, no indications of aggressive action were observed. At 11:15 a.m. the all clear was signaled. There would be no enemy ground assault at La Cude.

By 1:00 the same afternoon news broke concerning artillery damage north of La Cude. The German shelling had destroyed a dugout housing Americans from Company G., 60th Regiment, killing three, wounding three, and gassing twenty-four. Immediately following the gas attacks, two separate German assaults on American positions were quickly repulsed by vigorous machine-gun and rifle fire. The Americans did not counterattack. French positions were less fortunate—their positions absorbed more direct artillery hits and they suffered a far larger number of casualities than did the Americans, but French positions held, no Allied lines were breached.

By no means did this aggressive German action constitute a major offensive. It did, however, disturb the recent calm and seemed to forewarn of bellicose action in and along the quiet sector lines. Not only had the French-American divisions been teased, taunted, by German artillery bombardment, they had been warned. Future enemy infantry penetration was certainly possible. By accurate concentrations of artillery fire, the Germans made it clear they knew the locations of the American replacements, and they understood how to attack fortified French positions and to make it hurt. Clearly, the Germans had sent a message.

On Friday, June 21, at 2:00 in the morning the Allies responded to the earlier German aggression. Following two hours of Allied artillery bombardment, combined American and French forces launched a direct frontal assault against the German front lines near La Cude. Company L., Elzie's unit, was one of three companies spearheading the attack. Somehow enemy forces had been forewarned and had withdrawn their front-line forces beyond the objectives of the Allied raid. Fearful of entrapment or ambush, the Allied forces immediately stopped advancement and withdrew to their own lines. A token counterattack by the Germans was beaten off handily. The 61st suffered no casualties, but the near fiasco put Allied intelligence in question.

The absence of front-line German troops perplexed Allied command until late day intelligence indicated a possible massing of German infantry directly opposite the American lines at La Croix-Aux-Mines, the Headquarters of the 61st Regiment. This massing of troops explained the shifting of German forces. With Regimental Headquarters at risk, French and American troops were redeployed to shore up defensive positions near La Croix-Aux-Mines. However, redeployment thinned the ranks of infantry firepower at the outer portions of the sector. Although the Allies were well aware that Germans were masters of military deception and often deployed diversionary tactics, the Americans could not gamble the Germans were bluffing. Command had to protect Regimental Headquarters.

As part of the redeployment a French infantry company of seasoned combat veterans replaced Company L. in the La Cude Sector. The Americans were repositioned in the line one mile south nearer Regimental Headquarters. Third Squad was temporarily detached from Company L., more specifically they were ordered to remain in the outpost near La Cude, and were to be supported by the French company of replacements. Elzie, John, and the other four members of the little triangle were part of the twelve man squad. Their orders were clear: Secure the outpost, observe enemy movement, resist enemy encroachment.

Precisely at 1:00 a.m., Saturday, June 22, German artillery opened fire on positions held by the French-American amalgamated unit. In less than thirty minutes Allied artillery returned fire. Germans principally used their 7.7 cm, fifteen-pound shell, long range field guns. Allies used the French 75 mm, sixteen-pound shrapnel shell, and both sides targeted opposing trenches with close range mortars. The four-hour artillery barrage ended as abruptly as it started, and was followed by numerous launchings of observation flares over no-man's-land. No front-line soldier escaped the agony, the ordeal of massive artillery fire. No trench was deep enough, strong enough to assure safety.

Elzie went back out to scout no-man's-land, to make an assessment of damage. Within minutes of his departure, German artillery resumed fire. Dawn was less than one hour away.

CHAPTER 19

A BLANKET AND A BOTTLE

T exas."

"Illinois," answered John as he gave the counter password. "Get in here! Where the hell have you been? Shells landing all over the place and you're out in no-man's-land like you're on a Sunday picnic. We've all been worried—thought something might have happened to you."

Darkness still dominated the sky, although it was only minutes before dawn. Elzie hurried, as much as one can hurry while avoiding the entanglements of barbed wire, to get back safely into the outpost housing the other eleven men. In only a few minutes the first rays of the emerging sun would supply sufficient light to make Elzie an easy target for snipers.

"How long... has it been since they lifted... the artillery fire?" inquired a panting Elzie as he spoke before he had recaptured his breath.

"Are you nuts? Listen! Does that sound to you like they have lifted it?"

"I don't mean the fire on the line, I mean here, right where we are right now," Elzie said in disgust as he pointed his finger to the ground. "How long?"

John looked perplexed. "No shells have landed right here at all. About one-half hour ago the trench back there took a big hit. I think that was the last shell to land near here." Now John was pointing to the ground. "No shells right here, none at all." John became very concerned when he saw the worried expression on Elzie's face. "Why, what's wrong? Damn it, man, speak! What's wrong?"

"We've got problems," Elzie announced as he pushed John aside. "Corporal, Corporal Higgins," he shouted. "Where in the hell is the corporal?"

"Over here, Moore, what's wrong?"

"There are a bunch of things wrong. They're back, the Krauts are back. Listen

351

to me and listen well, because we must act fast. The Germans are back in their trenches and I'm talking about the trenches right over there." He turned to point at the German trenches but kept talking. "When we made our raid yesterday the Krauts weren't there, but they are now, and it looks to me like they're preparing to come here."

"The Germans are where, coming where?"

"God damn it, corporal, will you listen to me? Germans are in that trench, that trench right there, the one about one hundred and fifty yards from where I am standing this very minute." He pointed to the trench as he carefully enunciated each word. "The Germans have reoccupied their trench." He paused for another deep breath before he resumed speaking. "Get a runner back to our guys, tell them the Germans are back and we need cover to withdraw." The runner heard Elzie and not even waiting for orders he left for the primary trench. "There's more. The Krauts are not hunkered down, some are out of their trenches. It looks to me like they are preparing for assault. There's more. John said no artillery had hit this area in the last half hour. That makes me think the Germans have lifted their fire in this area, so that they can attack. Look down there, south of us. They sure haven't lifted it down there. We need to get ready. I think they intend to come right at us."

"How many are there?"

"Not sure. I would guess I saw maybe fifty to seventy infantry. Could be more, I'm not sure. I'll bet more Krauts are up there, somewhere. They might attack with only seventy men, but I wouldn't think so. I'll bet I just didn't see them all. Pretty dark out there."

The other men had heard Elzie's report and were already setting up defensive positions, checking ammunition. The first indirect rays of sun began to peek over the mountain. Dawn was coming.

"I wish it would hurry and get light. I'll feel better when I can see. I sure don't want any surprises." John's face revealed his anxiety.

"I'm not sure light is our friend on this day."

"You mean to tell me that you think they would attack in broad daylight. Why would anybody attack in daylight?"

"Not sure, unless they have something particular in mind."

"What do you mean, particular?"

Elzie never answered the question, because before he could speak, the runner returned, shouting, "Corporal, corporal!"

"What?"

"They're gone, the French are gone."

"What do you mean? Are they dead?"

"No, they're not dead, they've pulled out. The trench is deserted, there is no one there. We have no support."

The corporal looked as though he was trying to fit the pieces of a puzzle together. "Where did they go?"

The runner looked disgusted, wondered if the corporal believed him. "How in the hell would I know. The French support troops are gone, there is no one in that trench. If we withdraw, we do it without cover."

The corporal started to speak, but was preempted by shouts from John. "Jesus Christ, they're here! Get ready, here they come!"

The Germans were trying to sneak past the perimeter of the outpost. John's sharp eyes detected some ground movement and he realized the Germans were on the move. John opened fire. Others in the outpost joined the firefight, although not all saw their targets until the Germans returned fire. The attacking troops were not massed in a group, rather their attack formation resembled an arc with soldiers scattered and low to the ground in front of and to the side of the American position. They were attempting to encircle the outpost. The nearest enemy soldier was no closer than eighty yards from the outpost but there were so many of them, and they were so dispersed and well concealed that they were not easy targets. The ensuing firefight lasted less than five minutes before the Germans ceased firing and reassumed totally concealed positions. Because they were so well protected in the outpost the Americans suffered no casualties. It was impossible to determine if American fire had inflicted any German damage. All they could do was hold their position and wonder why the attack ended.

"We've got to get out of here, back to the trench," the runner said to the corporal.

"Too late. If we move now, we're sitting ducks. They would pick us off one at a time. Nobody would make it."

"Somebody has got to hear all this rifle fire. Our boys will be here in a few minutes, won't they?"

"They will if they hear it. I doubt if they can hear it with all that artillery fire. Maybe they will. Just hang in there a minute or so until we decide what to do." The corporal crawled to Elzie's position and spoke in a whisper. "Elzie, you got any ideas? I'm sure we can't make it back without cover fire."

"I agree, we can't. I think we're better off to stay here. They can't get us in here unless they get in behind us. We can't let them get behind us."

"I've got four men covering our rear, I don't think they can get behind us."

Elzie thought for a minute. "You know something? I think they could take us if they really wanted to. I think they want us alive, that's why they backed off in the first place. Otherwise a few rounds of carefully placed mortars would take care of all of us, it would all be over. Most likely, they're working on a way to penetrate our position and force some of us to surrender. Right now they're so scattered out there that some of them will get us no matter what we do, although they will pay a dear price if they do try. So here is what I think. We stay put, keep a close watch, hope some help comes. But here is the kicker. If no help arrives, we've got to act. If they do attack we must counterattack before they get to us, or behind us. Do you agree?"

"Yes, I think I understand, but how do we counterattack with only one squad?"

"Do you see that ridge over there next to the hill, about thirty or so yards from here?"

"I think I see what you are talking about. I can't see behind the ridge."

"That's the idea. Neither can they, nobody can. That's the route I use to get back here at night. I know the area. If they attack, we've got to counterattack long enough for me and three or four other men to reach that ridge. If we do that we've changed the situation. Once there we would have position to fire into the middle of the attackers. In essence, our fire from the ridge, plus fire from the outpost will put them in a cross fire. If we do it quick enough, they will have to retreat some, and that will divide their attacking forces, and anyone trying to get in behind us will be cut off from their own line. Then our guys in the outpost can concentrate their fire on them, hopefully wiping them out. In any event they won't get behind us that way. Then they have no choice but to call off the attack. Either they try again or they drop in the mortar shells. Surely by that time our reinforcements will be here. Do you understand what I am saying, does it make sense?"

"I think, but I'm not sure. Who mounts the counterattack?"

"We do, me and a few other guys. We break through their lines and take up position on the ridge. The rest of you stay in position here and give us cover during our counterattack."

"I got it, but how do you get back?"

"We don't until reinforcements get here. If reinforcements don't come, we're all goners anyway. If we can get to that ridge, they can't attack us without being in your line of fire, and they can't attack the outpost without being in our line of fire. If they try, we have them in a cross fire. I don't think they will take that risk. All we need to do is hold them off until help gets here. If need be, we wait until dark to get back. Hopefully, we don't have to wait that long. Sooner or later somebody on our side has got to figure out what is going on out here. Sooner I hope. Better yet, I hope the Germans don't attack. Since we already know their attack position they might decide to call it all off anyway. If I have a choice, I would rather stay right here until help comes. Believe you me, I don't want to counterattack. I don't see any other options, do you?"

"None."

Elzie sort of tilted his head and gave a superficial grin. "You do know that if they use their mortars, it's all over anyway."

"Yeah, I know. Why do you think they haven't attacked yet? Maybe they did call it off. What are they up to? How did they know the French were gone before we knew it? Something is not right."

"Good questions. I don't have the answers, but the fact is they did know the French were gone. Makes me mad, too. Why did the French pull out in the first place, and how did the Germans know it before we did? I can only guess. I suspect that they are specifically targeting us. I really think they are after us, after American prisoners. Otherwise, I can't think of what they would want, it makes no sense. You would think if they wanted us dead we would be dead. Sending men across open ground to surprise us is not the best way to kill us. There has to be something else on their minds. Anyway, we need to forget all of that, concentrate on what we talked about. If I go charging out there to counterattack, I want good cover. Make sure the best shots are covering us. You need to explain our plan to the others, and make sure they understand. If it's all right with you, I'll take half the squad with me. That will leave six men in the outpost. Is that enough?"

Nobody in the outpost cherished the idea of a forward, middle of the line counterattack, although they agreed there were few options. They had to execute the plan if, in fact, they were about to become surrounded by enemy forces. Without primary trench support, it seemed to be the only alternative to perhaps the most dreaded of all fates. The decision became final. Now, the isolated American soldiers were left to watch the open ground for enemy movement and to hope and pray that reinforcements were already on their way. The time was 6:10 a.m.

Remarkably, the squad of men remained calm. Wait was all they could do. During training these men had become soul mates, confident that every man in the squad could depend on the others to do all that was needed; and, if the counterattack became necessary, their allegiance to one another, their skills as infantrymen surely would be put to the test. The proposed counterattack was an extremely dangerous, daring maneuver, and their first major obstacle was getting past their own wire. The wire was not cut, not cleared for offensive assault, and anyone who got caught up in the wire faced certain death from German fire. There was one exit through the wire that the scouts used, but the others did not know the exact path or necessary precautions. The counterattacking group would need to follow Elzie, single file through the wire to the forward area, and they had to successfully make it or the plan would not work. With little success Elzie tried to explain the only way past the wire, but the procedure was so complex, intended to be difficult, that his explanation was worth little to anyone not trained for it or with such limited time to learn it. There was no alternative—the group had to follow Elzie.

At 6:15 a.m. an English-speaking German, concealed from view, addressed the Americans in the outpost. "We have you surrounded, you have no chance. If you lay down your arms and surrender, you will be well treated, the war will be over for you. If you resist, you will not know tomorrow. You have exactly two minutes to decide."

The Americans gave no official response, never really considered the German offer. John answered and spoke loud enough for all to hear. "When will those stupid bastards learn? It's we, not ve. It's well, not vell." In response a German soldier stood, fired his rifle and shouted orders. Other German soldiers, fifty-five men strong, initiated a frontal assault on the American outpost.

Elzie shouted, "Now!" and the six men, with strong cover fire breached their own wire and counterattacked the middle of the attacking enemy line. Almost unbelievably, without injury the six successfully broke through the German line and took up position on the reverse slope of the ridge. The Germans were taken by surprise, the Americans had achieved their first objective. Now they put down heavy rifle fire into the middle of the German line, hoping to break the attack and to isolate the most advanced German attackers.

Within minutes the Americans had achieved their second objective—to split the German line of attack. Meanwhile, the Americans in the outpost concentrated their fire on the Germans who might gain access to their rear. Very quickly the Germans suffered heavy casualties, were forced to take cover and, effectively, the situation was radically altered—the German advance was broken. German forces, still greater in number, were on open ground with little cover, while the fewer number of Americans all benefited from adequate cover. The Germans could not advance, nor could they retreat. In order to secure the safety of their own trenches they would be forced to cross the American line of fire. Judiciously, the Germans stayed put, stayed down and returned fire. The next eleven minutes the battle raged as rifles blasted away and the battle became a stalemate. Now, neither side dared attack, dared retreat.

The final leg of the American plan called for the doughboys to hold their positions, wait for Allied reinforcements; but it was not to be as the Germans quickly took the initiative. In a strengthened effort to give their stranded soldiers retreat cover, the Germans laid down heavy mortar fire on both American positions, the outpost and the ridge. Unprepared for mortar attack, especially those near the ridge, the Americans were forced to seek cover, thereby voiding their minority power position. As the Germans retreated to their trenches they hurled multiple stick bombs at both American positions, and although no hand grenades reached the American positions, their deployment did force the splintered group of Americans to seek more protection, to take deeper cover from exploding shrapnel. The Americans had lost their advantage, the stranded Germans were now back in their trenches. Americans in the outpost enjoyed adequate protection during the mortar attack, their comrades on the ridge were not as fortunate. Although many incoming rounds landed near their ridge position, one mortar shell found its exact target, and with disastrous results the shell accomplished all the Germans needed. The mortar shell landed on the crest of the ridge within feet of the American position, almost on top of John's position. The explosion decimated the Americans, violently hurling the bodies of all six men. The men on the ridge position were down. Soon thereafter the mortar attack ended, rifle fire ceased. The Germans had withdrawn.

Someone from the outpost shouted, "It's over, they're gone." The men in the outpost quickly tried to establish verbal contact with the men on the ridge, but their shouts went unanswered. Minutes later Corporal Higgins with two other men bravely left the outpost to assess the ridge situation, to render assistance to their men. Hopes were dashed when they found four dead, one suffering from critical wounds. Boldly, one gave medical aid to the wounded man and carried him back. Requiring two separate trips, the other two men dragged the bodies of their fallen comrades back into the outpost.

The corporal shouted, "Where's Moore?"

"He got it. I saw Moore's body fly through the air and land somewhere behind the hill."

Another private spoke up. "As I was getting what was left of Wagner's body, I saw Moore in the distance, face down. He's dead."

Uncharacteristically hesitating, looking as if he were in shock, the corporal said nothing. Attempting to regain his composure as he spoke, he uttered, "All right, all right, let's see now. Is he still out there? God no, he's still out there, isn't he? Why? If you saw the body, why didn't you get it?"

"Now wait a minute, corporal. It's not my fault. You were out there too."

"I'm sorry, I didn't mean that. Why didn't we get the body? Are we positive he's dead?"

"Not one hundred percent positive. I don't know how he could have lived through the blast. Just look at Wagner's body, half of it is still out there. Moore couldn't have made it, he must be dead."

Another private stepped forward to offer affirmation. "Corporal, we couldn't get to Moore, he was too far out. He was at least twenty yards beyond Wagner's body, he must have been on the forward position. If we would have got to him, we would have been in the German line of fire. He's dead, corporal, he's dead."

The confusion of battle eliminated certainties. No one in the outpost knew exactly what transpired on the ridge, they could only speculate. The corporal was correct that they should have retrieved the body, but the private was equally correct in asserting that such an effort would have placed them in harm's way. The American survivors of the German attack had done all they could do at that time. They had done the right thing, and they all knew it. The corporal, in one last attempt to understand the sequence of events, cried out. "Anybody see what happened?" No one answered.

There was nothing more for them to do about the ridge. The corporal was in command, and that meant the safety of the survivors had to be top priority. He reacted accordingly. "Let's get the hell out of here while we can. We've got to get back to the trenches. We'll deal with Moore's body later, after support gets here." He pointed as he spoke. "You four lead. Take Upton first, then the bodies. Go, we'll cover you! I'm sure the Krauts are gone, but just in case, be careful. When you get back you signal us and we'll follow. You cover us. Got it?" The hastily devised plan worked. The American soldiers not only made it back to the trench, they managed to transport one wounded man and four dead bodies. Six men from the twelve man squad in the outpost safely returned to the trenches. Although they did not know for certain, they suspected that Private William Upton had suffered mortal injuries. Private John Wagner, Private Tony Cimino, Private Alpio Souppo, and Private Antonio Wolpi were dead, killed in action. Private Elzie Moore's body remained in the field.

Reinforcements still had not arrived. Corporal Higgins sent a runner to secure medical personnel. He specifically ordered the runner to locate the captain of Company L., and to bring him back, and not to return until he did. The corporal wanted an officer to take charge as he did not know if the fight was over or not. They prepared for possible German attack.

Private Moore's face down, motionless body laid abandoned in the bloody field of battle but a short distance from where he had earlier engaged his enemy; and his location, his fallen position was not clearly visible from either trench. It was only logical to assume the fallen soldier was dead, anyone would have, but for what happened next. Only the most discerning observer would have noticed when the fingers on his left hand began to move, if ever so slightly. Private Elzie Moore was alive. His battered body had absorbed a horrendous shock, but now he was slowly reawakening, beginning to regain consciousness. Akin to arousal from a deep sleep, his body began to have feeling, his mind began to function. Gradually, agonizingly, he became aware of his injured body; he sensed warm spots on his left leg, felt a sharp pain in his left hand, his whole body hurt as if he had been physically beaten. Fearing additional movement might cause further injury, he became intentionally deliberate and cautious. He remained face to the ground and, little by little, he continued to evaluate his physical condition until, ultimately, various movements confirmed his body was intact. Indeed, he was capable of movement, he could physically function. Only then did his sluggish mind begin to comprehend his precarious predicament. Elzie did not panic. He opened his eyes, moved his head, and attempted to sit up, but instinctively froze when he heard the most terrifying sound—nearby soldiers speaking German.

Instinctively, he returned to his prone position. He harbored a desperate hope that the Germans might not notice his limp body, or if they did, might assume him dead. Prior training advised him to remain motionless while he devised a plan for escape. If only they would believe him dead, he had a chance. Faking his death was degrading but what other choice did he have. He became consumed with worry that his breathing might reveal his fraud. His mind was groggy, his thoughts muddled. He could only worry about what would happen if they found him alive, what would they do, or what would he do. He had to have a plan, he had to think.

Try as he might Elzie could devise no plan, no course of action. Seconds ticked away, one minute seemed like an eternity until finally he could wait no more; he could no longer endure not knowing what was happening around him and was compelled to open his eyes, to look around, to assess his situation. He had no choice, he had to know. Slightly moving his head, squinting his eyes, he saw German soldiers comforting and aiding their fallen comrades; but it became a most frightful thought when he realized these soldiers were too far away to make the sounds he was hearing. The enemy was all around him. As voices increased in number and the sounds became more distinct, he recognized there was nothing he could do. There were no alternatives, no viable options, no need for a plan. He was a downed, unarmed soldier in enemy territory. Armed German soldiers, the very men he had just engaged in combat were all around him. It was useless to concern himself with escape. Elzie had little choice other than to remain motionless, to continue his deceit.

Abruptly, the deception ended when the tip of a sharp object jabbed Elzie in the butt, and he flinched. They knew he was alive. An enemy soldier placed his rifle to the back of Elzie's head and shouted something in German. Elzie made no movement. Another German spoke in English, "Get up!" and when Elzie did not answer he kicked him in the ribs, and used his foot to roll Elzie onto his back. Apart from his tattered uniform, abrasions and splotches of dried blood, the Germans observed no major wounds to his body. Considering what the American soldier had just endured, Elzie looked uninjured. The marauding Germans now had the prize they had come in search of—an American prisoner of war.

Five German soldiers stood above him, observing the fallen soldier in his helpless predicament. There was nothing for Elzie to do but stare back. He was not going to show fear. Two soldiers reached down, grabbed Elzie, and brought him to his feet. Now things occurred so fast that the young American's groggy mind could not properly process all that was happening. The Germans were talking among themselves. Some talked to him, their manner of speaking seeming to indicate a pride in their humiliation of Elzie. Others were approaching to get a better look. Elzie felt shame knowing he would become the first man in the 5th

Division to be taken prisoner from the field of battle. They were holding him by the arms to keep him on his feet, perhaps to display him. He resented it and jerked his arms free, but never attempted to move from the place he stood. It was bad enough to be at their mercy, worse to be the focus of their ghoulish attention. Elzie was disgraced, humiliated. He saw no recourse but to remain standing in front of them, offering no resistance.

Elzie turned to see if he could determine his exact location or, heaven forbid, the fate of his fellow comrades. What Private Moore saw horrified him. Where his friend, John, had stood in battle he saw only a shell crater. Beyond the crater he saw discarded rifles, scattered American helmets, and a grimly scarred landscape strewn with body parts. Quite to the contrary, there were no indications that his comrades might have survived. Elzie's feelings of humiliation changed to guilt. Had the young warrior led his friends to their deaths in his scheme to counterattack? Vexatiously, he turned to his German captors as though he expected them to give some explanation of what had happened; and what he perceived was anything but explanatory. The German soldier holding Elzie's arm sported a heinous, contemptuous smile as though he were pleased with what Elzie had viewed. Elzie's guilt changed to anger as he looked into the eyes of the man partially responsible for the violent deaths of his friends. Other German soldiers broadly smiled, openly displaying their pleasure in Elzie's agony. Four soldiers talked to one another, the fifth soldier continued to look at Elzie and to smile.

The sequential feelings of humiliation, guilt, anger, and agony now gave way to hatred. The captured American soldier disgustedly looked away from his antagonist, and it was then that he saw the instrument of his salvation. One German soldier was carrying a side arm, an automatic Steyr pistol. The loaded pistol was housed in an unfastened holster and its safety was off. Elzie made his move, and in less time than it takes to blink an eye, Elzie grabbed the pistol out of the holster and commenced firing at his captors. His first shots brought down two men, wounded another, and Elzie managed to fire two more shots before the other German soldiers could partially restrain him. In seconds Elzie had killed three and seriously wounded two other enemy soldiers. A fierce, final struggle ensued where Elzie fired one more shot before he was totally subdued. He continued to struggle as the Germans overpowered him, and Elzie's reluctance to release his clutch on the pistol forced the Germans to maneuver the pistol barrel up and under Elzie's chin. A powerful German soldier maneuvered his finger over Elzie's trigger finger and applied the necessary pressure to fire the pistol a final time. The expelled bullet entered Elzie's head through his chin, passed through his mouth, teeth, bone, into his brain, and embedded in his skull. Instantly, Elzie died.

Elzie's lifeless body fell to the ground. His motionless limbs were twisted in unnatural, grotesque positions, and his face was bloodied beyond recognition.

His American blood freely spilled into the French soil where he had so valiantly resisted his enemy. Elzie's fight, his war, was over.

Making no secret of their arrival, Company L. reinforcements arrived one hour after Corporal Higgins and the remnant of his 3rd Squad had evacuated the outpost. German soldiers remaining in no-man's-land wisely retreated, but in doing so they were forced to leave many of their own dead on the field, an act most uncommon for either side.

The captain immediately questioned Corporal Higgins. "What the hell happened here?"

The corporal, relieved that reinforcements had finally arrived, took a drink from his canteen before he answered. He needed to gather his wits. "We were positioned in the outpost as ordered. When our scout returned shortly before dawn he informed us German infantry was in position to attack. I sent a runner to notify our French support troops of the situation, but they had pulled out, they were not in place. I repeat, there were no support forces protecting our rear. We had no support."

"Why? Where were they, where did they go?"

"That's what we want to know."

The captain looked angry. "I will find out, and when I sort this all out I will personally get back to you. Now, go on, finish your report. What happened next?"

"Private Moore worked out a plan of defense for the outpost, and as crazy as it might sound, the plan worked. Otherwise I wouldn't be giving a report now. We had to hold position, we dared not withdraw with no rear support. Had we tried they would have cut us to pieces. But if we were attacked by superior forces we were still in deep shit. That's where the plan came in. We couldn't allow the enemy to take up position behind us. If they did take position behind us, somehow we had to isolate those behind us from their main force. The only way to do that was to counterattack, to position some of our men on the ridge, thus severing their attacking line into two parts. Half counterattacked, the other half of us covered them. The amazing thing was the damn thing worked, the Germans were caught by surprise. We got them in a cross fire, we eliminated the enemy behind us."

"Who fired first? Why didn't you wait for reinforcements?"

"We did wait as long as possible, and it's a good thing we didn't wait any longer or you would be here now trying to figure out what happened, and I would be out there dead. There was no first shot, per se. We were under attack. I guess Moore fired the first shot. I don't remember for sure."

"Why did he fire?"

By now the corporal was becoming impatient with the meaningless questions. "When I think about it, Moore didn't fire the first shot, Wagner did. What difference does it make, anyway? Who gives a damn about first shot?" The corporal waited for a response, but the captain gave no answer. "Wagner fired because he saw enemy troops approaching our position. Moore fired because a German officer stood and ordered the others to attack. Private Moore's shot brought him down. His body is still out there. Look! Come over here and you can see him."

"See who?" the captain asked without moving to look.

"The German officer."

The captain looked although he did not understand what he was seeing. He hesitated, started to speak, and then he saw a sight which added new meaning to the corporal's report—several dead American soldiers were laid out in the trench. The captain had not been informed about casualties, nor had he asked. The story was coming together, the events were beginning to make sense. He glanced at the medical personnel applying aid to the wounded American. "How many did we lose?"

"Five dead, one wounded, and I doubt if he makes it."

There was a lull in the conversation as the captain was stunned. He saw only four dead. "Do we have all the bodies?"

"No, sir. Private Moore is still out there."

"Jesus Christ, corporal. Why? Why would you leave him out there, are you sure he's dead? Did you see him get it?"

"Now wait a minute, captain. You don't understand. No, I did not see him fall, however, three of us saw his downed body." The captain's questions had put the corporal on the defensive. "Listen to what I'm saying." The corporal meticulously repeated his report of the German attack on the outpost and the American counterattack. Finally, the captain understood why Private Moore was still on the field of battle.

"Very well, corporal, don't you worry about it. We'll retrieve his body after dark. All of you should stand tall for a job well done. I will write the account accordingly. Is there anything else I should know?"

"No, sir, although I did hear something else, but I don't think it relates to us. About twenty minutes ago we heard some small arms fire. Actually, it sounded like a pistol. At first we thought it might be another attack, but it wasn't. You know how sound carries in these hills. I'm never sure where it comes from. Far as I know the noise I heard could have been five miles from here."

The captain showed little interest in identifying the location or the origin of the small arms fire. "Forget about it. We've got other things to deal with. You get back to your position. You never know what those damnable Germans will do. They might be planning another attack right now." The captain walked away while talking with a lieutenant. "Get the death squad up here on the double. We've got to get rid of those bodies and fast. I don't want the men looking at them."

Hence, no additional attacks occurred near La Cude. That same night at 10:23

p.m. a squad of men was dispatched to retrieve the body of Private Moore. Concurrent to the American retrieval, the Germans were actively retrieving their dead. Although there were no hostile incidents, both sides knew the other was nearby, sometimes within hearing distance. Nighttime recovery of fallen soldiers in no-man's-land was always a tense time for those involved. The Americans were so eager to return to their trenches that they paid little attention to surrounding details, nor did they put forth any effort to reconstruct what had occurred at the site of Private Moore's death. Any evidence left by the Germans concerning Elzie's final struggle went unnoticed. The objective was to retrieve the body for proper burial, and that is exactly what they did. The captain had made arrangements for the death squad, the Ambulance Corps, to receive the body upon arrival in the trench. Private Moore was identified by name and serial number from the identification tags worn around his neck. A visual identification confirmed the tag information, although in this situation, visual identification was difficult at best. The identifier was Private Henderson, Company L., 61st Regiment. Identification was done in the dark of night, and subsequently performed again by the light of morning. Interestingly enough and perhaps indicative of the tense situation both identification tags were left with Elzie's body. Normally one tag was left with the body and the other tag was kept by the company officer for purposes of paper work. At this point in time American officers were inexperienced in dealing with dead soldiers. Proper procedure was something they would learn in the future.

Members of the death squad wrapped Elzie's uniformed body in a blanket and stored it for the night in the back of the ambulance. The others, the fallen buddies, had already been buried. In the a.m. of June 23, the ambulance drivers transported Elzie's body to the rear of the lines. Since no official American cemeteries currently existed in this area of the Vosges, the French government agreed to provide needed burial space for Americans in French military or local cemeteries.

By early afternoon the ambulance vehicle arrived at a French military cemetery near Ban de Laveline, France. The East Field Staff map, Colmar number 86, indicated the location of the cemetery as, on road south of hill number 905, Ban de Laveline. Burial was designated for grave number 4, Section number 399, Cemetery number 1868. Private Moore was the first American soldier to be buried in this French cemetery. During the afternoon of June 23, the grave was dug and a standard military wooden cross was placed in position. The United States Army required a corked bottle containing military information about the soldier be buried with the soldier. The information read:

Private Elzie Moore, 2388592.
Company L., 61st U.S. Infantry, 5th Division.

June 23, 1918.

Killed in Action June 22, 1918.
Killed by shell fire at La Cude-Violu.

Theodore O. Schmidt, Captain
Commanding Officer

Private Moore's body, dressed in the same uniform he was wearing at the time of death and wrapped in a wool blanket, was placed in a wooden coffin. The metal identification tags were placed on his chest. The bottle was placed on the right arm next to the chest. The lid to the coffin remained unnailed, awaiting confirmation of details by the chaplain. At 5:30 p.m. Chaplain John Mulligan, 61st Regiment, checked for accuracy, comparing the information in the bottle against his information from headquarters. The coffin was sealed, the body was lowered into the grave. The chaplain said a prayer before the caretaker filled the grave with dirt.

Before the grave was completely filled in, Corporal Higgins arrived at the burial site. "Private Moore, Company L.?"

The chaplain answered. "That is correct. May I be of assistance to you?"

"No, sir. I'm here to observe the burial, unofficially representing 3rd Squad, Company L. Just wanted to confirm that everything went all right."

"Private Moore must have been a good friend."

"He was a buddy, a comrade in arms. I am alive today because of Private Moore."

The men at the grave site did not understand the full meaning of the words spoken by Corporal Higgins. They did not ask, nor did he explain. Instead Corporal Higgins placed the greatest monument ever paid to a fallen soldier when he stuck Elzie's bayonetted rifle, helmet placed on top, at the head of his grave.

The massing of German troops at La Croix-Aux-Mines had been a diversionary tactic, and the American-French command had fallen for it. The actual objective of the German maneuver had been to engage a small unit of American troops at La Cude-Violu for the purpose of taking American prisoners. German Command needed to test American combat readiness, to determine how 5th Division doughboys would perform in tactical combat. On June 22 the Germans took no American prisoners, but they successfully determined 5th Division combat effectiveness.

American Command labeled the La Cude military engagement as an incident in the quiet sector. In the scope of possible future war events, this incident was deemed not worthy of special mention. Cause of death for all six Americans who died June 22, 1918, at La Cude, France, was officially listed as killed in action resulting from enemy artillery fire. Private Upton died from his wounds and was included in the body count.

The military records of enemy engagements on June 22, 1918, differed.

The American account:

> La Cude-Violu Sector.
> Six enlisted men killed in action, resulting from enemy artillery fire during a German attack on American-French lines.

The German account:

> German soldiers repelled strong American resistance at La Cude. Twenty-two enlisted men, one officer killed in action, thirteen wounded in ground fighting.
> For bravery in combat, fifty-five German soldiers nominated for Iron Cross, of the second class.

CHAPTER 20

CALL TO ARMS

I don't like this bridge one little bit," Helen emphatically stated as she reached for her husband's hand. "Come to think about it I don't like any bridge across water, especially when I'm the one on a train crossing that bridge. The mere thought of it scares me, let alone actually doing it."

Jesse desperately searched for words of comfort as the young couple crossed the Illinois River on the final leg of their journey. "Don't worry, Helen, it's safe. People who build railroad bridges know what they're doing. Besides, look, the river is frozen."

"Is that supposed to make me feel better? What do you think is underneath the ice? It's the water I don't like. How deep do you think the river is here, out in the middle?"

"Oh I don't know, not real deep, maybe fifteen or twenty feet."

"Now that is just wonderful. Not real deep my foot. I don't like water any deeper than bathtub level. As far as I'm concerned it might as well be six hundred feet deep. I wouldn't know the difference, because if I fell in I would have a heart attack before I drowned. I appreciate rivers from the shore not crossing them on a bridge built high above the water."

Normally Jesse would have found amusement in such a verbal exchange, but not this morning. He deemed it critical that Helen should have only positive experiences, good impressions when they arrived in Peoria as moving from the farm to the second largest city in Illinois was a major transition with many uncertainties for both of them. The sensitive husband offered diversion. "Helen, look ahead, that's downtown Peoria. What a sight to behold!"

"You look ahead, I can't. My eyes are closed tight. Tell me when we arrive on good, solid land."

Amused at her comments Jesse responded with a firm, reassuring hand grip. "Hang on, almost... almost, yes, we made it, we're over good, solid land! Open your eyes, look at the city! This is it, Helen, Peoria is where we are going to live. Yes, sir, Jesse and Helen Moore are going to live in Peoria, Illinois, as man and wife with baby in the hopper."

"Oh, Jess, you're so silly. Baby in the hopper is no way to say it. Oh my, look at the sign. Can you believe that 76,121 people actually live in this city? Gosh, that's a bunch of people. This place might not be such a bad place after all, providing we stay on good solid land away from the river." Her last statement was really Helen's way of announcing to Jesse that all was well, she was fine.

The conductor walked through the passenger car announcing, "Peoria, River Front Station. Fifteen minute stop. This is your stop, folks, baggage claim is located inside the terminal. You better bundle up, Missus, there's a mighty cold wind out there."

The air inside the terminal was warm. Helen waited near the heating stove, sitting in one seat while saving the adjacent seat by placing her purse on it as Jesse secured the two suitcases and one bundled package. Helen became sort of excited as she thought about all that was happening in her life. This was a first for her. She and husband were preparing to start anew in a strange city far away from family and friends. Helen liked how she felt as she waited for the love of her life to return on that cold February day in 1918. She was so much in love with her man, and her blind confidence in his ability to deal with life would allow her to follow him anywhere, even across the river to Peoria.

Jesse had gone outside. Upon return he wasted little time getting to Helen and near the fire. "It's one cold day, I can tell you that. I guess when you think about it, we're farther north now. I don't know if it's valid thinking, but I've always felt the air near the river was colder, full of dampness, usually windier."

Helen was more concerned about the practical matters at hand. "Where are the suitcases?"

"I made arrangements to pick them up later. I don't want to fool with luggage now."

"What happens now?"

"Well, we've got lots to do. First, I want to locate Holt's to make sure I have a job. I know they said I did, but I want to check it out to make sure; and if I do have work, I need to find out when I start. Tomorrow, I hope. Then we need to buy a local newspaper and look at the classified ads. We've got to find a place to live, a place that's already furnished. Once we get all that done, hopefully we'll still have time to find a grocery store and stock up. Those sandwiches you made aren't going to last forever. We also should get to a dime store, buy some sheets and a few

367

household supplies. We've got lots to do, and I suspect things and procedures in the city will be different. I've never lived in any large city before, so we'll need to learn as we go. Are you up to it? If so, let's go, let's get something done."

The transition could not have gone smoother. Indeed, the move to Peoria was bold, although seemingly a wise one as a job at Holt's was waiting where Jesse was slated to become an apprentice machinist. Holt's was under government contract to produce the first American-made armored tanks, and Jesse was sort of excited knowing that he would become a worker in such a production, even though at this point he did not yet know what a tank looked like. Production was already behind schedule, workers were needed. He was told to report for work the next day.

Helen and Jesse located a modest second-story, two-room furnished apartment in downtown Peoria. The first night in Peoria offered a grand beginning, however, the following day brought forth the reality of relocating when Helen was left alone to do errands and to function in the city on her own. Fortunately, neither suffered from the delusion that life in the big city was always going to be rosy. They were innocents with much to learn as they lived in a totally new environment. Most uncertain about the nature of outside influences of the big city, or how they might be influenced by such, both proceeded cautiously. It was their nature.

The city was an exciting place, offering more entertainment and more variety in social activities, but the need to pursue a frugal life style prevented them from availing themselves of most urban opportunities. They chose to spend less, save more by engaging in such activities as walks on the river walkway or in park areas, visiting the many sights of downtown Peoria, and sometimes attending a film theater. Their frugality was for a reason—they hoped to save enough money so that one day they might purchase a small farm of their own.

Peoria weather influenced outdoor activities more than they dreamed. The long, hard winter of 1917-1918 held its cold grip well into March, and early spring saw frequent cold rains. By April, Helen, a woman of small frame, was in her seventh month of pregnancy, and outside activities progressively became more difficult for her, forcing the young couple to slow down their recreational pace, spend more time in their small abode. As a result frugality became easier, but Helen's spirits were dampened. Jesse worked long hours forcing Helen to endure the blunt of necessary household errands which severely fatigued the expectant mother. When her husband was home she was too tired for much recreational activity. In a short time the city lost its lure.

Friday, May 10, the postman delivered an official government letter postmarked May 8, 1918, Jacksonville, Illinois. The correspondence was a summons ordering Jesse to report for military induction. His physical exam was scheduled for June

16, his induction June 28. Jesse was not totally surprised by the summons, but his wife became most distressed over the unexpected message. Following her tears a self-imposed calmness descended on Helen before she quizzed her husband about the conscription process. Calmly she inquired in her natural soft-spoken voice. "I was told that certain men were exempted from the draft. I thought single men were drafted first, men with children would not be drafted at all. Furthermore, I thought men who worked in defense-related industries, such as Holt's, were automatically granted deferments. You need to help me understand what is happening. You are married, you will be a father in five or six weeks, you work at a defense plant—why are they drafting you? Do you know something I don't know and, if you do, will you explain it to me?" Clearly uncomfortable with the question Jesse squirmed in his seat, placing his hands together with his fingers touching the opposite fingers as he delayed answering her direct, encompassing question. A few minutes of dead silence elapsed. "Well, I'm waiting. Can you explain to me why you got that letter, why are you being drafted?" Helen impatiently snapped as her anger began to show.

Jesse cleared his throat, sat very straight in his chair before he attempted to address his spouse's concerns, which made Helen all the more aware that her husband was uncharacteristically uneasy with her question. "I don't know if I can fully explain it or not. As you know when I registered for the draft I was not yet married. On the line about marital status I wrote single."

Helen's anger mounted. "After we were married you did go down and correct it, didn't you? We talked about it, I reminded you, and you said you would take care of it."

"I know I did. Needless to say I didn't notify them."

"And of course you did not notify them about our future child."

"I did not."

"What about work? Does the draft board know you work in a defense plant?"

"No. There is a place in the office to request deferment, but the worker must initiate it, it's not automatic. I picked up the form but decided not to fill it out."

"You decided, huh? Did it ever cross your mind that we should discuss that very important issue of deferment, or at least you should tell me what you were doing about it?"

"Of course I thought about it. To be honest I never thought I would get drafted. But, Helen, there is another issue here, it's very difficult for me to explain. I wasn't sure if you would understand."

"We'll never know will we? Now is your chance, you just explain away. You have my full attention, I assure you."

"I'll try if you'll calm down, no use talking to you when you're mad." Refusing to respond to that last remark, Helen sat still, looked into his eyes and waited for some explanation. Jesse lowered his head and searched for the right words before he finally spoke. "I hope you understand what I'm about to say. I never intended to withhold information from you, I simply never figured out what to say or how to say it. Men all over the world, common men like me, have answered their country's call to arms. When their country called, they answered. Now I know that not all men respond the same, some go to great lengths to get out of it. At this point in my life I would feel nothing but shame if I became associated with those who intentionally avoid service. I can't explain it any better than that. It's just not me to run away from service to my country. What kind of man would I be if I let others fight in my place? What would you think of me? All my life I have tried to meet my responsibilities head on. I hate it when others avoid their responsibilities. I won't do that, it's just not me.

"There is something deep inside a man that helps him distinguish right from wrong. I don't know about the rightness or the wrongness of any war, but I know it would be wrong for me to sit back and have some other man serve in my place. Who am I to tell Uncle Sam he should find someone else? I don't want to go but that's not the point. If I had wanted to go, I would have enlisted. The only question now is can I live with myself if I avoid the draft. Simply worded, I don't think I can live my life with the thought that some other man had to make the sacrifice because I decided that I didn't want to go. That is too much to ask of me. Since I have been called, I've got to go."

Jesse apprehensively waited for Helen's reaction, but none was forthcoming other than she sat in her chair with watery eyes, deep in thought. Helen required time to absorb her husband's expressions before, eventually, she released a few of her own thoughts. "In no uncertain terms I am hurt, I am disappointed. I hate what is happening. What have you done to us?"

Jesse had no answer, and Helen's words forced him to realize how selfish he had been by not considering the full equation. He had made a decision not fully factoring in the wishes of his wife, the well-being of his child, and possible repercussions on his marriage. He felt responsible for the crisis, helpless to resolve it.

Temporary resolution to the crisis came from Helen, not Jesse. She left her chair, walked over to her husband and took his hand. "You are my husband and I will abide by your wishes. I accept what you say, Jess, not because I agree with it, but because you are who you are, and I love who you are. I'm not clearheaded enough right now to think this all through, but I do anticipate considerable hardship for me and our child. I must accept it because of your chosen path, but I want you to know that I think the consequences of your inconsiderate decision sit squarely on your shoulders. Be that as it may we both now have much to consider with little time for thought. Tonight this is all I can say, the best answer I can come up with. I don't know about tomorrow. I can't help but to believe that we are

370

shaping our future by what we decide in the next couple of weeks. We need to plot a fitting course, be wise in our decisions."

Jesse retired to bed at his usual time, although sleep did not come easily. Helen's words wore heavily on his mind. Deep in thought Helen remained in her chair the entire night. She resolved to accept, to cooperate with her husband's wishes, if he would agree that in the future she would become an active participant in any and all such decisions. On this she was firm. Helen had always been blessed with incredible inner strength, and somehow this night she was able to draw on her reserve abilities. One overriding issue remained foremost on her mind—how would she cope with the consequences of Jesse leaving for the Army?

Helen prepared breakfast and made ready Jesse's usual sack lunch. His normal workday was long, lasting from 7:00 a.m. to 6:00 p.m. on weekdays, 7:00 a.m. to 12:00 noon on Saturday. Additional overtime was sometimes available and Jesse usually availed himself of the opportunity. Today the Saturday shift was extended until 9:00 in the evening for those who wanted to work. Every morning before Jesse left the house it was customary for him to advise Helen of his overtime intentions, and on this morning when he announced he would work late, Helen did not try to convince him otherwise. She looked forward to the time alone. Jesse returned home from work at 9:30 p.m., very tired from working the extended shift.

It was too late in the evening for a full supper, so Helen prepared a light, late night meal. On that night they retired together with the promise of a picnic in the park the following day. They fell asleep as husband and wife.

The Illinois River showed a gentle current, but those who knew the deceptive river were aware of its deep turbulence. The winter freeze had yielded to the spring thaw, the water level was high. The seasons were in change, cold winter had passed, spring had unleashed its beauty. The ground was dry, the air temperature was pleasant. It was a suitable day for a serious picnic.

The lunch was exquisite. Helen tidied the picnic area as Jesse found a comfortable spot for an after lunch visit. Wasting no time Helen spoke right to the point. "Have you given any thought to where I will live while you are in the service?"

"Of course I have."

"Where?"

"I've given thought to it, I haven't made a decision. You and baby will need to be near family where someone is around to render assistance."

"That's an understatement. I'll need more than assistance, I'll need direction since you won't be there."

"Oh, Helen, don't make it sound like I'm deserting you. I'm just going to the Army for a while. I will be back, you know."

Jesse's last comment bothered Helen because neither he or she knew for certain that he would return safely. She hesitated before answering, and ultimately when she did speak it was not in response to his comment. "I'll be direct. I need to live near the folks without question. I know this is going to be a tough time for me, and I want them nearby if I need to lean on them. I can't do it alone, I know that much. If you have no objection, I will write, request to live with them while you're gone. If they refuse, or if they're not crazy about the idea, I think both of us should find a suitable place for me to live in Jacksonville, not far from them, even if cost of housing requires us to use the money we've saved. Give me your thoughts."

Jesse looked relieved. "That's a wonderful idea. Your parents are such caring people. I had entertained similar thoughts, but I felt it was not my place to suggest it. It's perfect."

"Let's hope they think it's perfect too. I'll write tonight."

With some resolution at hand Jesse started to think about the future. His unstructured thoughts were revealed in his rambling words. "Let me see, today is May 12, tomorrow is Monday, the thirteenth. If I give notice at work, that's plenty of time. Hopefully, the landlord will give us back our deposit, he ought to. I wonder where I give my notice at work. Yes, sir, I think we can do it. Tie up things here by the first, and move either on the first or second. What day of the week is the first? Hum, the first is Friday I think, but that's all right because we can leave on Saturday, the second. That's still more than two weeks notice at work, and it leaves us time to square away everything in Jacksonville before I report. We need to really scrub the apartment. Hope we get the deposit back." He now looked at Helen as though she had not heard a word he had spoken. "Helen, that's a good plan. I think we have plenty of time to put our affairs in order, and enough time to get settled in Jacksonville. Let's go home, sit down and make out a list of all the things we need to do. Are you ready?"

Helen became tickled watching her husband think about transitional details. Helen was the one who thoughtfully had taken the bull by the horns, her husband was merely responding to her plan. Jesse's positive reaction offered more than support, it served to give Helen more confidence in her own judgment, something she undoubtedly would need much of in her near future. She addressed her husband with a sheepish grin. "Yes, sir, let's go home and make a list. Jess, you have the best ideas."

"Thank you."

"You're welcome," she muttered with satisfaction. "Next time we have a problem, I know what to do. Go on a picnic and give you time to think it out, time to solve the problem."

CHAPTER 21

A BIG HURRY

Tuesday, June 17, 1918, was a joyous day, a blessed day. Jesse Albert Moore, Jr., was born in Jacksonville, Illinois. Eleven days later Jesse Albert Moore, Sr., was scheduled to depart from his family for military service in the United States Army.

The breakfast dishes were done, the house was in order as representatives from three generations, son, mother, and grandmother gathered at the kitchen table. Mrs. Kelly was seated across the table from Helen who was holding Junior as his baby sounds entertained both adults. It was a sight to behold as both grandmother and mother effervesced with admiration and love for the newest addition to the family. Jesse was in the backyard tending the family garden. Mr. Kelly had long since left for work at the cemetery.

Helen, sensing that her mother wanted to hold the baby, proudly passed her infant son to her mother. It was pure delight for Helen to observe her child in the arms of his adoring grandmother, and the baby cooed as though he approved of his mother's act of sharing. Helen walked to the opened kitchen window so that she might observe her husband hoeing the garden. She watched as Jesse skillfully manipulated the hoe, but most of all she was looking at the man, admiring his firm stout body as he worked.

With a sadness in her voice Helen softly spoke so that Jesse could not hear. "I wish Dad could have waited to say good-bye to Jess. He left the house so early this morning."

The grandmother, made wiser by time, assuredly offered an acceptable explanation to her daughter. "I know, dear, but it's just as well that he did. You do know that your father is not big on good-byes. Parting from people he cares about has always been difficult for him. I suspect he said his good-byes last night, only none of us knew when he did it."

Helen was in awe of her mother's perceptiveness. "I hope that one day I can become just half the mother and half the wife that you are. I worry about it—that I won't measure up."

A modest Mrs. Kelly appreciated the sentiment from her youngest daughter. "Put your mind at ease, Helen. You have such good instincts, you have all the necessary qualities. All you lack at this time is experience, and that is coming to you in waves. Believe me, Helen, you have no reason to doubt."

"I hope you're right. At this moment I can think of no greater calling. I was born to be wife and mother."

Jesse entered by the back door. "Hello, folks. I think things around here are in order. Can you think of other outside work that needs to be done before I leave?"

"No, we can't," Helen quickly responded. "Jess, you sit down right here. Mother has a proposition. Tell him, Mother!"

Mrs. Kelly smiled. "I don't know if proposition is the right word or not. Instead, I will call it an offer, and before you accept my offer, Jesse, I want you to know that Helen approves." Mrs. Kelly now gave a bigger smile. "Not that I expect that to influence your decision."

"Oh, Mother, just tell him."

"Be patient, I will tell him as soon as I find the right words. I know you two have some work around the house you want to finish, but I'm not certain that you need to be concerned about it. The unfinished work will wait for another time. It's more pressing that you and Helen spend time alone, and that time should be without interfering, old fogies around. Helen and I have worked out a short list of need-to-do things and if you start reasonably soon, you can be done, out of here within the hour. That early departure will give you young folks a little time to be alone before the ceremonies begin. No argument now, because I've already packed a picnic lunch for you. Helen can feed Junior before she leaves, and I have plenty of fresh milk for a bottle. I know you both want the baby to nurse, but I'm quite confident that this little amount of bottle feeding won't hurt a thing. Junior and I will have a grand time while you and Helen take some needed time for yourselves. No reason for all of us to go downtown. Helen can observe the ceremonies and see you off at the train station."

Initially, Jesse was elated, but quickly his thoughts changed to concern. "What about you, Helen? Do you feel up to it? That's a long walk downtown, a long time to be on your feet. It's only been eleven days. How would you get back? You might not make it back by dark. I don't know if you're up to it. Are you?"

Helen shook her head, looked at her mother. "I told you what he would say, didn't I?" Diverting her full attention to Jesse, she continued. "Mother and I have talked about all your concerns. I will be all right. There are plenty of places to stop and rest if need be. Dad has agreed to meet me at the train station afterwards where, together, we will take the streetcar home. If those puny concerns are your only ones, I suggest you get ready. Time is wasting."

Jesse offered no more resistance, because this plan was considerably more preferable to him than was the original plan. He was ready to leave in less than one hour. Jesse's last few minutes at the Kelly house were spent holding Jesse, Jr. Holding the infant created such obvious satisfaction for the adoring father, and the sight of such only stirred admiration from those who watched. "Good-bye, little boy, I'm off to fight the Huns and, hopefully, I will be back in time to hear your first words and to observe your first steps."

Walking hand in hand carrying picnic basket and satchel, the proud couple started their brief journey to downtown Jacksonville. "I don't know about you, Helen, but I'm still in awe of the entire process."

"What process?"

"I used the wrong word, and I'm uncertain of the proper words. I'm talking about the miracle of birth. I look at that boy of ours in wonderment. I still am amazed that he came from you and me—a product of our love. I'm overwhelmed with the miracle of birth. I know no other way to say it."

Helen was pleased by her husband's words, and proud that he was willing to openly express such precious thoughts. "There might be another way to say it, but as far as I'm concerned you said it well." No additional words were needed because each understood the intensity of the other's feeling. Holding hands, being together was a sufficient expression of their love for one another.

"What a special gift your mother has given to us. Was it your idea or hers?"

"Her idea after I planted the seed."

"That's what I thought. Thank you very much to both of you." He squeezed Helen's hand expressing further confirmation of his delight. "I have a few thoughts that I need to express. Okay?"

"You first, then I will share my thoughts."

"I hope I can express my feelings. Well, here goes. This last month or so I have given considerable thought to my departure. As you know, I might have been able to get a deferment, had I tried, but that's water under the bridge. Now here's the important stuff so you listen carefully! I have already made the most important decision of my life, the decision to marry you. That decision was the wise one, the most important, the best decision in my life. First and foremost I am a husband and a father, and anything else pales in importance. I have agonized over this moment. I feel so foolish because when I leave today I will leave behind all that I have ever wanted. You are my world but..." Jesse delayed his speaking as though his mind was stuck, or as if he needed to turn a page on his thoughts. "I must go. I have already explained the reasons, and I won't go over them again. Simply put, as a man, I must go. The person I am compels me to help in this war. My question to you is, will you forgive me?"

Helen was philosophical. "Already done, no more explanation is necessary. In fact, although I hate to say it, I admire you for going. The qualities I have always admired in you are the same qualities that compel you to go. I still don't like it, but I do admire that."

Helen's comforting words, her expressions of respect helped relieve Jesse's feelings of guilt. "Separation will be difficult for both of us, and we both know that; but we both must learn to deal with it. I will be back! I repeat, I will be back. We must look at this separation as no more than a detour in our lives, not a destination. From the moment I leave until the moment I return, you and baby will be foremost on my mind. I will do nothing that will jeopardize my much anticipated life of joy with you and family. Do you understand, do you accept it?"

"I understand and I do believe you. The same goes for me. I regret that you are leaving, but I accept it. Above all, I am a wife and mother. I support you, my husband, one hundred percent. Junior and I will count the days until your return. Do you understand my feelings?"

"I understand, and thank you for saying what you did."

Helen unsuccessfully tried to contain her smile. "To be totally honest, Jess, I think we both understood all of what we have said, before we said it.

Jesse threw his head back and let loose a huge laugh. I should have known. You were already miles ahead of me in your thinking, but I'm glad I said it anyway. After all, I've been working on that speech for three nights. I committed it to memory, and while saying the words I forgot some of it. Do you want to hear it again, word for word, except the right way this time? I can say it, if you want."

"No, thanks, but since you're in the mood for mushy stuff, I might as well take advantage of the opportunity. I have prepared something for you. First, let's find a place to sit, a fitting spot."

"You don't need to give me anything more. You already have given me everything." Helen did not respond. "Are you tired, do we need to stop? We can stop anytime."

"No, no, I just want to stop at the proper place. I also want to give you my speech, the one I have committed to memory." Helen's words evoked another smile from both of them.

The young couple continued their slow paced stroll, hand in hand. They were only two blocks from the town square when they found a location and bench suitable for the occasion. Helen opened her purse and removed a neatly folded handkerchief. Carefully, she unfolded it and revealed two items—a wallet-sized photograph of herself and a lock of her hair, shaped in the form of a heart. "I hope you like them. Mother helped me get the photograph, but the lock of hair is all my doing. My hope is that you will carry these items with you while you're away."

The strong, manly Jesse gave way to the emotion of the moment and shed tears of joy and pride—joy because of the love he sensed, pride because he was married to such a caring and remarkable woman. A sensitive Helen allowed her husband time to emotionally compose himself before she continued. "I have something else. The other day I read a poem. At the time I read it I believed it must have been written for us. Bear with me as I read it aloud.

Life's Riches

Others have more wealth than I,
That never worries me,
I find so much contentment
With the flowers and the trees.

Some folks have great cars to drive
And famous is their name,
Though I find more enchantment
Down a shady country lane.

Others have great riches,
And coins of a golden hue,
But I think I am the millionaire,
Cause I am loved by you."

Her inflection was perfect as she read the words aloud. The poem precisely said it all, expressed what she wanted her husband to hear. Although both were normally reserved, private individuals, and although many other people were in the immediate vicinity, they threw caution to the wind. Helen and Jesse embraced in a public place.

Many more people than usual were about town on this day. A crowd already was gathering near the square where a local band was playing patriotic songs. Thirty large American flags were flying at full mast around the square, and patriotic paper banners were displayed in storefront windows. Large canvas banners, positioned at the four main entrances to the square, expressed the sentiment of the town. "Going Away And Safe Return. In Honor of Morgan County Boys."

By any measure this was to be a grand send-off. The Opera House was packed with spectators and the area outside the building was crowded to overflowing. The registrants, the men who had been selected for military service, occupied the parquet seats, while the dignitaries were invited to sit on the stage. The program ran on schedule.

Following roll call the drafted men exited the Opera House and reported to the west side of the square for a photographer to take a group picture. Afterward the men were placed in marching formation on the east side of the square. East State Street, roped off from the square to the train station, was lined with men in uniform from Company C., Illinois State Guard. The 270 inducted men began their march of the half-mile parade route to the train station.

Leading the parade was the official standard bearer. Following were members of the Women's Relief Corps, followed by a Boy Scout troop, followed by two marching bands, followed by the 270 men. Indubitably, the parade was a grand procession of pomp.

A roped space at the depot was provided for the inducted registrants, and an adjacent area was the designated area where individual recruits were granted a brief time for good-byes. Jesse's name was called and he gave his final farewell to Helen.

Jesse found a window seat. He admiringly watched his wife as she fought the crowd to find a better position to wave to her husband, to visually bid him adieu. Once she found her position, she and Jesse maintained eye contact, continuously waving or signaling to one another. It may have appeared strange to some, but to Helen this final process was important. She cared little what others thought.

At precisely 7:00 p.m., June 28, 1918, the train pulled away from the station. Apart from Helen for the first time since marriage, Jesse began his tenure as a soldier boy.

As promised Mr. Kelly arrived at the train station to escort a very tired Helen back to the house. Helen spoke with a disconcerting tone to her voice. "Dad."

"Yes, Helen, what can I do for you?"

"Nothing really. Already you have done more for me than anyone could expect. I'm ready to get home and visit with Mother. Dad, do you know the saddest sound I have ever heard? Of course you don't know, but I'm going to tell you. It's the sound of a train whistle."

Mother was waiting on the front porch for Helen to return. Quietly the two sat a few minutes until, gradually, they got around to exchanging thoughts. "Strangely enough, Mother, today I was happy for Jess. He really enjoyed the send-off. It surprised me. I really think he valued all the attention more than I thought he would, and I say to that, good for him because he deserves it. I was thinking that he is already twenty-two years old, and in all his life he has had little praise. Well today he got some praise and there is no doubt that he and all the men deserve it. I was just surprised at how much he seemed to enjoy it.

"I noticed another thing too. He sure knows a lot of people. All day different people kept coming over to say good-bye to him, and that's not all. I could tell by their tone that they admired him. I knew he was highly thought of, I just didn't know how much. These two thoughts might sound contradictory, but they aren't. They are very different. Isn't it interesting that you never really know all there is to know about someone?"

Mrs. Kelly smiled. "It is interesting, and I would guess we will always feel that to be true, even after a lifetime together."

Mother and daughter spent several hours on the porch visiting with each other on that warm Friday night in June. Many thoughts were pondered and shared. Mother sat in the rocking chair, Helen the porch swing. The conversation was predominantly much needed girl talk.

Three stops to pick up additional recruits plus the darkness of night made for a long train ride. Arriving at 2:30 p.m., Saturday, June 29, the troop train delivered more than one thousand draftees from Illinois to Camp Zachary Taylor, Kentucky, for the purpose of basic training. The Army camp was well prepared for the onslaught of new recruits, and in less than one hour the new arrivals had been officially greeted and were in line to be fed. Before the day was over the men were assigned quarters, issued military clothing and bedding, and were fed another meal. The camp was so organized, the staff so efficient, that the men from this train, plus men from another arriving troop train, were in their barracks with lights out by 10:00 p.m. The following day mustering-in activities resumed at 5:30 a.m.

The century old Camp Taylor could rightfully boast of its long tradition as a superior Army training camp. Strategically located southwest of Louisville and situated on the banks of the Ohio River, this camp now was primarily a reception center, a basic training facility for National Army conscripts. The monuments, the ornamental public display of older U.S. artillery attested to its history, as the recently constructed, well equipped modern training facilities spoke to its contemporary purpose. The recent arrivals had every reason to believe they would receive only the best available military training.

Sunday, the first full day of training, set the torrid pace of training which was expected to become the norm. Although the men were given an opportunity to attend early chapel, that was the only option they were offered. The remainder of the day was filled with structured events, hurry-up and wait-in-line activities. The recruits underwent physical exams, shots, immunizations, and detailed instructions on personal hygiene. They were lectured on the fundamentals of military protocol, learned proper military marching formations, and were exposed to military procedures, discipline, and expectations. They were taught to identify and respect rank, and to precisely follow orders, while drill instructors harshly evaluated their performances.

Monday was test day. Intelligence tests, aptitude tests, interest surveys, and personal, one-on-one interviews consumed the entire day apart from meals, personal hygiene activities, and housekeeping tasks. The written tests were revealing. No less than twenty-four percent of the draftees tested were deemed illiterate. The men were not informed of their individual results, no recruit was rejected or exalted.

Tuesday and Wednesday the draftees underwent physical testing. Without prior training or preparation all draftees were pretested and evaluated on their agility, endurance, and overall physical fitness. Results of the two-day test indicated that twenty-nine percent of the draftees were physically unfit and would require considerable training. The remainder were classified as probable candidates to meet minimum physical requirements in standard training time. It was pointed out that no recruit would complete his basic training until minimum standards of physical fitness were met.

The M1917 Enfield .30 caliber rifle was currently the standard issue weapon for all men in training, and trainees were required to qualify on the camp firing range with the rifle. There were no exceptions. Once a soldier qualified with the rifle, daily practice was no longer required during basic training. Jesse qualified at his first shooting, as did many others.

Thursday, the recruits were presented with all other basic training expectations and evaluation procedures used to meet these expectations. Primarily, basic training was to physically prepare the men for service in the Army, but it also served another important function—it gave a reliable basis for making determinations, recommendations of future military placement. In short, the Army identified its needs and matched the talents of its recruits with appropriate placement in the military. Every trainee, regardless of natural ability, possessed some talent which could be utilized. Once the man had arrived at training camp, and if he maintained his health, he had a valued place in the Army. The unknown variable was the length of training time required for each individual. Basic training might take longer for some, less for others.

After one week of training the recruits were regrouped. Men from five different states were intermingled and assigned new quarters. No explanations for the change were offered, but everyone assumed this reshuffle to be selective grouping for basic training acceleration. Since the Army urgently needed more soldiers in France, reduced training time became acceptable to Command for a variety of reasons. The new standard of military thinking placed more importance on appropriate placement after basic. Thus it was determined, regardless of training time, once a soldier could meet the minimum physical standards of basic training, he was ready for advanced training.

Jesse had few frustrations with his basic training, had little trouble meeting the minimum standards. He found the rigors of training not too demanding, the goals attainable with reasonable effort. He believed the instructors were fair and well suited for their task, just as he felt the amenities in the camp were more than adequate for the likes of him. In every letter to Helen he mentioned how good the food tasted, and often made reference to the physical comforts at his disposal. Jesse, unaccustomed to personal luxuries and a man of simple taste, found Camp Zachary Taylor to be a fine, modern camp. He had no quarrel with the way the Army treated him.

Wednesday, July 17, Jesse was notified that he had met the standards of basic training. Friday was designated graduation day when he was to march in review with three hundred other graduating soldiers. His brief tenure at Camp Taylor ended in less than twenty days, and was regarded as early completion even for the revised standards. Effective Saturday, July 20, his new orders were for him to report at Fort Benjamin Harrison, Indiana, for combat engineer training.

Jesse's pleasure in his completion of basic training was severely tempered when on the same day he received his new orders, he also received official notice of his brother's death. In addition, he was personally presented with a note from home, a confirmation letter from Helen. Enclosed in the letter was a clipping from a Pittsfield newspaper, *The Pike County Democrat*. The newspaper article was on the front page of the small town newspaper.

FIRST!!!
MILTON BOY IS KILLED IN ACTION.
ELZA HUBERT MOORE FELL IN BATTLE ON JUNE 22;
WORD CAME TO FATHER YESTERDAY.
Pike County's first soldier boy has fallen in battle. To Milton is the honor of placing the first gold star upon the service flag.

Jesse's emotional reaction was guarded. Carefully he folded Helen's letter and placed it in his pocket. He requested and was granted permission from his sergeant to seek solitude in the post chapel, where Jesse spent most of the night grieving alone and in his own way. Jesse reported back to duty at sunrise the following morning. Deliberately, he locked his feelings within himself, shared them with no one.

Camp Benjamin Harrison, situated northeast of downtown Indianapolis, was a fine, modern training camp, a fact not lost on Jesse. Positioned in a modern urban setting, the training camp sported clean, spacious grounds and emitted a businesslike atmosphere, somewhat reminiscent of a corporate headquarters. Troops were so efficiently received that two hundred incoming troops were quartered and fed in less than three hours. Written individual orders were issued on an alphabetical listing posted outside the mess hall. As ordered Jesse reported at 8:00 p.m. to a large lecture hall for orientation.

The mood in the lecture hall was unusually subdued as the attending soldiers were all strangers to one another and most harbored real concern about expectations for combat engineers. The common thread of the group was that each man was a draftee who recently had completed basic training and had been selected for this training; but that fact alone did little to ease their tensions. They waited patiently, apprehensively for the process to get underway. Most men quietly stared ahead at two chairs and one podium positioned on the large stage. Indeed, the unfamiliar circumstances provoked intrigue.

At 8:15 two officers walked to the stage. Major Wilcutts formally introduced himself as a civil engineer and referred to Captain Coultas as his colleague and their company commander. The major, a distinguished looking man approximately fifty years of age, was slender in build with graying hair, and spoke with a quiet dignity. "Good evening, men. My purpose tonight is to advise you of what lies ahead." He paused momentarily as though he was looking for the exact words. "I suspect your concerns paralleled mine when I first received this assignment. What is a combat engineer? What is the training? Tonight we will attempt to answer those and other questions. I suppose by now you have determined that I am not Regular Army. I am an engineer by vocation, now an Army training officer placed here because of need. Captain Coultas is the military person. Captain, will you explain?"

The captain stood and approached the podium. "You men are Company L., 22nd Engineers. In this Army we have two types of engineers—construction engineers and combat engineers. The 22nd Regiment is designated as a combat engineering unit, and the designation of combat engineer says it all. A combat engineer is a field engineer, trained and armed to fight with infantry as infantry. When not engaged in combat you will undertake engineering tasks of construction or destruction, always mindful that you are combat soldiers prepared to fight the enemy. You must become physically tough, infantry ready and also proficient in your engineering tasks. Whether or not our Army succeeds depends a lot on how much better you are at your job than the enemy engineer is at his. My orders are to oversee your training.

"In our 3,000,000 men Army we have fewer than 300,000 engineers, of which less that half are combat engineers. One field regiment of combat engineers is assigned to every division. At this point in time the Army has 40 divisions. In addition, one field regiment of combat engineers is attached to every corps. At present our Army has five corps. As of today my orders are to prepare you men, Company L., for corps attachment. If, in fact, we are given corps duty, our assignment may be a tougher, more demanding one. Corps engineers are territorial rather than tactical. Corps engineers operate in smaller units, usually by company, although sometimes in units as small as squads. We do what is needed when it is needed. We have no home base, we have no regimental headquarters, we are engineer soldiers at large. To simplify that concept, you may not know where you are or why you are there until you need to know. Don't expect explanations, because you won't get them. When command calls for engineers, they expect you to know your job. Corps engineers must be jacks-of-all-trades, plus fighting soldiers. Our training orders are clear—learn the basic elements of engineering while you learn how to be combat soldiers. The Army will place us where and when we are most needed. If the Army needs us to engineer, we will engineer. If they need us in the trenches, we will fight alongside infantry. If they need us to do both, we will.

"The 22nd Engineers is designated a specialist unit in light railway. Three companies of the 22nd, of which Company L. is one, are newly established companies and will train until we get orders to ship out, which very well could be before winter. Company L. is a minimum strength company, comprised of four commissioned officers and 120 enlisted men. The Army manual recommends that combat engineers should be trained for 19 weeks. Regretfully, you men will not receive the full 19 weeks. Learn well, men of Company L., for we have much to learn, little time to do it. Your life, as well as the lives of others, may hinge on how well and how fast you learn your job." The captain abruptly stopped talking and resumed his seat. He had defined his task, given a timeline, and shared his heavy burden of needing to quickly transform recruits to combat engineers. The captain's words were powerful, he had expressed ideas worthy of additional thought. The men in the room remained very quiet.

The major took charge. "Very eloquent, captain. You said what needed to be said, you wasted no words, and you sugar coated nothing. I hope all of you men took heed to his words of warning. With that said I will proceed with your intended schedule: First week—engineer's tools and elementary rigging with rope and wire. You will learn to use 47 different hand tools, understand their importance and care. Second week—field fortifications and barbed wire. Third and fourth week—camouflage, explosives, and demolition. Thereafter, and strictly from a demolition engineering view, we learn the basic mechanics of destroying fortified positions, roads, bridges, boats and rafts, railroads, and learn reconnaissance. If time permits we will explore elementary field construction. Gentleman, we all have much to do.

"Tonight you will be issued the standard combat engineer kit—a pocket knife, wire cutters, and an engineers soldier's handbook, a basic field manual. You are never to be without these three items and they are never to get wet. I repeat, never. You will eat with the kit, sleep with the kit, the kit will never leave your side. Keep the tools sharp and study that handbook until you know it by memory, and then study it some more."

Training progressed according to schedule. The men of Company L. endured six hours a day of standard infantry training and eight hours a day of engineering training. Infantry tactics were not emphasized, firing range qualifications were less stringent; however, combat engineers were required to qualify with two additional weapons: carbines and side arms.

Thus was the Army way of putting together eleventh hour training for badly needed combat engineers. Training was not deemed improper or inadequate, it simply was all that could be done in the allotted time. Techniques of practical battlefield application took priority over theoretical knowledge. The combat engineers would need to improvise, to think on their feet. Practical problem solving was the goal at hand and in this regard the engineer instructors were good teachers, the trainees were good learners.

The accelerated training schedule was demanding, providing little free time and no personal leave. Every infantry division requested more combat engineers, putting the trainees at Fort Benjamin Harrison in great demand. Almost 90% of the men drafted were placed in infantry regiments and few military experts disagreed with this allotment. However, if the war continued into 1919, more combat engineers would certainly be trained and made available for front-line duty. Until that time the Army had little choice other than to maximize the use of the men they had, regardless of training.

Before soldiers were sent abroad they were entitled to government insurance. Jesse, who had requested life insurance and an allotment for Helen, was patiently waiting for his interview. "Private Moore, Captain Coultas will see you now."

Jesse hesitantly entered the office, as a personal meeting with any officer was most unusual; and his company commander, Captain Coultas, was perceived as a direct, no nonsense type of person. "Private Moore, reporting as ordered, sir," he said saluting.

"Good evening, Private Moore. How are your wife and son? Do you hear from them often?"

Jesse seemed pleased that the captain had inquired. "My wife writes me everyday, if you can believe that. They both are very well, considering I'm here, and they're there."

"Do you have your completed forms with you?"

Jesse responded, "Yes, sir," as he passed the forms to the captain.

The captain briefly examined the papers. "All right, everything is in order. Here is how it works. You have requested 50% allotment for your wife. Private's pay is $30 per month, but since you are sending 50% home you are entitled to two dollars more. You get $16 a month and she gets $16. Pretty good deal, I think. Are you certain you can get by on $16 a month? That's not much."

"More than enough for me. The Army takes care of everything I need. I fully expect to have money left at the end of the month and I intend to send it to my wife. We've been saving our money for a while now. We hope that one day we can buy a small farm."

"Sounds good to me. Now for the insurance. You want $10,000 life plus disability. Is that correct?"

"Yes, sir."

"You do know that insurance premiums will be deducted from your pay? You will now get $14.50 a month."

"Yes, sir."

"Life insurance remains valid, unless you drop it, as long as you're in the Army. Once you're discharged, the insurance ends. Same is true of allotment. The disability insurance is different. If you are totally and permanently disabled as a result of your service in the Army, you will receive $30 a month for life. If you understand this, sign your name on both forms. The insurance is effective immediately. The allotment starts next month."

Jesse signed both forms. "Thank you, sir. Is that all?"

"One comment before you leave. Thought you might want to know that August 23-25 will be designated family visitation days here at the base. If your wife and child are nearby, they can visit with you, on base, for one hour each day. Official notice of such goes out tomorrow."

The passenger train from Jacksonville, Illinois, arrived at the Indianapolis military base at 8:00 a.m., August 23. Among the many passengers aboard the train were a young wife and an infant son. Helen and Jesse, Jr., had arrived for a visit with Jesse. Civilian lodging was available near the base, and a military bus provided transportation to the reception center. Helen had withdrawn savings in order to make the trip, but there was no doubt in her mind that it would be money well spent if, in fact, Helen and baby made connections to see Jesse. The Army gave no guarantees and offered a one hour visit for each of the three days as the best possible scenario. Helen judged the possibility to be worth the effort, and Jesse also understood that all might not work out. Both were hopeful.

The methodical ordeal of getting permission to visit the base was a frustrating process. First, Helen had to explain the purpose of her visit to a military police-man, a sentry protecting the base; then she was escorted to a restricted area where she and baby, along with other visitors, remained confined until a sergeant arrived to individually interview the wives. It was he who determined, or at least he in-formed her, if the meeting was even possible. Helen did not understand the crite-ria used, nor was it explained. At 3:30 p.m., after three hours of procedure, Helen was granted permission to visit with Jesse at 7:00 in the mess hall. She was given a one day visitor's pass signed by Colonel Thomas, but Helen had no doubt that the sergeant was making the decision.

Wives, the ones who obtained consent, were informed of the exact visitation process. First, the wives were presented with a written copy of the visitation rules of conduct. The visits would be supervised and no inappropriate display of affec-tion was permitted. They would be escorted together to the mess hall where the husbands would be waiting. To Helen, the restrictions were reasonable, and she willingly signed the form, agreeing to abide by the guidelines. Helen was going to see her husband.

Initially, Helen was elated, but her joy was soon tempered once she found out that she would need to repeat the entire process each day. Likewise, she was fur-ther disappointed once she determined that not all wives were granted visitation permission. A compassionate Helen could see no reason for the military to deny any wife visitation rights with her military husband. The more she thought about it the more she thought the policy unreasonable.

At 6:45 over 50 wives were escorted into the mess hall, or as Helen put it, "they were marched in." Although only two months had lapsed, it seemed like an eter-nity since Jesse and Helen had said good-bye on the train station platform in Jacksonville. The first few minutes of the allotted hour were consumed by one long embrace and many verbal expressions of love and happiness. Jesse lovingly, protectively held Junior in his left arm as he used the full expanse of his right arm to embrace Helen; as Helen, adoringly looked at, kissed, and spoke to her hus-band. Reunification was a precious experience for both.

Although neither was eager to break the embrace, Jesse did. The couple sat opposite one another at a table, Junior on Jesse's lap and Helen affectionately holding Jesse's free hand with both of her hands. Helen spoke first. "I don't want to dwell on it, Jess, but I must express my sorrow for the loss of Elzie. I think I know how much he meant to you, and I can only imagine the pain you must feel."

Soberly, Jesse nodded his head, his answer was direct. "I have come to terms with it, and if you don't mind, I would prefer not to discuss it, at least not today. I don't want to use our limited time in that way."

Helen was moved by Jesse's words and with a tearful acknowledgment she concurred. There was not a dry eye between the two of them, but the sadness was quickly lifted when Junior started to cry. Helen smiled as she spoke. "I don't know if he's crying because of what you said, or because he's hungry, or maybe he just wanted to get into the conversation. What do you think?"

"I think our son should be allowed to cry all he wants when he wants, and he doesn't need a reason. However, I suspect he's hungry."

Helen's visit with her husband actually lasted almost two hours instead of the allotted one hour, although it didn't seem like it. They parted company with high hopes of another visit the following day. Outside the base gates Helen encountered another woman, a disappointed wife, who had been unable to secure a visitation pass. Helen offered encouragement to the wife and tried to convince her that tomorrow still held promise. The conversation, a kind, sensitive exchange of thoughts between two wives, continued as they returned to the hotel; and even after the wives separated, Helen's sympathetic thoughts remained foremost on her mind. When no others were nearby, Helen spoke at Junior. "My heart goes out to that poor lady. No wife should be denied the right to see her husband. It just isn't right." Although these words were somewhat of a poetic statement about the personal sanctity of marriage, they also were an expression of contempt for nonsensical Army rules and restrictions.

Later that evening many wives congregated in the hotel lobby, visited with one another, shared stories. Helen mostly listened. Some tales were sad, some tragic, some humorous, a few were pretentious, and on occasion a story might become borderline vulgar. Whatever the individual stories revealed about the tellers of the stories, Helen found it less important than the common thread of suffering present in all the wives' tales. Although the stories were professions of love, all tales contained a theme of agony, of hardships created by military husband-wife separation.

All the wives had come to Fort Harrison with one purpose in mind—to grant a spousal farewell before their husbands were transported to the killing fields of France. Certainly the wives feared for the safety of their husbands, longed for a safe and speedy return, but these thoughts remained unspoken. Regardless of how repressed these thoughts might have been, the concerns, the undertones surfaced from time to time. The casualty list was mounting daily and the pace of the war was accelerating. The possibility of a husband's death loomed large.

Not all concerns were for the husbands. Many wives harbored doubts about themselves, fearing they might not adjust, might not be able to handle all the responsibilities at home without their husbands. A few wives faced living alone for the first time in their lives, few had been taught to run households. Most married women were simply unprepared to live alone. They were no more eager to face the trials of married life alone, than the husbands were eager to leave. Interestingly enough most wives shared their husbands' fears while few husbands even knew their wives' fears. Most men thought of their military service as an act of patriotism and sacrifice, and few men thought of family sacrifice beyond that. If they considered it at all, most men thought of their wives in supportive roles for them, rather than in the role of a wife left alone to survive the best she could. Many wives would be forced to make critical economic decisions on their own or to face loneliness as never before. Some were terrified of what their lives would be. Fearful they might needlessly alarm their spouses at a critical time, few shared these personal thoughts with their husbands.

The following day the wives endured repetition of the same military screening process. They waited for an interview with the sergeant, the only opportunity to plead their case for visitation rights; and not all wives would be granted permission to visit. Mothers with children by their side would be given priority, and Helen was now wiser to the process. She arrived early at the sergeant's office and again was granted permission to visit, slated to see Jesse at 7:00 p.m. As she left the office by way of the waiting room she observed many anxious wives waiting, pleading to see the sergeant. Helen looked down at her baby, the most precious person in the world, and she wondered, she pondered until she arrived at a bold decision. Helen took a seat next to a soldier's wife, the same wife she had visited with the previous day. The two quietly exchanged thoughts for several minutes, they became friends of a type. Both wives sported huge smiles when Helen handed Junior to her new friend to hold in her arms, and when the friend's name was called she entered the sergeant's office carrying Junior. Within minutes the friend returned to the waiting room with baby in arm and a visitor's pass in hand. Helen was filled with joy and pride. In one bold action she had helped a friend to see her husband and had bypassed a silly Army regulation. Before the morning was over, the process of lending Junior was successfully repeated four more times.

Saturday, August 24, at 7:00 p.m. Helen gained access to her husband. Although the time was limited to one hour, every moment was savored. Married one year and two months, the couple was still very much in love. One hour was not long, but it was an hour, and hopefully there was tomorrow's visit.

During the Saturday visitation Helen chose not to share with Jesse her story of lending Junior. She probably should have told him, he was destined to discover the story anyway, but she remained tightlipped. Later that same night a grateful husband told Jesse about Helen's defiant action. Jesse's only response was, "Yep, that's my wife all right." If possible, Jesse felt even more pride, not only because of his wife's deed, but because of the person she was. He loved the story and what it said about Helen.

Sunday was the final day at Camp Harrison for the wives to visit their husbands. The unofficial word was that the 22nd Engineers were about to leave for

France. No one in authority would confirm the rumor, although almost everyone believed it to be true. Helen was first in line at the sergeant's office. When the sergeant opened the door he immediately saw Helen and frowned. "Come in, Mrs. Moore." He wrote out the pass without asking his usual questions.

"Thank you, sergeant. You're a nice man, today."

"Well I'm glad you think so. Perhaps that will entitle me to ask you a personal question."

"Certainly, what is the question?"

"Exactly who does that baby belong to?"

Rather indignant, somewhat apprehensive, Helen retorted, "He belongs to me of course. His name is Jesse Albert Moore, Jr., and he was born June 17, 1918, in Jacksonville, Illinois."

The usually sober, grumpy sergeant responded with a grand smile. "Just asking, no need for concern. As a point of reference and for your information, all wives, with or without a baby, will receive a pass to see their husbands today. I thought you might want to know that early in the day."

"Thank you, sir, I do appreciate knowing that." As Helen left the room she turned and waved to the still smiling sergeant.

The sergeant was correct. Over 100 very happy wives met with their soldier husbands for one hour in the mess hall at 2:00 in the afternoon. Although the room was crowded and the noise level was high, no one seemed to mind. Husbands and wives were together, and everything else seemed secondary.

In the first five minutes of visiting three soldier husbands came over to thank Helen for her kindness. Helen was very pleased with herself, Jesse was just plain proud.

After the usual greetings and questions, Helen changed her tone. "Jess, I have three questions I want to ask before I leave today. They might seem like silly questions so I want to get them out of the way. First, why did the sergeant not let all the wives see their husbands all three days? Some of them made great sacrifices just to get here. You know it's not easy for a woman to travel alone, one must put up with a lot of inconvenience, nonsense. I had no unusual problems because I had a baby with me, but you should hear some of the stories of what some women had to endure. It's not easy for a woman to function alone in our society, especially if she's married and alone. Does the Army not know all of that?"

Having feared a disturbing question, Jesse was almost relieved by what he heard. "To be honest I don't know. I'm somewhat certain the Army has a reason, but I don't think you or I will ever know it. It's just the Army way, and I suspect they never thought much about women traveling alone. I wouldn't have."

Helen didn't like his answer. "Well, for what it's worth, I don't care much for the Army way and I'm disappointed in you. It's not easy being a woman alone." Jesse gave no response. Helen paused and then continued. "Second question: What can I send you while you're away? Is there something you need like socks, or sweater, or something to eat? I'll send anything you want."

"Bless your heart for such nice thoughts. The simple answer is I need nor want nothing, the Army takes care of all my basic needs. Food is good and there is plenty of it. Clothing is taken care of. As a matter of fact, the quality of my Army clothing is probably better than I wore at home. So, I need nothing. Maybe some homemade cookies, if you want."

"Okay then, but if you do need something I assume you will let me know. Third question: I wonder if I should be doing something more for the war effort, other than what I'm already doing. Let me explain. Everybody is doing something. For example, Dad has the victory garden. We go wheatless and meatless, three days a week. We intend to conserve on coal this winter. We try not to waste any food, and we already have given all extra metal scraps to the government. They have a big bin on the square where they collect donations of any material that might be used for the war. We've stopped using sugar. While canning this summer we only used fruit sweeteners or molasses, or we didn't use any sweetening at all. But I think everybody is doing that. At least I hope so.

"Here are my other options. Do you think I should be doing volunteer work? The newspaper is full of organizations wanting you to donate your time, such as Y.W.C.A., or Red Cross, or women's auxiliary groups. Some groups do sewing for the Army, some make bandages for overseas. There are all kinds of services one can volunteer for if they want. What do you think?"

"Of course, you can do any of those things you want. My preference is that you do none of them. I would prefer that you spend any extra time with Junior, or time writing me letters, or helping your parents. Let me be plain spoken. I think we are doing enough, more than our share. I'm sure there are many people at home who will never feel this war except to read about it. Let some of those people volunteer. Our family already has paid a high price. Anyway, that's my feeling. If you still feel a need to do something, it's all right with me. You might ask your parents what they think. I'll bet they'll agree with me.

"With that said I do have one other thing you might consider doing for me. How about keeping a scrapbook, or diary, or something like that? It doesn't need to be anything formal or special, just something to note daily, local events. Then after the war, we can sit down and you can go over with me everything I missed at home. Come to think about it, I really like that idea. Let's both do it. I don't know if I can keep up with it or not, but I'll try to keep at least a mental record of where I have been and what I have done. Together, we can go over things when I get home."

Helen was pleased with the thought. "Great idea."

Private Jesse A. Moore
Company L., 22nd Combat Engineers

"But please don't stop the letters. They mean so much to me."

Helen was pleased with her husband's comment. "I won't. I will write something to you everyday, post card, letter, or something. I think about you all the time. I have already set aside one hour every night to write you. I'll try to keep it up."

The pressing issues resolved, soldier and young wife sat at the table holding hands, gleefully sharing thoughts, attempting to hide their feelings of sadness. They embraced and said their farewells. Born from fear of creating unnecessary distress for her husband, Helen had promised herself that she would not openly weep when she left Jesse's side. She could not retain her composure, nor could he. They both cried. Helen's final words were plain and direct. "We love you, always remember that." She pointed her finger at her husband and emotionally stated, "You come home, you come back." In a stronger voice she repeated, "You come back home to us, Jesse Moore." After one final embrace, Helen profusely wept as she and child exited the room.

Jesse hurried back to his barracks for a second-story vantage point to watch Helen exit the post gate. Helen did not know he was watching. Even at this far distance he could not help but notice her beauty and her dignity of personal style. He felt so fortunate that he was married to a wonderful, sensitive person, who by any measure was wise beyond her years. In admiration he watched until wife and baby were gone from sight, and then he watched longer just to make certain. He sat on the side of his cot, placed his finger tips together and tried to sort out his feelings and to organize his thoughts.

Jesse reflected about the many times in his life that he willingly, or unwillingly, chose or was forced to leave on his own. He thought about the many times he was left behind. His thoughts made him sad. "I will come home, Helen. I will come home."

At 5:00 p.m., well after the departure of all visitors, the camp gates were locked, prohibiting all entry or exit. Extra sentries were posted. No doubt something significant was about to transpire. At 6:00 p.m. new orders were posted. Shortly before daylight the following morning all 22nd Combat Engineers were to board a train for Hoboken, New Jersey. They were shipping out. Jesse had trained for a mere total of 55 days.

The sky was a beautiful blue on Saturday morning, September 1, 1918, when the 22nd Engineers boarded a transport ship at the military port of Hoboken, New Jersey. Downstream and across the river stood the skyline of Manhattan, New York, and every soldier was on deck to view the magnificent sight, to gain a final glimpse of his beloved country before he left its home shores. Under tug and tow the massive transport ship slowly inched south on the Hudson River to open waters. The grand view disappointed no one as the ship proceeded past the southern tip of Manhattan, past Ellis Island, and on to that which every soldier wanted to view—the Statue of Liberty on Liberty Island. Indeed it was a moving sight, but in a short time the final glimpse of American shores faded into memory as the transport ship hastened to assume its proper place within the waiting convoy.

Thousands of American soldiers were now on the final leg of their journey to join the swelling ranks of other American Expeditionary Forces already in place preparing to wage war on the battlefields of France. These men represented the best America had, and they understood their destiny. American forces, under American Command, were about to mount their first major offensive of the war, and these men in transport were slated to participate, to become part of the final thrust to shatter the German Army. It seemed there were no more inspiring words suitable for this occasion as already these men had heard it all. These soldiers did not lack confidence, did not need more encouragement, because they were already primed to do their part in bringing this terrible war to a rightful conclusion. Like the Army, like most Americans they, too, were in a big hurry.

CHAPTER 22

INTO THE BREACH

That is one big ocean! Whoever first said across the pond either had no imagination or a mighty big one."

Jesse could not help but smile. "Or he could be like you, Zach, with a tendency toward dry humor, if humor is the right word."

Zach groaned. "Humor is the perfect word, at least in my dry opinion it is." Zach started to say more but a beautiful sight diverted his attention. "Look at that, would you? Look at that! I have just assumed the land we have been seeing was England, but now I know where we are for sure. Look, Jesse, that's Dover. No other place in the world puts out a welcome sign like that. Yes, sir, feast your eyes, because you're looking at the White Cliffs of Dover."

The rails of the ship were crowded with khaki-clad soldier boys, all looking in the direction of the approaching cliffs. The possibility that the ship might drop anchor raised their spirits, but it was difficult to assess if the men were elated to be in Europe or, if merely, they were joyful that the voyage was over. For these American soldiers had crossed the Atlantic Ocean free of hostile incident. Whatever their reasons, the men were pleased.

Private Jesse Moore stood in awe. "What is that on top of the cliffs? You don't suppose that's a castle, do you? Do they still have castles in Europe?" His expressions were really comments, rather than questions. "Maybe we'll get off here for more training, and since it's our first night abroad they might give us a pass to see the sights of Dover. There is a big Army base here, or at least I think there is. You always hear of American soldiers docking at Dover. How about it, Zach? If we get off here, I'll spring for your first cup of British tea, or maybe a pint of ale."

Equally excited, Zach responded. "I'll have my spot of tea on the cliffs, if you don't mind. Could be we'll find some English bloke to chat with, and we might just have ourselves a bloody good conversation."

Unfortunately, no level of personal excitement, no amount of wishing could make it happen. These two impassioned privates, full of youthful spirits bent on exploring the port city of Dover, were not to disembark at this most famous of ports. Hundreds of other soldiers would depart the ship for additional training, but not these two. Instead of walking on British soil, they were relegated to a passive role of observation from the deck of their transport ship, where they waited for sixteen hours watching other soldiers walk the gangplank to shore. Then, following a night's sleep, they watched another six hours as different soldiers boarded their ship. The two privates were left to wonder what opportunities they might have missed, or what adventures there might have been. The orderly transference of men and material made no sense to them. Some left, some stayed and the reasons for the exchange remained unknown to them. As privates they had no need to know. Jesse cloaked his displeasure with a frivolous comment. "Maybe they have British tea in France. I know they have beer. We've got to get off somewhere."

The following morning the convoy of troop ships sailed across the English Channel to Le Havre, France. The 22nd Combat Engineers received their land transportation orders en route. They would be attached to the IV Corps of the First Army, and would be used as front-line replacements for men in the 84th, one of the units which had spearheaded the American offensive at the Saint Mihiel Salient. Replacements were needed at once, and all efforts were directed to that end with deliberate speed.

The men of Company L. disembarked the ship, assembled in columns and marched directly to the rail yards where the now famous 40 men, eight horses boxcars were waiting. So efficient was the movement of soldiers that their troop train departed the port city of Le Havre six hours after the ship had docked. The train traveled at a high speed for five hours before departing the major track for a stop at a large military camp. It was 3:00 a.m. Friday, September 13, when the soldiers in transit were fed a hot meal, and were granted a two-hour acclimation break before re-boarding. The Company L. doughboys were not advised of their exact location, although it did not take long for the rumor mill to sort it all out. They were on the outskirts of Paris. Once back on the major track, the train followed another troop train which followed another and by early dawn the train convoy entered Paris proper. The ever curious Americans jockeyed for viewing positions in the cramped transport cars, all wanting to see the Eiffel Tower and other famous Paris sights. The Parisians who were inconvenienced by the slow moving train put aside their usual impatience, showed their gratitude by waving and welcoming the fresh American troops. It was all unofficial but the gracious greeting, nevertheless, was sort of like a ticker tape parade in their honor. With a feeling akin to conquering heroes the soldier boys not only felt welcomed, they felt appreciated.

By 9:45 a.m. the train departed the confines of Paris bound for Bar-le-Duc, a destination almost 200 miles away. Private Andrew Foster was the man of the hour in the crowded transport car. Normally, Andy was rather reserved, preferred to listen rather than talk; but today he freely shared his thoughts. For reasons not yet known to the other men of Company L., Andy knew French history and obviously appreciated French culture. The more Andy talked the more the others appreciated his incidental tidbits of information, his knowledge. It seemed to the listeners that Andy knew everything about France and, if asked, he would share his wisdom. His answers seemed to be no more, or no less, than what the others wanted to know. Andy's expressions were more than knowledgeable, more than interesting, they were fascinating. Although Andy was as critical of French history and culture as he was praising, he somehow conveyed his information without judgmental interpretation. When Andy spoke, you got the straight scoop, and such a rare quality only endeared him to others. Jesse was as surprised as anyone. He had known Andy for six weeks, and thought he knew him reasonably well, but Andy's knowledge of the French people provided a new dimension to the man.

The train's next stop was near a French military camp approximately four hours east of Paris where an American kitchen wagon was waiting to serve hot food to the hungry, fatigued men. The American soldiers dined on mulligan stew, fresh baked bread, baked apples, coffee, and two chocolate bars for dessert, which all suited Jesse just fine. Time remained for stretching and for much needed attention to body functions. Zach directed his speech to Jesse, but it was intended for Andy's ears. "Sure is nice to have the tour director back with the group, isn't it, Jesse? Our friend here is in real demand. If we want to keep him as part of our group, we may have to chain him to our arms, or he might end up as an aide to General Pershing."

Jesse grinned in lieu of a verbal response, although Andy quickly answered his teasing buddy. "I don't know which would be the worst fate—chained to you guys or to serve as an aide to Pershing."

Jesse thought the response was good. "I'd rather be an aide, myself. By the way, where did you learn all of that stuff about the French and their history? You were impressive."

Modestly, Andy said, "Oh, just here and there. My grandfather was French." His reply was sufficient for the moment, no other inquiries were made. Jesse knew that if Andy wanted to reveal more, he would in his own way and time. Andy appreciated the lack of personal questions. "It's hard to believe that we are just standing here eager to get back on the train, the same train we couldn't wait to get off of about an hour ago."

Jesse offered perspective. "We're going to get there one way or another, and the train sure beats walking. I don't mind waiting. It's sort of like crossing the Atlantic. It wasn't first class passage, but it wasn't a problem either. We just kind of sat back and watched while others did all the real work. Thus far, I have actually enjoyed all that we have seen while on the ship and the train. We better take advantage, because it won't be long until we'll need to get about shank's mare. Besides, Uncle Sam is footing the bill. Can't beat that."

Zach grinned. "Jesse, you make it sound like the Army is taking us on a sight-seeing tour of France. One way or another this trip will cost us. Although I suppose you have a point. We might as well enjoy while we can. I'll bet this easy travel all ends soon enough. I'll tell you what is interesting to me, and I don't know if you noticed it or not. It's the marred terrain. This land is so battle scarred, almost barren, and the farther east we go the worse it gets. The land looks ravaged to me. I would guess those big craters in the ground were caused by artillery. Just look at the surrounding countryside. Even the trees look puny, the ones left standing that is. Oh, look there! Look at the old wire and rifle pits. No doubt there was some big time action here sometime. I'm surprised the train can still make it through here, surprised the tracks are not destroyed. Probably destroyed and repaired a bunch of times. I'll bet at one time this area was pretty to the eye, loaded with farmhouses and such. You sure can't tell it now, not by looking anyway."

"It's God awful, all right," Andy said. "If we think about it we shouldn't be surprised. Much of this war has been fought in France and has been going on for four years. Even Paris came under attack at times. Modern armies can cause a lot of destruction in four years, and I'll bet we haven't seen the worst of it yet. Wait until we get to the front!"

Interrupting the conversation the sergeant yelled, "We're moving out, back on the train."

Zach could not help himself, he had to say it. "We better hurry, lads. Don't want to delay Andy, the tour conductor. He might have enough pull to secure some real comforts. Jesse, will you speak to the porter about our sleeping accommodations for this evening? Andy, will you check with the dining car about dinner reservations?"

Andy gave the gesture of a formal bow. "By all means, Sir Zachary. At your disposal and for your convenience at all times. Now get your ass on the train, you clown." All three shared a laugh.

Timing was perfect. It started to drizzle just as the train pulled away, and a few minutes later the light drizzle changed to a heavy downpour. At first the rain served as an incentive to securely close the boxcar doors, but eventually the unpleasant body aroma served as a bigger incentive to reopen them. Most men felt fortunate for a roof which protected them from the driving rain, yet many resented the close and uncomfortable confinement. Not too much was said because the situation could always get worse, as they often were told. They were all in this together and they understood that individual comfort for soldiers was not high priority. So they did·what they had to do—they adjusted.

The slow moving, rough riding train plowed ahead on its priority mission to transport fresh replacements to relieve the battle weary doughboys fighting in the Saint Mihiel Salient. Apart from some nervous chatter, conversation waned as time passed. Conversations competed with the clanking noise of the moving train until the train noises won out all together. Zach leaned over and whispered to Jesse. "Have you ever heard this group so quiet?" Without waiting for an answer he continued. "I think I know why. These guys are probably like me, they're worried about what lies ahead."

"I suspect you're right. That's exactly what I was thinking. We all know that every passing minute we've got to be getting closer to the trenches. Until the actual time comes, we all harbor doubts. Many of us probably have good reason to worry." Jesse looked straight ahead, softly spoke. "Let's be quiet, okay? I'd rather think."

It might have been the rain, or maybe the relative proximity of the battlefield, or possibly it was merely the nature of man. Whatever their reasons the soldiers in that rail car suddenly became reflective, consumed with self doubts. Rightfully, they had concerns. Their thoughts, seemingly spontaneous, were personal, private. It remained absolutely silent, but the mind could hear what the ears could not. *What measure of man am I? What about courage, do I have it? Will I be brave or act like a coward? Can I handle fear or will I fall to pieces? What will others think of me? Will I carry my own weight or will others need to help me?*

These were painful thoughts for young warriors. Questions beget more questions. Perhaps most frightening of all was the lingering thought that, one day, they might really learn the answers. The closer the men came to battle, the greater their doubts.

The sergeant's voice was loud and convincing, as though he knew what others were thinking. "Don't worry about it. Don't think about it. Before long you will know. If it helps, I'm scared too. If somebody is not scared, I don't want them on my train. We'll be all right, just relax, don't worry." In a strange way his disconcerting words provided comfort to the worried lot.

The slow moving rail car temporarily had shut out the outside world, had given them opportunity to ponder, but when the train did stop and the doors opened a new reality became the forefront of all thoughts. The train had stopped at a large military camp situated on the outskirts of Bar-le-Duc. The men of Company L.

were hurried off the train, ordered to fall in with packs and were marched to the east side of the camp. The rain had stopped.

Military police directed traffic and patrolled the area. Everything seemed so organized and efficient, while the individual soldier understood nothing of the whole picture and merely did as he was told. The wind was getting stronger and a mist was back in the air. The men double timed with full field packs to where a convoy of trucks awaited their arrival; and in the darkness of night they boarded, sixteen men and equipment to each canvas covered truck. Again, with no outside view the men were forced to rely on their mental images, their imaginations to guess about the next leg of their journey. Apart from occasional chatter the only distinct sound was the steady hum of the truck engines, and it became so quiet that a rare grinding of a transmission was a welcome sound of audible diversion. Without benefit of headlights the trucks continued to advance at a very slow pace on a well traveled, rain soaked road. There were no military police, or readable signs, or directing sounds; merely, each truck closely followed the truck in front, assuming the lead truck knew the proper course. The convoy stopped only once for a fifteen minute stretch break and feeding, but this time there was no hot food. The men were issued field rations of hardtack, a small piece of cheese and bread to consume as they traveled, rough ride permitting. Their journey continued.

"Out, get out now! All men out of the trucks!" was the cry from a passing sergeant. "Fall in with packs, single file. Hurry, men! We've got to get these trucks turned around, camouflaged, before full light." In single file and with full packs weighing almost 98 pounds including rifle and ammunition, the men of Company L. marched on a water soaked path leading to a nearby woods. They stopped their advance somewhere deep in the woods and sat on the cold, damp, inhospitable underbrush and waited for further instruction. "Use your slickers, sit on them, keep yourselves and your packs dry," was the order issued too late to be useful. The back sides of their uniforms were already soaked. "Fall in, move out in single file," was the order given right after the rain increased in intensity. It rained so hard that it was hard for them to see their hands in front of their faces. In a short time everything not under the slicker got thoroughly soaked, but they trudged on.

Jesse became amused with himself as he uncharacteristically struggled with the elements. He spoke to no one in particular, although he looked toward Zach. "Strange orders when we march in the rain, and rest when it doesn't rain. It's raining so hard I can't see anything, let alone walk anywhere without slipping. I know there has got to be a sun up there somewhere, but I can't find it. What direction are we headed? Does anyone know?"

A nearby sergeant heard the question and answered so that all nearby could hear. "We're going east, soldier. We're going to the front, and we don't want to announce our arrival to the Germans. We march when it's most difficult for Fritz to see us."

The sergeant's explanation made perfect sense to Jesse. From now on he hoped he had enough sense to keep his mouth shut, let somebody else ask the stupid questions. By afternoon the sun broke through the clouds, and the men of Company L. scurried to the nearest woods. A treetop canopy provided adequate protection from aerial observation, just as the dense perimeter of the forest prevented detection by enemy ground forces from afar. The ground residue was damp and moldy, and emitted a voracious smell of decay. Here they rested approximately four hours until nightfall when, once again, they resumed their forward movement; and with occasional rest breaks they marched throughout the night. At first light they bivouacked and rested in another wooded area. Shortly before noon another low pressure front moved into the area. Soon intermittent showers and a constant blanket of low lying clouds provided the necessary cover to advance. Capitalizing on the weather they broke camp and continued their forward trek free from aerial detection. By late afternoon the fatigued, rain soaked men arrived at a military encampment in close proximity to a small French village. The camp's location, situated on open ground clearly observable from air or from ground afar, made no sense to Jesse, but on the heels of his last doltish inquiry, he was not about to ask why. Hundreds of American soldiers were moving in and out of the area by way of one of the three roads in or out of the small village. Zach asked. "Where are we sergeant?"

"This is Manonville Junction, it's a jumping off point. This is our last stop before we venture into the breach. Forget about trying to make sense of it all. The intent is to confuse the Germans. One day when you're old and gray, sitting on a front porch in your rocking chair, you can find Manonville Junction on a map and show your grand kids where you entered the trenches. That is, you'll be able to tell them, if today you have enough sense to keep your head down. Stay down and you might stay alive." The sergeant spoke matter of fact without emotion or humor. It was almost as if his advice to keep their heads down was an absolute, his final proclamation.

The sergeant's explanation again satisfied the curious men. Jesse was pleased that someone else had asked the question.

The men marched to the edge of the village, followed a road north for almost a mile until they arrived at a place that surely was once a treasured rural home site. Now, its structures lay in ruins. A crumbling stone fence enclosed the old farm site. The cottage and several outbuildings had been totally destroyed by shell fire, and the former barnyard was dominated by two large shell craters partially filled with rain water. The barn was the sole building remaining erect although it, too, had suffered artillery damage. Near the barn was an Army kitchen wagon, a makeshift eating area. At this moment the thought of a hot meal and a full night's sleep under a roof was as gratifying as any thought could be. Already the men were exhausted.

Not all had heard the sergeant's explanation concerning the camp's location. Andy questioned why they were stopping in the open. "It seems strange to me that we were required to take such precautions getting here, but once we're here it makes no difference if the enemy knows of our presence. Will somebody smarter than I am explain it to me?"

Zach jumped at the opportunity, speaking as though he had figured it out. After his explanation he pointed at Andy. "It's a hot meal, isn't it? It's a place to put your head down, isn't it? View it as a gift, and never look a gift horse in the mouth." Although Zach's explanation did not make much sense, Andy was satisfied, and Jesse was amused.

Infantry guarded the camp's perimeter and before the men of Company L. were totally squared away, two squads of machine gunners took up positions behind the stone fence. Company L. was well protected from ground attack.

The men secured individual sleeping areas in the barn, first come, first choice. The interior of the barn, stripped of equipment and stalls, presented a large open area strewn with straw. The open loft, the area of choice for sleeping, provided additional straw and was made easily accessible by a homemade ladder. Sleeping positions were staked out by individual pack placement, quickly followed by a selfish gathering of additional straw for bedding. With space to spare the barn easily accommodated the minimum strength company of men.

Necessary facilities, including latrines, were already in place. Obviously, this location had housed other soldiers and probably would house many more in the future. With quarters provided, security arranged, there was little more for the replacements to do other than eat and rest.

A grand meal of hot beef stew, canned peaches, fresh bread, cheese, milk, fresh apples, chocolate bars, and hot coffee was made more special by the cook's proclamation, "Take all you want, eat all you take." Plans called for the company to move forward early the following morning, departure time depending on weather and cloud cover. Confined within the secured perimeter until the full company moved forward, the men were free to fill their own time until dawn, fourteen hours hence. While a few men played cards, rolled dice, or played other games, most rested, worked on correspondence, or visited with their buddies.

Andy, Jesse, and Zach secured a comfortable, somewhat isolated place near the south end of the crumbled stone fence. Intrigued by the surrounding operational farm land, Jesse seemed more interested in watching a group of French farmers than he was in conversing. Less than fifty yards from where the men sat, four women, one older man, and two children gathered a fresh cut of hay. From past experience Jesse knew the work to be tedious manual labor and he marveled at the French workers persistent, steady approach to their job. Suddenly, he became amused. "Will you look at that! In all my life I've never seen such as that before." The other two looked and immediately identified the source of Jesse's astonishment. One of the French women had laid down her hay fork, lifted her dress, squatted, and urinated within sight of the other workers. Once she finished her business the three American soldiers applauded and shouted approving cheers. Unaffected by the attention she calmly turned, acknowledged their cheers with a two-handed wave and returned to work. Jesse got the biggest kick out of observing a woman tending to such a private matter in such an open nonchalant way. "That's pretty good. That's what I call bold."

Andy was quick to answer. "Yeah, I suppose so. It's really just the French manner, not intended to be audacious in any way."

Zach had to interject his two cents worth. "Pray tell, how can a woman take a piss in public, not be embarrassed, and you tell me to think nothing about it? If you expect me to swallow that, you had better explain your logic to this simple mind."

"It does seem strange to us, I know, but it's really no more than a cultural difference. Most behavior and personal habits are acquired from our cultural background. What is proper one place may not be proper elsewhere, and vice versa. It's cultural. The French might think it strange that we go hide to take a piss."

"How do you know all this stuff?" asked a puzzled Jesse. "Are you formally educated, or have you just read a lot? Come on, out with it. How do you know?"

A modest Andrew was put on the spot. "Well, I don't know if I'm going to answer you or not." He paused and stared at his curious friends. "This is personal stuff and I don't want any of the others to know it. If I tell you, do I have your word that you won't tell the others?"

"You have my word."

"What about it, Zach, do I have your word too?"

"I suppose, if it's all that important to you. What's the big secret?"

"It's no secret, I just don't want to broadcast it. Before the war I used to teach World History at a prep school in Vermont, but that was my life before the Army got me. Now, I'm a combat engineer and I want to be judged accordingly. I don't want others to know I used to be a teacher, that's all."

"I believe I would be proud of that," Jesse retorted. "You should be proud, not secretive about it. I would tell the world."

Zach chimed in, "I better watch my p's and q's around you, I don't want you to keep me after school. If I had an apple, I would give it to you, teach."

"That's exactly what I'm talking about. Others need not know or I will have to put up with such crap all the time, plus I don't want people making smart remarks like—didn't they teach you that in college? I just don't want the abuse, I don't want to put up with it. I just want to be a regular combat engineer."

Jesse accepted Andy's explanation and wanted to further discuss the intriguing cultural difference concept, although he had little success getting Andy to open up. Zach remained amused and smiled every time he looked at Andy. Andy did not appreciate Zach's smile.

By 9:00 p.m. most men were in the barn under their blankets. Sleep would come easy this night. Zach got in the last words. "Good night, Jesse. Good night, Professor Andrew." Neither directly responded but Jesse made a crackling sound as he smiled. Andy remained silent.

The following morning no reveille was needed. The men were all awake before dawn, a few had already exited the barn. Zach spoke in anguish. "I don't know what I got into last night, but I itch all over. It's driving me nuts. Feels like I've got fleas."

Andy responded. "I would say it serves you right for that remark last night, but I can't because I've got them too, and I don't think they are fleas. They're lice. God damn it, we've got cooties. They must have been in the straw."

"I thought you got lice in the trenches. I sure never thought about getting them out here in the open. I'm going outside and pick them off," Jesse said without thinking. When he looked around and saw others already outside attempting to rid themselves of the pesky vermin, he realized the magnitude of the infestation. Knowing there was little he could really do about the lice, he still made the effort and gave a halfhearted, mocking laugh as he picked away at his many itchy spots. "Guess we're all going to live with them, I don't think we have much choice."

Zach appeared to suffer the most. "Well, I have a choice. I'm going to get rid of them if I have to kill every one of them with my bayonet," he proclaimed before he scurried outside dragging his pack behind him.

This time Andy laughed. "Good luck, itchy." Zach's angry look back caused Andy to laugh harder. It was quite a sight watching the entire company engage in its first shirt hunt—the name given to the futile process of searching for and removing cooties.

Breakfast consisted of hot oatmeal sweetened with real molasses, fried bacon, bread and butter, hot coffee, and another chocolate bar. The meal was not fully appreciated as it should have been as most men had not yet adjusted to their new personal companions, the body lice and, probably, most never would. Willingly, many would have traded their breakfast for a delousing if given the opportunity. All suffered from the lice, although some were severely affected.

Overnight the weather had changed. The morning air was crisp and dry, the sky was a cloudless blue and the surrounding small parcels of scattered woods displayed their red and yellow autumn leaves. The slight breeze cleansed the open

403

areas of unpleasant smells so commonly found near closely massed soldiers. Unfortunately, the beautiful setting was more suited for aesthetic appreciation than for forward movement. Word was that once they left their camp they were deemed to be within enemy artillery range. With such excellent long range visibility, orders were issued to stand down as any forward movement would surely be detected.

"I wonder how much longer they are going to keep us out here in the open," Andy asked as he looked at the distant woods. "We know we're moving up, don't we? Otherwise why would they issue us spare bandoliers of ammunition and six days of rations and hold us perched here like we were about to start a hundred yard dash. There must be some reason."

Zach ventured a guess. "Look at those observation balloons way out there! I can't see the markings, can you? I assume they are ours, but I'm not sure. Maybe our waiting has something to do with those balloons or, who knows, maybe they don't want us up there yet. Whatever the reason I'm perfectly content right here behind this stone wall. What about you, Jesse, are you anxious to move out?"

"I don't know what to think. I'm like Andy in that we're pretty exposed right here. On the other hand, and if we're going in the direction I think we are, I guess the wooded area to be about 500 yards from where we sit. I'd sure hate to get halfway there and find somebody in that woods hellbent on stopping us. I just don't know what to think. So far the officers seem to know what they're doing. I'm sure there must be good reason. Speak of the devil, look over there! The lieutenant wants us."

The lieutenant waited until the full platoon was gathered. "Listen up, we've had a change. We're going to split up the company, move out at different times. The captain is fearful of moving the whole company together because of such good visibility. Last report the Jerries have seven balloons and three airplanes up watching. That makes it dangerous for us. As the crow flies our objective is nine miles forward, much of it is across open country. Needless to say we must leap frog from woods to woods as long as their balloons are up. We're going in the only way we can. We move out in single file, avoid bunching up. Keep track of the man in front and the man behind you. Never let either man out of your sight. Believe me, you do not want to be lost out there. No matter what we encounter, we've got to be there by midnight tomorrow night, hopefully sooner.

"Orders are for us to link up with units from the 84th. Those boys spearheaded this attack, and have been fighting for six days straight. They need relief. From the beginning they've caught hell from the Germans, and they're still catching it. Command thinks the Jerries are planning a counterattack and we've got to get there before that happens. This is the real thing, boys. Once we cross this open area we're in the fire zone. Our approach has been cleared, but command thinks a few stray Germans might still be out there. Stay alert! I will take point with the scout, and sergeants will stay evenly spaced out. We'll move as fast as possible, but we won't leave anybody stranded. We move as a unit, communicate with hand signals only, no talking. If the head of the column stops, slows down, speeds up, or whatever, the entire column follows suit. We move or stop in unison. Try to keep five to ten yards between you and the man in front of you. If he takes cover, you take cover. Remember to keep track of the person behind you as well. If someone goes down, get assistance to him, but you keep moving. We have medical corps with us and they will tend to the wounded. Keep your heads down and remember your training. Good luck, men, I'll see you in the trenches."

Spaced out in single file the platoon crossed the stone fence and followed a muddy trail. Emotions ran high after the lieutenant's warnings, but you would not have known it by watching the men who advanced like seasoned veterans. The time required to reach the nearest tree cover was thirty minutes, although it seemed much longer to the exposed soldiers. The lieutenant had done his job, the anxious men were cautiously careful.

The advancing unit made it to the woods and beyond without incident. Once back on the open trail they quickly moved in the direction of a small village occupied by other Americans. Rather than passing through the village, the platoon circumvented it by a distance of about one hundred yards. Located on the far side of the village was an American aid station housing several dozen wounded soldiers. The men tried to see what was transpiring within the compound, but multiple aid tents prevented a clear view. Then they saw eleven men on stretchers outside the station, presumably waiting for medical attention. It was intimidating as the advancing men got their first glimpse of combat casualties, especially when they clearly could observe the wounded soldiers, two noticeably bloodied, one vocally agonizing. As ·if the sight of wounded men were not bad enough, the advancing unit quickly encountered another foreboding sight—an American Army temporary cemetery, created to deal with the many fallen American soldiers recently killed during the first stage of the offensive. The cemetery, not really small in size, had a huge impact. If ever so briefly, the passing soldiers now had been exposed to a darker side of war—the burial of fallen comrades. It was not known if the unit deliberately bypassed the village to avoid a close view of the aid station and cemetery or for other more practical reasons. Most were content with the bypass of the village, whatever the reason. They had seen enough.

The sun was fading, dark clouds were approaching. Rain was imminent as another low pressure weather system was about to descend. Zach commented. "It must rain every day in France. God, I hate the rain." The men wondered but did not know if more rain would enhance or restrict their forward movement. They knew for sure that rain would make it more difficult for them to walk with their heavy packs, and once it started to rain it poured. Drenching rain, or not, the forward bound military unit continued its erratic course over wet, slippery terrain in and out of small forests over road and trail.

How close in distance they were to where it all started! Arrival at the far side of a small wooded area placed the advancing troops in position to view where the battle for Saint Mihiel Salient had commenced. The battlefield looked exactly as the replacements thought it would—opposing strong defensive lines of deep, heavily fortified trenches separated by a vast, battle scarred stretch of open space called no-man's-land. Since October, 1914, these older trenches had been the front lines of battle in four years of a brutal, stalemated war. Now more as a monument to a bloody past than anything else, these once important trenches defiantly remained. To American soldiers this particular field of battle was almost sacred ground as it symbolically marked the launching of the first major offensive under American Command. Additionally, to the French it symbolized American might and all that was possible with effective deployment of fresh American troops in the ongoing Allied effort to cripple the mighty German military machine. Just looking at the old trenches reminded the replacements of why they were so hurriedly brought to bear.

The tired and weary French soldiers who now sparsely manned these older trenches still found the energy to make way, to openly smile and wave as the American replacements walked across the temporary plank foot bridge of the once mighty fortification of French trenches. The French gestures made the Americans feel like heroes for the cause, and they perked up, put pride in their steps, as they waved back to the grateful French soldiers. Appreciation abounded from men in both armies as the Americans departed across the dreaded terrain once called no-man's-land. The vast, open ground, pitted with shell craters, spent ammunition, and used articles of war, lay in waste showing no indications of vegetation or life. A few splintered tree trunks dotted the landscape, and attested to recent battle's unimaginable gore and brutality. The Americans wasted no time crossing the unseemly site.

The old German trench had been destroyed, or at minimum had been rendered ineffective. German equipment and personal military items were strewn about the area, and the American soldiers having been previously warned of the dangers of war contraband, took heed. Training had taught that German soldiers knew all the many ways to kill or maim their foes, and these tempting souvenirs could well be booby trapped. Surely, ground ahead would present better opportunities to gather enemy mementos, to engage in the forbidden act of gathering seductive, tantalizing items of war.

Beyond the old trenches near the path of their advance lay a dead German, mostly covered with dirt except for the head, feet, and one disfigured limb. The soldier's face was grimaced, and his open eyes blankly stared at the sky. Whether other soldiers once had quickly tried to bury him or if dirt from an exploding shell had engulfed him was not easily discernible. The grotesque display may have been intentionally left for others to view. Whatever the reason, the conspicuous sight was witnessed by every peering American soldier; and thereafter, for each soldier to wonder the circumstances of death that befell the pitifully placed fallen soldier. Strangely, many reveled in the sight of a dead enemy, and only a few lamented the death of a fellow human being. In this regard the many were well trained.

The spectacle of the dead enemy soldier again brought death into focus. Literally, these Americans now had looked into the eyes of a dead enemy combatant. Necessarily, soldiers were taught that it was preferable to kill without looking into the eyes of the enemy, for hesitation to kill might mean the loss of one's own life. Death was a risk of war and this war made killing less personal as new military technology made the task of killing from afar much easier to accomplish, easier to endure. But here and now was the close-up sight of a fallen soldier where death was death, and life was life.

The trail transformed into a gravel road before it reverted back to a dirt trail. Artillery shells had so destroyed the road's surface and its drainage ditches, plus the recent rains had so saturated the ground, that most of the men were pleased to be walking on anything that resembled a distinguishable hard surface. Old rusting barbed wire, probably having been dispersed by shell explosions, abounded everywhere. American, French, and German infantry items lay abandoned alongside the trail. Articles from packs, helmets, ammunition belts, mess kits, bayonets, and even a few rifles were among the many discarded commodities of engaging armies. Intriguingly, these ordinary army issue items, these personal remnants of past fighting, were now the lost components of a soldier's story that might never be told. The scene became symbolic of what many men feared most about combat—death without explanation. No matter where the men walked the symbolic items were ever present to remind them of what lay ahead, and the sights became fuel for already active imaginations of men about to enter combat.

Less than ten yards off the road lay another reminder of recent battle—the ruins of a German machine gun nest—which warned of danger ahead. Three dead German soldiers lay face up, presumably positioned where they fell. The machine gun was a damnable weapon feared by all soldiers, but especially dreaded by the Allies because of superior German deployment. The three-man machine gun nest, a defensive mainstay of German infantry, was perhaps the most effective defensive weapon used through out the war by the Germans. Referred to as the widow makers, German machine gunners seemed to have mastered its use, always knew where to deploy it, and appeared to have an unlimited supply of these modern killing machines. Even in retreat the Germans often left scattered machine gunners to effectively fend off a pursuing force.

German machine gunners were legendary for their bravery and skill. Every American soldier had heard the story about German machine gunners protecting a retreating army in the Aisne-Marne region in June, 1918. A lone machine gun nest stopped the advance of a full American infantry company for almost three hours before the machine gun fell silent. The story went that as the American soldiers finally charged past the machine gun position the gun was still smoking from its prolonged use. Some said they could feel the heat from the gun as they moved by it. The advancing soldiers were so awed by the gun's effectiveness that they failed to check the physical condition of the three German gunners laying face down in the dirt. Once the American company was past the nest, the same three German gunners got up and turned the now cooled machine gun on the Americans who were all positioned in open country. The Americans were forced to turn around and retake the same German machine gun position. Recapture required the loss of thirty additional American lives. The lesson taught was that American soldiers were never to pass a German machine gun nest without making certain the gunners were dead, and if possible, the gun destroyed.

The men of Company L. thought of the story as they passed the German machine gun position, but other American soldiers presumably had also heard the story. These German gunners all had multiple bullet holes in their chests and the barrel of the gun had been spiked. Once again, it was almost as though the German machine gun nest had been intentionally left intact as a warning to remind other Americans of the story.

The ever winding trail passed through open land over hill and dale before it ended in a grove of trees. Since less than one hour of daylight remained and standard procedure dictated that advancing troop movement should occur at night to avoid the watchful eyes of the enemy, the men were granted a well deserved respite. In the small woods the men assumed protective cover, ate, drank, and rested as they waited for nightfall. No cooking fires were permitted. Rather than seeking sleep as expected most men wanted to converse, to share their personal reactions about all they had seen. It was not surprising for they had observed much these last four hours.

Soon they were on the move again. Advancing in the dark of night over unfamiliar terrain was difficult, and made more difficult by other American troops traveling in the opposite direction. Just as they were advancing to the trenches, others were withdrawing, and by necessity all were required to use the same trails or face the frightful possibility of becoming lost at night. The process was inefficient movement of troops, made necessary by concerns of safety. Occasional flares forced everyone to the ground, just as occasional nearby small arms fire forced all to move forward with extreme care. The men simply followed the man in front and seldom did they know how far they had progressed or the identity of those nearby. Forward movement at night required blind trust, most unsettling to say the least, which forced the advancing men to show confidence that someone in command knew what was going on. That confidence was not always easy to muster, to maintain.

At approximately 3:00 in the morning the advancing unit was brought to a complete halt, not by the enemy activity but by orders. The men simply were too fatigued to continue, and exhausted replacements were of marginal value in the front trenches. Although unofficial word proclaimed that the front lines were less than one hour away, the ranks remained dubious. Once again they were told to seek cover, to eat and drink, and to get some rest; and this time most of the men were determined to get some sleep.

Jesse and Andy located a relatively dry portion of ground and used their entrenching tool to dig a shallow foxhole. Zach was sarcastic about the actions of his two friends. "By the book, huh. Not me, I'm going to lean up against this tree, it's good enough for me. I'm not digging any more holes." Zach put his nose to the air, sniffed, and then snickered as he spoke. "I'm not sure what that smell is, and I'm sure not going to dig in the ground and stir it up."

"Suit yourself. Besides, I don't smell anything any worse than I have smelled all day," Andy retorted.

The men in the platoon, camped no more than twenty yards from the trail, could hear the sounds of nearby troop movement but could not see well enough to identify the particulars. Although the movement was unsettling at first, the resting men soon adjusted. Through experience most were learning what to ignore and when to become concerned. Slowly but surely, the replacements were acquiring the basic skills of combat soldiers.

Minutes before dawn Jesse and Andy were awakened by Zach's anxious words. "Jesus Christ!" Zach jumped to his feet and drug his pack away from the tree, and as he moved away something from behind the pack fell to the ground. He turned and looked toward the tree and spoke with anger. "You son of a bitch. I've been next to you all the while. I knew I smelled something."

Fully aroused by now, Jesse asked, "What are you talking about? Who are you talking to?"

While pointing and shaking his finger, Zach answered. "I'm talking to that dead son of a bitch right there. It's a God damn horse." With every passing second the sky got lighter until Jesse could almost see about what Zach was talking. Jesse jumped up to see the source of Zach's irritation and, eventually, he was able to identify the object in question. It was a dead horse, lying on its side with all four legs extended out, stiff as boards. Zach had slept next to the dead horse, and Zach's pack had been wedged against the horse's head. The ridged head of the horse was unnaturally positioned on the ground with eyes wide open. A large open wound in the belly revealed the stomach interior, which had already been discovered by maggots and hundreds of hatched flies. Caked, dried blood covered much of the horse and surrounding ground. Although it was a putrid sight, Jesse could not help but laugh at the thought of Zach, who earlier had been too lazy to dig a hole, spending the last five hours sleeping next to a dead horse, especially one who gave off such a strong, offensive odor. Jesse tried to express his conjecture about what had occurred but his words were interrupted by his laughter. "Wounded... artillery shell... wandered in here... died." He finally gave up trying to speak and, instead, he looked at Zach and laughed.

Now fully awake, Andy joined the conversation. "Why are you mad at him? Did he pull covers, or did he snore? Are you about ready for breakfast?" As Andy spoke he became so amused at his own words, that he laughed, uncontrollably. With limited success Jesse tried to restrain himself. Andy did not and showed little compassion for Zach.

"Keep it down over there, you fools," cried an unidentified voice. "You want every Kraut around to know we're here?" Jesse and Andy took heed but their facial expressions remained the same. They were so amused and Zach was so angry that there was no need for further ribbing. Facial expressions said it all.

When the column exited the woods later that morning, Andy started walking stiff legged, his arms out straight, and his head cocked back with eyes opened wide. Jesse mimicked Andy. Zach tried to ignore both of them. Later Zach turned his head to sniff his pack, Andy saw him and the laughter was rekindled. Fortunately, humor prevailed and, eventually, even Zach became amused and joined in the mocking laughter.

The five hour rest had helped, forward movement was progressing well until the unmistakable sound of a rifle shot echoed overhead. The lieutenant had been brought down by sniper fire. The men scurried, tried to take cover on the open ground. A second shot fatally wounded the scout as he attempted to assist the downed lieutenant. The sniper squeezed off two additional shots and Zach heard a thud as the soldier in front of him took a hit to the chest. In the open and one hundred yards from good cover the platoon was pinned down. The sniper's position remained unknown. For over thirty minutes the men desperately hugged the ground as their eyes futilely scanned the woods and other areas thought to be the source of the rifle fire. Scared and frustrated the confined men continued their visual search, fearing all the while that any movement on their part might disturb the surrounding tall uncut field grass or that they might do something which revealed their exact location to the sniper. Some remained frozen where they fell, while others maneuvered for better vision. Wisely, no one returned fire. Finally, they heard the comforting sound of Enfield rifle fire quickly followed by the sound of something heavy hitting the ground. Still, no one moved even after a distant voice shouted, "It's okay, guys. We got him. Move out!" Having earlier been advised of German trickery, not one man from the pinned down unit moved. An American soldier stepped out from a distant tree and reiterated his command. "Company L., 1st Platoon, get your asses up here. We got the sniper." A sergeant near the position of the fallen scout was the first to stand, and others eventually joined him until all the men were on their feet and moving. The unit reassembled in a clump of trees and were checked for injuries. In a short time the platoon resumed its forward trek, minus three men.

By 9:30 a.m. they had advanced less than one additional mile. The men wondered where they were going and when they would get there. Hopefully someone was in charge who understood the big picture, because they did not. A light shower came and went, the sun was trying to break through the clouds, and the wind was increasing in intensity. Their wool uniforms were water soaked from three days of outside exposure, and every time the men hit the ground for protection or sat on the ground for rest, the uniforms became muddier. Much of the time the men were chilled, and when the sun came out and the humidity increased, they suffered. "It's one thing to fight the Germans, another to fight the elements. I'll bet I'm carrying five extra pounds of mud," Andy disparagingly expressed. "I'm cold now and in ten minutes I'll be hot."

Zach was equally agitated. "I'll carry your mud if you'll carry my cooties. I itch so bad I'm about to go crazy. When you're cold you can get warm. When you're hot you can usually find a way to cool off. But what the hell do you do out here when you itch? There is no end to it. You just keep itching. I've got to figure out a way to get rid of these cooties." Squinting as he looked in the direction of the sun, Zach removed his helmet, scratched his head, looked mystified. "If I'm reading the sun right, we're generally moving in a northwest direction. That doesn't make any sense, unless they want us back in Paris."

Jesse unleashed one of his controlled laughs. "I'm glad to hear you say that, because I've been confused about where we are, where we've been since Paris. I'm a country boy, used to knowing north, south, east, and west. Moving only at night or under cloud cover gets me all messed up. It seems to me that we go forward, sideways, backwards, or in circles. I never know where I am. The Army needs..."

A sergeant's shout ended their chatter. "Double time. Let's go, we've got to move now." The men hustled about two hundred yards back to the same grove of trees they had just passed. "Dig your pits, deep and fast, we're going to be here awhile." Rocky soil and tree roots rendered the entrenching tool somewhat ineffective, but the men continued to throw dirt in spite of the conditions. Jesse, Andy, and Zach worked on a common foxhole with one man tugging on the larger roots while the other two chopped and dug. In less than ten minutes they had produced a wide, shallow hole large enough to afford slight protection. They looked at the hole, thought about it and decided to dig it deeper, taking care to carefully pile the removed dirt around its perimeter, in essence making the pit deeper. Their real quandary was how deep was deep enough.

A sergeant hurriedly moved about inspecting foxholes. "What's up sergeant?" Andy asked.

The sergeant only slightly paused to answer. "Better make that hole a little deeper. Stay in it, but keep digging. Our artillery boys are going to drop a few rounds on the Germans, and we can expect return fire. Keep your heads down. Lately the Krauts have been firing shrapnel shells, and you don't want to be in the open if one detonates near you. Make that hole deeper." His words, his near panic were all the motivation the three needed. With more intensity they resumed digging.

They finished their hole took cover in it and waited, but nothing out of the ordinary happened. They ate the field rations, smoked, rested, or did what they could within the confines of the pit. Most of all they scratched away at the annoying, ever increasing number of louse bites. With adequate light and good eyes one could actually see the little vermin as they moved about. Blood was the source of life for the lice, and one single critter was capable of inflicting multiple bites within a brief time. It seemed to the soldiers as if the lice were hell-bent on longevity and could instantly proliferate. Those who could see the cooties would try to catch them between their thumb and finger and squeeze them, or better yet, squash them with a finger pressed against a bayonet blade. The latter method guaranteed destruction, but already the men knew that they could not win the battle with the cooties. Only delousing would eradicate the dreaded vermin, and that process only worked for a short while because the lice were everywhere and on everyone.

The calm was broken by an opening salvo of friendly artillery fire and, other than stay down, there was little the foot soldiers could do but wait it out. The Artillery launchings and the whine of the overhead missiles in flight was clearly audible to the dug in Americans. Suddenly all hell broke loose when German artillery returned fire. For three or four minutes a countless number of explosions were all about the woods, three explosions near enough to Jesse for him to feel the aftershocks and a slight trembling of the ground. The Germans were returning fire with a vengeance. Soon, the explosions became fewer in number until eventually the shelling became an occasional firing, seemingly random in target. It all made little sense to the men on the ground. The overall logic escaped Jesse of why the Allies would initiate artillery fire which only incited the Germans to return fire. Apparently, at this time the need to shell the enemy was greater than the need to get replacements to the front line. Jesse was learning very early in his combat experience that he was not about to understand the overall strategy of waging war.

In fact, he understood very little. Then he laughed. Why his frustrations became a source of personal amusement at this particular time he did not understand, but Jesse became so tickled he could not hide his feelings.

Zach looked at Jesse in wonderment. "If you're enjoying this, one of us is nuts, and I don't think it's me."

"I don't think it's you either. I'm the nut. I'm laughing at my own stupidity. It's finally dawned on me. I really don't have much control over my life, especially out here. I'm stupid, I'm the nut because it took me so long to understand a simple fact. Out here the objective is far more important than the person. In war, do what needs to be done, whither the individual."

Zach's response was clear. "I don't even know what the hell you're talking about. You didn't take a hit to the head, did you?"

Jesse laughed. "Could well be." He found no resolution to his questions and wisely decided that hereafter he should never mention his strange thoughts to others, and he should stop worrying about all the things that were out of his control. He should do what he was told, forget about understanding, and let others worry about analyzing overall strategy. These conclusions forced him to become more amused with himself. He spoke to no one in particular. "My life is on tenterhook and I should not worry. Sure, that's a good one, now tell yourself another one!"

Without warning an incoming shell exploded at tree top height less than twenty yards from Jesse's foxhole. The noise was deafening, the very ground shook. Tree tops splintered and fell to the ground as small pieces of shell fragments dispersed in all directions. A loud thud vividly recorded the implanting of a jagged piece of iron in the trunk of a nearby tree. Nearby, cries of men in agony abounded, but thanks to their deep foxhole Jesse and his buddies had been spared injury. The explosion had altered the landscape, had carved a huge hole in the treetop canopy and unobstructed sunlight beamed directly on the forest floor. Nearby trees were popping and crackling as though the whole forest might collapse and, yet, most larger trees remained rooted and upright while smaller limbs and other forest debris dropped or filtered down to the ground. As though the enemy had hit their intended target the shelling ceased as abruptly as it had started. German artillery effectively had greeted the replacements, had given them a warning of things to come. Dozens of Company L. Combat Engineers had borne witness to the incredible damage that one shell was capable of inflicting. The warnings to keep their heads down and to dig the hole deeper had been words to the wise. Another lesson was well learned.

This time the three buddies were lucky. Jesse saw that Andy and Zach were without injury, although all three were visibly shaken. Others were hurt, some seriously. They were ordered to stay in their foxholes as medical personnel surveyed the area and scurried about tending to the wounded. The three did as instructed and remained hunkered down as others assessed the overall damage and rendered assistance. It was difficult to stay down and out of the way of others, but they did as told. They remained in place and fretted.

The late hour neared sunset when the platoon moved out. They exited the wooded area in the same manner of marching that they had left Manonville—single file, following the man in front, but this time they spread out even more. Before long it was totally dark and, again, there was a slight mist in the air. For three hours they walked never knowing direction or location until about eight o'clock they ended their advance near a large encampment where soon thereafter they were fed a hot meal and resupplied with field rations and fresh water for their canteens. Little did they know that had it been daylight they could have seen the front-line trenches from where they took their meal. Without additional rest the replacements departed the encampment at 9:15.

On a dark moonless night the Combat Engineers of the 22nd Regiment moved into the trenches, took positions along a five-mile front. The remaining forty-nine men of 1st Platoon, Company L. were spread out in an area covering one hundred fifty yards in length. They assumed rifle firing positions and were ordered to hold at all cost. Shortly following their front-line emplacement a slow burning flare exploded high in the sky, almost as though the Army intentionally wanted to present the arriving men with their first glimpse of no-man's-land. The men looked and absorbed as much as they could before the slow burning flare totally burned away into darkness. Their trench position was somewhere in Lorraine, France, the time was 9:30 p.m., and the date was September 19, 1918.

Zach whispered to Jesse, "Are you all right, buddy?"

"Yeah, what about you?"

"Not so good."

CHAPTER 23

THE TEST OF BATTLE

What an experience last night was! I'm not certain what I felt, other than fear, but there was something about it that I liked. I'm exhilarated. I've never felt like this before, and I'm not sure if I ever want to feel like it again. Do you guys know what I'm talking about, did you feel it?" Corporal Pedigo enthusiastically asked. So eager in his excitement he could not wait for an answer. "I loved it!" For some unidentifiable reason the experience of his first night in the trenches had served to stimulate the corporal's emotions, to energize him. To others it was as though he had enjoyed his experience.

With no regard to rank Zach responded. "Corporal, you've lost your marbles. Jesse, Andy, don't you even think about answering his question. Make him think about what he just said." Others remained quiet while Zach became even more annoyed by the corporal's facial expression. "I'll tell you how I feel, and I'm sure you don't want to hear it. I think you are n..."

"Whoa, whoa, you're right, private, I don't want to hear it. I didn't mean to get your dander up, I was only sharing a personal feeling. I sure didn't mean to antagonize you. Sorry I said anything, just forget it all." The indignant corporal picked up his gear and moved far enough away so that he could not hear or see Zach.

Andy wasted little time in his effort to cool down his angry friend. "You need to calm down, Zach, you're out of line."

"Out of line hell. I'm not the jerk talking about how exciting it all is. I don't care if he's a corporal or not, I'm fed up with jerks telling me how brave they are."

"Zach, you're missing the point," inserted a baffled, concerned Jesse. "I think the corporal was scared, just like the rest of us, and he merely was wanting to talk about it. There was no harm in what he said. You overreacted."

"If that's the way you feel about it, I'll leave you alone and maybe the corporal will come back and you can all visit about your wonderful war experiences." Uncharacteristically, and not wanting any additional conversation, Zach defiantly left his position and assumed an unassigned position farther down the line.

Andy was flabbergasted. "Well, I'll be. What in the world got into him? That is so unlike Zach."

"I agree," Jesse said. "He has concerns right now and needs to deal with them. Something is eating at him that's for sure. I think he will be all right after he cools down. He needs to deal with it himself, alone."

"I hope you're right, although I'm not so sure. I think he is experiencing new feelings, and up to this point, he doesn't know how to deal with them. Normally Zach finds humor in everything. I hope he still can. I hope it isn't something bad. Whether we want to admit it or not, down deep we're all pretty fragile."

Andy's words wore heavily on Jesse. Andy was usually very perceptive, and his implication was that Zach was adversely affected by battle stress, or God forbid, something worse.

Attention was diverted elsewhere when an infantry sergeant approached. "We've got replacements. As soon as you are relieved, you guys stand down, find something to eat, get some shuteye. If you hear the whistle, get your butts back here in a hurry."

Traditionally, exposure to battlefield conditions elevated the status of any soldier. An encounter with the enemy and one full night in the trenches qualified the engineers as combat veterans, and in the eyes of the arriving green recruits, these engineers had endured the test of battle. Almost a rite of passage, combat veterans offered words of wisdom to virgin soldiers. As the replacements entered the trenches, Andy played the role of a veteran warrior. He winked at Jesse. "I'm not as good at this as Zach is, but since he's not here I will do my best." With hands shading the eyes and staring into no-man's-land Andy spoke so the green recruits could hear his every word. "Take your defensive positions, men. You hold these positions at all cost, and I mean at all cost. I don't care if the whole German Army comes at you, hold your positions. Me and my buddies are leaving you in charge. We are going to get some well deserved sleep. It's been a long week up here." Andy tapped Jesse and said, "Let's go, soldier, we've earned some rest." Once the two men were well past the hearing range of the replacements, Andy spoke with a cockiness about him. "How did I do? I know I don't have the flair of a Zach, but I thought I did a pretty good job."

Jesse's retort was appropriate. "Little flair, but most adequate."

Once away from the front, the first order of business was food. Zach ate alone refusing an offer to join his friends. Uncertain as to what they should do for Zach,

Jesse and Andy kept their distance, remained polite, but concerned.

It was another warm day and thus far, dry. Although the reserve trenches were not the height of comfort, they were considerably more desirable and much safer than the front ones. Most trenches in this sector were constructed in 1914 and were all interconnected with passage ditches. The reserve trenches served not only as the living and sleeping areas for the soldiers, they also served as the field supply and command center. The reserve areas were beehives of activity, small temporary communities in their own right made necessary by a war steeped in defensive strategy. The area served the needs of the fighting men, plus it provided a necessary respite from the constant tensions endured in the most forward positions. There were a lot worse places to be.

The evening meal was a stew of meat and potatoes, bread, butter, and coffee. If the soldiers got to the serving area soon enough, the meal was served hot, and other than reference to hot coffee, no other positive words were applied to the meal. For those who came late no complimentary adjectives were used at all. "It's nourishment, and it beats field rations," Jesse said.

A nearby sergeant chuckled. "Your description is kinder than anything I might have said. I see you boys are engineers. What division are you with?"

"No division, we're assigned to IV Corps. Just got here last night."

"I see. Better not get too comfortable then. As corps engineers you will be all over the place. At least you arrived on a quiet night."

The infantry sergeant's manner of speaking made the surrounding privates feel at ease, as well they should have. The older sergeant wore the full stripes of a battalion sergeant major; and his weathered appearance indicated experience as a combat soldier. Endearingly, others referred to him as Pop. The privates assumed he was career Army assigned to a National Army unit because of his military expertise. Without question, the sergeant's appearance and demeanor commanded respect from all in the field, particularly from drafted privates. His words were meaningful, his presence was imperious. Jesse ventured a question. "Say, sergeant, we've been wondering something, and maybe you can help us."

"I'll try."

"We're trying to figure out exactly where we are. Do you know?"

At first the experienced sergeant's reaction to the naive question was constrained amusement. His level of seriousness quickly changed, however, when he looked into the eyes of the eager to learn soldiers who were struggling to make sense of their new found predicament. The sergeant smiled as he said, "Well, we're somewhere in eastern France, called Lorraine." No one responded. "Sorry, boys, I couldn't pass that one up. No, I don't know where we are for sure." Using his finger to point, he said, "Paris is that way, Metz is the other way, and we're somewhere in between. Why? Why do you want to know? It doesn't make any difference. Even

417

if you find out exactly where you are, you'll be lost again as soon as you move. Other than command and a few Frenchies, I doubt if anyone really knows where he is, and sometimes I doubt if command really knows."

It was Jesse's turn to smile. "Since you put it that way, I guess we don't need to know."

The sergeant's voice became more serious. "If you really want to know where something important is, I'll tell you." Jesse gave an affirmative nod rather than speaking. "You boys were there last night—the front trenches. I doubt if you know it, but opposite your position last night was the mighty Hindenburg line, the strongest fortified trenches the Germans have. They have been preparing those strongholds for near twenty years. Of almost four hundred miles of German trenches, the brass believes this area is the best prepared against attack, and probably the most important trench to the German Army. For behind these trenches lies the most direct route into the heart of Germany. Yes, sir, lads, when you peer out across no-man's-land you're looking into the heart of the German military machine. If you are wise, you will take heed to what I have said. Remember this location always requires extreme caution and is no place for personal heroics. A word to the wise, you be wary up there."

His descriptive words of the German trenches, his warning, made more than a strong impression on the soldiers. His grasp of the situation, his interpretation of the significance of these exact trenches, awed them. It more than awed them, it terrified them. This sergeant, a soldier appearing incapable of fear, was speaking from the heart, from experience; and he offered concise words cloaked with warning. The privates were so taken aback by the sergeant's admonishment that they remained passively quiet, almost dumbfounded. No worthy questions followed his remarks. Instead, the benumbed group remained quiet, drank their coffee, and thought about those things that frightened men often think about. "Sorry, men," the soft spoken sergeant muttered. "I should have kept my mouth shut. I only thought it wise to forewarn you."

"No, not at all. We're appreciative," interjected Andy. "But tell us, what makes this part of the line so special? What's different here?"

Almost reluctant to supply additional information, the sergeant dissuasively asked, "Do you really want to know? You do know that I have never been on the German side to see anything first hand. What I know is mostly from scouts, aerial reconnaissance, and other bits of loose information."

"Sure we want to know!"

"The Hindenburg line is designed for defense of Germany. Out in front of their trenches lies four or five rows of barbed wire strategically placed and laced with scattered land mines. The trenches themselves are deep, reinforced with support walls, connected together by elaborate passages and underground shelters. They are well manned with infantry supported by trench mortars. The machine guns are entrenched in reinforced concrete bunkers. Field artillery positioned well behind the trenches and well camouflaged is protected by its own trench system with more concrete machine gun nests, more infantry. Between the two lines are the reserves with their own trench structure. Last I heard they had four infantry divisions in reserve, and I'm rather sure they have many more available troops if they need them because behind their reserve position lies a rest camp. Accordingly, the line is impenetrable, but we all understand better. With enough men and fire power any line can fall."

"Surely, they won't have us attack such a position. Can't we flank it?" asked a distressed private.

"You can flank any line with enough men. However, and for whatever it's worth, I don't believe we'll need to attack."

"Oh, my God. You mean they're going to attack us?"

Not hesitating at all, the sergeant replied, "No, no, that's not what I meant at all. Naturally, they will send out patrols, raiding parties, and will use diversionary attacks to test our readiness, our resolve. Remember I said the strength of their line was in defense, not offense. They would risk too much by a major attack which could leave their defensive positions exposed. On the other hand, my experience tells me that the only absolute about German Command is that you never know what they will do next. Part of their strength is how well they deceive. You can never be sure of anything over here!" The sergeant's last sentence did not set well and he recognized it. "Here I'm talking like I know something. What a joke. What I should have said was that I don't think we will attack the center of this line at this time. Reason, there is too much associated activity around here right now. Too many men coming and going. More specifically, I think more men are leaving this sector than arriving. Thus, I suspect we are preparing for another offensive, at some other location. But you never know anything for certain. Things change too fast."

Andy felt a strong need to pursue it further. "How do you know all of this?"

"Good question, son!" the sergeant quickly and humbly stated. "As I said in the beginning I don't know anything for sure. It's all guess. I suppose if I was as smart as I think I am, we would not need General Pershing, now would we. I'm just thinking out loud, boys, don't pay me any mind." His final words ended with a modest chuckle, almost of self-ridicule.

"No, sergeant, no, I didn't mean that at all. What I should have said was how did you put all of this together?" The sergeant's response was to modestly shrug his shoulders and open his hands, carefully avoiding the use of any boastful words.

Sensing the sergeant's embarrassment, Jesse imposed a diverting question. "I was wondering how our boys managed to push the Germans all the way back here. We were advised that the Germans took this area back in 1914, and the French have been trying to get it back ever since. What did we do that the French couldn't? Are Americans that good?"

The diversion worked and forced the sergeant to laugh. "I don't know about that. I doubt if we're really any better, though we are fresher. Remember, this war has been raging for four years. Lots of changes in any army which fights for that long. Plus, the area we took to get here was not the Hindenburg line. The Saint Mihiel Salient, as this area is called, is no more than a big protruding bulge in the line. I call it a big German tit, and you know how American boys like big tits." This assessment relieved all tension, evoking laughs from most, and smiles from even the most sober soldiers.

"So let me see if I've got this right," said another soldier. "American troops came to France, and in their first major offensive they licked a big German tit." Everyone appreciated this humorous expression which resulted in a rare sight—laughter near the battlefield.

"I like your wording better than mine," replied the amused sergeant. Laughter continued.

"What was it like, sergeant? You were there, weren't you?"

"Indeed I was, though I don't know if I really understood what happened, even though I was there. The captain calls it the fog of battle. Each soldier does what he needs to do, almost unaware of other things around him. You know what you did, though you can't always account for what others did, and you seldom know the overall scheme of events. That's the way I feel. They say the salient, shaped like a triangle, was more than twenty-five miles wide at its base and extended more than sixteen miles into Allied lines, and basically we took it all in seven days. No wonder we're foggy. As strange as it sounds, even though I was there, I really don't know what all happened."

"Any advice for us rookies, sarge?"

"My advice, for whatever it's worth, is keep your heads down. Pure and simple, keep your heads down. Be alert and keep your heads down. In this war there are a lot of ways to get hurt, many ways to die." The sergeant continued talking, although his thoughts were not necessarily sequential, and as though he still was preoccupied with the fog of battle concept. "I guess the fog of battle really means it's hard to see the overall picture of events. Nothing is certain in battle. Maybe someday a general will write a book and tell us what really happened out there, that is if there are any generals who really know."

His eyes shifted toward the ground, and his tone of speaking became more reflective than descriptive. He spoke from the heart again, more as a man, less as a sergeant. "The last few days have been terrible in this area we call the salient. The Germans had trenches out there, but they were not what I expected. They were not continual or as strongly fortified as they are right here, but they were better concealed, often without an opposing trench. The Germans nestled in good defensive positions, places we had trouble routing them, like hill tops and river banks. Some Germans took position in elaborate smaller trenches, like near the crest of a hill, protected by barbed-wire entanglements, multiple machine gun emplacements, and sometimes they had concrete shelters. Before we attacked we used a lot of artillery, though once we attacked you wondered if it did any good. I can tell you one thing for sure—those damned Germans know how to fight. They are mighty warriors. I can tell you another thing too. German soldiers are not reluctant to kill. Yes, sir, years of war have made them hardened warriors."

His tone shifted again, and now he sounded more like a sergeant. "A few things you can always depend on. If you're wise, you'll put these thoughts in the bank. The Germans always counterattack, and they always have reserves who come at you when you least expect them. They retreat in an orderly fashion, never in disarray, and usually they leave some troops behind to support their retreat. They know what they're doing, they're good. I will never forget..."

The sergeant was interrupted by a captain who was approaching the area shouting out the sergeant's name. "Where the hell have you been, I've been looking for you?"

"Been right here, captain, visiting with some replacements."

"Get your ass over to the colonel's dugout, he wants to see you right away."

"Yes, sir." Instead of moving immediately, as expected, the battalion sergeant lingered a few minutes. "So long, guys. Good luck out there, and remember to keep your heads down. Maybe we'll meet again." As the sergeant slowly got to his feet and walked away, his physical movements revealed a sore and exhausted body. In spite of the captain's plea for urgency, the sergeant asserted his independence and walked at his own pace; and the men watched in disbelief. A colonel had sent a captain to summon a sergeant, and the sergeant took it all in stride. One had to question, exactly who was this sergeant that had taken his time to bestow fatherly advice on new replacements?

The men from Company L. reassembled near an old French underground shelter. Found inside the shelter were uneven rows of cots supporting thin mattresses and lumpy pillows. A sufficient number of cots provided each man a single place for sleeping with additional nearby space for packs and equipment. Indeed, the sparse comforts looked heavenly to the fatigued soldiers. The men were told that they had four hours to sleep, not withstanding any unforeseen emergencies; and then, almost in a sadistic manner, the first mail call since their arrival in France was announced. "Anyone who is interested," said as if no one would be interested, "can pickup their mail outside the shelter in ten minutes." The supply lieutenant, the man in charge, seemed to enjoy that the men who wanted their mail right away would sacrifice sleep to get it.

Jesse received nine letters from Helen, and immediately read each letter in order of postmark. The correspondence provided him immeasurable pleasure. Although he got less than two hours of sleep, his decision to read all the letters at once was not regretted. Helen and baby were well, and all was fine on his home front.

Following less than six hours for eating, sleeping, and other necessities the men reassumed front-line positions. Unlike their first trench duty, this time they were there in daylight. The advantage of light provided more than an unrestricted view of a massive portion of the vast no-man's-land—it opened a mental window to the very soul of Jesse. For as he peered at the site of battles past, he harbored doubts about his own manhood, about his ability to survive it all. Surely it was this place, or others like it, where he would determine what measure of warrior he was. His destiny to personally participate in battle, to play a part in the cruelest endeavor known to mankind was virtually assured, although his own level of courage, his fate in battle, were still well beyond his level of understanding. Momentarily, the stark realization that this location might be the exact site of his death overpowered the other and lesser emotion of common fear. Although it was no more than an abstract, an activity of the mind, he was thinking about, he was sensing the ultimate fear of man—an end of life. Had he only known that he was not alone in his fears as many other men were also looking deep into their own souls. But he had no such comfort. Unquestionably, this moment and the memory of it would serve him well.

Although the vivid view of the dismal, scarred field of battle was most disconcerting, it was better than being in the trench at night as vision by flare light left too much to the imagination. Occasional rifle fire from both sides was the constant reminder that war was at hand, although no prompting was really necessary. They, the men in the trenches, fully understood that they were the constant target of enemy fire.

"Private Moore, Private Foster, down here on the double," cried a nearby voice from within the trenches. "Both of you hightail it to trench sector five and report to a sergeant in Company A. They need you now." With no inkling as to their mission, Jesse and Andy departed immediately.

The sergeant from Company A. was anxiously awaiting the arrival of the two combat engineers. "Took you long enough. Do you have your equipment with you?"

"What equipment?"

"How should I know what you need? Here's the trench map. Figure out where you'll cut and mark it, and for God's sake stay with the plan."

By now the two men were more than anxious; they were perplexed, and Jesse could no longer hold his questions. "What are you talking about? We were told to report to Company A. and nothing else. What's this map for?"

The sergeant mumbled something, and his facial expression clearly revealed his annoyance with the privates reporting to him, uninformed of task. He unfolded the map, pointed to a particular map location and spoke with a curtness. "Listen, I only have time to explain it once. This is a map of our sector. This is our location, here are the trenches, and these broken marks represent wire. You figure out where you are going to cut the wire and mark the cuts on this map. You are to cut in a zigzag manner through five rows of wire which, if done right, will allow our men to get out and back in, and so that the Krauts can't figure it all out. Remember, you will go back out and repair all the cuts as soon as our boys are back, so do it right. No mistakes. First, determine your pattern. Second, mark this map. Third, give the map back to me so that I can get the plan to the scouts. We will send out nine patrols tonight, and if any men are lost because of you, I will have your hides."

"What time do the patrols leave?"

The question further antagonized the sergeant. "You stay in the trench, look at the map, and then study the wire." He now pointed as he emphatically spoke. "See that wire right out there? We need to cut that wire so that our men can get out to scout the enemy trenches. The reason you are here, instead of back at headquarters, is so that you can see the map and the wire at the same time. You need to diagram your cuts from here, memorize where the cuts are, give the map back to me, go out under the cover of darkness and make the cuts. Then you crawl back here undetected by the enemy, and tell me about any problems, but there better not be any. Tonight you stay right here, all night, and you keep your heads down, and when I tell you it's time, you will go back out and repair the wire. Once all of us have the exit route committed to memory, we send the map back to headquarters. And then we might do the same thing tomorrow, all over again. Do you understand?"

Both responded, "Yes, sir." Jesse, while conferring with Andy, held the map as though he understood what he was doing. The sergeant departed, leaving the men to complete the preliminaries. "Kind of grumpy, wasn't he? Were you ever trained to do this?"

Andy answered with certainty. "No. I know how to cut and repair wire, but I've never put it to map before."

"I think we better just do it and pretend we know what we're doing," Jesse said, ending his sentence with a chuckle. "I wonder what the sergeant would say if I asked to borrow his wire cutters." Andy looked horrified. "Just kidding, just kidding."

The two combat engineers put their heads together and came up with a wire exit diagram they deemed adequate. Surprisingly, the map was accurate. They selected to cut two separate identical routes to better accommodate the unusually large number of patrols. Not trusting their memories, Andy made a copy of the diagram on a piece of scratch paper, and returned the completed map to the sergeant. "Just say when, and we'll get it done." The sergeant studied the diagram and his reply was an approving grunt. Once back, the two men worked out the details as to their individual positions and their method of operation. If they went over the details of the plan together once, they went over it ten times. It had to be done right. They felt up to the task.

The gray, overcast sky offered good protection for cutting wire as a cloudy night brought total darkness, no reflections. They went over the details of their plan one more time as they waited for darkness, and in less than one hour after sunset the orders to cut were issued. Separated from each other by a distance of less than twenty yards Andy cut the north passage, Jesse the south. Jesse had butterflies in his stomach as he went over the top and crawled out toward the nearest row of wire. It was a different feeling than he had expected—it was darker than he thought it would be, he was completely unable to see or hear his partner, and he felt more exposed, more vulnerable than he thought he should. His movements were deliberately slow and cautious as he crawled parallel to the first row of wire, counting the posts until he reached the determined site of his initial cut. He rolled on his back, made the first cuts taking great care to bend the wire exactly as it needed to be. The distant noise of a click made by wire cutters gave him indications of Andy's location and proof that both of them were progressing on schedule. His fear of exposure did not diminish, but stayed under control. Understanding the significance of his task, he continued to cut and place wire, always with slow, deliberate movement and extreme care. His confidence increased after a long forty minutes of successful work. With one more cutting he would complete his task, and then he could retrace his movements back to the relative safety of the trenches. Most mindful that he was alone, out of the trenches, and always at risk of exposure, he accelerated his pace of work. In his haste he prematurely cut a strand of wire that made a distinct clicking sound as it snapped back against other wire. He froze his movement, fearing the worst. Fortunately, the sound must have gone undetected as there was no enemy reaction. Now less confident he vowed to slow down, to be more careful as he made his last cuts.

Like a bolt from the blue an abrasive sound of metal against metal echoed above Jesse. Either Andy, in an unguarded moment, had accidentally banged his wire cutters against another piece of metal or someone else was out in the wire perimeter. Neither thought was comforting. Jesse was on his back, twisting and folding the last strand of wire, but the sound, and the need to identify the source of the sound, forced him to freeze in that precarious position as his eyes unsuccessfully searched for some explanation. He waited several minutes in dead silence and detected nothing, so he resumed his work. Abruptly, an explosion high in the sky was followed by a burst of bright light. Someone had fired a night flare, and the burst of bright light following total darkness instantly illuminated his exposed position. Jesse could see Andy as he moved on the ground, almost as clearly as if he were watching him in daylight. Near panic, Jesse rolled over face down and hugged the ground. Seconds later he heard American machine-gun fire originating south of where he lay. Sporadic fire from the American side continued for several minutes. Although he remained terrified that enemy eyes might already know his location, once it was dark and quiet again Jesse had little choice but to resume his task. Now he maneuvered with renewed urgency, and once he completed his work, he carefully retraced his route to the trenches, crawling as low to the ground as possible, mindful of another possible flare.

Andy was in the trench waiting for Jesse. "Get your butt in here. Are you all right?"

"Oh, I'm fine other than scared senseless. I've never seen such a bright light and I never care to see one again, especially when I'm out there instead of in here. God, what an experience! I did get it all done and checked. What about you?"

"I was mighty scared too. I didn't double check, but I was careful as I cut. It's done and done right, don't worry."

"You boys okay?" asked the sergeant as he moved nearer to get their report. "Did you get it done?"

Andy answered. "It's done and done right, but as a matter of reference it did get kind of hairy out there. Which fool shot off that flare?"

The sergeant's answer was matter of fact. "Some German fool, I assume. Which American fool made the noise that caused the German fool to send up that flare?"

A sheepish Andy had to answer. "I accidentally clanked my wire cutters against a spent shell, but I doubt if that caused them to send up a flare."

"Well, just as a matter of reference, we accidentally fired at the Germans which I suppose might have diverted their attention from you boys," the sergeant sarcastically retorted. "We're most fortunate to have so many innocent accidents all at once, don't you think? You are positive you got the exits cut and cleared, aren't you? If you didn't, I want to know it now."

"All clear, we're positive."

"Okay. Stay here and try to get some sleep. I'll notify you when it's time to put the wire back."

Later that evening the patrols went out and returned without incident. Jesse and Andy repaired the wire, also without incident. The sergeant was waiting for them when they returned. "All done?"

"All done!"

"Hell of a job, boys! At first I had my doubts but you proved me wrong. Hell of a job! Get on back there and get some food. I want both of you back here at noon. Hell of a job!"

It did not matter where the two men were located, something was always happening near the front lines. Once the Saint Mihiel Salient was declared secured, the entire area became a beehive of frenzied activity; replacements poured forward to relieve fatigued front-line soldiers, direct secure supply routes permitted needed war material to be ushered in, field kitchens and rest areas became integrated with front positions, aid stations gave way to field hospitals with adequate medical corps personnel, and engineers worked to repair war damaged infrastructure.

What few soldiers did know was that although the number of military personnel in this sector was rapidly increasing, the number of infantry soldiers was decreasing. To the experienced American warrior, presumably, another offensive was in the works. The not too distant German city of Metz, a highly fortified command center, was considered a likely military objective for the fresh Americans. If the Americans could lay siege to the city, they would be attacking Germany proper, achieving a long time Allied objective. The Germans had to consider all possibilities, and under no conditions could they allow Metz to fall.

"Change of plans," barked the Company A. infantry sergeant as he met with Privates Moore and Foster. "The patrols discovered some interesting stuff last night. Mainly, they believe the German lines are on hold and won't attack us, not right away anyway, so our boys can cut their own wire tonight. Now, that brings me to you. We need to spruce up this place a little bit, and guess who gets to do the sprucing. No, you don't need to guess, I'll just tell you. You do, and we're going to start with the trenches. I assume you noticed last night that things are in disrepair. I'm sure you noticed all the mud. Well, we need a new duckwalk in this sector and you're just the men to do it. Figure out what you need, go to the supply depot and work out the details with them. The depot is located about three hundred yards that direction, so go now, and get started on it right away. Also, secure material to build seven or eight new ladders for the deeper trenches. Be certain they're the right length, because we don't want them sticking up but they've got to be tall enough and strong enough to last. Help is on the way, should be here sometime this afternoon, and they're bringing tools with them. Now go to it. Report back to me when it's done. Remember to keep your heads down. Krauts love to shoot our engineers. That's why you boys were sent here—snipers got most of our engineers."

The duckwalk, a simple construction, was a slatted wooden walk built to prevent trench soldiers from sinking into the mud. The only complication in the construction was that they were best built on site and in daylight. The work was not difficult, merely dangerous.

In spite of the front-line location and much to the surprise of Jesse, the depot had ample material available for their use. Conditions must have radically changed during the last few days, as it would have been impossible to bring in supplies over the route they had used. Much to the dismay of Jesse the construction material had already been selected and hastily loaded on a flatbed wagon. Since no mules were available, a quartermaster lieutenant recruited several unwilling men who acquiesced under protest to push and pull the wagon across open ground to the trenches. It seemed that everyone, other than the lieutenant, understood that any slow moving, awkwardly loaded wagon would certainly be a tempting target for enemy artillery.

Sure enough, after about twenty yards of forward movement a German artillery shell exploded near the wagon. Soon thereafter a thick gray cloud formed and hovered near ground level, which warned that the cloud contained gas rather than smoke. The gaseous mixture refused to dissipate, stayed as a continuous cloud hugging the ground, and powered only by a variable breeze the cloud slowly moved directionless but following the contour of the land. The gas alarm sounded, forcing every soldier within hearing range to don a gas mask or to scurry from harm's way. The men sought outdoor shelter, preferably not in low places, as the heavier than air gas would sink and linger in low places. All nearby activity came to a halt until ever so slowly the gas cloud moved on. Eventually the all clear sounded.

Once out of physical danger the soldiers unleashed their emotional reactions. They thought from the beginning the lieutenant's order was stupid and greatly resented the enemy use of gas, especially mustard gas. Jesse removed his mask, looked with anger toward the German line and sniffed the air. He looked at Andy and spoke while shaking his head. "Do you smell that? That's mustard gas. Those bastards. They fired at us with mustard gas." He would have expressed more except a familiar voice from afar beckoned them.

"Hey, guys, wait a minute." The beleaguered voice belonged to Zach. "Are you all right, did any of that stuff get to you?"

"We're okay, no thanks to the bastard Germans. How about you?"

Zach, inquiring more out of courtesy than concern, had observed his buddies were uninjured before he asked. "I'm fine. I was over there when the shell exploded, and I saw the mist form and it looked like it came right over you, and then it sort of broke up as the cloud moved away. I watched it all from a safe distance. I saw you scramble to get your masks on. I didn't recognize you for sure until you took them off. That's when I yelled at you." Zach talked so fast and was so excited that the other two just listened without saying anything. Then Zach realized he really was not saying anything. "You guys have all the fun," he said in a teasing voice, hoping to divert their concern. "I had to sit over there and watch it all. I didn't get in on any of the fun."

"Yeah, poor you, what are you doing here anyway?" Andy responded in a harsh tone. "Last time I saw you, you bit my head off."

"I was ordered here. I just arrived with five others, we're supposed to help build duckwalks for the trenches." Before the words were out of his mouth he saw the supply wagon and put it all together. "I guess they figured you guys couldn't handle it without me."

Andy, still peeved at Zach, used his sarcastic tone. "At least it's good that you got your sense of humor back."

Zach almost looked guilty. Instead of making a flippant retort, or responding as expected, he offered a conciliatory diversion. "Let me help with this load. Where are you going with it?"

Sensing the awkwardness of the situation, Jesse intervened. "I think we ought to get this wagon under cover, and just carry the supplies by hand. It would be easier, and a lot safer, than lugging this wagon." The group agreed with the suggestion and transported the supplies by hand, continuing to curse both the Germans and the lieutenant as they worked.

That evening, while alone with Zach, Jesse used the opportunity to visit with his friend. "What's wrong buddy, something is eating at you? Did we do something to annoy you?"

"No, no, no. It's me, not you. If I thought I could explain it, I would, but I know I can't. It's something inside me."

"Try. Do you mean you're sick?"

"Not sick in the body, maybe somewhere else. I want to explain it, I just don't know how to. Do you remember the dead horse incident?" Jesse's part grin eliminated any need for a verbal answer. Once again agitated, Zach continued. "See, that's what I mean. You won't understand."

"Try me," Jesse pleaded as he straightened his facial expression.

Pausing before he resumed, he studied Jesse's face. "Okay, but if you laugh, I'm going to hit you right in the chops. The incident was funny at first, then I got to thinking. That could have been a soldier, and no one would have known or even cared. That carcass could have been me, or you, and that bothered me. Then, that sniper had us pinned down in the open. I know you remember that. Well, I was scared and I stayed scared, and it's not just one or two things that scare me, it's everything. It's everything that happens here. I'm not sure that I can handle it all."

"We all were scared, Zach. That's nothing to be ashamed of."

"Maybe, maybe not. Fear consumes you, nothing else matters when you're really scared, and it doesn't just leave you after you get out of the situation. Fear stays with you. That first night in the trenches I almost went nuts, and there was nothing I could do about it. I got so scared that I actually messed my pants. I simply could not overcome my fear, nor could I escape it. It's with me all the time. I get scared now just remembering it.

"My fear doesn't pass, it compounds. After you guys left the other day there was an incident in the trenches. There was an accidental explosion, a hand grenade I think, and it blew a guy's hand off. His shirt was shredded and you could see his wounds. He had skin hanging loose and an open wound between his chest and stomach. Blood was spurting everywhere. He died right in front of us and there was nothing anybody could do. Oh, they tried, but we knew it was useless. He was awake during it all and his expression almost made me sick. He was in real agony, but he also looked surprised and bewildered as though he didn't know what had happened. He looked like he wanted to ask a question, except that he couldn't determine what to ask. The man died right in front of us all and for no reason, no purpose. He died because he was here. It was a senseless, foolish accident that killed him.

"I can't get that image out of my mind. I shook for the next few hours because watching him made me more scared. The crazy thing is I don't know what I'm afraid of, unless I'm afraid of death. It seems to me that danger lurks everywhere on or near the battlefield and we really don't have any control over what happens. If it isn't a battle casualty, it's an accident. There is no safe zone." Zach stared at the ground the whole time he talked. Eventually he looked up at Jesse, hoping his friend might have some explanation. When Jesse said nothing, Zach continued. "I guess I'm a coward. I never thought of myself as a coward, but I think the word must fit me. Jesse, this fear is an awful thing, and I don't know what to do about it. I can't control my fear, I can't shake it."

"You're not a coward," Jesse adamantly stated. "Anybody that stays in the trenches feeling like you do is anything but a coward. You remember that. You are not a coward." Zach heard the words, but to him they were not convincing words. "Another thing, Zach, and this may be the most important of all. I'm not certain that you have any more fear than the rest of us. We're all terrified. Perhaps some of us are merely better at repressing it. Maybe we push it away, or conceal it better than you. Maybe you're more honest with yourself than most of us." It became obvious to Jesse that his words and thoughts were of little value. Zach wanted more help than Jesse knew how to give.

"In light of what you have told me perhaps you need to tell someone, but I don't know who—maybe a doctor, or a chaplain, or maybe the captain. They might be able to help." Jesse's advice fell on deaf ears. Zach had already considered such options.

"No, I don't think so. I heard some fellows talking about some men at head-quarters who either froze in battle, or ran away, I don't know which. They were taken out of the lines and given work detail. Sewn on the back of their uniforms was a yellow patch with the words coward, deserter. I know I can't handle that. Somehow I'm convinced there is only one alternative for me. I've got to live with it. Think about it. We haven't been here two weeks yet, and I'm already a mess. Only one way, I've got to deal with it."

Zach looked Jesse straight in the eyes as though he had found resolution, or at minimum, he had chosen his path of action. "I assume you understand what I have shared with you is private information, not for public consumption."

"Of course. I only wish I knew some way to help." Jesse's level of compassion was high, although he felt useless to render assistance. Was he, somehow, at fault? Had he been remiss as a buddy? What could he do to help Zach? As a friend Jesse felt like a failure.

"There is something you can do. Will you talk to Andy and explain it to him? I think if the two of you know the situation, and maybe try to understand why I'm so moody, it might help. Allow me to draw from your strength. I never want anybody else to know, just you two. Will you do that for me? Andy is such a good person, and perhaps if he understands, he might tolerate me."

Jesse found himself in the deplorable situation of agreeing with his friend's dire conclusion—he simply had to live with his fears if, in fact, it was possible to exist that way. As far as he knew the Army had made no prior provisions for such situations, although surely there were other men in similar conditions. To the best of his knowledge there was nothing he could do for Zach. "I will explain to Andy, and there is no doubt that he will support your efforts. Meanwhile we need to take one day at a time and maybe, just maybe, you will conquer the demon."

At dawn the next day the combat engineers took their turn at manning the front trenches. Zach took position between Andy and Jesse.

Clearly, something was askew, not of the ordinary. The number of American scouting patrols doubled while German patrols seemed fewer in number. During daylight hours and often in locations which easily could be observed by enemy, Allied trenches were structurally reinforced, necessarily exposing many doughboys to danger from German snipers. Whole companies of infantry would march to the woods at night, and in daylight and under danger of enemy artillery fire, they would return to the trenches. Incoming shipments of supplies to the front lines decreased in number, strategically placed artillery emplacements behind the trenches increased. Every soldier's time was utilized at maximum level either in trench duty or work detail. Field headquarters was alive with officer comings and goings, enlisted men were pushed to new levels of frenzied activities of which much seemed nonsensical or counterproductive. Adding to the confusion, many soldiers believed they were preparing to exit the area while others were convinced they were preparing to hunker down. Company officers gave no explanations if, in fact, they knew any. It was almost as if command were attempting to accomplish nothing, in order to convince the Germans they were planning something big.

In the early morning hours of September 25, every fighting man in this particular sector of the Saint Mihiel front was placed in ready combat position, either in the trenches or in reserve position. All company grade officers, and a few field officers, assumed front-line positions in the trenches alongside the men. Beginning at dark and continuing all through the night, and at considerable risk to the men, strong patrols and raiding parties were sent out to harass the front German lines and to capture prisoners for interrogation. At daybreak the Americans initiated a trench-to-trench, machine-gun firefight, and trench mortars laid siege to the enemy reserve positions. Quickly, the Germans responded. For soldiers on both sides the entire experience was nerve racking, let alone dangerous for life and limb, although the protective structure of the trenches did keep casualties to a minimum. Fortunately, no soldiers were sent over the top for direct frontal assaults.

Precisely at 7:00 p.m. long range Allied Artillery commenced firing, laying down a heavy barrage on forward German positions. Two hours later the Germans returned fire in kind. The continuous Allied bombardment lasted nine full hours, German fire ended after four hours and was less intense. At dawn Allied aircraft took to the air and dominated the overhead skies. Medical Corps and other support troops were placed in forward areas, and it seemed that all Allied forces at hand were brought to bear.

From past engagements the veteran soldiers recognized a familiar pattern to this foreboding sequence of events—heavy artillery fire followed by infantry attack. The Americans mentally prepared to leave the safety of their trenches, to venture across the dreaded no-man's-land, to participate in a deadly frontal attack on the highly fortified German trenches of the Hindenburg line. At 6:15 a.m. it looked like a go and soldiers waited for the shrilling sound of the whistle that initiated the attack. The combat engineers of Company L. were positioned in the forward trenches, dead center of the line. The troops hunkered down, waited for orders.

Then events began to change. Something was not right. Machine-gun fire slowly abated, trench mortars became silent, and rifle fire was reduced to sporadic intervals, until it too, entirely ceased. The whole battlefield became silent. The sudden absence of man-made explosive sounds following the twenty-three hours of heavy firing, created an eerie silence which prevailed throughout the entire bellicose area. No soldier escaped the silence, and no whistles blew.

"Stand down, pass the word," was the muffled order whispered throughout the trenches. "Stand down, pass the word. Stand down, pass the word," was repeatedly heard until the words became faint, eventually inaudible.

Having maintained attack formation for almost twenty-six hours, the men were exhausted, their nerves were frayed. Zach was trembling so much that he could hardly speak. "Is the attack off or delayed?" Neither Jesse or Andy answered, because they, too, were uncertain. "What the hell is going on? I'm going to peek, I've got to know."

Andy immediately grabbed Zach's arm. "No, you're not, a sniper will have your head. We have scouts and observers to do that. Stay put, we'll know something in a minute."

As though Andy was prophetic, a sergeant approached with news. "The attack is canceled. Every other man fall back to reserve position. This was no more than a diversionary demonstration to the Germans, there is no attack, we never intended to attack." Zach was told to and more than willingly fell back. Jesse and Andy were ordered to remain in position.

In a short time explanations were forthcoming. Granted the explanations were all by way of the rumor mill, but that was the common soldier's normal source of information, and more than not, the information was reasonably accurate. The forces at the Saint Mihiel Salient had participated in a diversionary demonstration and the ruse had worked. The Germans had been forced to keep a large contingent of crack forces in position at the salient to protect against a possible attack on Metz. Although German High Command believed such a bold move by the Americans would be costly, it was possible. Still uncertain about the exact nature of American strategy, and fully aware of past American boldness and aggressiveness, the Germans simply could not gamble on no attack. Having once underestimated the Americans in the Saint Mihiel offensive, they could little afford to do it again.

The diversion worked. On September 26, the Americans had mounted a major offensive to the far north between the Meuse River and the Argonne Forest. The diversionary maneuvers at Saint Mihiel had forced the Germans to keep three reserve divisions in place instead of shifting them to the north to oppose the American offensive. This three-day delay in movement of German infantry reserves played a vital role in the initial success of the American breakthrough in strongly fortified northern German lines. General Pershing had pulled a fast one.

This bold Meuse-Argonne offensive, coordinated with a simultaneous British and French offensive west of the Meuse-Argonne, proved devastating to the Germans. The simultaneous, combined Allied attack, the first in three years, was staged along a hundred mile front, and put German forces in retreat and on the defensive. German Command incorrectly had deemed the defensive positions in the Meuse-Argonne, the frontier to the German homeland, sufficiently strong to thwart any attack. The Germans expected an offensive, but not along such a wide front, and certainly not in the Meuse-Argonne area. The German High Command had underestimated the boldness of Allied Command, and specifically, the audacity of the Americans.

Significantly boosting American morale, the substantially accurate rumors continued to spread like wildfire among the men at the salient. In less than one month after the first American offensive, the war had taken a turn in favor of the Allies. Indeed, for the first time since the early months of the war, an Allied victory seemed possible. However, it was well understood that the key to any victory would only be found in the immediate success of the combined Allied offensive. The Americans needed to win the Meuse-Argonne offensive before the onset of winter.

Another American offensive, presumably against Metz, could not be ruled out, and any lasting jubilation by the boys at Saint Mihiel was tempered by this fact. One raiding party contended that during the diversionary demonstration they actually engaged German forces in the city of Metz. American Command believed the raiding party was mistaken about its location, although many who spoke with members of the party became convinced they actually had been in Metz. No matter about the exact truth concerning the raid or future offensive on Metz, real danger was in the future for anyone who believed the German Army was near collapse. Command fully understood that any future offensive against Metz would be costly to the Americans, but so would any other major offensive. No soldier was yet ready to celebrate future war events.

Neither Andy or Jesse talked much as they consumed their hot food. Eating was more for nourishment, less for pleasure. Following the meal they cleaned their mess kits, got a refill of coffee, and secured a reasonably quiet place to relax away from the crowd. Jesse sipped his drink. "Times have changed. I used to really enjoy food, now I just eat it, and hope I have some rest time. Even rest doesn't come easy. Every time I try to rest, I start itching again."

"Yeah, I'm in the same boat. I can't keep my underwear clean nor my socks dry. My uniform is filthy, and all clothing in my pack is lice infested. I hate it. I've scratched so much that my skin is raw. Surely, we're due for a rest and new uniforms. I don't know how long we've been up here, but it seems like about a year. With that said, I'm not going to complain anymore, because I'd still rather look at cooties than Germans."

The comment warranted a chuckle from an equally exhausted Jesse. "Plus, we forgot something. I know I haven't been dry in four or five days. Everything I own is soaked. I need a hot bath, clean uniform, and a nice soft bed. Maybe I should tell my woes to the captain, he might not be aware of our complaints." Another chuckle followed his words.

"Good luck. While you're there tell him about my discomforts too, will you? I can hear him now. Soldier, don't you remember your Army manual? It says to keep all clothing clean and dry while in the field. Why haven't you done that? Can't you just hear him, and the problem is he probably would wonder why you haven't done it."

The ever present sergeant located the two combat engineers resting under a tree. To their dismay he joined them. "I have another job for you guys." Neither responded nor objected, both thinking they would be assigned the task regardless of what they said. They were correct. "After you finish your little siesta, and as of now it's officially over, you've got work to do. First, you need to study this map. I've marked a wooded area that separates our position from the boys in the 2nd Division. This area was checked out last week, so I doubt if there is anything in there that shouldn't be there, but I want you two to confirm such."

"What do you mean by anything? Germans or obstacles?" Andy asked.

"Either, both, I mean anything," snapped the sergeant. "The entire area has taken some heavy artillery hits, and I don't know how bad this particular area is messed up. There is a trail clearly marked on the map here that needs to stay clear. We might need to move troops through there tomorrow. Check it out. If there is any wire, or anything else for that matter, clean it up, get it out of the way. The trail has got to be clear. I don't think there is any real concern, but look for any signs of snipers, past or present. Look for any indications that Germans might still be in the woods. Lieutenant says that if we send men through there tomorrow, he wants clear access. Got that? Be back by dark."

Andy was agitated. "I don't like his tone. I'd feel better if we had a couple of infantry boys with us. Do you think he really believes there might be Germans in there, or is he keeping us on our toes?"

"Keeping us on our toes, I hope."

The woods, approximately twenty acres in size, appeared similar to most other small forests in Lorraine. The old, large trees provided a protective canopy which reduced light and restrained undergrowth. Having been used by the locals for years, the trails were well defined. The natural beauty found within such wooded areas of Lorraine was worthy of note, and had it been another place, another time, Jesse and Andy surely would have admired it.

Although they faced a dreaded task, their first glance into the woods hinted at good news. The trail looked passable, mostly free from encumbrance. "This doesn't look so bad," expressed a relieved Andy. "How do we want to do this?"

"How about we try something. I'm not anxious to wander in the woods down an open trail," Jesse reluctantly confessed. "So let's walk opposite sides of the trail, say maybe each of us about twenty feet or so back into the woods, but still where we are able to see the trail. If we need to clear an area we both come up and clear it, cut the wire or whatever, and then return to our walking pattern. What about it? Good idea or is it foolish? Am I too concerned about safety?"

"Impossible to be too concerned. My only qualm is can we get it done in time? As you can tell I'm not sure about much, other than I want out of these woods by dark, and dark in here will be well before dark in the open. Do you think we have enough time?"

Jesse released another chuckle. "We're a fine pair, aren't we? I'm afraid of Germans, and you're afraid of the dark. Good thing the sergeant can't hear us now. Let's try it my way, and if we see we're running short of time, we'll finish by walking the trail."

Surprisingly, the two men made unimpeded progress, and in less than one hour they had checked and cleared most of the trail. Generally, the trail was unobstructed, other than easily removable nuisance litter. Just as they were about to prematurely proclaim the task completed, they saw a major obstacle—multiple strands of wire strewn across the path. The older, rusted barbed wire had been deliberately placed across the trail, with the ends wrapped around a few trees instead of stretched and attached to posts. Obviously, someone had done a hasty job of stringing wire, designed more to slow men rather than to stop them. Removing the wire and debris would not be difficult, merely time consuming. Somewhat disconcerting, it was impossible to identify which side had placed the wire across the trail. It might be a German trap.

"Wouldn't you know it? I knew it was too good to be true. We need..." Andy's words were interrupted by not too distant machine-gun fire. Soon, additional rifle fire erupted from the same vicinity. It sounded as though there was a limited firefight near the edge of the woods, presumably in the area held by the 2nd Division. "I don't like this at all. Let's get this stuff cleared, and get the hell out of here."

Jesse was anxious too. "Good idea. You start cutting and clearing while I look ahead. I want to make sure this is the last barrier. I'll be right back." Jesse cautiously advanced, remaining well off the trail, as Andy began to remove the wire. Within minutes Jesse was out of Andy's sight.

Jesse heard a shot from a Mauser rifle that sounded nearby, and instinctively dove to the ground landing behind a large fallen tree trunk. While in flight he heard another shot and thought he felt a slight impact on his left foot. Believing he had been shot, although feeling no pain, he looked at his foot expecting to see blood or something worse. He saw no blood, but remained unconvinced he was injury free. Mindful that any body movement whatsoever might reveal his location, he froze. A third rifle shot was fired and landed nearby. He was under sniper fire. Convinced he was reasonably well protected, he nudged closer to the large, downed tree trunk and waited until he could figure out what to do. As he lay in fear he spotted a curious object on the nearby ground and, startlingly, he realized it was the heel from his shoe. The sniper's second shot had separated the heel from his shoe, presumably as he dived for safety. His quick reaction to the sound of the first shot probably had saved his life.

Momentarily safe, Jesse's concern turned to the welfare of his friend, but since he was concealed so low to the ground he had no vantage point to determine

Andy's location. He could not cry out as any sound might jeopardize his own well being. His predicament left him utterly powerless to locate or help Andy. He became distraught as his mind conjured up different images. If Andy needed medical assistance, Jesse could not render it. He could do nothing but wait in concealment for the safety of nightfall. Perhaps, hopefully, Andy was employing the same tactic. Convinced he had no other options, Jesse reluctantly waited in the same position without movement or sound; and all during the prolonged ordeal, he could not perceive any activity from Andy's location, nor could he determine the sniper's position. Thus, cloaked in fear and uncertainty, he followed his only option—he waited. As he waited he listened to the continuing, distant sporadic small arms fire indicating the nearby firefight was still in progress.

Time seemed to slow down during Jesse's wait for darkness, his best opportunity to escape the clutches of the sniper. Only minutes of daylight remained in the dense forest. He studied the ground near him as he planned his exit route in the dark. Suddenly, he realized that the slope of the land near him might serve to his advantage. If he could crawl undetected following the full length of the tree trunk to a nearby ravine, he might have a better position from which to locate the sniper. Jesse agonized over the wisdom of the option as he considered the possible consequences. No doubt it was a calculated gamble, but one he felt compelled to take. He carefully crawled toward the ravine with rifle in hand. Undetected, he made it to the bank of the shallow ravine. He quietly and gracefully lowered his body to the deepest and darkest part of the terrain, and then slowly crawled about twenty feet, following the shallow embankment until he found a new place of concealment which also allowed him to observe. Still Jesse could not locate Andy, and in vain, he methodically searched the tree tops for the sniper. He saw nothing, and darkness was quickly approaching.

Just as Jesse was about to abandon the visual search, he heard a noise, the sound of a lowered rope ladder banging against a tree. During training he had made and used such rope ladders. He knew the sound. He heard the voices of two men that sounded more like gibberish to him than an intelligible language, then he saw a German soldier using the rope ladder to descend a tree. With darkness so near and light so precious, it was only prudent for Jesse to instinctively react. He took aim at the German on the ladder and just before he pulled the trigger he saw another German begin his exit from the same tree. Jesse had no choice but to fire immediately. The German's body jerked and fell from the ladder, which gave evidence of a clean, accurate shot. As quickly as he could, he bolted his rifle, took aim, and fired at the other man. The second German's top half was almost completely back in the tree shelter before the bullet was fired, but a brief pause in the German's movement gave reason to suspect that he also was hit. However, Jesse was left not knowing the exact condition of the second German, or if in fact, he had hit both snipers. "God forbid," he muttered as it crossed his mind that there could be a third sniper in the same tree now taking aim on him. Since Jesse's position was now revealed, he had no choice but again to seek cover low to the ground, and to hastily retreat under the protection of impending darkness.

The forest became dark, it was time to go. The open path was still too risky, forcing Jesse to move parallel to the trail through the undergrowth and in the direction of Andy's last known whereabouts. Fearing that Andy might not know who was approaching, Jesse softly called his name. "Andy, Andy Foster. It's Jesse." There was no answer. Then in desperation and in disregard to his own safety, Jesse shouted. "Andy, Andy Foster, where are you? Are you hurt? Andy! Andy." Again, there was no reply. Jesse's search became frenzied. In spite of his calls and desperate search in somewhat open area, Andy was no where to be found. Jesse searched near the wire entanglements, despairingly clinging to the hope he could find his lost, possibly injured, friend. But total darkness had descended and he could see nothing when abruptly he stepped on an object. He had found Andy's wire cutters. "Andy. Andy. Where are you?" Jesse continued his relentless search with no success. Andy was not to be found, and Jesse could only wonder if his friend were nearby in need of help. What was Jesse to do, other than not give up, dark or not? Time passed, hope faded, but Jesse clung to the thought that if he would only look harder, there was an outside chance he would locate his friend. For the better part of an hour Jesse blindly searched, continuing to call to his friend until a bleak realization finally penetrated his whole being. His efforts were to no avail. Andy could not be found.

Uncertain of the exact procedure he should follow after arrival at camp, the dejected doughboy located the sergeant who had sent them on the mission. Before Jesse could speak, the sergeant yelled at him. "Where the hell have you been? We've been looking all over for you. Your outfit pulled out over an hour ago. You're reassigned. You guys follow this road and catch up with them. Where's your buddy?"

Jesse's answer revealed his desperation. "I don't know. We got pinned down by a sniper and got separated. I don't know if he got out, if he got hit, or what. I looked and couldn't find him. I don't know where he is. I was hoping that you might know."

"Calm down. There's nothing we can do about it now. He probably got out. Some men from the 22nd were looking for you earlier, and they didn't say anything about looking for Foster. He probably had them looking for you. You better leave at once if you're going to catch your unit. Is the trail clear, or not?"

Jesse explained to the sergeant about the wire obstacle. The sergeant was not very pleased, and was not sympathetic to Jesse's concern about Andy. The sergeant was abrupt. "Stop worrying about him. Odds are he pulled out with your unit.

Now you get going."

"Sergeant, I don't think I better. I need to wait for daylight and go back in the woods, just to be sure."

"Like hell you will! Private, you don't have a choice. Your orders are to leave now and catch up with your unit."

"No, sir, I can't do that."

The open defiance, regardless of its noble intent, did not sit well with the sergeant. "This is a direct order, there is no discussion period. I will say it one more time. You are to immediately join your unit. There is nothing that you can do here. Tomorrow, I'll go in and take a look, and if he's there I'll find him, but I know it's a waste of time. I tell you he's with your outfit. Go!"

The sergeant's harsh words, his assertive actions weighed heavily on the despondent soldier. Still defiant, Jesse remained motionless until, in a particular moment, he seemed to find resignation. He became less defiant, almost reticent, as though he finally understood the sergeant might be correct. "Yes, sir," Jesse answered forlornly. "I understand. One way or another, Andy is gone."

CHAPTER 24

MUSTARD GAS

Y ou look like you need a rest. You must have been out there a long time, huh?"

Jesse appreciated the uncommon expression of concern denoted in the quartermaster sergeant's question. His exaggerated answer, "It seems like a lifetime," was expressed not to be factual as much as it was to provide the sergeant with useful information. The sergeant's official task was to replace needed soldiering gear for men in the field and his routine questions served that end. Nonetheless, the combat engineer found it personally rewarding that in the midst of war there were still a few fellow soldiers who found time to express humanitarian concern. In some small way the unsolicited concern signified a true camaraderie of sorts. "I guess when I think about it in terms of days, it really hasn't been all that long. I've been over here a little more than a month, not quite four weeks on the front."

"In terms of front-line duty that's a long time all right. Is this your first extended rest?"

"Yes."

"Well, enjoy it, you've earned it. What can I get you?"

"Actually a bunch of things, if you have them. Clothing wise, I need replacement shoes, socks, flannel shirt, and drawers. I was told to trade this jacket in for a heavy trench coat; plus, I need a new poncho. It got messed up in the wire. Toilet items, I need a cake of soap, toothpaste, and towel."

"Before you go any further, you have been deloused have you not?"

"Yes, sir, just came from there. I'm lice free for the first time since arriving," he answered with considerable satisfaction.

"Clothes and everything have been disinfected, right?"

"Affirmative."

"Then you're in business, you've done what you were supposed to do, and we've got what you need. Allow me to look and estimate your proper sizes."

"No need, I know my sizes. I wear size eight and one-half medium width shoes and..."

"Not so fast," interrupted the sergeant. "I need to determine your sizes, not you. They've got to be the right fit. A lot of boys just sound off the sizes they wore before the war, not realizing their sizes might have changed. You do know that marching with full packs can change your shoe size, or for that matter, some men just change in dimensions with time." The sergeant meticulously measured width and length of Jesse's feet, muttered "Aha," and proceeded to measure his waist and chest. "Just as I suspected, your shoes are size nine, wide, your poncho and coat, large, and I would guess medium drawers. We only have wool drawers, no cotton. Hope that's okay. Do you know the proper way to break in these shoes?"

Jesse regarded the question as meaningless, borderline condescending, but the sergeant had asked so he was going to answer. "I suppose you put them on and wear them," he flippantly retorted.

"No, no, no. What kind of training sergeant did you have? Do that over here and you'll regret it in a big way. Just wearing them is a big mistake, you've got to take proper care of the feet. Shoes need to be properly broken in." As the sergeant imparted his special knowledge he spoke with an instructional pride of concern, conveying his intent to be helpful rather than bossy. "Break them in this way: alternate wearing them with wearing of your old shoes and wear the new ones for seven or eight hours a day, for as many days as possible. While wearing your new shoes stand in about two and one-half inches of water for five minutes or until the leather is thoroughly pliable and moist. Let the shoes dry on your feet, forming to the irregularities of your feet. Then walk a ways. Use these shoe stretchers, see the adjustable knobs, to stretch any part of the shoe that puts pressure anywhere on your foot. Afterwards, rub a small amount of Neat's foot oil into the leather which will prevent hardening and cracking. Then, waterproof them. Shine them every-day, using your finger to rub in the polish. Always wear woolen socks, never cotton, with new shoes. If your feet get tender, use foot powder daily. I have a little kit for you that has everything you need. Bring the stretchers back when you're done. Follow my directions and you'll save yourself hours and hours of agony. Got that?"

Struck by the sergeant's sincerity and the details of his instructions, Jesse's answer was more of a grunting nod than a spoken word.

"Now, this is all you asked for. Need anything else? What about head cover?"

"No, that's all I need, thank you. I do appreciate the advice."

"Remember, keep your feet dry, and good luck out there. Next."

The newly constructed American rest-camps were unlike any other Army camps.

Necessitated by soldiers stationed in the field for long periods of time, they were by design intended to be different. The life of a soldier in the trenches presented both physical and psychological challenges, as this grueling war showed time and time again that prolonged combat could destroy mind as well as body. As a late comer to the war the U.S. Military benefited from the experience of other belligerents, and upon the advice of their allies, the U.S. Army adequately provided a place for weary soldiers to rest. The establishment of such camps was proving to be a wise decision.

Although the encampments were officially designated rest-camps, no American dared use the term rest-camp. The doughboys had developed their own special language to describe the unique conditions of war, and in doughboy slang, rest-camp meant battlefield cemetery, going west meant going home dead. Subsequently, the Army changed the name of their rest-camps to R & R facilities, and since most of them were situated west of the trenches, they were described by number rather than direction.

The location of Jesse's camp for rest and recuperation was situated less than one mile southeast of Saint Mihiel, on land occupied by the enemy less than five weeks past. This camp was so recently constructed that few combat soldiers had yet arrived, although many more were expected in the near future. This somewhat less crowded facility suited Jesse fine. He was assigned bunk 24 in tent A, one of the twelve oversized barracks tents. With all four sides enclosed the massive tents contained multiple rows of individual cots, and provided shelter for more than one hundred men. Kitchens provided three hot meals a day, and food was served in a mess tent with tables and chairs. A nearby commissary was a virtual supermarket of snacks and personal items at bargain prices for all military personnel. The quartermaster supply center and a reading center were open twelve hours a day. Doughgirls, female civilian volunteers, doling out free coffee, donuts, and cigarettes twenty-four hours a day gave witness that the Y.M.C.A., Red Cross, and other support services were already in place. A small infirmary provided medicine and medical assistance. Military police patrolled the immediate area, infantry protected the surrounding countryside. Perhaps best of all was the standing order for combat soldiers assigned to rest and recuperation area, Number 16, Saint Mihiel—no guard duty, no kitchen duty, and no responsibilities other than to rest the body and ease the mind.

On Thursday, October 10, no mail was posted for Private Moore, so he wandered about camp looking for, but not expecting to find, a suitable thinking place without others nearby. As if it were an act of providence, he sighted a majestic, giant oak tree standing alone in a somewhat deserted, open area near the southern perimeter of camp. Jesse liked this location where an old oak defiantly stood erect and undamaged as though the weapons of war had dared not touch it. Its thick, tall trunk ably supported a crown of strong branches and golden-hued leaves. Jesse had found his place to think.

The summer heat had abruptly departed. The daylight hours were fewer, the air was cooler, and the fall sun was now the best source of outside heat. He sat under the tree positioned so that the oak's thick trunk could shelter him from the cooler, moving air. The low-lying sun permitted the tree to cast a dark elongated shadow, distorting its true dimension. In the distance the uneven ground presented tenebrous patches of coalesced light, giving even a greater distortion. Oh what a glorious place he had found.

Lo and behold as Jesse lifted his eyes he saw a lad of five or six years of age standing in the open ground watching him sit under the tree. The lad squinted from the sun's glare as he stood with his hands on his hips and his right leg crossed the left between the knee and ankle with the toe of the shoe on the ground. Jesse wondered how the boy maintained his balance. Each curiously looked at the other without benefit of words. The lad, in his unnatural pose, and with his mildly aggressive invasion of Jesse's space, and with his seemingly insatiable curiosity, so reminded Jesse of his younger brother that Jesse continued to stare at him instead of conversing with the lad as he normally would have done.

The lad placed his opened hand upward and moved his entire arm to wave. "Hello, to American man," he shouted in his broken English.

Jesse raised his hand and returned the salutation. "Hello, French boy." He then motioned for the boy to come closer, but the youngster was naturally reluctant to approach any stranger, let alone an American soldier. "Hello, French boy, please come here for me to meet you." The boy indicated his lack of understanding by shrugging his shoulders while he stayed positioned where he was. Jesse had such a quandary. Did he dare approach the boy, or should he wait for the lad's curiosity to take hold? Hoping to entice the boy, Jesse devised a ploy and held a chocolate bar in the air and announced, "Chocolate bar. Chocolate bar for you."

The enticement worked and the lad scampered over to Jesse. "Chocolate bar, yes." Jesse handed the candy bar to the lad. "Thank you, American. Chocolate, thank you." He sat on the ground next to Jesse, immediately unwrapped the bar, and slowly ate it savoring every bite. Watching the lad consume the chocolate bar was such a delight for Jesse that once the lad finished eating it, Jesse offered him his last remaining candy bar. He was convinced the lad would enjoy it more than he would. Jesse was correct and the French boy followed the identical procedure as he consumed the second chocolate bar.

Most likely the French lad had led an austere life with limited opportunities to acquire such simple items as candy. Jesse first pointed to the boy and then to the tree as he spoke, clearly pronouncing each word as though it would help the boy understand English. "You stay here, and you wait. I will be back. You stay here."

The boy shrugged his shoulders and answered in French, and of course, Jesse did not understand. "No, you stay here. I will be right back." Jesse left for the camp, and when he returned ten minutes later, he found the French boy gone. Jesse was smitten with disappointment. Here Jesse was alone again but instead of appreciating his solitude he now lamented the absence of his new French friend. Because of his failure to properly communicate with the lad, he had botched a grand opportunity.

A few minutes into his reminiscences he was taken by surprise again. This time three people, two women and the young boy, were rapidly walking toward him. One woman held the boy's hand while the second, older woman walked a few steps behind both of them, and not one of the three sported a pleased expression. Assuming he was about to be chastised for having given candy to the young lad, Jesse prepared himself for a French tongue-lashing. Jesse humbly stood motionless near the tree, smiled at the boy, and issued the only proper greeting that came to mind. "Good day, folks."

On closer view the two women appeared more determined, less displeased, which offered immeasurable relief to Jesse. The younger of the two women extended her open hand to Jesse, addressing him in English but with a heavy accent. "Hello, nice American soldier. You are most kind to my son with chocolate. He speaks no English, and wants to say thank you to you. Thank you from him and from me. These times we see little kindness. Kindness is a good thing. You are kind. We like Americans and you are first American we know." She vigorously shook Jesse's hand, and with her other hand she handed him a small bundle wrapped in what appeared to be a lightweight cotton gauze. "Please, our gratitude you take this cheese. How do you say in English, ah, milk from farm animal, like sheep with, ah, short tail? Maybe, go cheese?"

Jesse hesitated before it finally dawned on him what she had said. "Goat cheese," he proclaimed.

"Ah, goat cheese."

He held the bundle to his nose, and quickly withdrew it. Smiling, he added, "Most certainly, goat cheese."

"You keep it, eat it, it is good cheese. We make it here. It is most good cheese."

"I love goat cheese, but you need not give me anything. I like your son, and he was polite to an American stranger. He's the one who deserves a reward, not me."

"Yes, he is good boy, and you are kind man. Please accept cheese, from me, my son, and my mother." Jesse looked at the older woman, and she granted him a large, toothless smile. She said something in French and immediately extended her hand forward. She too wanted to shake Jesse's hand, to show she also approved. Jesse could not help but to be moved by the friendly gestures of two French women and one young boy, all looking at him with big smiles, and in their own way trying to tell him that he was appreciated. Surely, they had less, had suffered more than he, but were willing to share what they had.

"I will accept the cheese on one condition."

"Condition? What does condition mean?"

Jesse loved to hear her speak. He knew nothing about the French language or accents, although he appreciated her attempting to speak English, and was fascinated by her pronunciation. He wanted to communicate. "This is condition," he replied as he reached in his pocket to pull out twelve chocolate bars which he had bought at the Red Cross canteen specifically for the French lad. He handed the chocolates to the boy. "I will accept cheese if he will accept chocolate. That is condition. Okay?"

"No, no. This is too much. You eat chocolate and cheese."

"No, the condition is, I will accept the cheese if you folks will accept the chocolate. It's an old American custom—chocolate for cheese." Jesse extended his hand, first shook the boy's hand, next the mother's hand, then the grandmother's hand. "Chocolate for cheese is fair exchange."

Following a brief discussion among themselves they graciously accepted. "Thank you, Mister American soldier. We accept condition." Their contented facial expressions made one think the foursome had forged a major business transaction. As though the three had other urgent business at hand they were preparing to depart when the mother turned toward Jesse and spoke in a stern voice. "You be very careful. It is dangerous place. Germans still here in Saint Mihiel. Danger for kind American." She gave no further explanation, but clearly, she had issued a warning to her newly befriended American soldier.

The French trio departed, and as they walked away the young boy, holding his mother's hand with one hand while using the other hand to contain the stack of chocolates against his body, turned, smiled, and shouted, "Good-bye, American soldier."

Jesse gave a huge, full arm wave. "Good-bye, French friends. Thanks again for the cheese."

In spite of Jesse's earlier proclamation, Jesse ate goat cheese for the first time that evening. Much to his delight the cheese was better than good, it was delicious. In retrospect, he was pleased with his experience that day. Just as the three had very well represented the French people, he believed he had well represented Americans. He hoped so. Before he retired that night, Jesse spoke aloud to himself. "I've got to remember the details. The folks back home will get quite a ha-ha from the whole story. Milk from sheep with short tail. Go cheese."

Shortly after midnight, all soldiers in camp were awakened by sounds of a loud explosion followed by rifle fire. The sounds were in close proximity to the camp, if not in the camp itself, and seemed to be getting closer with every passing minute.

All American soldiers in camp were ordered on alert and to make preparations for a possible enemy raid. Somehow a numerically large German raiding party had entered the city of Saint Mihiel, had blown up a French ammunition dump, and had exchanged gunfire with French forces. Both the French and American forces had been caught off guard by the German engagement. Sporadic rifle fire continued throughout the night, although no Germans were believed to have entered the American held area, nor were there any direct attacks on American positions. Finally, an all clear was issued at dawn, and American troops stood down. Needless to say, it was most troublesome to the Americans that the enemy had penetrated a secure area, conducted a raid, and managed to escape with only light casualties. Apparently, there was no such thing as a secure safe-zone in the Saint Mihiel Salient. Perhaps safe-zone was a misnomer anywhere in France.

Three days of almost total rest at the Saint Mihiel R & R camp ended all too soon for Jesse, although surprisingly his youthful body seemed to be rejuvenated. Two squads comprised of twenty-six privates, one corporal, and one captain all from the 22nd Engineers were ordered to assemble and prepare to move out. They crossed to the west bank of the Meuse River and joined a huge northward advancing column extending in both directions as far as the eye could see. West and parallel to the marching column was a prodigious but slower moving supply line headed in the same direction, indicating that something of major proportions was in the making. Rumor had it that the advancing soldiers were replacements for the beleaguered troops leading the attack on the Meuse-Argonne front, and the supplies were preparations for another major offensive.

Private Moore really did not expect to be informed of his mission as secrecy was the military way. What truly disappointed him was that he would leave the Saint Mihiel area, possibly for a far distant zone, without word from his Army buddies, Zach and Andy. The whereabouts and well-being of both men remained a troubling mystery to Jesse, and would continue to be troubling until he learned of their fate. Then and there Jesse made an unusual commitment, a solemn promise to himself. In the future he intended to be a good buddy in arms, to work hard, and to cooperate with the other men. What he did not intend to do was to become emotionally attached to any of his fellow soldiers. Because of recent past experiences, he had determined close battlefield friendships were unwise, not suitable for his own well-being.

Twenty miles north of Saint Mihiel the two squads of combat engineers detached from the main column and linked up with French units working on rail repair along a narrow-gauge track of light railway. The Americans really served as observers more than workers. The captain explained. "You are looking at the railway which made it possible for the French to hold Verdun in 1916. For eleven months they held out against German attack and this railroad line was the major source of French supplies. The supply line is every bit as important to any army as is its infantry. Supply lines must be kept open. Our mission is to link up with the American front in the north, not as infantry but as combat engineers to assist in the effort to keep the supply lines open. One source of supply transport is this narrow-gauge rail. It's the only type of railway in the area. So, you watch the French, and learn. We may need to repair tracks like this. The only other possible supply route is use of the existing roads. We may need to rebuild some old roads, repair some, or find alternate routes. Keep your eyes open and learn all you can. The more you know about rail lines, roads, ditches, and all the other components of a supply route, the better off we will be. We are a team, and we must work together." The captain paused in his lecture long enough to take a deep breath. "That, in a nutshell, is our mission. Any questions?"

No one knew how to respond. Their exact mission still was unclear but they knew this explanation was all they were going to get. Sensing the men's uneasiness the captain continued to explain but with less of a lecturing tone. "We will not be part of the primary attack force, but we will be right behind them. We'll be between the fighting and the reserve positions. Our job is to closely follow the forward lines and make sure that supply lines remain open. Needless to say, this is dangerous work. As bad as we want the lines open, the Germans want them destroyed. I'm not sure what we will encounter, other than I'm sure we will encounter German resistance, one way or another."

Second in command, Corporal Adams, openly expressed his concern. "We're not doing this alone are we? I mean it takes more than 28 men to keep supply lines open."

"Heavens no, corporal. There are units like us all over the place. We're just one small spoke in one very big wheel. However, that doesn't take away from our importance. Our job is critical."

"I don't mean to push the point, but what can we really do?" inquired the unsatisfied corporal.

The captain's expression was almost as though he was about to fess up to withholding information. "Before the war I was an engineer, I used to build bridges. Now I'm just like you, I'm a combat engineer. I do what they tell me to do when they tell me to do it. Command wants us to make assessments about rail lines, roads, bridges, or anything else that needs to be done in order to establish supply lines. It's just that simple. We are the assessment team. A unit from the signal corps will be close behind us. They will run telephone wire, thus linking us with headquarters. We're supposed to have infantry protection whenever we need it. I really don't think our mission is all that bad, considering other alternatives. We'll just do our job"

By any measure their mission would be difficult, made more difficult because the two squads of combat engineers were not attached to any particular American unit. In short, they were on their own. They pitched their tents and slept where they stopped, ate what and where they could, and were accountable more to each other than to a larger unit. If other units were nearby, the engineers could avail themselves of the conveniences, but they could not totally count on others for supplies and support. They were expected to be self-sustaining when necessary. The two squads were totally officer dependent, and the captain was still an unknown entity leading an unclear mission. His behavior was that of a demure man, but not a detached man. So far he seemed fair, reasonable. Certainly, he was knowledgeable, and convincingly his actions resembled that of a man in the military know.

Saturday, October 12, was a full day of forced march. That night the squads slept in a dilapidated outbuilding, somewhere south and west of Verdun. No open fires were allowed which meant more cold food for the hungry men. Adding to their misery a late evening thunderstorm dropped over an inch of rain and an Arctic front ushered in a strong cold air mass resulting in a temperature drop of thirty degrees. The cooler air was certainly fresher, if not outright frigid, for soldiers accustomed to weeks of heat; but the real downside was that rain soaked ground made rapid marching even more difficult. It seemed that most good happenings had a negative tradeoff, although by now the soldiers were accustomed to hardships, and few complaints were heard as they pushed forward. By noon they reached their destination and made contact with an infantry company from the 1st Division. They were where they needed to be—directly behind the forward assault forces. Command representatives and a squad of signal corps troops were already at location waiting for their arrival.

The captain met with command. The two squads of combat engineers, desiring an update on the war from the men in the trenches, attempted to amicably communicate with the battle weary men of the 1st Division. Somewhat surprisingly, the fatigued warriors from the 1st seemed reluctant to share their experiences. The infantrymen had just witnessed the ugly face of war and they had not yet had time, nor the inclination, to understand what they had just endured, let alone talk about it. The engineers understood, and quickly backed off with their questions. Temporarily, the engineers seemingly had lost their sensitivity to men returning from hand to hand combat and, if from nothing else, they should have known better from their own experiences. Instead of looking elsewhere for an update of war news, they remained together, ate their first hot meal in two days, sat around the fire drinking hot coffee and waited for orders.

Jesse noticed a sergeant exiting the command center tent who seemed to be heading toward them. It created great delight when Jesse recognized him as the same battalion sergeant major, the one they called Pop, who had visited with them when they were about to enter the trenches at the Saint Mihiel front. "Hello, boys. I was watching and saw what happened. Sorry for the cool reception. Those boys from the 1st just got back here about an hour before you arrived, and they have had one wicked, tough week. I'm sure they didn't intend to be so harsh." He looked directly at Jesse and said, "Hello, soldier, do you know where you are yet?"

Jesse was gratified that the sergeant remembered him. "Yes, sir, I do. Paris is that way, Metz is the other way, and I'm somewhere north of in between."

The sergeant smiled. "I'd say that's pretty good. You're a fast learner. By chance, you're not the engineers who are assigned to scout the supply line, are you?"

"Yes, how did you know?"

"Well, it's a small world. I'm going with you guys, at least for a few days. That's great, I like working with engineers. Say, where is your buddy, the doubting Thomas, the one with the good questions?"

Jesse's usually gentle face distorted to a look of agonizing sadness as he reluctantly told the sergeant the story of Andy's disappearance in the woods. The spellbinding story, made more intriguing by the emotional telling, demanded attention and interest even from those who had not personally known Andy. For some reason war stories fascinated most soldiers and, ironically, the telling of the story seemed to help Jesse purge his feelings of guilt. With full emotional composure Jesse made a final optimistic statement which struck a strange chord to those listening, for it was incongruous with the forlornness of the story. "Not to worry, sergeant, I suspect that Andy found his way out. He's most likely out there somewhere running around worrying about me."

"I hope so," was all the sergeant could say in response.

"What's up, Pop? Do you know why we're here, what's going on? You were right on target last time," Jesse asked in an effort to divert attention elsewhere. "This all looks like a big operation."

Almost as though the sergeant knew Jesse's intentions, he chuckled and then started talking to the group. "Big is an understatement. This is the battle we've been waiting for, the battle we Americans have got to win. Over 600,000 American boys are fighting this one, and before the month is over, the number will be over 1,000,000. As fast as they can get our boys over here they are sending them up here. That's why you guys are here. It takes a lot of effort to supply and keep that many men in the field. Service of Supply claims they can do it. There are no real railways in this area, no water routes, so we need to land transport all the supplies. Our mission is to lay out one of those land routes.

"Know it or not you combat engineers are in real demand, the men of the hour. Every division wants more of you without enough of you to go around. If we win this battle we infantry and the artillery boys will get all the credit, but let me assure you, we all know a lot is on your shoulders. Do it right and you are our heroes."

Once again, Pop, the battalion sergeant major, commanded such respect that all the soldiers within hearing range intently listened to his every word. Whether Pop was a visionary or merely a man-in-the-know made no real difference. He knew things, he put things together, he somehow uniquely grasped the whole picture. Although he spoke in a subdued tone, his words created excitement in the imagination of those who listened. Akin to a classroom situation, a question was shouted by an eager to learn, unidentified combat engineer from the back of the group. "Why is this battle so important?"

The sergeant did not hesitate. "Command calls it the Meuse-Argonne Campaign, because we're fighting between the Argonne Forest and the Meuse River. The whole area is a German stronghold, one they've got to hold at all costs. At the northern tip, where the forest and the river meet is the city of Sedan. Sedan is a critical rail center for movement of supplies to Fritz. If we take the area, the Germans can't supply any of their troops west of there, and that is where most of their troops are. If we win this battle, we have broken their main supply line. In essence, we will have broken their back, and then we will take the war into Germany itself. If we win this battle, and win it before deep winter sets in, the war might be over. If we don't win before winter, we'll be here another year, at best. Yes, sir, boys, we've got Fritz on the run, and there is a slight chance the war might end before long. Think of that—home by Christmas." He paused in his speaking and unleashed a huge smile. "Anyway, that's why I think this battle is so important. Home by Christmas, sure sounds good to my ears." All could tell the sergeant was finished with his insightful dissertation, although no one else spoke fearing their questions might preempt or prevent more insightful expressions from the sergeant. Somehow his words had lifted morale, had added purpose to their mission, and his listeners were more than eager for more expressions. But now his thoughts had shifted, he was ready to relax a bit. Extending his cup, he politely asked the private nearest the fire, "Any of that coffee left?"

Sensing an increase in prestige from simply knowing the sergeant, Jesse asked another question hoping to reenergize the sergeant's mind. "Wonder what is taking the captain so long."

The sergeant gave a direct, factual answer. "He'll be a while, they need to work out the logistics. If I was you, I wouldn't be in any hurry. Right now is about as good as it's going to be for awhile. Relax, it's a long, hard road ahead." Jesse took the advice.

Two more hours passed and the captain still had not returned. While the men were relaxing, patiently waiting for orders, a young infantry lieutenant joined the group and sat next to the sergeant. Believing the lieutenant was about to brief the sergeant, the anxious men from the two squads conspicuously gathered within hearing range. "Here is your map," the lieutenant said curtly. "Stay in the woods, near the edge, but always stay in the woods except when the captain orders you out. Don't forget that although we recently secured this area, German artillery is still very active. Don't make yourselves a target."

"We'll try not to, if possible. Seems to me we don't have much choice," the sergeant answered, somewhat flippantly.

"Whatever, just be careful. Remember the lost battalion?"

"No one will forget the lost battalion, ever. Nice of you to remind us." Uncharacteristically, the sergeant's sarcasm bordered on disrespect. His curt manner revealed a different side of the usually amiable sergeant, and the men were more than taken aback by the sergeant's tone. The lieutenant gave a hateful glance, but departed without additional words.

Jesse had to ask. "I take it you know that lieutenant from before."

"I do, sorry to say. It's too bad he doesn't fight for the other side. Then, for sure, we'd be home by Christmas." Officers were often the target of ridicule by enlisted men, but it was unusual to hear a sergeant go after one, particularly this battalion sergeant. He minced no words. "The lost battalion happened because of officers like him."

"What exactly was the lost battalion? Did they get lost in the forest?"

The sergeant's face revealed his surprise. "No, no, no. I thought everyone knew by now. They weren't lost in location, they were written off as lost, dead. It all happened not more than five or six miles from where we now sit, in that forest right over there. It was a nightmare that should never have happened. Let me start at the beginning.

"On October 2, men from the 77th were advancing deep into the Argonne Forest. Some jerk of an officer from headquarters gave the order to advance until the objective was reached, dig in, and hold, regardless of exposed flanks. It was a stupid order and whoever gave it was stupid beyond belief. The 700 men battalion, a motley assortment including the 77th and elements from the 306th, 307th, and 308th, secured their objective and dug in for the night on the reverse slope of the hill. They did everything by the book but, somehow, the Germans slipped in behind them, thus preventing any withdrawal, and all night they pounded our boys with trench mortars and machine-gun fire. Nothing our guys could do but hunker down. The battalion was cut off from their own forces, surrounded by enemy troops, and about to run out of supplies and ammo. By evening of the second day the battalion, hungry, cold, and exhausted, was depleted by over a hundred men. The commander, Major Whittlesey, sent a message to headquarters by carrier pigeon that they could not hold out much longer. Command at headquarters ordered two regimental attacks, but neither could penetrate the German lines." The sergeant paused and became visibly upset as he thought about the following sequence of events. "Mind you now, they knew where the battalion was, they just didn't get to them. Headquarters knew their location, their exact coordinates."

He spoke faster. "Divisional artillery opened up, and instead of hitting the Germans, our artillery dropped a barrage directly on the battalion's position. Some jerk at headquarters misread the coordinates. Needless to say, unnecessarily, casualties mounted. Hours later, another American rescue ground attack failed. That night they air dropped in supplies and not one landed on target. The Germans got them. The next day shells from the southwest, from where the French were positioned, began shrieking into the battalion's position. Apparently the French used the same faulty coordinates. After the French guns lifted fire, the Germans came charging up the slope, and I don't know how, but the battalion beat them back again. The next day, remember this was their fourth day out there, the Germans attacked again using grenades and flame-throwers. Our boys still held out.

"October 6 was the last day of resistance, and both sides knew it. Only 250 men were left standing and they were almost out of ammunition. The entire battalion was in dire straits. The whole fiasco was one hell of a mess—men were close to dying from hunger, thirst, and exhaustion while the wounded, some delirious from pain, were not properly cared for and gangrene was setting in. By mid morning headquarters finally got the coordinates right and American artillery opened up with another barrage and this time it hit the Germans as they were massing for an attack. It really pounded the Germans. That night some of our men left their foxholes to strip German dead of rifles, ammunition, food, and water. They got enough to last one more night." The sergeant stopped talking and shook his head in disbelief. "Isn't that one crazy, incredible story?"

"What happened? That surely isn't the end of the story. Did they get out, or not?"

"They finally got out, some of them did, that is. The 307th Infantry got to them the next day. Only 231 men out of the over 700 in that battalion walked out. I don't have any idea how many survived." The sergeant's face showed relief when he concluded the story. It was hard enough for him to hear the story, let alone tell the story of the lost battalion.

"Let me tell you something, men. There's much more here than is apparent on the surface. The battalion never should have been there in the first place. Help should have reached them sooner. There were too many errors made by officers back at divisional headquarters, more blunders than I can list. I hope these facts live on with the story. All the men suffered immeasurably, the dead ones before they got it as well as the ones who made it back, and needlessly in my judgment. That young lieutenant you saw talking to me awhile ago—that son of a bitch was one of the officers back at headquarters."

The hour was late evening on October 13, when Jesse started to compile a written list of daily events to later jog his memory so he could be more accurate when he shared his story with Helen after he returned home. In essence, he intended to write down daily reminder notes, a journal of sorts.

As he worked on his list he found the task more difficult than he had imagined. He wrote about such general events, the ones he would remember anyway, that the list seemed useless, impractical. Astonishingly, the vivid details of recent combat experiences were already fading from memory. He had lost the intensity, his feeling of the moment which is what he had hoped to share. He could not believe that he had forgotten so much emotional detail about such relatively recent events, but he had. Doubts emerged and he even questioned if he were verbally capable of describing past feelings, or current ones for that matter. Was it within him to find words worthy of his emotions and experiences. Starting today he needed to write daily notes, mentioning events, people, impressions or anything else that could capture the emotion of the moment. Helen would want details.

Jesse's vain desire to maintain good penmanship complicated the process. The pen was best for writing, but ink was in short supply so a pencil and a commissary note pad would have to suffice for the transient soldier. To be thorough but not wordy was his goal. Across the top of the first page he wrote: Notes for Helen. The title seemed fitting.

10/13 Sunday—Arrived at an infantry camp in the north near a small village called Varennes on edge of Argonne Forest. We made camp a few miles farther north, near a four street village with a name bigger than the whole village. Entire area called Meuse-Argonne Sector. Scene of some terrible fighting before I got here. Pop assigned to our unit. Hurrah!

Good, hot food and, finally, time to rest. Leave tonight at dark. Captain is nervous. Why?

Jesse determined that his message was still too brief. Somehow he needed to develop a more suitable style. He tried again.

10/13 continued. Observed an interesting event during late afternoon. A one mule wagon on its way to the cemetery passed through the village. It transported three fallen boys from the 1st I'm not sure of the regiment but every infantry soldier stood and saluted as the wagon passed. I observed a quivering hand of a nearby soldier as he saluted in respect. I think I saw tears in his eyes. The driver was caught off guard, and I know he felt very awkward; but, nevertheless, he slowed the pace. I don't know how those boys died, not sure I want to know. Their bodies certainly commanded respect from officer and enlisted man alike. It was a moving sight.

Interesting personal thought—finding out how a soldier died may be more painful than just knowing he died, especially for family. Of course, having expressed such a thought, you know who this made me think of. I see so many young soldiers who remind me of him. It is all so sad. I will never talk to Elzie again. No one will! There are a lot of boys over here who will never go home, but none of us know who they are.

Jesse continued to write when he could.

10/14 Mon. Terrible, terrible experience last night. We all got lost in the woods. Forest is no place to be at night. Germans all around. Remind me to tell you about the stupid thing I did.

Now the weather is turning worse. Not sure what the winters are like here (don't think I want to know.) I think we've gone from summer to winter. Hope not.

It seems our task is to evaluate the condition of this country road for possible use as a major supply line (Pop thinks so.) Captain isn't talking about what we're doing. Not everything we do makes sense. Today we built two sets of wood supports so that the road could pass over an old trench, one road for each direction of traffic. Captain was not pleased because he wanted sandbags for base. Instead trench will be filled with rock and dirt, but fortunately for us others will fill it. Pretty nice, huh. Every time we get to the point of hard physical work, the wagon carrying our tools catches up with us and a group of other men do the grunt work. This time I think German prisoners will dirt fill our last project. I think that strange but Pop says it's common nowadays. We see lots of German prisoners. Up close and out of uniform, they look no different from us. During battle they look so tenacious, but as prisoners they look less formidable. Sometimes I almost feel sorry for them.

We will sleep tonight in tents already pitched for us. Food wagon in sight, which means hot food. All the comforts of home (ha, ha.) When I read this to you remind me to tell you how much I love you. I miss and think of you all the time, but more so at particular moments. Don't know why, or what sparks my sadness.

Sorry I forgot your birthday.

10/15 Tue. Cold rain came down in buckets, and air is close to freezing temperature. Awful thought—what happens if all this water freezes? We moved forward in the rain on a terrible road.

We passed through a village totally destroyed by artillery. Nothing left but debris and partial foundations. No people. Saw several dud shells, and believe me I kept my distance. I can't distinguish the different types of shells, so I'm leery of all types. Captain thinks that's funny. He is a very professional man, not in the army sense, but in an engineer sense. He knows a lot, but he is not a good teacher.

The land here is all reasonably good farm land, or could be. Many farms positioned right next to the forest. Why I don't know. I think most are animal farms with crops grown only for feed. Land sort of reminds me of eastern Pike County. Another time, different conditions, I might like it here.

Wow. We got shelled this afternoon. I think Fritz was specifically targeting engineers. No one else around. No injuries, just scared us. I never thought of myself as a scaredy-cat until now. Enemy shelling convinced me I am. Fear one way or another is always with me. I can't escape it. I think everybody feels it.

Worked most of day on road drainage ditch. No grunts around today, so we had to do the work. Not much fun. After a rain these roads are left in terrible shape. I question if these roads ever can be used for supply route. Captain says otherwise.

Small villages everywhere. I think if there are two or more buildings, the French call it a village. Most village name markers are gone, and if they do stand I can't pronounce them anyway. French must be a complex language.

Tonight we'll sleep in the woods. I ate a can of tomatoes and some hard bread for supper. I can't seem to get enough food in me, hungry all the time.

10/16 Wed. Worst day yet. Fritz shelled nearby area at daybreak with mustard gas. Engineers had no casualties, but 5 infantry boys got it. Not sure, I think they died from shell explosion, not gas. They were dead by the time we got to them. Captain sent one of ours back to notify someone. One was so very young. He didn't even shave yet.

Another sad thought. Written on the faces of all five dead was an expression of agony. They were not peaceful deaths, if there is such a thing.

Poison gas is terrible stuff, especially mustard gas. You have no options, you must have a mask on or it will get you. It gets your lungs first, and enough of it in your eyes will blind you permanently. The gas seeps through your clothes and blisters any skin it comes into contact with unless you move out of it right away. Not sure what else it does. Pop says even the doctors don't know much about it. We all fear it. They say it stays around until the wind pushes it on. Don't know after that. I do know how the gas got its name. It smells like mustard and leaves a mustard taste in your mouth.

The gas masks are hard to wear, at least for me. They're tight and hot, they make it hard to get enough air, and the lens often fogs on me. You can only see what is directly in front of you, and I think the lens gives a distorted view (sort of magnifies and garbles) of everything, near and far. If Germans are around, you worry that you won't see all you need to see. Also, masks are impossible to carry on your person while you work. Our group usually stacks all of them in a pile together, near our work or where we eat or sleep. Hardly a day passes without an artillery shell of gas landing somewhere near us. Yesterday we had to don masks five times. Germans favor mustard gas, and I hate the stuff. Pop says there are three types of artillery shells, and they're all equally bad. Concussion (high explosive) shells that blow you to pieces, shrapnel shells that tear up your body, and gas shells that make you wish you were dead. They all scare me. You can hear most of them coming, but not always. Germans sometimes use a whiz-bang shell you never hear coming. I hate all artillery.

Today we worked to reinforce a damaged German observation tower. Why, I don't know. We made camp less than a mile from last night's camp. Indications are that we're going to be here a while. I think this is a critical place to command, but I don't know where we are. Still hungry. Although we always eat something, we never get enough. Some in squad are becoming grumpy.

10/17 Thursday. Big day, with more to do than we can get done in a week. Captain split us into two work groups. I'm with Pop's group. Other crew is constructing plank road sections for low places on main road which is really nothing more than a wide dirt path with shallow ditches. Our group is repairing two small bridges, one of wood the other of stone, across good-sized creeks. Neither bridge has taken a direct hit, but artillery has done its damage. Supplies will arrive tomorrow, today we dig and clear out junk debris.

Spitted rain all day and air stayed cool. Had a rare treat today. Late afternoon three of us sought shelter from wind and moisture under a bridge, and what did we find but a discarded German pack containing a can of syrup. We didn't hesitate. We opened the can, used our fingers, and ate every drop. Best tasting syrup I've ever had. Most interesting was that we never thought about sharing with others until it was gone.

Best story yet. Once we got back near our tents we start...

"Get your packs and rifles, we're moving out. Infantry needs us now." Although the sergeant's order had an urgency about it, his tone of speaking revealed more panic than urgency. His panic was what most concerned the men.

"Why? Move out where? What's wrong?"

"Follow me, now!" The engineers begrudgingly prepared to leave the comforts of their camp, and when the men moved too slowly to suit the sergeant's liking, he reiterated, "Confound it, I said move, now!" This time the men took heed to both the orders and the tone of instruction. All twelve men fell in behind the sergeant, hustling and blindly following their leader across open ground into the bleak darkness of night. No one further questioned purpose or destination, rather they struggled to keep pace with the man many years their senior. Stowing his gear as he moved, Jesse carelessly shoved his notes into his coat pocket because he had not yet thought about where he should safely store them while in rapid transit.

"Second Squad, Combat Engineers, where do you want us?" asked the sergeant.

"Take up position in the rifle pits. Hurry, the flares go up in minutes! Reinforcements are on the way, we've got to hold until they get here," instructed an anxious captain.

During the early evening hours American infantry scouts had discovered that German infantry was massing for assault. Every man in uniform within summoning distance who could fire a rifle was hastily put in front-line position to resist the expected German attack. The Germans had caught the Americans unaware—no one had anticipated a major enemy offensive in this sector. The dense Argonne Forest protected the American left flank, but it also prevented any organized American retreat to the west. Less than one mile on the right flank, Hill 263, a fortified German position, also prevented escape. The American position was vulnerable to a frontal assault and any withdrawal would most likely be disorganized, chaotic, perhaps disastrous. The choice for command was simple—hold their position at all cost or face calamitous retreat. Command chose to hold and defend.

The somewhat shallow rifle pits protected the squad of engineers from German view when American flares suddenly lighted the sky. Although the engineers could see no enemy forces, they could determine that their position was front line. The open ground in front of them appeared desolate, void of life or objects, when the apprehensive and wretched hunkered down warriors curiously, perilously peered from their concealed positions. The forward open ground was deemed no-man's-land and the collective rifle pits, not protected with barbed wire or parapets, now served as the primary trench, the Americans first and only line of defense. The distant sounds of German entrenching tools working the earth gave evidence to what the eye could not detect—the Germans were digging in for some reason, either preparing for attack or making arrangements to repulse counterattack. Most likely no man on either side, save the senior officers planning the aggression, knew the battle plan. To the engineers it was a moot issue because they clearly understood their role—they were to hold their position or die trying.

Three long hours elapsed without attack. Machine-gun fire and faint noises from men using entrenching tools occasionally broke the silence of an otherwise quiet but frightening, eerie night. The American reinforcements had arrived, and were integrated into the line while reserve forces took up rear positions. The delayed German attack had served the Americans well, and by 5:00 a.m. they were prepared, as much as they could be prepared, for the German assault. The stage was set, the troops awaited the opening act. Other than fret, there was nothing more to do but to remain vigilant.

The last minutes of the final hour before dawn tore at the very souls of the readied warriors. Hundreds, perhaps thousands of warriors on both sides were clustered side by side, and yet in a real sense, every soldier felt alone. With death looming large it could be no other way.

As anticipated a predawn German artillery barrage commenced, immediately followed by return fire from Allied artillery. Not anticipated was the sudden lifting of German artillery fire after only fifteen minutes of light shelling, which coincided precisely with the earliest light of dawn. The light barrage had altered little and made one question why it was deployed at all. Abruptly, a field of German soldiers clad in their gray uniforms and low fitting helmets rose from their entrenched positions aggressively and forcefully charged the American position. Protected only by the smoky haze resulting from forward slung smoke bombs, hundreds of German soldiers made a human wave direct frontal assault against the expecting American positions. The Americans opened fire with every weapon at their disposal. Machine guns virtually decimated the most forward German troops, and still the Germans continued to advance, sending wave after wave of soldiers to their certain grave. The supply of attacking German soldiers seemed endless, and already they were within 50 yards of the American position. Then defying all logic, the advance ended. The Germans did not regroup, they simply stopped their assault and sought cover on the open ground. In a desperate effort to provide cover for their stranded soldiers German trench mortars opened fire, as their artillery unleashed a series of smoke bombs; and gas canisters were hurled indiscriminately throughout the battlefield. Effectively, many Americans were forced to seek cover as others fired blindly into the enemy position. Fearing but not knowing what to expect once the gas and smoke cleared, the vigilant Americans maintained their positions, fixed bayonets, and prepared for hand-to-hand combat. When the smoke finally cleared the Americans were surprised. The German soldiers were in full retreat, many already back undercover in their trenches. The German assault had been successfully repulsed. The battle on this day and in this place was over. Methodically, the Germans retreated from their attack trenches to their rest-reserve position near Hill 263 leaving the defense of their forward position to artillery, machine gunners, and a skeleton crew of infantrymen.

"Thanks for lending a hand," said the infantry captain. His manner of speaking was indicative of the pride he felt for his role in organizing the defensive line. Sergeant, you can take your squad back to whatever you were doing, cause I don't think we'll hear from those bastards again. We gave them a good whipping. I suspect they will be back tonight to retrieve their dead, but that is not our concern. By then we'll have a whole regiment here. Hot food and bathing facilities will be available late tonight, if you are interested."

"We'll be there, captain. I can assure you we're more than interested. What are the numbers, did we take many casualties?"

"Don't know for sure yet, thought to be light."

"Good! Incidentally, do you know where the other squad of engineers is? I assume they were in the line too."

"No idea. Didn't know there were others."

The sergeant concealed his concern. "No worry, we'll find them, thanks anyway. The boys and I are going to find some coffee and something to eat. We deserve a little special treatment. Follow me, men, and I'll follow my nose, it never fails me. We'll find something to eat."

The sergeant was correct about his nose, because he led them directly to a makeshift chow line. "Look here, boys, hot victuals. How about that? Looks like we're going to eat two hot meals in one day. Yes, sir, this is better than getting money from home without sending for it. Let's get in line but stay together. Get your food and we'll meet in that shell hole right over there. Thanks to Kraut artillery, we'll have a private dining room."

Although the men were exhausted, they were not too tired to eat a hot meal. Still too tired for meaningful conversation they hastily ate in the shell crater without uttering a sound. As anticipated the food rejuvenated them.

Normally a slow eater, Jesse varied his habit; he kept pace with the fastest of eaters, and after the meal he also kept pace with the fastest smokers and the biggest coffee guzzlers. He wanted to make sure he got his fair share. Identifying a rare opportunity to tap the sergeant's wisdom, Jesse stopped his rapid consumption long enough to ask a question. "Tell me something, sergeant. I don't understand what just happened. Why did the Germans come right at us, right into the throat of our fire? No cover or anything, they just charged."

Another private in the squad answered without waiting for the sergeant's response. "Because they're stupid, that's why." Boastfully, he continued. "They didn't know that if you fight Americans, you'll reap the whirlwind. I took down my share, I'll tell you that much, and Jesse you were something else. I saw you empty clip after clip, and when your shoulder tired you started firing from the left side. Damn, I've never seen that done before, shoot right or left handed. How many do you think you brought down?"

Jesse ignored both the intended compliment and the ridiculous question. "What about it, Pop, usual German tactics or unusual blunder? Why did they attack under those conditions in broad daylight?"

Pop abandoned his normal reserved tone and his definite answer lacked his usual disclaimers of real knowledge. He spoke with anger in his voice. "There is no way in hell that anybody here can accurately answer that question at this time. Very few German military actions are conducted as isolated events, not associated with an overall plan. I keep telling you guys that these Germans are warriors. I don't know if it's in their culture, or in their blood, or where it comes from, but they are good warriors, and don't you forget it. Let your guard down and they will kill you in an instant. And one other thing—they're not stupid. Haven't you ever wondered why Allied armies, twice the size in number, still can't defeat them. It's not because they're stupid, mean maybe, but not stupid."

Humbled by the sergeant's remarks, the private apologized and tried to redeem himself. "Sorry, sergeant, I didn't mean to rile you. What I meant was the attack seemed to be a foolish attack without possibility of victory."

"Forget it, son. My fault. My distemper kicked in I guess. I don't know, perhaps what I saw scared me." The privates did not understand what might have scared him, nor did they ask. Many had believed the sergeant was incapable of fear. A brief lull followed the sergeant's words, but his alarming words kept ringing in the privates' ears. Whether they had too much respect for the man or they feared his wrath was not known. Questions abated, silence ensued.

Eventually, Pop resumed speaking, and this time he spoke more in his usual non-presumptuous manner. "I'm not certain how to answer your question, Jesse. I can only guess as to why. Perhaps the whole thing was diversionary, to make us get men here so they could attack elsewhere. Maybe it's not over yet. Maybe that attack was testing us. You know they did retreat at a strange time during the attack. They were almost on top of us. Could be there is still a full regiment out there somewhere just waiting for us to feel over confident before they come at us again." It was obvious to the men that the sergeant lacked his usual clarity and was thinking about explanations as he was talking.

"Also, it could well be that I'm over reacting. Other possibilities—maybe the attack was simply ill conceived and they underestimated our troop strength. Who knows, it could be that their commander was inexperienced, or that his troops were. They did look mighty young. Some of those boys looked like they ought to be at home going to school rather than in the army." His observation was absolutely amazing to the men—that the sergeant had the capacity to humanize an attacking enemy, or to observe personal characteristics. "Of course, there is always one other possible explanation—we've defeated them, we've broken their spirit, and they feel the war is a lost cause. It could be we're nearing the end." Although the expression, nearing the end, was unrealistically joyous in nature, it nevertheless was a deep-felt, indelible thought, one the men appreciated, savored. Seeing what he had done the sergeant burst their bubble of hopeful thinking when he added, "But I doubt it."

Then it happened. A familiar, terrible screeching sound of incoming artillery destroyed all thoughts of victory or war's end. Scattered shells aplenty were landing distant and nearby. "Keep your heads down, let me do the looking," the sergeant yelled as he peered over the top of the shell crater. "Those sons of bitches. It's not an attack barrage, these are shells with a message. They're telling us they can shell us anytime they want, those sons of bitches. Oh my God, take cover, now!"

No sooner had the sergeant himself taken cover than the men in the crater heard the worst imaginable sound that any hunkered down soldier could hear— the whine of an overhead shell descending on his exact position. Just as the screeching sound had forewarned, the shell hit almost on top of them, very near the sergeant's exact location. The explosion delivered an awesome shock that vibrated the very ground and spewed forth disturbed earth in all directions which instantly covered the engineers with a shallow layer of expelled soil. Had the shell contained more explosives, the men would have been totally buried, if not blown to bits. Those on the far side of the old crater were forcefully ejected from the hole and propelled a considerable distance through the air, while those protected from the direct blast were left incapacitated in the crater. All the men in the squad were down or disabled. Those very men who, only moments ago, had sought the protection of the crater and celebrated as they consumed their first hot meal in three days, now lay partially covered with dirt, supinely reposed at the bottom of an old shell crater. In less time than a blink of the eye, their youthful bodies were altered to a state of motionless, helplessness. In a brief time, a cloud of gray mist gathered overhead, hovered, and lingered over the downed, incapacitated men.

Suddenly the German random shelling of the American position was over. The shelling had been no more than a message, but indeed, what a powerful message it had been. The gas alarm sounded and verbal warnings of "gas" could be heard from all directions.

The cloud of poisonous gas stubbornly lingered near its location of release, gradually settling in the craters and other low areas. To a casual observer the gassed area might appear similar to a small body of water emitting fog on a cold morning; but, in fact, the cloud contained a toxic chemical capable of depriving man of life itself. It took no more than a simple slight breeze with sufficient force to bring about the gradual departure of the poisonous cloud. Only the deep, low lying areas retained any remnant of the gaseous cloud, as the languid breeze reached the low areas not at all. The gas lingered in the various bomb craters and refused to dissipate.

The all-clear signal sounded and the soldiers anxiously stripped off their bulky, vision restricting masks. "We've had casualties," cried a voice of command. "Get out and assess the damage, help the wounded!"

"Help!" was the nearby cry of another voice, only this voice was far more desperate than the sound of the first voice. "Help! We need help over here, now." An infantry private peered into the horrendous sight of the crater containing the downed men. "The engineers are down. Get the Medical Corps. Oh my God, it's still in the air, I can smell it," he said between coughs. "Wear your masks. There is mustard gas in the crater and the men are still there. Hurry, one is convulsing."

CHAPTER 25

WAR'S END

W ake-up, private, wake-up," nurse Stanton shouted as she shook the arm of the groggy, semiconscious soldier. "Wake-up, if you can, it's time to take off the bandages. Can you talk? If you can, say something, grunt, make any kind of sound." The soldier made a sound that resembled a faint exhale more than a word. "Good, now keep trying to talk, make sounds. The words will come in a few minutes. Will you move your fingers for me? That a boy, now move the hand, now the arm, that's right. Don't worry about the eyes, we'll get those bandages off in a few minutes."

After two unsuccessful tries to emit words, Private Jesse Moore found limited success. "Who...," was followed by a deep breath, then "Where..."

Your name is Private Jesse Moore, your serial number is 3706157, you are at a Red Cross Field Hospital. I am nurse Stanton. Can you hear me? If you understand me, say yes or squeeze my hand."

"Yes."

"You were knocked out by an artillery shell and exposed to a large dose of mustard gas. You are all right now, you are recovering and you will feel much better after a few more days of rest. Your eyes are not damaged, but we flushed them with water just in case. The bandages are to protect your eyes from light. You are all right. Do you understand what I just said?"

"Yes." This time his tone was stronger, clearer. Nurse Stanton detected hope.

"If you will assist me, I will help you to sit up in bed. Then I will give you a quick check over before we take off those bandages." Jesse exerted some effort and made his first body movement with his arms. "Very good." The two worked together until Jesse was in a sitting position leaning against the iron rails at the head of the bed. "This is a cup of nice, cold water. You need to take a few sips if you can." She watched as Jesse drank the entire cupful and returned the empty cup to her by holding it out with arms extended in front of his chest. "Very good. I would say you are even better than I thought. Now hold still, I need to check your vital signs and quickly examine your body. I'm not going to hurt you, okay? I will be careful I just need to check a few places." Jesse remained quiet, passive as the nurse went about her business of checking the vital signs, the gas burns on his legs, and the various bruises and contusions about his body and head.

Nurse Stanton stood steadily erect for several minutes as she recorded the recently observed data on her chart. Initially Jesse considered her to be painfully quiet, although quickly he came to appreciate her professional demeanor of efficiency and thoroughness. She had a good nurturing manner. "Now, we need to look at the eyes. Keep your eyes closed while I remove the bandages, and open them only when I tell you to do so. We must protect them from light. Do you understand?"

"Yes."

Carefully, gently she removed his head wrapping. "Bear with me, be indulgent as I clean the eye lids and surrounding area. Your eyes have been flushed with water so many times that accumulated eye matter has matted, what you would call sleepiness in the eyes. There, that's better, now go easy, but try to open your eyes. At first they might seem stuck or glued down but eventually they will open, and remember, don't open too fast, or too wide. You need to protect your eyes against too much light until the eyes have adjusted. You will know when to fully open them. Start opening them now, please. Gently, gently, gently."

The wounded warrior followed the nurse's instruction to a tee, until both eyes were fully opened. He gave no verbal indication that he had vision, although his eyes moved about the room focusing on both near and far objects. Jesse was undaunted when his sensitive, gray-blue eyes first watered and then became teary as he gazed about the room. With absolute delight and with a smile from ear to ear he proclaimed, "I can see, I can see!"

"Of course you can see, but exactly how well do you see? Can you distinguish objects, is your vision sharp, do you see colors?"

Squirming to get on his side, Jesse looked directly at the nurse. "Everything is sort of cloudy, as though I am looking through a mist, but I think I can see everything in the room. Objects are kind of faint, maybe dark, but I can see them. I assume the watering will end after my eyes adjust."

"Wonderful! Don't be concerned about the watering, it's perfectly normal. Describe to me what you see!"

"Well, beside my bed I see one very concerned nurse, somewhere in her twenties I would guess. She's wearing a white long dress and a funny looking white hat that comes to a point in the front. Also she wears a long white apron, starched stiff as a board. Her face..."

"That's enough, I think your vision is just fine, not to mention what passes for a sense of humor. That's good. Take a minute and move your body to see if you have any sharp pain anywhere. I expect you to be somewhat sore, but mostly I'm interested in pain. Do you have any?"

In a more serious manner Jesse moved, felt, reached, probed and contorted until he was satisfied he knew the answer to her question. "No real sharp pain, just sore and stiff. My head has a sharp pain when I turn too quickly. My whole body feels greasy. My legs, below the knees, feel very sensitive, almost like I got burned. Why are they wrapped in bandages?"

"Private Moore, you are most fortunate. Apparently, nothing is broken or out of place. No skeletal or muscular damage. You should expect to be sore for a few more days. Your headache is no surprise, you probably suffered a concussion and your headache will most likely ease up in a few days. Your legs are as you surmised. You have gas burns below the knees, which will heal with time, maybe with some minor scarring, but no permanent injury. Your entire body is oiled to assist in the healing of any minor burns. At the dressing station they washed and oiled your body, flushed out your eyes several times and wrapped your eyes, all standard treatment for gas exposure. In essence, we've done the same thing here."

Almost as though the mind had been in selfish remission since regaining consciousness, something mentally clicked and Jesse remembered eating with the other engineers in the crater. That was his last memory. He had no recollection of the explosion although he was positive there had been one. He became excited, agitated, his breathing accelerated. "What happened? Where are the others? Anybody else hurt? Dressing station, what dressing station? Where are the others, what about the sergeant? Oh, my God, are the others all right? Are they here?"

"Calm down, private. I don't know what happened other than that you were exposed to a pretty good dose of mustard gas and you were delivered here from a dressing station. I'm not certain if anyone else was injured or not. We have several men here suffering from gas exposure, and I'll inquire as soon as I can. Meanwhile, you stay calm. If you work yourself into a frenzy, you will only complicate your recovery. Stay calm, do you understand?"

"This is no calm situation. Those were buddies, and I need to know. I hope I didn't leave them in a lurch."

"What a ridiculous concern, you're the one injured. I'll try to find out what I can; meanwhile, you put aside any concern about leaving someone in the lurch. You're not well yet, so you listen to me, stop thinking about others. I mean it, you listen to me, listen carefully to my instructions. Be attuned to your body, watch for changes or other symptoms. You need to move your body as much as possible.

Wiggle your toes, test out your body, try to get everything moving. You need to stretch out your muscles. Later, if you feel like it, get out of bed and move around. You also need nourishment. We'll get food to you as soon as possible. Eat all you can, and if you feel you can eat more, ask for it. Drink all the water you can, your body needs liquid. Let me know as soon as you have a bowel movement. You've got to make your bowels move. If they don't move on their own, we'll need to make them move, and I know you don't want that. You do exactly as I tell you, and you'll be good as new before you know it. I'll get back to you as soon as I know anything about your buddies. Until further notice you follow my directions. Are we in agreement?"

Nurse Stanton's reassuring words served to soothe, if not pacify. "We're in agreement for now and I will not forswear. I will try to calm down, if possible, and follow your instructions. But you can bet on one thing for sure—I won't totally calm down until I find out what happened out there." Nurse Stanton started to exit the area when Jesse spoke again in a noncontentious voice. "Nurse, thank you for your kindness. I do appreciate it."

"You're welcome, soldier boy."

Evening and morning passed before Jesse had contact with additional medical personnel. An elderly, non-English speaking orderly kept food and drink in supply as Jesse precisely followed his instructions. Within hours Jesse was out of bed and made every effort to walk out his soreness and stiffness, although he met with little success. His vision remained imperfect, better at certain times. The eyes continued to water and Jesse, try as he might, was unable to determine neither the cause or the pattern of the watering. More than his other injuries, his eyes were of most concern to him. Two more days passed.

During the late hours of the following morning the field hospital erupted into a hubbub of added activity. Motorized vehicles arriving from numerous dressing stations delivered a surplus of soldiers in need of medical care, as hospital staff struggled to provide needed medical attention and adequate housing. To the credit of the Army Medical Corps and the efforts of many local volunteers, the situation did not become a crisis.

Nurse Stanton made a return visit to Private Moore during the early evening hours; and, although she endeavored to conceal her fatigue, her appearance and her curt manner reflected the strain of her day. "How are you progressing, Private Moore?"

"I'm doing well and following your directions. I'm better. How are you?"

She offered no answer to his polite inquiry. "I see you're up and around. Had your bowel movement yet?"

"Yes, this morning, and again this evening. It was almost like..."

"Do you have any pain or discomfort that you didn't have yesterday?"

"None to speak of other than..."

"Good! We need your bed so you must vacate this ward and move to one of the nearby temporary facilities. Shortly, someone will be here to assist and direct you. Keep up the good work, eat properly, get all the exercise you can, flush your eyes with water every four hours, and try to get some fresh air. Sit, I want to remove the leg wrappings and oil your legs." Without her usual sensitivity she quickly unwrapped the bandages and oiled his legs. "Legs look good. Wrapping is no longer necessary, just oil. Be certain to bathe the entire body once a day, and gently rinse any burn areas in lukewarm water and re-oil after each bathing. Just to be safe you probably should oil your entire body once a day. A doctor will see you when he can, most likely two days henceforth. If a doctor doesn't get to you by then, you seek one out. Any questions?"

Annoyed by her manner Jesse answered her in a forbearing tone. "Two questions. One, what happened to my unit and two, where are my clothes and personal possessions?"

Nurse Stanton was surprised, somewhat dismayed by Jesse's manner. "I'm sorry, have I offended you?"

"Yes, you have, if you really want to know, but I'm not going to take your precious time explaining. Please, just answer my questions."

"Again, I'm sorry. At a less busy time I will try to make amends. I have not had time to check on your friends. When you are feeling better you can look around or you can check with the desk of hospital records and they can tell you if your buddies are still here. However, I doubt if there will be any record, assuming they have been dismissed. You must understand that we are becoming overwhelmed with casualties from the offensive, and for now our records are not what they should be. I don't know what else to suggest other than after you return to your unit, your company commander should know. This terrible war is taking its toll on all of us." Her eyes pleaded for compassionate understanding, but the patient showed no indication of tolerance, let alone understanding.

Rudeness was unbecoming to Jesse. He, nevertheless, spoke bemoaningly. "You've got that right, nurse. This war is taking its toll on a bunch of us. Now, what about my second question?"

Nurse Stanton understood she had offended her patient, but so be it. Almost at wit's end she felt she had no other recourse than to drop the issue. She could spend no more time attempting to console the beleaguered, wounded warrior, so she prepared to move on. "Whoever takes you to your new bed, will give you your belongings. However, I do warn you that most arrive here with nothing in their possession. The first thing they do to gas victims at the aid station is decontaminate everything. We try to dispose of everything after exposure to gas unless, of course, it can be sanitized. Good luck, Private Moore." Offering no other thoughts to Jesse, she donned the same fatigued look she had when she arrived, and proceeded to another bed and greeted a patient. "Good evening, Private Taylor. I hope you are feeling better, as we desperately need your bed."

"Well I'll be a monkey's uncle, look who I see. If that isn't Jesse Moore sitting there feeding his face. We were just talking about you."

"Well I'll be, it's Zach," Jesse exclaimed as he stood to physically greet his dear friend. "You're a sight for sore eyes. I've been worried sick about you, how have you been? Tell me about yourself."

Smiling and shaking his head Zach was quick to respond. "You have been worried about me, how have I been? If that doesn't take the cake. We heard that you boys took a direct hit, sending all of you to the hospital, and you want to know how I am. Nothing has happened to me, I'm just fine. Tell me about you, what happened up there?"

Jesse was not going to answer his questions until he penetrated the exact information Zach already knew. "I got knocked out, don't remember much, and know nothing about what happened. I woke up at a field hospital, but no one there knew anything either. You said they all were in the hospital, nobody died, right? Both squads, the sergeant, all are okay?"

At once Zach became evasive. "No, I didn't say that, I just told you what I heard. Two days ago the captain sent a replacement squad to link up with the other squad still up there. We heard you guys were gassed and assumed the other squad didn't get a scratch. That's all I know, don't count on me for accurate information. I only know what I hear."

"Kind of pisses me off," Jesse plainly stated. "Last night I reported for duty to the captain, and I asked him if he knew anything about the others, and he said he didn't. Told me he would let me know if he found out something. Pisses me off, he knew the whole time. When I get the opportunity I'm going to visit with him about it, see if I can't get a straight answer. I've got a right to know, I was there."

"Don't get mad at me, get mad at the captain or the Army, not me. Now tell me, were you gassed or not? Are you all right?"

"Sorry, I didn't mean to get my dander up with you." Jesse mellowed, sat down and prepared to brief Zach about his ordeal. "I'm okay, I think. Yeah, we got gassed big time, but I don't remember much about it. I woke up in a field hospital. They said I got there from a dressing station, and my eyes were wrapped with bandages and I had a few gas burns. I still don't see right, but they told me not to worry about it, that full vision would be restored in time. I was sore, had headaches, threw up a few times. I was weak, coughed up my lungs for a few hours.

467

First day or two I was very tired and had no appetite. I'm feeling better now. I must be fine, because in essence they kicked me out of the hospital."

"Astonishing. They kicked you out?"

"Not really, I suppose, they did give me a choice. The doctor told me I could go to the gas hospital at Rarecourt if I wanted, although he sure put some qualifiers with it. He said that after they neutralize the gas they really don't know what else to do for gas injuries, other than rest, exercise, and nourishment. So, why go? He also told me that the war might be winding down, maybe near its end, if we can get enough men on the front to convince the Germans that they're whipped. So my choices were go to Rarecourt, where they couldn't really do anything for me, or go back in the lines and help win the war. They told me where our company was so I linked up with some boys from the 81st who were heading this way. I assumed the sooner the war ended, the sooner we all would get to go home. So I chose to come back and here I am. What would you have done?"

Zach was straight forward with his answer. "Without question I would have gone to Rarecourt, and in my answer you will find the real difference between you and me. The first legitimate opportunity to get off these lines, I'm gone. Pure and simple, I'm gone."

Zach's no nonsense declaration reminded Jesse of their last meeting. "Enough about me, what about you? The last time we talked you were expressing doubts. Have you overcome that?"

"Hell no, I'm still scared shitless everyday. The only difference now is that I have learned to live with it. I either deal with it or I become a nut case, what the Army now calls suffering from shell shock, and believe me there is no future in that. They treat shell shock victims like they are nuts. I believe once I'm out of here, I'll be just fine. I wouldn't be surprised, heaven forbid, if some of those poor, shell-shocked boys end up in an insane asylum. It's like gas, Jesse, the Army doctors have no treatment for shell shock either. I really wouldn't be surprised if they simply lock them all up after the war. They can't help them, they don't know how to help, they don't understand it. Think about that one for awhile!" The mere thought of the horrible fates awaiting shell-shocked victims sent shivers down Zach's spine. "Don't get me going on this one, we've got to change the subject. I can't talk about it."

Zach's expression changed, and Jesse knew not what to say. Quickly, Zach resumed speaking. "When I came upon you I was on my way to the village, do you want to go? I'll show you the seedy side of life at the front."

The tone, more than the question itself, set well with Jesse, at least in terms of evaluating his friend's mental well-being. He sounded more like the old Zach, the one who found humor and adventure in all phases of life. "Love to go, Zach, but I just got here last night. I better wait around, they might need me, and I don't even have my duty assignment yet."

"Yes, you do, everyone here has the same duty. We're reserves for the 81st. Our time is our own as long as we stay rested and healthy and are always available for call. There is this little village about a twenty minute walk from here where everything is set up to help us relax. The Army doesn't care if you go there as long as you sign out and write down where you are. The village is a great spot. They have everything: Y.M.C.A. and Red Cross trucks, personal supply depot, shops, mess halls, delousing mill, and for those faint of heart," he moved closer and sort of whispered, "they have soothing music concerts." He knew music would tempt his friend. "Everything is free except for the whores and they only cost two dollars. There is this one little French whore who I love to listen to." He cocked his head and looked upward as he spoke in an imitating manner. "Come close, Yank, I have what you need. Two dollars, half hour, every clothes off pay 25 cents more. I satisfy."

Jesse roared with laughter at the humorous imitation, but still showed reluctance to accompany Zach to the village. He worried that Zach was beguiling him. Enticed by the music concerts, put off by the presence of prostitutes, he was intrigued by the thought of visiting such an interesting area. He deceptively gathered more information. "Do you pay the asking price for the whores?"

"No, I don't, I'm not going to pay to be with a woman. God might forgive me but my wife wouldn't if she ever found out, and knowing her, she would find out. I just like the place. Stay away from the gaming rooms, bars, and whorehouses, it's actually a good place to be. Come on, go with me or else I will stay here and pester you all day. The Army knows about it, there's no harm. I don't know if they condone everything that goes on there, they don't condemn it. The only major street in town, the one with the houses of ill-repute, has been renamed Pershing Avenue. Can't be all bad, can it?"

The enticement worked. Jesse accompanied Zach to the village, not only on this day, but on several future occasions. The innocent adventures, village escapes, as they came to call them, served a good purpose—they helped the two men to relax, to temporarily think about something other than their own predicaments; and, more importantly, the outings allowed the two men an opportunity to renew their friendship.

Over time, Jesse informed Zach about the unknown status of Andy and eventually he described his northern exploits in detail. Zach, with Jesse's assistance, continued his fight to overcome his demons of fear. Gradually, Zach appeared to be healing. Jesse was less fortunate as he made little progress toward full recovery, although those around him were basically unaware of his struggles. His failure to regain good eyesight continued to plague him most of all.

One of Jesse's priority tasks was to compose a letter to Helen. Taking pains not to alarm his family, he wrote a succinct letter to Helen informing her that he had been gassed, had been in a hospital, but was now back on the front lines. His company commander read the letter before posting and assured Jesse that the letter would pass the censors. Strangely, Jesse continued to find it most difficult to write letters, to write anything about the war. Having lost his written narrative for Helen, he made no attempt to regain his thoughts, made no effort to continue with his diary. Valid or not, he concluded that many of his war experiences were much too awful to share with anyone, let alone with his wife, and after he returned home he would recall to his wife only those events worthy of sharing, without benefit of notes. Somehow, Jesse found peace of mind in not sharing his thoughts concerning the ugliness of war.

"Why do they need all these ladders anyway? If we keep building ladders we'll end up with one ladder for every two men. Not to mention all the effort, it's kind of wasteful isn't it?" Zach's words were spoken more to vent his frustration than in expectation of any meaningful answer. All front-line duty was stressful and the recent move by the engineers to the forward trenches only added to the stress and to the possibility of personal danger. "Will someone explain all of this to me? I'm tired of all the crap."

Corporal Black, the squad leader, retorted, "Who knows why we do anything. I'm tired too, but bellyaching doesn't do any good. Just shut up and do your work!"

"Now that isn't fair, corporal, Zach's only letting off steam. You have no call to talk like that," Jesse responded in defense of his friend. "All these ladders do seem a bit foolish, corporal. Have you ever been in a trench that needed this many ladders? What's up, does anyone know?"

"Sorry, private, I guess I too am bellyaching only in a different way. No, I don't have a clue. Something is afoot, that's for sure. To my way of thinking things have been different the last week or so, ever since we heard that Kaiser Bill had accepted Wilson's Fourteen Points."

Acceptance of the Fourteen Points was news to Jesse. "What does that mean? Is the war about to end? That's what we were fighting for, wasn't it, acceptance of the Fourteen Points? Has anyone else heard about this? How come I didn't know? Zach, did you know?"

"Yeah, I heard about it, and I put as much stock in the truth of it as I do in all the other rumors I hear almost everyday. I heard the Krauts have not attacked us because they are afraid of the mighty American Army. I also heard we're kicking German ass in the Meuse-Argonne, and the British and French are advancing toward Germany, kicking more German ass as they move. I heard that Austria-

Hungary is about to surrender, and that there is a revolution about to erupt in Germany. And if you believe any of that crap, I've got this bridge in Brooklyn that I would like to sell you. It's rumors, all rumors, not worth repeating."

"I'm inclined to agree with Zach," confessed the corporal. "I think someone at headquarters starts those rumors thinking it will boost morale, otherwise it doesn't make any sense to me. If only a small part of what we hear was true, the war would be winding down, and we know that isn't true. For the last week everything we have done is geared toward an offensive, not a cease fire. Fresh troops and supplies are pouring in everyday. Have you noticed all the officers mounting those periscopes and charting information? Have you noticed all the forward observers, additional artillery and Signal Corps men around here lately? And what about all these ladders? Yes, sir, it sounds to me more like a major offensive than any cease fire. I think if the war was about to end we would be flooded with field officers wanting to be at the front in time to take all the credit. Anyway, that's what I think about the whole thing. Home by Christmas is hogwash."

The hogwash statement pleased Zach. "Corporal, you sure have changed your tune. Maybe you're not so naive after all. I guess if we stay here long enough, we all become a little cynical. I detest deliberate lies, and both sides do it, I know they do. I still carry the propaganda leaflet the Germans dropped a couple of weeks ago. The more I read it, the madder I get."

"I guess I'm out of it. What are you talking about, Zach?" asked a confused Jesse.

"I'm talking about the effort by both sides to win with lies on paper what they can't win on the battlefield. It's all over the place. When you were gone the Germans dropped a bunch of leaflets from one of their planes. Let me read you a couple of paragraphs and you'll see what I mean.

HOW TO STOP THE WAR

Do your part to put an end to the war. Put an end to your part of it. Stop fighting. That's the simplest way. You can do it, you soldiers, just stop fighting and the war will end of its own accord. You are not fighting for anything anyway. What does it matter to you who owns Metz or Strassburg, you never saw those towns nor knew the people in them, so what do you care about them? But there is a little town back home in little ole United States you would like to see and if you keep on fighting here in the hope of getting a look at those old German fortresses you may never see home again.

The only way to see home again is to stop fighting. That's easy. Just quit it and slip across no-man's-land and join the bunch that's taking it easy there waiting to be exchanged and taken home. There is no disgrace in that. That bunch will be welcomed just as warmly as you who stick it out in those infernal trenches. Get wise and get over the top.

There is nothing in the glory of keeping up the war. But think of the increasing taxes you will have to pay the longer the war...

"Quick put that away, here comes the lieutenant. We better get with it because he doesn't look happy."

Zach continued talking as he stuffed the paper in his pocket. "You can read it tonight, there are several more paragraphs. It gets better. Those Germans lie, lie, lie."

"What's going on here, men? Do you think you're members of a sewing circle or something? You better get those ladders done, now. Save your chatter until you get back to reserve. Get with it, there's work to be done."

Once the lieutenant was beyond hearing range Zach muttered mockingly, "Sewing circle, chatter, get with it. I'll give one dollar to anyone that can prove me wrong. That lieutenant is inept. He's a sorry son of a bitch. That's the reason they made him an officer. Why I'll bet he could not drive one of these nails straight if his life depended on it. Any takers?"

Jesse laughed. "You won't get any takers here, I'm sure. Speaking of nailing straight, I'm having problems seeing the nails here in the shadows. How about if I assemble, and you nail? Or maybe we can..."

Like a thunderbolt from nowhere a soldier from no-man's-land came crashing into the trenches where the engineers were working. He landed on his feet and his eyes instantly surveyed the nearby men and surrounding conditions before he assumed a position leaning against the dirt wall and closed his eyes as though he intended to take a nap. He said nothing.

A startled Jesse jumped away from the intruder. "Where in the hell did he come from? Who is he, do you guys know him?"

An amused Zach was only too happy to explain. "That's Pierre, or at least that's what we call him. He's a French soldier, sort of. You don't fool with him, he's top dog around here."

Unsatisfied, Jesse inquired further. "What do you mean, top dog? He came directly out of no-man's-land in broad daylight. Nobody can do that without being seen. How did he do that? What's he doing here? Does he talk?"

"He does whatever he wants to do. I suspect he talks, but I don't think he speaks

English. I've never heard him make a sound. He's legendary in these parts, been here ever since the Battle of Verdun. They say he lived near here before the war and knows the terrain around here like the back of his hand. He's known hereabouts as the Hun killer. Goes over to their lines whenever he wants, day or night, and kills Germans. No one sees him until it's too late, just like right now. All of a sudden he's there."

The other men were enjoying Zach's description, forcing Jesse to wonder if it all was a joke at his expense. "Is he joshing me?"

Corporal Black answered. "He's telling the truth, at least what we think the truth to be. He's real all right, look at him, he's not imaginary. They say the captain was ordered to let him come and go as he pleases, and we supply him with whatever he wants. He gets his ammo here, eats here, sleeps here, and as far as I know he answers to no one. As Zach said, the captain calls him the Hun killer. Some say he is evil incarnate. I'm scared of him. Look at him!"

Pierre was an unusually large man, clad in a tattered, woolen French trench coat, American officer boots, American gloves, and a German helmet. Dirt was caked to his outer garments and nothing about him was clean, certainly not his face. His facial features, somewhat concealed by matted and filthy facial hair, were not particularly distinct other than his dark bushy eyebrows which shadowed his brown colored sunken eyes. Unusually large ears and a sloped nose protruded from his full, rounded face. Pierre was convincingly ferocious in appearance and expelled an aura of evil. He so blended into the natural surroundings as he leaned against the side of the trench with his eyes closed, that one questioned his actual existence. The mere presence of this unconventional warrior served to evoke fear in the bravest of men.

Jesse sort of grinned. "I'm convinced, he can have all the space he needs as far as I'm concerned. I'm glad he's on our side." Sort of joking but not entirely, he continued, "He is on our side, isn't he?"

"As far as I know he is. If he kills Germans, I think that puts him on our side. My God, just look at him! He's so dirty you can hardly see him leaning against the dirt. He's in perfect camouflage." The men all stared in wonderment before the corporal continued. "I'll bet there is an interesting story behind this man. I can't vouch for the truth of it; but, I heard that he was a farmer before the war and lost his whole family to German artillery during the first few days of fighting. They say he has been like this ever since. They say he prefers to kill Germans with his knife, and that he is somewhat fond of throwing hand grenades, especially at German officers; but that no matter what happens out there, he won't come back until he takes out someone. Captain said that he has already killed enough Germans to have a cemetery named after him." The corporal paused to laugh before he continued. "Maybe they will name it Pierreville Cemetery."

473

As they all laughed at the sick humor, Jesse thought he saw Pierre open his eyes to look at the person who had most recently defamed him; but Jesse lost eye contact with the Frenchman when a burst of machine-gun fire forced all of them to seek cover. When Jesse looked back to view how the Frenchman reacted to the fire, he could not find him. No one had heard nor observed any movement, but somehow Pierre had exited the area while under fire. "He's gone," Jesse said. "Just like that he is gone. Are you guys sure he doesn't speak English, or maybe understand a little English?"

"I'm not positive, but I don't think so. Why?"

"Oh, I just wondered. I'm not as sure as you are."

"Don't worry about it. Even if he understood you, you wear the wrong uniform."

"Maybe, I hope you're right. You may find this weird but I have a strange question. What happens to someone like that in peace time? Can you ever go back to what you were?"

Zach was perplexed by Jesse's questions. "Weird, I guess. Why would you ask such a question, where do you get such strange thoughts?"

"Oh, I don't know for sure. Who knows what this war will do to us, will do to anyone. I was just wondering if all of us might have a Pierre in us."

Zach was the only man to venture a response to such a disturbing thought. "I don't have any answers to questions like that, and I'm glad I don't know." He momentarily hesitated as though he had second thoughts. "God, I hope not."

Generally, the first week of November was little different from any previous week in the trenches east of the Meuse River. Soldiers did what front-line combat troops do in war—they fought, prepared to fight, or tried to rest. Although there was no such thing as a normal day, by midweek the days became less routine. Something seemed vastly different as the pace of routine military operations intensified, accelerated. Soldiers sensed a new urgency mounting. Some event of military significance was surely in the offing. Change was in the air.

Prodigious numbers of troops and supplies arrived daily, and yet command gave no indications, no inkling that another major Allied offensive was imminent. The skies were alive with Allied pursuit and reconnaissance aircraft while few German aircraft patrolled over Allied territory, giving credence to the claim that Allied aircraft controlled the skies. Daily foot patrols into enemy territory progressively increased in number, and in response German machine-gun fire became more pervasive and was of lengthier duration. Enemy artillery fire picked up, sometimes targeting the trenches but not always. For no obvious reason enemy artillery delivered harassing fire on nearby roads and villages, as canisters of poisonous gas were randomly, indiscriminately hurled at different troop positions. American and German casualties mounted as American artillery returned fire twofold for all enemy invasive action; and apart from general enemy harassment, the maneuvers made little sense. Surely some monumental event was about to unfold. Little wonder the men in the trenches fretted as they prepared for the worst and hoped for the best. Troops on both sides knew something was awry.

The unsettled weather made a turn to the worse. Temperature sometimes dropped below freezing, and low level visibility remained poor much of the daylight hours, somewhat negating Allied air superiority. It was precisely under such conditions when the pieces came together, when it all started to make sense. Sunday, November 3, command ordered American forces to mass in attack positions. Over one million American forces in the Meuse-Argonne and the Saint Mihiel sectors prepared for a coordinated assault along a 90-mile portion of enemy lines. All other combat forces, including the 22nd, Combat Engineers, took up reserve positions as an attack was scheduled to commence as soon as the troops were in position. The attack was to follow a massive artillery barrage on the enemy defensive positions; and it was ordered and understood that Allied artillery would continue its heavy shelling during the ground attack. Instructions were clear—soldiers had better be where they should be. Using ladders to climb over the parapet the leading assault wave was to exit the trenches spaced no more than three-yards apart, to cross the cut wire at the predesignated locations, to advance across no-man's-land, to break through the German wire and to penetrate the German trenches. The bold tactical order was to bayonet, shoot, or bomb any resisting enemy and for Americans to take possession of all enemy trenches. There was to be no retreat, and if there were contingent plans for retreat, they were not shared with the attack forces. As soon as the assault forces secured the enemy primary trench the reserves were to follow, advance beyond the secured positions, capture and hold the secondary trenches. Unlike former battlefield strategy, this plan required the immediate use of reserves. This was the big one.

Packs were reduced from sixty to twenty pounds, bayonets were fixed, and the troops waited for the signal. If German machine guns were still in place and operational, the lead American forces faced decimation and it was of little comfort when command assured the junior officers that all German machine guns would be diminished, if not disabled, by artillery before any attack. The junior officers and the enlisted men knew better but there was no backing down now. There was nothing more to do but wait for the whistle. Each minute passed ever so slowly for the American assault forces on that cold night in November as they waited in the trenches for the order to go over the top. Perplexing, if not bewildering, the Allied artillery barrage did not commence before dawn as scheduled. Something was wrong.

New information was at hand. The assault forces were ordered to stand down as command reevaluated. Minutes before the scheduled artillery barrage was to begin an American patrol of five men returned with more than one hundred German prisoners, including five officers, who had all surrendered on their own accord. Although Intelligence tried to conceal the news of the unusual surrender until they had time to interrogate the prisoners, it did not happen. Before the men on the patrol were muzzled they were already back in the trenches spreading the intoxicating message to their fellow comrades about the German prisoners and how they had surrendered. The word spread like wildfire as regimental runners made unauthorized jaunts announcing the news to men in other trenches. Rumor had it that Germany was considering surrender and that mutually acceptable terms for a cease fire were close at hand. Before the prisoners were delivered to Intelligence they willingly shared their disillusionment, their disappointment in the Kaiser's government, with their captors. More poignantly the prisoners openly expressed their desire not to be included in the ranks of German soldiers killed in action during the final days of the war. In essence, the prisoners admitted they were deserting a defeated army. The dejected Germans emphatically stated that their cause was lost, and if given the opportunity, there were hundreds more, just like them, willing to surrender. Divisional Field Command was obliged to postpone the American assault until they could pass on the acquired information to General Headquarters.

When the news hit the trenches, the war-weary Americans became overjoyed but restrained in their celebration, as these men had faced disappointment too many times in the past to accept any news as factual until the rumor was confirmed by action or deed. Instead of outright jubilation most men clung to their hope with guarded optimism. Regardless of past experiences, Jesse was borderline elated. "Zach, ole boy, I've got a feeling this time and it's a good feeling, running from the top of my head to the tip of my toes. Yes, sir, home by Christmas!"

Almost nonchalantly, a cynical Zach answered. "You might be right, but I wouldn't bet the farm on it. You know the Krauts, it all might be a ploy. I wouldn't put it past them to sacrifice a few men to entice us to let our guard down and then pounce on us. It's probably all a ruse, and if I was you, I'd keep that rifle pointed."

Although Zach's words were those of a combat-experienced sage and his message did not fall on deaf ears, his words did not dampen all hope. Instead, Jesse reserved judgment, appeared subdued, as he thought about the rumor and about Zach's cautious interpretation. "Yeah, you might be right. I'll stay alert and keep my rifle pointed in the right direction, but while I'm doing that I'm going to hope the rumor is true. Do you have any objection or discouraging thought to that?"

"Nope, hope away, I'm all for it, buddy. It's just that I'm not going to waste what little bit of hope I have left, if you don't have any objection to that."

Word reached American Command in time to abort the attack and stand-down orders were issued. Ankle deep in mud in freezing temperatures the men were truly exulted. Following the stand-down orders all combat engineers were reassigned to reserve status and only infantry manned the forward positions. Although reserve positions offered no shelter to escape the elements, no beds with warm blankets to sleep in, no hot meals to relieve the bland taste of uncooked field rations, and no free time to relax, the engineers believed they had been given a reprieve. For five, consecutive days the men in Company L. 22nd Engineers held such reserve positions, but in comparison with the conditions suffered by the men in the forward trenches, it was easy duty.

Indications persisted that an Allied victory was close at hand. The Germans sent out fewer patrols and launched no offensives. German prisoners in transit to G.2. Headquarters, many surrendering on their own initiative, became a common sight. "You might be right, Jesse," expressed a less cynical Zach. "It just might be this war is about to end. Almost a week of no real action, other than watching German prisoners march by, suits me fine. For every German who surrenders, there is one less to fight."

An annoyed Jesse was in no mood to agree. "Tell that to those boys out on reconnaissance patrols every night. Tell it to the guys who took that damned mustard gas last night. This is not my idea of no real action," he said with anger in his voice.

Concerned, Zach sought conciliation. "Yeah, that gas was kind of close. I already had my mask on by the time I heard the alarm. You didn't have any problems with that gas did you? When I looked at you, everything seemed all right."

Uncharacteristically, Jesse openly revealed his aggravation. "Well, even if I looked all right, I wasn't. I had my mask on too, but not before I got a good dose of it, and I had to sit there and take it. I thought it was going to burn my eyes out. Then my lungs started burning. You ever try to cough with a mask on? It hurts. It hurts as much as hurt can hurt. That's why I left the area. What did you think, I was out for a stroll or something? I had to get away from it. I hate that stuff."

"Sorry, guy, I didn't know. Next time say something or give me a signal and I'll help you."

Jesse calmed a little. "Forget about it, there is no way you can help me. I guess my body is just saturated with chemicals. Even a little breath of it hurts and just the smell of it makes me throw up. I just have lost all tolerance for the stuff. I hate it, but there is nothing I can do about it. Healing will just take more time."

"You're still sick, Jesse, you ought to report your condition and get the hell out of here."

That comment aggravated Jesse all the more. "Report to who? You think I ought to go tell the C.O. that I don't like gas? I bet he would be very sympathetic, probably advise me to take a month of leave, relax on a beach. All he will say is go to the dressing station. They would only flush out my eyes, oil my body, and tell me I'm fit for duty. I'd be right back here tomorrow. There is nothing they can do, they have no idea how to treat gas injuries. I doubt if there is any doctor in the world who knows how to treat it. They all probably say the same damn thing, just give it time. And if you're going to tell me that I should ride it out in some hospital, you might as well save your words. There are many boys out here in a lot worse condition than me. I'm here and I'm going to see it through."

Late morning the lieutenant gathered the platoon for a briefing. "We've got new orders, men, urgent orders, and these are from the top, the Allied Commander, Marshall Foch, himself. Listen carefully! Negotiations are presently underway to end the war, we've got the Germans where we want them. At noon today a coordinated Allied attack will commence all along the entire 400-mile front. The objective is to push the enemy back, to put the German Army in retreat, all along the Western Front and he is to be given no time to rest or reorganize his troops. Nothing will be held back. We'll hit the bastards with everything we've got.

"Company L. will remain in reserve. We will not engage the enemy unless forced to do so. We are to support infantry units only if they are forced to retreat. We are mop-up. I repeat, we are support only. Hopefully, today is the last day you will see these damnable trenches, because once we leave from here there is no turning back. Gentlemen, it is my pleasure to inform you that you are a player and you will personally participate in the final defeat of the German Empire.

"If a cease fire is arranged, additional orders will be forthcoming. Otherwise, we intend to give them all we've got and to hurt them as much as possible for as long as we can. Men, this is a proud day. Good luck. God bless America."

For two hours United States forces were given reason to hope that the attack would not be necessary, that a truce was at hand. However, as so often occurs during wartime, events proved the promise of a ceasefire to be a foolish hope. The delayed attack plan was reaffirmed, scheduled to commence mid-afternoon, and no explanation was offered to the soldiers. Rumors abounded as all troops prepared to move out. It was said: "Germany had sued for peace, the German Navy had mutinied, the German people were revolting in Munich and Berlin, Kaiser William II had abdicated and a democratic government in Germany was now in place." Ostensibly, if the rumors were correct, all that remained was to destroy the German Army in the field.

Exactly at 2:30 p.m., November 9, a cold, dry Saturday afternoon, the Allies initiated their final offensive with a two-hour artillery barrage. The 81st Division spearheaded the attack east to capture Abaucourt, a German stronghold. Fierce fighting ensued, resulting in heavy casualties for both sides, until the German stronghold ultimately fell to the Allies during the final hours of November 10. The Germans did not fight like a defeated army, refused to surrender the city;

rather they engaged in a hasty retreat destroying what they could in the process. The Americans occupied the city and made preparations to pursue the retreating German Army at first light the following day, November 11. Contingents, including Company L. of the 22nd Engineers were held in reserve and saw no action.

American Command deemed this assault a success. In less than thirty-six hours this one American force, considered relatively small compared to the total forces in action that day, penetrated almost three miles into German held territory and occupied a German city. This action was a clear military victory, although in terms of American casualties it had been very costly.

Although not directly involved in the battle, the reserves in the march to Abaucourt were exposed to a rare, up close, unhampered view of the immediate aftermath of battle, the personal throes of warfare. Human carnage, mutilation, agony, and prolonged suffering of men who had fought and fallen on both sides were far too common. Such an untouched overall view of the ugly aftermath of combat presented more raw images than even the hardened veteran should be forced to endure. Those in close pursuit of the front forces were witnessing the worst side of war, man's inhumanity to his fellow man. The daunting sights on the road to Abaucourt would surely forever carve a deep imprint on the psyche of all who were forced to bear witness to such ghastly sights.

At 5:00 o'clock the following morning, November 11, 1918, the Armistice was signed and was scheduled to take effect at 11:00 a.m. on the same day. At 8:00 a.m., three hours after the signing, all American forces were notified of such, and contained in the same notification was a Field Order for Divisional Commanders, from General John J. Pershing, Commanding Officer, A.E.F.

1. All other orders from these headquarters are revoked.
2. Hostilities will cease along the whole front at 11 hours, 11 November, 1918, Paris time.
3. No Allied troops will pass the line reached by them at that hour and date until further orders.
4. All communication with the enemy, both before and after termination of hostilities, is absolutely forbidden. In case of violation of this order, the severest disciplinary measures will be taken.
5. Every emphasis will be laid on the fact that this arrangement is an armistice only and not a peace.
6. There must not be the slightest relaxation of vigilance. Troops must be prepared at any moment for further operations.
7. During the armistice should anyone from the enemy's posi-

tion approach our line with a white flag, he will be received by an officer, blindfolded, and conducted to the nearest battalion P.C.

8. Special steps will be taken by all commanders to insure the strict discipline, and that all troops are in readiness and fully prepared for any eventualities.

This official announcement of a scheduled armistice probably brought more joy to more people on any single day than any other event in the history of the world. For not only was the intended armistice announced to the military forces, five hours later it was to be announced to the people of the world.

Three hours remained to wage war and Allied Command capitalized on the opportunity. Item 3 specified that no troops were to pass beyond the line at that 11:00 o'clock hour, and presumably the more land occupied, the better the bargaining chips at the final peace settlement. Subsequently, at 9:00 a.m., the American forces at Abaucourt were ordered to pursue and engage enemy forces using all resources and military forces available to command. In a little more than one hour's time the Americans penetrated an additional one-half mile of enemy held territory where, again, the casualty rate was high on both sides. All hostilities ceased at 10:54 a.m.

Exactly at five minutes before 11 o'clock in the morning, Paris time, the entire western front fell totally quiet. Wisely, common soldiers on both sides stayed low and took all necessary precautions to assure their own safety as the final seconds ticked away. Soldiers had endured much to reach this point and no one wanted to be the last man to die in the war. Anxious officers peered through their field glasses and handheld periscopes searching for enemy movement or other indication that all was not well as they waited for the eleventh hour of the eleventh day of the eleventh month to arrive. The hour came and passed and, yet, nothing happened to indicate war's end, nor did any field soldier know what to expect; so soldiers in both armies at Abaucourt waited for some official process to begin. Suddenly, surprisingly, and unofficially one unlikely event put the entire process into motion. A single German soldier in clear view slowly rose to his feet and allowed his rifle to drop at his side before he discarded his helmet. He looked toward the heavens and locked his clasped hands in front of his chest as though he were giving praise. His benign action signified less a movement of surrender, more a recognition of an end to fighting. All eyes remained on the one lone soldier as he appeared frozen in time. Ironically, had he committed such a bold move only moments earlier, he would surely have been killed; but now he stood as a common leader, a giant of men, alone and tall in an army of men perched for battle. Slowly and gracefully he scanned the American position before he turned to discern his fellow ranks. His actions, his very movements conveyed a spirit of mitigation, not repudiation; peace, not war, and only moments passed before another lone German soldier stood, then another, then another, until legions of German soldiers were on their feet, using actions rather than words to acknowledge that the fighting had ended, that the brutal beast of war had been caged.

A few brazen Americans, totally disregarding orders, rose to their feet in a like manner. Likewise, the American posturing was perceived less like a victory stance, more like a formal nod of reconciliation. In an odd but moving way, the behavior of a select few American soldiers spoke for many as they stood in recognition of war's end and respectfully acknowledged enemy soldiers who had valiantly fought for life and country. In effect, they professed a camaraderie among all fighting men and, indeed, the gesture was presented and perceived as a tribute from the heart.

One officer from each side moved forward from their ranks, met and saluted one another in the open space of the war's final no-man's-land. For several minutes the two opposing officers exchanged thoughts of which not one word was heard by the ranks of men, although the conveyed message of the words was never in doubt. The curious at Abaucourt were left to wonder what action elsewhere, what first gesture officially notified other forces that a ceasefire was at hand. Here at Abaucourt there was no doubt—the German Army had capitulated, the war was over.

CHAPTER 26

ARMY OF OCCUPATION

W hat's up, corporal, find out anything? Are we going home or what?" Seriously annoyed after four days of waiting in the trenches without confirmation of a German surrender, Zach was in no mood to accept more nebulous answers. He wanted details. In truth he really spoke for most soldiers as the surrender issue pressed heavily on their minds. Was the war over or not? With no ordered stand-downs American troops remained offensively deployed in a state of combat readiness. German troops had withdrawn, but where had they gone? Had they disarmed and dispersed or were they regrouping elsewhere? Soldiers fretted that something was awry and, understandably, they feared the worst. As front-line troops they were entitled to know their current status, to know something about the terms of surrender, or to be properly informed if the armistice were no longer valid.

"Relax, boys, all is well," replied Corporal Black. "No problems at all, we're right on schedule." His words offered comfort but stopped well short of revealing information.

Zach's annoyance gave way to anger. "Corporal or not, if you know more and you're deliberately holding back just to taunt us, I'm going to be pissed. I've heard enough bullshit, I'm not listening to it anymore. Understand?"

"Is that a threat, private?"

Timely, Jesse intervened. "No, it's no threat. Zach is just venting the same frustration we all feel. Tell us if you heard something. Is the fighting officially over? What do you mean when you say all is well?"

"I mean just that. Give me a minute to organize my thoughts, and I'll tell you what I know. Relax, nobody is withholding information." The corporal paused, found a sitting position, and retrieved a note pad from his pocket which he read as if he were memorizing something. Minutes later he spoke. "Everything is on schedule, the Armistice has been signed, the Germans have surrendered, it's official. Our forces are out there collecting enemy weapons as we speak. It all takes time because everything needs to be done by the book, according to the terms in the armistice. And no, we're not going home, not just yet anyway. The brass is still working out final details of the surrender, and the German Army is preparing for an unarmed withdrawal back to Germany."

"Well, if that doesn't beat all. We win the war and the Germans get to go home first."

"Zach, if you'll just shut up a minute, I'll finish, then you can talk, okay? There is a lot more to it and I need to get the details exactly right, so that all of you clearly understand our orders. Listen up as this is important stuff. Apparently, the American Army finds itself right in the middle of a fifty-year-old, sticky political situation which brass says we need to handle with kid gloves. Brass refers to a French vendetta from a war that ended almost fifty-years ago when the Germans served up a humiliating defeat to the French. Something about a Franco-Prussian War that I don't know anything about, let alone understand. I don't need to know the politics, the history of it all, and neither do you. Far as I'm concerned we need to know our orders, nothing more, nothing less."

Zach was near his limit of patience. "Goddamn it, answer our questions, quit pussyfooting around."

"Go to hell, Zach! I'll take all the time I need." Following a brief stare down, the corporal resumed. "After the Krauts surrender their weapons they are to immediately evacuate all invaded territories like Belgium, France, and Luxembourg. The area of Alsace-Lorraine is considered annexed French territory rather than German territory. Hell, I thought we already were in Germany, but not according to brass. They say the soil of Lorraine is all French, not German. The city of Metz lies in Lorraine, as does all the land between here and there. Simply put, our orders are to pursue German forces as they exit Lorraine and to make certain they all have gone. Once accomplished, at some point our forces will hand over to the French any annexed area that we control. We're not invaders of Germany, boys, we're liberators. We've liberated the people of Lorraine from German control. That's as clear as I can make it."

Zach spoke again using his all too common rudeness. "Too bad Andy isn't here, he would explain it so we all would understand." Others were now becoming annoyed with Zach's interruptions, so Jesse addressed Zach with a harsh, cold stare. As he should have, Zach felt foolish, immature. "Sorry, corporal, I'll keep my mouth shut."

"Good, then I'll go on! The Germans have been given fifteen days to evacuate

Alsace-Lorraine, thirty days to get east of the Rhine River. That's where we come in. Instead of French forces, Americans will follow the Germans to Metz, because brass fears the French may want immediate revenge against the German people. There is to be no retribution against Germans. American Infantry is ordered to prevent it and to ease tensions, if possible. We are specifically ordered not to engage in any activity that might increase tensions on either side. I repeat, no tense situations. Americans should defuse, not create, situations.

"Tomorrow, November 17, at 5:30 hour we pursue the Kraut Army for the purpose of making certain they return to Germany in timely fashion. Now listen carefully, because these are our exact orders: We are to peaceably pursue. The scouts, with limited infantry support, will form our lead force and we combat engineers will follow close behind. Company L. is going straight to Metz. The entire 1st and 3rd Divisions will be right behind us, and they are to handle all disputes, not us. Orders are for us to check out the physical conditions—conditions of roads, bridges, barriers, unused ordinance, or other obstacles that might hinder troop movement or endanger American lives. Also, command needs our assessment of existing railroad tracks and the present conditions of local coal and iron mines. We're not to repair anything, just report condition and location. Check out everything! If we identify any dangerous, unsafe situations, we post the site, notify an officer, and stay put until someone arrives to verify, or assess the problem. Our job is to make certain that the terrain is hospitable and safe for our advancing infantry.

"We move forward during daylight hours only. At dark we reassemble with the company, make our reports, and get briefed for the next day. We've got a tough job. The days are down to less than eight hours of daylight so we need to work fast, but it needs to be done, done right, and in an orderly fashion. We take one day at a time. Got that?

"More orders. Although I don't think these are priority concerns for us, there is always to be a safety zone of ten kilometers between us and the retreating German columns. If the Germans stop, we stop, no exceptions. If we encounter any German stragglers, they become prisoners of war and should be treated as such. If we encounter armed individuals or groups, civilian or military, we offer them one chance to surrender before we shoot to kill. Take all necessary precautions, do not endanger yourself or others. All adult, male civilians must have identification, and if they don't, they're probably deserters and need to be held for interrogation. If we come across any German officers bearing communication documents, we immediately escort them to a superior officer or to Divisional P.C., if nearby. And as always, no fraternization with any Germans, male or female.

"One more item of concern. Command is worried about distribution of Bolshevik propaganda, whatever that is. We are to seize any pamphlets being distributed in English other than official military printed material. If we encounter written pamphlets or other printed propaganda we are to confiscate and prevent distribution to either military or civilian personnel. We confiscate all documents in circulation written in a foreign language. Whatever we confiscate we send back to headquarters for scrutiny.

"Now, as far as I know, that's all. Remember we are to follow these orders exactly. If we don't know procedure for a given situation, we do nothing until we get clarification other than we always protect ourselves. Be ready to move out with field packs at dawn tomorrow. Every man carries his weapon, a full ammo belt and field rations. Any questions? Good. By the way, all of you received a promotion to Private First Class, effective November 1. Pay is one dollar a month more. Private Moore made corporal November 11th, but don't celebrate yet because all promotions after November 10th have been rescinded. Word is they have too many noncoms and officers arriving in France and they want to keep the proper ratio of men to officers. Thought you might enjoy that little tidbit of information. Sorry, Moore.

"Better get some rest tonight. Tomorrow we start for Metz, Germany. Excuse me, I mean Metz, France."

On November 17, 1918, at 5:00 a.m., without benefit of daylight, the combat engineers departed the most forward American trenches to pursue the Germans in their withdrawal to the Rhine River. Scouts had already departed. Exactly at 5:30 a.m. American Infantry Regiments followed. The post-armistice, Allied advance to the Rhine River through the disputed territories was officially underway.

It required seven and one-half days of careful, deliberate pursuit before the Americans reached the heights on the Moselle River overlooking the outskirts of Metz. Confirmation was sent to headquarters that American forces were positioned on the west bank of the Moselle River, all was quiet on the front, and their advance had met with minor incidents, no organized resistance. They awaited further orders.

Jesse considered his new quarters more than adequate. "Talk about the good life, these barracks are better than the ones we had in the States. Electric lights, good heating stove, individual beds, is right downtown to my way of thinking. If we have got to stay here, it's fine with me that we're quartered in these old German barracks. Good thing too, because it's getting mighty cold outside. Standing guard this morning I about froze my ass off."

Zach was in agreement. "Fine with me too. It's okay with me if I stay here until I get orders to go home. I'm just happy the weather waited to turn this cold until we got here. God, I hate to think about what it would be like in a trench tonight. It makes me shiver to think about it. The other night I wiped my nose with my glove, and a few minutes later the snot froze on my glove. Can you imagine how cold your hands would get if you were in a trench and had to hold your rifle all night? On second thought, don't imagine because we don't have to. We're inside. Hallelujah!"

"I wonder what the temperature would be in that German Command bunker tonight. Not bad, I bet."

A buddy from a different squad heard the conversation. "Are you guys talking about that German bunker on the down slope? Were you guys in that bunker? Was it really all they say?"

Almost in a proud manner, Jesse answered. "And more. I've never seen anything like it before, and never expect to again. Just getting to it was something else. I'm glad we didn't need to take that place under enemy fire, because I don't think we could have. It would have been a two-mile assault up a steep hill against dozens of those heavy machine guns, 7.92 caliber I think. That place was something all right! Zach and I measured the thickness of the outside wall to be four feet, solid concrete. Even before you got to the bunker you had to get past an interlocking maze of rifle pits, concrete traps, and gun emplacements woven into the landscape. Only one entrance to the bunker, one way in and the same way out, and it was a three-inch steel door. Zach thought it was impregnable. Until the defenders ran out of food and ammunition, no army could have taken it. It was the granddaddy of all fortresses."

"What was the inside like?"

Zach could not wait to give his description. "All the comforts of home and more. We assumed it was command center, or at minimum it was quarters for command staff officers. Listen to this: running water, electric lights, piped drainage, steam heat, upholstered furniture, wall decorations, long conference tables and, believe it or not, a piano. Even had two small cook stoves, I suppose to keep their coffee hot in between piano concerts. Those Krauts sure do know how to fight a war in comfort."

"Awe come on, I don't believe it."

"Believe it, buddy, it's true," said Jesse. "They even had a wine rack that ran the length of the wall. On the other side of the room they had stacked cases of beer. Everything was organized and in its place. When I think about that, I shouldn't be surprised. Germans are organized. Remember passing those German campsites on the way here. Even in retreat they took time to put everything in its proper place."

"Tell him about the lower level!"

"You tell him, I couldn't see all that well in the dim light."

"What dim light? It was lighted up in there like a Christmas tree. The lower level housed the sleeping quarters. About 60 beds I'd guess. Looked more like a hotel than military quarters. Best part was that in one closet I found a stack of shoe boxes containing women's shoes and perfumes." Zach stopped talking long enough to sport a large grin. "I'll bet you those officers didn't get cold at night."

"Damn, you think our side has anything like that?"

"Could be but I doubt it. Most likely, construction on that place took ten to fifteen years. I think the Krauts counted on war a long time ago. Don't know that, I just think it."

Jesse considered Zach's conclusion valid. "I'll bet you're right about the Germans, but I'll bet the French prepared too. When I was near Verdun I saw something I will never forget. I didn't get to see on the inside of it, but the French also had constructed a massive underground shelter called The Citadel. My last day at the hospital I went to look around Verdun and right on the edge of the city stood this massive, underground, fortified structure. Verdun lay in ruins while The Citadel looked like it hadn't been touched. Since the entire area around The Citadel was restricted, I couldn't get up close so I only saw the outside of it. It looked to me like they carved out the inside of a mountain. With any imagination at all you really didn't need to be near it to know what it was—it was headquarters for French Field Command."

"How big was it?"

"It was, oh, I would guess about ten city blocks square, maybe larger. No idea how deep it was. I was told later that it housed thousands of French soldiers and stored enough supplies to keep an army in the field for a year. It took years and years to build, I am certain of that. Yes, sir, the French also used some foresight." Jesse's final expression about French intent gave others pause for thought.

"Kind of makes me mad," blurted Zach. "Has it ever crossed your mind that other than the men who ended up fighting the battles, everybody knew a long time ago that there was going to be a war between Germany and France? Somebody got hoodwinked. The more I think of that possibility, the madder I get. I wonder how we got locked up in this war. Do you think other countries were aware of such contrivance? I'll bet there is more to the story than we know. I'll bet there is a lot more."

"Too late to worry about it now, the war is over," interjected Jesse. "I'd rather not think about such things, if you don't mind. If I start thinking about things like that, I'll get mad too. I want to think about good stuff, like going home. Speaking of home, I guess you heard the mail finally caught up with us. I got two more letters today from Helen and she wrote some interesting news. They've canceled the draft back home. All draftees still in the states are getting discharges, don't even have to finish training, so the Army can clear out all the training camps to make room for us. They've designated the training camps as mustering out sites for when we get back. She described a picture in the local newspaper of infantry soldiers boarding a transport ship in New York Harbor, and when they heard the war ended they made them get off because they don't want any more Americans over here. Supposedly, Uncle Sam is sending all the ships they can locate over here to get us. When we get home they intend to give us a hero's welcome, have us march through the streets of the big cities and things like that. Helen wrote that Jacksonville is going to bring out a brass band and welcome every soldier when he returns home. She wrote they intend to greet all soldiers, if they made it over here or not. If that's true can you imagine the reception our hometown friends will give us combat veterans when we get home? What a splendid thought!" Jesse stopped talking and others stopped listening as their minds wandered to images of home. Sounds yielded to silence, thoughts became fantasies; and not surprisingly, these comforting thoughts, these mental images warmed the hearts of these victorious combat engineers so far from home.

Following the evening meal there was an unscheduled barracks inspection. The men sort of resented it, but since it was the Army way they went along, offered no objection. Later that evening the captain posted the following day's duty roster before he verbally broke disturbing news. The men were informed of an immediate reorganization of American forces in France for the purposes of establishing an Army of Occupation in the German Rhineland. The American Occupation Army would be comprised of nine full divisions with ten divisions held in reserve. The 22nd Regiment was to be splintered by company and attached to infantry divisions as needed in the Allied march to the Rhine. Company L. Combat Engineers remained quartered in the former German barracks on the heights, west of the Moselle River, and were temporarily attached to the French Army in and around Metz. The date was Wednesday, November 27, 1918, the day before Thanksgiving.

"What does a combat engineer do when there is no combat, no war to fight, no army to disarm? What do you think, Zach? How long will American forces maintain an Army of Occupation? All this reorganization stuff is hard for me to understand. I guess we're needed over here until Germany totally disarms, however long that takes, and then we go home. What do you think? Are we talking weeks or months?"

"I think I don't know. I have no idea about what we will do or how long we will do it. I guess it could be worse, at least no one is shooting at us. Besides, we're in barracks. I'd rather be here than under canvas. I know for sure I would rather be here than outdoors with the troops marching toward the Rhine. At night it's cold out there, warm in here."

Jesse quickly answered. "I suspect you're right, although I was thinking more about time than location. I suppose home by Christmas is out of the question. It seems to me that some of those boys who arrived too late for combat would jump at this opportunity, and we worn out guys could be sent home to our families."

Comprehending that his buddy was distressed, Zach attempted to offer words of encouragement. "It will all work out, everything will be okay. We'll get home one day soon. We just need to view this as easy duty, bide our time, and take advantage of the situation. Come on, buddy, we can do it."

Normally Jesse was ,not one to openly express his woes, preferring instead to seek resolution from within, but once again his anger openly emerged. In a tart tone he lashed out at Zach. "What do you know about it? I know we can do it, we can do a lot of things. I just don't want to do it. Besides, I'm sick and tired of dealing with the continuing effects from that damn mustard gas. Apart from my poor vision it's hard to describe how I feel. It's not the same symptoms but it's kind of like having a bad cold. Usually by the second or third day you start to feel a little better, and in a few more days you know recovery is only a few days down the road. Well, I can't get past the second day. I just don't seem to get better. I can't go home less of a man than when I left, can I?"

Jesse's expression revealed more about the man than his mood—it gave insight into his inner fears. For the first time since the gassing, Zach grasped the magnitude of Jesse's injuries. He was beginning to understand the underlying fear harbored deep within his friend. Jesse was not recuperating from his injuries as he was told he would.

In relative terms the men of Company L. served easy duty as occupation forces. By late December they realized their temporary assignment near Metz was rather permanent, at least by Army standards it was; and most likely, save an unforeseen crisis, they would serve their final tour of duty in their present locale. However, because of the harsh winter weather, they spent more time patrolling the entrances to the city of Metz than they spent on engineering tasks. The extreme cold prohibited most outdoor repair or construction jobs, although they did engage in a few demolition projects. Mostly, they stood guard on the heights which controlled the all important western access to the city of Metz.

Little did American politicians suspect that in many ways the doughboys stationed in Lorraine were pawns in a French political game of revenge. The French agenda from the start of the Great War was to regain the lost territories of Alsace-Lorraine, and to finalize achievement of this objective they now needed direct assistance from the American military. President Wilson's idealistic 14 Points carried little weight with the leaders of France, Great Britain, and Italy. Most Allied nations viewed The Armistice as recognition of a total German defeat and German agreement to an unconditional surrender. Idealism be damned, the Allies felt Germany should accept total blame for the war, and certainly believed Germany should be punished accordingly. Likewise, always the victorious European Allies always wanted any postwar agreement to favor territorial change which benefited their respective nations. The European Allied intentions were not noble, their goals not easily attainable.

The first Allied priority was to disarm Germany. France preferred total, immediate German disarmament, assuring complete destruction of the existing German Army, and thus diminishing the likelihood of their rebuilding any armed force capable of future aggression. More specifically, German disarmament meant Germany would be forced to accept any terms of an eventual peace treaty. The unanswered question of whether an unarmed Germany could survive in the modern world was not a factor in their calculations.

While French forces supervised German disarmament, France needed American forces to help occupy the mineral-rich Rhineland. France also insisted on an immediate, unqualified return of Alsace-Lorraine and expected full American support in this endeavor. Since most American forces were already located in Lorraine, the French wished the Americans to hold this territory for as long as it took French forces to achieve their other non-territorial, postwar objectives. The American government felt a military obligation to help with the disarmament process, but held no territorial ambitions for itself, and instead, favored a just and permanent peace. Thus, the American military was placed in a difficult position of working with other military forces who did not share the same political postwar objectives.

The American soldier was not privy to the details of postwar politics, although he was perceptive enough to identify the political chicaneries which occurred right under his nose. For Americans the military process of occupation was not desirable duty, awkward at best. Occupation duty brought little personal danger, not much demanding physical work, but such service resulted in soldier weariness and discontent. Adding to the problem the entire area was to remain under military law until the peace process resolved the political issues at hand. Until resolution was reached, the French authorities temporarily removed many local officials from office, creating, in effect, a civil need for martial law. American occupation soldiers quickly had to play a new role—they became policemen instead of soldiers. Having no training for such, the American soldiers stationed in Lorraine merely performed as ordered without any real understanding or appreciation of the complex social, political situation.

"Zach, can you figure out what's going on here?" asked a confused Jesse as he stretched out on his bunk. "For the life of me I can't understand why we don't help some of those refugees. They're hungry, and they want to go home, that's all. Does it make sense to you or am I just too damn dumb to understand?"

On hearing the question Corporal Black snickered. "Figure that one out and they will put you in charge of the whole mess. What we see here is the aftermath of war, no more, no less. I don't think soldiers are expected to understand. I've already decided for myself. I'm going to put in my time while here and not worry about solving the world's problems, which I can't do anyway. For whatever it's worth my advice to you is you ought to do the same."

"That's pretty easy to say as we return to our warm barracks from our third meal of the day. Those people are cold and hungry."

Zach wasted little time responding. "He's got it right, Jesse, and you know he does. We can't get caught up in these local problems. There is nothing we can do, even if we could figure out what to do which we can't. Besides, things aren't as bad for the people in Metz as they are for the refugees trying to get into the city. If once in a while you would come with us to see the sights of Metz you would know that. Life goes on there, although I will admit, their lives are abated. To be honest with you, I don't think there is any real solution to the refugee problem."

Other soldiers lent an ear to the conversation. The issues under discussion were more than casual, they were interesting to these uninformed occupiers of a strange land. From across the room came a question. "What makes this area so special? Why all the fuss?"

"It's disputed land. Two different countries want it."

"I know that, but why is it disputed? Is there something other than space that makes it valuable? Why fight for it? I'm certain the men who fight the wars are not the ones who end up with the land. We all know that. Why do countries fight wars for this land? I don't understand."

"I've been told the land is full of coal and iron. Maybe that's why," a different speaker inserted.

"Perhaps, but I'll bet it's not that simple, although I would bet wars have been fought for less." Imparting a doleful expression Zach looked at Jesse. "We know who could answer our questions if only he were here, don't we? Andy would say, look at the history, boys, look at the history. I thought of him the other day when we were visiting the Cathedral Museum in Metz. They had exhibits there I couldn't believe. Did you know that Julius Caesar, himself, was once here in this exact place and fighting to control this land? They contend the Romans fought many ferocious battles right here close to where we are. They say Attila the Hun camped at Metz for over a year. There was something on display about Charlemagne dividing up his empire from the city of Verdun, and he considered this area the most valuable part of the empire. They even claimed that Joan of Arc lived a stone's throw from where we fought earlier. I ran out of time and energy and didn't finish the exhibit even though I only got up to the 1400's. If I would have stayed with it, I'll bet there were more famous names we might know. I really don't know anything about all those famous people, but I know they were important for some reason. Anyway, this is my point. Must be sufficient cause for all those wars, and I'll bet it's not fighting a war to end all wars. It's beyond me, although I know enough to know there was some good reason. I'm just not smart enough to figure it out. Anybody here know?"

No one offered answers and the discussion probably would have ended had Jesse not led the discussion in a different direction. "The answer to that question is well beyond all of us. But I have a question I'll bet somebody here can answer. Why are some former German soldiers wearing those red armbands? Is it like a white flag or something?"

Corporal Black emphatically answered, "No! It means they support some type of revolutionary government for Germany. The other day the lieutenant ordered me to keep count of all the red bands I saw. I think the ones who wear red are in sympathy with the Bolsheviks, the same group that fought in the Russian Revolution. They overthrew the Czar of Russia you know. I'm not sure what Bolshevism is, other than I do know that some powerful people out there fear the Bolsheviks. They fear the ideas will contaminate the people of Germany."

Exasperated, Jesse raised his hands in the air. "Isn't anything simple here, is everything really that complicated? Let me ask something else. Why are all those ex-prisoners of war trying to get here to Metz? I don't mean refugees, I mean former soldiers. Some are Russian, some Italian, and all kinds from eastern Europe. Why are they still here, and why can't we let them in? Why haven't they been sent back to their homeland?"

"I can answer that one," said Zach. "The Krauts kept prisoner camps near here because the area was so secure during the war. Probably didn't want civilians, or anyone for that matter, to know about them. The war ended and the guards just left. Since their countries haven't been here to claim them, the war prisoners, some call them deserters, were never officially informed of war's end, were left to survive by their own wits. Sergeant told me that the other day."

"Then why don't they just go home, or why not let them in our perimeter, so that we can help them get home if they need help? My God, Zach, they were soldiers, they fought on our side."

"Sergeant didn't tell me that, nor did I ask. I doubt if he knew."

American soldiers had little choice but found a way to make the regional issues weigh gentle on the mind. Simply, they were soldiers in the sunset of their military careers with one final job to complete—disarming Germany and restoring order to an unstable region. They had accomplished what their country had asked of them and, now, they thought of themselves less as warriors, more as peacekeepers in uniform and, overriding all other concerns, was when would they get their orders to go home.

Long days became long weeks. February arrived and the men of Company L. found themselves still stationed near Metz, still performing the routine duties of an Army of Occupation. Although the occupation soldiers witnessed little change in their daily lives, the area of Lorraine underwent major change. French desideration prevailed. The liberated area of Alsace-Lorraine sounded and functioned more like a French province than a German one. Germany was more than aware of the recent changes, but remained powerless, unable to prevent the French makeover.

General Pershing ultimately assumed a more aggressive stand against the French postwar philosophy. In February he proclaimed that the existing American military role in France was about to terminate and, soon thereafter, announced that a withdrawal of all American forces from France would commence immediately with a target date for complete withdrawal to be no later than July 1, 1919. France balked at the American suggestion of withdrawal, accusing the Americans of not meeting their postwar responsibilities and proclaiming that Allied occupation troops would be needed for years to come. With the backing of the United States Congress, and the support of the American people, General Pershing stood steadfast. American troops were coming home.

The news of the withdrawal quickly spread among the occupation forces, reaching Metz the day following announcement. The normally cold, wet winter weather of Lorraine had eased during the second week of February prompting one American to profess that the fine change in weather was a parting gift from Mother Nature, her way of showing approval for an American job well done. The bright sun only added to that already particularly pleasant day for the enlisted men who manned the guard post at the summit of the Moselle heights. The men grouped and visited near the retractable traffic barrier which was located exactly at the apex of the mountainous road. From that position the men held a commanding view for miles in two directions. "Kind of nice having to check only for contraband rather than turning people away," expressed Jesse as he waved a truck forward. "I suppose you heard the news last night. I heard Pershing ordered all commanders to prepare at once for withdrawal of American troops from France. I tell you that was music to my ears."

Zach abandoned his usual cynicism. "Maybe, let's hope it's true, however, past experiences prevent me from getting too excited. Think about what it must require to disassemble this two million A.E.F. Some troops have got to leave first and some have got to leave last. Hope we're first, but I'll bet we're not. I heard the French are so mad that they won't provide the trains necessary to get us to the coast. That's all right, the hell with them. I'll walk. I'll gladly walk, if that's what it takes to leave France. I've tried not to pester you, Jesse, so I haven't asked. How are you feeling these days? I know you're not seeing well, but you look good. In general, is your health okay?"

Jesse snickered at the question. "You sound like an Army doctor. Ignore the eyes and tell me how you feel otherwise. Yeah, I guess I'm okay. I have good days and bad days. Sometimes I have what I call short bouts of illness, mostly general fatigue. Today is a good day."

Weeks earlier Zach had realized it was usually wiser if he made few inquiries into his friend's health. Jesse preferred it that way because he often became frustrated in his futile attempt to accurately describe his malaise. Although his condition was symptomatic, the symptoms varied with the day and he feared his inconsistent descriptions sounded more like repetitious complaining than an accurate assessment, especially to medical personnel and to those who did not personally know him. Therefore, his usual answer to health inquiries assumed the form of a general, nondescriptive reply. More than not, Jesse was not totally forthright about his deteriorating health, not even with Zach."

Jesse's friend realized it was time to change the subject. "Look at that down there, isn't that a sight to behold? See the Moselle River? See that tall, massive structure near the river? That's the cathedral and that big empty space near it is the cathedral square. Civic buildings and stuff like that, I think. See that other square about one block north? That's my hangout." Zach paused as though he were attempting to identify other landmarks. "Hey, buddy, I've got a great idea. Let's you and me celebrate. You've never been inside the city of Metz, and I think you are really missing something. Let's see if we can get a two-day pass. What do you say? It might be our last opportunity to explore a real European city."

Jesse thought a few moments. "Partner, that's a good idea. I've been moping around here far too long. Apart from the train ride through Paris, I have yet to see a real French city, if in fact, Metz is a French city." He paused long enough to give a cocky smile. "Let me paraphrase. I agree it's about time that I visit a European city. We'll call it our own celebration in recognition of going home, but I don't want to say that too loud, because with our luck somebody might hear me and throw a wrench into the works. Yes, sir, I might even buy you a beer or two, or three, or four. Let's check on that pass tonight."

Their top sergeant had been instructed to reduce the number of overnight passes as extended passes seemed to promote promiscuousness among the boys too long away from home. Jesse's small group was granted an eighteen-hour pass, and the following Saturday morning five excited men embarked on an adventure to visit the European city, Metz.

The splendid outing did worlds of good for Jesse, but the best news came three days after the Metz adventure when the men of Company L. received the news that they all were waiting to hear—they were moving out, withdrawing from occupied territory. Orders did not specify destination, but not a single man doubted that this move was the first leg of the highly anticipated trek home. It was a cold, snowy night as they prepared their gear for final departure and, although they still needed to police the barracks and grounds one final time, nothing could dampen the spirits of these soldiers. They had done all, if not more, of what their country had asked of them. They had answered the call to arms, they had fought the war, they had helped restore order to a volatile world. They had served their country honorably, bravely, now it was time to go home.

"I may not have another opportunity so I want to say it now. Zach, you have been a good friend. Thank you!"

"No need to thank me, you were the real friend. Had it not been for your moral support and words of wisdom, I probably would be locked up in some looney bin in some God forsaken place."

"That is not true and you stop saying that. It's a wonder that any of us are sane after all we have been through. We'll just call it even and leave it at that although, once again, thanks. I want to express appreciation for pushing me to see Metz. I do believe that was the best time I've had in months. It was exactly what I needed." Jesse's eyes rolled upward and a look of pleasure came over his face. "It's going to be a while before I forget French food. What did they call it, quiche Lorraine or something like that? Afterwards I figured we ate five full meals in eighteen hours. Isn't that something? The French certainly know how to prepare their food. Back home I would say, I have been to hog heaven. I'll never forget walking down those winding streets and sitting around drinking beer in those plaza sidewalk cafes. Those buildings were something else. What beautiful architecture! These Europeans sure build things to last. I still wonder where all those people live and how they get any furniture in those cramped buildings. It's a lot of people in little space. And that cathedral was as grand as grand can be. I still can't believe it took them over two hundred years to build. What perseverance. I bought a bunch of post cards in Metz, and when I got back I realized every one of them had the cathedral in it somewhere. I guess I did like it. Thanks, Zach."

Zach felt such delight in seeing Jesse as he talked and acted like he once did in earlier days . "Yeah the food was good but you know what impressed me the most? The people did. They sure were receptive to American soldiers. At the time I sort of wondered if some of those men at one time might have been in enemy trenches shooting at us. Interestingly, take the uniform off a man and you can't tell if you should hate him or not. Sounds stupid to say, even though it is true. And oh, those French mademoiselles. With one of them in your bed, these winters wouldn't seem cold at all. God, the French are good-looking, fun loving people. Good thing I'm already hitched or I might be out looking." He stopped talking and started visualizing.

"Why, Zach, do I detect a note of lust in your heart?"

"Perhaps you detect lust, but it's not in my heart—it's lower." His silly comment offered a good note by which to end the conversation on their last night near Metz. The date was February 23, 1919. Jesse had turned age twenty-three exactly one week ago this day.

Two days hence, the men of Company L. arrived at Manonville Junction. The once rural area, now a busy, noisy place dominated by a hubbub of military movement, was the exact place where they had spent their first night in a combat zone, lodged in a dilapidated barn and, not inconsequential, where they first picked up cooties. Although their prior stop here had occurred a mere six and one-half months earlier, it now seemed a lifetime ago. Jesse and Zach nostalgically searched but were unable to locate the barn and stone fence. Apparently, six and one-half months was sufficient time for the Army to totally recast the layout of this once quaint place. Together they laughed when they remembered their first terrifying ordeals as inexperienced soldiers blindly following others to the trenches. In light of their many recent experiences, the once horrible nightmare of trench entry was now an amusing memory of lost innocence, of young men about to be forever altered. Thankful they had endured the war, their Manonville stop became a monumental milestone in their journey from civilian to soldier to warrior to peacekeeper. While they were grateful for their own personal survival they were also deeply saddened by the memory of many comrades who, for one reason or another, were not returning home.

Compared to most days of their military tenure the following two days were easy to take—they slept indoors, ate three hot meals a day, endured routine physical examinations, filled out administrative forms, and were issued new uniforms. These activities of hurry-up and wait procedures were, in fact, reminiscent of their early days in training, but now were easier to accept and were taken in stride. Although he told no one, Jesse continued not to feel well. He ran a low grade fever and, at times, his vision became more impaired.

Following breakfast the men of Company L. fell in for an unscheduled second roll call. The captain reassembled his company in an open field, recited a short list of names which included Jesse, and ordered those identified men to assemble at a designated indoor location. The remaining column of men formed new ranks and marched two miles east where the column linked up with truck transportation destined for the rail center. These men were going home.

The other small group of men remained isolated indoors, unaware of the whereabouts of the column. As ordered they stood at attention until they were put at ease about one hour later. In a brief time, a Colonel Madison arrived, formally addressed the indoor assembled unit, and informed the men that they had been separated from their former regiment and were reassigned to a casual detachment. Jesse was not going home.

CHAPTER 27

NON-SERVICE CONNECTED

Early March, 1919, the casual detachment arrived at an American military base near Dijon, France.

The base at Dijon was primarily an Army administrative center, not a repatriation facility. Clean and modern, the quarters, administrative buildings and warehouses were equipped with central heating, electricity, and indoor plumbing. The base hosted numerous facilities including a large hospital, a research and war-data collection center, and a storage center for unused war material. It was at this base where command was attempting to reconcile a final tally, a historical reckoning, a written blueprint documenting the role of the United States Army in the Great War. From a common soldier's perspective this American military camp was little more than a military center for bureaucratic nonsense, manned mostly by officers who had not personally participated in the war.

A squad of men from the Manonville Casual Detachment waited several hours in an interior room of a large building where they had been ordered to report for a routine physical examination. Stripped down to their underwear they impatiently waited in three rows, arm's length apart, until a youthful looking medical doctor, Captain Butler, made his entrance. "Good morning, men, let's get started," he cheerfully greeted the men, giving the impression that he was looking forward to his work. "This is a routine physical. I will examine you one at a time and I expect you to inform me of any physical complaints you presently have or any injuries you have suffered in the past."

Before Captain Butler could initiate an exam, a tall, brawny man stepped forward. "Permission to speak, sir?" Since the man was dressed only in his underwear the captain was unaware of his rank. The other men knew his identity—he was

497

Regular Army, a decorated 1st sergeant with extensive combat experience.

"What is it?" Captain Butler answered in an impatient manner.

The sergeant surprised everyone when he spoke. "What the hell are we doing here? I don't need any Goddamn physical, I just had one three days ago, as did every man here. What the hell is going on, sir?"

A shocked captain turned and faced the speaker. "Identify yourself, soldier."

"Sergeant O'Malley, Casual Detachment, formerly Company E., 61st Infantry Regiment, 5th Division. Respectfully, sir, will you answer my question?"

"I don't have an answer to your question. I'm an Army doctor, under orders the same as you. Ask your C.O., he knows the answer."

"I would, sir, but presently he is assigned elsewhere. It is my understanding that he is on leave in Nice, competing in a tennis tournament. I can't ask him or I would. I have asked other company officers and not one knows, or rather, that is what they tell me. I ask you again, sir. Why are we here getting another physical? Why do we remain in casual detachment?"

Captain Butler was aware that some officers were away competing in athletic events. Likewise, he was more knowledgeable than he had indicated about why the men were in casual detachment. The captain stood without speaking, looking first at the sergeant, then at the other men, then deliberating in silence four or five minutes. "Gentlemen, have a seat. I don't know the precise answer to your question, but I will tell you what I know." Surprised by the captain's response, the underwear clad group of soldiers broke ranks and assumed sitting positions. "First of all allow me to reiterate—I do not know for sure why you are here as casuals other than at one time or another all of you were treated at military hospitals. Furthermore, all soldiers in casual detachments are, or were, classified in one of four groups: Class A. Casuals includes hospital evacuees who are fit for combat service. Class B. Casuals is a temporary classification. Class C. Casuals are soldiers not likely to return to their units for two months or longer. Class D. Casuals are those not likely to return to their units for an indefinite time. All of you are designated Class B. or C. I assume each of you revealed or showed indications of a lingering physical problem at the time of your Manonville medical exam. I don't know that, I only assume it.

"General Pershing gave clear orders. Every soldier will undergo a physical exam to determine fitness before transport to the states. Healthy soldiers will be cleared for departure and others will remain here for further examination. More precisely, we will not send infirm soldiers back to their homes without medical evaluation for proper care, short and long term. The American public would not stand for it, and it would be improper for the Army to do so. I say again, my job is to medically evaluate you and to make recommendations, nothing more, nothing less. My job is to determine your level of medical fitness for travel back to the States. There are many illnesses or injuries with long-term medical complications, some of which we don't totally understand. The Army expects us to resolve these medical issues, once and for all."

The captain's words shocked the men, but no one interrupted. "For example, take the issue of the influenza pandemic, one I'm sure you are all aware of. That flu erupted overnight and although we're not certain about its point of origin, we believe the first outbreak was at an American military base back in the States. Influenza killed millions of people at opposite ends of the earth in less than eighteen months. One could wake up healthy and be dead by nightfall. Strangely, it seemed to strike healthy people, mostly between the ages of 20 and 40. Some recovered, some died from it. Just as quickly as the epidemic started, it ended, at least we hope it did. We know it was a virus and that is all we know for certain. Now have any of you men had the flu?"

All, individually answered they believed they had not.

"Okay. Since arriving in France have you been afflicted with high fevers, delirium, nose bleeds, diarrhea, or fluid in the lungs?"

The sergeant answered. "Of course, we have. Every soldier at the front has been sick or has had dysentery at one time or another. That doesn't mean we were sick with the flu."

"Exactly, but can we be certain the epidemic is over? Is it possible that some soldiers still carry the virus in some mutated or dormant state? Might this virus one day re-emerge and spread to others, perhaps cause another epidemic? I doubt that any of you carry the virus, I'm simply offering that as a possibility, as reason to undergo further examination. In addition to the influenza our soldiers have been subjected to numerous diseases, and that is why I am examining each of you. It only makes sense, doesn't it? Think about the catastrophic result if soldiers with a contagious disease boarded a ship crowded with other soldiers. Think about the consequences if you returned home with a contagious illness. Just think about it. Again, my purpose is to give you a clean-bill-of-health, so that you might return home. No one wants to keep you here any longer than necessary. Clearly put, you men aren't going anywhere until you are deemed medically fit.

"Gentlemen, that is the only answer I have. It is my belief that in a few days most of you will be reassigned and this experience will be but a bad memory."

A youthful, wise captain had defused an awkward situation. His sensitivity to their potential medical problems and his clear explanation of the dangers of a contagious disease were valid explanations which helped the men derive some logic out of a nonsensical situation. The Regular Army sergeant with impeccable credentials had been the right man to demand an explanation. His veritable inquiry made clear to other enlisted men that they were not alone in their predicament.

The sensitive captain went beyond the customary military procedure when he arranged for individual interviews following the physical examinations. Privately, each soldier had the opportunity to describe any personal medical concerns they harbored, and in return, the doctor could unofficially, or off the record, advise each soldier. For some reason Jesse had confidence in the doctor and was candid during his interview.

"You are convinced these symptoms are all a direct result of your exposure to mustard gas? Is that correct, private?"

"Yes, sir, I am."

"You had no other eyesight problems prior to that time? No stomach problems? No bouts of sickness prior to the gassing?"

"No, sir. You ask as though you doubt me. Do you?"

"I do not. I only wanted to affirm what you said."

Jesse felt relieved. "How much longer before all this stuff clears up? Can you give me a good guess?" His question served to stir his own anxiety. "This won't keep me from going home will it? You said our conversation was private, otherwise I wouldn't have been so honest. You will clear me to go home, won't you?" The following silence disturbed Jesse even more. "Sir."

"I'm thinking, I'm thinking. We have a situation here that I don't exactly know how to deal with. Gas injuries are not my specialty and to be honest I don't know how to answer your question. We just don't understand the long term effects of gas. I'm sorry to say it, but I have no idea of the time required for full recovery or, in fact, if full recovery is even possible. I don't know enough to give a valid medical answer." The captain said no more, and a terrified soldier apprehensively waited for a more reassuring response. Several minutes passed.

In an attempt to better understand the full story the captain pursued a different line of questioning. "If you were gassed, why do you not wear a wound chevron on your right sleeve?"

Jesse did not hesitate. "I didn't know there was such a thing for gas injuries. I've not seen any. Perhaps it will be granted later. Don't the field hospital records document all that?"

"At best, field hospital records are incomplete. They indicate you were there and when, but that's about all. Why did they not immediately send you to one of the gas hospitals? Why did you go back to the line? Were you ordered back?"

Almost offended by the implication contained within the question, Jesse briefly paused before answering. "I need to be careful how I answer those questions. I don't want to unfairly upbraid the medical group that treated me. So please, sir, permit me to be factual, deliberate. I was informed that I could receive treatment at Rarecourt, a gas hospital. I was also told they expected that in time I would fully recover on my own, that they expected no complications. They did not order me back to combat, they allowed me to choose—Rarecourt or back to my unit—so I chose to go where I was needed at the time. The very day I made my decision to return to the lines, the hospital was receiving massive casualties from another offensive, and the incoming soldiers certainly were in more need of attention than I was. At least in my judgment they were. Let me rephrase that; most were in dire need of medical help, and I thought the best thing I could do was get out of the way. At the time there was no question but that I had made the proper decision. Now allow me one more thought which is in direct response to your implication. Am I 100% positive that today I am suffering from the ill effects of gas? The answer is yes. For sure that gas damaged my eyes. I can't be sure about the other symptoms, but I didn't have any of them until I got gassed. Sir, that is the best answer I can give. In return I would appreciate an honest answer from you. Do you believe that my physical condition on this day, my poor eyesight included, is a direct result of my exposure to mustard gas, or do you think it was caused by something else?"

The doctor was moved by the simple, eloquent presentation. Private Moore had more than answered the doctor's questions, he had posed a professional dilemma for the medical officer. Captain Butler understood that he could not go on record as having diagnosed a soldier as suffering long term effects from gassing other than blindness. Medically there was no such condition. He certainly could not offer a prognosis with any certainty. He, likewise, believed the soldier deserved an honest medical appraisal of his persistent troubling physical condition. "Off the record my answer is an unqualified affirmative. You are suffering from injuries caused by mustard gas and I don't know when you will totally recover. On the record I regret I can not medically answer your question. Simply, I don't know. However, I can do this much for you. We have a doctor on staff who has experience treating chemical injuries. In fact, he served at Rarecourt for a while. I will consult with him and others about your condition and even arrange for you to see him if he considers it advisable. At some point I will attempt to come up with a prognosis. Understand, I will ask for assistance, but I promise nothing. You may believe I am passing the buck, but I am not. I will state it again. We understand the chemical agents involved in mustard gas, we understand the chemical process, but we do not understand the long term effects on the human body. Officially, exposure to mustard gas can cause permanent loss of vision or death. If neither occurs, most victims begin immediate recovery. Seldom do men with gas injuries receive any additional or any different treatment than you received at the field hospital. That is to say, the agents are immediately neutralized and the patient is given rest and nourishment. If the patient has made it that far, he usually gets better and is expected to fully recover. Few victims are kept under medical watch and, as far as I know, no medical records are kept on the long term effects of gas injuries and little research, if any, is underway. That is my honest answer to your question.

"When I have more time I will make my inquiries and will get back to you. I repeat, I will initiate contact with you, not the other way around. Do you understand?"

"Yes, sir, I do not contact you."

"Correct. For now you must accept the only medical opinion I can give. Sorry to say this, I deem you medically unfit for transport home. You are hereby ordered to undergo weekly examinations until you are determined physically fit to make the voyage. Dismissed."

Three weeks passed without contact from Captain Butler. A different doctor gave him his weekly physicals. Jesse's days were occupied with routine military duty and nights became opportunities for rest and recovery. Jesse Moore was physically and emotionally feeling better. Perhaps the doctors were correct all along—time was the healer.

On March 28, Captain Butler ordered a recall visit for Private Moore. Only the two men were present during the meeting, and the doctor offered no pleasantries or military formalities. "I consulted with other doctors as I said I would; and I'm fearful that I don't have much good news for you. Here it is. We are uncertain as to the exact cause of your medical condition. Most likely, you suffer from the effects of gas, but we have no way of knowing with certainty. If your condition is the result of exposure to mustard gas on the field of battle, the Army has the responsibility to keep you here under observation until we can help you. Do you understand what I just said?"

"Yes, sir. How long?"

"An indefinite time at best. I'm not certain that we ever will have the means to help you."

"Does that mean you will immediately authorize my return home?"

"No, it doesn't, it means just the opposite."

Bordering on anger Jesse snapped back. "If you can't help me, why would you keep me here? That makes no sense to me."

"It makes sense to the Army. If your condition is a result of combat, the Army has an obligation to treat that condition. Otherwise, we clearly would be remiss in our duty and responsibility to our soldiers."

"Why not treat me back in the States?"

"We cannot return sick soldiers home, not until we can prescribe a proper medical treatment for recovery.

"Captain, I need an honest answer. If my condition is a result of gas, in your opinion will I recover in due time? Will I regain my health, will I get my vision back?"

"My honest answer is I don't know. One of the doctors I consulted believes that, in time, you may recover. The other doctor, and this is totally off the record, believes that anyone subjected to mustard gas for any substantial period of time, has already suffered irreparable damage, and that no length of time or no application of current medical treatment will result in recovery. He believes the damage is done and recovery is not possible, at least not at this time."

These despairing words bit deeply. Although Jesse somewhat expected this prognosis, he was not prepared to hear the words. Almost stupefied he sat for minutes, motionless, before he regained his outward composure. Then he briefly reflected on what the captain had said. The captain remained quietly in his seat, compassionately observing Jesse. Without emotion Jesse asked, "What happens if I decide that gas has nothing to do with my condition? Will I go home?"

"Medically, I cannot answer that question, nor will I attempt to shape your thinking."

Striking a demeanor of full composure, Jesse pursued additional information. "I understand I must decide for myself, but whatever I finally decide affects others too. Heaven help me, I have a wife and small child at home; and everything I do from now on affects them in a most serious way. I can only imagine how this ordeal has already preyed on her mind. Can I appeal to your sense of compassion? Will you give me your best guess about what lies ahead? Will I recover or not?"

Without question the doctor was moved by the impassioned plea. "You're very persuasive, private, but I don't know if I can do what you want. I just don't have the answers." Jesse remained attentive as though he was certain the doctor had more to say, and the doctor waited for Jesse to respond to his declaration of ignorance. The captain relented first. "Very well, private. Against my better judgment I will yield to your appeal. I will tell you what I think, not what I know. Do you clearly understand that what I say is a personal guess, not a medical fact? Do you accept that I am speaking as a fellow human and not as an Army doctor to patient?"

"Yes, sir, and I accept all as such."

"All right, here it is and it's not pretty, brace yourself. If indeed you were exposed to enough gas for a sufficient period of time, you will most likely never recover, certainly you will never recover your sight. In fact, if you were exposed to enough gas, it ultimately could be fatal, probably will be. We just don't know for sure. On the other hand, there is a chance that in time you may totally recover and suffer no long-term ill effects whatsoever apart from diminished vision. My best guess is that if you survive the first year of this affliction, with affliction in quotes, you are likely to survive many more years. However, you may have less than one year to live."

Stoically, Jesse remained in his chair saying nothing. With his hands in front of his chest he sequentially touched his fingertips to the opposite finger as though the slight movement helped him sort through what the doctor had said. Finally, he spoke. "Thank you, sir, I appreciate your honesty."

Jesse's thoughts were tantalizingly obscure, but the doctor's feelings were on display—he showed regret for having been the bearer of such sad news. "Given your present condition I cannot medically clear you for passage home. However, there is another option for your consideration. I only notify you of it, I do not recommend it. There is a simple procedure that bypasses medical release for transport home. It is a standard medical form called, non-service connected. It declares that any injury or illness that you now have is non-service connected. In other words, your signature on this form releases the Army from all responsibility, now or in the future, for any affliction that you may have. If you sign this form you forever forfeit any claim to future benefits. Assuming you have no contagious disease, your signature and proper filing of this form preempts the need for medical clearance for return to the States. You request this form from your company commander. I say again, I do not recommend it, I only advise you of its existence."

"Thank you, sir, I appreciate your forthrightness. May I be dismissed?"

Jesse was disturbed by what he had just heard, he needed time to think. His future was in doubt and his confused thinking bordered on panic. He found it difficult to accept the doctor's thoughts that his present physical situation might not improve. He had always believed in a better tomorrow and had never considered the possibility that he might not recover. The mere thought of the non-service connected disclaimer made him angry, so he barely considered the possibility of signing it. It seemed to Jesse that his life was out of his control. He bordered on abject despondency. His emotions ranged from anger to self-pity, from contempt of military institutions to doubts of personal worthiness. He needed time to think, to control his emotions, to sort out his own muddled thoughts.

The following day Jesse received a lengthy letter from Helen. In all her wisdom Helen beautifully composed her thoughts to express how much she wanted her husband by her side, and she reaffirmed that no amount of physical injury to her husband could diminished her love, her need for him. She spoke of how fortunate each was to have the other and that she was looking forward to their resumed life together. In that one letter Jesse sensed more love directed his way than many men would feel in a lifetime. He had a remarkable wife.

Enclosed in the letter was a clipping from *The Pike County Democrat*, dated November 6, 1918. Helen wrote that she believed Elzie would have approved of the article, and would have received great pleasure knowing that his big brother would read it.

HOW ELZIE HUBERT MOORE WAS KILLED IN BATTLE

Headquarters of Asst. Chief of Staff
To: Erastus L. Moore, Milton, Illinois.
Subject: Elzie Hubert Moore.

1. Elzie Hubert Moore was an Intelligence Scout and was killed when the enemy made an attack on the place where he was, in the latter part of June. The attack was preceded by very heavy shelling on that immediate locality. He was one of a group of less than ten. The number of enemy who attacked was fifty-five and they were to surround the group.

2. Over a month later the enemy's story of the fight came through a prisoner of war who had participated in it. He said that the German attack failed partly because the small American group vigorously counter attacked.

3. The body of Elzie Hubert Moore was found twenty yards in advance of the barbed wire which was protecting the position where he was. His body was more advanced than those of any of his fellows and showed that he led this counter-attack. That the Germans considered their men who participated in it worthy of mention was shown by the fact that they were all given iron crosses of the second class. The action of this small group of American soldiers was much more noteworthy and was worthy of the highest tradition of the American Army. The position where your son's body was found shows that his part in it was most conspicuous and something of which his family may ever be proud.

4. As head of the Intelligence Section of the General Staff of the Division I share with you in sorrow for the loss of him in the way in which he met his death. It is such as he, who are winning this world war for democracy.

Herbert Parsons. Lieut. Col., G. S. G. 2.

Jesse studied the letter. It struck him as strange that, during an intense period of American fighting, the Fifth Division Chief of Intelligence had taken time to inform the family about the particulars of Elzie's death. Normally a family was officially informed of a soldier's death by telegram and, other than noting killed or missing in action, standard military policy restricted release of additional information. Convinced there was more to this letter than met the eye, Jesse shared the letter with and sought advice from his acquaintance, Sergeant O'Malley, Casual Detachment formerly Company E., 61st Regiment, 5th Division. Although the sergeant had not been personally acquainted with Elzie, he had heard the story about the heroic counterattack at La Cude. He informed Jesse that the battle of La Cude, the place and time where the 5th Division suffered its first fatal casualties of the war, was legendary among all men in the 5th Division. He described in detail the story of the valiant stand and the only discrepancy between his version and the colonel's letter was that the sergeant believed a corporal, not a young private, had led the attack; and he further stated that after reading the colonel's letter he was now convinced that Elzie was the leader in question. Once the rugged, Regular Army veteran determined that Jesse was Elzie's brother he formally saluted his fellow casual out of respect for Elzie. Thereafter, he gave additional details describing what the prisoner of war had said about Elzie's final struggle.

Jesse was proud but saddened by Elzie's final adventure but for now he could dwell little on the past event as he had greater, more pressing concerns about his own survival; and as he often had done in the past he took a walk hoping to further sort out his muddled thoughts. It was only by chance that Jesse, with head hung low, walked west to a section of camp not ventured to before by him. The near perfect, pleasant weather on this spring day was wasted on the usually weather conscious soldier. The low, late afternoon sun brilliantly beamed its low angle rays casting elongated shadows, and Jesse noticed the shadows more than he minded his location or climate. He walked slowly, without purpose, for he carried a heavy burden, perhaps too much for any one man.

The road dead-ended but the sidewalk guided him around a corner to a beaten down grass and gravel pathway. He had left the main thoroughfare and might never have noticed had he not heard the roar of laughter from afar. To identify the distraction he was forced to look about; and almost as though he was annoyed by the sounds of laughter, he glared toward its direction. To his surprise the laughing men were patients, wounded American soldiers in the Army hospital recovering from combat related injuries. From where Jesse stood the low sun served him well as he could observe the soldier patients placed outside for sun and fresh air, while they would have difficulty seeing him. He stared at the men, partly in shock, partly in sympathy. The soldier patients, numbering almost a hundred, were dressed alike—Army-issue pajamas, olive green robes, and brown slippers. A few wore

Army-issue caps, jackets or sweaters. A few men were in wheelchairs, some were lying on their backs in portable beds, while others were moving about encumbered by bandages, casts, or crutches. Nine men had no sight and walked with the aid of white canes or with assistance from others. Closer inspection revealed more emotionally disturbing details. Among the men laughing were amputees, two were paraplegics. Some wore head bandages while one soldier's entire body was covered with wrapped bandages. A few men showed burn scars, a few revealed twisted or mutilated limbs. One man with one ear and one eye had total scarring on the left side of his head and he was conversing with another man who had no chin and was wearing a rigid neck brace to support his head in an upright position. Some men sat immobile. Many were too distant to identify their specific injuries, but it was evident they all suffered from combat related injuries.

Overwhelming to Jesse who was presently somewhat engaged in self-pity, was the spectacle of soldiers, surviving victims of a brutal war, laughing as though they had no cares at all, joyful to be alive. But a few short years ago on almost any beautiful spring day like this, most likely, many of them were youthful adolescents playing with family or friends in the backyard waiting for mother to announce meal time. Yet, on this day these incapacitated soldiers with questionable futures were outdoors conversing with others, appreciating the beautiful weather and, perhaps, appreciating life itself. If anyone of the observable patients felt despair or self-pity, he did not show it.

Jesse sensed shame, guilt about his own depressed thoughts. Shame because he was better off physically than most of the observed men, but he was the one obviously wallowing in pity. His feelings of guilt were every bit as strong but more difficult for him to reconcile. He tried to understand his feelings but could not.

He continued his walk on the path, albeit with a different perspective. Directly ahead was a fence surrounding a compound which was guarded by soldiers within the fence. Jesse assumed the inmates were prisoners of war not yet repatriated, until closer inspection revealed disquieting evidence to the contrary. The men were American soldiers suffering from shell shock. Two patients stood close to one another near the fence, yet each seemed unaware of the other's presence. Jesse walked toward the two men but stopped his advance well short of them. He felt compelled to offer some greeting, some type of personal communication. "Hi, guys, perfect day for an outside stroll, isn't it?" Neither man answered. One man stood with a blank stare on his face and acted as though he had not heard the greeting. The other man moved away as though he was frightened, occasionally looking back to confirm that Jesse was not pursuing him.

Jesse turned, slowly moved away. The behavior of both men had disclosed the reason for their confinement—they were shell-shocked soldiers under guard for their own well being. An unknown number of former soldiers were now de facto prisoners of war, not a result of enemy capture but a result of mental anguish. The compound offered living proof that minds as well as bodies could be altered by man's participation in the savage conflict called war. Jesse could not help but wonder if the world understood that many of those who survived the war remained broken in health or spirit, perhaps both.

The grass path continued onward and regardless of where it lead or additional exposures that lay in store, Jesse felt compelled to pursue its future revelations. Soon the path gave way to a more traveled, stone walking path which circumvented a small frame building situated on the crest of a small hill. Certain that he had not walked beyond the secured perimeter, Jesse approached a large stone monument with a carved inscription. He was approaching hallowed ground, a resting place for those never scheduled to return home.

> American Military Cemetery
> Dijon, France
> Here Rests In Honored Glory
> A Comrade In Arms

Here, under an American flag, a two-acre cemetery hosted hundreds of white, wooden crosses neatly placed in linear rows, positioned an equal distance apart. Jesse hesitated, not knowing if he should dare enter such sacred ground. He chose to enter, to pay his respects to the many fallen, interred soldiers. For anyone ever having fought on a battlefield, perhaps for any compassionate human being, the imposing sight was a moving but devastating view which brought forth a realization that each cross represented a youthful life lost in service of country while fighting thousands of miles from home shores. So clearly illustrated was one simple truth—that here these American soldier boys lay buried in foreign soil, and would forever stay ageless, remembered more for what they did than all they might have become.

Jesse had to exit the cemetery, he could look no more, but even upon departure he was constrained to read the inscriptions on each imposing cross as he passed. One particular inscription caught his eye, forced him to tarry.

> Private Samuel T. Mulvaney
> 22nd Engineers, Company L.
> September 26, 1918

Jesse had not personally known the individual, although he recognized the name. This soldier had entered the trenches at the same time and with the same men as Jesse. It was possible that they had fought side by side, and Jesse was most regretful that he could not recall a face.

He would have made his exit but near the outer perimeter of markers he, again, was given reason to pause.

Private William Fay
5th Div., 61st Infantry, Company L.
August 16, 1918

At once, Jesse recognized this fallen soldier was 61st Regiment, Company L., the same as Elzie. Jesse's body began to tremble, his emotions consumed his very existence, and he fell to his knees, placed his hands to his face and sobbed uncontrollably. He had lost control, his defenses were gone. He wept and continued to weep until there were no more tears to shed, but that did not end his grieving, so there he remained.

The hour was near dark when the cemetery caretaker approached. "I'm sorry to disturb you, sir. The cemetery closes at sunset." Jesse apologized to the caretaker, exited the cemetery, and returned to his barracks.

The following day Jesse received another letter from Helen—Jesse, Jr., had taken ill, was suffering from double pneumonia. One would think that such a rapid series of disturbing events would break the spirit of one restrained so far from home. Conversely, the combination of recent events—the shocking news from the doctor, his unexpected tour of the many different casualties of war, his discussion with the 5th Division sergeant about Elzie's last stand, the news about his son—only served to help Jesse regain a proper perspective about his own mission in life. He drew from Helen's strength, from her earlier declaration of love and unqualified support for whatever path he chose. He found resolution. He had everything to live for, a future with wife and family, and nothing to gain from dwelling on past problems and mistakes. Not only did the man find the courage to positively pursue life, he also found the strength of mind to believe it possible. From some place deep inside the soul of the man an inner strength emerged, and using this strength he developed a resolve, a strong will to persevere.

That same day Private Jesse Moore met with his company commander and signed the non-service connected injury form. Three days later Jesse received notice of his transfer to Le Mans, a repatriation center for homeward bound troops.

April 15, Jesse arrived by train at Le Mans, a small city near Paris. The American Army base at Le Mans was another fine modern military facility where Jesse had no quarrel with his accommodations or food. Just as the Army asserted that soldiers needed acclimation to wartime conditions in France, they also insisted that soldiers needed adjustment time before returning to civilian life. Only this time they enforced their guidelines, and the process was called repatriation. All soldiers undergoing repatriation were given light duty and, in fact, their major responsibilities were centered around completing paper work and meeting designated repatriation obligations and deadlines.

The United States military was shouldered with the awesome responsibility of safely returning over two million American soldiers to the States for eventual discharge. By mid April, 1919, less than one million American soldiers had set sail for home ports. With the limited number of available transport ships, embarkation had to be gradual and prioritized. Likewise, the government wanted regiments to return as a unit to their point of induction or enlistment so that they would properly and ceremoniously be welcomed. Apart from those who needed stateside hospitalization, casual detachments were not given priority of return and were often incorporated in other regiments for transport. Except for five divisions remaining in occupied Germany, all American soldiers were slated to leave France by July of 1919.

Since the base at Le Mans housed over 250,000 American men, the Army placed considerable effort on establishing educational courses, lectures, sporting events, and numerous other activities for the bored soldiers awaiting return home. Apart from music concerts Jesse participated little in structured recreational activities. Although the opportunities for American soldiers to travel to Paris or other places of interest were many, only once did Jesse avail himself of any such travel opportunity. He made one, four-hour visit to Paris and avoided most other structured recreational activities. By his own design Jesse directed all his energy and effort into the process of physical recovery, acquiring sufficient rest and proper nourishment. Although he accepted his sight limitations, he held steadfast in his belief that he would ultimately make a full recovery and enjoy good health once again.

April 21, Jesse received wonderful news from Helen. Jesse, Jr., was past the critical stage and was slowly recovering from his bout with pneumonia.

Jesse gave thanks for his son's recovery, for the blessings of family, and for all the love that had been bestowed upon him. Perhaps he underwent a religious experience of a type, as for the first time to his memory the soldier engaged all the mental abilities he could muster in the pursuit of a single quest—the search for a spiritual meaning to life.

The long days of waiting passed slowly and sometime during late April Jesse's fragile health made a turn to the worse. He lacked energy, required more rest and even the most mundane daily tasks required concentrated effort. Fortunately, Helen's faithful daily correspondence offered solace and he mostly survived by continuing to draw from her strength. Somewhat embarrassed by his own deteriorating handwriting, Jesse mostly answered her letters with picture post cards and short messages instead of informative letters. Although he knew his son would not be aware of it, Jesse also started sending post cards to Junior. Probably, the cards to Junior were more for Jesse than for the child.

In late April Jesse mailed a card to Helen with pictures of Paris landmarks. The card was titled, Souvenir de France, 1919.

> Dear Wife Helen,
> I received your six letters last night. Sure was glad to hear from you and glad to hear of you both. No I still don't have any idea when we will start home. It looks as though we are here for good. It's quite a proposition to write you a letter any more. I hope you understand. I still love you and am true.
> I remain yours only,
> Jesse

Another card was postmarked May 11, 1919.

> Dear Wife Helen,
> Just a card today. How are you and baby? It sure is warm here today. Well it's the middle of May and we are still here. Looks like we are a long time getting started home, don't you think. A card is about all I can write any more seems like.
> Your Husband True,
> Jesse

Helen could read between the lines—her husband was in failing health. Although she never revealed to anyone her deepest concerns, she prepared herself for the unknown. She never wavered in her daily writing responsibilities, and never did she give up hope. Her letters were always encouraging, loving. She showed her strength and Jesse continued to draw from it.

Mysteriously, during the third week of May Jesse's health made a turn for the better. He slowly regained his strength, began to develop endurance. On June 7, 1919, Jesse received his embarkation orders. After fifty-two days stationed at Le Mans, he was to leave the following day for St. Nazaire, the port city for embarkation.

During the four days at St. Nazaire every soldier in the casual detachment was given a physical, received his final disinfection treatment, and was issued a new uniform before boarding the Princess Matoika, a cruise ship converted to a troop transport ship. At noon, Paris time, June 12, the Princess Matoika set sail for home shores. Jesse was going home.

Only eighteen days later the last ship carrying American soldiers home from France would depart the same harbor. The last units of the American Expeditionary Force to leave France were all on their way back to the United States.

The ocean crossing required ten days and each glorious day of sailing toward home lifted Jesse's spirits immeasurably. Upon reaching American territorial waters, soldiers lined the decks of the Matoika for a glimpse of home shores. Spirits could not have been higher. Jesse's new shipboard friend made polite conversation as they waited for tug and tow. "I thought we would land in New York. That's where we embarked from."

Jesse replied, "Yeah, me too, but to be honest I don't care where we dock as long as it's American soil. Charleston Harbor looks mighty fine to me."

"Yeah, I agree. I heard that the eagle flies as soon as we land—back pay and all. I heard we even get a bonus for having served in France. Pretty good, huh! I wonder if the Army has planned a grand reception for us at the docks. They say the whole route home is lined with brass bands and cheering crowds. We're heroes, Jesse, we whipped the Germans, saved the world from evil." The comment got no response from Jesse. "I would think in light of all that is about to happen, you might show a little excitement. You know, a big hurrah or something."

The comment evoked a grand smile from Jesse. "Those thoughts do strike a good chord. Once we're back on American soil I'll give you all the hurrahs you want. In fact, I'll go you one better. If we have time and opportunity while in Charleston, how about we go to town, go out to a restaurant maybe see the sights? I need a celebration. Is it a deal?"

"It's a deal, I'd love to celebrate with you. Of course, first we need to parade around a little to allow the local people a chance to welcome us home. Who knows, some grateful person in Charleston may even treat us to a meal."

"That would be fine with me. I think I might enjoy a little appreciation, a little attention. What I'm most looking forward to is the reception I get when I get off the train in Jacksonville, my home town. I've got a wife and family and all kinds of friends there. When we left, almost the whole town showed up to sent us off. Yes, sir, I can hardly wait. It wouldn't bother me any if right away they put me on a fast train going home. Who knows, maybe we won't have enough time to celebrate here. I don't know what they have in mind for us."

"Yeah, me either, but I think we both better keep our britches on. You know the Army, I wouldn't count on anything happening too fast."

Both of the returning soldiers were wise to expect delay, to guard against disappointments. The receiving docks held no civilian crowds to cheer their return, and there was no other troop welcome. Troop ships had been arriving at Charleston Harbor since November, 1918, and the civilian desire to welcome the troops home had long since faded. If anything, the townspeople were tired of the returning soldier boys. The city had been flooded with battle hardened soldiers, many of whom were ready and anxious to let off some steam. Some local townspeople were quite vocal in their desire to be rid of carefree returning soldiers. So in terms of a welcoming celebration, the soldiers' arrival and transport to the temporary barracks were major disappointments. Regardless of how long the war had been over, it seemed to Jesse that returning troops should have been officially welcomed, if only in some small way.

Their fourth night in Charleston was the first opportunity to leave the base. Jesse and five other returning soldiers, dressed in uniform, exited the base bound for downtown Charleston. Proud as punch they walked the downtown streets thinking of themselves as conquering heroes and anticipating a red carpet treatment; but only street venders and prostitutes paid them any mind. Others resented or at best ignored their presence. Dismayed, they decided to locate a suitable restaurant, eat a sit down, served meal and call it a short evening. The downtown restaurant they selected appeared perfect—not too fancy, not too plain, and not too crowded. Upon entering the restaurant the six soldiers received the surprise of their lives—they were coldly, if not rudely received and were told by the hostess that she preferred they find a more suitable restaurant. Angered, they demanded to speak with the owner. The curt owner offered no explanation other than the restaurant was too small to accommodate such a group. Defiantly, the soldiers offered to split into two groups, but were advised the restaurant still could not accommodate them without prior reservations. The soldiers knew the score, understood what was happening and stubbornly insisted on service, and even talked openly among themselves about a destructive protest if they were not seated. The owner would not relent and threatened to notify military officials of their rowdy behavior if they did not leave immediately. Meanwhile a local crowd was gathering and it became more than obvious to the soldiers the crowd was not sympathetic to their cause. Wisely, they departed, but not without caustic parting comments.

The entire ordeal was unfortunate. It never should have happened, but it did, and these proud veterans were troubled by it. Rightfully, they resented their treatment and harbored ill will toward Charleston. Perhaps what hurt the most was that they never understood the reasons for the maltreatment. Jesse assumed the rude behavior was a social snub from the proprietor or that someone in management must have perceived the soldiers as acting above their station. In addition to spoiling their celebration, the experience served as an early wake-up call that not everyone was happy to see them, and not everyone respected them for the sacrifices they had made. Jesse managed to keep his perspective and referred to the incident as another bump in the road. What else could he do?

The following day, Friday, June 27, the troop train departed Charleston in the late p.m. and arrived at Camp Zachary Taylor early Monday morning. Camp Taylor, Jesse's former basic training site, had been converted to a postwar discharge center, and keeping with the unit discharge concept, all soldiers were to receive their discharge at their training site and be sent home together. The 84th Division received basic training at Camp Taylor, but once in France the division was used as replacements for other front-line divisions. Therefore, the men had no particular loyalty to the 84th, nor did the Army try to reassemble them in cohesive units. It really made little difference for the purpose of discharge other than it meant soldiers were not returned to their hometown as a group. Had Jesse not been with the casual detachment, he most likely would have been sent for discharge to Fort Harrison, Indiana. Jesse considered the discharge process as the more important issue, not the location.

The converted training camp was a most efficient separation center, hindered only by the masses of men stationed there for discharge. Hundreds more continued to arrive daily prompting Jesse to jokingly discern, "The entire 84th Division plus a few sister divisions must already be here." Camp command followed an orderly procedure—discharges were processed in a priority order based on the date and hour that the men arrived at Camp Taylor for separation. Thus, all soldiers had no choice but to wait their turn. Until discharge was granted the soldiers were still in the military with regulations strictly enforced. One notable exception was enlisted men were given freedom of movement provided they were readily available for processing. Amazingly, the system worked.

Tuesday evening Jesse remained at the barracks. He cared not to see Louisville. While Jesse was shining his shoes a soldier from across the room approached. "Hi, buddy. If you want to be alone, that's all right. If you want company you are welcome to join us. Tonight most men are in town or out being processed. We misfits decided to stay here and share our thoughts with each other. We've had enough excitement in our lives."

Politely Jesse answered. "Very kind of you, but I do prefer to be alone if it's all the same to you. I have a lot to think about."

"As do we all. That's the reason we misfits are here talking, rather than in town."

"What does that mean? Why do you call yourselves misfits?"

"I use the term misfits because it applies to us. We call ourselves the orphans of the military because we all have one thing in common—one split second decision in combat changed our lives forever. Look over there, I'll show you what I mean! There are about twenty or thirty of us gathered tonight, and we're preparing ourselves to go home. We've got a lot to talk about. See the tall man on the left? He was a machine gunner, now he can't sleep at night for thinking about all the men he has killed. See the man next to him? He froze in combat at Saint Mihiel, and he feels that his inaction caused the death of a dear buddy. See the big guy near the door? He shot one of our own and then held the boy in his arms as he died crying for his mother. Every man over there has a story. We're all haunted by memories of what we saw, what we did, or what we didn't do. Myself, I let my whole squad down and most of them are still in the hospital. I'll bet there isn't one man in this Army who saw combat who doesn't have a story to tell. We believe that it helps to share the story with someone who understands. Shall I go on, or do you want to come hear for yourself, maybe share some of your thoughts? Strange as it may sound there is comfort in sharing. It helps to hear other stories."

He was so emotionally moved by the man's explicit expressions that Jesse could muster no words of his own. Instead he nodded no, and stayed where he stood. Although Jesse did not participate and pretended to be unconcerned, he did try to listen without being obvious. He heard one personal gut-wrenching story after another from men adversely affected by combat. One participant, a former artillery man, sadly referred to himself as a butcher in uniform. Jesse listened until he could listen no more. He left the building. Once outside he spoke to himself. "God, will it never end? How many more stories will there be, how many more casualties of war can there be?" For over two hours Jesse walked about the camp pondering his own queries.

That evening Jesse did not sleep well, his mind would not allow it. He had to put this war behind him. Sometime during the night, somewhere in his mental process, Jesse made a mental transfiguration, a commitment of sorts. No longer could he concern himself with what might have been, or what if. Men like the ones he listened to the night before were the true casualties of war, not he. They suffered mortal wounds to the mind and soul, the type of wounds that might never heal. Jesse's physical wounds to the body paled in comparison to the suffering they endured, and undoubtedly would continue to endure. Jesse could not be like that for he knew such feelings would take him under. Jesse made a vow. From this day forward he would not consider his physical limitations as a liability, but as an asset. With the proper attitude, the right frame of mind, his war experiences should only serve as a source of strength in his future life.

Jesse A. Moore, 3706157, Grade: Private First Class, Casual Detachment, last assigned Company L., 22nd Engineers, received his honorable discharge from the United States Army July 12, 1919. It was noted in his record that he honorably served in the A.E.F. His character was deemed "excellent." In his exit interview he gave the following answers: to wounds in battle, he listed "none," to physical condition at the time of discharge, he answered "good."

Jesse was given two months back pay, paid a $60 bonus for service in France, $2 travel allowance, and was issued a railroad ticket to Jacksonville, Illinois. Jesse departed Camp Taylor by train July 13, scheduled to arrive in Jacksonville in the a.m. Monday, July 14, 1919. By this date over ninety percent of all men already had been reintegrated to civilian life.

The Private Jesse A. Moore returning home by train was not the same man he was thirteen months earlier. He returned a physically weaker man but spiritually and emotionally stronger. He considered himself a better, a wiser man. Outwardly he showed the strain's of war as his gaunt face gave the appearance of a man aged by ten years of life. His wavy black hair was streaked with strands, patches of gray, and his hairline was noticeably in recession. He still stood straight and proud, but his firm physique weighed fifteen pounds less. His blue-gray eyes lacked their earlier sparkle, frequently watered, and provided decreased vision, although the casual observer seldom noticed. His body was whole, his mind retained its sharpness.

Jacksonville, Illinois, U.S.A., deceptively appeared the same as when he left. However, it was the edifices, the physical that remained the same, not most of the people. To those at home the Great War in Europe had ended long ago, and their memory of it was becoming distant, not a current issue of concern. The vast majority of local soldiers already had returned, and had been ceremoniously and properly welcomed by the town's leaders and citizens. Understandably, most townspeople were emotionally beyond the war, now more concerned with the pressing issues of personal living in a postwar world. Soldier and civilian alike were ready to put the strains of war behind, and who could blame them? That which was unfair from the start of war was still unfair—not all men, families were equally affected by the war and a natural dichotomy of war memories would forever exist. While many would soon forget the agony of war, some were doomed to remember.

Unlike Jesse's ceremonious departure from Jacksonville, his return was not officially recognized. No brass bands, no welcoming committees, no cheering crowds lay in wait at the train station. Apart from a waiting wife, no one at the station showed any awareness that a local boy was on this train returning home from war.

The weather on this summer day was near perfect when the train slowed and pulled into the East State Street Station and the conductor announced, "Jacksonville, arriving in Jacksonville." Along with several civilian passengers Jesse prepared for his exit, although he was clearly more excited as demonstrated by his position at the front of the departing line. Once he saw Helen waiting on the platform he almost could not contain himself, and with each passing second his level of excitement only increased in intensity. The moment he dreamed about was at hand, was all that mattered as he now understood that it was only Helen and family that gave his life its true meaning.

Jesse was the only man in uniform scheduled to disembark the train at Jacksonville. When the door opened, Jesse was crowding the conductor and Helen was so close to the train that the conductor hardly had room to secure the stepping platform. In one quick movement the returning soldier jumped off the train and into the arms of his adoring wife. Her embrace was proof that at last he was home. Jesse knew what he wanted to say, but when the exact moment to speak arose Jesse forgot his prepared words, and instead, he passionately embraced and kissed his wife without benefit of a single word. Likewise, Helen was so emotional, so happy that no words could pass her lips either. Simply, they stood locked in the arms of the other, both unaware that because of where they stood no one else could exit the train; and compassionately, not one person verbally objected to the blocked passageway. It was as if the crowd understood and approved of the emotions, the needs of the reunited couple and time passed before the conductor reluctantly encouraged the returning soldier to move aside. The couple slowly moved away, never breaking their embrace.

When the couple did exchange words it was not at the expense of a lost embrace. Jesse refused to release his hold and that suited Helen. Private whisperings were more than sufficient for now. As if words were unnecessary, when they did separate their bodies it was not to speak, but to visually admire one another. It was Jesse who broke the silence. "Let's go home."

The returning soldier in uniform and his adoring wife walked home hand in hand. Their joint presence reeked of happiness, and they exhibited a pride worthy of notice from all in their path. For only two in number, neither large in stature nor arrogant in demeanor, they stood immense in spirit. For in their own way they already had become giants among men, this son and daughter of commoners, this husband and wife of love, this father and mother of commitment. For it surely must be people like them who now and forever are destined to keep their nation great.

EPILOGUE

August, 1920, Erastus Moore received official correspondence from the Office of Quartermaster General, United States Army, notifying him that the next of kin to all fallen soldiers buried in Europe were entitled to select a permanent interment site. Erastus was to state his preference for one of three cemeteries to serve as Elzie's interment site. The selection of site was final. His options were: 1. American military cemetery on foreign soil, designed, constructed, and maintained specifically to honor in perpetuity the dead of the war. 2. Arlington National Cemetery, Arlington, Virginia. 3. Local cemetery selected by next of kin. In November of the same year Erastus notified the authorities that he wished the body shipped home for burial in Montezuma Cemetery, Pike County, Illinois. December 4, 1920, the official process was placed in motion.

December 17, Elzie was disinterred from his battlefield grave #399 in cemetery #1868 commune of Ban-de-Laveline, Vosges, France. His buried body was in uniform, wrapped in a blanket in a wooden box. The remains were so badly decomposed that on site positive identification was impossible. Both identification tags were so corroded that they could not be read. However, the bottle buried with the body contained information identifying name, rank, and serial number of Private Elzie Moore. Cause of death was listed as killed by artillery shell. The body was visually examined to determine estimate of height, weight, hair color, and other noticeable characteristics. Noted wounds were a large cavity extending from chin, through the lower left bicuspids, through the roof of the mouth and the skull was shattered. Since the identification tags could not be read and the visual observation of the body was not consistent with the listed cause of death, the body was reburied in the same grave awaiting future instructions for further identification.

Instructions from the War Department's Grave Registration Service were crystal clear—confirmed positive identification was essential before any bodies were

519

returned home. Subsequently, Elzie's remains were slated for additional identification and verification. Until further notification by proper authorities the soldier's remains were to stay buried in the battlefield cemetery at Ban-de-Laveline.

Two months later, February 25, 1921, the Grave Registration Service ordered the body disinterred and shipped to the military morgue in Saint Die. Here the body was examined by Army medical experts, prepared for shipment, and sent by rail to Toul, France, for additional examination. The coffin was labeled, Private Elzie H. Moore, 2388592, 61st U.S. Infantry, Co. L. Case of questionable identity.

At Toul, additional information was gathered: Elzie's medical records, dental records, and all physical reports were obtained from Jefferson Barracks, Missouri. Casualty records from the 61st Infantry Regiment were collected from Dijon. The commanding officer of Co. L., 61st Regiment was ordered to evaluate and reaffirm all data and to forward his official records concerning death and burial. The chaplain present at Elzie's burial was ordered to do the same. Emphasizing urgent priority, the written orders to gather this precise information were signed by Robert C. Davis, Adjutant General, G.H.Q. Acquisition of any other pertinent data was authorized, including the form filled out by the informant from Co. L. at the time of death at La Cude-Violu Sector, on June 23,1918. It was the informant's information which designated the cause of death as killed in action by artillery shell.

Medical and dental records confirmed the remains as belonging to Elzie H. Moore. The C.O. of Company L. and the chaplain's reports both listed the cause of death as gunshot wound to the head. The medical examination at Toul confirmed the large cavity in the mouth and shattered skull to be consistent with death caused by a gunshot fired from a small caliber weapon. A bullet had entered the body through the chin and shattered the skull. This finding made the manner of death consistent with injuries to the body. Positive identification was confirmed—Private Elzie H. Moore was killed in action, resulting from gunshot to the head.

Immediately, the remains were prepared for shipment home. April 30, 1921, the body was shipped by rail to Antwerp, Belgium, for ship transport to the United States. Elzie's body, along with hundreds of other fallen soldiers, was ceremoniously loaded on U.S.A.T. Wheaton and sailed for home shores. Without incident or delay the Wheaton crossed the Atlantic Ocean, sailed around the southern tip of Manhattan, and arrived Saturday evening, July 2,1921, at the New York City receiving port on the Hudson River at Hoboken, New Jersey.

July 16, 1921, 177 bodies of returning soldiers brought home for burial, were loaded on the Erie Railroad for shipment to Chicago, Illinois. This single contingency of bodies represented soldiers from eight Midwestern States.

August 5, 1921, the body of Elzie Moore arrived by train in Pittsfield, Illinois, and was received by his father, Erastus L. Moore, and J. Smith, Mortician. Elzie's body was escorted by Private Teddy Wojcioska, Co. H., 52nd Regiment, and his orders required him to remain with the body until burial. Elzie arrived in Milton the following day, Saturday, August 6, 1921, where his closed coffin was placed on display in the funeral home.

On Sunday the usually quiet small town of Milton was crowded with visitors, including numerous former servicemen from all parts of the county and a few from nearby counties. In full dress uniform a thirty-man American Legion honor guard stood watch outside the funeral home and church.

The funeral was scheduled to begin at 3:00, Sunday afternoon. Upon arrival the family members were obligated to make their way through a quiet, respectful crowd extending from the town's square to the church; and as they entered the church they found an overflowing sanctuary with all seats occupied save five rows reserved for family. Droves of people were standing in the rear of the church and outside the building. Two ministers were seated near the alter as eight military pallbearers stood at attention guarding the flag-draped coffin positioned front and center in the sanctuary. Side by side Erastus and Aunt Mary were seated near the center aisle of the first row, and in order of descending age Elzie's four oldest siblings and spouses filled the first row. Frieda sat next to Helen and Jesse in the second row. The remaining reserved section was completely filled by other family members.

Reverend Edwin Priest of Pittsfield opened the service. In addition to paying homage to Elzie he spoke to the value of patriotism and personal sacrifice. His brief inspiring message ended with the concluding words: "He was Pike County's first boy killed in action. Less than eighteen when he enlisted he was one of the youngest of the boys who fought to make the Stars and Stripes the greatest banner under the sun. He wanted to go. He gave to Montezuma Township the honor of placing the first gold star on Pike County's service flag." The reverend's tribute was followed by two prayers and a soloist singing a religious song.

Reverend Harkins, the pastor of the Christian Church in Milton and himself a Y.M.C.A. man who saw service in France, delivered the personal eulogy, a discourse aimed at the hearts of the multitude in attendance. He spoke as only one who personally knew Elzie could speak of him. He spoke of the family's struggle to survive after the death of the mother. He spoke of Elzie's struggles in his early life and about the likable nature of the boy; and he described the personal qualities of Elzie as a young adult. He spoke of the many stories of Elzie's bravery on the field of battle and of the mystery surrounding his death. He made reference to the high esteem held for Elzie by the military and by his fellow soldiers. He identified Elzie, the boy from Pike County, as an American military hero who made the ultimate sacrifice for his country. On this day and at this period in time, there were no higher tributes for one's fellow man.

The military pallbearers, accompanied by the thirty-man honor guard plus many family members, walked the three and one-half miles to the Montezuma Cemetery. Elzie's body was slowly conveyed to the cemetery in an automobile hearse. Other family and friends followed in automobiles and buggies.

The pallbearers carried the coffin on their shoulders the eighty or so yards from the road to the cemetery. Out of necessity the ceremony at the small cemetery was closed to the public, restricted to family, pastors, and men in uniform. A large, respectful crowd observed from the roadside. Reverend Harkins said a few final words, gave a final prayer before a seven-man firing squad faced east and fired a three-shot volley representing the traditional military 21-gun salute for heroes. The 21-gun salute was followed by an Army bugler masterfully playing taps. Members from the honor guard neatly folded the flag which had draped Elzie's coffin, and the commander presented the properly folded flag to Erastus, saying as he presented, "In honor of our fallen comrade we proudly present to you this flag of the United States of America which covered the coffin of your son who died in service to his country. Sir, I salute you." He then backed away, faced the coffin of his fallen comrade, and on command, the entire honor guard gave one final hand salute to Elzie. Three years and two months after his battlefield death, Elzie was ceremoniously and respectfully laid to rest in Pike County, Illinois.

Elzie was home.

———————

Today, Montezuma Cemetery is abandoned and neglected. Only a handful of family members remain aware of Elzie's life, his valor.

October, 1937, Jesse was granted a $360 annual pension for non-service connected total and permanent disability. Most of the men who had received gas injuries during the war and had signed the non-service connected form had already died by the mid 1930's.

———————

At the time of Jesse's death Helen and Jesse had been married for almost 63 years. They had 10 children.

Jesse A. Moore died March 2, 1980, at age 84.

Mary Helen Moore died March 30, 1986, at age 83.

About the Author

David G. Moore received his B.A. degree from Illinois College, his M.A. degree from the Univeristy of Illinois. He taught History at Galesburg High School for 31 years. *Forgotten Valor* is his first publication.

Printed in the United States
28058LVS00002B/13-15

9 781594 081088